DANIEL IN THE LIONS' DEN

The

Story of the Bible

BY

CHARLES FOSTER

CONTAINING OVER 300 ILLUSTRATIONS
AND
COLORED PICTURES

A. J. HOLMAN CO.
Publishers
1222-1226 ARCH STREET, PHILADELPHIA

TO EVERY READER OF THIS BOOK

SINCE the publication of the "STORY OF THE BIBLE," a great many good people have read and approved of it. But some few have found fault ; they say they do not think the words of the Bible ought to be changed as they are in this book. Especially they object to any change where the words are spoken words.

To show you what I mean :—On the seventh page, in the account of the creation, we read that God said, "Let there be light." In this place there is no change. These are the exact words that we read in the Bible. But on page four hundred and twenty-nine, where we are told how God sent the prophet Ezekiel to speak to the captive Jews, we read that God said to him, "I send thee to them because they are a disobedient people ; both they and their fathers have disobeyed me. Yet thou shalt tell them my message, whether they will hear, or whether they will not hear." In this place the words are changed. They are not the same words that are given in the Bible, as you will see by turning to the second chapter of Ezekiel and reading from the third verse.

Now, because some persons object to such changes, I wish to give my reason for making them. I do it because children, and others for whom this book was written, would not understand the words in the Bible. I have found when reading the Bible to them that they want to have those words explained. Therefore I have tried to use in this book simpler words, such as they can understand, and not only understand, but read for themselves.

But although I have changed the words, I have tried to give their true meaning. In doing this, (praying at the same time that God would help me to do it), I hope I have not done wrong, nor what is displeasing to him. Yet I think it is well for me to tell every one who reads the book, here in the very beginning of it, that these changes have been made, and that the "STORY OF THE BIBLE" is not the Bible, nor meant to take the Bible's place. On the contrary, it is meant to interest those who read it in the things that the Bible teaches, so that they will want to read about those things, and study them in the Bible itself.

CHARLES FOSTER.

2

PREFACE

The author of this book, during many years' experience as a teacher of the Scriptures, both in the Sunday-school and the home circle, felt the need of a simple version of the main portions of the Bible, which would give not only its stories, its precepts, and its doctrines in a continuous form, but would also show the connection and unity between the Old and the New Testaments. Being unable to find such a work, he has endeavored to prepare one; and in this volume offers the result of his labors, hoping it may supply a want which he believes others have felt equally with himself.

In writing this book, his object has been—

First. To include all of Scripture that may most profitably be included in a work of its character and purpose.

Secondly. To follow closely the Sacred Narrative, adhering to its details and maintaining a reverential spirit.

Thirdly. To add no more of comment than is necessary to the elucidation of the text; and

Fourthly. To employ such simple language and forms of expression as, (while not undignified, nor displeasing to more mature and cultured minds), shall be intelligible to children without further explanation.

CONTENTS

CONTENTS

THE OLD TESTAMENT

THE
STORY OF THE BIBLE

THE BOOK OF GENESIS

CHAPTERS I, II (1, 2)

GOD MAKES THE EARTH AND THE SKIES IN SIX DAYS: HE MAKES ADAM AND
THE WOMAN, AND PLACES THEM IN THE GARDEN OF EDEN.

A VERY long while ago, before anybody can remember, God
made the world. Yet it did not look at first as it does now,
for there was nothing living on it—no men, nor animals, nor
birds; and there was nothing growing on it—no trees, nor
bushes, nor flowers; but it was all lonely and dark everywhere.

Then God made the light. He said, Let there be light; and
the light came. And God saw the light and was pleased with it,
and he gave the light a name; he called it Day. And when the
day was gone and the darkness came again to stay for a little

while, he called that darkness Night. God did these things on the first day.

And God made the clouds, and he made the sky up above the world where the clouds should be; and he gave the sky a name; he called it Heaven. God did this on the second day.

And God said that the waters should go into one place by themselves; and when they had gone into that one place, and were very deep and wide there, God gave the waters a name; he called them Seas, and the dry land he called Earth. And God made the grass to grow up out of the earth, and the bushes and the trees, that have fruit on them. And the grass and the bushes and the trees were to bear seeds, so that, when those seeds were planted in the ground, some more grass, or other bushes or trees would grow there. God did these things on the third day.

And God made two great lights, the sun to shine in the day, and the moon to shine in the night; he made the stars also. And he set the sun and moon and the stars up in the sky, where we see them now. God did this on the fourth day.

And he made the great whales, and all the fishes that swim about in the sea; and the birds also, some to fly over the water and swim upon it and live near it, like ducks and geese; and some to live all the time upon the land and in the woods, like eagles, robins, pigeons, and wrens. God made these on the fifth day.

And God made the animals, those that are wild and that live out in the forest, such as elephants, lions, tigers, and bears; and those that are tame and useful to men, and that live where men live, such as horses, oxen, cows, and sheep. And he made the little insects that creep on the ground, and the flies that fly about in the air.

And God made man and spoke kindly to him, and told him that he should be master over the fish of the sea, the birds of the air, and over every thing that was living on the earth. And God told man that the fruit which grew on the trees and on the bushes should be his food. The animals were given the grass and the leaves of the bushes to eat.

And God looked at all the things he had made, and was pleased with them; and this was the sixth day.

So the earth and the skies were finished in six days: the seventh day God rested from all his work, and the Bible tells us he sanctified the seventh day; that is, he separated it from the other days of the week and made it a holy day.

THE GARDEN OF EDEN

Now we have been told how the earth and the skies were made; God made them. And he made every bush and every tree; for there had been no rain to make them grow, and no man to plant them; but after God had planted them, the trees, the bushes, and the grass took root and grew by themselves.

And God made man out of the dust that lies on the ground; and he breathed into him, and then the man breathed, and moved, and was alive, because God had breathed into him. And the Lord

God planted a garden for the man he had made.   It was called the garden of Eden; in that garden God made to grow every tree that was beautiful to look at, and that bore fruit good to eat. A river flowed through the garden and watered it.

And God took Adam, the man he had made, and put him into the garden to take care of it; God told him he might eat of the fruit of every tree in the garden except one; that one was called the Tree of the Knowledge of Good and Evil.   God said he must not eat of that tree, for if he did eat of it he should surely die.

And God said it was not good that the man should be alone, therefore God made some one to be with him and help him.   He caused Adam to fall into a deep sleep; and while he was sleeping, God took out of his side a piece of bone, and of that bone he made a woman.   And God brought the woman he had made to Adam, and she was his wife.

And all the animals and the birds came to Adam; God sent them to him that he might give them their names, and whatever Adam called each one was its name.

CHAPTERS III–V (3–5)

THE SERPENT TEMPTS THE WOMAN TO EAT OF THE FORBIDDEN FRUIT, AND
    SHE TEMPTS HER HUSBAND.   ADAM AND HIS WIFE ARE DRIVEN OUT
    OF THE GARDEN OF EDEN.   CAIN AND ABEL ARE BORN.   THEY BRING
    OFFERINGS TO GOD.   CAIN KILLS ABEL.   ENOCH AND METHUSELAH.

Now there was a serpent in the garden of Eden.   And the serpent spoke to the woman, yet not of itself; but Satan, that wicked Spirit that comes into our hearts and tempts us to sin, went into the serpent and tempted the woman to sin.   The serpent asked her, Has God said you shall not eat of every tree in the garden?   The woman answered that they might eat of all the trees except one, but of it God had commanded them not to eat, lest they should die.   Then the serpent told her they should not die, and that God had forbidden them to eat of the tree because it would make them wise.

The woman listened to what the serpent said, and when she saw that the tree was beautiful to look at, and that the fruit seemed good to eat, and remembered that the serpent had said it would make her wise, she took some of the fruit and did eat of it, and gave also to her husband and he did eat.

After they had eaten they heard a voice in the garden; they knew it was God's voice, yet they did not come when they heard

ADAM AND EVE ARE DRIVEN OUT OF THE GARDEN

it. They were afraid, and hid themselves among the trees. But God spoke again, and called to Adam, saying, Where art thou? Adam answered, I heard thy voice in the garden, and I was afraid and hid myself. And God said, Hast thou eaten of the tree I commanded thee not to eat of? Then Adam began to make excuse, and blame the woman; he said, The woman whom thou gavest to be with me, she gave me of the fruit, and I did eat. And God said to the woman, What is this that thou hast done? The woman answered, The serpent deceived me, and I did eat.

And God was angry with Adam and the woman, and with the serpent. The serpent, he said, should be punished by having to crawl on the ground, with its mouth in the dust, all the days of its life. He told the woman, also, she should have sickness and sorrow. And God drove Adam and his wife out of the beautiful garden, and would let them live there

ADAM AT LABOR

no longer. And he sent cherubim, or angels, that kept watch, and a fiery sword that turned every way, to prevent them from going into the garden again. And to Adam God said, that because he had listened to his wife's voice, and eaten of the tree which the Lord commanded him not to eat of, the ground should not any more bear fruit for him by itself, and without his labor, as it used to do in the garden of Eden, but it should send up thorns and thistles. And Adam would have to work very hard, as long as he lived, to raise food to eat; and when he should die, God said, his body would go back to dust again, like the dust out of which the Lord had made him.

Yet God prepared a way for Adam and his wife to be saved from any more punishment after they should be dead. They could not be saved from sorrow and trouble while they were living in this world, but after they should die, and their souls should go into the next world, God prepared a way for them not to be punished there. And this is the way: He promised to send a Saviour who would be punished in their place; so that if Adam and his wife repented of their sin and believed in that Saviour, they would be forgiven, and, after they died, taken up to heaven, where they would be as happy as if they had never sinned at all. And this Saviour was not to be punished for them alone, but for their children also. For since Adam and his wife had sinned and made their own hearts wicked, their children would have wicked hearts too; because children must be of the same nature as their parents.

Adam gave his wife a name; he called her Eve. And God made coats for them out of the skins of animals.

After they had been driven out of the garden of Eden, God gave Adam and Eve two sons; the elder one was named Cain, the younger one Abel. When they grew up to be men, Cain was a farmer or gardener; Abel was a shepherd and kept a flock of sheep. And they both had wicked hearts, like their parents, which often caused them to sin. But Abel repented of his sins, and believed the promise which God had made to send a Saviour. And one day he brought a lamb from his flock and offered it to God. The way he offered it was to kill it first, and then burn it on an altar. An altar was a pile of stones, or earth, with a flat top, heaped up as high as a table. He put some wood on this altar, all cut and ready to burn; then laid the lamb, after it was killed, on the wood; next he set fire to the wood, and that burned up the lamb, so there was nothing left on the altar but ashes.

God was pleased that Abel should worship him in this way, because the lamb that he brought was like the Saviour that God had promised. It was gentle, and patient, and innocent, like him; and when Abel killed it, and offered it on the altar, it seemed like that Saviour who was coming, after many years, to die for his sins. The lamb meant the Saviour, or represented him, and therefore God was pleased with Abel and his offering.

But Cain did not repent of his sins, nor believe God's promise to send a Saviour; and when he brought his offering it was not

CAIN AND ABEL OFFERING UP SACRIFICES

a lamb, but some fruit, or grain, taken out of the field, or from the trees of his garden; and God was not pleased with Cain or his offering. When Cain saw this, he was angry, and showed plainly, by his looks, that he was angry with God. Yet God spoke kindly to him, and asked why he was angry. If Cain did right, God said, he would be pleased with him; and if he did not do right, the fault was his own.

And Cain hated Abel, because God was pleased with Abel's offering, but not with his. And one day when they were out in the field together, he rose up and killed him; and the blood ran out of Abel's wounds and sank into the ground. After Cain had done this, God spoke to him, and said, Where is Abel, thy brother? Cain answered, I know not. Am I my brother's keeper? Yet God saw all that Cain had done, and now, he said, as a punishment for killing Abel, Cain should be a fugitive and a vagabond in the earth; that is, he should flee about the earth from one place to another, as a person who was always afraid, and who had no home to stay in.

God said, also, that when Cain planted anything out in the field to bear food, it should not grow well. It would die, or briars and weeds would come up and choke it, or it would bear leaves, but no fruit; so that Cain would have hardly enough to eat. Then Cain said, that as God had driven him away and would no longer take care of him, every one who should meet him would want to kill him. But God said that whoever killed Cain should be punished with a very dreadful punishment; for God chose to punish Cain himself, and not that any man should punish him.

And God set a mark on Cain. We are not told what sort of a mark it was, but it was something which other people could see; and when they saw it, they knew Cain, and remembered God's command that no one should kill him.

Adam lived a great many years after this, and God gave him other children beside Cain and Abel. But when he was nine hundred and thirty years old he died, and his body went to dust again, as God said it should when he ate of the forbidden fruit in the garden of Eden. Nine hundred and thirty years was a very long time for a man to live, but God allowed men to live much longer then than they do now.

And Adam died, and his children, but their children lived still. We are told the names of some of the men who lived in those days. One of them was called Enoch. The Bible says of him that he walked with God. This means that he loved God, and remembered him all the time, as if he had been walking beside him, with his hand in his, listening to what God said, and trying to please and obey him in every thing he did.

After Enoch had lived three hundred and sixty-five years, God did a wonderful thing for him; he took him up to heaven while he was alive. Enoch did not die like other men; but God took him up without his dying, just as if he were to take up one of us now.

Enoch had a son named Methuselah, who, when he died, was nine hundred and sixty-nine years old. We are not told of any other man as old as this; therefore Methuselah is called the oldest man that ever lived.

CHAPTERS VI–IX (6–9)

THE PEOPLE GROW VERY WICKED. GOD SAYS HE WILL DESTROY THEM BY A FLOOD. HE COMMANDS NOAH TO BUILD AN ARK AND GO INTO IT. NOAH OBEYS. THE FLOOD DESTROYS EVERY THING THAT LIVES ON THE DRY LAND. NOAH COMES OUT OF THE ARK AFTER THE FLOOD.

AFTER a long while, when there came to be many more people living in the world, they grew very wicked. Their hearts were filled with sinful thoughts and all their acts were evil, for they did not care to please God, or even try to obey him. Therefore God was angry with them, and said he would punish them by sending a flood that should cover the earth with deep water, and drown all the people, the animals, the birds, and every thing that lived upon the ground. For almost all the people in the world were very wicked, and yet not quite all; there was one good man whose name was Noah. The Bible tells us he was a just man, and that he walked with God, as Enoch did. Therefore God loved Noah, and told him of the flood he was going to send.

And God commanded Noah to build an ark. This was a great boat. It was to be very large, with rooms in it, and a window, and a great door in its side, and was to be three stories high. And God told Noah that when the ark was finished, he and his sons and their wives should go into it. And he commanded Noah to take in with him some of every kind of beast, and of every

CAIN KILLS ABEL

kind of bird, and of every kind of insect, to keep them alive while the flood should be on the earth; for all that were not in the ark would be drowned.

Then Noah began to build the ark. It took him a great while to build it, perhaps more than a hundred years; but, as we have read, men lived much longer then than they do now. And Noah not only worked at building the ark—the Bible says he was a preacher; he used to speak to the people about God, and about the punishment that was coming upon them for their sins. But they would not repent, nor believe what he told them; so that he had to hear their wicked words and see their wicked acts all the time he was building the ark.

ENTERING THE ARK

Yet he worked on patiently, until at last he finished it as God had commanded him.

Then God spoke to Noah and told him to come, with all his family, into the ark; for God said he had seen him to be a good man among all those wicked men who were living on the earth. And God told Noah to bring the birds and the beasts also with him into the ark, for in seven days he would send the rain on the earth, and every thing that was living on the dry land should be drowned. And Noah did as God commanded. He was six hundred years old when the flood came on the earth. And he went with his wife, and his three sons and their wives, into the ark, and took the beasts, the birds, and the insects in with him. When they were all safe inside, God shut them in.

After seven days the rain began, and it rained, without stop-
ping, forty days and forty nights. The Bible says the windows
of heaven were opened; this means that the rain came down not
only in little drops, as we see it come, but it came as if poured
out of great windows up in the sky. And the springs, the creeks,
the rivers, and the great ocean, all began to rise up and overflow
the land. After a while the water came to where the ark was,

THE FLOOD

underneath and around it; it rose higher and higher till the ark
floated and was lifted up from the place where Noah had been
building it so long, and the ground everywhere began to be covered.

What now were those men to do who would not obey God, nor
listen to the preaching of Noah? Before the rain came they
thought there would be no flood, and that Noah wanted only to
make them afraid. Now the flood had come, and they saw that
all he had told them was true. How glad they would have been

to go with him into the ark, but it was too late. No doubt they climbed up to the highest places on the hills and mountains; but the hills and mountains were covered at last; there was no other place for them to go, and all the people in the world, except those few in the ark, were drowned. And every beast and bird and little insect, except those in the ark, were drowned also. Then all the earth was covered with water. There was no land to be seen anywhere; only the ark could be seen floating alone, with the water all around it and the sky above.

But God remembered Noah, and took care of him and of those who were with him, through all that dreadful storm. He kept the ark safe till the rain stopped, and the waters began to flow back again into the seas and rivers and springs underground, where they were before the flood.

After Noah had been in the ark a hundred and fifty days, the waters were gone down so much that the ark rested on the top of a mountain called Ararat. There it stood, resting on the top of the mountain, for more than two months. By that time the waters were lower still, and the tops of other mountains could be seen peeping above them.

THE TOPS OF THE MOUNTAINS APPEAR

And Noah opened the window of the ark and let a raven go; and the raven flew about over the water and roosted at night on the tops of the mountains, or on the roof of the ark, but never came back to Noah again. Then Noah sent out another bird; it was a dove. He sent it that it might fly off and see whether the waters had left the ground dry yet. But they had not left it dry. Although the tops of the mountains were not covered, the rest of the ground was; and the dove found no pleasant place with trees and flowers, where she would like to stay away from her mate; so she came back to the window of the ark, and Noah put out his hand and took her in.

Then Noah waited seven days longer and sent her out again, and in the evening she came back to him as before, but this time with a leaf in her mouth, plucked off from an olive tree. When

NOAH RECEIVES THE DOVE

Noah saw the leaf, he knew that the waters must have gone down greatly, or the dove could not have found it. God had taught the dove to pluck that leaf and carry it to Noah, so that he might know the ground would soon be dry. And he waited another seven days and sent the dove forth once more; but she did not come back to him again. For by this time no doubt the woods were pleasant to fly about in, much pleasanter than the ark where she had been shut up so long. And beside, God kept the dove from going back to Noah, so that he might be sure it was almost time for him to come out of the ark.

And Noah looked and saw that the ground was dry. And God spoke to him, and told him to come out of the ark, and to bring out also his wife and his sons and their wives, and the animals, the birds, and the insects that had been in the ark

NOAH OFFERS UP A SACRIFICE

with him. So Noah came out and brought every living thing, and they walked on the dry ground. And Noah built an altar, as Abel had done, and offered up animals and birds upon it to the Lord, who had saved him and his family from the flood while all the other people in the world were drowned.

And God spoke kindly to Noah and his sons, and said they should be masters over every thing living on the earth: and God told them they might kill the animals for food. He had given Adam only the fruits which grew on the trees and the bushes for food; but now, after the flood, he said that men might kill and eat any animal they chose.

And God promised that he would never send another flood on the earth to drown all the people as this one had done. And he gave Noah a token; that was something to make him remember and believe God's promise, so that he never need be afraid of a flood any more. This token was a beautiful thing, and God set it up in the sky, where Noah could often see it, and as often as he should see it he would think of God's promise. The token that God gave Noah was the rainbow.

Noah lived after the flood many years: but when he was nine hundred and fifty years old he died.

CHAPTERS XI–XVII (11–17)

THE PEOPLE BEGIN TO BUILD THE TOWER OF BABEL; THEY ARE MADE TO SPEAK IN DIFFERENT LANGUAGES, AND ARE SCATTERED OVER THE EARTH. ABRAM AND LOT COME INTO THE LAND OF CANAAN. LOT GOES TO LIVE ON THE PLAIN OF JORDAN. ISAAC IS PROMISED. ISHMAEL IS BORN.

AND God gave to Noah's sons children of their own. They, when they grew up, had children too, so that after a while there came to be a great many people in the world once more.

Now we should think that these people would have been very careful not to offend God. They knew how the men who had offended him before were punished, and though God had promised never to send another flood, there were many other ways in which he might punish them. He might send sickness upon them, or give them no food, and leave them to starve; or he might send down fire from heaven to burn them. But they seemed to forget this, and as their hearts were wicked, they went on as the men before the flood had done, sinning against him.

There was only one language in the world then. The people all talked alike, and could all understand each other; and as they journeyed from the east they came to a plain in the land of Shinar, and stopped there. And they said one to another, Let us make brick and build a tower whose top may reach up to heaven. And they began to build it. We are not told why they wanted to build this tower. But God, who saw their hearts, knew that it was for some wicked purpose. Perhaps they did not believe God's promise, that he would never send another flood on the earth, and thought, if he should send one, this tower would be so high that the waters could not overflow it, and they would climb up into it and be safe. Or perhaps they built it as a sort of temple, or church, not to worship God in, but idols.

And the Lord came down from heaven to see the tower which the people were building, and he saw it and was displeased.

BUILDING THE TOWER OF BABEL

Then he did a wonderful thing to stop them. He made them, all at once, begin to speak in different languages, such as they had never spoken before. They could not go on building now, because they were not able to understand each other's words. Therefore they had to cease building before the tower was done. After that they would not all of them wish to live together any more. Only those would wish to live together who spoke the same language, and they would go off to some place where they could be by themselves. This is the way that people, at first, were separated from one another and came to live in different parts of the world.

The tower which they tried to build, but which God would not allow them to finish, was called the tower of Babel. Babel means confusion. When the people began to talk in different languages, so that they could not understand each other, it made confusion there. Therefore this tower was called the tower of Babel.

Many years after these things, there lived in the land of Ur a man named Abram. The people of that land worshipped idols. And God told Abram to leave his home and his relations, and go to another land which he would show him. Abram did not know what land it was, yet he left his friends and his home as he was commanded to do. For he had faith; he believed that God would bring him to the land he had told him of.

Abram was seventy-five years old: and he took his wife, whose name was Sarai, and his brother's son, whose name was Lot, and they started to go to the land which God had promised to show him. It was a long journey there; he had to cross over wide rivers and a desert, where the country was lonely and wild. Yet God took care of him and of those who were with him, and brought them safely to the promised land. It was called the land of Canaan.

And Abram came to a place in Canaan called Shechem. While he was there God spoke to him and told him he would give all the land of Canaan to his descendants. Abram's descendants were his children and his children's children, who should live long after Abram himself was dead. They were to live in the land of Canaan, and it was to be their land. And Abram built an altar at Shechem. Afterward he left Shechem and came to a mountain, and there built another altar and offered up a sacrifice to the Lord.

And he went on journeying through the land. Other people were living there then, but God kept them from doing him any harm. And there was a famine in the land. It is a famine in any place when the grass and the corn will not grow there, so that the people have nothing for themselves or their cattle to eat. And now there was a famine in Canaan. Therefore Abram went into another country called Egypt, and Lot, his brother's son, went with him. Egypt was a good way from Canaan. Abram did not go there to stay, but only to wait till the famine should be over in Canaan, and after it was over he and Lot returned again. And they came to Shechem, where Abram had first built an altar in the land; and there, again, he offered up a sacrifice to the Lord.

Now Abram was very rich: he had much silver and gold and

a great many cattle. Lot had cattle, too—herds of cattle and tents; for he and Abram did not live in houses, but in tents. It was better for them to live in tents than in houses like ours, because they moved so much oftener than we do. After they had been long enough in one place for their cattle to eat up the grass there, they left it and went to another. Then they took down their tents and carried them wherever they went. Beside, they did not need houses as we do, because it was never so cold in that country as it is here.

Abram and Lot had, each of them, a great many cattle, and they had men called herdsmen to take care of their cattle; and these men quarrelled. Abram's herdsmen and Lot's herdsmen quarrelled with each other. When Abram heard this, he spoke to Lot about it. And how did he speak? Did he say, This is my land; God has given it to me, and you must move away somewhere else? No; he spoke kindly to Lot and said, Let there be no strife between me and thee, and between my herdsmen and thy herdsmen. Then Abram told Lot he might go to any part of the land that he chose to live in, and Abram said he would go to another part.

And Lot chose the plain of Jordan. The Jordan is a river, and the plain of Jordan was the level country through which the river flowed. Then Lot took his cattle and his herdsmen and went away from Abram to live on the plain of Jordan. And some cities were there; one of them was named Sodom. The men of Sodom were very wicked, yet Lot went to live in that city. He was not a wicked man himself, he served God; but he went to live among wicked men, because there he might have better pasture for his cattle and so increase his riches. He should not have done this, and we shall see afterward how much trouble it caused him.

After Lot had gone, the Lord spoke to Abram and told him he would give all that land, as far as he could see it, to him and to his descendants. And God said he would make Abram's descendants so many that no one could count them. Then Abram moved his tent and came to a place called Hebron, and there he built an altar to the Lord. This made three altars he had built since he came into Canaan; so we see, as he journeyed from one place to another, he loved to have an altar near him that he might offer up sacrifices and worship the Lord.

And there was war on the plain of Jordan. Four kings came there with an army, and fought against the city of Sodom where Lot lived, and they gained the victory. Then they went into the houses and carried off the spoil, that is, food and money and clothing, and everything that they wanted. They took some of the people, and Lot also, away with them as captives, or slaves. When Abram heard of it, he gathered his servants together and followed after them. The Bible tells us he had three hundred and eighteen servants. This was a large number for one person to have, but Abram owned great flocks of sheep and herds of cattle and camels, and he needed many servants to take care of them. And beside his servants some of the men of the land, who were his friends, went with him to help him against the four kings.

And he came up with them and fought with them, and God gave him the victory. Then he took all the captives and the spoil which they had carried away, and brought them back to Sodom. As he was coming there, Melchizedek, the king of a city called Salem, who was also a minister of God, came out to meet Abram, bringing him bread and wine. And Melchizedek blessed Abram, that is, he asked that God might bless him and be good to him; and he thanked God for giving Abram the victory. And Abram gave Melchizedek a tenth part of all the things he had taken from his enemies. When the king of Sodom saw how Abram had brought back the captives which the four kings had carried away, he said to him, Give the captives to me that I may send them to their own homes again, but keep the spoil for thyself. But Abram said he had made a promise to God not to keep anything for himself. The men who had gone with him to help him might take their share of the spoil, he said, but he would take nothing.

After this God spoke to Abram and told him that he was his friend. But Abram said that God had never given him a child. Then God promised to give him a son. And he brought Abram out and told him to look up at the stars as they shone in the

sky, and asked him whether he could count them.   And God said
that Abram's descendants should be as the stars, so many they
could not be counted.   God told Abram also that his descendants should live in another country that was not theirs, and
that the people would treat them cruelly for many years.   Yet

MELCHIZEDEK BLESSES ABRAM

God said he would punish the people who treated them so, and
afterward would bring Abram's descendants out of that land
with great riches.   But this was not to happen until long after
Abram was dead, for God told him he should live to be an old
man and should die in peace.

And Sarai, Abram's wife, had a handmaid; that is, a woman

who was her servant. The woman's name was Hagar; she came from Egypt, perhaps when Abram came from that country after there had been a famine in Canaan. But Hagar displeased her mistress Sarai, and Sarai was angry with her and punished her. Then Hagar fled into the lonely wilderness where no one lived, so that she might not be punished again.

And the angel of the Lord found her there by a spring of water; and he asked where she came from and to what place she was going. She answered that she had fled from her mistress Sarai. Then the angel told her to go back to her mistress and obey what she said to her; he told Hagar also that she would have a son whose name should be Ishmael, and that he would be a wild man: he would fight against other men, and other men would fight against him. So Hagar went back to Sarai, and afterward God gave her a son whose name was called Ishmael.

When Abram was ninety-nine years old God talked with him again, and Abram bowed down with his face to the ground while God talked with him. And God told him again that his descendants should be very many, and some of them, he said, should be kings. And God made a covenant, or agreement, with Abram and his descendants, and said that he would be their God. And he promised again to give them the land of Canaan for their own land. And he said to Abram, Thy name shall not any more be called Abram, but thy name shall be Abraham, which means the Father of a great many people. And Sarai's name, he said, should be Sarah, which means Princess. So the Lord changed both their names. And he promised again to give Abraham and Sarah a son, whose name should be Isaac. Then, after the Lord was done talking with him, he went up from Abraham toward heaven.

CHAPTERS XVIII–XXI (18-21)

THE LORD SENDS TWO ANGELS TO DESTROY SODOM AND GOMORRAH. LOT AND HIS TWO DAUGHTERS ARE SAVED, BUT HIS WIFE IS CHANGED INTO A PILLAR OF SALT. ISAAC IS BORN. ABRAHAM SENDS HAGAR AND ISHMAEL AWAY. THE KING OF GERAR AND ABRAHAM MAKE A COVENANT TOGETHER.

ABRAHAM was sitting one day at his tent-door, in the hot part of the day. And he looked up and saw three men standing near him. Then he ran out to meet them and bowed down before them toward the ground, for so they used to welcome strangers in that

EASTERN SALUTATIONS

land. And Abraham asked the men to rest under the tree, and to let some water be brought that they might wash their feet.

In those days people did not wear shoes such as we wear now: they went with bare feet or else wore sandals. Sandals were like the soles of our shoes, and were tied on with strings. They kept the feet from being hurt by sharp stones, but did not keep off the dust and dirt as shoes do. Therefore it was pleasant for a person, after he had been walking on a warm day, to take off his sandals and wash his feet in cool water. And Abraham asked these three men to have water that they might wash their feet. He said he would bring them some bread also; and they told him to do as he said.

And Abraham made haste into the tent to Sarah, and told her to bake some cakes quickly. And he ran to the herd and brought a calf that was tender and good, and had it killed. Then he took butter and milk, and the calf that had been cooked, and set them before the men, and they did eat, and

Abraham stood by them to wait on them, under the tree. After they had eaten, they rose up and went toward the city of Sodom, and Abraham walked with them.

ABRAHAM WAITS ON THE ANGELS UNDER THE TREE

And yet, although we call them men, these three persons were not men. Two of them, we believe, were angels, and the other one was the Lord. You may ask, Could it be the Lord who looked and talked like a man? Yes, for he could come down to this world in the form of a man. And further on in the Bible we read, several times, of his coming, and staying for a little while, and speaking to men. And long afterward, he came and stayed many years, and walked about on the earth as a man, and made sick people well, and dead people alive, and died on the cross for our sins, and then went up to heaven again.

And now the Lord was going to send his angels to burn up Sodom and Gomorrah. Gomorrah was another city near to Sodom; the Lord was going to burn up both these cities because the people who lived there were so wicked. And he was willing to tell Abraham what he would do; for Abraham loved God, and obeyed him, and taught his family to obey him. But when Abraham heard that Sodom, the city where Lot lived, was to be burned up, he felt grieved; for he feared that Lot might be burned up also. And he spoke to the Lord and said that perhaps there were some righteous persons living in the city, and he asked whether the righteous should be destroyed with the wicked. The Lord answered that if there were fifty righteous persons in the city, he would not destroy it. Then Abraham said perhaps there might be a few less than fifty; there might be forty-five. The Lord told him that if there were but ten righteous persons in Sodom, he would not destroy it.

When the Lord was done talking with Abraham, he went from him, and Abraham came back to his tent.

And Lot was sitting at the gate of Sodom in the evening. For in that country the cities had walls around them, to keep out robbers or any enemies who might come to do the people harm. And these walls had gates which were shut at night or whenever there was danger. Lot was sitting at the gate of Sodom, and two angels came there, but they looked like men. They were, we suppose, the same that had been with the Lord at Abraham's tent. When Lot saw them he rose up to meet them, and bowed down with his face toward the ground. And he asked them to come into his house and stay there all night and to wash their feet; in the morning, he said, they should go on their journey. They answered, No, we will stay in the street all night. But Lot begged them until they consented; so they came, and he set out food for them, and they did eat.

Afterward they asked whether he had any sons or daughters in the city beside those who were with him in the house; if he had, the angels said, he should go and take them out of Sodom, for the Lord had sent them to destroy it. Then Lot went and found his sons-in-law, who had married his daughters, and said to them, Up, get you out of this place, for the Lord will destroy

LOT FLEES FROM SODOM

the city. But they would not believe his words, and Lot went back to his own home without them.

When it was morning the angels said to him, Arise, take thy wife, and thy two daughters, and make haste away, lest you be burned up with the wicked people of the city. And because Lot stayed a little while, perhaps to save something out of his house, the angels caught hold of his hand, and of his wife's hand, and of his two daughters' hands, and brought them out of Sodom.

3

After they were brought out, they were commanded not to stay near, nor go slowly away, but to go very quickly, that they might not be burned. They were commanded not even to look behind them, but to make haste to the mountain where the fire could not reach them.

Now there was another city near Sodom, named Zoar; it was a little one. And Lot prayed that it might not be destroyed, because he would rather go there than up on the lonely mountain, where wild beasts or wicked men might kill him. Therefore God did not destroy that city. And Lot and his daughters fled toward Zoar, but his wife looked back toward Sodom, which she had been commanded not to do, and she died there because she looked back; and she was turned into a pillar of salt. But Lot came to Zoar, he and his daughters; the sun was risen up when they entered into Zoar.

Then the Lord rained down fire and brimstone out of heaven upon Sodom and Gomorrah, and destroyed those cities, and all the plain where they stood, and the people who lived in them, and the things which grew on the ground. Yet he saved Lot and his two daughters alive, though his wife died for her disobedience. But of all his riches that he took with him when he went from Abraham, we are not told that Lot had anything left.

Early the next morning Abraham went out from his tent and looked toward Sodom and Gomorrah, and he saw the smoke going up from the place where they had stood, like the smoke of a great furnace, but those wicked cities were not there. Then Abraham knew that God did not find even ten righteous persons in Sodom, because he had promised that if he found them he would not destroy the city.

And Abraham moved away to another part of the land of Canaan, named Gerar, where a people called the Philistines lived. And the king of Gerar gave Abraham a present of sheep and oxen, and also men-servants and maid-servants, to wait on him and work for him. And the king told Abraham he might live in any part of the land he chose.

And God gave to Abraham and Sarah the son he had promised them, and Abraham called his name Isaac, as God had

ABRAHAM SENDS HAGAR AWAY

35

commanded. Abraham was one hundred years old when Isaac was
born; and he and Sarah were glad, because God had given them
a son.   And the child grew, and when he came to be a larger
boy, Abraham made him a feast.   And Sarah saw Ishmael, Hagar's son, mocking Isaac.   Therefore Sarah was displeased with
Ishmael, and she asked Abraham to send him and his mother

THE ANGEL SPEAKS TO HAGAR

away.   But Abraham did not wish to send them away, and it
troubled him when Sarah asked him to do this.   Then God
spoke to Abraham and told him to do as Sarah had said.   So
he rose up early in the morning and took bread, and a bottle
of water, and gave them to Hagar, Ishmael's mother.

The bottles of that country were what we would call sacks, or
bags.   They were made of goat-skins, folded over and sewed
tightly together around the edges, except at the neck, which
was left open for the water to pass through.   And when Abraham

had given Hagar some bread, and a bottle of water, putting this on her shoulder, he sent her and her son away.

Then Hagar took her boy and went into the wilderness. And when all the water in the bottle was gone, and they had no more to drink, the child grew weak, and Hagar thought he would die. And she laid him under a bush, in the shade, and went a little way off and sat down and wept, for she did not want to see her boy die. And God heard her weeping; and the angel of God called to her out of heaven and said, What aileth thee, Hagar? Then the angel told her not to be afraid, but to lift up Ishmael from the place where she had laid him, and to hold him in her arms. And God showed her a well of water that was there in the wilderness, and she went to it and filled the bottle and gave her son drink, and he became strong and well again. After this God was kind to Ishmael, and he grew and lived in the wilderness and was an archer; he shot with a bow and arrow. And his mother took a wife for him out of the land of Egypt, where she used to live.

Now the king of the Philistines, in whose land Abraham was staying, saw that God was kind to Abraham and was his friend. Therefore he came and asked Abraham to promise that he would never do him or his children any harm. And Abraham promised that he would not; yet he found fault with the king because some of his servants had taken away a well of water which Abraham's servants had digged. For the rivers and streams did not run through the fields in that country as they do in ours. People had to dig in the ground to find water, and when they had found it, and made a well, that well belonged to them, and they valued it and did not like to have it taken from them.

And now Abraham said that the king's servants had taken away his well. But the king answered that he did not know who had done it and that he had never heard of it before. Then Abraham took seven lambs from his flock and set them in a place by themselves. When the king saw them, he asked why they were there. Abraham replied that those seven lambs were for the king that he might take them and keep them for his own, to make him remember that it was Abraham who had digged that well.

So the king and Abraham made an agreement, or covenant, together, to be friends with each other. And Abraham called the name of the place Beer-sheba, which means the well of the oath, or promise; because there he and the king had promised that they would do each other no harm. And Abraham planted a tree at Beer-sheba, perhaps to give a pleasant shade about the well. And there he worshipped the Lord. And he stayed in the land of the Philistines many days.

CHAPTERS XXII–XXV (22–25)

GOD COMMANDS ABRAHAM TO OFFER UP ISAAC. ABRAHAM MAKES READY TO OBEY, BUT IS FORBIDDEN BY THE ANGEL. SARAH DIES AND IS BURIED. ABRAHAM'S SERVANT IS SENT TO FIND A WIFE FOR ISAAC. ABRAHAM DIES. JACOB AND ESAU ARE BORN. ESAU SELLS HIS BIRTHRIGHT.

WE have read that Abel offered up a lamb to God, and that God was pleased with him for offering it. Noah also offered burnt offerings after he came out of the ark, and Abraham himself had built three altars in the land of Canaan and offered sacrifices upon them all.

But one day God spoke to Abraham, and said, Abraham. He answered, Here am I. Then God said, Take now thy son, thine only son Isaac, whom thou lovest, and get thee unto the land of Moriah, and offer him there for a burnt offering upon one of the mountains which I will tell thee of. Yes, Abraham was commanded to offer up Isaac upon an altar; to kill him and lay him on the wood, and let him be burned up, as if he had been a lamb. How could Abraham do this? How could he kill his own dear son? Yet God told him to do it; Abraham heard him speak. He knew that he should do whatever God said, and he knew also that even if Isaac were killed and burned on the altar, so that nothing was left but his ashes, God could take these ashes and make him alive again as he had been before.

So Abraham rose up early in the morning and saddled his ass and took two young men, who were his servants. with him.

and the wood, ready cut to lay on the altar, and Isaac his son;
and he started to go to the mountain which God had told him
of. And he journeyed that day and the next, and did not come
to the place; but on the day after, he looked up and saw it a
good way off. Then he told the young men they need go no
farther. He and Isaac, Abraham said, would go to the moun-

ABRAHAM OFFERS UP ISAAC

tain and worship and come back to them again; for he did not
wish them to see him offer up his son. And he left the ass with
the young men, but took Isaac with him, and Isaac carried the
wood. Abraham took some fire also to light the wood, and he
carried a knife in his hand; and he and Isaac went on together.

Now Isaac did not know what God had commanded his father
to do, nor what his father was taking him to the mountain for.
He knew they were going to offer up a burnt offering, for they
had the wood to burn it with, and the knife to kill it; but he

did not know that he was to be that burnt offering himself. So, as they walked together, he said to his father, My father, see the fire and the wood, but where is the lamb for a burnt offering? Abraham answered, My son, God will find himself a lamb for a burnt offering.

And they came to the place which God had told him of; there Abraham built an altar and laid the wood on it. And he bound Isaac and laid him on the wood; and Abraham put out his hand and took hold of the knife to kill his son. But just then the angel of the Lord called to him out of heaven, and said Abraham, Abraham. He answered, Here am I. And the angel told him not to hurt Isaac, for now he knew that Abraham feared God, because he was willing to offer up his only son when God commanded him. And Abraham looked and saw behind him a ram caught fast in the bushes by its horns. God had sent it there for a burnt offering instead of Isaac; and Abraham took it and killed it, and offered it up on the altar.

And God was pleased with Abraham; and the angel of the Lord spoke to him again out of heaven, and told him that because he had obeyed God, and been willing to offer up his son, God would bless him. And the angel promised him that his descendants should be like the grains of sand on the sea-shore, which no one can count, there are so many of them. The angel said to him, also, In thy seed shall all the nations of the earth be blessed. This meant that the Saviour whom God had promised should be descended from Abraham. So Abraham brought Isaac and came to the young men who were waiting for him, and they went back together to Beer-sheba where Abraham lived.

After these things Abraham left Beer-sheba and came to Hebron. And Sarah, Abraham's wife, was a hundred and twenty-seven years old, and she died there in the land of Canaan. Then Abraham mourned and wept for her. And he spoke to the people of that country, and asked them for a place where he might bury Sarah. They answered that he might bury her in any of their sepulchres that he chose.

Sepulchres are places in which dead persons are buried. In that country they were made by hollowing out a cave in the side of a rock. After this was finished, a great stone was rolled against the door to shut it up. When any one died the stone was taken away and the dead person was laid in the cave. Then the stone was put back again and the cave shut up until some one else was to be buried there. It was very kind in the men of the country to tell Abraham he might bury his wife in any of their sepulchres. But this was not what he wanted; he wanted a sepulchre of his own.

And there was a man in that land whose name was Ephron. He owned a field; this field had trees in it, and at one end of it was a cave. Abraham thought he would like to have that cave for the sepulchre. So he asked the people to tell Ephron that he wanted it, and would give him money for it. When Ephron heard this he said that Abraham might have the cave for nothing, and not the cave only, he would give him the field also.

But Abraham bowed himself down before Ephron and the men who were with him, and answered that he would rather buy the field and pay for it; he did not want to take it for nothing. Then Ephron said he was willing to sell it;

ABRAHAM BUYS THE CAVE OF EPHRON.

and Abraham gave him four hundred shekels of silver for the field, and the trees that were in it, and the cave. Shekels were money; so Abraham paid for the field, and the trees, and the cave, and they were his own after that. And he made the cave his sepulchre, and there he buried Sarah.

And Abraham was old, and the Lord had blessed him in all things. And when Isaac was grown up to be a man, Abraham, his father, did not wish him to take a wife from the women who lived in the land of Canaan, for they worshipped idols. He wanted Isaac to have his wife from that country where Abraham used to live, and where he had relations still living who feared the Lord.

Now that country was a long way from Canaan; so Abraham called his oldest servant, who took care of his silver and gold, his flocks and his herds, and all that he had, and asked him to promise that he would go to that country and bring back from there a wife for Isaac. Then the servant said that, perhaps, the woman would not be willing to come. But Abraham told him that God would send an angel before him, to help him, and that he would be able to find there a wife for Isaac. Yet if the woman should not be willing to come, Abraham said, he would excuse the servant from his promise. And the servant promised to do as Abraham commanded.

So he took ten of Abraham's camels and some beautiful presents, and went on his journey to the land where Abraham had sent him. And he came near to a city in that land and made his camels kneel down by a well of water that was just outside of the city. Camels are used in that country to ride upon, as horses are here; they carry heavy loads also on their backs, and go a long way without resting. Before they start upon a journey they kneel down to have their loads put on them, and when they come to the end of it, they kneel down to have them taken off.

It was evening, the time when the women of the city came out to draw water from the well. Then Abraham's servant prayed that God would help him, and make him know which of those young women that came to draw water should be Isaac's wife. But how would the servant know? In this way. He was going to ask one of them to give him some water out of her pitcher. If she answered him kindly and said, Drink, and I will give thy camels drink also, then she was to be the one whom God had chosen for Isaac's wife. But if she answered unkindly and would give him no water, she was not to be the one.

So while he was praying, a beautiful young woman, named Rebekah, came out of the city, carrying her pitcher upon her shoulder, and she went down to the well and filled it with water and came up again.   And the servant ran to meet her and said, Let me drink a little water out of thy pitcher; she answered, Drink, and I will draw water for thy camels also.   And she let down her pitcher from her shoulder and gave the man drink;

ABRAHAM'S SERVANT MEETS REBEKAH

afterward she ran to the well and drew water for the camels, and they drank too. Then the servant stood still, wondering whether she was the one whom God had chosen to be Isaac's wife or not.

After the camels had done drinking, the man took an earring of gold and two bracelets of gold, and gave them to Rebekah. And he asked whose daughter she was, and whether there was room at her father's house for him and the men who were with him to sleep there. Then Rebekah told him that she was the daughter of Bethuel; she said also that they had room at their house, and food and straw for the camels. When the servant heard that she was Bethuel's daughter, he knew she was one of Abraham's relations, for Abraham was Bethuel's uncle. And he was glad, and bowed down his head and worshipped the Lord, and thanked him for helping him to find his master's relations who lived so far away.

Then Rebekah left the servant and ran to her home and told her mother about all these things. And she had a brother whose name was Laban. When Laban heard what she said, and saw the earring and the bracelets, he ran out of the city to the man, and found him standing by his camels at the well. And Laban asked him to come to their house, and said he had made it ready for him, and that there was room for the camels. And the man went with Laban, and Laban helped him to unload the camels, and gave him straw and food for them, and he gave the men water to wash their feet. Afterward there was food set before Abraham's servant that he might eat. But he said he would not eat until he had told them what he came to their country for.

Then he said that he was Abraham's servant, and that the Lord had blessed Abraham and made him great. He had given him silver and gold, and flocks, and herds, and camels, and asses; and he had given him a son also. And all his riches, the servant said, Abraham had given to his son Isaac. And he told them that Abraham had sent him into their country to find a wife for Isaac. And he had come to the well that day, and prayed that God would make him know which was the young woman who should be Isaac's wife; he had prayed that she might answer him kindly when he should ask her for a little water to drink, and so he would know that she was the one. And while he was praying, he said, Rebekah came out, and when he asked her for drink, she answered him kindly, saying, Drink, and I will give thy camels drink also.

Then the servant asked them whether they would let Rebekah go home with him to be Isaac's wife or not. They answered that

it was the Lord who had done all these things, Rebekah might
go.   When the servant heard this he was glad, and bowed himself down to the ground and worshipped the Lord.   Afterward
he brought out more beautiful presents, jewels of silver, and
jewels of gold, and raiment, and gave them to Rebekah.   And
he gave her mother and her brother presents also.   Then he did

REBEKAH SEES ISAAC IN THE FIELD

eat and drink, he and the men that were with him, and they
stayed at Laban's house all night.

When they rose up in the morning, Abraham's servant wanted
to take Rebekah and go on his way back to the land of Canaan.
But her mother and her brother did not wish to part with her
so soon; they said, Let her stay with us a few days, at least ten,
after that she shall go.   But the man begged them not to keep
him, because, he said, the Lord had helped him to do what his

master sent him for; therefore he wanted to make haste home to his master again. They said, We will call Rebekah, and ask her. And they called her and asked, Wilt thou go with this man? She answered, I will go. So they sent away Rebekah, and her nurse went with her, and they rode on the camels after Abraham's servant.

And they came into the land of Canaan. It was toward evening, about the time the sun goes down, when they came to the place where Isaac was. And Isaac had gone out into the field to walk there, and think by himself alone. Perhaps he wondered whether the servant would soon be back, and whether the Lord had helped him to find the woman who should be his wife. And he looked up and saw the camels were coming. As they came nearer Rebekah saw Isaac, and she asked the servant what man it was walking in the field to meet them. The servant told her it was Isaac. Then she took a veil and covered her face with it, and came down from the camel; and Isaac brought her into the tent that used to be his mother's, for his mother was dead. And he took Rebekah and she was his wife, and he loved her.

And Abraham gave all that he had to Isaac. And when he was a hundred and seventy-five years old he died, and was buried in the cave which he had bought from Ephron, where he had buried Sarah.

After Abraham was dead, God was very kind to Isaac and blessed him. And he gave Isaac and Rebekah two sons, whose names were Jacob and Esau; Esau was the elder, and Jacob was the younger. Now in those days the eldest son in every family had what was called the birthright. This made him the chief one among all the children; he was greater than any of the others. And when his father died he got more of the silver and gold and cattle that had been his father's than the others did; he got twice as much as any of them because he had the birthright. And Esau was Isaac's eldest son, and therefore had the birthright.

When Esau and Jacob grew up to be men, Esau was a hunter; he went out into the fields and woods, and killed deer, and brought the meat home to his father, because his father loved to eat of it. But Jacob lived at home in a tent, and helped to take care of his father's flocks. And one day Jacob made food called pottage. And Esau came in from his hunting very weary and faint, and he asked Jacob to give him his pottage. Jacob told him he would do so if Esau would sell him his birthright. Then Esau, because he felt weak and sick, said that he was going to die, and that his birthright would do him no good, so he sold it to Jacob, and Jacob gave him the pottage for it. It was wrong in Esau to sell his birthright; God had given it to him, and he should not have sold it; and it was wrong for Jacob, in this way, to take it from him.

CHAPTERS XXVI–XXXI (26–31)

ISAAC GOES TO GERAR AND AFTERWARD TO BEER-SHEBA. JACOB TAKES AWAY ESAU'S BLESSING. HE FLEES FROM ESAU; HIS DREAM. HE COMES TO LABAN'S HOUSE AND MARRIES LEAH AND RACHEL. HE STARTS ON HIS JOURNEY BACK TO CANAAN. LABAN FOLLOWS HIM.

THERE was a famine in the land of Canaan, and Isaac moved away to Gerar. It was the same place his father Abraham had moved to, many years before, after Sodom was destroyed. And when Isaac came to Gerar, the Lord spoke to him and told him to sojourn, or stay for a while, in that part of the land, and the Lord said he would bless him. And Isaac sowed seed out in the field, and when the grain grew up, he reaped a hundred times as much as he had sowed, because the Lord made it grow well and bear a great deal for him.

And the Lord made him very rich and great, and gave him flocks of sheep and herds of cattle, and a great many servants. But the people called Philistines, who lived in Gerar, were not pleased to see him so much richer than themselves; they envied him, and wished they had his flocks and herds for their own. And the king of the country came to him and told him to go away from them.

So Isaac went away from that place and came to a valley and set up a tent there. And he found the wells that his father

Abraham had digged when he was in Gerar, but the Philistines had filled them with earth, so that he could get no water from them. Then Isaac took the earth out of them; and his servants dug a new well, but the herdsmen of that country came and said it belonged to them, and they quarrelled for it, and took it for their own. And so they did with another well that Isaac dug. Then he went to a different place and his servants dug a well there; the herdsmen did not take this one from him. Afterward Isaac moved to Beer-sheba, which was the place where his father Abraham had once lived, and where he had digged a well. And in the night the Lord spoke to Isaac and told him not to fear, for he would be with him to take care of him and bless him. And Isaac built an altar and worshipped the Lord, and set up his tent there.

And the king of the Philistines came from Gerar, with two of his friends, to visit Isaac. Isaac asked them why they came to him, when they hated him, and had sent him away from their country. They answered that they wanted him to promise he would do them no harm; for they saw, by all the good things the Lord did for him, that the Lord was his friend. And Isaac was kind to them. He made a feast for the king and the men who were with him, and they did eat and drink, and stayed all night. And Isaac promised he would do them no harm, and they promised to do him none. So Isaac and the king made a covenant together; then the king and his friends went away to their own homes.

And Isaac's servants digged a well at Beer-sheba, and they came to him and said, We have found water. They were glad, for sometimes the water was very deep in the ground, and they had to dig a long time before they found it.

And Esau, Jacob's brother, when he was forty years old, took two of the women of Canaan for his wives. But his father and mother were much grieved because he did this; for, as we have been told, the women of Canaan worshipped idols.

Now Isaac was old and could not see, and he called Esau and told him to take his bow, and go out into the field, and hunt a deer; and to cook the meat in the way that Isaac loved, and bring it to him that he might eat of it. Then, Isaac said, he would bless Esau before he died; that is, he would ask God to be kind to him, and would tell Esau of the things he should have after his father was dead. For Isaac meant to bless Esau before he blessed Jacob, and to give him the best things, because

JACOB TAKES ESAU'S BLESSING

Esau was his oldest son and had the birthright. And Esau went out into the field to hunt the deer for his father.

But Rebekah heard what Isaac said and she was not pleased, for she did not wish Esau to be blessed first, although he was the oldest son; she wished Jacob to be blessed first, because she loved him the best. So, after Esau had gone for the venison, she told Jacob to go to the flock and bring her two little kids: and when he brought them, she cooked them, making nice food of them that tasted like the venison which his father loved.

Then she put on Jacob some of Esau's clothes that were in the house, and told him to take the food to his father, and to say it was Esau who brought it.

So Jacob came to his father with the food which his mother had cooked. And his father asked who it was. Jacob said it was Esau and that he had brought the venison which his father told him to bring. And Isaac could not see; he put his hands on him and felt the clothes and believed it was Esau, so he ate of the meat and blessed Jacob. It was wicked in Jacob to do this, and in his mother to help him; for although Esau had sold him his birthright, Jacob should not have deceived his father.

As soon as Isaac had done blessing Jacob, Esau came in from his hunting, with the venison he had killed. And Isaac said, Who art thou? Esau answered, I am Esau, thy oldest son. And Isaac was surprised and afraid, and he trembled a great deal, and asked who it was that had been there before, and brought venison and taken Esau's blessing. Then Isaac knew it must have been Jacob, and he told Esau that his brother had been there before him and taken away his blessing.

Then Esau was in great trouble. He cried with a loud voice and begged his father to bless him also. And Isaac did bless him, but he had promised the best things to Jacob, and now he could not take them from him. And Esau hated Jacob for what he had done, and said to himself, My father will soon die and then I will kill Jacob. For Esau was not a good man, he did not love God.

When a good man has been tempted, and done some wicked thing, after he has done it he repents of it and asks God to forgive him, and tries to do so no more. But when a bad man has done wickedly, he does not repent and ask to be forgiven; he goes on and does as wickedly again. Though Jacob did evil at this time, he was afterward a good man; he loved and served God as long as he lived, and God forgave him his sin. But Esau was not willing to forgive Jacob; he said he would kill him after his father should die. When Rebekah heard this she sent for Jacob, and told him to leave his home and go

JACOB'S DREAM

to that country where she used to live, to the house of her brother Laban, so that Esau might not find him.

And Rebekah said that the women of Canaan gave her much trouble, for Esau had taken two of them as his wives; and she asked what good her life would be to her if Jacob also should take a wife from among them. Then Isaac called Jacob to him and blessed him again, and told him that he should not take for his wife a woman of Canaan, but he should take one of Laban's daughters to be his wife. And Isaac sent Jacob away, and he went out from his father to go to that country where Laban lived.

As he journeyed he came to a place where he stopped to rest for the night, because the sun was set. And he took some of the stones that were on the ground for his pillow, and lay down to sleep. And he dreamed, and thought he saw a ladder set up on the earth; the top of it reached to heaven, and angels were going up and down on it. And the Lord stood above it, and spoke to Jacob, and told him that he would give the land of Canaan to him and to his descendants, and that his descendants should be a great multitude of people. And the Lord said he would be with Jacob to take care of him wherever he should go, and would bring him back to Canaan again.

And Jacob awaked out of his sleep and was afraid, because the Lord had been there and spoken to him in his dream: and he rose up early in the morning and worshipped the Lord. He called the name of the place Bethel, which means, The house of God. And Jacob promised that if the Lord would take care of him, and give him bread to eat and clothes to wear, and keep him from harm, so that he should come back safely to his father's house again, then he would obey the Lord; and of all the silver and gold, the flocks and the herds, which God should give him, he would give a tenth part to the Lord. Jacob could not give these things into the Lord's hand, but he could help the poor and the sick with them, and build altars and offer burnt offerings with them, and that would be the same as giving them into the Lord's hand.

And Jacob went on his journey until he came near to Haran.

where Laban lived. And he saw there a well in a field, with three flocks of sheep lying down by it, and the shepherds were with their flocks. A great stone was rolled over the mouth of the well, to cover it; but when the flocks had come in from feeding, the shepherds used to roll the stone away and draw up water for the sheep. After they were done drinking, the stone was rolled back again over the mouth of the well.

JACOB MEETS RACHEL

And Jacob asked the shepherds where their home was. They said at Haran. Then he said, Do you know Laban? They answered, We know him. And Jacob asked if he was well. They said, He is well; and look, Rachel his daughter is coming with the sheep. While they were speaking, Rachel came with her father's sheep, for she took care of them. And Jacob went near and rolled away the stone and watered the flock for her; and he kissed Rachel, and told her he was her relation and Rebekah's son, and she ran and told her father.

When Laban heard that his sister Rebekah's son was come, he made haste and ran out to meet him, and put his arms around him and kissed him, and brought him to his house. And Laban spoke kindly to Jacob, and Jacob stayed at his house for a month. Then Laban asked Jacob how much he should pay him to stay and live there, and take care of his flock. And Laban had another daughter beside Rachel, whose name was Leah; but Ra-

LABAN ENGAGES JACOB

chel was more beautiful than Leah. Now Jacob loved Rachel, and he told Laban he would stay and serve him for seven years if, after they were ended, Rachel might be his wife. And Laban said she might be; therefore Jacob served Laban seven years for her, and they seemed like only a few days to him, because of the love he felt for her. But when they were ended Laban would not give him Rachel, because she was the youngest. He gave him Leah, and said that Jacob must serve seven years more for Rachel; for the youngest, he said, must not be married before the oldest. So Jacob stayed and served Laban seven years longer, and he had both Leah and Rachel for his wives. And God gave sons to him.

After this Jacob asked permission of Laban to take his wives and his children, and go back to the land of Canaan. For he wanted to see his father and mother if they were still alive; and he thought, perhaps, that after so long a time, Esau would forgive the unkindness he had done him when he took away his blessing.

But Laban was not willing to let Jacob go. He had found, he said, that the Lord blessed him because Jacob was with him, and he asked what wages he should give Jacob to stay longer. Jacob said that if Laban would give him some of the cattle which he took care of, he would stay and feed his flock as he had done before. Therefore Laban gave Jacob some of his cattle, and he stayed and took care of Laban's flock. Then Jacob had sheep and goats of his own. These he kept separate from Laban's, and put them in a different place. It took three days to go from Laban's flock to the place where Jacob kept his flock. And Jacob's flock grew to be a great many, so that after a while he was rich, and had herds of cattle, and his sons took care of them. And Jacob had men-servants and maid-servants, and camels and asses.

But one day Jacob heard Laban's sons speaking unkindly of him. They said he had taken away their father's cattle, and that was the reason he had grown so rich. And Jacob saw that Laban did not look on him as kindly as he used to do. His face was changed and he looked displeased.

And the Lord spoke to Jacob and commanded him to go back to the land of his fathers; that meant, to the land of Canaan, where Abraham, his grandfather, had lived when he was alive, and where Isaac, his father, was living still. And the Lord said he would be with Jacob, to take care of him and keep him from harm. Then Jacob sent and called Rachel and Leah to him while he was out in the field with his flock. He wanted to talk with them there, so that Laban could not hear what he said

When they came he told them that their father did not look kindly on him as he used to look, and that the Lord had commanded him to go back to Canaan. And Rachel and Leah told him to do as the Lord commanded.

And Jacob made ready to go. He set his wives and his children upon camels, and took all his cattle and every thing that belonged to him, and started on his journey toward the land of

JACOB RETURNING TO CANAAN

Canaan. But Laban had gone away from his home to shear his sheep, and he did not know when Jacob left, because Jacob had kept it a secret from him. But on the third day after he had gone, some one told Laban of it. Then Laban took men with him and followed after Jacob. No doubt he was angry, and wanted to do him some harm; but in the night. in a dream, God spoke to Laban and told him not to harm Jacob nor speak unkindly to him. And Laban did not overtake Jacob until he had been following him seven days; for Jacob had gone a long way, across a river and through a wide lonely country, to a mountain called Gilead. There Laban came up with him.

Now Jacob had set up his tent at mount Gilead, and when Laban came there he set up his tent also. And he asked Jacob why he had gone away secretly, and carried Rachel and Leah and their children with him, without letting him know; for Laban said, he had not allowed him to kiss his sons and his daughters before they went. Jacob answered that he had gone away secretly because he was afraid Laban would take Rachel and Leah from him if he knew he was going. And Jacob was displeased at Laban for coming after him, and asked why he had followed him. Jacob said that he had served Laban for twenty years, taking care of his sheep and his goats. He had been out in the night and in the day, when it was cold and when it was hot, watching over them. And now, he said, if God had not been with him to help him, Laban would have sent him away without giving him anything for all the work he had done.

Then Laban spoke kindly to Jacob, and said, Thy wives and thy children are the same to me as if they were my own, and I would not do them any harm. Let us, therefore, be friends and make a covenant together. And they piled up stones and made a heap of them in that place, and promised they would do each other no harm. That heap was always to stay there to remind them of the covenant they had made. If ever they should be angry and want to harm each other, then, as they were going to do it, when they came to that heap and saw the stones there, they would remember their covenant and turn back, and never harm each other any more.

And Jacob built an altar and offered up a sacrifice on mount Gilead, and he and Laban, and the men who were with him, ate bread together, and they stayed all night in the mount. Early in the morning Laban rose up and kissed Rachel and Leah and their children and blessed them, and then went back to his own home.

CHAPTERS XXXII–XXXVI (32–36)

JACOB SENDS MESSENGERS, AND A PRESENT, TO ESAU. HE WRESTLES AT
PENIEL. THE MEETING OF JACOB AND ESAU. JACOB COMES TO BETHEL
AND AFTERWARD TO HIS FATHER IN CANAAN. BENJAMIN IS BORN.
DEBORAH AND RACHEL AND ISAAC DIE. ESAU MOVES AWAY TO EDOM.

JACOB left mount Gilead, and went toward Canaan. As he
went some angels met him. Jacob called them God's host,
or army. Perhaps God had sent them to take care of him on his
journey. And he came near to the place where his brother Esau
was, and sent messengers to tell him that he had been living with
Laban until that time, and had oxen and asses and flocks, and
men-servants and maid-servants. He sent to tell Esau about it,
he said, so that Esau might not be angry with him. For Jacob
was afraid of Esau. Though it had been twenty years since he
deceived his father and took away Esau's blessing, yet Jacob remembered his sin and it made him afraid.

And the messengers returned to Jacob and told him that Esau
was coming with four hundred men to meet him. Then Jacob
was in great fear; he took his flocks, and his herds, and his
camels, and made two companies of them instead of one large
company; and some of Jacob's men went with one company and
some with the other. And Jacob told them that if Esau came
to hurt or kill one company, the other must make haste and
flee away.

And Jacob prayed that God would save him from Esau; for
he was afraid that Esau would kill him, and his wives, and his
children. Jacob said that the Lord had been very kind to him,
and that he did not deserve the good things which God had
given him; for when he left Canaan, twenty years before, he had
only the staff which he carried in his hand. But now, when
he was coming back, he had two companies, or bands, of men,
with flocks and herds and camels. Then he was very poor, but
now God had made him rich.

Jacob stayed in that place all night. And he took some of
his cattle and sent them as a present to Esau: two hundred and

twenty goats, two hundred and twenty sheep, thirty camels with their colts, forty cows and ten bulls, and twenty asses with ten little ones. But he did not send all of these together; he made different droves, or flocks, of them, and sent each drove by itself. Then when Esau should meet the first drove, and ask the man who was driving it whose cattle they were, and where they were going, the man was to say, They are thy servant Jacob's; it is a present he has sent to my lord Esau. When Esau should meet the next drove, and ask the same questions, the man driving it was to answer as the first had done. And so they were all to answer, till Esau should have seen every drove. Jacob sent them to make Esau feel kindly toward him, so that he might not hurt him, or his wives, or his children, or take his flocks or his herds from him.

And Jacob rose up in the night, and sent his two wives and his eleven sons over the stream of water that was there; and he was left alone. And there came a man and wrestled with him, putting his arms around him and trying to throw him down, and Jacob put his arms around the man. So they wrestled together till the light of the morning shone a little in the sky. When the man saw that Jacob did not fall, but was strong, and wrestled on still, he touched Jacob's thigh; and just by his touch Jacob's thigh was put out of joint, and he was lame.

And the man said, Let me go, for the day breaketh. But Jacob said, I will not let thee go, except thou bless me. The man asked, What is thy name? and he told him, Jacob. Then the man said, Thy name shall no more be called Jacob, but Israel; which means, A Prince of God: and the reason he changed Jacob's name was that Jacob wrestled with him so long to get his blessing. For this man was the same as the one who had talked with Abraham, and told him he would destroy Sodom and Gomorrah: this man was the Lord. And Jacob said to him, Tell me, I pray thee, thy name. But the Lord answered, Why dost thou ask after my name? And the Lord blessed Jacob there. And Jacob said, I have seen God. And he named that place Peniel; which means, The face of God. For Jacob said, I have seen God face to face. And as he crossed the stream the sun rose up, and he was lame in his thigh where the Lord had touched him.

And Jacob looked up and saw Esau coming, and four hundred men with him. Then he took his eleven sons, and gave some of them to the two handmaids and the others to Rachel and Leah, that they might bring them to Esau when he should

JACOB WRESTLES WITH THE ANGEL

come near. But Jacob went on first by himself to meet his brother, and, as he went, he bowed down to the ground seven times before him. Then when Esau saw this he ran to meet Jacob, and put his arms around him, and leaned on his neck and kissed him; and they both wept.

We have read that when God commanded Jacob to leave Laban's house and go back to Canaan, he promised to be with him and keep him from harm. And we have seen how God kept his promise; for, first, he would not let Laban hurt, or even speak unkindly to Jacob, and now he made Esau, that angry brother who had wanted to kill him, feel so kindly toward him that when they met, he ran to him and kissed him, and wept, leaning on his neck.

When Esau saw the women and the children, he said, Who are these with thee?   Jacob answered, The children whom God

THE MEETING OF JACOB AND ESAU

hath given thy servant.   Then the handmaids, and Leah, and Rachel came near, bringing the children with them, and they bowed down before Esau.   And Esau asked Jacob what he meant by all those cattle he had met.   Jacob answered he had sent them as a present, so that Esau might be pleased with him. And Esau said I have enough, my brother; keep what thou hast to thyself; for Esau had flocks and herds of his own.   But Jacob said, I pray thee take my present; and he begged him till Esau took it.

Then Esau wanted Jacob to go on his journey and wait no longer at that place. If he would do this, Esau said he would go with him. But Jacob told Esau that his children were young and weak, and might easily be made sick; and that his flocks and herds had to be driven very carefully, because if they were made to go too far or too fast, for only one day, many of them would die. And he begged Esau to go on first by himself, and Jacob said he would come after him more slowly, as the children and cattle were able to bear it.

Then Esau offered to leave some of his men with Jacob; they could help him to drive his cattle, or defend him if robbers should attack him by the way; but Jacob said that he did not need them. So Esau left him and went away to his own home. After he had gone Jacob went on his journey till he came to a place called Succoth; there he stopped and made booths for his cattle to rest in. Booths were sheds, or huts, made out of the branches of trees. When his cattle had rested Jacob left Succoth and came into the land of Canaan.

And God spoke to him, and told him to go up to Bethel and build an altar there. Bethel was the place where Jacob had his dream, and saw the ladder reaching to heaven, with the angels going up and down on it. God had promised in that dream to be with him wherever he should go, and to bring him back to Canaan; and now God brought him back. Although it was more than twenty years since he went away, the Lord had taken care of him all that time, and at last brought him safely to his own land. And God told Jacob to go up to the place where the promise was given him, and there to build an altar to the Lord.

Then Jacob said to Rachel and Leah, and to his sons, Let us go up to Bethel, and I will build there an altar unto God. And he told them how kind the Lord had been to him many years before, when he was in trouble, and was fleeing from his brother Esau; and how the Lord had been with him ever since that time to take care of him in the way that he went. And Jacob, and his wives, and his sons journeyed toward Bethel. There were cities in the land they passed through, but God made the people who lived in them afraid, so that they did not come out to do Jacob any harm.　And he came to Bethel, he and all who were with him, and there he built an altar and offered up a sacrifice to the Lord.

And Rebekah, Jacob's mother, had a nurse, named Deborah. Perhaps she was the same that Rebekah brought with her when she came into Canaan with Abraham's servant, to be Isaac's wife. And Deborah, Rebekah's nurse, died, and they buried her under an oak at Bethel.

And God spoke to Jacob, and blessed him, and said again, Thy name shall not be called Jacob any more, but Israel shall be thy name.　God told him also that he would give the land of Canaan to him, and to his descendants after he should die, and that his descendants should be so many there would be whole nations of them, and that some of them should be kings.　After he was done talking to Jacob, God went up toward heaven. And Jacob set up a pillar of stone at Bethel, so that it might always be remembered as the place where God had spoken to him.

And Jacob left Bethel, and came near to Bethlehem, and God gave him another son, whose name was called Benjamin. But Rachel, the little boy's mother, died before they came to Bethlehem, and they buried her on the way there.　And Jacob set up a pillar upon Rachel's grave to show where she was buried, and that pillar stood there for hundreds of years.

After these things Jacob came to Hebron, where his father lived; for Isaac, Jacob's father, was still alive.　Though it had been so long a time since he was old and blind, and since he had sent Esau for the venison, that he might bless him, because he thought he was going to die, yet God had kept Isaac alive till Jacob came again.　But after Jacob had come, and when Isaac was a hundred and eighty years old, he died, and his sons Jacob and Esau buried him in the cave where Abraham and Sarah were buried.

And Esau took his wives, and his sons, and his daughters, and his cattle, and all that he had in the land of Canaan, and went away to live in another country, called Edom.　For he and Jacob had so many cattle that there was not food enough for them all in the land where they both had lived.

CHAPTERS XXXVII–XLI (37–41)

JOSEPH IS HATED BY HIS BRETHREN. THEY SELL HIM TO THE ISHMAEL-
ITES, WHO CARRY HIM INTO EGYPT. POTIPHAR PUTS HIM IN PRISON.
HE INTERPRETS THE DREAMS OF THE CHIEF BUTLER AND BAKER, AND
OF KING PHARAOH; AND IS MADE RULER OVER EGYPT.

JACOB had twelve sons: Benjamin, who was born near Bethlehem after Jacob came back to Canaan, was the youngest of
them all, and Joseph was next to the youngest. Joseph was
seventeen years old, and one day he went out in the field with his
brethren to feed his father's flock. And he came home to his
father and told him of some wicked thing that his brethren
had done. It was right in him to tell of it, so that his father
might speak with his brethren about it, and command them to
do so no more.

Now Jacob loved Joseph more than all his other children, because God had given Joseph to him when he was an old man.
Yet it was not only for this he loved him the most, but also because Joseph was more obedient and kind than his other children.
And the Bible says that Jacob made him a coat of many colors.
We cannot tell what kind of a coat this was, except that it was
different from the coats his brethren wore and more beautiful
than theirs.

When his brethren saw how much their father loved Joseph
they hated him, and could not speak peaceably to him. And
Joseph dreamed a dream, and told it to his brethren, and they
hated him yet the more. He said to them, Hear, I pray you,
this dream which I have dreamed. We were binding sheaves
in the field (sheaves are large bundles of grain), and my sheaf
rose and stood up, and your sheaves stood round about and
they bowed down to my sheaf. Then his brethren were angry,
because, if their sheaves bowed down to Joseph's sheaf, it seemed
to mean that they were to bow down to Joseph. And they said
to him, Shalt thou, indeed, rule over us?

And he dreamed yet another dream, and told it to his brethren, and said, I have dreamed a dream more. The sun, and
the moon, and the eleven stars bowed down to me. Now there

were just eleven of Joseph's brethren, so they thought the eleven stars meant them, and the sun and moon meant their father and mother. And they were displeased at Joseph, because it seemed as if some day he would be greater than they. He told this dream to his father also, and his father found fault with him, and said, Shall I, and thy mother, and thy brethren come to bow down ourselves to thee to the earth?

And his brethren went to feed their father's flock at Shechem; Shechem was a good way from Hebron, where Jacob lived. And Jacob said to Joseph, Do not thy brethren feed the flock in Shechem? Come, and I will send thee to them. And Joseph was willing to go. Then his father said, Go see whether it is well with thy brethren, and well with the flocks, and bring me word again. So Jacob sent Joseph away from Hebron to Shechem, where his brethren fed the flock.

And Joseph came to Shechem, but his brethren were not there. As he was wandering in the field, a man found him, and said to him, What seekest thou? Joseph said, I seek my brethren; tell me, I pray thee, where they feed their flocks? The man answered, They are gone from here, for I heard them say, Let us go to Dothan. Dothan was still farther off than Shechem: so Joseph went after his brethren and came toward Dothan. And when they saw him coming, even while he was yet a good way off, they began to talk with each other about killing him. They said to one another, See, this dreamer comes; now let us kill him, and throw him into some pit, and we will say some evil beast has devoured him, and we shall see what will become of his dreams.

When Reuben, one of his brethren, heard what they said, he wanted to save Joseph from them; so he persuaded them to put him into the pit without harming him: he said, Lower him into this pit that is in the wilderness, but do not hurt him. Reuben thought that afterward he would come back, when the others were gone, and take Joseph out and bring him home to his father. So they concluded to do as Reuben said. And when Joseph came to them, they stripped off his coat of many colors that was on him, and took him and put him into the pit: there is often water at the bottom of deep pits in the ground, but this one was dry, there was no water in it.

And they sat down to eat their food. But looking up, they saw some men, called Ishmaelites, coming that way with their camels: these men were merchantmen who carried things to sell, and they were going down into Egypt. When Judah, an-

JOSEPH SOLD BY HIS BRETHREN

other of Joseph's brethren, saw them, he asked what good there would be in killing Joseph. Come, let us sell him to the Ishmaelites, he said; and his brethren were willing to do it.

Then the Ishmaelites with their camels came by, and Joseph's brethren lifted him out of the pit, and sold him for twenty pieces of silver; and the Ishmaelites took him and carried him down into Egypt. But Reuben, the one who had wanted to take him back to his father, was not there when his brethren sold him;

afterward he went to the pit to find Joseph, and when he could not, he was greatly distressed: and he came and told his brethren, and said, Joseph is taken away; and I, where shall I go?

And Joseph's brethren took his coat, and killed a kid and dipped the coat in its blood. Then they brought it to their father, and told him they had found it; he could tell, they said, whether it was Joseph's coat or not. And Jacob knew it, and said, It is my son's coat, an evil beast has devoured him. Joseph is, without doubt, torn in pieces.

Then Jacob rent his clothes. The men of that country dressed in clothes different from ours. They wore a long coat, or sack, made of linen. It reached from the neck down below the knees, and was fastened around the waist with a belt or girdle. Over this coat they wore a loose garment, like a shawl or blanket. When in great distress they sometimes took hold of the linen coat, and tore it from the neck down to the girdle. This was called rending the clothes. And Jacob rent his clothes, because he thought Joseph was torn in pieces. He put on sackcloth also. Sackcloth was a dark, coarse kind of cloth, which persons wore to show they were in trouble. Jacob was in great trouble for many days, and no one could persuade him to stop mourning; for he said that he would mourn till he should go down into the grave to Joseph; he meant till he himself should die.

EASTERN GARMENTS

And the Ishmaelites brought Joseph down into Egypt. The king of that country was named Pharaoh, and he had an officer in his army whose name was Potiphar. Potiphar bought Joseph of the Ishmaelites, and Joseph was Potiphar's servant, and lived in his house. And the Lord helped Joseph in serving his master, so that his master was pleased with him, and set him over his other servants. Joseph had the care of his house, and of every thing in it, for his master trusted Joseph with all that he had. And the Lord blessed Potiphar, because Joseph was with him.

But after a while Potiphar's wife persuaded her husband that Joseph was a wicked man. Then Potiphar took him and put him in prison, where the king's prisoners were kept. But the Lord was kind to Joseph, and made the keeper of the prison his friend, so that he set Joseph over the other prisoners as Potiphar had set him over his other servants. The keeper gave the care of all the men in the prison to him, neither did he watch over them any longer himself; he let Joseph do it for him. And the Lord helped Joseph to do all things well.

And two of king Pharaoh's servants offended him; one was his chief baker, who attended to cooking his food, and the other was his chief butler, who carried his wine-cup to him when he wanted to drink. Pharaoh was displeased with them both, and put them into the prison where Joseph was, and Joseph had the care of them there. And each of these men dreamed a dream the same night, and when Joseph came in to them in the morning, he saw they looked sad. Then he asked them, Why look ye so sadly to-day? They answered, We have dreamed a dream, and there is no interpreter of it; that is, no one to explain what it means; for an interpreter is a person who explains to us something which we do not understand. And Joseph asked the men if God could not interpret all things; and he told them to tell him their dreams.

So the chief butler told his dream to Joseph. He said that he thought he saw a vine, and on the vine were three branches. While he was looking, there came out buds on the branches, and very soon these buds changed into bunches of ripe grapes. And the butler thought he was holding Pharaoh's wine-cup in his hand, so he took the grapes and pressed the juice out of them into the cup, and gave the cup to Pharaoh that he might drink. This was the chief butler's dream.

And Joseph interpreted it to him, for God showed Joseph what the dream meant. He said the three branches which the butler saw on the vine, meant three days; for within three days, Pharaoh would send and take him out of prison, and bring him to the king's house again.   And there he should wait on the king and give the cup into his hand, as he used to do when he was butler before.   Then Joseph asked the chief butler to remember him when he should come to the king's house, and to speak to Pharaoh about him, so that he might be brought out of the prison; because, Joseph said, he had been stolen away from the land of the Hebrews, that is, the land of Canaan; and since he had been in Egypt he had not done anything that they should put him in prison for.

When the chief baker saw that the butler's dream meant something good, he told Joseph his dream.   He said that he thought he was carrying three baskets on his head, one above the other. In the highest basket were all kinds of cooked meats for Pharaoh, and the birds flew down and ate the meats out of the basket.   Then Joseph told him that this was the interpretation of his dream.   The three baskets meant three days.   Within three days, he said, shall Pharaoh hang thee on a tree, and the birds shall eat thy flesh from off thee.   This meant that in three days Pharaoh would put the baker to death, and afterward would let him hang where the birds could fly down and eat his flesh.

And it came true as Joseph said.   For after three days was the king's birthday, when he made a feast to all his servants. And he sent and brought the chief butler back to his house again, so that he gave the wine-cup into Pharaoh's hand, as he used to do when he was butler before.   But he hanged the chief baker as Joseph had told him.   Yet the chief butler, when he was taken back to the king's house, did not remember Joseph and speak to Pharaoh about him; he forgot all the kindness that Joseph had shown to him while he was shut up in prison.

After Joseph had been in prison two whole years, Pharaoh dreamed a dream.   He thought he stood by the river that was in Egypt, and saw seven cows come up out of the water.   They were fat and well looking, and they went into a meadow and ate the grass there.   After them came up seven other cows, but these

JOSEPH INTERPRETS THE DREAMS OF THE CHIEF BUTLER AND THE CHIEF BAKER

were thin and starved looking. And the thin and starved looking cows ate up those that were fat and well looking. And
Pharaoh awoke.

And he slept and dreamed again. He thought he saw seven
ears of corn grow up on one stalk. They were all good and
filled with grain. And after them came up seven bad ears, that
were spoiled and had no good grain in them. And the seven
bad ears did eat up the seven good ones. And Pharaoh awoke
and found it was a dream.

In the morning he was troubled, and sent and called for all
the wise men of Egypt, and told them his dreams; but they
could not interpret them. Then the chief butler spoke and said,
that he remembered when Pharaoh was angry with him, and
with the chief baker, and put them both into prison, they each
of them had a dream in one night, and a young man who was
in the prison interpreted their dreams, and what that young man
told them came true.

Then Pharaoh sent and called for Joseph; and they brought
him quickly out of the prison, and he shaved himself, and put
on other clothes, and came to Pharaoh. And Pharaoh said to
Joseph, I have dreamed a dream, and none can interpret it
and I have heard of thee, that thou canst understand a dream
to interpret it. Joseph answered, that it was not he, but God,
who would tell Pharaoh the things he wanted to know. And
Pharaoh told Joseph his dreams: the one in which he thought
he stood by the bank of the river, and saw the seven bad cows
eat up the seven good ones; and after they had eaten them, no
person could have told they had eaten anything, for they were as
thin and starved looking as before. And Pharaoh told Joseph
his dream about the ears of corn also.

Then Joseph said that the king's two dreams both meant the
same thing, and that God had showed Pharaoh in these dreams
what he was going to do. The seven good cows and the seven
good ears of corn, he said, meant seven years; and the seven
bad cows and the seven bad ears of corn, meant seven other years.
For first there would come seven good years in Egypt, when the
corn would grow well, and there would be plenty for the people

to eat. But after those seven good years would come seven bad years, when the people would want bread, because there would be a famine in all the land.

Then Joseph told Pharaoh to look for some wise man, who could attend to saving up the corn for him in the seven good

JOSEPH INTERPRETS PHARAOH'S DREAM

years, so that, when the bad years should come, the people would have bread to eat and not starve. And the king was willing to do as Joseph told him; and he said that as God had taught Joseph how to interpret his dreams, and showed him all these things which were to happen, Joseph was the wisest man and the best one to attend to saving up the corn for him.

So Pharaoh would not let Joseph go back to the prison any more, but he made him a great man.   He took off his ring from his hand and put it on Joseph's hand, and dressed him in rich clothing and put a gold chain about his neck.   He made him ride also in the chariot next to the king's chariot; and as he rode

JOSEPH IS MADE RULER OVER EGYPT

along the people cried, Bow the knee.   And Pharaoh made him ruler over all the land of Egypt.

And Pharaoh said that every man in Egypt should do as Joseph commanded him; and he gave Joseph a wife whose name was Asenath.   Joseph was thirty years old when he interpreted Pharaoh's dreams.   And he went out over all the land and attended to saving up the corn for Pharaoh.   In the seven good years it grew well.   When it was ripe and cut down, the people had much more than they could eat.

Then Joseph took a part of it and had it carried into those cities which were near to the fields where it grew. And he put it away in houses called store-houses, that it might be kept safe until the seven years of famine should come. He saved up in this way very much corn, until he stopped counting how much, for there was more of it than any one could tell. And God gave Joseph two sons, one of whom he named Manasseh and the other Ephraim.

And the seven good years were ended and the seven bad years began. The famine was not only in the land of Egypt, it was in other lands beside: but in Egypt there was bread, because Joseph had saved up the corn before the famine came. When the people had nothing to eat, they cried to Pharaoh for bread, and Pharaoh said, Go to Joseph, and what he says to you, do. And Joseph opened all the store-houses where the corn was kept, and he sold it to the Egyptians. And people came from other countries also to buy corn, because the famine was in the countries where they lived.

CHAPTERS XLII–XLV (42–45)

JOSEPH'S BRETHREN COME INTO EGYPT TO BUY CORN. HE PRETENDS NOT TO KNOW THEM, AND KEEPS SIMEON WHILE HE SENDS THE OTHERS BACK TO CANAAN FOR BENJAMIN. THEY BRING BENJAMIN. HE MAKES HIMSELF KNOWN TO THEM AND SENDS FOR HIS FATHER.

Now Joseph's brethren were still living in the land of Canaan. It had been many years since they sold him to the Ishmaelites, and they did not know what had become of him, but they thought he was dead. And as the famine was in Canaan, they wanted bread for their father and their little children to eat. They looked at one another as if they did not know where they should get it, or what they should do. Then Jacob said to them, Why do ye look one upon another? I have heard there is corn in Egypt; go down there and buy some for us, that we may live and not die. So Joseph's ten brethren left their home to go. But Benjamin, his youngest brother, stayed with his father in Canaan, for his father was afraid that some evil might happen him if he should go with them. And Joseph's brethren came down into Egypt, with many other persons to buy corn, for the famine was in all the countries around Egypt.

Now Joseph was governor over Egypt; it was he who sold corn to the people. And his brethren came and bowed down before him with their faces to the earth. Joseph saw them and knew them, but pretended he did not. He asked them, saying, From whence do ye come? They answered, From the land of Canaan, to buy food. But though Joseph knew his brethren they did not know him, nor think at all that it was their brother whom they had sold to the Ishmaelites so many years before. Then Joseph spoke roughly to them, and said, Ye are spies (that is, enemies), who are come into the land to find out something which you ought not to know. But his brethren answered, No, my lord, but to buy food are thy servants come. We are all one man's sons. We are true men (that is, men who speak the truth); thy servants are no spies.

Yet Joseph seemed not to believe them, and said again they were spies. But it was not because he was angry that he spoke roughly to them. He did so that they might not know him. He was soon going to be very kind to them, for Joseph was a good man and willing to forgive his brethren their unkindness to him. Then they told Joseph that they were all brothers, and that their father had twelve sons. One of them, they said, was with their father, in the land of Canaan—that was Benjamin;— and one, they said, "was not." They meant he was dead. The one who they told Joseph, was dead, was Joseph himself.

Yet Joseph still pretended not to believe them, and said he would find out whether they spoke the truth or not, and this was the way he would do it. One of them should go home to Canaan to bring their youngest brother down to Egypt, but all the rest must stay till that one should come back; and he put them in prison three days. On the third day he spoke to them again; but this time he said that only one need stay. The rest might go home to take corn for their families to eat. Yet they must leave one, so that Joseph might be sure the others would come back and bring their youngest brother with them. When his brethren heard him say this, and saw that he was in earnest and meant to do as he said, they were in great trouble. They did not know it was Joseph who spoke with them and had put them in prison, yet they thought that God was punishing them for their sin in selling their brother to the Ishmaelites so long ago. And they talked with each other about it and said how wicked they had been.

And Reuben (the one who had intended to take Joseph out of the pit and bring him back to his father) said to his brethren, Did I not speak to you, saying, Do not sin against the child; but you would not listen to me? That was the reason, Reuben told them, why such trouble had come on them now. And Joseph heard them talking together, for they thought he could not understand what they said, because he had talked with them only in the Egyptian language, and when he did so, had an interpreter to explain what he said. Yet Joseph understood every word they spoke, and he had to go away from them that they might not see him, for what they said made him weep. Afterward he came back and talked to them again. Still he pretended to think they were spies. Then he took Simeon, one of his brothers, and bound him, and all the rest saw him do it, for Simeon was to stay in Egypt while the others went home after Benjamin.

Then Joseph commanded his servants to fill his brothers' sacks with corn, and to put the money that each one had paid back again into his sack; but he did not tell his brethren of this, and they did not know that their money was put back. So when their asses were loaded, all of them except Simeon started on their journey to their home in Canaan. And they came to the inn on the road, where travellers stopped to rest. Here as one of them opened his sack to give his ass some food out of it, he saw his money, for it was in the sack's mouth. And he said to his brethren, My money is given back to me; it is in my sack. Then they were afraid, for they did not know who had put it there.

And they went on their journey, and came to Jacob their father in the land of Canaan, and told him of the things that had happened to them while they were gone.   They said, The man who is the lord of the country spoke roughly to us and took us for spies.   And we said, We are no spies, but are true men. We are twelve brethren, sons of our father; one is not, and the youngest is this day with our father in the land of Canaan. And the man, the lord of the country, said to us, This is the way I shall know whether you are true men: leave one of your brethren with me, and take food for your families and go and bring your youngest brother unto me.   Then I shall know that you are no spies, but true men; and I will give your brother up to you again, and you may buy corn in the land.

And when they came to empty the corn out of their sacks, they found every man's bundle of money, that he had paid for the corn, put back into the sack.   They and their father saw the bundles of money and were afraid.   And Jacob was troubled, and said to his sons that they had taken away his children from him; for Joseph was gone and Simeon was gone, and now they wanted to take Benjamin away.   Then Reuben, who had two sons of his own, spoke to his father, saying, Slay my two sons if I do not bring Benjamin back to thee; give him to me and I will bring him to thee again.   But Jacob said that Benjamin should not go down into Egypt; for Joseph was dead, and if any harm happened to Benjamin, it would be a greater trouble than he could bear.

Now the famine was very dreadful in the land of Canaan. And when they had eaten up the corn which they brought out of Egypt, Jacob said to his sons, Go again, buy us a little food. And Judah told his father they would go down and buy food if he would let Benjamin go with them, but if he would not let Benjamin go, they would not go down; for the man, the lord of the country, had said to them, Ye shall not see my face except your brother be with you.   Then Israel, that was Jacob, for now he had two names, asked his sons why they were so unkind to him as to tell the man they had another brother.   But they answered, The man asked us, saying, Is your father yet alive? have you another brother?   Could we know that he would say, Bring your brother down?

THE MONEY FOUND IN THE MOUTH OF THE SACKS

And Judah told Israel, his father, to send Benjamin with him, and under his care; then, he said they would arise and go, that they might not starve, but have food for their father and themselves and their little children.   Judah said he would watch over him, and that no harm should happen to him.   His father should trust Benjamin to him, and if he did not bring him back safely, then he would bear the blame forever.   For if they had not stayed so long they would have been to Egypt and come back by that time.

Then their father, Israel, told them that if it must be so, if they must take Benjamin, they had better take also a present to the man.   Do this, he said, take some of the best fruits of the land, and carry down the man a present, a little balm, and a little honey, spices and myrrh, nuts and almonds: and take more money with you, and the money that was brought back in the mouths of your sacks, perhaps it was a mistake.   Take also your brother, and arise and go again unto the man.   And Israel prayed for his sons, that God would make the man kind to them; for, he said, if his children were taken away from him, he would be left lonely and sorrowful indeed.

So they took the present, and the money, and Benjamin, and went down to Egypt and stood before Joseph again.   And when Joseph saw Benjamin with them, he said to his steward who took care of his house, Bring these men home and make ready, for they shall eat dinner with me at noon.   And the servant did as Joseph commanded; but the men were afraid when they came to Joseph's house.   They said to one another that it was because they had carried the money home in their sacks the first time they were brought there, and that now Joseph was going to blame them for it, so that he might make them his slaves and take away their asses from them.

And they came near to Joseph's steward, and talked with him at the door of the house, and said, O, sir, indeed we came down the first time only to buy food.   And they told him that as they were going home to Canaan, when they stopped at the inn, they opened their sacks and found the money they had paid for their corn put back into their sacks.   Every man's money was in the mouth of his sack. And now, they said, they had brought that money back with them, and other money beside to buy food. But they could not tell who had put their money into their sacks when they went home before.

Then Joseph's steward told them not to fear. And he brought Simeon out to them, the one who had been left bound in Egypt while they went home to Canaan. And the steward gave them water to wash their feet, and he gave food to their asses. And they made ready the present which they had brought for Joseph, to give it to him when he should come home at noon, for they had heard they were to stay and eat dinner there. When Joseph came, they brought his present into the house, and bowed themselves down before him to the earth. And he spoke kindly to them, and said, Is your father well, the old man of whom ye spake? Is he yet alive? They answered, Thy servant, our father, is in good health, he is yet alive. And they bowed down to him again.

Then Joseph looked and saw his brother Benjamin, and said, Is this your younger brother of whom ye spoke unto me? And he said, May God be good to thee, my son. Then Joseph made haste to find a place where he might go and weep, and he went into his chamber and wept there, because he was so full of joy at seeing his brother. But afterward he washed his face, and came out, and kept back the tears, so that his brethren could not tell he had been weeping.

And he told his servants to set bread on the table, and they set on bread for Joseph in one place, to eat by himself, and for his brethren in another place, to eat by themselves: for the Egyptians would not eat with the Hebrews (that is, with the sons of Jacob), and Joseph wanted now to pretend that he was an Egyptian. And when his brethren came to take their seats, they found that the oldest one had the first seat, and the next oldest the next seat, and so they were all placed according to their ages. Then they wondered who could have known how to place their seats in that way.

And Joseph sent food to his brethren from his own table, but to Benjamin he sent five times as much as to any of the others.

He loved Benjamin more than the others because Joseph and Benjamin had the same mother. All of them had the same father, but they had different mothers; and Joseph and Benjamin were the only ones who had Rachel for their mother. Rachel, as we have read, died long before, and Jacob buried her on the way, as he went toward Bethlehem. And Joseph's brethren ate and drank with him in his house, but they did not know it was Joseph.

And Joseph commanded the steward of his house to fill the men's sacks with food, as much as they could carry, and to put every man's money back in the mouth of his sack, as had been done when they came down into Egypt before. And put my cup, the silver cup, he said, in the sack of the youngest. And the steward did as Joseph commanded. In the morning, as soon as it was light, the men started on their journey back to Canaan. When they had gone out of the city, but were not far off, Joseph told his steward to follow after them, and ask why they had taken his silver cup. So the steward followed after them, and when he came up to them, asked as Joseph had told him.

Then the men were very much surprised, and wondered why the steward spoke such words to them. God forbid, they said, that they should do such a thing as steal Joseph's cup. They had brought back the money which they found in their sacks, when they went home to Canaan the first time; they could have kept it had they chosen to do so, but they brought it back of their own accord. And if they had done this, they asked, would they now take from Joseph's house silver or gold which did not belong to them?

Then they told the steward that if any of them had taken the cup, he might put that one to death, and all the rest would be his servants. The steward answered, that the one who had taken the cup should be his servant, but the rest should not be blamed. Then each of them quickly took down his sack from the back of the ass, and rested it on the ground; and every man opened his sack so that the steward could look into it. And he looked, beginning with the sack of the oldest, and leaving off with the sack of the youngest, and he found the cup in Benjamin's sack. Then they rent their clothes, and loaded their asses, and returned with him to the city.

And they came to Joseph's house, for he was still there, and they fell down before him on the ground. And Joseph pretended to think they had really stolen his cup, and he asked if they did not know he would find it out. Then Judah spoke to him, and said, What shall we say to my lord? or what shall we do that we may not be punished? God has found out our wickedness; we are all my lord's servants. But Joseph answered that only the one who had the cup should be his servant; as for the rest they might go home to their father.

Then Judah came near to Joseph and begged him not to be angry, but to let him speak. Judah said that when they came down to Egypt the first time Joseph asked them, saying, Have you a father and a brother at home in the country where you live? And they told him they had a father, an old man, and also a brother who was a little child yet; and that their father loved the boy, for his mother was dead and his brother was dead. And Joseph told them to bring that younger brother down to Egypt that he might see him. Then they had answered that the boy could not leave his father, for if he should do so his father would die. But Joseph told them that if they did not bring their brother down, they should never see his face again. So when they went home to their father, they told him what Joseph had said. And after a while their father wanted them to go down to Egypt again to buy a little more food. But they said to him, We cannot go unless our youngest brother be with us, for we may not see the man's face unless Benjamin be with us. Then their father told them that if they took Benjamin, and any harm should happen to him while they were gone, he would die with sorrow.

So now, Judah said, that if he went home without Benjamin, when their father saw that Benjamin was not with them, he would die. For Judah had promised to bring him back safely to his father, and had told his father that if he did not bring him back he would bear the blame forever. Then Judah begged

6

Joseph to let him stay and be his servant in Benjamin's place and to let Benjamin go home to his father.

Then Joseph could hide himself from them no longer, and he commanded all his servants to go out of the room, so that no one was left there but Joseph and his brethren. And he wept out loud, and his brethren heard him and saw him weeping. And he said to them, I am Joseph; does my father yet

JOSEPH MAKES HIMSELF KNOWN TO HIS BRETHREN

live? But they were afraid and could not answer him. And Joseph said to them, Come near to me, I pray you. And they came near; and he said, I am Joseph, your brother, whom ye sold into Egypt.

Then he told them not to be troubled, nor angry with themselves, because they had sold him, for God had sent him into Egypt to save people alive, and to keep them from starving in the famine. Joseph did not mean to say that his brethren did right when they sold him, but that God had made good to come out of the evil which they had done; Joseph told them this so that they might not be unhappy and afraid. For he loved them, and had forgiven their unkindness to him, and did not want them to be unhappy now when he was so glad to see them once more.

And Joseph told them that the famine had been in Egypt two years, and would be there five years longer. In these years there would be no harvest nor planting of seed in the ground, for God had said the famine should last that long. And Joseph told his brethren that God had sent him into Egypt before them to save them from starving. And he said to them, Make haste and go back to my father in Canaan, and say to him, Thus saith thy son Joseph, God has made me ruler over all Egypt. Come down to me, and thou shalt live in the best part of the land, and shalt be near to me; thou and thy children, thy flocks and thy herds, and all that thou hast. And I will take care of thee, lest thou and thy family should come to be poor.

And Joseph said to his brethren, Your eyes see and my brother Benjamin's eyes see that it is my mouth that speaketh unto you. You shall tell my father of all my greatness in Egypt, and of all that you have seen, and you shall make haste and bring down my father here. And Joseph leaned on his brother Benjamin's neck and wept, for he was more glad to see him than he could tell; and Benjamin wept on his neck. And Joseph kissed all his brethren and wept on them, and afterward they talked with him.

When Pharaoh heard that Joseph's brethren had come, it pleased him well. And he told Joseph to tell them they should load their beasts and go back to the land of Canaan, and get their father, their wives, and their little children, and bring them to him. They should take wagons for their wives and their little ones to ride in, and they should bring their families and come; but they need bring nothing else, Pharaoh said, for it was the same as if all the good things in the land of Egypt belonged to them.

And Joseph's brethren did so; and he gave them wagons, as Pharaoh had commanded, and food to eat while they were gone.

And to all of them he gave raiment; but to Benjamin he gave more than to any of the others, and also three hundred pieces of silver. To his father he sent twenty asses loaded with bread and meat, and good things from the land of Egypt. Then he sent his brethren to their own home, and told them to be careful lest they should quarrel with one another by the way.

So they went up out of Egypt and came to their father in Canaan, and said to him, Joseph is yet alive, and is governor over all the land of Egypt. But it seemed too wonderful to be true, and Jacob did not believe them; yet when he heard all the kind words that Joseph had spoken, and saw the wagons which Pharaoh had sent to carry him, Jacob believed what his sons told him; and he said, It is enough. Joseph, my son, is yet alive; I will go and see him before I die.

CHAPTERS XLVI–L (46–50)

ISRAEL COMES DOWN INTO EGYPT. JOSEPH BRINGS HIM TO PHARAOH AND HE BLESSES PHARAOH. THE ISRAELITES LIVE IN THE LAND OF GOSHEN. JACOB DIES. HIS SONS CARRY HIM UP TO CANAAN AND BURY HIM THERE. JOSEPH DIES.

AND Israel left his home in Canaan and went on his journey to the land of Egypt. When he came to Beer-sheba, where Isaac his father had built an altar many years before, Israel stopped there and offered up sacrifices to God. And God spoke to him in the night and said, Jacob, Jacob. He answered, Here am I. God said, Fear not to go down into Egypt, for I will there make of thee a great nation. A nation is a great many people who live together in the same country, and have one king, or ruler, over them. And God said he would make Jacob's descendants so many, while they were in Egypt, that they should be a great nation there. And he told Jacob he would go down with him to take care of him, and that when the time came for him to die, Joseph should be by his side.

So Jacob left Beer-sheba; and his sons took him, and their wives and their children, in the wagons which Pharaoh had sent to carry them. They took their cattle, also, and all that belonged to them in Canaan, and came into Egypt—Jacob and all his children with him, his sons and their sons and daughters; they did not leave one behind. There were sixty-six of Jacob's descendants, that is, of his children and his children's children, who came with him. Joseph and his sons made three more—that was sixty-nine; and Jacob himself made seventy, altogether, of the family of Israel that came into Egypt.

And Jacob sent Judah, his son, to go on before him and tell Joseph that his father was coming. When Joseph heard it he made ready his chariot to go out and meet his father. And when he met him he came to him, and leaned on his neck, and wept on his neck a good while. And Israel said to Joseph, Now let me die, since I have seen thy face, because thou art yet alive. He was so glad to see Joseph, and to know he was still alive, that he felt as though there was nothing else he need stay for in this world; he felt willing to die.

Then Joseph said to his brethren that he would go and tell Pharaoh they had come, and had brought their flocks and their herds with them. And he said that when Pharaoh should call them to him, and ask what kind of work they had been used to, they should tell him they had always taken care of cattle, and that their fathers had taken care of cattle also. Joseph told them to say this because it was the truth, and because he wanted Pharaoh to let them live in Goshen, which was the best part of the land of Egypt for feeding cattle.

And Joseph came to Pharaoh, and said, My father and my brethren, and their flocks and herds, and all that they have, are come out of the land of Canaan, and they are in the land of Goshen. And Joseph took five of his brethren and brought them to Pharaoh, and Pharaoh asked them what kind of work they were used to. Then they answered him as Joseph had told them. And they said that they had come to stay for a while in Egypt, because there was no food for their flocks in the land of Canaan, the famine was so dreadful there. And they begged Pharaoh to let them live in Goshen. And Pharaoh spoke to Joseph, and said that his father and his brethren might live in the best part of the land of Egypt, they might live in Goshen And Pharaoh told Joseph that if any of his brethren were in dustrious men he should make them rulers over his cattle; for Pharaoh had cattle of his own.

After this Joseph brought Jacob, his father, to Pharaoh, and Jacob blessed Pharaoh. And Pharaoh asked him how old he was. He answered that he was a hundred and thirty years old. Jacob called these hundred and thirty years the years of his pilgrimage. A pilgrim is a person going on a journey. Jacob was going on a journey all those hundred and thirty years. To what place was he going? To his home in heaven, for he loved and served God. So Joseph gave his father and his brethren a place where they should live, in the land of Goshen, as Pharaoh had commanded him. And Joseph was very kind to them, and gave them and their little children as much food as they needed.

But the famine was very dreadful in Egypt and in Canaan, and the people had no bread to eat. And they came to Joseph to buy corn until they gave him all their money, and he gave it to Pharaoh. After they had given all their money, the Egyptians still came and asked for bread, for, they said, they had no more money. Then Joseph told them to bring their cattle; and they did so, and for their cattle he gave them bread—enough to last through that year.

When the year was ended they came to Joseph again, and told him their money was spent, and they had given him all their cattle; so they had nothing left but their lands and themselves. And they said they would give their lands to Pharaoh, and be his servants, if Joseph would let them have bread. Then Joseph gave them more bread, and so he bought all the land of Egypt for Pharaoh. Afterward he sent the people to the different cities to be fed there, for he had saved up the corn in the cities.

But at last the seven years of famine were ended, and Joseph gave the people seed to plant in the ground, because he knew that now the corn would grow again. And he told the people that as they had sold all their land to Pharaoh, it was not their own any longer; yet Pharaoh was willing they should keep it if, when the corn grew, they would give a fifth part of it to him.

JOSEPH MEETING HIS FATHER

The people answered that Joseph was the one who had saved them from starving, and therefore they were willing to do as he said; they were willing to give a fifth part of the corn to Pharaoh.

So the famine was over in Egypt, but Joseph's brethren still lived in the land of Goshen; and they and their children came to be a good many people. And Israel, their father, lived with them for seventeen years; then the time came near for him to die. And he called Joseph, and told him that he did not wish to be buried in Egypt, but in Canaan; and he made Joseph promise that he would carry his dead body up to that land and bury him there.

After this some one came to Joseph and said, Thy father is sick. Then Joseph took his two sons, Manasseh and Ephraim, and went to the house where his father was. When Israel heard that Joseph had come, he made ready to see him, and sat up on his bed. And Jacob talked with Joseph, and told him how God had spoken to him, and blessed him many years before, when he had his dream in the land of Canaan. Then Jacob told Joseph that Ephraim and Manasseh were like his own sons to him; that is, Jacob took Joseph's sons to be his sons. And when Israel knew that the boys were there, he asked Joseph to bring them to him that he might bless them. Now Israel was very old, and his eyes were dim; and when Joseph brought his sons near, Israel put his arms around them and kissed them. And he said that he used to think he would never see Joseph again, but now God had let him see not Joseph only, but his children also.

And Joseph bowed down with his face to the earth before his father, and he took his two sons and brought them near to his father. And Israel stretched out his hands, and laid his right hand on Ephraim's head, and his left hand on Manasseh's head, to bless them. And Israel blessed both the sons of Joseph, and he blessed Joseph also. And he called all his other sons, and blessed each one of them, and told them he was going to die, but that God would be with them, and bring them back to the land of Canaan; and he commanded his sons to bury him in that land, in the cave that was in the field which Abraham had bought of Ephron the Hittite. There, said he, they buried

braham, and Sarah his wife; there they buried Isaac, and
Rebekah his wife; and there I buried Leah. And after Jacob
had done speaking with his sons, he lifted up his feet into the
bed and died.

Then Joseph put his face down to his father's face and wept
over him and kissed him. And he commanded his servants,

JACOB'S BURIAL

the physicians, to embalm his father. To embalm a dead person was to put spices and such other things into his body as
would keep it from decaying and going to dust; and Joseph's
servants embalmed Israel. And the Egyptians mourned for
him seventy days.

And Joseph sent word to Pharaoh that his father, before he
died, had made him promise not to bury him in Egypt, but in his
own sepulchre in the land of Canaan. And he asked permission

of Pharaoh to go and bury him there; afterward, Joseph said
he would come back to Egypt. And Pharaoh told him to do
as he had promised. Then Joseph went up to bury Israel,
and with him went all Pharaoh's servants and many great men
from the land of Egypt. Joseph's brethren went also; only
their little children and their flocks and their herds stayed behind. And there went up chariots, and men riding on horses,
and a great many people. So Israel's sons did as he had commanded them, for they carried him into Canaan and buried him
in the cave which Abraham had bought of Ephron the Hittite.
Afterward Joseph came back into Egypt, he and all those who
had gone up with him.

When his brethren saw that their father was dead, they began
to fear Joseph again, and said that now he would surely punish
them for all the evil they had done to him. And they sent a
messenger to tell him that his father left word, before he died,
asking Joseph to forgive them. When Joseph heard their words
he wept, for he knew they had sent that message because they
were afraid of him. And they came and fell down before his
face, saying, We are thy servants. But he told them not to
be afraid, for though they had intended to do him harm, God
meant to do good by sending him into Egypt, that he might
save many people from starving in the famine. And Joseph
said to his brethren, I will take care of you and of your little
ones. And he spoke kindly to them and comforted them.

Joseph and his brethren stayed in Egypt, and Joseph lived
till Ephraim's sons and Manasseh's sons were grown up and
had children of their own. But after many years, he told
his brethren that he was going to die; yet some day, he said,
God would certainly come to the children of Israel (that is, to
all of Jacob's descendants), and would bring them out of Egypt
into that land which he had promised Abraham, and Isaac, and
Jacob to give them; he meant the land of Canaan. And he
made the children of Israel promise that when God should bring
them there, they would carry up his dead body with them.

So Joseph died when he was a hundred and ten years old, and
they embalmed him, and put him in a coffin in Egypt.

THE BOOK OF EXODUS

CHAPTERS I–VII (1–7)

THE CHILDREN OF ISRAEL GROW TO BE A GREAT MULTITUDE OF PEOPLE.
A NEW KING IS CRUEL TO THEM.   MOSES IS BORN; PHARAOH'S DAUGHTER
TAKES HIM FOR HER SON.   HE KILLS AN EGYPTIAN AND FLEES TO MIDIAN.
GOD SPEAKS TO HIM FROM THE BURNING BUSH, AND SENDS HIM AND
AARON TO BRING THE CHILDREN OF ISRAEL OUT OF EGYPT.   AARON'S
ROD IS CHANGED INTO A SERPENT, AND THE WATER INTO BLOOD.

AFTER Joseph died his brethren died also; but their descendants lived and grew to be a great multitude of people. And a new king ruled over Egypt. His name was Pharaoh, like the one who had been so kind to Joseph; but this Pharaoh had never known Joseph. And when he saw how many there were of the children of Israel, he was afraid of them. He thought that some day, when his enemies should come and make war against him, the children of Israel would help them, and afterward would rise up and go out of his land; he did not want them to do this; he wanted them to stay and be his servants.

So this wicked king persuaded the people of Egypt to treat the children of Israel very cruelly; they set taskmasters over them, and made their lives unhappy by forcing them to labor as slaves, in building houses and doing all kinds of work out in the field. But the more cruelly the Israelites were treated, the more there came to be of them, for, as we have read, God had promised Jacob, when he was coming down into Egypt, to make his descendants a great nation there; and now God was doing as he had promised. He was making them so many that they would be a great nation.

And Pharaoh told the women who took care of the Israelites' little children, to kill all the boys as soon as they were born. The girls he was willing to let live, because they would never be able to fight against him. But the women feared God, and would not obey the king. They let the little boys live also, and God blessed them for doing it. Then Pharaoh gave all his people permission to take the little boys that belonged to the children

of Israel, and to throw them into the river, to drown them; bu
the little girls, he said, they should save alive.

There was a man among the Israelites named Amram. Hi
wife's name was Jochebed, and God gave them a son. The chil
was very beautiful, and his mother loved him, but she fearee

ISRAELITES AT LABOR

that some of Pharaoh's servants would come and take him fro
her, to kill him. Therefore she hid him for three months aft
he was born, but then found she could hide him no longer. S
she took a little ark, or boat, made out of the long weeds th
grew by the river, and daubed it over with pitch to keep out t
water. And she put her baby into the ark and laid it careful

nong the bushes at the edge of the river. But the little boy's
ster waited, not far off, to see what might happen to him.

And the daughter of king Pharaoh came down to bathe in
te river, and she and her maids walked along by the river's
de. When she saw the ark among the bushes, she sent one of

PHARAOH'S DAUGHTER FINDS MOSES

em to bring it. The maiden brought it, and as Pharaoh's
ughter looked into it, the little boy wept; and she pitied him,
d said, This is one of the Hebrews' children. Then his sister,
o had been watching, came near and spoke to the king's
ughter, saying, May I not go and call one of the Hebrew
men to nurse the child for thee? She said, Go. And his
ter went and called her mother. When she came, Pharaoh's
ughter said to her, Take this child away and nurse it for me,

and I will give thee thy wages. So his mother carried him back to her own home and nursed him there.

But after a while Pharaoh's daughter sent for the child. Then his mother brought him to her. And Pharaoh's daughter took him into her house to be as her own son, and she called his name Moses, which means, "drawn out," because, she said, I drew him out of the water. Yet, when he was grown to be a man, he knew

MOSES SLAYS THE EGYPTIAN

that he was not the son of Pharaoh's daughter, but was one of the children of Israel; and although he might have been rich and great if he had stayed with her, he chose rather to go and live with his own people.

And Moses went out one day to the place where the Israelites worked for the Egyptians. There he saw a cruel Egyptian striking a Hebrew. Then Moses looked this way and that, and, when he saw no one near, he killed the Egyptian and hid his body in the sand; for Moses believed that God had sent him to set the children of Israel free, and he supposed they would understand this. And he went out another day, but this time he saw two of the children of Israel quarrelling together. And he spoke to the one who did wrong, and asked him why he struck the other. He answered, saying, Who made thee a ruler over us? Wilt thou kill me as thou didst the Egyptian yesterday? Then Moses was afraid, for he thought that other persons must know of what he had done.

When Pharaoh was told of it, he tried to kill Moses; but Moses fled out of Egypt to the land of Midian, where Pharaoh could not find him. And he sat down by a well in that land, and some women came to draw water. There were seven of them who were sisters. They wanted to draw water for their father's flock, but some shepherds drove them away. Then Moses helped them and gave their flock water. When they went home to their father, whose name was Jethro, he asked them, How is it that you are come so soon to-day? They answered, An Egyptian saved us from the shepherds, and also drew water for the flock. Then Jethro asked where the man was, and why they had left him. And he told them to go and call him, that he might have something to eat. So they called Moses, and he went to Jethro's house, and he lived there many years, and he took one of Jethro's daughters for his wife.

While Moses lived in the land of Midian, Pharaoh, the king of Egypt, died. But the people of Egypt were still very cruel to the children of Israel, and the children of Israel cried to the Lord because of their sufferings, and the Lord heard them and looked down from heaven and pitied them.

Now Moses took care of Jethro's flock, and he led it out into the wilderness, to find pasture, till he came to a mountain called Horeb. On this mountain the Lord spoke to him. For there came up fire out of a bush that grew on the mountain; and when Moses looked, he saw that the bush was not burned, though the fire came up out of it. Then he said, I will turn and see this wonderful sight—why the bush is not burned. And when he turned, God called to him out of the bush, and said,

Moses, Moses. He answered, Here am I. And God told him not to come near, but to take his shoes from off his feet, because the place where he stood was holy ground. It was holy, and Moses was not to come near because God was there. God said to him, also, I am the God of thy father, the God of Abraham, the God of Isaac and the God of Jacob. And Moses hid his face, for he was afraid to look upon God. Then God told him that he had seen the affliction of the children of Israel, and heard their cries and had come down to set them free from the Egyptians.

MOSES AT THE BURNING BUSH

Now the king who ruled at that time in Egypt was named Pharaoh, like those who had lived before him, because the Egyptians called all their kings by this name. And the Lord told Moses he would send him to Pharaoh, that he might tell Pharaoh to let the children of Israel go; and the Lord said that Moses should lead them out of Egypt, and bring them to that mountain where he was then talking with him. But Moses was afraid to go; he said, Who am I that I should go to Pharaoh and bring the children of Israel out of Egypt? God said to him, Certainly I will be with thee to help thee.

And God commanded Moses to go and tell the children of Israel that the Lord God of their fathers, the God of Abraham, the God of Isaac, and the God of Jacob, had sent him to bring them out of Egypt to a good land, where they should have milk to drink and honey to eat. After Moses had told them this, he was to speak to Pharaoh and ask him to let them go. But

Moses answered the Lord, and said that when he should come into Egypt and tell the children of Israel these things, he was sure they would not listen to him, nor believe that the Lord had spoken to him at all.

Now Moses held a rod in his hand, and the Lord said to him, What is that in thine hand? Moses answered, A rod. The Lord said, Cast it on the ground. And Moses cast it on the ground, and God made it change into a serpent, so that Moses was afraid of it and fled away before it. And the Lord said, Put out thy hand and take it by the tail. And Moses took it and it was changed back again into a rod in his hand.

And the Lord said to Moses, Put now thy hand into thy bosom. Moses put his hand into his bosom, and when he took it out, it was white as snow; for it was covered with a dreadful disease called leprosy, which made it look white like snow. And God said, Put thy hand into thy bosom again. And Moses put it into his bosom, and when he took it out it was well and covered with leprosy no more.

God gave Moses power to do these two wonderful works, or miracles, so that when the children of Israel should see them, they might believe that God had sent him. But if they would not believe after he had done them both, then, God said, Moses should take some water out of the river that was in Egypt and pour it on the dry ground; and the water should be changed into blood on the ground where Moses had poured it. Still Moses did not want to go, and he began to make excuses for no going. He was not eloquent, he said, that is, could not speak well before the people. But the Lord commanded him again to go, and said he would teach him what to say. Yet Moses begged the Lord to send some one else. Then the Lord was angry, because he was still unwilling to go.

And Moses had a brother named Aaron. God said that Aaron could speak well, and that he should go with him into Egypt; Moses should tell Aaron what to say, but Aaron should tell it to the people. And God said he would teach them both what they should do; and he told Moses to take his rod in his hand, for with it he should do wonderful things. All this time, while God was talking with Moses, Moses was on mount Horeb by the bush that burned with fire. He had gone there, as we have read, with Jethro's flock. When the Lord was done talking with him, Moses went to Jethro's house again and asked permission to go back into Egypt, that he might see his brethren, the children of Israel, and Jethro gave him permission to go.

And the Lord commanded Aaron, Moses' brother, to come out and meet him at mount Horeb; and Aaron came there and met Moses, and he was glad and kissed him. And Moses told Aaron of all the words that God had spoken. Then Moses and Aaron went into Egypt and spoke to the children of Israel. They could not speak to all of them at once, there were too many to hear; so they sent for the chief men among them, called elders, and told them, and the elders told the people. They showed them the miracles, also, that God had given Moses power to do. When the children of Israel saw these, they believed that God had sent Moses and Aaron, and that he was coming, as he had promised, to take them out of Egypt.

After they had spoken with the elders, Moses and Aaron went to Pharaoh, and said, Thus saith the Lord God of Israel, Let my people go that they may hold a feast unto me in the wilderness. But Pharaoh answered, Who is the Lord that I should obey him? I know not the Lord, neither will I let the children of Israel go. Then Moses and Aaron told him that it was God who had spoken to them, and they begged Pharaoh to let them go, lest, if they should not, God might punish them for their disobedience. But Pharaoh was angry when they said this to him. He asked why they kept the people from their work by telling them they were to go out of Egypt, and he told Moses and Aaron to go and work themselves.

Now the children of Israel were digging clay out of the ground and making bricks with it, for that was the work which Pharaoh made them do. These bricks were not burned in the fire, as ours are, to harden them; they were only baked in the sun. But to make them tougher and stronger, the clay they were made of was mixed with pieces of straw. This straw was gathered out in the fields by men, who brought it to the children of Israel, for them to work it up with the clay before they made the bricks. But Pharaoh was so angry with the children of Israel for wanting to go out of Egypt that he said they must go and gather the straw themselves; and yet that they must make as many bricks as they used to make when it was gathered for them. For they were idle, Pharaoh said, and that was the reason they cried, Let us go and serve the Lord.

Then the taskmasters went and told the children of Israel that Pharaoh said, I will not give you straw. Go get straw where you can find it. So these poor men went out into the fields, after the grain had been reaped, and gathered up the straw that was left, and carried it away to make bricks with. But though they worked very hard, they could not make as many as they had made when the straw was brought to them, and some of them were beaten because they did not. Then they came to Pharaoh and told him that the fault was not theirs. Pharaoh answered, Ye are idle, ye are idle; that is the reason you say, Let us go and sacrifice to the Lord. And he told them to go and work, for no straw should be given them.

Then the children of Israel were in great distress, and some of them went to Moses and Aaron, and said that they had done them harm and not good, for they had made Pharaoh hate them, and treat them more cruelly than he treated them before. And Moses went and told the Lord, and asked why he had sent him to speak with Pharaoh; for, Moses said, since he had spoken to him, Pharaoh had done evil to the children of Israel, and yet the Lord had not set them free. The Lord answered that Moses should see what he would do to Pharaoh to make him let the children of Israel go. And he commanded Moses to tell them that he would bring them out of Egypt, and take them to be his people, and would lead them to the land which he had promised their fathers, Abraham, Isaac, and Jacob, to give them.

And Moses went and told the children of Israel what God said, but they would not listen to him. Then the Lord sent Moses and Aaron to speak with Pharaoh again. Moses was eighty years old, and Aaron was eighty-three, when they went to speak with the king. And the Lord said that when Pharaoh should ask them to do a miracle for him to see, Aaron should take the rod and throw it on the ground, and it should be changed into a serpent.

So Moses and Aaron went to Pharaoh, and Aaron threw down his rod and it was changed into a serpent. And Pharaoh called for his servants, the magicians, or wise men of Egypt. And they came with rods in their hands, and when they had thrown them down, their rods also were changed into serpents, because the Lord let the magicians do as Aaron had done. Then Aaron's rod swallowed up all the other rods, but Pharaoh would not let the children of Israel go.

And the Lord told Moses to stand in the morning by the river's side, and when Pharaoh should come there, to speak with him and say, The God of the Hebrews (that is, of the children of Israel) has sent me to say to thee, Let my people go that they may offer up a sacrifice to me in the wilderness. And Moses did as the Lord said. He went to the river, and when Pharaoh came there, told him the words that the Lord had spoken. But Pharaoh would not let the people go. Then the Lord commanded Aaron to take his rod and strike the waters with it, that they might be changed into blood. And Aaron took the rod in his hand and struck the waters, and Pharaoh and his servants saw him do it. And all the water in the river was changed into blood, and the streams and ponds of water, all over the land of Egypt, were changed into blood. And the fish that were in the river died, and the Egyptians could not drink of the water.

And Pharaoh's servants, the magicians, came, and they, too, turned water into blood, because the Lord let them do again as Aaron had done. And Pharaoh went home to his house, yet he would not let the people go. Then all the Egyptians digged in the ground about the river, to find water that they could drink. And the blood stayed in the river seven days.

AARON'S ROD IS CHANGED INTO A SERPENT

CHAPTERS VIII–XII (8–12)

MORE PLAGUES ARE SENT UPON PHARAOH AND THE PEOPLE OF EGYPT;
AFTERWARD THEY LET THE CHILDREN OF ISRAEL GO.   THE ISRAELITES
KEEP THE FEAST OF THE PASSOVER.   THE MEANING OF THIS FEAST.

AND the Lord commanded Moses to tell Pharaoh that if he would not let the people go, frogs should come over all the land.   And Pharaoh would not let them go.   Then God said that Aaron should hold out his rod over the waters of Egypt. And when Aaron held it out, the frogs came up out of the waters, so many of them that they covered the land.   They went into the houses of the Egyptians, into their ovens, and into their kneading-troughs where they made their bread; they went into Pharaoh's house, and up into his bed-chamber, and on his bed. And Pharaoh's servants, the magicians, also brought up frogs, for God allowed them once more to do as Aaron had done.

But Pharaoh and the people of Egypt were in great trouble because of the frogs; and he called for Moses and Aaron, and asked them to pray to God that he would take the frogs away; then, Pharaoh said, he would let the people go to sacrifice in the wilderness.   Moses said, When shall I pray for thee?   Pharaoh answered, To-morrow.   And Moses and Aaron went out from the place where Pharaoh was.   Afterward Moses prayed to the Lord, and the Lord did as he asked; the frogs that were in the houses, the villages, and the fields died, and the people gathered them in heaps, and the smell of their decaying bodies was all over the land.   But when Pharaoh saw that the frogs were dead, he would not let the children of Israel go.

Then the Lord commanded Aaron to strike the dust on the ground with his rod.   And when Aaron had done so, the dust was changed into very small insects, or creeping things, called lice, that crept on the people and on the cattle.   And Pharaoh's servants, the magicians, tried to bring up lice, but they could not, because God would not let them do as Aaron had done any more.   Then they told Pharaoh that it was God who did these things for Moses and Aaron; but Pharaoh's heart was wicked and he would not listen to them, neither would he let the people go.

And the Lord told Moses to rise up early in the morning, and stand where he would see Pharaoh when he came out to the water. There, the Lord said, Moses should command him again to let the people go, and if he disobeyed, should tell him that the Lord would send swarms of flies over all Egypt. And Moses did as the Lord commanded, yet Pharaoh would not let the people go. Then the Lord sent swarms of flies, and they came over all the land. They crept on Pharaoh, and on his servants, and on the people; they went into their houses, so that the houses of the Egyptians were full of swarms of flies, and the ground was covered with them. But in the land of Goshen, where the children of Israel lived, there were none, for the Lord did not send them there.

Then Pharaoh was troubled because of the flies as he had been because of the frogs. And he called Moses and Aaron to him, and told them they might offer sacrifices to their God, but they must not go into the wilderness to do it; they must do it in Egypt. But Moses asked him whether the Egyptians would not be offended if the children of Israel should offer sacrifices in Egypt; for the Egyptians used to worship idols that were formed like oxen and calves, and if they had seen the children of Israel killing those animals and burning them on the altar, they might have been angry and tried to kill the people. Moses told Pharaoh they would go three days' journey into the wilderness, where no one could harm them, and there they would offer sacrifices to the Lord, as he should command them.

Then Pharaoh said he would let them go, only they must not go very far. And he asked Moses to pray for him, that the flies might be taken from the land. Moses said he would pray that they might be taken away on the morrow, but he told Pharaoh not to deceive them any more by refusing to let the people go. Then Moses went and prayed to the Lord, and the Lord took away the swarms of flies from Pharaoh, and from his servants, and from his people, so that there was not one left. When Pharaoh saw that the flies were taken away, he made his heart wicked this time also, and would not let the people go.

And the Lord commanded Moses to tell Pharaoh that if he

would not let the children of Israel go, the Lord would send, on the morrow, a great sickness to destroy the cattle of Egypt, but that he would not send it among the cattle of the children of Israel, for none of them should die. And Moses told Pharaoh this, yet he would not let the people go. Then the Lord sent that sickness; and the cows, the horses, the asses, the camels, and the sheep died all over the land. But not one of the cattle of the children of Israel died. And Pharaoh sent to see if any of their cattle were dead; when he found they were not, his heart grew more wicked, and he would not let the people go.

And the Lord told Moses and Aaron to take handfuls of ashes from a furnace, where fire had been burning, and to sprinkle them up in the air so that Pharaoh could see them doing it. And those ashes, the Lord said, should go like dust over all the land, and cause sore boils to come on the men and on the animals that were still left in Egypt. So Moses took ashes and stood before Pharaoh, and sprinkled them up in the air; afterward boils broke out on men and on beasts over all the land. And the magicians could not come to try and do as Moses had done, for the boils were on them also. But Pharaoh's heart was still wicked, and he would not let the people go.

And the Lord commanded Moses to rise up early in the morning and stand before Pharaoh, and say that on the morrow he would send a great storm of hail, such as had never been in Egypt. And Moses was to tell Pharaoh to bring into his barns all his cattle from the fields, for every man and beast that should be out in the storm would be killed. And Moses did so. Then those Egyptians who feared the Lord made their servants and their cattle come quickly into the houses and barns, where the hail could not hurt them; but the others let them stay out in the field.

And the Lord told Moses to stretch out his hand toward heaven, that the hail might come. And he stretched it out, holding up his rod; and the Lord sent thunder and hail, and there was fire, also, running along on the ground. So there was hail, and fire mixed with the hail, very dreadful, such as had never before been in the land. The hail came down on the fields, killing the men and the animals that were there, and it broke the bushes and every tree that was growing in the field. And all the grain that was grown up was broken and spoiled by the hail. But some of it was not yet grown up above the ground; this was not spoiled. Yet in the land of Goshen, where the children of Israel lived, no hail came.

Then Pharaoh sent and called for Moses and Aaron, and said to them, I have sinned; the Lord is good, and I and my people are wicked. Pray to the Lord that he may take away the mighty thunder and hail, and I will let you go and you shall stay no longer. Moses answered that as soon as he should go out of the city he would pray to the Lord, and the thunder should cease and there should be no more hail. Yet, he said, he knew that Pharaoh and his servants would not obey the Lord. And Moses went out from Pharaoh into the terrible storm; but God kept the hail and fire from harming him. And when he had gone out of the city, he lifted up his hands and prayed to God, and the thunders ceased, and the hail came down no more. Then when Pharaoh saw that they had ceased, he made his heart still more hard and obstinate, both he and his servants, and they would not let the people go.

And Moses and Aaron came to him again, saying that if he would not obey the Lord, on the morrow the locusts should come into his land. Now Pharaoh's servants were afraid to be punished any more. They remembered when the river was turned into blood, so that they had no water to drink. They remembered, also, the frogs, and the lice, and the flies; the sickness of the cattle, the boils, and the hail, which had been sent into Egypt already. Therefore they begged Pharaoh to let the children of Israel go, that no more punishments might be sent upon them.

Then Moses and Aaron were brought before Pharaoh, and he said to them, Go, serve the Lord your God; but who are they that shall go? Moses answered that all the children of Israel would go—the young and the old, with their sons and their daughters, their flocks and their herds; for they must hold a feast to the Lord. But Pharaoh said that only the men might go—the women and children must stay in Egypt. And Moses and Aaron were driven away from the place where they talked with Pharaoh.

And the Lord told Moses to stretch out his hand for the locusts to come. Then Moses took the rod and held it out; and the Lord made an east wind to blow on the land all that day and all that night, and in the morning the wind brought the locusts. They went up over all the land of Egypt, and covered the ground so that it could not be seen for them. They filled Pharaoh's house, and the houses of his servants, and the houses of all the Egyptians. They ate up the fruits which the hail had left, and every green thing, until there was not a leaf to be seen on the bushes or on the trees through all the land.

Then Pharaoh made haste to call for Moses and Aaron, and said, I have sinned against the Lord and against you. And he asked Moses to forgive him only this once, and to pray that God would take away the locusts. And Moses went out and prayed to the Lord. And the Lord sent a very strong west wind, which blew away the locusts and cast them into the Red Sea, where they were drowned, so that there was not one locust left in all Egypt. But when Pharaoh saw that the locusts were taken away, he would not let the people go.

And the Lord commanded Moses to hold up his hand toward heaven, that it might be dark in the land. And Moses held up his hand, and there came a great darkness over all Egypt, so that the Egyptians could not see one another, nor move from the places they were in, for three days. But in the houses of the children of Israel there was light. Then Pharaoh called for Moses, and said, Go, serve the Lord; only let your flocks and your herds stay. Let your little children go with you. But Moses told him their flocks and their herds must go also, that they might have sacrifices and burnt offerings, for they did not know how many of these they would need till they should come into the wilderness. The Lord would tell them there what animals they must kill and offer up to him. But when Moses said this, Pharaoh would not let the people go; and he told Moses to leave him and come before him no more, for if he should see his face again Moses should surely be put to death.

Then Moses told Pharaoh of one more punishment; he said that the Lord himself was coming into Egypt; he would come,

Moses said, about the middle of the night, and would cause the oldest son in every house to die. Pharaoh's oldest son and the oldest son of all his servants should die on that dreadful night, and there would be a great cry of trouble and grief over all the land, such as had never been before and would never be again. But not even a dog should harm one of the children of Israel. None of their sons should die, so that Pharaoh might know that he and his people were the ones whom the Lord intended to punish, and not the children of Israel. After this punishment, Moses said, the Egyptians would come and bow down to him, and beg him to take the people and go out of the land. And when Moses had told Pharaoh this, he went out from him in great anger.

And the Lord commanded the Israelites, both the men and the women, to ask the Egyptians for their jewels of silver and their jewels of gold; their necklaces and earrings, and whatever ornaments they wore; and when the children of Israel did so, the Lord made the Egyptians willing to give them a great many of these things.

And the Lord told Moses and Aaron that every man among the children of Israel should take a lamb from the flock, and keep it four days. Afterward he was to kill it in the evening. And he was to take a bunch of a plant called hyssop, and to dip it in the blood of the lamb. Then he was to go to the door of his house, and strike the hyssop upon each side of the door, and over it, so that there would be three marks of blood outside of every house where the children of Israel lived. When the man had done this, he was to go into the house again, and no one was to come out of it until morning.

And the lamb which had been killed was to be roasted with fire, and every person in the house was to eat of it that night. This is the way they were to eat of it: with their clothes girded around them, their shoes on their feet and their staves in their hands, all ready to go out of Egypt. They were to make haste while they ate of it; because the Lord would go through the land that night, and would cause the oldest sons of all the Egyptians to die, so that Pharaoh and his people should let the children of Israel go. But he promised that, when he saw the marks of the blood on the houses where the children of Israel lived, he would pass over those houses, and not harm any one in them. Therefore the supper of the lamb, which the children of Israel ate that night, was called the Lord's passover. And the Lord commanded them at this supper, and for seven days afterward, to eat only one kind of bread. It was called unleavened bread, because there was no leaven, or yeast, in it.

And Moses called the elders of the children of Israel to him, and told them what the Lord had said, and the elders told the people. Then every man took his lamb, and kept it four days. Afterward he killed it in the evening, and dipped the bunch of hyssop in its blood, and struck the wood outside of his door, so that there were three marks of blood on every house where the children of Israel lived. And those who were in the house ate of the lamb that night; they ate of it with their clothes girded around them, with their shoes on their feet, and with their staves in their hands, all ready to go out of Egypt.

And that same night, in the middle of the night, the Lord passed through the land. And wherever he saw the marks of the blood on a house, he passed over that house and did no harm to any one in it. But on the houses of the Egyptians there were no marks of blood, and the Lord sent his destroying angel into every Egyptian's house, and caused the oldest son there to die. Pharaoh's son and the sons of his servants died. And the king rose up in the night, and all his people, and there was a great cry of distress through all the land, for there was not a house where there was not one dead.

And Pharaoh called for Moses and Aaron, and told them to go out of Egypt and to take all the children of Israel with them. He said, Take your flocks and your herds, and be gone. And the Egyptians begged them to go, and to go quickly, for they were afraid that the Lord would cause them all to die. And the children of Israel went, carrying their clothes bound up with their kneading troughs on their shoulders. And the Egyptians gave them jewels of silver, and jewels of gold, and raiment also, so they went out with great riches. And many other persons who were not Israelites went with them.

THE DESTROYING ANGEL PASSING THROUGH EGYPT

We have read in the book of Genesis where God told **Abraham** that his descendants should live in a strange land for many years, and that the people there would treat them cruelly. Yet God said he would punish the people who treated them so, and afterward would bring the children of Israel out of that land with great riches. It had been more than four hundred years since God spoke those words to Abraham, but now he made them come true.

The lamb which the children of Israel killed at the supper of the passover was like the lamb which Abel offered up on the altar. We have read how Abel's lamb meant, or represented, the Saviour. So this passover lamb represented him. The passover lamb died for the people, and the Saviour was coming, after many years, to die for them. When the Lord came into Egypt in the night, he did not punish those who had the marks of the lamb's blood on their houses. And when he shall come to the earth on the Judgment day he will not punish those who have the marks of the Saviour's blood on their hearts, that is, whose hearts have been cleansed from sin by his blood.

CHAPTERS XIII–XXIV (13–24)

GOD GOES BEFORE THE CHILDREN OF ISRAEL IN A PILLAR OF CLOUD. THEY PASS THROUGH THE RED SEA. THE EGYPTIANS, FOLLOWING THEM, ARE DROWNED. THE ISRAELITES MURMUR, AND MANNA AND QUAILS ARE SENT, AND WATER OUT OF THE ROCK. THEY FIGHT WITH THE AMALEKITES. GOD SPEAKS THE WORDS OF THE TEN COMMANDMENTS.

AFTER Pharaoh had let the children of Israel go, the Lord led them toward Canaan. Yet not by the shortest way, which passed through the land of the Philistines, lest the Philistines should make war against them and they should be discouraged and go back into Egypt. The Lord showed them another way, toward the Red Sea. And Moses took the dead body of Joseph with him, because, as we have read, Joseph, before he died, made the children of Israel promise that they would carry him up when they should go back to Canaan.

And the people journeyed to a place called Etham on the edge of the wilderness. There they set up their tents and made a camp. As they journeyed, the Lord went before them in a cloud to show them the way. The cloud was shaped like a pillar, reaching up toward heaven. They could see it all the time. In the day it was the color of a cloud, but at night it was the color of fire. It gave them light at night, so that they could journey both in the day and in the night when the Lord commanded. And the Lord did not take away the pillar of cloud in the day, or the pillar of fire in the night, from before the people.

But after the children of Israel had left Egypt, Pharaoh and his servants were sorry they had let them go, and they said, Why have we let Israel go from serving us? Then Pharaoh made ready his chariot, and took with him all the chariots in which his soldiers rode out to battle, and went after them. And he came up to them while they were encamping by the sea. When Pharaoh came near, the children of Israel looked back and saw the Egyptians marching after them. Then they were greatly afraid and cried out to the Lord. They blamed Moses also for bringing them away from Egypt. It would have been better for them, they said, to stay and work for the Egyptians than to be slain there in the wilderness. But Moses told the people not to fear. He said to them, Wait, and see how the Lord will save you; for the Egyptians, whom ye have seen to-day, you shall see no more forever. The Lord will fight for you, and you need do nothing but be still.

And Pharaoh and his army followed after the children of Israel until they had almost come up with them. Then the cloud which went before the children of Israel changed its place and came behind them. It came between Pharaoh's army and the children of Israel. That side of it which was turned toward Pharaoh's army grew very dark, so that the soldiers could not see to come any nearer to the children of Israel all that night. But the other side of the cloud, which was turned toward the children of Israel, was bright like fire and gave them light in their camp.

And the Lord said to Moses, Speak unto the children of Israel, that they go forward. And lift up thy rod and stretch out thy hand over the sea, and the children of Israel shall go

on dry ground through the sea. Then Moses lifted up his rod
and stretched out his hand over the sea. And the Lord sent
a great wind all that night, which blew the water away from
that part of the sea, so that the bottom of the sea was left dry.
And the children of Israel went down into it, and walked on
the bottom of the sea on dry ground. The waters were piled
up high on each side of them like a wall; yet they did not

THE EGYPTIANS ARE DROWNED IN THE RED SEA

come down to drown them, all the while they were walking
through the sea.

And that is the way the children of Israel went out of Egypt.
They walked through the Red Sea on dry ground till they all
came safe to the other side. When Pharaoh saw they had gone,
he and his chariots and his horsemen followed after them, for
he thought that they would be able to pass through the sea
as the children of Israel had done. But in the morning the
Lord looked out of the pillar of fire and of the cloud on the

Egyptians as they were marching through the sea. And he made the wheels of their chariots come off, so that they could drive but slowly, and he troubled the Egyptians. Then they were afraid and said to each other, Let us make haste back, for the Lord fights against us and he fights for the children of Israel. But before they had time to go the Lord told Moses to stretch out his hand over the sea once more. And Moses stretched out his hand; and the waters came together again and covered the Egyptians in the bottom of the sea. Then all Pharaoh's horses and his horsemen, and all his army were drowned. Not one of them was left alive. And the children of Israel saw them lying dead upon the seashore, where the waters washed them up.

But Moses and the Israelites were safe on the other side of the Red Sea. There they sang a song of praise to the Lord for saving them from Pharaoh. And Moses brought the people into the wilderness, and they journeyed for three days and found no water. And they came to a place called Marah. There they found water, but when they had tasted it they could not drink, for it was bitter. Then they complained against Moses, and said, What shall we drink? And Moses prayed to the Lord, and the Lord showed him a tree which he took and threw into the water, and the water was made sweet so that the people could drink of it.

And they journeyed and came to Elim, where were twelve wells and seventy palm trees. And they journeyed again, and came to the desert of Sin. And the people, because they were hungry, spoke wickedly to Moses and Aaron. They said that while they were in Egypt they had plenty of bread and flesh to eat. They wished that God had made them die there, for Moses and Aaron had brought them out in the wilderness on purpose to kill them with hunger. And the Lord told Moses he had heard their complainings, and that in the evening they should have flesh to eat, and in the morning as much bread as they wanted. Then they would know that it was the Lord who took care of them.

And the Lord did as he promised; for in the evening, about the time the sun was going down, great numbers of quails came flying up to the camp, so that the people could catch them. And in the morning, after the dew was dried, there was left, spread all over the ground, a small, white, round thing which looked like the frost. When the children of Israel saw it they did not know what it was. But Moses said to them, This is the food which the Lord has given you to eat. And the Lord commanded the people to go out and gather it, each man as much as he and his family would need for one day. But the Lord said they must not

EASTERN QUAIL

gather any to keep till the next day, for by that time there would be more on the ground for them; and the Lord wanted them to trust him, each day, for their daily bread. Yet some of them disobeyed the Lord and kept part of what they gathered till the next morning, and by that time it was spoiled and had worms in it.

After that the people went out every day and gathered the food which the Lord sent for them. When they had gathered enough, and the sun had grown hot, all that was left on the ground melted away. But on the day before the Sabbath the men gathered twice as much as they did on other days, and what they saved of this was not spoiled by the next morning. For the Lord sent none on the Sabbath, because he did not want the people to go out and gather it or to do any work on that day. Therefore he sent them enough for two days on the day before the Sabbath. Yet some of them went out to gather it on the Sabbath, but found none. And the Lord was displeased because they went; so after that they did not go out, but rested on the Sabbath day.

The people called this new food Manna: it was small, and round, and white, like the seed called coriander seed, and tasted like cakes made with honey. And Moses told Aaron to take a

GATHERING THE MANNA

pot and put into it as much as one man would eat in a day. And that pot of Manna, the Lord said, must always be kept, so that the Israelites who should live long afterward might see what kind of food the Lord had given the children of Israel.

when he led them through the wilderness to the land of Canaan. And the people ate manna until they came into that land.

And they journeyed and came to a place called Rephidim, but found no water there. Then they found fault with Moses

MOSES BRINGS WATER FROM THE ROCK

and said to him, Give us water that we may drink. Moses asked why they found fault with him. They answered that he had brought them out of Egypt to kill them, and their little children, and their cattle with thirst. Then Moses cried to the Lord and said, What shall I do to these people? For they are almost ready to stone me.

Now by this time they had come near to the mountain called Horeb, where Moses saw the fire burning in the bush, and where the Lord told him he should bring the people. And when he asked what he should do, because they were almost ready to stone him, the Lord commanded him to take his rod in his hand and go on before the people, until he came to a rock that was

AARON AND HUR HOLDING UP MOSES' HANDS

in Horeb, and the Lord said that Moses should strike the rock with his rod and then water would come out of it. And Moses obeyed the Lord. He took the rod in his hand and struck the rock, and water flowed out of it, and the children of Israel drank of the water.

And a people, called the Amalekites, came and fought against them. Now there was among the children of Israel a brave man named Joshua, and Moses said to him, Choose men, and go out to fight with the Amalekites; to-morrow I will stand on the top of the hill with the rod of God in my hand. And Joshua did as Moses told him. He chose men and went out and fought with the Amalekites, and Moses went up to the top of the hill, and Aaron, and a man named Hur, went with him. Then Moses held up the rod, and as long as he held it up the children of Israel overcame the Amalekites, but whenever he let it down the Amalekites overcame them. And Moses' hands were tired with holding up the rod so long, therefore Aaron and Hur took a stone and put it under him, and he sat upon it. Then they held up his hands, one on the one side, and the other on the other side, till the going down of the sun, and God gave the children of Israel the victory. But God was displeased with the Amalekites for making war against them, and he said that the time should come when that people would all be destroyed, and no one would remember them.

In the third month after the children of Israel went out of Egypt, they came near the mountain called Sinai, and encamped before it. And Moses went up on the mountain and the Lord spoke to him there. He told him to say to the people that they had seen how he punished the Egyptians for their sakes, and afterward brought them out of that land. And now, the Lord said, if they would obey his commandments he would love them more than any other people.

And the Lord said he would come down in a thick cloud and speak with Moses on mount Sinai, so that the people should hear him; and he commanded Moses to tell them to wash their clothes and make themselves clean, and to be very careful not to sin, but to be ready for the third day, when the Lord was coming down before them all on mount Sinai. On that day, God said, none of them might go up on the mountain, for whoever should go there would surely be put to death. But when they should hear the great sound of a trumpet far up on the mountain, they should come and stand at the foot of the mountain.

After the Lord had spoken these things, Moses went down and told the people, and they washed their clothes, and were careful not to sin. And on the third day, in the morning, there were thunderings and lightnings and a thick cloud on mount Sinai. And the trumpet, which, no doubt, an angel blew, sounded very loud, so that all the people trembled when they heard it. Then Moses led them out of the camp, and they came and stood near the foot of the mount. And all the mountain smoked, because the Lord came down in fire upon it, and the smoke went up like the smoke from a furnace, and the mountain shook greatly. And when the trumpet sounded long, and grew louder and louder, Moses spoke, and God answered him, and called him to the top of the mount.

And God spoke, on mount Sinai, the words of

THE TEN COMMANDMENTS

I

THOU SHALT HAVE NO OTHER GODS BUT ME

This means that we must love God more than anything else; for if we love anything more than Him, then that is our idol that we set up in His place, to serve instead of Him.

II

THOU SHALT NOT MAKE ANY GRAVEN IMAGE, NOR BOW DOWN TO IT NOR WORSHIP IT

There are a great many people in the world who believe that an image of gold, or silver, or wood, or stone can help to save them. But in this commandment God forbids every man to make such an image, or to bow down to it and worship it; for God is the only one who can save men, and they are to worship Him alone.

III

THOU SHALT NOT TAKE THE NAME OF THE LORD THY GOD IN VAIN

This means that whenever we speak God's name, we must do it reverently, remembering how great and holy a name it is. For if we speak it carelessly or thoughtlessly we offend Him.

IV

REMEMBER THE SABBATH DAY, TO KEEP IT HOLY

We keep the Sabbath holy when we do not take that day for work nor for week-day employments, but spend the time in worshipping God, in reading His word, in thinking and talking about His kindness to us, and in doing good to others.

V

HONOR THY FATHER AND THY MOTHER

Next to obeying God, we should obey our parents; not putting off what they tell us to do, nor even waiting to be told, if we know their wishes already. But doing, out of love to them, such things as they approve; for this is God's commandment.

VI

THOU SHALT NOT KILL

We break this commandment not only when we kill a person, but when we feel as if we would be glad for him to die; because then we have the wish for his death in our hearts, and God looks at our hearts.

VII

THOU SHALT NOT COMMIT ADULTERY

When a man leaves his wife to live with another woman instead of her; and when a woman leaves her husband to live with another man instead of him, they commit adultery. God forbids us to commit this sin. He commands us, also, to be pure in all our thoughts, words, and actions.

VIII

THOU SHALT NOT STEAL

We must not take anything for our own that belongs to another. If we have ever done so, whether by mistake or on purpose, God commands us to give back, or to pay for, the things we have taken.

IX

THOU SHALT NOT BEAR FALSE WITNESS AGAINST THY NEIGHBOR

This means that we must never say anything about another person which is not true. And when we are saying what is true, we must be very careful how we say it, lest we leave out a little or add a little, and so make it different from the real truth.

X

THOU SHALT NOT COVET ANY THING THAT IS THY NEIGHBOR'S

To covet a thing is to wish that it was ours. We must not covet what belongs to another. God gives us all just what we ought to have, and he knows best whose everything should be.

And all the people heard the thunderings, and the sound of the trumpet, and they saw the lightnings and the mountain smoking. They heard God's voice, also, and were afraid. Then they said to Moses, Speak thou with us and we will hear; but let not God speak with us, lest we die. But Moses told them that God had not come to cause them to die, but to make them fear to sin against him. And the people stood a good way off from the mountain, but Moses went up to the mountain near to the dark cloud where God was.

There God talked with him, and gave him many more laws for the children of Israel to obey. Afterward Moses came down from the mount, and wrote th se laws in a book, and read them out to the people. When the people heard them, they promised to obey all the words that the Lord had spoken.

CHAPTERS XXIV–XXXI (24–31)

GOD CALLS MOSES UP ON MOUNT SINAI AGAIN, AND PROMISES TO GIVE HIM TWO TABLES OF STONE WITH THE TEN COMMANDMENTS WRITTEN ON THEM. HE COMMANDS THAT THE TABERNACLE SHALL BE BUILT, AND SAYS THAT AARON AND HIS SONS SHALL BE PRIESTS.

AND the Lord told Moses to come up on mount Sinai again. He said that he would give him tables of stone with the Ten Commandments written upon them. And Moses went up on the mount, and Joshua went with him; Joshua was his servant or minister. And there came a cloud and covered the mountain for six days. On the seventh day the Lord called to Moses out of the cloud, and Moses went up into the cloud and stayed on the mountain forty days and forty nights. And the children of Israel saw the glory of the Lord on the top of the mount, like a bright burning fire there.

And the Lord spoke to Moses and told him that the children of Israel should build a tabernacle, or church, where they should worship him; and he showed Moses a pattern of this tabernacle like which they were to build it. It was to be very beautiful, and to have many beautiful things in it and around it, some made of gold, some of silver, and some of brass. There were to be curtains of fine linen also, with rich work embroidered upon them. It would take a great deal of gold and silver, of brass, and of linen to make all these things; but God told Moses to ask the people for them, and whoever wanted to bring an offering to the Lord might bring whatever he chose.

God commanded Moses to have an ark made, which was to be placed inside of the tabernacle. This ark was a chest, or box, made first of wood and then covered over with gold; both the inside and outside were covered with gold, so that the wood could not be seen. After it should be finished, Moses was to put into it the two tables of stone which God would give him.

A cover, also, was to be m.de for the ark, of pure gold, with two golden cherubim, or angels, upon it; one at one end, and the other at the other end. These cherubim were to have their faces turned toward each other and their wings spread out. The cover, with the cherubim upon it, was to be called the Mercy-seat.

And a table was to be made of wood, covered over with gold, to stand in the tabernacle; a golden candlestick, also, which should burn and give light there.

And God told Moses how the tabernacle itself should be made. As the people were to carry it with them on their journey to the land of Canaan, it would have to be made in such a way that they could take it down and put it up again, something like a tent. The sides of it were to be of boards covered with gold; these boards were to stand on end and be fastened together. Over their tops curtains were to be spread, from one side to the other, for the roof. The door was to be a curtain hanging down in front; and there was to be another beautiful curtain, called the veil, hanging across the inside of the tabernacle, so as to make two rooms there. Moses was to bring the ark, with the mercy-seat upon it, into one of those rooms; in the other he was to set the golden table and the golden candlestick.

And he was commanded to make a wall, or fence, around the tabernacle, a little way off from it, that there might be a yard around it. The yard was called the court. And an altar was to be made, which should stand in the court, before the door of the tabernacle. It was to be made of wood first, and then covered over with brass, and was to be very large; because oxen and sheep and goats were to be offered upon it. For until the Saviour should come into the world and be offered up on the cross, the children of Israel were to offer up these animals on the altar to show that he was coming.

And the Lord told Moses that Aaron and his sons should be ministers, or priests, at the tabernacle. Aaron was to be called the high priest, for he would be the chief one; his four sons were to be called priests.

Beautiful garments were to be made for Aaron; a linen cap, or turban, called a mitre, for his head, with a plate of gold fastened to its front, having these words written on it, HOLINESS TO THE LORD. This would remind Aaron that God commanded him to be holy. It would remind the people, also, whenever they saw it, to honor him as God's high priest.

HIGH PRIEST

Next his flesh Aaron was to wear a coat made of embroidered linen, with sleeves to it; this coat was to reach to his feet.

Over the linen coat he was to wear a coat, or robe, of blue, that had no sleeves. Around the lower edge of this robe were to be hung pomegranates made of blue, and purple, and scarlet. Pomegranates are a fruit something like an orange. Those on the robe were not real pomegranates, but ornaments made to look like them. Between the pomegranates were to be hung golden bells.

And over the robe of blue Aaron was to wear a third coat. It was to be shorter than the robe of blue, and, like it, was to have no sleeves, but was to be of different colors; it was called the ephod.

On his breast Aaron was to wear the breastplate. This was a square piece of richly embroidered cloth, with twelve precious stones set upon it. These stones were of the most beautiful kinds, such as the ruby, the sapphire, and the diamond. Aaron's dress was to be very splendid; and his four sons were to have dresses made for them also; but their dresses were not so beautiful as Aaron's, because he was to be the high priest.

And the Lord told Moses that after the tabernacle should be finished, he should bring Aaron and his sons to the door of it. There he was to wash them with water. And he was to put on them the garments which had been made for them, and to pour oil on Aaron's head and anoint him. Afterward he was to offer up sacrifices for them. These things Moses was to do, so that Aaron and his sons might be consecrated, or made priests, for the children of Israel. And after they had been made priests, they were to offer up two lambs every day on the great brass altar, one in the morning and the other in the evening, for the sins of the people.

And God commanded Moses to make another altar, not of brass like that for the burnt offerings, but of wood covered over with gold. It was to be smaller than the brass altar, and was to stand inside of the tabernacle, in the room with the golden table and the golden candlestick. This altar was not to have animals burned upon it, but incense. Incense was made of gum from a tree, mixed with some spices which the Lord told Moses of. When burned, it sent up a smoke that was sweet to smell.

We have read that the animals which were burned on the brass altar meant, or represented, the Saviour. Now the incense, sending up its sweet smoke from the golden altar, is supposed to have meant the prayers of God's people going up to heaven. Aaron was commanded to burn incense on the golden altar every morning and evening, at the time he should come into the tabernacle to trim and light the lamps on the golden candlestick.

And God commanded Moses to make a laver, or great basin, out of brass, to hold water. It was to stand in the court, outside of the tabernacle and near the great brass altar.

After the Lord had given Moses all these commandments about the tabernacle and the things that should go into it, he told him who should attend to making them. This was a man named Bezaleel, one of the children of Israel, whom the Lord said he had taught to work in silver and gold, in brass and precious stones, and to make all kinds of beautiful work. Another man named Aholiab was to help him. Beside these there were others whom God taught, as many as were needed to make all the things which God had commanded should be made.

And when the Lord was done talking with Moses, he gave him the two tables of stone with the ten commandments written upon them, which God had written there with his own hand.

CHAPTERS XXXII–XL (32–40)

THE PEOPLE WORSHIP THE GOLDEN CALF. MOSES BREAKS THE TWO TABLES
OF STONE. THE LEVITES SLAY THREE THOUSAND MEN. GOD WRITES
THE TEN COMMANDMENTS ON TWO NEW TABLES. THE TABERNACLE
IS MADE AND SET UP. THE CLOUD RESTS UPON IT.

Now all the time that God had been talking to Moses, and telling him of the things that were to be made, Moses was on mount Sinai; he stayed there, as we have read, forty days and forty nights. But the children of Israel were in their camp at the foot of the mount. And when they saw that Moses stayed so long they grew impatient, and came to Aaron, and said, As for this Moses, the man that brought us up out of Egypt, we know not what has become of him. And they asked Aaron to make idols for them, such as the heathen nations worshipped. Aaron said, Break off the golden earrings which are in the ears of your wives, and of your sons, and of your daughters, and bring them to me. So the people brought them, and Aaron took them and put them into the fire, and melted them, and made an idol in the shape of a calf.

Then the people said that the calf was their god that had

brought them up out of Egypt. And Aaron built an altar before it, and told them that the next day they should hold a feast. And early in the morning they rose up and offered burnt offerings to the calf, instead of to the Lord, and they had a feast and ate and drank before the idol. While they were doing these things Moses was still on the mount. He

MOSES BREAKING THE TWO TABLES OF STONE

could not see them, but the Lord saw them, and told him to go down, because his people had done wickedly. They have made a calf, the Lord said, and worshipped it and sacrificed to it, and called it their god.

And Moses turned and went down mount Sinai, with the two tables of stone in his hand. Joshua, his servant, was with him, and as they came near the camp he heard the noise of the people shouting, and Joshua said to Moses, There is a noise of war in the camp. Moses answered that it was not the noise of war, but the noise of singing he heard. When they came nearer Moses saw the golden calf and the people dancing before it. Then he was in great anger, and threw the two tables of stone out of his hands, and they were broken in pieces as they fell down below the mount.

And Moses took the calf and burned it in the fire, and ground it up into very small pieces, like powder or dust. Then he strewed the dust on the water that they drank, and made the children of Israel drink of the water. And he asked Aaron why he had helped them to do this great sin. Then Aaron tried to excuse himself, saying that the people were determined to do wickedly, and they asked him to make an idol for them, and brought him their gold, and when he put it into the fire, it came out in the shape of a calf. But it would not have come out so unless Aaron had given it that shape. And when the people asked him to make them an idol, he who was to be their high priest should have told them how wicked it would be, instead of helping them to do it.

And Moses stood at the gate of the camp, and said that all the men who were on the Lord's side should come to him. Then all the men who were the descendants of Levi, one of Joseph's brethren, came to him. And he told them that God commanded each one of them to take his sword and go through the camp from one end of it to the other, and slay every man he should meet. In this way God would punish the people for their wickedness. And the Levites did as Moses told them, and they slew that day about three thousand men of the children of Israel.

The next day Moses spoke to the people, and said, that although they had done a great sin, he would go and pray to the Lord for them, and perhaps their sin might be forgiven. And he went and prayed to the Lord, saying, O, this people have sinned a great sin, and made an idol of gold. And he begged that God would forgive them. But God said he would punish those who had sinned against him, and that he would not go with them in the cloud, as he had done before, to show them the way to Canaan. Then Moses prayed very earnestly that he would go, and the Lord heard his prayer, and promised that he would still go with the children of Israel.

And God told Moses to make two tables of stone like those he had broken. God said he would write on these new tables the same words that were written on the first tables. And he commanded Moses to be ready in the morning, and come up to the top of the mount. But no man was to come with him, or to be anywhere on the mount, and no flocks or herds were to feed there. So Moses cut out of the rock two tables, like those he had broken, and he rose early in the morning and went up on mount Sinai, with the tables in his hand. And the Lord came down in the cloud and passed by before him, so that Moses could hear his voice. Then Moses made haste, and bowed down to the earth and worshipped. And he prayed that the Lord would forgive the children of Israel, and take them to be his people again. And the Lord heard his prayer, and took them to be his people again, and promised that he would do wonderful things for them, and would drive out the wicked nations of Canaan, to make room in that land for the children of Israel.

And the Lord told Moses that he must be careful, when he should come into Canaan, not to make friends of those wicked nations. He must throw down the altars which they had built to their idols, and break those idols in pieces, because the children of Israel were not to worship idols, but the Lord. And Moses stayed on mount Sinai forty days and forty nights. In all that time, and in the forty days and forty nights that he spent there before, he did neither eat bread nor drink water. And the Lord wrote on the two tables of stone which Moses brought the words of the Ten Commandments.

After the forty days and forty nights were ended, Moses came down with the tables in his hand. And the skin of his face was bright and shining, because he had been so near to the Lord, though Moses did not know that his face shone. When Aaron and all the children of Israel saw his face shine they were afraid to come near him, but he called them to him. Then they came, and he told them the words that the Lord had spoken. But while he was speaking with them he put a veil on his face that it might not dazzle them.

And Moses called all the children of Israel together, and said that the Lord had commanded them to keep the Sabbath day holy; and now he also commanded them to bring gold and silver, and brass and wood, and whatever else was needed to build the tabernacle. Then the people brought whatever they chose to

MOSES SPEAKS TO ALL THE PEOPLE

give—bracelets and earrings, ornaments of gold and silver, brass and fine linen, and wood. Some brought precious stones also for the breastplate and oil for the lamp. Both men and women brought offerings for all the different kinds of work which the Lord had commanded Moses to have made. They did this willingly; and even after enough had been brought, they still kept on bringing more every morning, until Moses sent word through the camp that they should stop bringing. And he gave their offerings to Bezaleel, and Aholiab, and the other men whom the Lord had taught to do the work.

9

Then these men made curtains of fine linen, of blue and purple and scarlet, for the tabernacle; and curtains of goats' hair, and of goats' skins dyed red, to be spread over the tabernacle for its roof.   Also that beautiful curtain of blue and purple and scarlet, called the veil, that was to be hung inside of the tabernacle to make two rooms there; and the curtain that was to hang down in front for the door.   They made the boards also, covered with gold, which were to be set up and fastened together for the sides of the tabernacle.

And Bezaleel made the ark which God had commanded should be made, first out of wood, afterward he covered it, both on the inside and the outside, with gold.   And he made the cover of the ark, called the Mercy-seat.   There was no wood in this—it was all of

ARK   GOLDEN CANDLESTICK   TABLE OF SHEWBREAD

pure gold. And he made two cherubim, or angels, of gold, to be one on the one end of it and the other on the other end.   Their faces were turned toward each other and their wings were spread out.

And he made the table for the inside of the tabernacle ot wood covered with gold.   Around the edge of it was a golden border, like a little fence or railing.   He made dishes and bowls and spoons also for the table, all of gold.   And he made the golden candlestick with six branches out of its sides, three out of one side and three out of the other.   On these branches were shapes of almonds and flowers, worked in the gold.   There were seven lamps belonging to the candlestick, to hold oil and burn. And he made the altar of incense, out of wood first, and covered the wood over with gold.

And he made the oil which was to be poured on Aaron's head when he should be anointed as high priest, and the sweet incense that was to be burned on the golden altar. And Bezaleel made the altar of burnt offering, on which the children of Israel were to offer up sacrifices—oxen, lambs, and goats. First it was made of wood, and then covered over with brass. And he made the laver of brass, which was a great basin, or bowl, to hold water, for Aaron and his sons to wash their hands and their feet in; because God commanded them always to wash their hands and

ALTAR OF INCENSE   ALTAR OF BURNT OFFERING   LAVER

their feet before they went into the tabernacle, or came to the altar of burnt offering to offer up a sacrifice there.

And Bezaleel made the posts or pillars of brass, which were to stand around the tabernacle to make a court, or yard, around it; and he made the curtains that were to hang between those pillars, for a wall, or fence; also, the curtain that was to hang down in front of the court for its gate.

And Bezaleel and Aholiab made the clothes for Aaron; his linen coat, and the coat called the ephod, of blue, and purple, and scarlet. They took gold and beat it very thin, and cut it into little strips, and worked these strips in among the purple, the blue, and the scarlet, to make this coat more beautiful. And with it they made a belt, or girdle, of the same stuff as the ephod itself. This was to be fastened around Aaron's body over the ephod. And they made the breastplate with twelve precious stones upon it. Each stone was set in a piece of gold. Aaron was to wear this on his breast. It was to hang there by two chains of gold coming down from his shoulders.

And they made the robe, or coat, which Aaron was to wear underneath the ephod. It was all of blue, and around its lower edge were hung pomegranates of blue, and purple, and scarlet; and between them the golden bells, which were to ring as Aaron went in and out of the tabernacle. And they made coats of fine linen for Aaron's sons, and linen trowsers also; and the mitre for Aaron's head, with the plate of gold having these words written on it, HOLINESS TO THE LORD.

So the different parts of the tabernacle were finished, and ready to be put together. And they brought them to Moses, and he looked at all the work, and saw it was done as God had commanded.

And God spoke to him, and told him to set up the tabernacle. Then Moses set up the boards covered with gold, for its sides, and spread over them the curtains which had been made for its roof, and these curtains covered the tabernacle, and hung down on each side of it. And he put the two tables of stone with the ten commandments written on them into the ark, and covered the ark with the mercy-seat. Then he brought the ark, with the mercy-seat upon it, into the tabernacle, and hung up the curtain called the veil, so that it made two rooms there, and he left the ark in the innermost room.

And he stood the golden table, and the golden candlestick, and the golden altar in the other room, and hung up the curtain which was made for a door in front of the tabernacle. Outside of the door, but not far from it, he stood the altar of burnt offering, and he offered up a sacrifice upon it. He set the laver near to the altar and put water in it, and Moses and Aaron and his sons washed their hands and their feet at the laver. And Moses set up the brass pillars around the tabernacle, and hung up the curtains between them for a wall, and made the court around the tabernacle. And he hung up the curtain of blue and purple, and scarlet and fine linen, which had been made for the gate of the court.

So the tabernacle was set up, and the court; and everything was put in its place inside of the court, and of the tabernacle. Then the pillar of cloud, that went before the children of Israel to show them the way, came over the tabernacle and covered it. And the glory of the Lord filled the inside of the tabernacle, so that Moses could not go into it.

THE BOOK OF LEVITICUS

CHAPTERS I–XIX (1–19)

GOD SPEAKS TO MOSES OUT OF THE TABERNACLE. AARON AND HIS SONS ARE CONSECRATED. THE BURNT OFFERING AND THE PEACE OFFERING. NADAB AND ABIHU ARE SLAIN. ANIMALS CLEAN AND UNCLEAN. LAWS FOR THE LEPROSY. THE DAY OF ATONEMENT. OTHER LAWS ARE GIVEN.

AFTER the tabernacle was finished God did not call Moses up on mount Sinai again to speak with him, but he called him into the tabernacle. For God came into the tabernacle in a cloud, over the mercy-seat, where the golden cherubim spread out their wings; and he spoke with Moses there, and gave him many new laws for the children of Israel.

And God told Moses to bring Aaron and his sons to the door of the tabernacle to consecrate them, or make them priests. Then Moses brought them, and he called all the people that they might come and see what the Lord had commanded him to do. And while they stood around the door of the tabernacle he took Aaron and his sons and washed them with water; and he put on Aaron the beautiful garments that had been made for him. Then he poured oil upon his head and anointed him. He took Aaron's sons also and put their garments on them, and afterward offered up sacrifices to God. So Aaron and his sons were made priests, to stay at the tabernacle and burn incense and offer up sacrifices for the children of Israel. Before this time other men might offer up their own sacrifices, as Abel, Noah, and Abraham had done. But now that God had chosen Aaron and his sons to be priests, no one else might offer up a sacrifice; every man must bring his offering to the tabernacle, and let the priests burn it for him on the altar that was there.

After Aaron was made high priest, he took a lamb and killed it, and laid it on the altar as an offering for the sins of all the people, but he put no fire under it. Then the Lord sent fire that burned up the lamb. When the people saw the fire they shouted for joy, for now they knew that the Lord was pleased with their priest and with their offering. Afterward the priests always kept that fire burning on the altar, and would not let it go out, because the Lord had sent it there for them.

The priests were commanded to offer up two lambs every day, one in the morning and the other in the evening, for the sins of all the children of Israel. But God told Moses that if any man who was sorry for his sins wanted to bring an offering for himself alone, he might bring an ox, or a sheep, or a goat to the door of the tabernacle. There he was to lay his hand upon its head. This was as if the man put his sins away from himself on to the animal. Then he was to kill the animal; and Aaron's sons, the priests, would burn it for him on the altar, and God would be pleased with it for an offering. God would be pleased with the man's offering and forgive his sins, not because the innocent animal had died for him, but because the Saviour was coming to bear his sins and die for him, like the animal. The animal (like Abel's lamb and the passover lamb) was meant to represent the Saviour, and to show that he was coming. This was the only reason why God was pleased with animals for offerings.

There were different kinds of offerings. When a man brought one because he repented of his sins, and wanted to be forgiven, the priests took it and burned the whole of it on the altar. Therefore it was called a burnt offering. But when he brought one because he was thankful for some blessing which God had given him, or because he wanted some blessing which he was praying that God would send him, then the priest took the animal and burned only part of it on the altar, not all; some of it the priests kept for themselves to eat, and some of it they gave back to the man for him to eat. This offering, that was part burned and part eaten, was called a peace offering.

And the man who brought the peace offering, after the priest had given him back his part, invited his family and his friends, and perhaps his poor neighbors, and they feasted on it. For the man was not allowed to put his part by and keep it to eat at some future time; it must be eaten that same day or the next

HIGH PRIEST BURNING INCENSE

day. We often read in the Bible of the feasts which the people made with their peace offerings.

Aaron had four sons, who were all made priests when he was made high priest. It was their duty to attend to the worship of God at the tabernacle in the way that God commanded. We have read that God commanded incense to be burned on the golden altar. This incense was placed in a censer, which was something like a cup, made, we suppose, of brass. The priest first put coals of fire in the censer; afterward he carried it into the tabernacle and set it on the golden altar, and he sprinkled the incense on the coals, that it might burn and send up its sweet smoke there. The fire which he put in the censer was taken from off the altar of burnt offering, where God had sent it, and where, as we have read, it was never allowed to go out; for it was sacred fire.

But the Bible tells us that two of Aaron's sons, named Nadab and Abihu, put strange fire in their censers to burn incense. And God was angry at their sin and sent fire that burned them to death. And Moses called men to carry their dead bodies away from the tabernacle and out of the camp. And God commanded Aaron and his two sons who were still living not to rend their clothes, nor show any grief for Nadab and Abihu, because they had been put to death for sinning against God.

And the Lord told Moses what animals, and birds, and fishes the children of Israel might eat after they should come into the land of Canaan, for they were not to eat of every kind. They might eat of the ox, the deer, the sheep, and the goat; but not of the camel, the rabbit, or the pig. Of fishes they might eat all that had fins and scales on them, but those whose skins were smooth and without scales they might not eat. And they might eat of some kinds of birds, such as the dove, the pigeon, and the quail. But there were many others which were forbidden them, such as the eagle, the raven, the owl, and the swan. Those that they might eat were called clean animals, and those they might not eat were called unclean.

We have read of the leprosy which came suddenly upon Moses' hand, making it white as snow, and then was taken away again, leaving it well as it was before. God sent it upon Moses so that he might show the miracle to the children of Israel in Egypt. But the leprosy was a very dreadful disease that was sometimes sent upon persons for their sins. It was not taken away quickly then, but it stayed and often spread over their whole bodies, for no one could cure it but God.

And God told Moses and Aaron that when a man should have a spot or sore on his skin that seemed like the beginning of leprosy, he must be brought to the priest, that the priest might look at it and say whether it were leprosy or not. If it were, the man must go away from the camp, from his family, and from all the rest of the people, and live in some place alone until he should be made well. When God should make him well, he must be brought to the priest again. Then the priest would look at him and say that he was well. After that he might come back and live in the camp. But he must bring three lambs, or, if he were poor, and could not bring so many, he might bring one lamb and two doves or young pigeons to the tabernacle as offerings to the Lord who had healed him.

Now that room in the tabernacle where Moses had left the ark and where God came and dwelt, in a cloud, over the mercy-seat, was the most holy part of the tabernacle; it was called the most holy place. And the Lord told Moses that no one but Aaron, the high priest, might ever go there. And Aaron himself must not go often lest he should die. He might go but once every year, and then he must go very carefully. Before going he was to wash his flesh in water, that he might be clean, and he was to take off his splendid high priest's dress and put on a plainer dress of pure white linen; for he must go in humbly dressed before the Lord. He was to offer up sacrifices before going, for his own sins and the sins of all the people, and he was to take the blood of those sacrifices into the most holy place and sprinkle it, with his finger, before the mercy-seat; and there Aaron was to pray that the Lord would forgive him and all the people their sins.

And what was meant by the high priest doing these things? It was meant to show what the Saviour would do for us who trust in him. The high priest went to pray for the people into the most holy place on earth. The Saviour, after he was crucified, went to pray for us up in heaven. The high priest asked God to forgive the people for whom the sacrifices had died. The Saviour asked God to forgive us for whom he himself had died. Now the high priest has long since been dead, and can no more ask God to forgive us; but the Saviour still lives in heaven, and there he is asking God to forgive us every day.

On that day when Aaron went into the most holy place the

children of Israel were commanded to do no work, but to remember the sins they had committed. God said they should afflict
their souls for their sins, which means, they should think of them
and repent of them, with great sorrow. Whoever would not
do this, God said, should be punished; for that day was to be
the most solemn day of all the year to the children of Israel.
It was called the day of atonement.

God said that when the children of Israel should come into
Canaan and go into the fields, to cut down their grain and
bring it into their barns, they must not bring it quite all in,
they must leave a little. And when the grapes should be ripe
on their vines, and they should go out to gather them, they must
not take every grape, they must leave a few. They must do this
so that poor persons and strangers, who had no fields or vineyards of their own, might come and take what was left.

The Lord said that the children of Israel must not steal, nor
deceive, nor lie to one another. When a man had been working for them they should not tell him to wait until the next day
to be paid for what he had done; they should pay him that
same day for his work.

If a person were deaf, they must not speak against him
because he could not hear; or if he were blind, they must not
put things in his way to make him stumble and fall. If any
one knew some evil of another, he must not go about telling it,
he must not be a tale-bearer.

And the children of Israel were not to hate one another, but
they were to love each other as they loved themselves. When
one of them should see another do wrong, he must reprove him
kindly for what he had done; perhaps, then, he would repent
of his sin and do so no more.

If a stranger from another country should come to live among
them, they must not treat him unjustly, nor take away what
belonged to him. They must be as kind to him and love him
as much as though he had always lived with them and was one
of their own people.

CHAPTERS XX–XXIII–XXVI (20–23–26)

THE ISRAELITES MUST NOT GIVE THEIR CHILDREN TO MOLECH. THEY ARE
COMMANDED TO KEEP THREE FEASTS TO THE LORD EVERY YEAR. THE
BLASPHEMER IS STONED. THE SABBATH YEAR AND THE YEAR OF JUBILEE.
BLESSINGS PROMISED AND CURSES THREATENED.

THE heathen nations among whom the children of Israel were
going, worshipped an idol named Molech. We are told that

WORSHIPPING THE IDOL MOLECH

this idol was made of brass and had the face of a calf; and was
very large and hollow, so that a fire could be lighted inside
of it. After it was heated very hot those wicked people used to
put their little children into its arms, where they were burned to
death; while they were being burned the people beat drums, so
that their cries could not be heard. They burned their children in this way to please the idol, and they called it giving

their children to Molech. And God told Moses that if any man among the Israelites should give his children to Molech, he should be put to death; all the people should stone him with stones till he was dead. And if they should let him go without punishment, pretending not to know what he had done, God said that he himself would punish that man.

The Lord commanded the children of Israel to keep three feasts to him every year. The first was called the feast of the passover. We were told about this feast when they kept it for the first time on the night they came out of Egypt. And now, the Lord said, they should keep it once every year, eating of the lamb in the night as they did then, and for seven days afterward eating of unleavened bread. Through all those seven days it was called the feast of the passover. While the people were keeping this feast it would make them remember how God had punished Pharaoh for their sakes, and had set them free when Pharaoh was determined not to let them go.

Seven weeks after the passover, they were to keep the feast of harvest. It was to last but one day, and was to come after the grain had been gathered into the barn. Then the people would thank God for sending the rain and the sunshine, which had made their seed grow out in the field, and bear food enough for another year. At this feast, the Lord said, they should be glad and rejoice; they, and their sons, and their daughters, their men-servants, and their maid-servants, and all the people who lived in the land.

At the end of the year, when all the grain had been gathered in from the fields, all the fruits taken off from the trees, and all the grapes picked from the vines, they were to keep the feast of tabernacles. It was to last seven days. Then, the Lord said, they should cut off branches from the trees and make booths, or tents, of them; and they should come out of their houses and live in those booths for the seven days of the feast, because the children of Israel had lived in tents or booths while they were journeying through the wilderness. And the Lord wanted them to remember that time after they should come into Canaan and have houses there to live in. At each of these three feasts every man among the children of Israel was to come to the tabernacle and bring an offering to the Lord.

And God told Moses to command the people that they should bring olive-oil for the lamps in the tabernacle. Olives are a

FEAST OF HARVESTS

fruit that grows in Canaan. When they are bruised, or pressed, a very pure oil runs out of them. It was this oil the people were to bring for the seven lamps that belonged to the golden candle-stick. The Lord said that every day Aaron and his sons should trim the lamps, which were to burn all night in the tabernacle. None but the priests might trim them.

And God commanded Moses to take fine flour and bake twelve cakes, or loaves of bread. These were to be placed on the golden table which stood in the tabernacle near to the golden candlestick. He was to put them there on the sabbath day, and leave them a whole week, until the next sabbath. Then the priest was to take them away and put fresh loaves in their place. The priests were to do this every week. Aaron and his sons might eat of the old bread after it was taken away, but they might not carry it to their homes to eat it. They must eat it at the tabernacle, because it was holy bread; it had been set on the golden table before the Lord. These twelve loaves were called shew-bread.

Now there was, at this time, a man in the camp whose father was an Egyptian, but his mother was one of the children of Israel. He quarrelled with an Israelite, and, being angry, he blasphemed God's name; that is, he spoke wickedly of God. And they brought him to Moses; then they put him in some place to keep him safe until the Lord should tell Moses what his punishment must be. And the Lord spoke to Moses and commanded him to take the man out of the camp, and let all the people stone him. The Lord said that whoever blasphemed his name, whether it were one of the children of Israel or a stranger who had come to live among them, should surely be put to death; all the people should stone him till he was dead. And Moses told the people, and they took the man out of the camp and stoned him as the Lord commanded.

God said that after the children of Israel should come into the land of Canaan they should plant seed out in the field, and when it had grown, should cut it down and take it into the barn. They should do this for six years, but when the seventh year came they must not plant any seed at all, but must let the land alone. If any grain should grow by itself, without being planted, they must not cut it; or if any grapes should grow on the vines, they must not pick them, for this year, God said, should be a sabbath year, or year of rest, for the land. Every seventh year, he said, should be so. They were never to plant the seed nor take the grain into the barns, nor gather the grapes from the vines, in the seventh year. If any of the people were afraid they would not have food to eat, because they might not plant that year, the Lord told them that he would make enough grow the year before to last until the sabbath year had past, and the time had come again for them to sow their seed and reap their grain.

Once in fifty years was to come the year of jubilee. This was to be a glad and happy year; on the day that it began trumpets were to be blown through all the land. The people were not to sow nor reap in this year; God promised that he would give them enough food the year before, to last through the year of jubilee. Then, if any man had been very poor, so that he was forced to sell the field which his father had left him, when the year of jubilee came he was to have it back. The person who bought it must give it back to him, that it might be his own again; for the Lord said it must be given back to him. Or if any poor man among the children of

THE YEAR OF JUBILEE

Israel had been sold to be a servant, or slave, when the year of jubilee came he was to be a slave no longer; neither he nor his children, for the Lord said that then they should be free.

And God told the people that if they would obey his commandments, he would send rain on their land. Their grain should grow well, their trees should bear fruit, they should have plenty of bread to eat, and no man should hurt them. The Lord would destroy or drive away from Canaan the wild beasts that might do them harm; he himself would take care of them, and make all their enemies afraid of them.

But if they would not obey his commandments, God said they should have sickness and trouble. They would sow their grain, but it would do them no good, for when it had grown up their enemies would come and take it from them. Wild beasts would carry off their children and kill their cattle; and in the streets and roads where there used to be a great many people, only a few would be left. The Lord would send famine upon them, so that they should have no food, and pestilence, that they should die. Their enemies would make war on them also, and the children of Israel would be carried away from their own land to other lands, where the people would hate them. There many of them would perish. Yet if those who were left alive should confess that they had been wicked, and that it was God who had punished them, he would punish them no more, but would be kind to them, and bring them back to the land which he had promised Abraham, and Isaac, and Jacob to give them.

THE BOOK OF NUMBERS

CHAPTERS I–XII (1–12)

THE PEOPLE ARE NUMBERED. THE LEVITES ARE CHOSEN TO DO THE WORK AT THE TABERNACLE. THE CHILDREN OF ISRAEL LEAVE MOUNT SINAI. THEIR CAMP. THEY MURMUR FOR FLESH TO EAT. QUAILS ARE SENT, AND MANY OF THE PEOPLE DIE OF A PLAGUE. AARON AND MIRIAM SPEAK AGAINST MOSES.

MORE than a year had now passed since the children of Israel left Egypt, and they were still at mount Sinai, where their camp had been so long. For, first, they had waited there forty days and forty nights, while Moses was on the mount, when God gave him the two tables of stone with the Ten Commandments written upon them. But these were broken because the people worshipped the golden calf. Then they waited forty days and forty nights more while Moses went up with the two new tables which the Lord commanded him to make. Afterward they waited still longer while the tabernacle was building, and while God spoke to Moses inside of the tabernacle, giving him many new laws for the children of Israel to obey. But now the time was near when they should leave mount Sinai and go on their journey toward the land of Canaan.

The children of Israel were divided into great companies, called tribes. There were thirteen of these tribes. Each tribe was descended from one of the sons of Jacob or of Joseph. These were their names: the tribes of Reuben, Simeon, Levi, Judah, Zebulun, Issachar, Dan, Gad, Asher, Naphtali, Ephraim, Manasseh, and Benjamin. As they would have to fight against their enemies when they came into Canaan, the Lord commanded Moses and Aaron to number, or count, the men in the different tribes who were able to be soldiers and go out to war. And Moses and Aaron did so, and found there were six hundred and three thousand, five hundred and fifty of them.

But the men of the tribe of Levi were not numbered with the others, because the Lord did not want them to go out to war. He chose them to stay near the tabernacle and take care of it. When the children of Israel should go on their journey, the men of this tribe were to take the tabernacle down and carry the different parts of it, and when they should stop to rest and make a camp, these men were to set it up again. For the tabernacle and all the things in it were holy, and no one, except the priests and Levites, was allowed to come near them or touch them. If any other man did so, except when he came to offer up a sacrifice, or to worship, the Lord said he must be put to death.

After the other tribes had been numbered, the Lord commanded Moses to bring the men of the tribe of Levi to Aaron. He said that they should help, and wait upon Aaron and his sons. They should not only take down the tabernacle, and carry it and set it up again, on their journeys, but all the time that it stood in the camp they must do the work there; for there was much work to be done. Beside the two lambs, which the priests were to offer up every day, the people would bring many other offerings. Wood must be cut to burn these with; water must be

10

brought for the laver, where Aaron and his sons were to wash their feet and their hands, whenever they should go into the tabernacle or offer up a sacrifice; the ashes must be taken away from the altar, and the court where the offerings would be killed must be kept clean from their blood. Aaron and his sons could not attend to all these things, and now God chose the Levites to do it. And he commanded Moses and Aaron to number them; and they did so, and found there were of them, eight thousand

HIGH PRIEST   PRIEST   LEVITE

five hundred and eighty men. So, after they were numbered, the men of the tribe of Levi went to wait on the priests and do the work at the tabernacle. Now Aaron himself was of the tribe of Levi, but he and his family had been separated to be priests.

And twelve princes came from the other twelve tribes, bring ing presents to the tabernacle. They brought six covered wagons and twelve oxen to draw them; also dishes, bowls, and spoons, made of silver and gold, to be used at the tabernacle. Then Moses took the wagons and the oxen and gave them to the Levites to carry different parts of the tabernacle in, when the children of Israel should go on their journey. Two wagons were to carry the heavy curtains; and the other four, the boards covered with gold, that made the sides of the tabernacle, and the brass pillars that stood around the court. But he gave no wagons to carry the ark, the golden table, the golden candlestick, the golden altar, and the brass altar, for these were not to be carried in wagons, but on the Levites' shoulders.

Now the pillar of cloud was still over the tabernacle. In the day it was the color of a cloud, and in the night the color of fire. On the day that Moses set up the tabernacle it came there and stood over the most holy place. And after that it stayed there always, except when the Lord wanted the children of Israel to go on their journey. Then it was lifted up higher. As soon as it was lifted up the people knew they were to go, and as the cloud moved on they followed after it. As long as it moved they followed, but whenever it stopped they stopped, and made their camp in that place.

And when they had made their camp, they stayed there until the cloud rose up again from over the tabernacle. If it stayed only one day, they stayed one day. If it stayed two days, they stayed two days; or if it stayed a whole year, they stayed a year. But whenever the cloud was taken up, whether it were in the day or in the night, they went on their journey. For it was the Lord who made it to stay or to go, and he was in this way guiding them through the wilderness. And the Lord commanded Moses to make two silver trumpets for the priests to blow upon, when Moses wanted to call all the people together, and also when they were about to start on their journey.

While on their journey the children of Israel carried standards, or banners, with them, and marched like an army. Each tribe kept in its own place, and each one had a captain over it. In the midst of the other tribes went the Levites, carrying the different parts of the tabernacle. As soon as the people stopped anywhere to make their camp, the Levites set up the tabernacle there. Next to it they set up their own tents, and the other tribes set up theirs farther off. This was the way the children of Israel always made their camp.   The tabernacle was in the middle of it, the tents of the Levites were next, and the tents of the other tribes were farther off, but on every side of the tabernacle.   And they kept their tents in the same place until they took them down to go on their journey again.

And now the time was come for them to leave mount Sinai. The Lord spoke to them, and said they had been long enough at that place, they should go on their journey toward Canaan. Then the cloud rose up from over the tabernacle, and moved on before them, and they followed it for three days, until they came into the wilderness of Paran.   There it stopped and they made their camp.

We should suppose that when the people saw the cloud going before them they would have been thankful to God, and satisfied with whatever he chose to give them, until they reached that good land to which he was leading them.   But it was not so. Because they had no meat to eat in the wilderness they complained and said, Who shall give us meat to eat?   We remember the fish that we had in Egypt, the cucumbers, the melons, and the onions, but now we have nothing at all beside this manna. For they still went out every day and gathered the manna, and baked it, and made cakes of it.   Yet they complained and wept because they had no meat, and Moses heard them weeping at the doors of their tents.

And the Lord was very angry with them; and Moses was discouraged, because the people that he had the care of did so wickedly.   He asked the Lord why he gave him the care of them all.   It was too much for him, he said, and if the Lord was going to send him such great trouble, he begged he might die, so that he would have it no more.   But Moses sinned in speaking so; the Lord had always helped him when he was in trouble before and was willing to help him now; he should not have complained, but have trusted in him.

And the Lord commanded Moses to tell the people that they should have meat given them, for he had heard them weeping and asking, Who will give us flesh to eat?   They should have it, he said, not only for one day, nor five days, nor twenty days,

but for a whole month, until it should be loathsome to them, that is, until they could not bear to taste it nor see it. God would make it loathsome to them because they had been so wicked as to complain of the manna, and to ask why they had been brought out of Egypt.

But when the Lord told Moses that the people should have flesh for a whole month, Moses could hardly believe it; he said, Here are six hundred thousand men, and thou sayest, I will give them flesh that they may eat for a whole month. Must all the flocks and herds that we brought with us out of Egypt be now slain for them? Or shall all the fish of the sea be caught to give them enough? The Lord answered, Has my hand grown weak that I cannot do it? Wait and thou shalt see whether my words will come true or not. So Moses told the people what the Lord said.

Then the Lord sent a wind that brought quails from the sea, and they fell all around the camp. There were so many that the ground was covered with them. And the people went out and gathered them all that day, and all that night, and all the next day. But when they began to eat them, as soon as they had put the flesh in their mouths, the Lord sent a great plague among the people, and many of them died for their sin and were buried there in the wilderness.

And the cloud was lifted up again, and the people followed it until it stopped at a place called Hazeroth; there they stopped and made their camp.

Now Moses was the chief one among the children of Israel, because the Lord had chosen him to rule over them, and had talked with him, and given him the laws which they were to obey. Yet the Bible tells us he was more meek and humble than any other man who was then living on the earth. But Miriam, his sister, and Aaron, his brother, found fault with him because he had married a woman who was not one of the children of Israel. They said, too, that God had spoken to them, as well as to him, as if they, also, ought to be rulers over the people.

And the Lord heard what Aaron and Miriam said, and he commanded them to go with Moses to the tabernacle. When they had gone there the Lord came down in the pillar of cloud and stood by the door. Then he called to Aaron and Miriam, and they came before him; and the Lord told them that Moses was his servant, who was obedient in doing his will, and he asked them why they were not afraid to speak against him. Then the pillar of cloud in which the Lord was, rose up from the tabernacle; after it was gone Aaron looked on Miriam, and she was covered with leprosy, as white as snow. God had sent it upon her as a punishment for their wickedness. When Aaron saw it, he was greatly troubled and he spoke to Moses and said, We have sinned. And he begged that Miriam might be healed. Then Moses prayed earnestly to the Lord for her, saying, Heal her now, O God, I beseech thee. And the Lord heard his prayer and healed her of her leprosy. Then the people journeyed from Hazeroth to the wilderness of Paran.

CHAPTERS XIII–XXI (13–21)
(DEUT. 1, 21, 22)

THE CHILDREN OF ISRAEL REFUSE TO ENTER CANAAN. THEY ARE SENT BACK INTO THE WILDERNESS TO WANDER THERE FORTY YEARS. THE SABBATH-BREAKER STONED. THE REBELLION OF KORAH, DATHAN, AND ABIRAM. AARON'S ROD BLOSSOMS. MOSES AND AARON SIN AT THE ROCK. AARON DIES AT MOUNT HOR. FIERY SERPENTS ARE SENT AMONG THE PEOPLE.

Now the children of Israel had come near to Canaan, and Moses told them to go into that land and take it for their own, as the Lord had said they should. But they asked him first to send men as spies, who should go and search the land, and bring them word of what they saw there. And Moses sent twelve men, one from each tribe, and told them to look at the land, and see whether it were a good or a bad land, and what sort of people lived there; whether they were few or many, weak or strong, and whether they lived in tents or in cities with walls around them. Moses told them not to fear, but to go and bring back also some of the fruits of the land.

Then the spies went into Canaan, and walked through it

from one end to the other, for the Lord kept the people who lived there from doing them any harm. At a place called Eschol, where grapes were growing, they cut off from the vine a branch with a single cluster upon it. This cluster was so large that it took two men to carry it. They hung it upon a pole, or staff, and one man carried one end of the staff and another the other end, so that the cluster was carried between them. They brought with them also some pomegranates and figs.

RETURN OF THE SPIES

They were forty days in going through the land, then they came back to Moses and Aaron, and to all the children of Israel, and showed them the fruits they had brought. They said that in the land where they had been, the grain and the vines grew well, and there was plenty to eat and drink; but that the cities had walls around them, and were very great, and the people were very strong. They said this because they were afraid, and did not want the children of Israel to go there.

But two of the spies, named Caleb and Joshua, wanted them to go. They remembered that God had promised to give them the land, and they were sure that he would keep his promise, for they had faith in him. Caleb spoke to the children of Israel and begged them to go at once into Canaan, and said they were well able to take it for their own. But the other spies persuaded them not to go, and said that the people who lived there were giants, so large that the men whom Moses had sent seemed only like grasshoppers when they came near to them. So the children of Israel would not go. They all began to weep, and they cried that night, and murmured against Moses and Aaron, saying, We wish that God had let us die in the land of Egypt, or as we came through this wilderness. And they asked, Why has the Lord brought us up to this land, so that we, our wives, and our children should be killed by our enemies? Then they said to one another, Let us choose a captain instead of Moses, and go back into Egypt.

Then Moses and Aaron were in great distress. Joshua and Caleb, the two good spies, were troubled also, and they spoke to the people again, and told them that the land they had been through was a good land, and they begged them not to be afraid of the men who lived there; for the Lord would not help those men, they said, but he would help the children of Israel. But the people were angry at Caleb and Joshua for saying this, and wanted to stone them.

Then the Lord was greatly displeased with the children of Israel, and he told Moses that he would send a pestilence to destroy them, and would no longer have them for his people, but would make of Moses' descendants a greater nation than they were. But Moses spoke to the Lord, and said, that if he should destroy the people and not bring them into the land he had promised to give them, all the heathen nations who heard of it would say that it was because the Lord was unable to bring them in. Then Moses prayed that the Lord would not destroy the children of Israel, but would keep them for his people.

And the Lord heard Moses' prayer and promised not to destroy them. Yet he said that because they had so often disobeyed him, and would not believe his promise after all the wonderful things he had done for them, they could not go into Canaan, but must turn back into the wilderness, and there they should wander forty years, until all the men who refused to go in were dead. Then, after the forty years were ended, and all those men had died, God said he would bring their children into Canaan. And he promised that Caleb and Joshua, the two good spies, should live until that time and go in with them.

When the children of Israel heard this they were sorry for what they had done; and they rose up early in the morning, and told Moses that now they were willing to go. But Moses told them not to go, for the Lord would not help them, and if they should go they would be killed by their enemies. Yet they disobeyed him and went, and the people of the land came and fought against them, and chased them as bees chase persons who come near their hive. Then the children of Israel came back into their camp and stayed there many days. Afterward they all returned into the wilderness again.

While they were in the wilderness, some of the people found a man who was at work gathering sticks, on the sabbath day, and so disobeying the Lord's commandment. Then they took him and put him in some place to keep him safe, until they should know what the Lord would have done to him for his sin. And the Lord said to Moses, The man shall surely be put to death. All the people shall take him out of the camp and stone him with stones until he is dead. Then they took the man, and brought him out of the camp, and stoned him as the Lord commanded.

After these things three men, named Korah, Dathan, and Abiram, with two hundred and fifty more of the men of Israel, came to Moses and Aaron and spoke against them, saying that Aaron had no right to be high priest, and that Moses ought not to be the ruler over the people. Now Korah was one of the Levites who waited on the priests at the tabernacle, but he was not satisfied with doing this, he wanted to be a priest himself. That was the reason he came, bringing these men with him, to speak against Aaron. And Moses heard what they said, and told them that the next day each of them should take a censer and burn incense in it, as the priests did, and Aaron should do so

THE EARTH SWALLOWS UP KORAH, DATHAN, AND ABIRAM

too. Then, Moses said, the Lord would show which was the man he chose for high priest.

The next day Korah, Dathan, and Abiram, and the two hundred and fifty men, took censers and put fire in them, and sprinkled incense on the fire, as the priests did at the tabernacle.

And all the rest of the children of Israel came out with them to rebel against, or refuse to obey, Moses and Aaron. But the Lord was greatly displeased with the people for coming. He commanded them to go away from Korah, Dathan, and Abiram. So the people went away from them. Then Moses said, that if the ground should open and swallow up these men, the children of Israel would know that they had offended the Lord. And as soon as Moses was done speaking, the ground opened and swallowed up Korah, Dathan, and Abiram, with their tents, and all who were in them. And they cried out as they went down alive under the ground; and the earth closed over them. And all the people that were near them fled away, when they heard their cry, for they feared the earth would swallow up them also. At the same time that Korah, Dathan, and Abiram were swallowed up, the Lord sent fire that slew the two hundred and fifty men who had come out with them.

And on the morrow all the people murmured against Moses and Aaron, and said it was they who had killed Korah, Dathan, and Abiram, and the two hundred and fifty men. The people said, also, that these men were good men. Then the Lord was very angry with the children of Israel; he said to Moses and Aaron, Go away from them, that I may destroy them in a moment. But Moses and Aaron fell on their faces and prayed for the children of Israel. Yet the Lord would not hear them, for even while they were praying, he sent a great pestilence among the people, and many were already dying in the camp.

As soon as Moses knew it, he said to Aaron, Take a censer and put fire in it from off the altar of burnt offering, and sprinkle incense on the fire, and go out quickly and offer up the incense to the Lord for the people, because the plague has begun. And Aaron did as Moses said; he ran out among the people and stood, with the burning incense, between those who had died and those who were still living, and the Lord caused the plague to cease. Yet there died of it fourteen thousand and seven hundred persons, beside Korah, Dathan, and Abiram, and the two hundred and fifty men who were slain with them.

After this the Lord commanded each of the tribes of the

children of Israel to send Moses a rod. And he commanded Moses to write the name of the man who brought it upon every rod, so that the rods might be told one from another. Then Moses was to take them to the tabernacle, into the most holy place, and leave them there before the ark, all night. And one of them, God said, should grow in the night, and bear blossoms, as if it were still growing on the tree. And the man whose name

AARON'S ROD BEARS ALMONDS

was found written on that rod would be the one whom God chose for his high priest. God did this because the people had come with Korah to complain against Aaron, saying that he ought not to be the high priest.

So the people sent the rods to Moses. And after he had written the names on them, Moses took them into the tabernacle and left them before the ark all night. The next day he went and looked at them, and one of them had grown the blossoms and borne almonds; on this rod Aaron's name was written.

Then Moses brought out the rods to all the people, and they saw that none had grown but Aaron's. And God commanded Moses to take that rod and put it in the tabernacle again, to be kept there, so that the children of Israel might always remember that God had chosen Aaron for his high priest.

When Aaron and his sons should die, their sons who lived after them were to be priests; for all the men who should be descended from Aaron were to be priests for the children of Israel. And God told the people again that the men of the tribe of Levi should be with Aaron and his sons, to help them and wait on them, and do the work at the tabernacle.

And the Lord said that all the other tribes of the children of Israel must give to the priests and the Levites a part of their grain, of their fruit, and of their cattle. For when they should come into the land of Canaan the priests and the Levites would not have fields given them, where they could sow seed and plant vineyards, like the rest of the people. They would not have time to attend to these things—they were to stay at the tabernacle, attending to the worship of God. Therefore the other tribes were commanded to give them a tenth part of the grain, of their fruit, of their cattle, and of everything they should get.

And the children of Israel journeyed and came into the desert of Zin. And Miriam, the sister of Moses and Aaron, died and was buried there. And there was no water for the people. Then they spoke wickedly again to Moses and Aaron, saying, Why have ye brought us up into this wilderness, that we and our cattle should die? No figs grow here, nor vines, nor pomegranates, and there is no water for us.

And the Lord told Moses to call the people together at a rock which was near that place, and to take the rod in his hand, and go with Aaron and speak to the rock: then, the Lord said, water should come out of it. Now Moses and Aaron were very angry because the people had spoken against them. And when they came to the rock, Moses said to them, Hear now, ye rebels, must we fetch you water out of this rock? And he lifted up his hand and struck the rock twice with his rod, and water came out, a great deal of it, enough for all the children of Israel and their cattle to drink.

But Moses sinned when he spoke in anger to the people. He should not have said to them, Must we fetch you water out of this rock? As if he and Aaron were doing it. It was the Lord who made the water come out for the children of Israel, and Moses and Aaron should have taught them to thank him for it. But they did not; they took the honor to themselves. And the Lord was displeased with them for what they had done, and he said that because they had not honored him before the people, they should not bring them into the land of Canaan. The children of Israel should go into that land, when the forty years were ended which they must pass in the wilderness, but Moses and Aaron should not go in with them. They must both die before that time.

And the people came near to Edom, the country where Esau went to live. As we have read in the book of Genesis, Esau took his wives, his sons, his daughters, his cattle, and all that he had in Canaan, and went to live in another country called Edom. It had been more than two hundred years since Esau went there, and no doubt he was long since dead, but his descendants were living there still; it was their land. And now the children of Israel wanted to pass through it on their journey to Canaan; therefore Moses asked permission of the king.

Moses sent word to him saying, Thou knowest how our fathers went down into Egypt, and we have lived there for a long time; and the Egyptians treated us, and our fathers, very cruelly. But when we cried to the Lord, he heard us and he has brought us out of that land. And now, we pray thee, let us pass through thy country; we will not go through the fields to tread down the grain, neither will we drink the water out of the wells. We will go only by the king's highway, the road on which every one may go, until we have passed through thy land. But the king of Edom said they should not pass through, and he came out with his army to fight against them. So the children of Israel turned and went by a different way.

And they came to mount Hor. There the Lord spoke to

Moses and Aaron, and said that Aaron should be gathered to his fathers; this meant that he should die and be buried in the grave as his fathers had been. Then the Lord said to Moses, Take Aaron and his son Eleazar, and bring them up on mount Hor; and take off the high priest's garments from Aaron, and put them on Eleazar, for Aaron shall die there.   And Moses

MOSES LIFTS UP THE SERPENT OF BRASS

did as the Lord commanded. He and Aaron and Eleazar, Aaron's oldest son, went up on mount Hor, and all the people saw them going up. And Moses took the high priest's garments off Aaron, and put them on Eleazar his son, and Aaron died there on the top of the mount. So Eleazar was made high priest in the place of his father. And Moses and Eleazar came down from the mount. When all the people saw that Aaron was dead, they mourned for him thirty days.

But the children of Israel had yet a long way to go, and they grew weary of the journey, and sinned again, by speaking against God and against Moses. They said, There is no bread here for us, nor water, and we loathe this manna. And the Lord was angry, and sent fiery serpents into the camp, which bit the people so that many of them died. Then they came to Moses and said, We have sinned, for we have spoken against the Lord and against thee; and they begged Moses to pray that the serpents might be taken from them. Moses prayed for them; and the Lord commanded him to make a serpent of brass, like those which bit the people, and to set it up on a pole. And whoever was bitten, the Lord said, if he would look at that serpent of brass, should be made well.

So Moses made a serpent of brass and put it upon a pole, and when any one who had been bitten looked at it, he was made well. Yet the serpent of brass could not make him well. It was the Lord who did it, because that serpent, lifted up on the pole, meant, or represented, the Saviour who was to be lifted up on the cross. And it was intended to teach us, who read of it now, how we should look up to the Saviour, so that he may save us from being punished for our sins.

CHAPTERS XXII–XXXV (22–35)

THE CHILDREN OF ISRAEL ENCAMP ON THE PLAINS OF MOAB. BALAK SENDS FOR BALAAM TO CURSE THEM. THE PEOPLE SIN AND ARE PUNISHED BY A PLAGUE. THEY COME TO JORDAN. TWO AND A HALF TRIBES ASK PERMISSION TO STAY ON THAT SIDE OF THE RIVER.

THE children of Israel journeyed again, and came to the plains of Moab. A people called the Moabites lived there, whose king was named Balak. When Balak saw the children of Israel he was afraid, because he thought they had come to make war against him, and there were too many of them for his soldiers to fight with. Therefore he sent for a man named Balaam to come and curse them. We curse a person when we ask God to send some great evil upon him. The king of the Moabites wanted some great evil sent upon the children of Israel, and he thought that if Balaam asked for it God would send it, because Balaam pretended to have power with God.

So the king sent for Balaam, and told him that he would give him silver and gold, and make him rich and great, if he would come and curse the children of Israel. Now Balaam loved riches, and although the children of Israel had done him no harm, he was willing to curse them for the silver and gold which the king promised to give him. Therefore he rose up early in the morning, and saddled his ass, and started to go with the men whom the king had sent for him.

But God was angry with Balaam for going, and sent his angel to stand before him in the way, with a drawn sword in his hand. Balaam could not see the angel, but the ass saw him, and she turned out of the way into the field. Then Balaam struck the ass to make her go back. And the angel went on further, and stood in Balaam's path, at a place where there was a wall on each side of it. When the ass came to the place, she pressed up very close to the wall to get by, but she hurt Balaam's foot in doing so, and he struck her again. Then the angel went on further still, and stood in a narrow place where there was no room to turn to the right hand or the left. And the ass, because she was afraid, fell down upon the ground under Balaam. Then Balaam was very angry, and struck her with the staff that he had in his hand.

And the Lord made the ass to speak like a man, and say, What have I done to thee that thou hast struck me these three times? Balaam answered that it was because she had disobeyed him, and turned out of the way when he wanted her to go on. And Balaam said, I wish there was a sword in my hand, for now would I kill thee. Then the ass spoke to him again, saying, Hast thou not ridden upon me ever since I was thine until this day, and have I ever done so before? He answered, No.

Then the Lord made Balaam see the angel standing before him, with the sword in his hand, and Balaam bowed down with his face to the ground. And the angel said to him, Why hast thou struck thine ass these three times? Behold I have come out against thee, because thy way is wicked before me. And

BALAAM SEES THE ANGEL IN HIS PATH

the ass saw me and turned out of the path; unless she had turned from me, surely now I had slain thee and saved her alive. Then the angel commanded Balaam to go with the men whom the king had sent, but to speak to the king only those things which the angel should tell him.

So Balaam went with the men, and when the king heard of it he came out to meet him. The next day the king took him up on a high place, from which Balaam could look down and see all the camp of the children of Israel. And Balaam told the king to build seven altars in that place, and get ready seven bullocks and seven rams, to offer up as burnt offerings. The king did as Balaam said; he built seven altars, and they offered up a bullock and a ram on every altar. Then Balaam asked the king to stay by the burnt offering while he went away to a place alone, that he might see whether the Lord would speak with him, and let him curse the children of Israel.

And Balaam went away to a place alone, and the Lord came and met him there. Then Balaam told him of the altars he had built, and of the animals he had offered. But the Lord would not let him curse the children of Israel; he sent him back to the king and made him speak good things of them.

Then the king told Balaam to come to another place; and he took him up to the top of a mountain, and there he built seven more altars, and made ready seven bullocks and seven rams, and they offered a bullock and a ram on every altar. For Balaam thought that, by building so many altars and offering up so many sacrifices, he might persuade the Lord to let him curse the people. But it was wicked in Balaam to think so, for the Lord would not be persuaded to let any one do wrong, no matter how often he should ask, or how many offerings he should bring him.

Then Balaam told the king again to stay by his burnt offerings while he went away alone to speak with the Lord and ask permission to curse the people. And Balaam went away, and the Lord came and spoke to him, yet he would not let him curse the children of Israel.

And the king said to Balaam, Come, I will bring thee yet to

another place; perhaps the Lord will let thee curse them from there. Then he took him to a mountain called Peor, and built seven altars, and they offered up a bullock and a ram on every altar, as they had done before. Still the Lord would not let Balaam curse the people, for when he came to speak with the king the Lord made him say good things of them and bless them. And the king was angry at Balaam, and said, I sent for thee to curse my enemies, and behold, thou hast blessed them these three times. Then he told him to make haste and go back to his own home. And he sent him away, without any of the silver and gold which Balaam wanted so much.

When the Moabites found that they could not bring evil upon the children of Israel by seeking permission for Balaam to curse them, they tried another way to do them harm. They tempted them to sin and offend God. Balaam taught the Moabites how to do this. He told them, and another people of that country, called the Midianites, to invite the children of Israel to the feasts which they held to their idols. And the Moabites and Midianites did as Balaam said. They invited the children of Israel to their feasts, and the children of Israel came and ate with them and bowed down to their idols. Then the Lord was angry with the children of Israel, and sent a pestilence which killed many thousands of them.

And the children of Israel wandered in the wilderness forty years. But when those years were ended God brought them near to the land of Canaan again, and he commanded Moses and Eleazar to number them, and count how many of the men were able to be soldiers, and go to war, as Moses and Aaron had done while their camp was at mount Sinai. And when Moses and Eleazar went out and numbered them, they found that all those men who had refused to go into Canaan the first time had died in the wilderness, as the Lord said they should. But Caleb and Joshua, the good spies, were living still, for he had promised that they should live, to go with the people into the land.

And the Lord commanded Moses to make war against the Midianites, because they had tempted the children of Israel to sin and worship idols. Then Moses sent twelve thousand men, a thousand from each tribe, against them. And the men of Israel gained the victory over them and slew their kings, and Balaam also, who had taught the Midianites how to tempt the people. The men of Israel took away all the goods that belonged to the Midianites, and all their cattle; seventy-two thousand oxen, sixty-one thousand asses, and six hundred and seventy-five thousand sheep. And they burned their cities and

THE CHILDREN OF ISRAEL ON THEIR JOURNEY THROUGH THE WILDERNESS

their great castles with fire. After the battle was over, the officers of the children of Israel came to Moses and said, We have counted the men that went out with us to fight, and all of them are here, not one has been slain. Therefore we have brought to thee, for the Lord, the gold and the jewels which we took from the Midianites. And Moses, and Eleazar the high priest, took the gold and the jewels, and carried them into the tabernacle as an offering to the Lord.

And the Lord brought the people near to the river Jordan, there they made their camp. And they waited until he should command them to pass over, for on the other side was the land of Canaan. But while they were waiting there, two of the tribes of the children of Israel came to Moses and told him that they did not want to pass over Jordan. They wanted to stay in the land where they were then (which was called the land of Gilead), because it was a good land for feeding cattle, and they had a great many cattle.

Moses was displeased with them, for he thought they wanted to stay there because they were afraid to fight against the wicked nations in Canaan. He said to them, Shall your brethren go over to war, while you rest here? They answered him, We will build sheep-folds for our cattle, and houses for our wives and little children to live in; but we, who are men, will go over Jordan with our brethren, and help them fight against the nations who live there, until those nations shall be driven out and our brethren shall have the land for their own. After that we will come back, and have our homes on this side of the river. Then Moses said if they would do this, it should be as they wished. And he spoke to the rest of the people, and told them to let the two tribes have the land that they asked for. So the people gave them the land of Gilead.

And the men of the two tribes built folds for their sheep, and houses for their families to live in, till they should come back to that land again. These two tribes were the tribes of Reuben and Gad. And half the tribe of Manasseh, also, asked permission to stay and have their homes on that side of Jordan.

And the Lord spoke to Moses, and told him that when the children of Israel should go over into Canaan, they must drive out all the heathen nations that lived there. They must break down their idols, and destroy the places they had built to worship their idols in. They must take the land from those wicked nations and keep it for themselves, because the Lord meant to give it to them. Every man among the children of Israel was to have a part of the land given to him, where he might build his house, and sow his grain, and feed his cattle. But if they would not obey the Lord, and drive out all the heathen nations, then, the Lord said, those that were left would cause the children of Israel also to sin, and to worship idols, so that after a while the Lord would drive them out too, as he was now going to drive out those wicked nations.

The Lord told Moses how large the land was that he would give the children of Israel, and how far it would reach. And he named the men who would divide it among the people, and give each tribe the part it was to have. But the priests and the Levites were to have no land given them. Yet they would need houses to live in; therefore the Lord commanded the people to give them some of the cities of Canaan. They were to give them forty-eight cities, which should belong to them. And the priests and Levites were to take their wives, and their sons, and their daughters into those cities, and have their homes there.

THE BOOK OF DEUTERONOMY

MOSES SPEAKS TO THE CHILDREN OF ISRAEL. HE TELLS THEM OF THE
    GOOD LAND TO WHICH THEY ARE GOING, AND WARNS THEM NOT TO
    FORGET GOD WHEN THEY SHALL COME THERE. THE CITIES OF REFUGE.
    THE FIRST FRUITS MUST BE BROUGHT TO THE TABERNACLE. MOSES
    DIES ON MOUNT NEBO.

WHILE the children of Israel had their camp near the river Jordan, Moses spoke to them for the last time. He knew that he could not go with them into Canaan, but must die before they went, and he feared that after he should be taken from them they would forget the things that God had spoken to them and done for them. Therefore he told them again about many of those things. He reminded them of the time when they came near to Canaan before, but would not go into it, because the spies who had been through the land told them that the people were greater and stronger than they. And the Lord was angry with the children of Israel and sent them back into the wilderness, where they had stayed forty years. Then Moses said, as the end of that time drew near, the Lord commanded them to come toward Canaan again.

And as they came they passed by the land of Bashan, and Og, king of Bashan, came out and fought with them. But the Lord gave them the victory over him. They took from him sixty cities, which had high walls around them, with gates, and bars to keep the gates shut, when their enemies should come against them. The Lord gave the children of Israel, also, the land on which those cities stood, and all the cattle that belonged to the people. This Og, king of Bashan, was a giant; for the Bible tells us there were giants in those days, and Og was the last one left of them in that country. His bedstead was made of iron, and was twice as large as the bedsteads of other men.

And Moses told the people that he begged the Lord, at that time, to let him go over and see the good land to which they were going across Jordan. But the Lord would not let him go, and commanded him to speak of it no more. For he remembered how Moses and Aaron had sinned at the rock, where they were sent to bring out water for the people. Yet the Lord said that Moses should go up on a high mountain from which he could see that land afar off, but he should not cross over Jordan and go into it.

Then Moses asked the Lord to choose a man who should go over with the people and lead them as he had done, because if they should have no one to guide and take care of them, they might be scattered and lost, like sheep without a shepherd. And the Lord said that Joshua should go with them, and that they should obey him as they had before obeyed Moses.

And Moses told all the people that God said they should teach his commandments to their children, and talk with their children about them, while they were sitting at home in the house; when they went out, as they walked by the way; before they went to sleep at night, and when they awoke in the morning. They were to tell them often about God, how great and good and kind he was, and about his laws, so that they might learn to obey them.

And when the Lord should bring the children of Israel into Canaan and give them great and beautiful cities which they had not built, and houses full of good things which they had not brought there, and wells which they had not digged, and vineyards and olive trees which they had not planted; when they should have all these things given them, with as much to eat as they wanted, they must be careful lest they should forget the Lord who gave them these things.

They must remember, then, how he had led them forty years through the wilderness and fed them with manna. In all that time their clothes had not grown old, nor worn out, and though they had come so far, their feet had never swollen nor been sore with their journey. For God had led them through that lonely wilderness, where there was no bread to eat nor water to drink, that he might bring them into a better land, where streams ran through the fields, and springs of water came out of the ground, in the valleys and on the hills. In that good land the wheat grew and bore grain, and the vine bore grapes; the fig-tree, the pomegranate, and the olive bore their fruit. There the children of Israel should have bread enough, and never want anything. And under the ground, among the rocks, and in the hills they should find iron and brass, of which they could make many things that they needed to use.

After they should come to that good land, and their herds of cattle and flocks of sheep should grow larger, and they should be rich, and have very much of silver and gold, then they must not be proud, and say they had gotten these things for themselves, for it was the Lord who would give them to the children of Israel. And if they forgot him, and served other gods, they also would be destroyed like those nations which he was now going to destroy in the land of Canaan.

And Moses told the people that very soon they were to pass over Jordan, and the Lord would go before them. They would have to fight against the nations that lived there, but it was the Lord who would give them the victory. And when he should have given them the victory, and driven out those nations, the children of Israel must not say that it was because they were righteous he had done it. For it was not because they were righteous, but because those nations were wicked that God would drive them out; and because he had promised Abraham, and Isaac, and Jacob that he would give the land to the children of Israel. For the children of Israel had not been righteous, they had not obeyed the Lord. They should remember, and never forget, how often in the wilderness they had sinned against him, from the time they left Egypt until they came to that place where their camp was then.

And Moses said that the land of Canaan, to which they were going, was not like the land of Egypt from which they came. In Egypt it scarcely ever rained. A river, called the Nile, ran through the land. Once every year this river rose up higher than it was at other times, and flowed over the fields and gardens that were near it. But where the water from the river did not come, the people had to carry it or nothing would grow. This caused them great labor and trouble. But in Canaan rain fell from the sky and watered all the land. And now, Moses said, if the children of Israel would love God, and serve him with all their hearts, he would send them this rain as it should be needed, to make the corn, the vines, and the olive-trees grow, and grass also in the fields for the cattle to eat.

Now the people of Canaan served idols, and made places in which to worship them, on mountains and hills, and under trees. They built altars also on which they offered sacrifices to them: even their sons and their daughters they burned in the fire to their false gods. Moses told the children of Israel again, that they must destroy all the places where idols had been worshipped, and throw down the altars and the images. But the children of Israel must offer their sacrifices in only one place, which the Lord would choose for them after they came into the land of Canaan. There his tabernacle would be, and the people must bring all their burnt offerings there to be burned by the priests on the altar.

And if any man should try to persuade one of them to go away from the tabernacle and sacrifice to other gods, and not to the Lord, the one whom he persuaded must not go with him, but he must tell all the people of what the man had said, and the people must take that man out and stone him with stones till he was dead.

And the Lord commanded the children of Israel, whenever

there should be any poor man among them, to be kind to him, and lend him whatever he needed, even though they might think he could never pay them again. And they should lend to him willingly, not feeling sorry to do it, nor wishing in their hearts that he had not asked them; for on account of their being kind to the poor, the Lord would bless them in everything they did.

And God told the children of Israel that some of the cities in the land of Canaan must be cities of refuge; this meant cities where a man, who had killed another by accident, might go and be safe from punishment. God had said before that any person who killed another on purpose, and because he hated him, should be put to death. He would be a murderer, and the murdered man's brother, or his son, or his nearest relation was allowed to kill him wherever he found him. But sometimes a man might kill another without intending it. He might go to the woods to cut down a tree, and while doing it, the head of the axe might fly from the handle, and strike some one who was standing near, and hurt him so that he would die. Yet the man who killed the other would not be a murderer. But for fear the dead man's brother, or his son, or some relation of his might come in anger and kill him, he must make haste to the city of refuge.

And when he should come to the gate of the city, he must tell the elders who lived there of what he had done. And the elders would take him into the city and give him a place where he might live. And if the brother, or the son of the man he had killed, should come and ask for him, they would not give him up, because, although he had killed the man, he had not meant to do him any harm. But if some wicked murderer should come there, the elders would not take him into the city to save him from punishment, they would give him up to be put to death for his sin.

The Lord said that when the people should come into Canaan and live there, and have the land for their own, each man must take the first of the grain, and the first of the fruits, that should grow ripe in his fields, and put them into a basket and bring them to the tabernacle. And the priest at the tabernacle should

FLEEING TO THE CITY OF REFUGE

take the basket out of the man's hand, and set it down before the altar of burnt offering.   Then the man should say, I have brought the first fruits of the land which thou, O Lord, hast given me.   And there he should worship the Lord.   And the man was to leave the basket, with the first fruits in it, at the tabernacle; and the Lord said these should belong to the priest. For the Lord gave them to the priest, because the priests would

THE ISRAELITES BRING THEIR OFFERINGS TO THE TABERNACLE

have no fields, nor orchards, in which to raise grain and fruit for themselves.   And the Lord commanded each man among the children of Israel to bring his first fruits, every year, in this way as an offering to the tabernacle.

Moses told the people that on the day they should go over Jordan into Canaan, they must set up some great stones there and cover them with plaster.   And while the plaster was yet soft, they must write on it all the words of the law which God had given them.   Then when the plaster grew hard, those words would remain; and every one who passed by could read God's law written upon it.

And Moses said to the children of Israel that if they would obey the Lord, the Lord would make them greater than any other nation.   He would bless their children, their land, and their cattle.   Their enemies, who should come out against them, would be afraid and flee away before them.   And all the other nations of the earth should know that the Lord had chosen them for his people.   But if they would not obey him, they should have great trouble.   They would sow much seed in their fields, but reap only a little grain, for the locusts would come and destroy it; they would plant their vines, but should not gather the grapes, for the worms would eat them.   They should have sickness such as could not be cured.   And the Lord would send against them a fierce nation that would not pity the old or the young, but would take their cattle and their food, and at last carry them and their children away, as captives, to other lands, where the children of Israel should be slaves to their enemies, and, like their enemies, worship idols of wood and stone.

Moses said to the people that he had now set before them the good way and the evil way, and he begged them to choose the good way, so that they and their children might live and not die.   And he told them he was a hundred and twenty years old that day and could not go over Jordan with them, but Joshua, he said, would go.   Then he called Joshua before them all, and told them that he was to go with them, and lead them, and help them take the land.   And the Lord commanded Moses to come with Joshua to the tabernacle; and when they came there, the Lord appeared to them in the pillar of cloud, and he appointed Joshua to be ruler over the people after Moses should die.

Moses wrote down in a book the laws which God had given him.   And he commanded the priests and the elders, once in every seven years, to gather all the people together, the men, the women, and the children, and to read those laws out loud to them, that they might hear them and learn to obey them.   And he gave the book to the Levites who carried the ark, and told them to take it and put it in the side of the ark, that it might always be kept there.

After these things, the Lord spoke to Moses and commanded him to go up on a mountain called mount Nebo, and to look from there across Jordan into the land where the children of Israel were going. Then, when he should have seen that land, the Lord said, Moses should die on the mount, as Aaron had died on mount Hor. And Moses went from the place where

MOSES SEES THE PROMISED LAND FROM MOUNT NEBO

the children of Israel had their camp, on to the mountain which the Lord told him of. And when he came to the top of it, the Lord made him see very far over the land of Canaan, and told him that this was the land which he had promised Abraham, and Isaac, and Jacob, to give their descendants.

So Moses, the servant of the Lord, died there on the top of the mount, before the people came into that good land. And the Lord buried him in a valley, in the land of Moab, but no man has ever known the place where he was buried. He was a hundred and twenty years old when he died, yet he had not grown weak from age, but was well and strong until the day that the Lord took him.

After he was dead, Joshua ruled over the people, and they obeyed him as they had obeyed Moses. For the Lord gave Joshua wisdom, and made him able to teach them and guide them as Moses had done before. But there was never afterward any man among the children of Israel, whom the Lord talked with, face to face, as he did with Moses; or whom he sent to do such wonderful works as he sent him to do, in Egypt and in the wilderness.

THE BOOK OF JOSHUA

CHAPTERS I–VIII (1–8)

JOSHUA SENDS SPIES INTO THE CITY OF JERICHO. THE PRIESTS CARRY THE ARK BEFORE THE PEOPLE, OVER JORDAN. THE LORD SPEAKS TO JOSHUA. THE CHILDREN OF ISRAEL TAKE JERICHO. ACHAN'S SIN AND PUNISHMENT. AI IS TAKEN.

THE Lord spoke to Joshua, saying, Moses, my servant, is dead. Now therefore, do thou arise and take the children of Israel over Jordan, into that land which I give them. Be strong and brave, and very careful to obey all that is written in the book of the law, so that thou mayest do well and prosper. And fear not, for I will be with thee to help thee wherever thou goest. Then Joshua spoke to the officers of the children of Israel, and said to them, Go through the camp and command all the people that they make food ready to take with them, for within three days you shall pass over Jordan.

Joshua first sent two men as spies over Jordan, to look at the land before the children of Israel should go into it. And the men crossed over the river to a city of Canaan, called Jericho, and went into the house of a woman named Rahab. Then some one told the king of Jericho that two spies of the children of Israel had come into the city and were at Rahab's house. So the king sent to Rahab and asked her to bring out the men.

Now the roofs of the houses in that country were flat, so that persons could walk on them. And Rahab took the two men up on the roof of her house, and hid them under some stalks of flax which were spread out to dry there.

Then the king's messengers came, but could not find them. After the messengers had gone, Rahab went up and talked with the men. She told them that she knew the Lord had given the land to the children of Israel, for the people of Canaan had heard how he made the Red Sea dry for them to cross over it, and afterward helped them in fighting against their enemies. As soon as the people heard of these things, Rahab said, they were afraid of the children of Israel. Then she asked the two men to promise that they would remember her kindness to them, and not let her, or any of her family, be put to death, when the children of Israel should come to take the city of Jericho. And the men said that if she would tell no one of their coming, they would do as she asked.

Then they told her to fasten some scarlet thread, or cord, in the window of her house, so that they could see it from the outside, and know which house was hers, when they should come back with the children of Israel to take the city. And they promised that no one inside of her house should be harmed.

Now Jericho had a wall around it, and Rahab's house stood close to the wall, and was built up above it, so that there was a window in her house over the wall. And she let the two men down from that window, by a cord, outside of the wall, that they might flee from the city. For the gates of the city had been shut by the king's servants, to keep the spies from going out there. And Rahab told them to go and hide for three days in a mountain that was near, until the king's servants should cease looking after them. And the two men went and hid for three days in the mountain, as Rahab said, until the servants of the king had given up looking for them. Afterward they crossed over the river again, and went back to Joshua in the camp and told him of all that had happened to them.

Joshua and all the people rose up early in the morning and came to the banks of the river; there they stayed three

RAHAB HIDES THE SPIES

days. Then Joshua said to the children of Israel, Make yourselves ready; to-morrow the Lord will do wonders among you. For the priests shall carry the ark over Jordan before you, and it shall be that as soon as their feet stand in the river the waters shall cease to flow, and the priests shall walk through Jordan on dry ground.

And it came true as Joshua said; for on the morrow the priests took up the ark and carried it toward the river, and all

THE PRIESTS CARRY THE ARK OVER JORDAN

the people followed after them. When the priests came to the edge of the river, as soon as their feet touched the water, the water parted before them, and they walked out on dry ground into the middle of the river. There they stood with the ark, and waited while all the children of Israel passed over to the other side, into the land of Canaan.

The men of the two and a half tribes, who had asked to have their homes in the land of Gilead, went over also, as they had promised Moses to do, forty thousand of them, armed, to help their brethren fight against the nations of the land. After the people had gone over, the priests, carrying the ark, followed them. And as soon as they came up out of the river and stood on the shore, the waters flowed in the river again, filling it as full as it had been before.

The children of Israel made their camp at a place called Gilgal. There they found some of the corn that had grown in the land, and they parched it and did eat of it. And on the morrow, after they had eaten the corn, the manna ceased coming. For forty years the Lord had sent it to them in the wilderness, where no grain grew. But now they were in Canaan, where there was plenty of food for them, therefore the Lord sent the manna no more.

Joshua went out of the camp and came near to the walls of the city of Jericho. And he looked up and saw a man standing there, with a drawn sword in his hand. And Joshua came to him, and said, Art thou for us or for our enemies? The man answered, As captain of the Lord's army I am come. He called the army of Israel the Lord's army, and he meant to tell Joshua that he had come as their captain, to show them how they should gain the victory over their enemies. Then Joshua bowed down to the earth and worshipped him; for this man was the Lord; the same who came to Abraham's tent and told him that he would destroy Sodom; and that wrestled with Jacob when he was coming back from Laban's house into Canaan.

Now the people of Jericho had shut up the gates of the city, so that no one could go out or come in, because they were afraid of the children of Israel. But the Lord said he would give Joshua the victory over the king of Jericho; and he told him in what way the children of Israel should take the city. All their men of war, or soldiers, he said, should march around the city once every day for six days; and some of the priests should carry the ark around with them. Seven more priests were to go before the ark, and to blow on trumpets made of rams' horns. But on the seventh day the children of Israel were commanded to march around Jericho seven times, and the priests were to blow on the trumpets. Then, when the men of Israel should hear a long blast on the trumpets, they were all to give a great shout, and the Lord said that the wall of the city should fall down flat, so that they could go up into the city.

And Joshua told the children of Israel that only Rahab, and the persons who were in her house with her, should be saved alive; for the Lord had commanded that all the rest of the people of Jericho should be put to death for their sins. And

THE TAKING OF JERICHO

Joshua said that all the silver and gold, and the vessels made out of brass and iron, which should be found in the city, belonged to the Lord, and must be put into the treasury where the things were kept which were given to him. Joshua commanded the people not to take any of the silver or gold, or brass or iron, for their own, lest the Lord should send a great punishment upon them for their disobedience.

So the people did as the Lord commanded. On the first day

they marched around the city once, and after them came the priests that blew on the trumpets. Then followed the priests who carried the ark. On the second day they marched around the city again. So they did for six days. But on the seventh day they rose up early, before it was light, and marched around the city seven times. The last time, when the priests blew with the trumpets, Joshua said to the children of Israel, Shout, for the Lord has given you the city.

Then the people shouted, and as they did so the wall of the city fell down flat before them, and they went up into Jericho and took it. And Joshua told the spies, who had been at Rahab's house before, to go and bring out all the persons who were there, as they had promised to do. And they went and brought out Rahab and her father, her mother, her brothers, and all who were with her. Afterward the children of Israel burned the city; but the silver and gold, and the vessels of iron and brass were put into the treasury of the Lord. Joshua saved Rahab alive, and all her relations, because she hid the spies whom he had sent into Jericho. And after that she lived among the children of Israel.

And Joshua sent spies to another city of Canaan, called Ai. When the spies came back they told him that not many people lived there, and that only a small army of the men of Israel need go up to take the city. Two or three thousand of them would be enough, they said. So Joshua sent up about three thousand men. But when the men of Ai came out against them, the Israelites were afraid and fled, and the men of Ai slew about thirty-six of them.

Then Joshua was in great distress. He rent his clothes, and he and the elders of Israel bowed down with their faces to the earth, praying, until the evening. And Joshua cried to the Lord, saying, All the people of Canaan will hear how the children of Israel have fled before their enemies; and they will gather around us on every side and kill us, till none of us are left. But the Lord told him to rise up, and asked him why he lay with his face to the ground. There was sin among the children of Israel, the Lord said, and that was the reason they had

been afraid, and not able to stand before their enemies.   For
one of them had taken some of the silver and gold that was in
Jericho, and hidden it, instead of putting it in the treasury
of the Lord.   And the Lord said he would not be with them

ACHAN'S SIN.   FINDING THE HIDDEN TREASURE

to help them again, unless they punished the man who had done
this thing.

And he commanded Joshua to bring out all the people before
him, that he might show who the man was.   That man, the Lord
said, should be burned with fire—he and all that he had.   So

Joshua rose up early in the morning and brought out all the people, and the Lord showed him the man. His name was Achan. And Joshua said to him, Tell me now what thou hast done—hide it not from me. Achan answered that, when he had seen in Jericho a beautiful garment, and some silver money, and a piece of gold, he wanted them for his own; so he took them, and hid them in the ground under his tent.

Then Joshua sent messengers, and they ran to Achan's tent, and found the things hidden there as he said. They took them out and brought them to Joshua, and to all the children of Israel, and laid them out before the Lord. Then Joshua and all the people took Achan, and the beautiful garment, and the silver and gold which he had hidden, his sons also and his daughters, his tent and his cattle, and everything that he had, and brought them into a valley. There they stoned them with stones, and afterward burned them with fire. And over Achan's dead body they raised a great heap of stones, to show where it lay. Therefore the Lord was no longer angry with the children of Israel on account of this sin, because they punished the man who had done it. And the name of the valley was called Achor, which means Trouble.

Then the Lord said to Joshua, Fear not; take all the men of war with thee, and go up again to Ai, for now I will give thee the city, and the king of Ai, his people, and his land. And the Lord commanded Joshua to do to the people of Ai as he had done to the people of Jericho; they were to be put to death for their sins. But he said that the gold and the silver which the children of Israel should find there, they need not put into the treasury of the Lord; they might take it for themselves.

So Joshua, and all the men of war, arose to go up against Ai. But they did not all of them go together. Joshua chose thirty thousand brave soldiers, whom he sent away in the night to go around behind the city, and hide where the people of Ai could not see them. The rest went with Joshua in front of the city. When the king of Ai saw the men who were with Joshua, he thought they were all that had come, and he marched out with his army to fight against them. Then those who were hidden

behind the city, came into it and set it on fire. When the men of
Ai looked back, and saw the smoke of their city going up toward heaven, they knew not which way to go. Joshua and
his men were in front of them, and those who had set the city
on fire were behind them, so they could not escape. And Joshua
put them to death, as the Lord commanded. But the gold, and
silver, and the cattle which were in Ai the children of Israel
took for their own.

And Joshua built an altar of great stones on the mountain
called Ebal; and he covered the stones with plaster and wrote
on the plaster the words of God's law, as Moses commanded the
children of Israel to do before they crossed over Jordan.

CHAPTERS IX–XXIV (9–24)

THE GIBEONITES DECEIVE THE MEN OF ISRAEL. JOSHUA WARS AGAINST THE
CANAANITES. THE SUN AND THE MOON STAND STILL. THE MEN OF
THE TWO AND A HALF TRIBES RETURN TO GILEAD. JOSHUA SPEAKS
TO THE PEOPLE. HE DIES.

WHEN the kings who lived in Canaan heard how Joshua had
destroyed Ai, they gathered together to make war against
him. But the people of a city called Gibeon acted more cun-
ningly. They did not want to make war against Joshua, for
they knew that the Lord would give him the victory. Therefore they sent messengers to him who put on very old clothes
and worn-out shoes, and carried dry and mouldy bread with
them, to pretend they had come from another country, and had
been a long time on the journey. And they came to Joshua in
the camp and said to him, We have come from a country far
off from Canaan, for we heard of your God and of all the great
things he has done for you; therefore all our people sent us to ask
that you would make a covenant with them, and be their friends.

Then Joshua and the children of Israel did not ask the Lord
what they should do, as they ought to have asked him; they
promised at once to be friends with the men of Gibeon. But
after three days they heard that those men had not come from
a far country at all, for they lived near by, in Canaan, and were

among the wicked nations whom the children of Israel were
commanded to destroy. Then Joshua called the men of Gibeon
to him, and asked them why they had deceived him. They
answered that they were afraid for their lives, for they had heard
how the people of Canaan were to be destroyed and their land
given to the children of Israel. So the children of Israel did
not put the people of Gibeon to death, because they had prom-

THE GIBEONITES DECEIVE THE MEN OF ISRAEL

ised, before the Lord, to let them live. But Joshua said they
should be bondsmen, or slaves, and work for the priests and the
Levites, in cutting the wood and carrying the water which would
be needed at the tabernacle.

The king of a city, called Jerusalem, was angry with the
people of Gibeon for making friends with the children of Israel.
Therefore he and four other kings of the land gathered their
armies together and came to the city of Gibeon, to fight against
it. Then the men of Gibeon sent to Joshua, saying, Come up to
us quickly and help us, for the kings that live in the mountains

are gathered together against us. So Joshua and all the men of war went out against the five kings. Now the Lord made the kings and their armies afraid of the children of Israel, and they fled from them. As they fled, the Lord cast down great hail-stones upon them, out of heaven, so that more died from the hailstones than the children of Israel killed with the sword.

JOSHUA COMMANDS THE SUN AND MOON TO STAND STILL

But while the men of Israel followed after them, the sun was going down and the night was coming on. So Joshua feared that his enemies would escape in the darkness. Therefore he spoke to the sun, commanding it not to go down, and to the moon, com-manding it to rise no higher in the sky. And the sun stood still, and did not go down for many hours after the time that it went down on other days. So that day was longer than any other day. There was no day like it, either before or after it, when the Lord, at Joshua's prayer, made the sun and moon stand still that the children of Israel might keep on pursuing their enemies. The five kings, when their armies fled, hid in a cave, and it was told Joshua. Then he spoke to the people, saying, Roll great stones in the mouth of the cave, and set men by it to watch it, but do you go on following your enemies.

After the battle was over and the people had come back to Joshua in the camp, he said to them, Open the mouth of the cave and bring those five kings out to me. And they did so. Then Joshua said to the men of Israel, Fear not, but be strong and brave; for as the Lord has done to these kings, so will he do to all your enemies against whom you shall have to fight. And Joshua put the five kings to death as the Lord had commanded. In the evening, as the sun was going down, they took their dead bodies and cast them into the cave where they had hidden. And the men of Israel laid great stones in the cave's mouth again, to shut it up.

After this, Joshua gained the victory over twenty-four more kings, and yet there was much land left for the men of Israel to take in Canaan. For these kings did not rule over whole countries, like the kings that are living now; they ruled over cities only, or small portions of the land.

Now Joshua had grown old; he could not any longer lead the men of Israel out to war as he used to do. And all the people came to the city of Shiloh, to set up the tabernacle. They had carried it, as we have been told, all the way from mount Sinai, taking it down when they journeyed and setting it up when they made their camp. But now they had come into Canaan to stay and journey no more. And they brought the tabernacle to Shiloh, which was in the middle of the land, and set it up to let it stand there, because that was the place the Lord had chosen for it.

As we have read before, the men of the two and a half tribes who left their wives and little children in Gilead, had come over Jordan with the rest of the men of Israel, to help them fight against their enemies and take the land of Canaan. But, since they came over, the men of Israel had taken only a part of Canaan. The reason was they had grown tired of going out to war, and chose rather to rest and be quiet. But the Lord was not pleased with them for this, for it seemed as though they did not care to have all that good land which he was willing to give them. So the Lord spoke to Joshua, and said that a large part of the land which he had given to the people was not yet taken from the Canaanites.

CASTING LOTS FOR THE TRIBES OF ISRAEL

Then Joshua spoke to all the people, and asked how long it should be before they would go out against the heathen nations that were still living in Canaan. And he asked them to choose men whom he could send out as spies. Then they chose twenty-one men, and Joshua sent them through that part of the land which the children of Israel had not yet taken. He told them to go and see the land, and to write down in a book the description of it, and afterward to come back to him in Shiloh.

So the men went as Joshua told them, and walked through the land, and they wrote down in a book the description of it, and brought the book to Joshua in Shiloh. Then Joshua cast lots for the different tribes, so that the Lord might show what part of the land each tribe should have. And after the Lord had shown them this, Joshua told the men of Israel to go and drive out the heathen nations and take the land as their own; for Joshua promised that the Lord would help them.

And the Lord told the people to choose those cities which were to be cities of refuge, where any person who had killed another by accident, might flee and be safe from punishment; and the people chose six cities in different parts of the land.

We have read that the priests and Levites were not to have fields given them, in which to sow grain and plant vineyards, like the men of the other tribes, because God had chosen them to stay at the tabernacle and attend to his worship there. Yet God had said they should have cities to live in. And now the priests and Levites came to Joshua and the chief men of Israel, saying, The Lord commanded that cities should be given us. Then Joshua, and the people, gave them forty-eight cities in Canaan, where they should bring their wives and their children, and have their homes.

Now the men of the two and a half tribes had stayed with the children of Israel ever since they crossed over Jordan, and had gone out to war with them against many heathen nations in Canaan. Therefore the men of Israel had given the men of the two and a half tribes a share of the cattle, of the gold and silver, and of all the spoils which they had taken from those heathen nations. In this way the men of the two and a half tribes had gotten much riches. And now Joshua called these men to him and spoke kindly to them, saying, You have obeyed me in all that I said to you; for you have not let your brethren go out to war alone, but have stayed with them and helped them many days. Now, therefore, take with you all the riches you have gotten, and go back to your homes on the other side of Jordan. But be very careful after you shall come there to obey all the commandments which Moses gave you, and to love and serve the Lord your God with all your heart and with all your soul.

So Joshua sent the men of the two and a half tribes away, and they started to go back to their homes on the other side of Jordan. But when they came to the bank of the river, they stopped and built a great altar, shaped like the altar of burnt offering at the tabernacle in Shiloh. Now, as we have read, God had commanded the children of Israel to offer up their sacrifices on no other altar but that which was at the tabernacle. Therefore when the men of the other tribes heard what the men of the two and a half tribes had done, they were angry and gathered together to go out to war against them.

But first they sent Phinehas, the high priest, and ten of the princes with him, to go to the men of the two and a half tribes and ask why they had done this thing. So Phinehas and the princes came and spoke to them, saying, All the men of Israel have sent us to ask why you have built another altar to offer sacrifices upon, when the Lord has forbidden us to offer up sacrifices except on his altar at Shiloh? Do you not remember how he sent a great plague upon us, when some of the people disobeyed him, and went to the idols' feasts with the Midianites and the Moabites? Do you not remember, also, how he punished us when Achan, in the city of Jericho, took and hid the silver and gold which the Lord had commanded the people not to take? Why then will you, too, disobey the Lord by offering up sacrifices on his altar that you have built? For if you do so, he will not only punish you, but he will surely send his punishment upon us all.

Then the men of the two and a half tribes answered Phinehas and the ten princes, saying, The Lord our God, the Lord our God, he knows that we do not mean to sin against him. And the men of Israel shall know it too when they hear why we have built this altar. For we have not built it to offer up sacrifices on at all, but because we are afraid that after you and we are dead, and your children shall see our children living on the other side of Jordan, they will say that our children do not belong to the tribes of Israel, and that they shall not come to worship in Shiloh. Therefore we have built this altar, so that our children may answer your children, saying, Look and see the pattern of the altar which our fathers built when they came here, how it is shaped like the altar at Shiloh. This proves that they belonged to the children of Israel, and that we have a right to come to Shiloh, and worship your God there.

When Phinehas and the ten princes heard what the men of the two and a half tribes said, they went back and told it to the men of Israel. Then the men of Israel were glad, and they thanked the Lord because their brethren of the two and a half tribes had not disobeyed him; and they did not want any more to go out to war against them.

After these things, Joshua spoke to the people, and said that he was going to die. And he called them all to him, and told them how good the Lord had been to them, in driving out their enemies, and in giving them cities, and fields, and vineyards, and a land of their own to live in. He has done all this for you, Joshua said, now therefore, fear the Lord and serve him. Yet if you will not serve him, then you may choose for yourselves the idols that you would rather serve; but as for me and my family, we will serve the Lord. The people answered, God forbid that we should leave the Lord to serve idols. For it was he who brought us up out of Egypt, and gave us this land; therefore will we also serve the Lord, for he is our God.

Then Joshua took a great stone, and set it up under an oak that stood by the tabernacle in Shiloh. That stone, he said, should be for a witness, to remind them of the promise they had made there to serve the Lord. When he had done talking with them, the people went away, every man to his own home.

After this Joshua, the servant of the Lord, died, being a hundred and ten years old. And they buried him in the part of the land that had been given him for his own, on the side of the hill Gaash. The dead body of Joseph, which the children of Israel brought up out of Egypt, they buried at Shechem, which was the place where Joseph went to find his brethren, when his father sent him out to them, wearing his coat of many colors, nearly three hundred years before.

THE BOOK OF JUDGES

CHAPTERS I–VIII (1–8)

THE CHILDREN OF ISRAEL WORSHIP IDOLS, AND ARE PUNISHED BY BEING MADE SERVANTS TO THEIR ENEMIES. GOD CHOOSES JUDGES TO RULE OVER THEM: OTHNIEL, EHUD, SHAMGAR, DEBORAH, AND GIDEON.

AFTER Joshua was dead, the men of Israel went out to war against the heathen nations, as he had commanded; and the Lord helped them, and gave them the victory. Yet they did not persevere until they had driven out all those nations from Canaan; they allowed some of them still to live in the land. And the Lord spoke to the children of Israel, saying, I brought you up out of Egypt into the land which I promised to give you, and I commanded you to destroy the idols of the nations that lived there, and never to make peace with those nations. But you have not obeyed me. Now, therefore, I will not any more drive them out from before you, but those that are left shall stay in the land, and they will tempt you to sin, and cause you great trouble.

When the children of Israel heard these words they wept. Yet they soon forgot what the Lord had said, for they not only allowed many of the heathen to stay in Canaan, but they treated them as their friends. They even married among them; the men of Israel took heathen women for their wives, and the daughters of the Israelites married heathen men. Then the children of Israel began to worship the idols called Baal and Ashtaroth, that the people of Canaan worshipped. And the Lord was very angry with them, and sent enemies who fought against them and made them their servants. But when they repented, and asked the Lord for help, he heard them and gave them rulers called judges, who led them out to war against their enemies, and set them free. Yet as often as the Lord set them free, they forgot him and sinned again. So they went on sinning, and afterward repenting, for more than three hundred years. During that time fifteen judges ruled over them.

The first was named Othniel; he was Caleb's younger brother.

13

He went out to war against the king of Mesopotamia, who had made the children of Israel his servants for eight years. And God gave Othniel and the men of Israel the victory, so that they had to serve the king of Mesopotamia no more. And they had rest from war for forty years.

But after Othniel was dead, the people sinned again. Then the king of Moab brought an army against them, and made them his servants for eighteen years. The people cried to the Lord for help, and the Lord made Ehud judge over them. He was a man of the tribe of Benjamin, and was left-handed. The Lord sent Ehud to set them free from the king of Moab. So Ehud made a dagger, and hid it under his garment on his right thigh. Then he came to the king of Moab's house, while the king was sitting in his summer parlor. And Ehud said, I have a secret errand from God for thee, O king. When all the servants had been sent out, and Ehud was left alone with the king, he put forth his left hand, and took the dagger from his right thigh, and thrust it into the king's body, and the king fell down dead.

Then Ehud made haste to flee out of the house, and he shut the doors after him and locked them. Now the king's servants did not know what Ehud had done. So when they came and saw that the doors were shut, they said to themselves, The king himself has shut them because he wished to be alone; and the servants did not open the doors. Yet after they had waited a long while, and saw that the king did not open them, they took a key and opened the doors; and behold their master was fallen down dead upon the floor. But Ehud by this time had fled far away, so that they could not take him.

And Ehud went to mount Ephraim, in the land of Canaan, and blew a trumpet to call the men of Israel. When they came to him, he said, Follow me, for the Lord will give you the victory. And they followed him to the river Jordan; there they fought with the men of Moab and slew ten thousand of them, who were all brave and strong soldiers; they let not a man escape. So the children of Israel were set free from the Moabites: and they had rest from war for eighty years.

After Ehud, Shamgar was judge over the people. He fought against their enemies, the Philistines, and the Lord helped him, so that, by himself alone, with nothing but an ox-goad in his hand, he slew six hundred men.

And the children of Israel did evil again. Then the king of Canaan came against them, and made them his servants for twenty years. Now the Lord had chosen a woman to be judge over Israel at this time. Her name was Deborah; she lived in a house that stood under a palm tree near Bethel. And Deborah sent for a man named Barak, and told him that the Lord commanded him to take ten thousand of the men of Israel, and go to fight against Sisera, the captain of the king of Canaan's army. But Barak was afraid, and answered that he would not go unless Deborah went with him. Then Deborah said she would go, but that Barak should not have the praise of the victory, because a woman would put Sisera to death.

So Barak took ten thousand men and went out against Sisera, and Deborah went with him. Sisera gathered all the king of Canaan's army together, his soldiers, and his war-chariots made of iron, nine hundred of them, and came to fight with the children of Israel. Then Deborah said to Barak, Up, for this is the day in which the Lord has given Sisera into thy hand. So Barak with his ten thousand men, fought against Sisera, and the Lord gave them the victory. And Barak followed after Sisera's army, putting them to death with the sword; but Sisera got down out of his chariot and fled away on his feet, that Barak might not take him.

And he came to the tent of a woman named Jael, who was a friend to the children of Israel; and he said to her, Give me a little water, for I am thirsty. And she opened a bottle of milk and gave him to drink. Again he said to her, Stand in the door of thy tent, and when any one comes and asks if there is a man here, say No. And he went into her tent to hide, and lay down and slept. Then Jael took a great nail of the tent, that was used in fastening the side of the tent to the ground, and she went softly to Sisera while he was sleeping, and drove the nail into his forehead, so he died there. Soon afterward Barak came by, seeking for Sisera, and Jael went out to meet him, and said to him, Come, I will show thee the man whom thou art looking for. Then she took him into the tent, and there Sisera lay dead. So the children of Israel were set free from the king of Canaan that day, but Barak had not the praise of the victory, because Sisera, the captain of the king's army, was killed by the hand of a woman, as Deborah had said.

After this the people had rest from war forty years. But when the forty years were ended, they did wickedly and displeased God, and the Midianites came up against them and made them their servants and treated them very cruelly. For they drove the children of Israel from their cities, and their homes, so that they had to live in dens and caves in the mountains. The grain which they planted, after it was grown up, the Midianites destroyed, or carried away, till there was nothing left for them to eat. They took their oxen, their goats, and their sheep also, and the people grew very poor, and were in great distress because the Midianites did these things to them. Then they cried to the Lord to help them, as they had done before, but the Lord sent a prophet to tell them how wicked they had been.

Now there was a man of the children of Israel named Gideon who was threshing wheat one day, that he might hide it from the Midianites. And the Lord came, in the form of an angel, and spoke kindly to him. Then Gideon told the Lord of the troubles that had come on the children of Israel because of the Midianites. The Lord said to him, Thou shalt set the children of Israel free from the Midianites. Gideon answered, O my Lord, how shall I set Israel free? The Lord said, Surely I will be with thee, and thou shalt destroy their whole army, as if it were but one man.

Then Gideon said to the Lord, Stay, I pray thee, until I can go and bring thee an offering. The Lord answered, I will stay till thou comest again. So Gideon went and killed a kid and made it ready, and put the meat into a basket, and brought it out to him. The Lord told him to lay it upon a rock that was there, and Gideon did so. Then the Lord reached forth the end of the staff that was in his hand, and touched the flesh, and there rose up fire out of the rock and burnt up the offering. And the Lord went away from Gideon's sight.

Soon the army of the Midianites came, and made their camp in the valley of Jezreel. Then Gideon blew a trumpet, and called the children of Israel to go with him and fight against them. He sent messengers also through different parts of the land, and many of the people came.

THE ANGEL OF THE LORD APPEARS TO GIDEON

Now Gideon asked the Lord to do a miracle for him, so that he might know the Lord would certainly help him, when he should go to fight against the Midianites. Gideon said he would take a fleece of wool, and leave it out on the ground all night. If, in the morning, it should have dew on it, and the ground all around it be dry, then he should know that the Lord would surely help him to set the children of Israel free. So Gideon took the fleece of wool and left it on the ground all night, as he had said. And he rose up early in the morning and went to it, and found it full of dew, so that he wrung the dew out of it with his hands, and filled a bowl with water; but the ground all around it was dry.

Then Gideon spoke to the Lord again, and prayed that he would not be angry if he asked him to do one thing more. He said he would put the fleece out another night, and asked

GIDEON WRINGS OUT WATER FROM THE FLEECE

that this time it might be dry, but the ground all around it wet with dew. And he left the fleece of wool out another night, and in the morning, when he looked, it was dry, no dew was on it, but the ground all around it was wet with dew. So Gideon knew by these miracles, which the Lord had done for him, that the Lord would certainly help him when he should go out to fight against the Midianites.

Then Gideon and all the army of Israel rose up early and came near the camp of the Midianites. But the Lord spoke to Gideon, and told him there were too many men in the army of Israel. For if such great numbers of them should go to the battle and gain the victory, they would say they had gained it by their own strength, and not that the Lord had gained it for them. The Lord commanded Gideon to tell the men in his army that all who felt afraid might go back to their homes. When Gideon told them this, twenty-two thousand went from the camp of Israel, and there were left ten thousand men.

And the Lord spoke to Gideon again, saying, There are yet too many. Bring them down to the water, and I will shew thee there which of them shall go with thee to the battle. So Gideon brought them to the water. Now all the men were thirsty and began to drink. But they drank in different ways—some lifting the water in their hands to their mouths, and some stooping down and putting their mouths into the water. Then the Lord commanded Gideon to put those who drank out of their hands apart, by themselves; and when he had done so there were three hundred of them. It was the Lord who made them drink in this way, so that they might be separated from the others; for now he told Gideon that only these three hundred men should go with him to the battle.

That same night the Lord commanded Gideon to arise and go with his three hundred men against the Midianites; for, he said, he would give him the victory. But if Gideon were afraid to go with so few, then, the Lord told him, to go first with his servant, alone, near their camp, not to fight against them, but in the dark where they could not see him, that he might listen and hear what they said. And the Lord promised that after Gideon had done this, he should feel no more fear, but would be willing to go and fight against them.

Now the Midianites lay along in the valley like grasshoppers —there were so many of them—and their camels no one could number. And Gideon went down with his servant alone, in the night, and came near to their camp, and heard two of them talking together. One was telling the other of a dream he had dreamed. He said, I saw in my dream a loaf of barley bread come tumbling into our camp, and it struck against a tent and threw it down, so that the tent lay flat upon the ground. And the man who heard him answered, saying, That loaf of bread means the sword of Gideon; for the Lord is going to give all our host into his hand.

When Gideon heard this, he went back to the three hundred

GIDEON FIGHTING AGAINST THE MIDIANITES

men, and told them to rise up and come, for the Lord would give them the victory. Then he set them in three different companies, and put a trumpet in every man's hand, and a pitcher, with a lighted lamp inside of the pitcher. And he told them that when they should come near to the camp of the Midianites, they must look at him and do as he did. When he should blow with his trumpet, they must all blow, and cry out, The sword of the Lord and of Gideon.

So he came with the three hundred men near to the camp of

the Midianites in the middle of the night. Then suddenly they all blew with the trumpets, and broke the pitchers that were in their hands, and cried aloud, The sword of the Lord and of Gideon. When the Midianites heard the noise, and saw the burning lamps that had before been hidden in the pitchers, they cried out with fear and fled. For the Lord made them afraid of the men of Israel, and afraid of each other also, so that they fought among themselves all through their host.

And Gideon followed them to the river Jordan, and passed over the river after the two kings of the Midianites, who fled before him with fifteen thousand men—all that were left of their great army. Gideon and his three hundred men came up with them, and gained the victory over them, and took the two kings captives. So the Midianites were driven out of Canaan, and the children of Israel had to serve them no longer.

Gideon was judge over the people forty years. God gave him many sons, and he lived to be an old man. And he died, and was buried in his father's sepulchre.

CHAPTERS VIII–XII (8–12)

ABIMELECH IS MADE KING AT SHECHEM: HE IS SLAIN. TOLA AND JAIR ARE MADE JUDGES: AFTER THEM JEPHTHAH, IBZAN, ELON, AND ABDON. JEPHTHAH IS MADE CAPTAIN OVER THE ARMY OF ISRAEL. HIS VOW. HE FIGHTS AGAINST THE AMMONITES AND SETS THE PEOPLE FREE.

As soon as Gideon was dead, the children of Israel forgot how kind the Lord had been to them, in setting them free from the Midianites, and they turned away from him, to worship the idol Baal. Then Abimelech, Gideon's son, went to the city of Shechem, where the people had set up an image of Baal, and he asked them to make him their king; they did as he asked them and made him their king. They also gave him seventy pieces of silver out of their idol's temple; with these he hired wicked men, to go with him and help him in making himself king over all the rest of the people. And he went to the house where his father Gideon had lived, and killed all of his brothers except the youngest, who fled from him.

Abimelech did this because he was afraid that his brothers might be made rulers over the people instead of himself. And the men of Shechem helped him in slaying his brethren.

But after Abimelech had been king for three years, God sent trouble upon him and the people of Shechem. The Bible tells us that he sent an evil spirit between them. Then instead of being friends any longer, and helping each other, they became enemies and hated one another. And when Abimelech had gone away from the city, the people set men to watch for him, as he should come back, that they might kill him.

But the governor of the city, who was Abimelech's friend, sent word to him secretly, saying, The people of Shechem have rebelled against thee. Now, therefore, come up in the night, thou and the men who are with thee, and hide out in the field until morning. Then as soon as the sun has risen up, thou shalt bring thy men before the city, and when the people come out against thee, thou shalt do to them whatsoever thou thinkest best. So Abimelech did as the governor said. He brought his men up in the night, and hid them in the fields near the city. In the morning the people saw him and came out against him, and he fought with them, and chased them back to the gate of the city, killing many of them.

The next day they came out again. And Abimelech divided his men into three companies, and hid them in the field. As soon as the men of Shechem had come a good way from the gate of the city, one of the companies made haste to the gate and stood before it, so that the men of Shechem could not flee back into the city. And the two other companies ran upon them out in the field, and slew them. Then Abimelech and his men went into the city, and fought against it all that day; and he slew the people, and broke down the houses, and destroyed the city.

But some of the men of Shechem who escaped fled to the temple of their idol, and shut themselves in, where Abimelech could not reach them. Then he went up on a mountain, where wood was growing, and, taking an axe in his hand, he cut down the branch of a tree, and laid it on his shoulder, saying to his men, Make haste, each of you, and do as I have done. So every man cut down a branch. Then they followed Abimelech to the idol's house, and piled up the branches against the door and set them on fire. And the house was burned, and all the men who had shut themselves in there were burned up with it.

And Abimelech went to another city, named Thebez, and fought against it and took it. After it was taken, the men

DEATH OF ABIMELECH

and women of the city fled into a strong tower, and shut the door, and went up to the top of the tower. Then Abimelech came near the door to burn the tower, as he had burned the idol's house in Shechem. But a woman, who was on the top of the tower, threw down a piece of a mill-stone upon his head and broke his skull. When he knew that he must die, he called one of his young men and said to him, Draw thy sword and slay me, that the people may not say I was slain by a woman. For, because Abimelech was a man of war, and soldier, he was ashamed to have it said that a woman had put him to death. Then the young man drew his sword, and thrust it through Abimelech's body and killed him. So God brought punishment on him for slaying his brethren, and on the people of Shechem, also, for helping him to do that great sin.

After Abimelech was dead, Tola, a man of the tribe of Issachar, was judge over the children of Israel. The Bible tells us nothing about him, or about the things that he did, except that he was judge for twenty-three years; and that he died and was buried in the city of Shamir, on mount Ephraim, where his home had been.

Then Jair, a man of Israel, who lived in the land of Gilead, where the two and a half tribes lived, was judge over the people for twenty-two years. He had thirty sons that rode on thirty colts, and each one of them was governor over a city in Gilead. And Jair died; and was buried in the city of Camon.

And the children of Israel did evil again, for they turned away from serving the Lord to serve Baal and Ashtaroth, the idols their fathers had worshipped. Then the Philistines and the Ammonites made war against them, and the Lord did not help the children of Israel. Therefore their enemies got the mastery over them, and made them their servants for eighteen years.

In their trouble they cried to the Lord for help; but he answered that he had often before set them free from their enemies, yet afterward they had left him to serve their idols. Now therefore, he said, they might go to the idols they had chosen, and ask them for help. But the children of Israel still cried to the Lord, confessing their sins, and telling him to punish them in any way he saw best; only they begged that he would set them free from the enemies who were then ruling over them. They put away the idols they had worshipped, and served the Lord again; and he pitied them in their sufferings.

And the Ammonites gathered together, and made their camp in the land of Gilead, on the other side of Jordan. The children of Israel had their camp at a place called Mizpeh; and they wanted a captain for their army, and said, Who is the man that will lead us out to fight against the Ammonites? He shall be ruler over all the people of Gilead.

Now there was a man of the children of Israel named Jephthah. He was a great and brave soldier, yet the men of Israel had been unkind to him, so that he fled from the land of Gilead, where his home was, and went to live in the land of Tob. But when the people wanted a man to lead them out to war against their enemies, they remembered Jephthah; and the elders went to him in the land of Tob, and said, Come and be our captain, that we may fight against the Ammonites. Jephthah answered, Did you not hate me and send me away? Why then are you come to me now, when you are in trouble? The elders told him they had come that he should go with them to fight against the Ammonites, and be ruler over all the people of Gilead. Jephthah asked them whether, if he should go, and the Lord should give him the victory, they would indeed make him ruler over all the people. The elders promised, before the Lord, that they would.

So Jephthah went with them, and the people made him their captain. Then he sent messengers to the king of the Ammonites, asking him why he had come to fight against the children of Israel. The king answered that it was because they had taken away his land when they came up out of Egypt. Now, therefore, the king said, give me back my land. But Jephthah sent messengers again, saying that the land which they had taken was given to them by the Lord, and that whatever land the Lord gave them they would keep for their own. The children of Israel had done no wrong to the Ammonites, Jephthah said, but the Ammonites did wrong to the children of Israel in making war against them.

Yet the king of the Ammonites would not listen to his words. And Jephthah came, with the men of Israel, to the place where the Ammonites had their camp. And before the battle, he made a vow or promise, that if the Lord would give him the victory, he would offer up, as a burnt offering, whatever should come out of his door to meet him, when he went back to his own home. Jephthah did wrong in making such a vow, for he could not tell what might come out of his door to meet him; yet he made this vow to the Lord. Afterward he went and fought against the Ammonites, and the Lord gave him the victory, so that the children of Israel were set free from them.

When the battle was over, Jephthah returned to his home, and as he went toward his house, his daughter came out with music and dancing, to meet him, being full of joy at seeing her father, for she was his only child.   But when he saw her he was

JEPHTHAH MEETS HIS DAUGHTER

greatly troubled, and rent his clothes, and told her of the vow he had made.   Then she answered, My father, if thou hast made a vow to the Lord, do to me as thou hast said.   But Jephthah should not have kept the vow which it was wrong in him to make.   God had commanded the Israelites to offer up oxen, and goats, and lambs as burnt offerings, not their children.   The heathen nations offered their children to idols, and were punished for doing it.   Jephthah should have repented of his vow, and asked forgiveness for making it.   But the Bible tells us that he took his daughter, and did with her as he had promised, and all the young women of Israel mourned for her. Jephthah was judge over the people for six years; and he died and was buried in one of the cities of the land of Gilead.

After Jephthah was dead, Ibzan was chosen judge, and he ruled over the people seven years. After him, Elon was judge for ten years; and after Elon died, Abdon was chosen judge for eight years. Of these three judges the Bible tells us very little, except how long they ruled, and that they died and were buried.

CHAPTERS XIII–XVI (13–16)

THE CHILDREN OF ISRAEL SIN AGAIN AND ARE MADE SERVANTS TO THE PHILISTINES. SAMSON IS BORN. HE FIGHTS AGAINST THE PHILISTINES AND IS TAKEN CAPTIVE. HIS DEATH.

AFTER these things, the children of Israel sinned again and displeased the Lord, and the Philistines came out against them and made them their servants for forty years.

There was at that time a man of Israel named Manoah. Both he and his wife feared the Lord; and they had no child. And the angel of the Lord spoke to the woman, and told her they should have a son, and that he should be a Nazarite to God: this meant that he should be set apart for God, to serve him. He was never to drink wine, and his parents were to let his hair grow without ever cutting it, because persons who were Nazarites drank no wine, neither did they cut their hair as others did, for so the Lord commanded them. And the angel said that Manoah's son should be a Nazarite, and that he should be the one who would begin to set the children of Israel free from the Philistines.

Then the woman came and told her husband that a man of God, or prophet, had spoken to her, for she did not know it was an angel. Yet, she said, his face was like the face of an angel, but I did not ask him from where he had come, neither did he tell me. When Manoah heard what his wife said, he prayed, saying, O Lord, let the man of God whom thou didst send, come again unto us, and teach us, what we shall do to the child that shall be born.

And the Lord heard Manoah's prayer, and the angel came again to the woman as she sat in the field, but her husband was not with her. Then she made haste and ran to her husband, and told him that the man had come who came to her the other day. And Manoah rose up and went with his wife, and when he came to the man, he said to him, Art thou the man of God that spoke to the woman? He said, I am. And Manoah said, How shall we do to the child which thou hast promised us? The angel answered, All that I commanded thy wife when I came to her before, let her be careful to obey.

And Manoah begged the angel to stay till they should make ready some food for him; for they did not know that it was an angel. But the angel said, Though thou keep me, I will not eat of thy food. And Manoah said, Tell us thy name, so that when what thou sayest shall come true, we may know whom to honor. The angel answered, Why askest thou after my name, seeing it is secret? And Manoah took a kid and offered it upon a rock, as a burnt offering. Then the angel did a wonderful thing, for while the fire was burning on the rock, as the flame went up toward heaven, the angel of the Lord went up in the flame; and Manoah and his wife saw it, and they bowed down with their faces to the ground.

And Manoah said, We have seen God: and he was afraid, for he believed that this angel was the Lord; the same that came to Gideon while he was threshing wheat, and told him he should set the children of Israel free from the Midianites. Manoah said to his wife, We shall surely die, because we have seen God. But his wife said to him, If the Lord had intended to kill us, he would not have allowed us to offer up the burnt offering, nor told us that we should have a son.

After these things, God gave to Manoah and his wife the son he had promised them, and they called his name Samson; and the child grew, and the Lord was kind to him and blessed him. When Samson was grown up, he went to a city called Timnath and saw there the daughter of a man who was a Philistine. And he was pleased with her, and came back to his home and said to his father and mother, I have seen a woman in Timnath

who is the daughter of a Philistine. Now, therefore, get her
for me, that she may be my wife. Then his father and mother
asked him if there was not a woman among the children of
Israel whom he would take for his wife instead of this one, who
was the daughter of a Philistine; for the Philistines were enemies to the Israelites. But Samson was not willing to give

SAMSON KILLS THE LION

her up: he said to his father, Get her for me, for she pleases
me well.

So his father and mother went with him to Timnath, and they
came to the vineyards which were in that country. And a young
lion met Samson and roared at him; and the Lord gave him
strength to kill the lion as easily as if it had been a kid. He
did this with his hands alone, for he had no sword nor spear to
fight the lion with. Then Samson saw the young woman at
Timnath and talked with her, and still she pleased him well.

And he went to Timnath again, to marry her. On the way
he came to the place where he had killed the lion, and he turned

aside to look at its dead body; a swarm of bees had come into it, and made honey there. And he took some of the honey in his hands, and as he walked did eat of it. Afterward he gave some to his father and mother, but did not tell them that he had taken it out of the dead body of the lion.

Samson made a feast at Timnath, for so the young men, when they were married, used to do. The feast lasted seven days, and thirty of the Philistines came to it. Then Samson said he would give them a riddle, that they might find out what it meant and tell him. If they should do so before the seven days of the feast were ended, he promised to give them thirty suits of raiment, or clothing. But if they could not find out his riddle, they were to give thirty suits to him. The Philistines agreed to this, and asked him to tell them his riddle.

So Samson told it to them, and these were the words of it: Out of the eater came forth meat, and out of the strong came forth sweetness. It meant, Out of the strong lion that was ready to eat Samson, Samson had taken sweet honey for himself to eat. But he did not tell the Philistines what it meant; and they tried, for three days, to find out for themselves, but could not. Then they were angry; and on the seventh day they came to his wife, and told her that they would burn her and her father's house with fire, unless she helped them to find the riddle.

So she persuaded her husband to tell her, and wept before him, saying that he did not love her, but hated her, because he had given the riddle to her friends, yet had not told her what it meant. But Samson answered, I have not told my father or my mother, and shall I tell thee? Still, she wept before him all the time that was left of the feast, and at last he told her because she troubled him. When he had told her, she told the Philistines. Then they came to Samson on the seventh day, just before the end of the feast, and pretended they had themselves found out his riddle. They said, What is sweeter than honey and what is stronger than a lion? But Samson knew that his wife had told them.

And now the time was come when Samson should begin to punish the Philistines for their cruelty to the children of Israel.

The Lord had said that he was the one who should begin to set the children of Israel free. This was the reason why the Lord had made him so strong that he could tear the young lion as if it had been a kid. And Samson went down to a city of the Philistines called Ashkelon; there he slew thirty men, and took from them thirty suits of raiment, which he brought and gave to those who had told him his riddle. Then he went back to his own home, but his wife stayed with her father in Timnath.

At the time of wheat harvest, Samson came to Timnath to visit his wife, and to bring her a kid. But when he had come to the house, her father would not let him go in, and told him that she could be his wife no longer, for she was given to be the wife of another man. Then Samson was very angry, and he went and caught three hundred foxes, and tied fire-brands, or pieces of blazing wood, to their tails, and let them loose in the fields and vineyards of the Philistines. There they set fire to the grain, so that it was burned up, both that which had been cut and piled in shocks, and that which was still growing in the field. The grape-vines and the olive-trees were burned also. And the Philistines said, Who has done this? When they knew that it was Samson, they took his wife and her father and burned them with fire. Then Samson fought against the Philistines, and slew many of them. Afterward he went on to the top of a rock called Etam, and stayed there.

Then the Philistines came up to take him, and made their camp in the land of Israel. And the men of Israel said to them, Why are you come up against us? They answered, To bind Samson, that we may do to him as he has done to us. And three thousand men of the children of Israel went to the top of the rock Etam, where Samson was, and said to him, Knowest thou not that the Philistines are rulers over us? Why hast thou done these things? Samson answered, Because they have done evil to me, I have done evil to them. Then the men of Israel told him they had come to bind him, that they might give him to the Philistines. Samson asked them whether they would promise not to put him to death, if he should let them bind him.   They answered, We will not put thee to death, but will bind thee fast and give thee to the Philistines.

So Samson let them bind him with two new cords, and they took him to bring him to the Philistines' camp.   As he came near to it, the Philistines saw him and were glad, and they shouted against him.   But the Lord gave him such strength that he broke the cords off from him, as easily as if they had been burned by fire.   And Samson found the jaw-bone of an ass, and took it in his hand, and with it fought against the Philistines and slew a thousand men.   Then he said, With the jaw-bone of an ass, heaps upon heaps, with the jaw of an ass have I slain a thousand men; and he threw away the bone out of his hand. Afterward he was thirsty, and grew weak because he had no water to drink.   Then he prayed to the Lord, and the Lord opened a spring in that place, from which water flowed out, and when he had drunk of it, his strength came to him again.

And he came to a city called Gaza, and went into a house there.   Now the Philistines lived in Gaza, and when they heard that Samson had come, they shut the gates of the city, and watched by them all night, to take him as he should go out again.   They said, In the morning we shall kill him.   But in the middle of the night he rose up and came to the gates, and when he found them shut, he dragged up the two posts to which the gates were fastened, and took the posts, and the two great gates, and the bar which went across them on the inside, to keep them shut, and put them all upon his shoulders, and carried them a good way off to the top of a hill.

We have read that Samson was a Nazarite, and that persons who were Nazarites were commanded not to cut their hair.   Samson's hair had never been cut, and had grown thick and long. He was commanded never to cut it, because the Lord had chosen him to be a Nazarite as long as he lived.

Now there was in that land a woman named Delilah, and Samson used to go to her house.   When the lords of the Philistines knew of it, they came to her and promised to give her eleven hundred pieces of silver, if she would find out for them how they might bind Samson, and make him their captive, so

that they could do with him as they pleased.   Therefore, when
Samson came to Delilah's house, she begged him to tell her
what made him so strong, and how he might be bound so that
he would not be able to break loose again.

SAMSON CARRYING AWAY THE GATES OF GAZA

Samson should have given her no answer to these questions.
But instead of this he told her an untruth. He said that if he
were bound with seven green withes—that is, cords made out of
twigs, or thin branches of trees, twisted together—he would not
be able to break them, but would be as helpless as any other
man. Then Delilah told the lords of the Philistines, and they
brought her seven green withes, and Samson let her bind him

with them. Now she had men hidden in the room to take him if he could not break them. So when she had bound him, she cried out, The Philistines are coming to take thee, Samson. She did this to try whether he could break the green withes or not. And as soon as she had spoken these words, he broke them as easily as if they were so many threads.

Then Delilah said to him that he had mocked her and told her lies, and she begged him again to tell her how he might be bound. Samson answered, that if he were bound with two new ropes which had never been used, he would not be able to break loose again. So she took two new ropes and bound him, having men hidden in the room this time also; and after she had bound him she cried, as she did before, that the Philistines were coming to take him. But he broke the new ropes from off his arms as easily as he had broken the green withes.

And Delilah told him again that he spoke lies to her, and she begged him to tell her how he might be bound. Samson said that if she would weave, or plait, his long hair in a certain way his great strength would go from him, so that they could do with him as they chose. Then she plaited his hair, and fastened it as he had told her, and she cried out again that the Philistines were coming to take him. But when he heard these words, he rose up and went away, as strong as ever.

Then she said to him, How canst thou say, I love thee, when thou hast mocked me these three times? And she begged him every day to tell her, and would let him have no rest, but troubled him with her words until at last he told her the truth. He said that he had been a Nazarite ever since he was born; that his hair had never been cut, and that if it were shaven off from his head, he would be strong no longer, but as weak as other men. Why did Samson tell her this, and teach her how to take away the strength which the Lord had given him that he might fight against the enemies of the children of Israel? He did it because he had chosen a wicked woman for his friend, and, when she tempted him, he listened to her words until she persuaded him to do this great sin against God.

And now Delilah saw that he had not deceived her. So

she sent word to the lords of the Philistines, saying, Come but once more, for this time he has told me the truth; and they came to her, and brought the money they had promised. Then, while Samson was asleep, she called a man to shave the hair from his head; and after it was done, she cried out that the Philistines were coming to take him. And he woke from his sleep, and said he would go out against them, as he used to do when

SAMSON IS TAKEN BY THE PHILISTINES

she spoke these words to him before. He did not know that the Lord had taken away his great strength from him. Then the Philistines took him, for he could no longer fight against them, and they bound him with chains made of brass. And they put out his eyes, and shut him up in prison: there they made him work very hard, in turning a mill-stone to grind their corn.

And now, while he was shut up in prison, no doubt Samson repented of his sin, and prayed to the Lord whose command he

SAMSON IN PRISON

SAMSON BREAKS DOWN THE PILLARS

had disobeyed. And after a while, as his hair grew long again, the Lord gave him back his strength. But the Philistines did not know this.

One day the lords of the Philistines called the people together in their idol's house, to offer up a sacrifice to their idol, whose name was Dagon, and to rejoice because Samson was taken. The people came, and praised their idol, and thought it was he who had helped them to take Samson and make him their captive. They said: Our god has delivered into our hands our enemy, and the destroyer of our country, who slew many of us. And they were all pleased and merry. Then they said, Send for Samson, that he may make sport for us. So they sent for him, and brought poor, blind Samson out of the prison, and made sport of him, and set him between two pillars in the house of their idol.

Now the house was full of men and women, and all the lords of the Philistines were there. On the roof also were great numbers of the people, who looked down to see Samson, while those who were in the house mocked him, and made sport of him. A boy held him by the hand, to lead him, because he could not see. And Samson asked the boy to let him feel the pillars which held up the house, that he might lean against them. And the boy guided him, so that he could feel the pillars as he stood between them.

Then Samson prayed, saying, O Lord, remember me, I pray thee, and give me strength only this once. And he put his arms around the pillars, one around one pillar and the other around the other pillar; and he said, Let me die with the Philistines. And he bent down and pulled the pillars together with all his might, till they were moved from their places, and the house fell upon the lords of the Philistines, and upon all the people, killing great numbers of them. And Samson died with them, but the Lord helped him, so that in his death he slew more of the enemies of the children of Israel than he had slain in his life. And his brethren came and took his dead body and buried it in his father's sepulchre. Samson was judge over the people for twenty years.

THE BOOK OF RUTH

ELIMELECH AND HIS FAMILY GO FROM BETHLEHEM INTO THE LAND OF MOAB
   ELIMELECH AND HIS TWO SONS DIE THERE, AND NAOMI COMES BACK
   WITH RUTH TO BETHLEHEM.   BOAZ MARRIES RUTH.

IN the days when the judges ruled over Israel, there was a
famine in Canaan.   And a man of the children of Israel who
lived in the city of Bethlehem, went to stay for a while in the
land of Moab; he and his wife and their two sons.   The man's
name was Elimelech, and his wife's name Naomi.   After they
had come into Moab, the man died, but his sons took wives
of the women of Moab, and lived for about ten years.   Then
they died also, and their mother, Naomi, was left alone with her
two daughters-in-law.

And Naomi heard that the famine was over in Canaan, and
that the Lord had given the people food again; so she rose up to
leave the land of Moab, and go back to the city of Bethlehem.

Then she spoke to her daughters-in-law, and asked if they
would not rather stay in Moab, which was their own land, where
they were born, and where their relations lived.

When her daughters-in-law heard what she said, they were
troubled and wept; and one of them, named Orpah, kissed
Naomi, and bade her farewell, and went away to her own home;
but the other, whose name was Ruth, would not leave her.   Ruth
told Naomi not to ask that she should leave her, or go back from
following after her.   Where thou goest, she said, I will go, and
where thou livest, I will live; thy friends shall be my friends,
and thy God, my God; where thou diest I will die, and there
will I be buried.   And Ruth asked the Lord to punish her, if
she ever left Naomi as long as they both should live.   When
Naomi saw how much Ruth loved her, and wanted to go with
her, she did not speak to her any more about staying in the
land of Moab.

And they came into Canaan, to the city of Bethlehem, where
Naomi used to live.   The people remembered her, and all of
them spoke about her coming, and said, Is this Naomi?   But

she was very sorrowful, and answered, Call me not Naomi, which means pleasant; but call me Mara, which means bitter; because the Lord has dealt very bitterly with me. She meant that the Lord had sent her great trouble. For when she went away from Bethlehem, so many years before, her husband and her two sons were with her; but now, when she came back, they were all dead. It was in the beginning of the barley

NAOMI AND HER DAUGHTERS-IN-LAW

harvest, when the people were cutting their grain, that Ruth and Naomi came to Bethlehem.

Naomi had a kinsman, or relation, at Bethlehem, named Boaz, who was a rich and great man. And Ruth said to Naomi, Let me go now out to the field, and glean ears of corn. To glean in the field was to pick up the grain that the reapers had left. Only poor people gleaned, who had no fields of their own. It was not much they could gather, yet the men who were reaping always left a little for them, because the Lord had commanded the reapers not to take away all, but to leave

a little for the poor. And Ruth and Naomi were poor. Therefore Ruth asked her mother-in-law to let her go and glean in
some field where the man would give her permission to do it.
And Naomi said to her, Go, my daughter. Then she went and
happened to come into the field that belonged to Boaz, and
there she gleaned after the reapers.

And Boaz came out to the field and spoke to his reapers, and
said to them, The Lord be with you. They answered him, The

RUTH GLEANS IN THE FIELD OF BOAZ

Lord bless thee. And he asked his chief servant, that was set
over the reapers, Whose young woman is this? The servant
answered, It is the young woman that came with Naomi out
of the land of Moab; she said to us, I pray you let me glean
after the reapers; and we allowed her to do it. So she came into
the field, and hath kept on gleaning from the morning until now.

Then Boaz spoke kindly to Ruth, and told her not to go into
any other man's field, but to glean in his, for he had commanded
his young men to do her no harm. When she was thirsty, he

said, she should go to the pitchers which the young men had filled, and drink what she wanted. And Ruth bowed down to the ground before Boaz, and asked him why he was so kind as to take notice of her, who was only a stranger. Then Boaz answered that he had been told of all her kindness to her mother-in-law; how she had left her father and her mother and the land where she was born, and had come to live among the children of Israel. He asked that God might reward her, because she had done these things, and had left the land of Moab, where the people worshipped idols, to come into Canaan and serve the Lord.

And Boaz told her to come at meal-time, and eat and drink with the reapers. So she did as he said; she sat beside them, and Boaz reached her parched corn, and she ate and had enough, and afterward went out in the field again. And Boaz commanded his young men to let her glean, even among the sheaves that they had bound up for him; he said, also, Let fall some handfuls on purpose for her, that she may take them, and do not find fault with her.

So she gleaned in the field until evening, and beat out the grains of barley that she had gathered, and took them and went into Bethlehem. When her mother-in-law saw how much Ruth brought, she was glad, and asked the Lord to bless the man who had been so kind to her. And she asked her who the man was. Ruth said, The man's name is Boaz. Then Naomi told her he was a near kinsman to them. And Ruth said he had asked her to come again into his field and glean after the reapers, and to do so until they had ended all of his harvest. Naomi told her to do as Boaz said. So she went out into his field, and gleaned there until the end of the barley harvest and of the wheat harvest.

And Naomi said to Ruth, Boaz winnoweth barley to-night in the threshing floor. Barley is a grain something like wheat. To thresh it was to separate it from the long straw on which it grew. To winnow it was to separate it again from the small, broken pieces of straw which were left mixed with it after the threshing. These pieces could not be picked out with the hands, there were too many of them; but the reapers used to throw the grain and the small pieces of straw together, up in the air, while the wind was blowing. Then the wind would blow away the straw, because it was so light, but the grains of barley, being heavier, would fall down by themselves in a heap on the ground. A threshing floor was the smooth, level piece of ground where these things were done. Naomi had heard that Boaz was to winnow his barley that night, and she asked Ruth to wash and dress herself, and go to the threshing floor, and speak to Boaz the words which she told her.

So Ruth did as her mother-in-law said. She washed and dressed herself, and went to the threshing floor: and Boaz winnowed his barley, and then had a feast. After he had eaten and drunk, and had enough, she came near to him, and spoke to him, saying, Thou art our near kinsman: and she asked him to be kind to her. He answered, May the Lord bless thee, my daughter. Then he told her not to fear; he would do for her all that she needed, because all the people of Bethlehem knew that she was a virtuous and good woman. And he said to her, Bring here thy veil and hold it out. And when she brought it, he poured into it six measures of barley. Ruth carried it into Bethlehem, to Naomi, and told her of all that Boaz had done, saying, These six measures of barley he gave me, for he said, Go not away without taking something with thee for thy mother-in-law. Then Naomi told Ruth to wait and be patient, until she should see what else Boaz would do.

We have read that the cities of Canaan had walls around them with gates. Now it was at the gates that the people used to meet together. Whoever came into the city, or went out of it, passed through them. That was the place where the rulers came to hold their court, and try those who had disobeyed the laws, and to say what their punishment must be. Persons also bought and sold things at the gate, making a kind of market there. So that when any man wanted all the people to know of something he was going to do, he would go and speak about it at the gate, because there he found more of them gathered together than anywhere else.

The next day after Boaz had winnowed his barley, he went to the gate of Bethlehem, and sat down in a seat there. And he called to him ten of the elders, or principal men, of the city, and said to them, Sit down here; and they sat down. Then Boaz spoke to them, and to all the people, and told them that he was going to take Ruth, the daughter-in-law of Naomi, to be his wife. And he said to the elders, and to all the people, You are the witnesses: that is, you are the persons to whom I tell it, that you may know it yourselves and tell others also. And all the people and the elders answered, We are the witnesses. And they prayed that the Lord would bless Ruth, and make Boaz still richer and greater than he was then.

So Boaz took Ruth and she was his wife. Naomi was glad for her daughter-in-law, who had loved her, and come with her out of the land of Moab into Canaan, to live with the children of Israel and serve the Lord. After awhile the Lord gave Boaz and Ruth a son. Naomi took the child and laid it on her bosom, and nursed it for them. And they named the little boy Obed.

THE BOOK OF JOB

JOB'S GOODNESS AND RICHES. AFFLICTIONS ARE SENT UPON HIM. HIS FRIENDS' UNKINDNESS. JOB COMPLAINS OF HIS SUFFERINGS. GOD SPEAKS TO HIM AND GIVES HIM GREATER BLESSINGS THAN HE HAD BEFORE HE WAS AFFLICTED.

THERE was a man in the land of Uz named Job, who feared God, and was careful to do no evil. And God gave him seven sons and three daughters. He gave Job great riches also; for he had three thousand camels, seven thousand sheep, a thousand oxen, five hundred asses, and many men-servants and maid-servants, so that he was the greatest of all the men in that part of the world where he lived.

His sons, who were grown up, and had homes of their own, used to feast together, taking turns at each other's houses, and inviting their three sisters to come and eat and drink with them. When their feasts were over, Job always sent and told them, if they had done anything wrong, to repent of it; then he offered up burnt offerings for each of them, because he feared they might have sinned and displeased God.

But after Job had enjoyed his blessings for many years, God sent trouble upon him, to try whether he would bear it patiently, and be willing that his heavenly Father should do to him what he thought best. Therefore God allowed his riches and his children to be taken from him. For there came to him one

JOB RECEIVING EVIL TIDINGS

day a messenger, saying, While thy oxen were ploughing in the field and the asses were feeding beside them, a band of robbers drove them all away, and slew thy servants who were with them, and I am the only one left to tell thee.

While this servant was speaking, there came another, who said, A great fire has fallen from the sky and burnt up thy sheep and the servants who were taking care of them, and I alone am left to tell thee. While he was yet speaking, another came, and said, Some enemies have taken thy camels, and killed thy servants who were keeping them, and I only am left to tell thee. While he was speaking, there came also another, and said, Thy sons and thy daughters were feasting in their eldest brother's house, when there came a great wind from the wilderness that broke down the house; so that it fell on the young men and they are dead, and I only am left to tell thee.

When Job heard these things, he rent his clothes and bowed down to the earth and worshipped, saying, I had nothing of my own, when I was born as a little child into the world, and I shall have nothing when I die and go out of it. It was God who gave me my children and my riches, and it is God who has taken them away again. He knows what is best for me, and I thank him for all he has done. So Job did not sin nor speak wickedly of God, although his grief was so great and had come so suddenly upon him.

After this, to try Job still more, God sent him sickness and pain. Sore boils came on him and covered him, from his feet to his head, and he sat down on the ground in great distress. Then his wife, being angry because God sent him such suffering, came to Job, and said, Dost thou still trust in God? Do so no more, but speak against him and wish him evil, for afflicting thee, even though he kill thee for doing it. Job answered her, Thou speakest like a foolish woman. After we have had so many good things from God, shall we not be willing to take evil things? In all this Job said nothing that was wrong.

And he had three friends, who, when they heard of his trouble, came to talk with him and comfort him. But when they saw him, he was so changed that they did not know him. Then they rent their clothes and wept, and sat down on the ground near to him, but did not speak, because they could see that his grief was great. Now his friends thought his troubles had been sent upon him on account of some evil that he had done. And after a while they spoke to him, and said, If thou hast done wickedly, do so no more. Thou must have sinned, in taking what did not belong to thee, or in being cruel to the poor, or in not praying to God; yet if thou wilt repent of thy sins, God will forgive thee and take thy sufferings away.

But Job knew that he had not done the things which his friends accused him of, and he said to them, You came to comfort me, but what you say does not help me at all. I would rather you should be still altogether, and let me alone. Did I send for you, or ask you to talk to me? If you were afflicted as I am, I also could say many things against you, and call you wicked. But instead of this I would speak kindly, and try to make your troubles less.

JOB AND HIS THREE FRIENDS

Then Job spoke of his sorrows, and said, The Lord has sent great troubles upon me. Oh, that he would put me to death, that I might suffer no more. When I lie down at night, instead of resting in sleep, I toss upon my bed in pain and wish it were morning. Or, if I fall asleep for a little while, dreadful dreams frighten me, so that I would rather die than live. Oh, that I had some one to speak to God for me, for he does not listen to my prayers. Yet I know that my Saviour is living, and that after many years he will come on the earth, and I shall rise up from the grave and see God for myself.

But when Job saw that he could neither die, as he wished to do, nor be made well, but that he must still bear his pains, he grew impatient. He was willing to bear them for a little while, but not until God saw best to take them away. Then he began to find fault, and say that his troubles were too great, and that God was cruel to him. And his three friends, instead of trying to encourage him, still told him that he must have offended God. His troubles were a punishment, they said, and God did not punish the good, but the wicked; therefore Job must have done very wickedly. Then Job was displeased with them and answered them angrily, and they answered him angrily again. So they kept on, accusing one another and complaining against each other. After they had talked in this way for a long while, and had, each of them, said many things they ought not to have said, they heard a voice speaking out of a whirlwind that came by that place. It was the voice of God.

And the voice spoke to Job, and told him of the wonderful works God had done; that it was he who had made the earth, the sea, and the sky. It is God, the voice said, who sends the rain on the fields, to make the grass and the flowers spring up. He covers the rivers with ice, and the ground with snow, and sends the lightning from the sky. He gives the wild beasts their food, and feeds the young birds which cry to him when they are hungry. It is God who gave the beautiful wings to the peacock, and feathers to the ostrich. He made the horse that is so swift and strong, and that is not afraid in the time of war, when he hears the trumpets, and the shouting of the captains, but is eager to rush with them into the battle. He taught the eagle to build her nest on the high rocks, and to fly off and hunt food for her young ones.

When God had told Job of all these wonderful works, he asked whether Job was able to do such things, or whether he was wise enough to teach God what he should do? Then Job saw how he had sinned in finding fault with God. He said, I am wicked, and have spoken of things that I do not understand; therefore I repent of my sin, and bow down in the dust before thee.

And God said to Job's three friends, I am angry with you, for you have not spoken what is right to my servant Job, in his trouble. Now, therefore, lest I punish you, take seven bullocks and seven rams, and offer them up as a burnt offering, and ask Job to pray for you that you may be forgiven, for his prayers I will hear. So they did as the Lord commanded; and Job prayed for them and they were forgiven.

JOB IN PROSPERITY

After this the Lord took away Job's sickness. Then all his brothers, and sisters, and friends came to him, and they had a feast in his house. Every man gave him a piece of money and an earring of gold. And now the Lord blessed Job more than he had done before he sent his troubles upon him, and gave him twice as great riches. For Job had fourteen thousand sheep, six thousand camels, two thousand oxen, and a thousand asses. He had also seven sons and three daughters; and in all the land there were no women so beautiful as the daughters of Job. After these things he lived a hundred and forty years; and he died, being a very old man.

THE BOOK OF JONAH

JONAH FLEES FROM THE VOICE OF THE LORD. HE IS THROWN INTO THE SEA AND SWALLOWED BY A GREAT FISH, WHICH CASTS HIM OUT ON THE DRY LAND. HE PREACHES TO THE NINEVITES.

NINEVEH was one of the mightiest cities of the old times. In it were temples, palaces, and houses for a great multitude of people; and beautiful gardens, also, and green fields, where cattle were fed. Around the city were walls a hundred feet high. These walls were so thick that on their top three chariots, drawn by horses, might be driven side by side. And towers were built above the walls, all around the city. There were fifteen hundred towers, each one being two hundred feet high. On the top of the walls, and in the towers, the Assyrian soldiers stood, to shoot arrows and darts at their enemies when they came to fight against Nineveh. But Nineveh was a very wicked city.

And God spoke to the prophet Jonah, saying, Arise and go to Nineveh, that great city, and tell the people of the punishment that is coming upon them for their sins. But Jonah did not want to go, and he fled to Joppa, a city by the sea. There he found a ship that was going to a far country, and Jonah paid his fare and went into it, that he might flee to some place where he would not hear the Lord speaking to him.

But when he had sailed out on the sea, the Lord sent a strong wind and there was a great storm, and the ship was in danger of being broken to pieces. Then the sailors were afraid, and they prayed, each one to his idol, for help. They threw out, also, some of the loading of the ship, to lighten it and keep it from sinking. But Jonah did not know of the danger they were in, for he had gone down to the lower part of the ship, and lay there fast asleep. And the captain came to him and awaked him, saying, What meanest thou, O sleeper? Rise up and pray to thy God; perhaps he may pity us, and save us from perishing.

Then the men talked with one another, and said, Because some one in the ship has done wickedly, this storm is sent; and they said, Come, let us cast lots that we may find out for whose sake it is brought upon us. So they cast lots, and the lot fell on Jonah. Then they said to him, Tell us, what wicked thing hast thou done? where is thy country? and to what people dost thou belong? Jonah answered, I am a Hebrew, and am fleeing from the Lord who made the sea and the dry land, that I may not hear his voice speaking to me. And the men were greatly afraid, and said, Why hast thou done this thing? And they asked Jonah, What shall we do to thee, that the sea may be still for us? For the ship was tossed by the tempest. Jonah answered them, Take me up and cast me into the sea, so shall the sea be still for you, because I know that it is for my sake this danger has come upon you.

Yet the men did not want to throw him into the sea, and they rowed hard to bring the ship to land, but could not. Then they prayed to the Lord, whom Jonah had told them of, and they cried out to him, saying, O Lord, we beseech thee, punish us not for casting this man into the sea, as if we were putting to death one who had done us no harm, for thou, O Lord, hast sent the storm on his account. Then they took up Jonah and cast him into the sea, and the sea grew still and calm. The men wondered at this; and they offered a sacrifice to the Lord, and promised, after that, to serve him.

Now the Lord had sent a great fish to the side of the ship, to swallow up Jonah as soon as he should be cast into the sea. And Jonah was in the fish three days and three nights. And he prayed to the Lord while he was in the fish; he cried to God in his trouble, and confessed his sin. God heard him, and commanded the fish to cast him out on the dry land.

Then the Lord spoke to him again, the second time, and said, Rise up and go to Nineveh, that great city, and preach to the people the words that I shall tell thee. So Jonah arose and

JONAH IS CAST INTO THE SEA

went. And he came into the middle of the city, as far as he could walk in one day, and there he cried out with a loud voice, and said, After forty days Nineveh shall be destroyed, for the sins of the people.

When the king of Nineveh and the people heard this, they believed that God had sent Jonah, and that the words he spoke would come true. So the king rose up from his throne, and took off his royal robes and put on sackcloth. And the king

JONAH CAST OUT BY THE FISH

and his princes sent word through the city that all the people should fast. Let not man nor beast, they said, eat any food or drink any water, but let them be covered with sackcloth, and let every one pray with all his heart and cease doing wickedly; for who can tell but the Lord may forgive us and take his great anger from us, so that we perish not? And when God saw how they prayed to him, and ceased doing evil, he took away his anger from them and did not destroy the city.

But Jonah was displeased at this. He wanted Nineveh to be

destroyed because the people who lived there were enemies to the children of Israel. Jonah feared also being laughed at, and called a false prophet. Therefore he was angry and spoke wickedly to the Lord; he said, I knew that thou wouldst not destroy the city, and therefore I fled the first time, that I might not hear thy voice speaking to me. Now, I beseech thee, O Lord, put me to death, for I would rather die than live. Yet the

JONAH UNDER HIS BOOTH

Lord spoke kindly to Jonah, and asked if it were well for him to be angry.

And Jonah would not stay in Nineveh, but he went to a place outside of the city, and made a booth there, and sat down under it, by himself, to see whether the city would be destroyed or not. And the Lord caused a gourd, or vine, to grow up in one night over his booth; its thick leaves shaded his head, and Jonah was very glad for the gourd. But soon God sent a worm that gnawed at its root, and the next day it died. In the morning God sent a hot wind on Jonah, and the sun also beat upon his head, and as the gourd no longer shaded him, he was made sick by the heat and fainted. Again he was angry and wished he might die, and said, It is better for me to die than live.

And God said to him, Doest thou well to be angry? Jonah answered, Yes, I do well to be angry. Then God said, Thou art angry because I have destroyed the gourd, which was only a vine that grew up in a night and died in a night; and now wouldst thou have me to destroy Nineveh, that great city, where there are more than a hundred and twenty thousand little children, so young that they cannot tell their right hands from their left? So God taught Jonah how selfish and wicked he was in wishing that Nineveh should be destroyed, because the people were not friends to the children of Israel, and because he feared being laughed at and called a false prophet.

THE FIRST BOOK OF SAMUEL

CHAPTERS I–VI (1–6)

ELKANAH AND HANNAH SACRIFICE AT SHILOH: HANNAH PRAYS FOR A SON, AND SAMUEL IS GIVEN HER. SHE LEAVES HIM AT THE TABERNACLE. THE LORD SPEAKS TO SAMUEL. THE PHILISTINES TAKE THE ARK, AND HOPHNI AND PHINEHAS ARE SLAIN. ELI DIES. THE ARK IS SENT BACK TO THE LAND OF ISRAEL.

THERE was a man of the children of Israel named Elkanah, who went every year from the city of Ramah, where he lived, to offer up a sacrifice at the tabernacle in Shiloh. And his wife, whose name was Hannah, went with him. Now Elkanah loved his wife, and gave her a present whenever he went to offer up his sacrifice; yet she was unhappy, because the Lord had given her no child.

And she came to the tabernacle and prayed, and made a vow to the Lord that if he would give her a son, she would give that son back to him, and he should be a Nazarite, and set apart to serve the Lord all the days of his life. Eli was the high priest at that time. Hannah came with her husband to Shiloh and prayed at the tabernacle, and wept while she prayed. And Eli saw her lips moving, but could not tell what she said, for she spoke softly, so that her voice was not heard.

Then Eli thought she was drunken, and muttering words to herself, and he said to her, How long wilt thou be drunken? Put away thy wine from thee. But Hannah answered, No, my lord, I am a woman in trouble. I have drunk neither wine nor strong drink, but have been praying with my heart to the Lord. Then Eli answered her kindly, and said, Go in peace, and may

HANNAH PRAYS AT THE TABERNACLE

God give thee what thou dost ask him for. Hannah was glad at the high priest's words, and went away and looked sad no more. After this she and her husband left Shiloh, and came to their home in the city of Ramah.

And the Lord remembered Hannah's prayer, and sent her a son, and she called his name Samuel, which means, Asked of God; because she had asked God for him, and God gave him to her. After Samuel was born, the time came for his father to go

to Shiloh again, and offer up his sacrifice as he did each year.
But Hannah would not go; she said she would wait till the boy
was weaned, and then would take him up, that he might stay
there always. For she had given Samuel to the Lord, that he
might live at the tabernacle and wait on the priests, and serve the
Lord as long as he lived. And her husband told her to do as

HANNAH BRINGS SAMUEL TO ELI

seemed right to her; so Hannah stayed at their home until her
son was weaned.

When she had weaned him, she took him up to the tabernacle,
and she and her husband offered a bullock as a sacrifice. And
they brought the child to Eli, and Hannah spoke to Eli, saying,
O my lord! I am the woman that stood by thee here, praying
unto the Lord. For this child I prayed, and the Lord has given
me what I asked him for. Therefore I have given the child
back to the Lord; as long as he liveth, he shall be given to the
Lord. And she left Samuel to stay with Eli at the tabernacle.

Eli had two sons, whose names were Hophni and Phinehas; they were priests at the tabernacle. Now the Lord had said that the priests should be holy, because they were his ministers who offered up sacrifices to him; but Hophni and Phinehas were not holy, they were wicked men.

We have read that when any man offered up a peace offering, only a part of it was burned on the altar; the rest was given, some of it to the priest, for him to eat, and some of it to the man who brought the offering, for him to eat. But Hophni and Phinehas took more than their share of the peace offerings, and if any man were unwilling they should have so much, they would take it from him by force. Therefore the people did not care to come any more to the tabernacle with their offerings, because of the wicked things which were done by Hophni and Phinehas.

But Samuel, who was only a child, did what was right and pleased the Lord. And his mother made him a little coat, and brought it to him each year, when she came up with her husband to offer their sacrifice. And Eli spoke kindly to them, and asked that the Lord would bless them, because they had given Samuel to the Lord. So his parents came every year to Shiloh and worshipped, and afterward went away again to their own home; but Samuel stayed with Eli at the tabernacle.

Now Eli was very old, and he heard of the evil things which his sons did, and he said to them, Why do you such things? For he was grieved at their wickedness. Yet he did not punish them, nor put them away from being priests, as he ought to have done, but allowed them to go on in their sin. And there came a prophet to him with a message from the Lord. The Lord asked why he allowed his sons to take the best part of all the offerings that the people brought. Eli cared more to please his sons, the Lord said, than he did to please him; therefore the Lord declared that he would not have Eli for his high priest, but would choose another man who should do his will, and both of Eli's sons, the Lord said, should die in one day.

And Samuel stayed at the tabernacle, doing as he was bidden by the high priest. One night he lay down to sleep, and Eli lay down also. And Samuel heard a voice calling to him, and he answered, Here am I. Then he rose up and ran to Eli, and said that he had come because Eli called him, for he thought it was Eli's voice. But Eli said, I called not, lie down again; and he went and lay down.

And he heard the voice again, and arose and went to Eli, and said, Here I am, for thou calledst me. Eli answered, I called thee not, my son, lie down again. And Samuel heard the voice a third time, and went to Eli and said, Here I am, for thou didst call me. Then Eli knew that it was the Lord who had called the child; therefore he said to him, Go, lie down; and if he call thee say, Speak, Lord, for thy servant heareth.

So Samuel went and lay down. And the Lord came and called as before, Samuel, Samuel. And Samuel answered, Speak, for thy servant heareth. Then the Lord told him that he was going to do a thing which would make every one who should hear of it afraid; for he would punish Eli and his sons as he had said, because his sons had made themselves wicked, and Eli had not kept them from doing so; and though they should offer up sacrifices and burnt offerings for their sins, he would not hear them nor forgive them.

When the Lord was done speaking, Samuel lay still until the morning; then he rose up and opened the doors of the tabernacle. He was afraid to tell Eli of what the Lord had said. But Eli called him, and asked, saying, What is the thing that the Lord hath said unto thee? Hide it not from me. God do so to thee (that is, God punish thee too) if thou hide anything from me of all that the Lord has spoken. Then Samuel told him every word, and hid nothing from him. When Eli heard it, he said, It is the Lord, let him do what seemeth him good; that is, It is my heavenly Father who has said he will punish me. I deserve it, let him do to me whatever he thinks best.

And Samuel grew, and the Lord blessed him, and all the people knew that he was chosen to be a prophet.

The words which God spoke to Samuel came true; for the children of Israel went out to fight against the Philistines, and made their camp at a place called Ebenezer. The Philistines made their camp at Aphek, and they fought against the children of Israel, and slew of them about four thousand men. When the army of Israel came back to their camp after the battle, the elders asked why the Lord had allowed so many of them to be slain. Then they said to one another, Let us bring the ark out of the tabernacle to save us from our enemies. Perhaps they remembered how it was carried around Jericho, when the children of Israel took that city. But the Lord commanded them to carry it then; he did not command them to send for it now, and it was foolish to think that the ark could save them: the Lord alone could do that.

Yet they sent to Shiloh for the ark, and the two sons of Eli, Hophni and Phinehas, came with it. When it was brought into the camp, the people were glad and shouted with a great shout, and the noise sounded far off on every side. The Philistines heard it, and said, What meaneth the noise of this great shout in the camp of the Hebrews? They were told that the ark had come into the camp; and they were afraid, and cried, Who shall save us? Then they said to one another, Let us be strong, and fight like men, that we may not be servants of the Hebrews.

And they fought again with the men of Israel, and slew thirty thousand of them; they took the ark away from the Israelites also, and the two sons of Eli, Hophni and Phinehas, were slain. And there ran a man out of the army to Shiloh that same day; his clothes were rent, and he had put earth on his head to show his grief. Eli, the high priest, sat upon a seat by the way-side, watching; for he was afraid, since the ark had been carried to the battle, lest some evil might happen it, and he waited to hear what word should come.

Then the man came into the city, and told the people that the ark was taken, and they all cried out with fear. When Eli heard them, he said, What meaneth this noise among the people? Now Eli was very old, and his eyes were dim, so that he could not see. And the man came in quickly to him, and said, I am he that fled to-day out of the army. Eli asked him what had happened there. The man answered, The men of Israel have fled from the Philistines, and a great many of them have been slain; thy two sons, Hophni and Phinehas, are dead, and the ark of God is taken. When the man spoke of the ark, Eli fell off from his seat backward, down to the ground, and his neck broke, and he died; for his grief was greater than he could bear, when he heard that the ark was taken.

Eli was not only high priest, but he was judge also over the children of Israel forty years.

The Philistines took the ark and carried it to one of their

A MAN RUNS TO TELL THAT THE ARK IS TAKEN

cities, called Ashdod, where they had a house for their idol whose name was Dagon. They brought the ark into the house of Dagon, and set it down by the idol and left it there all night. But when they rose early in the morning, and came into Dagon's house, they found that the idol had fallen upon its face on the ground before the ark. Then they lifted it up, and set it in its place, and left the ark there another night. And when they came, early in the morning, Dagon was fallen down before the ark again; but this time his head and his hands were cut off, only his body was left.

After that, there came a great sickness upon the people of Ashdod, and many of them died. Then they said to one another, The ark of the God of Israel shall not stay with us. They said this because they believed it was God who had sent the sickness

DAGON FALLEN DOWN BEFORE THE ARK

among them, and thrown down their idol. Therefore they called all the lords of the Philistines together, and spoke to them, saying, What shall we do with the ark of the God of Israel? They answered, Let it be carried to Gath. Gath was another city of the Philistines. And they carried it to Gath, but there came a great sickness among the people of that city also. And the Philistines kept the ark for seven months, but during all that time the Lord sent great trouble upon them. Then they called for their wise men, and asked how they should send it back to the land of Israel, for they were afraid to keep it any longer.

Now in that country cows were used for drawing carts, as horses are here. And the wise men told the Philistines to make a new cart, and take two cows and tie them to it, but to bring their calves home from them. Then, they said, the people should lay the ark upon the cart, and send it away, letting the cows draw it wherever they chose, without any one to guide them. If the cows should go, of their own accord, away from their homes and from their calves, and take the ark into the land of Israel, the wise men said it would show that the Lord made them go there; and that he was angry with the Philistines for keeping the ark, and had sent all their troubles as a punishment upon them. But if the cows should not take the ark to the land of Israel, then it would show that the Lord did not want it sent back, and that he had not punished the Philistines for keeping it, but that their troubles had come by chance upon them.

The Philistines did as their wise men said. They took two cows and tied them to a new cart, but shut up their calves at home. Then they laid the ark on the cart and let the cows loose, to go wherever they chose—the lords of the Philistines following after them to see which way they would go. And as soon as the cows were let loose they went straight into the land of Israel, lowing as they went, until they came to a city called Beth-shemesh. The children of Israel who lived there were reaping their wheat harvest in the valley near to the city. They looked up and saw the ark, and rejoiced to see it.

And the cows brought it into the field of a man named Joshua, and stood still beside a great stone that was there. Then some men of the tribe of Levi came, and took the ark down from the cart and laid it on the stone. And they broke up the cart for wood, and killed the cows for a burnt offering, and offered them to the Lord. The Levites took the ark down from the cart, because, as we have read, the Lord had chosen them to take care of it, and of all the things in the tabernacle. If the men of any other tribe should come near to those sacred things, God said they must be put to death. But the men of Beth-shemesh disobeyed

God; they wanted to see the ark, and they came near to it, and looked into it, and many of them died for their sin.

THE ARK IS BROUGHT BACK TO THE CHILDREN OF ISRAEL

Then the ark was taken to the city of Kirjath-jearim, into the house of a man named Abinadab, and was left there for many years.

CHAPTERS VII–XII (7–12)

SAMUEL IS MADE JUDGE OVER THE PEOPLE. HIS SONS DO WICKEDLY. THE PEOPLE ASK FOR A KING, AND SAUL IS CHOSEN. HE SAVES JABESH GILEAD FROM THE AMMONITES. SAMUEL TELLS THE PEOPLE OF THEIR WICKEDNESS IN ASKING FOR A KING.

AFTER Eli was dead the Lord made Samuel judge over the people. He lived in the city of Ramah, where his father, Elkanah, and his mother, Hannah, had lived. We have read that after the tabernacle was finished, and the ark was put into it, every man among the children of Israel was commanded to bring his sacrifice there, that the priests might offer it up for him on the altar of burnt offering. But at the time we are now reading about the ark was not in the tabernacle; for the people had never brought it back to Shiloh, as they ought to have done, and we are not told that the priests stayed there any longer to offer up sacrifices. Then Samuel built an altar at Ramah, where he lived, and offered up sacrifices himself.

And the children of Israel sinned again, for they worshipped the idols Baal and Ashtaroth. Then the Philistines made war upon them. And Samuel spoke to them, saying, If you will put away your idols and serve the Lord, he will save you from the Philistines. The people obeyed Samuel; and he said to them, Come all of you to the city of Mizpeh, and I will pray for you. Then they came to Mizpeh, and there they confessed their wickedness, and said, We have sinned against the Lord.

When the Philistines heard that the people were at Mizpeh, they went up to fight against them. Then the men of Israel were afraid, and they said to Samuel, Cease not to pray to the Lord our God for us, that he may save us. Samuel took a young lamb and offered it up as a burnt offering; and he prayed to the Lord for the people, and the Lord heard him. While Samuel was offering up the lamb the Philistines came near, to battle. But the Lord sent a great storm of thunder and lightning upon them, that made them flee away in fear. Then the men of Israel came out of Mizpeh and chased them, killing many of them. So the Lord gave the men of Israel the victory. And Samuel set up a stone at the place where the Lord helped them, and called it Ebenezer, which means, The stone of help.

When he was grown old, Samuel made his two sons judges, that they might help him in ruling over the land. But they did not rule justly, as their father had done. For if two of the people disputed about anything, and came to them to decide which was right and which was wrong, they would say that the one was right who paid them for saying so. This was taking a bribe; and they took bribes from the people, allowing any one to do wrong who would pay them money for it.

And all the elders of Israel came to Samuel, at Ramah, and told him that he was now old, and that his sons did wickedly; and they asked him to choose for them a king, that they might be like the other nations around them. It was right in them to tell Samuel that his sons did wickedly, but it was wrong in them to ask for a king, because the Lord was their king, and Samuel was the judge whom he had set over them. Samuel was displeased when they asked him to choose a king, and he prayed to the Lord, that the Lord might tell him what he should do. Then the Lord said it was not Samuel whom the children of Israel wanted to put away, but it was the Lord himself whom they wanted to put away from ruling over them.

Yet the Lord commanded Samuel to tell them what their king would do to them, and how cruelly he would treat them, if they should have a king like the other nations. And Samuel did so. He told the men of Israel that the king would take their sons to be drivers of his chariots, and workmen in his fields, and their daughters to be cooks and bakers in his kitchen. He would take the best of their lands and of their vineyards, and give them to whomever he pleased. Their cattle and their sheep he would take away also; and they would cry out, Samuel said, in that day for the trouble their king had brought upon them, but the Lord would not hear them. Yet the people said, We will have a king like all the other nations, that he may rule over us, and go out with us to fight our battles. Then the Lord commanded Samuel to do as they asked, and choose them a king.

Now there was a man of the children of Israel named Kish, who had a son called Saul. The Bible tells us that Saul was a goodly young man; that is, he was well formed and handsome to look at: he was taller also than any of the rest of the people. And the asses that belonged to Kish, Saul's father, were lost. So Kish said to Saul, Take one of the servants with thee, and arise, go look for the asses. Then Saul took a servant and went to look for them: but after he had gone a long way and could not find them, Saul said to the servant, Come, let us go back, lest my father stop caring for the asses and be troubled about us. But by this time they had come near to a city of that land,

and the servant told Saul there was in the city a prophet whose words always came true. The servant meant Samuel. And he said, Let us go and ask him; perhaps he can tell us which way we shall look for the asses. Saul answered, Thy word is good: come let us go. Now there was to be a peace offering that day in the city, and the people were to have a feast upon the part of it which was not burned on the altar. As Saul and his servant went up the hill to the city, they met young maidens going out to draw water, and they asked them if the prophet were there. The maidens answered, Yes; he came to-day, for there is to be a feast of the people. As soon as you come into the city you shall find him. And when they had come into the city, Samuel met them.

Now the Lord had told Samuel he would send to him that day the man who should be king over Israel. And when Samuel saw Saul, the Lord said to him, This is the man I spoke to thee of. But Saul did not know Samuel, and he went to him and said, Tell me, I pray thee, where the prophet's house is. Samuel answered, I am the prophet. Then he told Saul to bring his servant and come to the feast, and stay there that day; on the morrow, Samuel said, Saul should go on his journey. And as for the asses that had been lost, he need think of them no more, for his father had found them.

Then Samuel took Saul and his servant, and brought them into the parlor, and made them sit in the best place, among those who were invited to the feast. Samuel told the cook to bring the food which he had bidden him save; and the cook brought it and set it before Saul, and Samuel told Saul to eat of it, because it had been saved for him. So Saul stayed with Samuel that day.

The next morning, very early, they rose up, and Samuel took Saul on to the roof of the house, where they would be alone, and there he talked with him; afterward he went with him toward the gate of the city. And as they were walking together, he said to Saul, Bid thy servant go on before us, but stand thou still, that I may show thee what the Lord has commanded me to do. When the servant had gone on before, Samuel took a

bottle of oil and poured it upon Saul's head, and anointed him.
We have read that Moses anointed Aaron when he was made
high priest; so they used to do to the one who was made king.
And now Samuel anointed Saul that he might be king over the
children of Israel, because the Lord had commanded him to do
it. But no one knew of it except Saul and Samuel, for the Lord

SAUL ANOINTED BY SAMUEL

did not mean to let the people know of it until he should choose
Saul again, before them all, for their king.

After these things, Samuel spoke to the people, and told them
that the Lord said he had brought them up out of Egypt, and
set them free from their enemies, yet they would not have him
to rule over them, but asked for a king. Then Samuel commanded them to come to the city of Mizpeh, that they might
have a king set over them. And they came to Mizpeh, and
there the Lord chose, from among them all, Saul to be king

over Israel. But when the people looked for him they could not find him. Therefore they asked the Lord where he was, and whether he would come to be their king. The Lord answered, He hath hidden himself among the stuff.

Then the people ran and brought him out, and as he stood among them, he was higher than any of them, from his shoulders and upward. Samuel said to them, See the man whom the Lord hath chosen; there is none like him among all the people. And they all shouted and said, God save the king! Then Samuel told them about the kingdom, and how Saul should rule over them, and he wrote it down in a book. Afterward he sent them away, every man to his own home. Saul also went to his home in the city of Gibeah.

After this the Ammonites came up to fight against the city of Jabesh-gilead. And the men of Israel who lived there were afraid, and promised that if the Ammonites would treat them kindly, they would be their servants. But the Ammonites would not; they said they would take every man and put out his right eye, and afterward would boast of having done it to all the rest of the people. When the men of Jabesh-gilead heard this, they asked the Ammonites to give them seven days, that they might send messengers to their brethren in other parts of the land. If, by that time, no one should come to help them, they promised to go out of the city and let the Ammonites do to them as they pleased.

Then they sent messengers to Gibeah, where Saul lived, and the messengers told the people what the Ammonites said; and the people wept when they heard it. While they were weeping, Saul came in with a herd of cattle from the field; and he asked, saying, What aileth the people, that they weep? And they repeated to him the words that the messengers had spoken. Then Saul took two oxen and cut them in pieces, and sent the pieces through all the land of Israel, saying to the people, Whoever does not come to fight against the Ammonites, so shall it be done to his oxen. When the people heard these words, there came to Saul more than three hundred thousand men. Early the next morning he led them out against the Ammonites, and they fought with them and slew them, until the middle of the day. Those that were not slain, fled and were scattered, so that no two of them were left together; and the children of Israel rejoiced over their victory.

After these things, Samuel spoke to the people and said, I have made you a king as you asked me, and your king is before you. And now I am old and gray-headed. I have been with you from my childhood to this day, and you know of all that I have done. Tell me then, whether, since I have been judge over you, I have ever taken away any man's ox, or his ass, or anything that belonged to another? or whether I have been unjust, or cruel to any man, or taken a bribe, and allowed the person who gave it to do wrong? For if I have done any of these things, I will now give back what does not belong to me. The people answered, Thou hast never been unjust to us, nor taken a bribe, nor anything that did not belong to thee.

Then Samuel told them they had done wickedly in asking for a king, because the Lord was their king, and they should have wanted no other. And he said to the people, Stand still, and see what the Lord will do before your eyes. Is not this the time of wheat harvest, when we do not have rain? But I will call to the Lord, and he shall send a great storm of thunder and rain, to make you feel how much you have offended him. So Samuel called unto the Lord, and he sent thunder and rain that day, until all the people greatly feared the Lord and Samuel. And they begged Samuel to pray for them, that they might not be put to death.

Samuel said, I shall not cease to pray for you, and to point out to you the good and the right way. Only fear the Lord, and serve him in truth with all your heart: for consider what great things he has done for you. Thus Samuel spoke kindly to them, and told them not to fear. They had sinned, he said, yet if they would obey the Lord, the Lord would forgive them and take care of them, because he had chosen them for his people. But if, instead of obeying him, they still should do wickedly, they would be destroyed, both they and their king.

CHAPTERS XIII–XVI (13–16)

THE PHILISTINES BRING AN ARMY AGAINST ISRAEL. SAUL DISOBEYS THE
LORD AT GILGAL. THE MEN OF ISRAEL GAIN A VICTORY OVER THE
PHILISTINES. SAUL, BEING SENT AGAINST THE AMALEKITES, AGAIN
DISOBEYS THE LORD. THE LORD SENDS SAMUEL TO BETHLEHEM TO
ANOINT DAVID.

AFTER Saul had been king two years, he chose three thousand
men for soldiers. Saul himself was captain over two thousand
of them, and his son Jonathan was captain over the other
thousand. And Jonathan fought against some Philistines,
who had come into the land of Israel. Then the Philistines
gathered a great army, and came up with thousands of chariots
and horsemen, and with so many soldiers that they could not
be counted. When the people saw what a great host had
come against them, they were afraid, and hid in caves, and
thick bushes, among the rocks, and on the mountains, and in pits
in the earth. Some of them fled over Jordan, into the land of
Gilead, where the two and a half tribes lived. The few who were
left followed after Saul their king, but they trembled with fear.

Saul came to Gilgal, for Samuel had promised to meet him
there, and had commanded him to wait till he should come,
that Samuel might offer up burnt offerings and peace offerings,
and afterward tell Saul what he should do. And Saul waited
seven days; then, when Samuel came not, he grew impatient and
said, Bring here a burnt offering to me; and he offered up the
burnt offering himself. As soon as he had done it, Samuel came,
and Saul went out to meet him. And Samuel said, What hast
thou done? Then Saul began to make excuse for offering up
the sacrifice, and said that he was afraid to wait any longer,
lest the Philistines should come against him. But Samuel said
that he had done wickedly and disobeyed the Lord, and therefore the Lord would put him away from being king, and would
choose another man in his place. Samuel did not mean that
Saul would be put away at once; but that the Lord had determined to do it some time, and that it was as certain to be done
as if it were done that very day.

Saul numbered the people who were with him, and found there were about six hundred men; and he and Jonathan came to the city of Gibeah, but the Philistines were at Michmash. Now the Philistines had for a long time made the children of Israel their servants; and they would not let the men of Israel have swords or spears, for fear they might rise up and fight against them. The Philistines had sent all the smiths out of the land, lest they should make these things for the people. So when the day for the battle came, it was found that among the children of Israel no man had either a sword or a spear except Saul and Jonathan.

In those days soldiers wore armor made of iron or brass. They carried shields also, made of strong boards covered with the skin of oxen. These they held up before them while they were in battle, that the arrows and darts of their enemies might not wound them. Jonathan, Saul's son, wore armor, and he had a soldier to carry his shield and spear for him, when he did not want to use them. This soldier was called his armor-bearer.

Now the Philistines had their camp near to the camp of the children of Israel. And Jonathan asked his armor-bearer to go with him over to the camp of the Philistines. For, he said, the Lord might help them, even Jonathan and his armor-bearer alone, to fight against all their great army; because the Lord could give the victory to whomever he chose, either to many or to few. And the armor-bearer said he would go. Then Jonathan told him that this was the way they would know whether the Lord intended to help them or not. They would go and stand where the Philistines could see them; if the Philistines should call out to them and tell them to wait, then, Jonathan said, they would go no further, for the Lord was not going to help them. But if the Philistines should say, Come up to us, they would go up; for the Lord would give them the victory.

And Jonathan and his armor-bearer went and stood at a place where the Philistines could see them. Then the Philistines made sport of them, and said, See, the Hebrews are coming out of the holes where they were hidden: and they called out, Come up to us, and we will show you something. When Jonathan

heard them say this, he told his armor-bearer to come, for the
Lord would give the children of Israel the victory. Then Jonathan climbed up over the rocks, on his hands and feet, to reach
the Philistines' camp, and his armor-bearer climbed after him.
When they came to it, they fought with them and slew about
twenty men. And the Lord made the earth shake under them,
so that all the host of the Philistines were afraid and trembled.

JONATHAN AND HIS ARMOR-BEARER ATTACK THE PHILISTINES

Now Saul and the men who were with him, did not know
what Jonathan had done; but Saul's watchman looked out
toward the camp of the Philistines, and saw fighting there, and
he told Saul of it. Then Saul counted over all his men, that he
might know which of them had gone against the Philistines; and
when he counted them, he found that Jonathan and his armor-
bearer were missing. And Saul and his men went over to join
in the battle. Many of those also, who before had been afraid,

and hidden in the mountains, came after them; and the Lord helped the children of Israel, and the Philistines fled from them. Yet the men of Israel suffered on that day, for Saul commanded that no man should eat any food until the evening, because he wanted them to go on pursuing their enemies. So none of the people tasted of any food.

And they came to a wood where honey was dropping on the ground, from a nest in the trees where the wild bees had made it, and the men were hungry, yet they were afraid to eat. But Jonathan did not know what his father had said, so he reached out the end of the staff that was in his hand, and dipped it into the honey-comb, and put the honey to his mouth. When Saul heard of it, he said, Thou shalt surely die, Jonathan; for he was angry, and would have slain Jonathan, because he had disobeyed his command. But the people asked, saying, Shall Jonathan die, who has caused us to gain this great victory? And they said that no harm should be done to him. So they saved Jonathan from being put to death.

After this, Samuel told Saul that the Lord remembered the wickedness of the Amalekites, in making war against the children of Israel when they came out of Egypt, although the Israelites had done them no harm. And now, Samuel said, the Lord commanded Saul to go out against the Amalekites, and destroy them, and their cattle, and save nothing of theirs alive. Then Saul gathered a great army of more than two hundred thousand men, and fought with the Amalekites, and overcame them and slew the people, but their king he let live. Also the best of their sheep, of their oxen, of their lambs, and all that was good, Saul and the men of Israel saved alive; but what was poor and worth nothing, they put to death. And the Lord was displeased with Saul, and he said to Samuel, I repent of having made Saul king, for he has not obeyed my commandments.

After the battle, Samuel came to Saul. And Saul said to him, I have done as the Lord commanded me. But Samuel heard the bleating of the sheep, and the lowing of the oxen, which Saul had taken from the Amalekites, and he said, What meaneth, then, this bleating of the sheep, and the lowing of the oxen, which I hear? Then Saul began to make excuse and say, that the people had saved them alive to offer them up as sacrifices to the Lord. But Samuel asked Saul whether the Lord was better pleased to have sacrifices offered up to him, than he was to have his commands obeyed. It is better to obey than to offer up sacrifices, Samuel said. For to go on doing what the Lord had commanded them not to do, was as wicked as to worship idols.

DAVID PLAYING THE HARP IN THE FIELD

Then Samuel told Saul again that because he had disobeyed the Lord, the Lord would put him away from being king.

And God told Samuel that he should go to the city of Bethlehem, to a man named Jesse, and should anoint one of Jesse's sons to be king. But Samuel answered, How can I go? for if Saul hear of it he will kill me. Then the Lord said that Samuel should take an heifer to offer up as a sacrifice there, and should ask Jesse to come to the sacrifice. Afterward, the Lord told him, he would show him what he should do. And Samuel did

as he was commanded.   He came to Bethlehem and made ready
his sacrifice, and invited Jesse and his sons to come to it.   When
they came, Samuel thought that Jesse's oldest son was the one
whom the Lord had chosen for king.   But the Lord told him
he was not the one.   Then Jesse called another, but the Lord
did not choose him.   And Jesse caused seven of his sons to

DAVID ANOINTED AT BETHLEHEM

pass before Samuel.   And Samuel said, The Lord has chosen
none of these.

Then Samuel asked, Are these all thy children? Jesse
answered, There is yet one left, the youngest, but he is keeping
the sheep.   Samuel said, Send and bring him.   And they sent
and brought him.   Now he had been out in the field, and when he
came in and stood before them, his cheeks were red and his face
was beautiful to look at.   And the Lord said to Samuel, Arise,
anoint him, for this is he.   Then Samuel took oil and poured

it on his head, and anointed him before all his brethren. So the Lord chose David, for that was his name, to be king over Israel. Yet he was not to be king at once, nor for a long while afterward, but when the Lord should put Saul away from being king.

And after David was anointed, the Lord sent his Holy Spirit

DAVID PLAYING THE HARP BEFORE SAUL

into David's heart, to make him good and wise; but he took his Spirit away from Saul.

We have read of the angels—those good spirits that serve God. The Bible tells us there are evil spirits also, that serve Satan. And now one of these went into Saul and troubled him. Then Saul's servants told him that he should look for a man who could play well on the harp, and when the evil spirit troubled him, that man, they said, should come and play before him, for then the evil spirit would go from him. So Saul said to his servants, Get for me now a man that can play well, and bring him to me. And one of them answered that he had seen such a man. He was the son of Jesse, the Bethlehemite. It was David of whom he spoke; for David knew well how to play on the harp.

Therefore Saul sent messengers to Jesse, and told him to send David, his son, who kept the sheep. Then Jesse took an ass, and loaded it with bread, and a bottle of wine, and a kid, and sent them by David as a present to Saul, but he did not let Saul know how Samuel had anointed David to be king. So David came to Saul, and stayed with him and waited on him, for he pleased him well. And when the evil spirit troubled Saul, David took a harp, and played with his hand and made sweet music that comforted him; then the evil spirit went from him. But after a while David left Saul's house and returned to his own home. Saul had many other servants, and he forgot David.

CHAPTERS XVII–XX (17–20)

THE ARMY OF THE PHILISTINES AND THE ARMY OF ISRAEL MAKE READY FOR BATTLE. GOLIATH DEFIES THE MEN OF ISRAEL. HE IS SLAIN BY DAVID. SAUL TAKES DAVID TO HIS OWN HOUSE, BUT GROWS JEALOUS OF HIM AND TRIES TO KILL HIM. DAVID MARRIES SAUL'S DAUGHTER. JONATHAN SAVES HIM FROM SAUL.

THE Philistines gathered their armies together to fight against Israel. And Saul and the men of Israel made ready for the battle. The camp of the Philistines was on a mountain on one side, and the camp of Israel was on a mountain on the other side, and there was a valley between them.

And there came out of the camp of the Philistines a giant, named Goliath of Gath. On his head was a helmet made of brass, and he wore a coat of armor; pieces of brass also covered his legs, so that no sword nor spear might wound him. He came into the valley between the two armies, where the men of Israel could see him, and he stood and cried to them, Choose you a man out of your army, and let him come down to me. If he be able to fight with me and to kill me, then we will be your servants; but if I kill him, then shall you be our servants. And the Philistine said, I defy, that is, I dare, the armies of Israel this day; give me a man, that we may fight together. When Saul and the men of Israel heard these words, they were greatly afraid; for no man in Saul's army was willing to go out and fight with the giant. And every morning and evening for forty days, he came out and defied all the men of Israel.

Now David was feeding his father's sheep at Bethlehem, but his three elder brothers had gone out with Saul to fight against the Philistines. And Jesse said to David, his son, Take now this parched corn and these ten loaves of bread, and run to the camp, to thy brethren; and carry these ten cheeses as a present to their captain, and see how they do. So David rose up early in the morning, and left the sheep with a servant, and went as his father commanded. He came to the camp just as the host was going out to fight, and all the men shouted for the battle. For the Philistines and the children of Israel had made ready, and they stood, one army before the other. David left the things he had brought with a man, to take care of them, and he ran into the army to speak with his brethren.

While he talked with them, Goliath came out between the two armies, and spoke the same words that he had spoken before, and David heard him. Then the men of Israel fled from him in fear. And David heard them say that if any man would kill the Philistine, the king would give him great riches, and he should have the king's daughter to be his wife. David asked them to tell him again what would be done for the man who should kill the Philistine.

Eliab, David's eldest brother, heard him asking, and was angry with him, and said, Why camest thou down here? and whom hast thou left at home, to take care of the sheep? I know the naughtiness of thine heart, for thou art come down to see the battle. But David answered his brother, saying, What wrong have I now done? Then David said, Who is this Philistine, that he should defy the armies of the living God? David called the armies of Israel the armies of God, because the children of Israel were God's chosen people; and he called God the living God, because all other gods are only dead idols. When the men who were near him heard the words that David spoke, they told them to Saul, and Saul sent for him. And David came, but Saul did not remember him.

And David talked with Saul, and told him that he would go out against the Philistine. David said, Let no man's heart be afraid because of him; thy servant will go and fight with this Philistine. Saul said to him, Thou art not able to go out against him, for thou art but a youth, and he has been a man of war from his youth. David answered, While I was keeping my father's sheep, there came a lion, and a bear, and took a lamb out of the flock; I went after the lion and struck him, and set the lamb free from his mouth. When he rose against me, I caught him by the beard and slew him. Thy servant slew both the lion and the bear; and this wicked Philistine shall be like one of them, seeing he has defied the armies of the living God. David said also, The Lord who saved me from the paw of the lion and the paw of the bear, he will save me from the hand of this Philistine. Then Saul said to David, Go, and the Lord be with thee.

And Saul gave David his own armor, his helmet of brass, and his coat of mail, and his sword. But David said, I cannot go with these; and he put them off from him. Then he took his staff, such as shepherds carried, and he chose five smooth stones out of the brook, and put them in his shepherd's bag; and his sling was in his hand, and he came near to the Philistine. And the Philistine came near to David. But when he saw him, he thought him not worth fighting with; for David seemed not like a soldier, strong and brave, such as Goliath expected would come out against him; but like a shepherd boy, gentle, and with a beautiful face, who had never seen a battle.

Then the Philistine said, Am I a dog, that thou comest to me with a staff? And he called on the idols that he worshipped to curse David, and told him to come near that he might kill him. David answered, Thou comest to me trusting in thy sword, thy shield, and thy spear; but I come to thee trusting in the God of Israel. For this day he will give thee into my hand, and I will kill thee and cut off thy head from thee; and the army of the Philistines shall be slain, and their dead bodies shall lie on the ground; the birds of the air and the wild beasts of the field shall eat them.

When the Philistine came near, David made haste and ran toward him, and put his hand in his shepherd's bag, and took out a stone, and slung it and struck the Philistine in his forehead, so that the stone sunk into his forehead, and he fell down upon his face to the earth.   So David overcame the Philistine with a sling and with a stone, for there was no sword in his

DAVID SLAYS GOLIATH

hand.   And David ran and stood upon the Philistine, and took his sword from him and killed him, and cut off his head with it. When all the Philistines saw that the man in whom they trusted was slain, they fled.   Then the army of Israel rose up and shouted, and followed after them and slew them, and many fell down by the way as they fled.   Afterward the men of Israel turned back from pursuing them, and went into the Philistines' camp, and took all the gold, the silver, and the raiment that they had left in their tents.

And David came from the battle with the head of Goliath in

his hand.   Then Abner, the captain of the army of Israel, took
him and brought him to Saul.   And Saul said, Whose son art
thou, young man?   David answered, I am the son of thy servant Jesse, the Bethlehemite.

Now Jonathan, Saul's son, was there, and when he saw David
and heard him speaking with his father, he loved him; the
Bible says he loved him as his own soul, that is, as much as he
loved himself.   It was the Lord who made him love David, so
that David might have Jonathan for his friend in all the troubles that were coming afterward upon him.

Saul took David that day to be with him, and would let
him go no more home to his father's house.   And Jonathan
made a covenant with David, and promised to be kind to him,
because he loved him as his own soul.   To show his love he
took off his robe, and the garments that he wore, and gave them
to David, and his sword also, and his bow, and the girdle that
was fastened around his waist.   David obeyed the commands
of Saul, and behaved himself wisely in all things, and Saul
made him a captain in his army.

After the battle with the Philistines, as Saul and David
passed together through some of the cities of the land, the
women came out with songs and dances, to praise them for their
victory.   But they praised David more than Saul; they said
that Saul had slain thousands, but David had slain ten thousands of the Philistines.   And Saul was greatly displeased at
their words, and from that time he was jealous of David, and
looked unkindly on him.   The next day an evil spirit came into
Saul's heart and troubled him, and David played before him on
the harp, as he used to do.   Saul held a javelin, or spear, in
his hand, and he cast it at David, intending that it should go
through his body and fasten him to the wall, for he wanted to
kill him.   But David saw it, and stepped aside out of the way,
and it did him no harm.   Saul cast it at him again, but he
stepped aside this time also.

And Saul was afraid of David, because he saw that the Lord
was with him, but he was not with Saul any more.   And Saul
sent David away from his house, with the soldiers that he had

made him captain of. The Lord helped David to do all things well, and all the people loved him. And Saul said to him, I will give thee Merab, my daughter, for thy wife if thou wilt go out and fight against the Philistines. Saul said this because he hoped the Philistines would kill him. And David went and fought with them, but when the time came that he should have Merab, Saul gave her to be the wife of another man.

After that, Saul's younger daughter, Michal, loved David, and they told Saul of it. Then he said that if David would go and slay a hundred of the Philistines, he should have Michal for his wife; for he hoped that, this time, they would surely kill him. So David went with his soldiers and fought against the Philistines, and slew them, but David himself was not harmed; then Saul gave Michal to him, and she was his wife. And Saul saw that the Lord was with David to help him, and he was yet the more afraid of him, and came to be his enemy, and hated him. He spoke to Jonathan, his son, and to all his servants, and commanded them to kill David. But Jonathan loved David, and told him of what his father had said, saying, My father seeketh to kill thee; now, therefore, go to some secret place and hide thyself. And I will talk with my father, and what he says I will tell thee.

And Jonathan talked with Saul, and begged him not to harm David, for he said that David had done no evil to Saul, but had done that which was good. He had risked his own life that he might kill Goliath, the Philistine, and after he had killed him, the men of Israel gained a great victory. Saul knew of all these things, and was full of joy when they happened. Why, then, Jonathan asked, would he do so wicked a thing now as to kill David, although David was a good man and had done nothing for which he deserved to die? And Saul listened to Jonathan's words, and promised, before the Lord, that David should not be slain. Then Jonathan called David from the place where he was hidden, and told him what his father had said. And he brought David to Saul, and David stayed at Saul's house as before.

Again there was war in the land, and David went out and

fought with the Philistines, and gained the victory over them. But Saul was not pleased that he gained the victory, because it made the people love him yet more. And the evil spirit came into Saul's heart, as he sat in his house with his javelin in his hand, while David was playing on the harp before him. Then Saul cast the javelin again at David, to kill him, but David

SAUL CASTS HIS JAVELIN AT DAVID

saw it and slipped away, as he had done before, and the javelin went into the wall and did him no harm; and he fled that night.

Saul sent messengers to David's house to watch that he should not escape in the night, and then to kill him in the morning. But Michal, David's wife, knew of it, and told him, saying, If thou save not thy life to-night, to-morrow thou shalt be slain. So she let him down through a window, where Saul's men could not see him, and he escaped from them. Then she took an image and laid it in his bed, and put a pillow under it, and covered it up, to make them think that David was there, so as to let him have time to flee far away. And Saul commanded his men to go up into the chamber and take him, but when they came there, they found an image in the bed, laid on the pillow. And Saul was angry with Michal for this.

David fled to Ramah, where Samuel lived, and told him of all that Saul had done. Afterward he came to Naioth, and someone told Saul of it, and Saul sent men to take him, but the Lord saved him out of their hands. Then he fled from Naioth to the place where Jonathan was, and went to him, and said, What have I done? What is my sin, that thy father seeketh to kill me? Now Jonathan had not heard that his father was trying to kill David; therefore he said to him, Thou shalt not die, my father will do nothing without first telling me of it. But David said it was true that Saul wanted to put him to death. Then Jonathan promised to do whatever David should ask of him.

Now the next day was to be a feast day, when Saul would expect David to come to his house and eat of the feast. But David was afraid to go, and he begged Jonathan to let him stay away for three days. When Saul should ask why he was not at the feast, Jonathan was to answer that he had given David permission to go to Bethlehem, where his father lived, that he might be with his family when they offered up their yearly sacrifice. If Saul should be angry when he heard this, David said it would show that he was determined to do him evil.

And Jonathan gave David permission to be away for three days. Then David asked, But who shall tell me what thy father says, when he hears that I have gone? Jonathan answered, Come, let us go out into the field. And they went out together into the field. And Jonathan told David that after the three days were past, David should come and hide in the field behind a rock that was there. Then, Jonathan said, he would come out at the same time into the field, pretending no one was there, and he would shoot three arrows from his bow, as if he were shooting at a mark, and would send a lad after the arrows to pick them up. If Jonathan should call out to the lad, The arrows are on this side of thee, David might know that Saul was not displeased with him, and would do him no harm.   But if Jonathan should cry out, The arrows are beyond thee, David would know that he must flee, and that Saul meant to kill him.   Jonathan took this plan because he feared he would be watched, and not be able to speak with David.

So David went away from Saul's house, and the next day was the day of the feast.   And Saul sat down to eat, as at other times, on a seat by the wall.   Jonathan, and Abner, the captain of the host, sat near him; but David's seat was empty.   And Saul asked nothing about David that day, for he thought something had happened to keep him away.   But the next day David's seat was empty again; and Saul said to Jonathan, Why comes not David to eat, neither yesterday nor to-day?   Jonathan answered, David asked leave of me to go to Bethlehem.   He said, Let me go, I pray thee, for our family has a sacrifice, and my brother has commanded me to be there; and now I pray thee, let me go and see my brethren.

Then Saul was very angry with Jonathan for allowing David to go, and told him that he ought not to love David.   Saul told him this because he wanted Jonathan to be king after he himself should die; but now, he said, that Jonathan would never be king as long as David lived.   Therefore, he said, Send and bring him unto me, for he shall surely be put to death.   But Jonathan asked, Why shall he be put to death?   What evil has he done?   Then Saul cast his javelin at Jonathan.   Therefore Jonathan knew that his father was determined to slay David.   So he rose up from the table in great anger, and would eat no food, for he was grieved for David, because his father had said these things of him.

The next day was the day on which David was to hide out in the field, behind the rock that Jonathan had shown him.   And Jonathan went out at the time he had said, and a little lad went with him.   And he sent the lad on before him that he might find the arrows he would shoot.   Then he shot an arrow that passed over the lad.   And Jonathan cried out loud, saying, The arrow is beyond thee; make haste; stay not.   And David heard the words in the place where he was hidden, and he knew from those words that he must flee, because Saul meant to kill him.

And the lad gathered up the arrows and brought them to Jonathan, but he did not know why Jonathan had shot them, and called out after him. Jonathan gave his bow and arrows to the lad, and said, Go, carry them to the city. As soon as he was gone, David came out from his hiding-place, and he bowed

PARTING OF DAVID AND JONATHAN

down with his face to the ground, before Jonathan, three times. Then they came together and kissed one another, and wept with one another. And Jonathan told David to flee, and he helped him to escape from his father; because he loved David, and they had made a covenant together that they would be kind to each other, and to each other's children, forever. Then David rose up and fled from Saul. And Jonathan went back to the city.

CHAPTERS XXI–XXV (21–25)

DAVID FLEES TO AHIMELECH, THE HIGH PRIEST. SAUL COMMANDS THAT ALL THE PHILISTINES SHALL BE SLAIN. DAVID AND JONATHAN MAKE A COVENANT TOGETHER. DAVID CUTS OFF A PIECE OF SAUL'S ROBE IN THE CAVE. NABAL OFFENDS DAVID. DAVID MARRIES ABIGAIL.

DAVID came to the city of Nob, where the tabernacle was at that time, for the people had moved it from Shiloh after the ark was taken by the Philistines. And Ahimelech, the high priest, asked David why he had come. Then David was afraid to say that he had fled from Saul, lest some one might send word for Saul to come and take him. So he was tempted to tell an untruth. He said that the king had sent him on a secret errand, but had commanded him to tell no one what it was. David sinned when he said this. The Lord who had saved him from the lion and the bear, and from Goliath the Philistine, was able to save him from Saul. He should have spoken the truth and trusted in him.

And some young men, who were the friends of David, had come with him. Therefore he asked Ahimelech for five loaves of bread, that they might have something to eat. Ahimelech answered that no bread was there excepting the shew-bread, which, as we have been told, the priests placed each week on the golden table. And Ahimelech gave this to David.

Now there was at the tabernacle a man named Doeg; he was not one of the children of Israel, but had come from the land of Edom; and was hired by Saul to take care of his cattle. Doeg saw David while he talked with Ahimelech. And David said to Ahimelech, Is there not here a spear, or sword, that I may have? for I have not brought my sword or my weapons with me. The high priest answered, The sword of Goliath, the Philistine whom thou slewest, is here, wrapped in a cloth; if thou dost want it, take it, for there is no other. David said, Give it to me.

And David arose and fled from the tabernacle, because he feared that Saul would find him. And he came to the city of the Philistines, called Gath. The king of that city was named

Achish. When his servants saw David, they knew him and brought him to the king, saying, Is not this David? Did not the women of Israel sing to each other, saying, Saul has slain thousands, but David has slain ten thousands of the Philistines? Then David was afraid, and pretended he had lost his senses: he scrabbled on the doors, and behaved strangely before them. And king Achish saw him, and said to his servants, You see the man is mad; why, then, have you brought him to me? Have I need of madmen, that you have brought him? Shall such a fellow as this come into my house? So they let him go.

And he fled from Gath, and went into a great cave, called the cave of Adullam, and lived there. When his brethren and his parents heard of it, they came to him, and others who were willing to help him came also, until he had with him about four hundred men. But David's father and mother were old, and he wished them to be in a better place than the cave where he was hidden, yet he would not send them back to their home in Bethlehem, because the Philistines were there. Therefore he went to the king of Moab, and said to him, Let my father and my mother, I pray thee, come and stay in thy land, until I shall find out what God will do for me. And the king said they might; so David brought his father and mother, and they stayed with the king of Moab as long as David was in the cave.

And David remembered the time when he used to live at Bethlehem, when he was a boy, tending his father's sheep, and before all his troubles had come upon him. And he thought of the well by the gate, that he used to drink of then. He longed for it, and said, O, that some one would give me a drink from the well that is by the gate of Bethlehem. Then three of his men who heard him speak, went and broke through the host of the Philistines and drew water from the well and brought it to David. But when he remembered how they had risked their lives to get it for him, he would not drink of it, but poured it out on the ground as an offering to the Lord.

And a prophet, named Gad, came to David, and said to him, Stay no longer in the cave, but go back into the land of Judah.

Then David went into that land, and lived in a wood. Now Saul was in the city of Gibeah; he rested there under a tree, with his spear in his hand, while his servants were standing about him. And he spoke to them, saying, that they were not his friends any longer, but his enemies, because they would not tell him what David and Jonathan were going to do against him.

DAVID POURS OUT THE WATER FROM THE WELL AT BETHLEHEM

Then Doeg, the Edomite, spoke to Saul, and said that he had seen David at the tabernacle, and that Ahimelech, the high priest, had given him bread, and the sword of Goliath the Philistine. So the king sent for Ahimelech, and for all the priests who were with him; and they came to the king. And Saul asked Ahimelech why he had helped David to rise up against him, and given him bread and a sword. Ahimelech answered that he had not helped David to rise up against Saul; for he did not know, when David came to the tabernacle, that he was fleeing from Saul, or that the king was seeking to slay him.

But Saul was very angry, and said, Thou shalt surely be put

to death, Ahimelech, thou and all thy relations. And he turned to the soldiers that stood near him, saying, Slay the priests, because they are on David's side, and when they knew where he had fled, they would not tell me. But the soldiers refused to obey him. Then he said to Doeg, the Edomite, Do thou slay them. And that wicked man rose up and slew eighty-five men who were priests. He went to the city of Nob also, where the tabernacle was, and where the priests lived, and slew all whom he found there. But one of Ahimelech's sons, named Abiathar, escaped and fled to David, and told him what Saul had done. David answered, I knew, when Doeg, the Edomite, saw me at the tabernacle that he would surely tell Saul. It is my fault that thy father and all thy relations have been slain. Then he asked Abiathar to stay there, and promised that no one should harm him.

After this, some one told David that the Philistines had come into the land of Judah, and were fighting against the city of Keilah, and robbing the people of their grain. Then David asked the Lord whether he should go and fight against them. The Lord answered, Go, and destroy the Philistines, and save Keilah. But the men who were with David feared to go. Then David asked the Lord again, and the Lord told him to go, for he would give him the victory. So David and his men went and fought with the Philistines, and overcame them, and saved the people of Keilah.

And it was told Saul that David had gone into Keilah. Then he said, I shall now surely take him, for my soldiers will surround the city on every side, so that he cannot escape. And Saul called all his army together to go down to take David. When David heard of it, he asked the Lord whether Saul would certainly come. The Lord said, He will come down. Then David asked whether the people who lived in Keilah, and whom he had saved from the Philistines, would fight for him against Saul, or whether they would give him up. And the Lord answered, They will give thee up.

Then David and his men (there were, by this time, about six hundred with him) went out of Keilah, to flee to any place they could find where they might hide from Saul. When Saul heard that David had fled, he did not go to Keilah after him. Yet he tried every day to find him, but God saved him out of Saul's hand. And David hid in a wood. One day Jonathan came to him there, and spoke kindly to him, saying, Fear not, for Saul, my father, shall not find thee, and thou shalt yet be king over Israel. And again they made a covenant together, promising never to harm one another. Afterward Jonathan went away to his own home, but David stayed in the wood.

And the people called Ziphites came to Saul, and said they would show him where David was. Then Saul and his men went with them to seek him. But when they had almost taken David, a messenger came to Saul, saying, Make haste and come back, for the Philistines have come into thy land. And Saul had to go to fight against the Philistines; thus the Lord saved David this time also; and he fled into the wilderness.

When Saul returned from following the Philistines, it was told him where David had gone. Then he chose three thousand of his soldiers, and took them into the wilderness to hunt for David among the rocks, where the wild goats lived. And he came to a cave. Now David and his men were hidden in the sides of the cave, but Saul could not see them. And Saul walked alone into the cave. While he was there, David's men wanted him to rise up and kill Saul. But he would not, for although Saul wanted to kill David, David did not want to kill him. Instead of this he was willing to obey him, and do all that he commanded, because Saul was still king. Therefore David would not slay Saul, yet he went up softly behind him, while he was in the cave, and cut off a piece of his robe and took it away in his hand, but Saul did not know it.

When Saul went out of the cave, David followed him and cried aloud, saying, My lord, the king. And Saul looked round to see who it was. Then David bowed down with his face to the earth before him, and asked why Saul listened to the wicked men who told him that David wanted to do him harm. On that day, David said, he might have killed Saul, and some of his men wanted him to do it, but he had told them he would not

kill his master, whom the Lord had made king. Then David
held up the piece of robe which he had cut off, and said, See this
piece of thy robe in my hand! Since I was so near thee as to
cut it off, but did not kill thee, thou mayest know that I would
not do thee evil. Yet thou art hunting me to put me to death.
Let the Lord judge between us, and see which one is doing
wrong, and let him punish thee for thy cruelty to me, but I will
not do thee any harm.

When Saul heard David speaking so kindly to him, the feeling of hatred went out of his heart, and he said, Is this thy
voice, my son David? and he wept. Then he said to David,
Thou art more righteous than I because thou hast done good to
me, but I have done evil to thee; and thou hast shown me kindness this day, for when I was in thy power thou didst not kill
me. May the Lord reward thee for the good thou hast done.
And now I know well that thou shalt some day be king over
Israel. Promise me, therefore, before the Lord, that thou wilt
not slay my children after I am dead. And David promised
that he would not. Then Saul went away to his own home, but
David and his men stayed out in the wilderness.

And Samuel died, and all the children of Israel gathered together to mourn for him, and they buried him at Ramah, the
city where he had lived.

After Samuel was dead, David went down to the wilderness
of Paran. And there was in that country a very rich man, who
had three thousand sheep and a thousand goats; his name was
Nabal, and his wife's name Abigail. She was a kind and a
beautiful woman, and acted wisely and prudently; but he was
ill-natured and foolish, and did what was evil.

Now David and his men had their camp near the place where
Nabal's flocks were feeding, and David's men were very good to
Nabal, for although they wanted food to eat, they never took a
sheep or a goat from him, nor allowed others to do so, neither
did they harm his shepherds. And Nabal went to shear his
sheep at Carmel. When David heard of it, he spoke to ten of
his young men, saying, Go up to Carmel and speak kindly to
Nabal, and ask if he will not give us some food? And they

went and spoke as David had told them. But Nabal answered, Who is David? There are plenty of servants now-a-days that run away from their masters as he has done. Shall I take my bread, and the meat that I have killed for my shearers, and give it to men who have come from I know not where?

So David's young men came back to him and told him all that Nabal had spoken. Then David said to his men, Gird on every man his sword; and David also girded on his sword, and there went up after him about four hundred men; for two hundred stayed to guard the things that were in their camp. And David was very angry, and told his men that he had kept Nabal's flocks safe all the time they were out in the wilderness, so that none of them were lost; yet now, when he spoke kindly to him and asked him for food, he would give none, but returned only evil for the good that had been done to him. And David said he would go to Carmel and punish Nabal with a very great punishment.

Then he started to go to Nabal's house. But before he had come there, one of Nabal's young men went to Abigail, Nabal's wife, and told her how David had sent messengers to Nabal, and how unkindly Nabal had treated them. Yet David's men were very good to us, the young man said, when we were out in the wilderness. We were not harmed by them, neither missed we anything, but they kept us safe by night and by day, all the time we were near them keeping the sheep. Then the young man told Abigail to think what she should do, because David would surely come and punish them for Nabal's unkindness.

Then Abigail made haste and took two hundred loaves of bread, and two bottles of wine, five sheep, ready killed, and five measures of parched corn; one hundred clusters of raisins, and two hundred cakes of figs, and put them upon asses. And she said to her servants, Go on before me, and I will come after you. But she did not tell her husband Nabal.

And it was so, as she rode on the ass, that she came by a shady place of the hill, and there she met David and his men coming toward her. When she saw him, she got down from the ass, and bowed before him with her face to the ground, saying,

I pray thee, let me speak, and hear what I say; but mind
not the evil words that Nabal has spoken. She said also, Let
this present, which I have brought, be given to thy young men.
And she begged that David would forgive her for coming to him.
The Lord would certainly bless him, she said, and save him
from Saul. And when the Lord should have done as he prom-

ABIGAIL BRINGS A PRESENT TO DAVID

ised, and made him king over Israel, then Abigail said, David
would not be sorry that he had listened to her, and let her persuade him to stay away from Nabal's house, and not go there to
put Nabal to death.

David listened to her words, and, when she was done
speaking, he thanked the Lord for sending her to meet him, and
for the good advice she had given him, because it had kept him
from going on in his anger to kill Nabal. So he took the present which Abigail brought, and spoke kindly to her, and sent

18

her safely away; and he and his men went back to their camp.

When Abigail came to her home, Nabal was holding a great feast there and was drunken. Therefore she said nothing to him until the morning. Then when she told him of the danger he had been in, he was greatly afraid, and all his strength went from him, so that he lay helpless and without moving, like a stone. And about ten days afterward he died. When David heard that Nabal was dead, he thanked the Lord again for keeping him from going to Nabal's house in his anger. David said, Blessed be the Lord, who has kept me from doing evil.

And David loved Abigail, and sent messengers to ask that she would be his wife. When they came to her house, they said, David sent us unto thee to take thee to him to be his wife. And she bowed herself with her face to the earth, and said, Let me be his servant. Then she made haste, and rode upon an ass, and five of her handmaidens went with her; and she followed after the messengers of David, and came to him and was his wife.

CHAPTERS XXVI–XXXI (26–31)

SAUL HUNTS DAVID IN THE WILDERNESS. DAVID, BY NIGHT, TAKES AWAY SAUL'S SPEAR AND CRUSE OF WATER. THE PHILISTINES BRING AN ARMY AGAINST SAUL. SAUL INQUIRES OF A WOMAN WHO HAS A FAMILIAR SPIRIT. HE AND HIS SONS ARE SLAIN.

THE people called Ziphites, who once before had helped Saul to find David, came again, and told him where David was hidden out in the wilderness. Now Saul's wicked heart was not changed; although the feelings of hatred had left it for a little while, when David spared his life at the cave, yet those feelings soon came back, so that he wanted to kill him as much as ever. Therefore, when the Ziphites told where David was hidden, Saul took three thousand men and went out into the wilderness to find him.

And David heard of it and sent out spies to watch for him, and they brought back word that Saul had come indeed. Then David went secretly near to the place where Saul made his camp; and he said to the men who were with him, Who will go down with me to Saul in his camp? And Abishai, David's nephew, answered, I will go with thee. So David and Abishai came down in the night. And Saul lay sleeping in the camp, with his spear stuck into the ground by his pillow; and Abner, the captain of Saul's army, and the rest of his soldiers were

DAVID AND ABISHAI FIND SAUL SLEEPING

sleeping around him. Then Abishai asked David to let him kill Saul. He would strike the sharp spear through his body into the ground, he said, and would not have to do it a second time. But David answered, Destroy him not, for who can kill the Lord's anointed without sin? He called Saul the Lord's anointed, because it was the Lord who commanded Samuel to anoint him as king.

And David told Abishai that the Lord might kill Saul, or

that the time might come for him to die, or he might be killed in battle, but that he would not kill him. Then David said to Abishai, But I pray thee take the spear that is by his pillow, and the cruse (or bottle) of water, and let us go. So they took the spear and cruse of water from Saul's pillow, and left him; and no man saw them, or knew of it, because the Lord had sent a deep sleep upon Saul and his men. Then David went and stood on the top of a hill, a good way off. And he cried to Saul's men, and to Abner, saying, Answerest thou not, Abner? And Abner awaked out of his sleep, and answered, Who art thou that criest to the king. David said, Why hast thou not kept better watch over the king, thy master, that no one should come into the camp to kill him? Now see where the king's spear is, and the cruse of water that was by his pillow.

And Saul heard David speaking, and knew his voice, and said, Is this thy voice, my son David? David answered, It is my voice, my lord, O king. Then David asked Saul what he had done, and how he had sinned, that Saul still followed after him to kill him. If he had been wicked, he was willing to confess his fault, and to offer up a sacrifice that he might be forgiven. But if Saul was following him only because evil men persuaded him to do it, David prayed that the Lord would punish those men; and he begged Saul not to slay him.

Then Saul said, I have sinned; come back, my son David, for I will no more do thee harm. I have done wrong exceedingly. David answered, See the king's spear, let one of his young men come over and take it. And David told Saul how he might have killed him that day, but he would not. Then David prayed to the Lord that he would save him out of all his troubles. And Saul heard him, and spoke kindly to him, and did not try to do him any harm. So David went away, and Saul came back to his own home.

But though Saul spoke kindly to him, David did not believe his words, for he had spoken so before, and wept, and called him his son, yet afterward had come out with three thousand men to take him. Therefore David thought that Saul would never stop seeking after him. He said to himself, He will surely find me some day, and kill me. There is nothing better for me to do than to flee into the land of the Philistines; then Saul will give up looking for me, so I shall escape out of his hand.

And David arose and went with his six hundred men into the land of the Philistines, to the city of Gath. And Achish, the king, when he saw them, hoped to make them his servants; therefore he let them stay in his land and gave them a city, called Ziklag, to live in. When it was told Saul that David had fled, he sought no more after him. David was in the land of the Philistines a year and four months. While he was there, all the Philistines gathered their armies together to fight against Saul. And Achish said to David, Thou shalt go out with me to the battle, thou and thy men. He wanted David to go with the Philistines and fight against Saul and the children of Israel. But David did not say he would go.

The Philistines came and made their camp at a place called Shunem; and Saul and all the men of Israel made their camp at Gilboa. When Saul saw the host of the Philistines, he trembled, for he was greatly afraid. And he asked of the Lord what he should do; but the Lord did not answer him, neither did he send any prophet to answer him.

Now there were at that time in the land of Israel, persons who had evil spirits that would come when they called them. Then they talked with the spirits, and questioned them about what would happen in the future, and asked the spirits to help them in doing things that were wicked. These spirits were called familiar spirits. It was a great sin to have a familiar spirit. The Lord commanded that all those persons who had them should be put to death, and he forbade the people from going to such persons to inquire, or ask any questions: and Saul had sent many who had them out of the land. But now he was in great trouble. He had asked the Lord what he should do against the Philistines, and the Lord would not answer him. Then he said to his servants, Seek for me a woman that hath a familiar spirit, that I may go to her and ask. His servants answered, There is a woman that hath a familiar spirit at Endor.

Then Saul put on other raiment, that no one might know him,

and took two men with him, and came to the woman by night;
but she knew not that it was Saul.   And he asked her to let the
familiar spirit bring up for him a man who was dead, but whom
he wanted to speak with.   Saul should have known that the evil
spirit could not bring up a man from the dead: God alone can
do that.   Yet Saul said, Bring up the one I shall name to thee.

SAUL VISITS THE WITCH OF ENDOR

The woman asked, Whom shall I bring up to thee?   Saul answered, Bring me up Samuel.   Then Samuel, who had been
dead and buried for years, rose up before them.   But it was not
the evil spirit that brought him up; the Lord sent him to speak
with Saul.   And Saul stooped with his face to the earth, and
bowed himself down to the ground.

And Samuel said to him, Why hast thou disturbed me to
bring me up?   Saul answered, I am sore distressed, for the
Philistines make war against me, and God has gone away from

me, and answers me no more; therefore I have called thee, that thou mayest tell me what I shall do. Samuel said, Why dost thou ask of me, seeing the Lord has gone from thee, and become thine enemy? For the Lord has done to thee what I told thee he would do; he has put thee away from being king, and made David king, because thou didst not obey him. And now he will give the Philistines the victory over thee, and over all the army of Israel; to-morrow thou and thy sons shall be with me among the dead.

Then Saul fell down to the earth, and was greatly afraid, because of the words that Samuel had spoken, and there was no strength left in him; for he had eaten nothing all that day, nor all the night before. And the woman came to him and saw his distress, and she said, I pray thee, let me set food before thee, that thou mayest eat and gain strength before thou goest on thy way. But he refused and said, I will not eat. Then his servants and the woman begged him, until he consented. So he rose up from the earth and sat upon the bed. And the woman had a fat calf that she made haste to kill, and she took flour and kneaded it and made bread. And she brought it and set it before Saul and his servants, and they did eat. Then they rose up and went away that night.

Now the lords of the Philistines gathered all their armies together at Aphek. And Achish, the king of Gath, came there and brought David and his six hundred men with him. But when the lords of the Philistines saw them, they said, What are these Hebrews doing here? Achish answered them, This is David, the servant of Saul, the king of Israel, who has been with me now for a long while, and I have found no fault in him from the time he came until this day. But the lords of the Philistines were angry at Achish for bringing David; they said to him, Make this fellow go back, and let him not come with us to the battle, lest he turn and fight against us to please Saul, his master. Then Achish called David and told him, saying, Therefore now go back, that thou displease not the lords of the Philistines. So David and his men rose up early in the morning and went away from the camp.

On the third day, they came to their homes in Ziklag, but they found their houses burned with fire, for the Amalekites had been there and destroyed the city, and carried away their wives and children captives. Then the men of Israel wept till they could weep no more; and David was greatly distressed, for his men were angry because he had taken them from their homes to go with Achish, and they talked about stoning him; but he trusted in the Lord his God.

And David called Abiathar, the high priest, and told him to ask the Lord for him, saying, Shall I go after the Amalekites, and shall I come up with them? The Lord answered, Go after them, for thou shalt surely come up with them, and get back all they have taken. So David went with his six hundred men, till they came to the brook Besor; there two hundred of them stayed, because they were so weary and faint they could go no further. But David followed on, he and four hundred men.

And they found a man who was sick, alone in a field, and they gave him bread and water, also a piece of a cake of figs and two clusters of raisins. When he had eaten he grew stronger, for he had taken no food for three days and three nights. And David said to him, From what place hast thou come? and to whom dost thou belong? He answered I am a young man of Egypt, the servant to an Amalekite, and my master left me three days ago when I fell sick.

Then he told David what the Amalekites had done, and how they burned Ziklag with fire. David asked him, Canst thou bring us to the place where they now are? The young man said, Promise me, before God, that you will not kill me nor give me back to my master, and I will bring you there. And David promised him. So he brought them to the place. When they came there, the Amalekites were scattered over the ground, eating, and drinking, and dancing, because of the spoil they had taken from Ziklag, and from other places where they had been to rob the people. And David and his men fought against them, and slew them, so that none of them escaped, except four hundred young men who rode on camels and fled. And the men of Israel got back their wives and their children, and all the spoil that the Amalekites had taken, as the Lord said they should. They took also the flocks and the herds which the Amalekites had with them.

David and his men returned to the brook Besor, and the two hundred men whom they had left there came out to meet them. Then some of David's men, who were selfish and wicked, said, Because these two hundred went not with us, we will not give

SAUL IS OVERCOME BY THE PHILISTINES AND FALLS ON HIS SWORD

them any of the spoil we have taken; except to every man we will give his wife and his children, that they may go away from us. But David answered them, Ye shall not do so, my brethren. Then he told them that all should share alike—those who were left behind and those who went down to the battle.

And the lords of the Philistines, after David had left their camp, went out and fought against Saul and the men of Israel. And the men of Israel fled from them, and many fell down slain on mount Gilboa. The Philistines followed hard after Saul; and they slew Jonathan and two other of Saul's sons. And the battle went greatly against him. The archers with their bows and arrows hit him, and he was sorely wounded by the archers. Then he said to his armor-bearer, Draw thy sword and put me to death, because I fear the Philistines may take me and treat me cruelly. But his armor-bearer was afraid, and would not. Then Saul took his own sword and stood it on the ground with its point upward; and he fell upon it, on purpose, so that it ran into his body and killed him.

When his armor-bearer saw that Saul was dead, he also fell upon his sword and died. So Saul died, and his three sons and his armor-bearer, and great numbers of his men, that same day together. And the Philistines gained the victory, as Samuel had told Saul they should. As soon as the children of Israel who lived in that part of the land heard how their army had fled, they fled also, and the Philistines came and lived in the cities they had left.

The next day, when the Philistines went to strip off the raiment of the men whom they had killed in the battle, they found Saul and his three sons lying dead on mount Gilboa. Then they cut off Saul's head and took off his armor, and sent word through the land of the Philistines, so that all their people might hear of it, and know that Saul was dead, and that the children of Israel had been driven out of their country. They put Saul's armor in the house of their idol, Ashtaroth, and fastened up his dead body, and the dead bodies of his sons, to the wall of the city of Beth-shan.

But when the Israelites, who lived in Jabesh-gilead, heard what the Philistines had done to Saul, all the brave men of that city arose, and went all night till they came to Beth-shan. And they took down the dead bodies of Saul and his sons from the wall, and brought them to Jabesh; there they burnt them, and then took their bones and buried them under a tree. For Saul had been very kind to the people of Jabesh-gilead many years before, when he came with an army and saved them from the Ammonites.

THE SECOND BOOK OF SAMUEL

CHAPTERS I–IX (1–9)
(1 CHRONICLES xiii (13))

DAVID HEARS THAT SAUL AND JONATHAN ARE DEAD.   HE GOES TO HEBRON,
AND IS MADE KING FIRST OVER JUDAH, THEN OVER ALL ISRAEL.   HE
TAKES THE CITY OF JERUSALEM AND BRINGS THE ARK THERE.   HIS
KINDNESS TO MEPHIBOSHETH.

DAVID was still at Ziklag.   He did not know that the Philistines had fought with the men of Israel, and gained the victory over them.   But there came to Ziklag a man with his clothes rent and with earth upon his head, as though he were in great distress.   When he saw David he bowed down to the ground before him.   And David asked him from what place he had come.   The man said, Out of the camp of Israel am I escaped. David asked him how the battle went.   He answered, The men of Israel have fled and many of them are slain, and Saul and Jonathan are dead also.

David said to the young man, How knowest thou that Saul and Jonathan are dead?   The young man answered, As I happened, by chance, to be upon mount Gilboa in the battle, Saul stood there leaning on his spear, while the Philistines with their chariots and horsemen were coming swiftly upon him to kill him.   When he looked behind him he saw me and called me; I answered, Here am I.   And he spoke to me, saying, Come, I pray thee, and put me to death, for I am grieved that my life is still in me.   So I went to him and slew him, because I was sure that he could not live.   And I took the crown that was on his head, and the bracelet that was on his arm, and have brought them to thee.

But what the young man told David was not true; for, as we have read, Saul had killed himself.   The young man said that he had killed him, because he thought it would please David, and that David would reward him for saying so.   But David was not pleased.   He took hold of his clothes and rent them; and all the men who were with him rent their clothes.

And they mourned and wept for Saul, and for Jonathan his son, and for the men of Israel, because so many of them had been slain. And David asked the young man where his home was, and to what country he belonged. He answered that he was not one of the children of Israel, but an Amalekite. Then David asked him why he was not afraid to kill Saul, whom the Lord had chosen to be king over the people. And David said that the young man should die for his sin, and that the fault was his own, because he had confessed with his own mouth that he had slain the king of Israel.

After this David asked the Lord whether he should leave the land of the Philistines and go back to the land of Israel. And the Lord said he should go. Then David asked to what part of the land he should go. The Lord told him, To the city of Hebron. Now David belonged to the tribe of Judah, and Hebron was one of the cities of that tribe; for as we have read, Joshua gave to each of the twelve tribes a part of the land for its own, and Hebron was in that part which he gave to the tribe of Judah.

And David, who was now thirty years old, went up out of Ziklag to the city of Hebron. And the chief men of the tribe of Judah came to Hebron and made him king over that tribe. But the other tribes did not come, because one of Saul's sons, whose name was Ish-bosh-eth, and who was not slain in the battle, still ruled over them. Ish-bosh-eth ruled over the other tribes for seven years after Saul was dead. Then one day, as he lay on his bed, about noon, two of his captains came into his house, pretending they wanted only to bring in some wheat, but when they had come into his chamber, they slew him.

And they cut off his head and fled away with it all night to Hebron, where David was. Then they brought it to David, saying, Behold we have brought thee the head of Ish-bosh-eth, the son of Saul, who was thy enemy, and wanted to kill thee. But David was greatly displeased; he told them that when he was living at Ziklag, and a young man came to him, and said he had killed Saul, thinking that David would reward him for it, instead of rewarding him he had put him to death. So now, David said, these two men who had killed Ish-bosh-eth, Saul's son, when he was doing no wrong, should be put to death for their sin. And he commanded that they should be slain. But he sent away the head of Ish-bosh-eth to be buried in a sepulchre.

When the other tribes saw that Ish-bosh-eth, who had ruled over them, was dead, they also came to David in Hebron, and made him their king. So, at last, David was king over all the tribes of Israel.

DAVID IS MADE KING AT HEBRON

David went with his army to the city of Jerusalem. The men of Israel had, before this time, taken a part of that city from the people of the land, but not all of it. There was a strong fort, or castle, on the mountain called Zion, in which those people still lived. But now David took this also from them, and went and lived in the castle himself, which he called the city of David. And he came to be a very great man, for the Lord helped him in all that he did. The king of a city called

Tyre was his friend. This king's name was Hiram. His people knew well how to work in wood and stone. And Hiram sent builders and carpenters to David, and they built a house for him in Jerusalem.

We have been told that after the Philistines sent back the ark to the land of Israel, it was carried to the city of Kirjath-jearim, and left there in the house of a man named Abinadab. It had been in Abinadab's house ever since that time—for more than seventy years—because the people had grown careless about it and neglected it. But now David spoke to them, and asked them to come with him and get it, and bring it to Jerusalem. Then David went, and the people with him, and they took the ark out of Abinadab's house and set it on a new cart, to bring it to Jerusalem.

Now the ark was a very holy thing. We have read that when it was first brought inside of the tabernacle, God came in a cloud, into the tabernacle, above the ark, and there he dwelt in the cloud over the mercy-seat. We have read also that when the children of Israel went on their journey through the wilderness, and took the ark with them, they were not allowed to put it into a cart, but it was carried on the Levites' shoulders. And the Levites themselves were not allowed to come near it, until the priests had covered it with the curtains of the tabernacle. For none but the priests were permitted to touch it or even to look upon it uncovered. All other persons were forbidden to do so, lest they might die. Therefore when David wanted to bring the ark up to Jerusalem, he should not have laid it on a cart. Yet he did this; and Uzzah and Ahio, the sons of Abinadab, drove the cart.

But when they came to the threshing-floor of Nachon, the oxen that drew the ark stumbled and shook it; and Uzzah stretched out his hand and took hold of it, which God had said should not be done. Then the Lord was angry with Uzzah for doing this, and put him to death there beside the ark.

And David was displeased because the Lord had put Uzzah to death. He was afraid, also, that some punishment might be sent upon him. So he took the ark no further, but stopped on the way, before he came to Jerusalem, and left it in the house of Obed-edom, a Levite. It was in Obed-edom's house for three months, and the Lord blessed Obed-edom and all his family while it was there. When David heard how the Lord blessed him because the ark was in his house, he called for the priests and Levites, and told them to make ready to bring up the ark, and put it into the tent which he had made for it in Jerusalem; for he

THE DEATH OF UZZAH BESIDE THE ARK

said, because they had not brought it up the first time, the Lord was displeased and Uzzah had been put to death.

Then David and all the people with him, went to bring up the ark out of Obed-edom's house. But now he commanded the Levites to carry it on their shoulders. David was clothed in a robe of white linen, and so were the Levites who carried the ark, and those who were chosen to sing praises to the Lord. And they brought up the ark with shoutings and the sound of trumpets, and cymbals and harps. As soon as the Levites who carried it had started and gone a few steps, David offered up sacrifices to the Lord. And the Bible tells us that he danced before the Lord with all his might; that is, he was so glad in being allowed to bring up the ark that he felt as though he could not walk quietly along, but must leap and dance for joy. But Michal, his wife, looked out of a window and saw him leap-

DAVID REJOICES WHEN THE ARK IS BROUGHT TO JERUSALEM

ing and dancing, and she despised him for it in her heart. And she told him that he, who was a king, made himself look mean and humble before his servants by doing so. But David said it was before the Lord he had done it, and that he was willing to make himself still more humble and mean before him.

So they brought the ark to Jerusalem and set it in the tent

which David made for it. Then David offered up more sacrifices, burnt offerings and peace offerings. As soon as he had done this, he blessed the people, and he gave to each one, to the women as well as the men, a good piece of flesh, a loaf of bread, and a cake of pressed grapes. And when they had received these things, they went away every man to his own home.

But as David sat in the beautiful house which he had built for himself at Jerusalem, and remembered how the ark was kept in a tent, he felt in his heart that he would love to build a house yet more beautiful than his own, in which to keep the ark. Now there was at that time among the children of Israel a prophet named Nathan, and David told Nathan of what he wanted to do. Nathan said to him, Do all that is in thine heart, for the Lord is with thee to help thee. But that night the Lord spoke to Nathan, and said that he should tell David not to build the house. Yet the Lord was not displeased with David for wanting to build it, but he said that David's son, who would be king after him, should build the house for the ark. So David did not go on to build it, but left it for his son to build, as the Lord commanded.

And David went out to war against the heathen kings around him, and gained the victory over them, and took from them great numbers of horses and chariots, and much gold and silver. Of the gold and silver, he gave a part into the treasury of the Lord. The Lord was with him to prosper him, wherever he went; and he ruled justly over all his people.

Now that he was grown so rich and great, David remembered how Jonathan, Saul's son, had loved him when he was poor and in trouble, and how they had made a covenant together to be kind to each other's children. Therefore David sent for a man named Ziba, who had been a servant to Saul, and he asked Ziba whether any of Jonathan's children were yet alive, because, if they were, he wanted to be kind to them for Jonathan's sake. Then Ziba told the king that one of Jonathan's sons was still living, who was lame in his feet. For on the day that Saul and Jonathan were killed in battle, when word of it came to Jonathan's house, the little boy's nurse took him up and fled. But as she made haste to flee away, he fell out of her arms and was hurt, so that ever since he had been lame. Now he was grown to be a man, and his name was Me-phib-o-sheth.

Then David sent for him, and when he came to the king he bowed down to the ground before him. And David said, Me-phib-o-sheth. He answered, Behold, I am thy servant. David said to him, Fear not, because I have sent for thee; for I will surely be kind to thee for thy father's sake, and will give back to thee all the land that belonged to Saul, thy grandfather. And thou shalt come and eat at my table. Me-phib-o-sheth said to the king, What am I, that thou shouldest take any notice of me? Then the king called Ziba, Saul's servant, and said to him, I have given Me-phib-o-sheth all the land that belonged to Saul. Do thou, therefore, and thy sons, take care of it, and bring all the fruits that grow on it to him. But as for Me-phib-o-sheth, he shall stay with me, and always eat at my table, and be as one of my sons. So Me-phib-o-sheth lived in Jerusalem, and did eat continually at the table of the king.

CHAPTERS XI–XV (11–15)

DAVID CAUSES URIAH TO BE SLAIN, AND TAKES URIAH'S WIFE TO BE HIS WIFE. THE PROPHET TELLS HIM OF HIS SIN. THE SON THAT IS GIVEN TO DAVID AND BATHSHEBA DIES. SOLOMON IS BORN. ABSALOM REBELS AGAINST HIS FATHER. DAVID FLEES FROM JERUSALEM.

THE captain of David's army was named Joab. And David sent Joab with his soldiers to fight against the Ammonites, but David stayed in his house at Jerusalem. He went up in the cool of the evening to walk upon the roof of his house, and he saw, a little way off, a beautiful woman. Then David sent a messenger to ask who she was. And some one told him that she was Bathsheba, the wife of Uriah, the Hittite, who had gone with Joab to fight against the Ammonites.

And David sent word to Joab, saying, Send Uriah, the Hittite, to me. And Joab sent him to David. When he had come, David asked him about the war, and spoke kindly to him, pretending to be his friend. But after three days he sent him back to the army with a letter for Joab. In the letter David told Joab that when the men of Israel went forth to battle, he should send Uriah with them, and put him in the most dangerous place. But as soon as the Ammonites should come out to meet them, all the rest must flee and leave Uriah alone to be slain. David did this, so that after Uriah was slain, he might take Uriah's wife to be his wife.

NATHAN TELLS DAVID OF HIS SIN

So Uriah went back to the army and gave Joab the letter which David had sent, but he knew not what was in it. And when the men of Israel went out to fight, Joab did as David commanded: he set Uriah in the front of the battle, and the Ammonites came out against him and slew him. And Joab sent word to David that Uriah was slain. Then David brought Bathsheba to his house and took her for his wife. But the Lord was displeased at what David had done.

And the Lord sent Nathan, the prophet, to David. Nathan came to him and said, There were two men in one city; one of them was rich, and the other poor. The rich man had many flocks and herds, but the poor man had nothing except one little lamb, which he had bought and taken care of; it grew up with his children, he fed it from his table, it drank out of his cup and lay in his bosom, and seemed to him like a daughter.

THE POOR MAN'S LAMB

There came to the house of the rich man a traveller, who rested there from his journey. Then the rich man would not take a sheep or a goat from his own flocks, though he had so many of them, but he took the poor man's lamb and killed it for the traveller to eat.

When David heard the story which Nathan told him, he was very angry, and said, The man who has done this thing shall surely be put to death, and he shall give to the poor man four lambs for the one he took from him. But Nathan had told this story to show David his own wickedness. Nathan said to him that he was the one who had done like the rich man. For the

Lord had chosen him to be king over Israel, and had given him wives and children, and made him rich and great. Yet he had caused Uriah, who was given so much less than himself, to be killed by the Ammonites, that he might take Uriah's wife to be his wife. Therefore, Nathan said, the Lord would send a dreadful punishment upon David. When Nathan spoke these words,

THE RICH MAN'S FEAST

David felt how wicked he had been, and he said, I have sinned against the Lord.

After this God gave a son to David and Bathsheba, and David loved the child. But the Lord sent a great sickness upon him. Therefore David prayed for him that he might not die. David fasted and ate no food, but lay down on the earth all night, crying to the Lord. Then the chief men of the city came to him persuading him to rise, but he would not; neither did he eat with them as he used to do at other times, when they came to sit at the table with him.

On the seventh day the child died. And David's servants feared to tell him that the child was dead, for they said, While he was yet alive we spoke to the king, but he would not listen to us; how great then will his sorrow be if we tell him that the child is dead. But when David saw his servants whispering together, he knew that the child was dead; therefore he said to them, Is the child dead? They answered, He is dead.

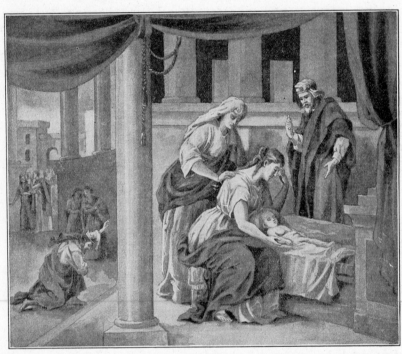

DAVID PRAYS THAT HIS CHILD MAY NOT DIE

Then David rose up and washed and dressed himself, and went out to the tent where the ark was kept, and there he worshipped the Lord. Afterward he came into his house and told his servants to bring food; and when they set it before him, he did eat. Then his servants were surprised, and asked him why he did these things. He wept and would eat nothing, they said, while the child was alive, but now, that it was dead, he rose up and did eat. David answered, While the child was alive, I fasted and wept, for I said, Who can tell whether God will be kind to me and let the child live? But now he is dead, why should I fast any more? Can I bring him back again? I shall go to him when I die, but he shall never return to me.

And God gave to David and Bathsheba another son, whose name was called Solomon, which means Peaceable; and the Lord loved him.

But David had other wives beside Bathsheba, who had children also. One of them had a son named Absalom. He was grown up to be a man, and among all the young men of the children of Israel, none was so much praised for his beauty as he. From his feet to his head there was no fault to be seen in him. His hair was so thick and long that when he cut it at the end of the year, it weighed as much as two hundred shekels of silver. But Absalom was a wicked man, for when his brother Amnon sinned against him, he killed him and fled to another country, where he stayed three years. Then he came back to his own house in Jerusalem. But David would not see him nor speak with him, because he had slain his brother.

After he had lived two years in Jerusalem without seeing his father, Absalom sent for Joab, the captain of David's army, because he wanted him to go with a message to the king. But Joab would not come. And Absalom sent a second time, and still he came not. Therefore Absalom told his servants to go into Joab's field, and set his grain on fire, and the servants did so. Then Joab came and asked him, saying, Why have thy servants set my field on fire? Absalom answered that it was because he would not come to take a message for him to the king. For, Absalom said, if he could not see the king, he might as well have stayed in that land to which he fled, and not have come back to Jerusalem at all. Now, therefore, Absalom said, let me come before the king, and if I be guilty let him kill me.

So Joab went to the king and told him. Then the king sent for Absalom, and Absalom came and bowed himself with his face to the ground before his father. But David did not punish him for his sin, as he ought to have done, for when he came to him he kissed him.

After this Absalom made ready for himself chariots and horses, and had fifty men to run before him when he rode out in his chariot, so that all the people might see him and think him a great man. He rose up early in the morning, also, and stood by the gate of the city, and when he saw any man coming into the city, to speak with the king and ask some favor of him, then Absalom called the man and talked with him, and said, that if he were only ruler over the land, the man should have all he wanted. And whenever any man bowed down to him, because he was the king's son, Absalom put out his hand and took hold of him, and kissed him. So he did to all the people who came to ask help of the king, and he made them think much of him, not because he was a good man, or really cared for them, but because he deceived them and made them believe he was their friend.

And he went to the king and said, I pray thee let me go to Hebron and pay my vow to the Lord. He pretended that he had made a vow to offer up a sacrifice at Hebron, and that now he wanted to go there and do it. And the king told him he might go, so he arose and went. But it was not to serve the Lord that he went, it was to have himself made king instead of his father. Therefore he sent spies through all the land to persuade the people to put his father away, and make him king. And the spies told the people that, on a certain day, as soon as they should hear the sound of the trumpets which Absalom's friends would blow, they should cry out, Absalom is king in Hebron. He took two hundred men with him out of Jerusalem to help him, and sent also for a great man named Ahithophel, who was David's counsellor, or adviser. And Ahithophel and many of the people went with him.

And there came a messenger to David, who told him how the men of Israel were going after Absalom. Then David was afraid, and said to his servants, Arise, and let us flee; make haste and go, for fear Absalom may come suddenly and fight against the city with the sword. His servants answered, We are ready to do whatever the king shall command. And the king fled in haste out of Jerusalem, he and his servants, and many of the people of the city, and they passed over the brook Kedron and went up toward the wilderness.

And the priests and Levites brought the ark to carry it with David wherever he should go, but David told them to take it back into the city again. He said that perhaps the Lord would be kind to him, and bring him back also, but if not, he was willing the Lord should do to him as he saw best. For David felt how wicked he had been in causing Uriah to be slain, and in taking Uriah's wife to be his wife. He remembered how the Lord had said that a great punishment should come upon him. And now a great punishment had come upon him, and David knew he deserved it, and he was willing to bear it. He went out of Jerusalem over the mountain called Olivet, weeping as he went, with his head covered and his feet bare. And all the men who were with him covered their heads; and they also went up, weeping as they went.

And some one told David that Ahithophel, his counsellor, had gone with Absalom, to help him, and advise him what he should do to make himself king. Then David prayed that Ahithophel's advice might be turned into foolishness, so that it would not do Absalom any good. And when David had gone a little way out of the city, Hushai, one of his friends, came to meet him and go with him, for he loved David and was not willing to leave him. But David told him to go back to Jerusalem and stay there till Absalom should come. Then, David said, Hushai could watch and see what Absalom would do, and send word secretly to him; and so he would do David more good than if he should go with him. Therefore Hushai went back, as David desired him.

CHAPTERS XVI–XXIV (16–24)

SHIMEI CURSES DAVID. ABSALOM FOLLOWS HUSHAI'S ADVICE, AND IS SLAIN IN BATTLE. DAVID GRIEVES FOR HIS SON; HE GOES BACK TO JERUSALEM. DAVID AND THE PEOPLE SIN AGAINST GOD. THEY ARE PUNISHED BY PESTILENCE.

Now David made haste to flee away from Jerusalem. When he reached a place called Bahurim, there came out a man

named Shimei, to meet him.   Shimei was one of king Saul's rela-
tives, and because David had been made king instead of Saul
Shimei hated him, and was glad now to see him in trouble.   And
as he came near, he cursed David and threw stones at him, and
at those who were with him.   When Abishai, David's nephew,
heard Shimei cursing him, he came to David, saying, Why should

SHIMEI THROWS STONES AT DAVID

this man, who is no better than a dog, be allowed to curse my
lord the king?   Let me go over to him, I pray thee, and cut off
his head.   But David would not permit him; for he said that
the Lord was allowing Shimei to curse him, and that it was part
of the punishment that the Lord was sending upon him.   And
David said, My own son Absalom is trying to take away my
life; how much more then, may this man, who is my enemy, be
expected to do me evil.

After David had left Jerusalem, Absalom came there, and

Ahithophel, the man who had been David's counsellor, was with him. And Absalom saw Hushai, David's friend, in the city, but he did not know that David had sent him. And Absalom asked Ahithophel to advise him what he should do to make himself king. Ahithophel answered, Let me choose twelve thousand men, and I will take them and follow after David this night, and will come up with him while he is weak and faint, and make him afraid. And all who are with him will flee, and I will kill him alone. Then, when they see that he is dead, those who have obeyed him will come and obey thee, and thou shalt be king over all the people.

Although this advice pleased Absalom, he would not do as Ahithophel said until he had asked Hushai what he thought was the best way. Then Hushai advised him not to go out with so few as twelve thousand men, but to wait until he should have a great army. Hushai said this because he hoped that while Absalom was gathering this army together, David would have time to escape to some place where Absalom could not take him.

And the Lord made Absalom believe that Hushai's advice was the best, because the Lord did not mean to let David be slain, but he meant to bring evil upon Absalom, and to punish him for his great sin in rebelling against his father. Then Hushai, as soon as he had done talking with Absalom, went to the priests in Jerusalem, who were David's friends, and spoke to them secretly, saying, Send a messenger quickly to David and tell him to make haste and cross over Jordan, lest Absalom's army follow after him, to slay him and all who are with him.

Now there were two young men, sons of the priests, who were hiding from Absalom at a place a little way out of the city, and a woman went and gave them Hushai's message; then they started to take it to David. But a boy saw them and told Absalom, and he sent out men after them. And the priests' sons came quickly to a house by the way, which had a well in the yard. They went down there to hide, and a woman spread a covering over the top of the well, and sprinkled corn on the covering, so that no one could see that a well was there. When

Absalom's servants came to the house to look for them, they could not find them, and they went back to the city again. Then the young men came up out of the well, and carried Hushai's message to David. And David, and all the men who were with him, passed over the river that night; by morning there was not one left who had not passed over Jordan.

When Ahithophel saw that Absalom would not do as he had advised him, he was so displeased and ashamed that he left him and went away to his own house. There he put all things in order, and then went and hanged himself. So he died, and was buried in his father's sepulchre.

After David had passed over Jordan, and come into the land of Gilead, Barzillai, an old man who lived in that land, and others with him, brought wheat and barley, flour, parched corn, honey, and butter, and sheep, for David and his men; because they said that David's men must be hungry and weary after coming so far through the wilderness.

But Absalom, as soon as he had gathered his army together, made haste to follow after his father. Then David counted the men who were with him, and set captains over them; Joab he made the chief captain. And David said, I will surely go with you myself also, to the battle. But the men answered, Thou shalt not go with us, for they will care more to take thee than they will to take all the rest who shall go out against them. David said, Whatever seems best to you I will do: so he stayed in the city of Mahanaim, where he and his people had come.

And he stood by the gate of the city while his men were going out to fight; as they passed by him, he spoke to all the captains, saying, Deal gently, for my sake, with the young man, even with Absalom. So the people went out, and the battle was in a wood. And God gave David's army the victory, for they slew of Absalom's army twenty thousand men. And Absalom rode on a mule, and the mule went under the thick branches of a great oak, and Absalom's head was caught among the branches. Then the mule that was under him went away, and left him there, hanging above the ground.

And a man in the army saw him, and came to Joab, and said,

ABSALOM'S DEATH

I saw Absalom hanged in an oak. Joab said to the man, Why didst thou not kill him? and I would have given thee ten shekels of silver, and a girdle. The man answered, Though I should have a thousand shekels of silver, I would not kill the king's son, because the king commanded us all not to harm Absalom. Then Joab said, I cannot stay here to talk with thee. And he took three darts in his hand, and went to the place where Absalom was, and thrust the darts into his body, while he was yet alive, hanging in the branches of the oak: afterward ten young men, who were servants to Joab, came and slew him.

Then Joab blew a trumpet for the people to come back from following after Absalom's army; because, now that Absalom himself was dead, there was no need that any more of his men should be slain. And they took Absalom and threw his dead body into a pit that was in the wood, and piled a great heap of stones over him. And all the men who had been with him fled every one to his tent.

After the battle was over, one of the priest's sons, whose name was Ahimaaz, came to Joab, and said, Let me run now into the city and tell the king how the Lord has punished his enemies. But Joab forbade him, and told another man, named Cushi, to go and tell the king. Then Ahimaaz said, I pray thee let me also run after Cushi. Joab asked him, Why dost thou want to go? But he answered again, Let me run. And Joab said to him, Run. Then Ahimaaz ran by another way, and came near to the city before Cushi.

And David sat at the gate of the city waiting till he should hear news from the battle. His watchman had gone up to the top of the wall to see if any one were coming, and he saw a man running toward the city alone. And he cried out and told the king: the king answered, If he is alone, he brings word from the army. While the man was coming near, the watchman saw another running, and he called, and said, Another man is running toward the city alone. The king said, He also bringeth news. And the watchman said, I think the running of the first is like the running of Ahimaaz, the priest's son. The king answered, He is a good man and is bringing good news to us.

Then Ahimaaz came to the king and spoke to him, saying, All is well. And he bowed down with his face to the earth before the king, and said, Blessed be the Lord who has given us the victory over the men who rose up to fight against the king. And the king asked him, Is the young man Absalom safe? Ahimaaz answered, When Joab sent me, I saw a great tumult in the army, as if something had happened, but I knew not what it was. The king said, Step to one side, and stand there.

Then Cushi, the other messenger, came and spoke to the king, saying, I have news, my lord, the king; for the Lord has this day punished all those who rebelled against thee. And the king said, Is the young man Absalom safe? Cushi answered, May all the king's enemies, and all those who wish to do him evil, be as that young man is. Then David knew that Absalom was dead. And he was in great distress, and went up into the chamber that was over the gate of the city, and wept; and as he went he cried, O my son Absalom! my son, my son Absalom! Would that God had let me die instead of thee, O Absalom, my son, my son!

And it was told Joab how the king mourned for Absalom. The people also heard of it, and they were afraid to come before David while he grieved so much for his son whom they had slain. Therefore they stole into the city by another way, that he might not see them, like persons who were ashamed and fleeing from the battle, instead of those who had just gained the victory. But the king kept on mourning; he covered his face, and cried with a loud voice, O my son Absalom! O Absalom, my son, my son!

And Joab was angry, and he came into the house of the king and said, Thou hast made ashamed, this day, all thy servants who have fought for thee and saved thy life, and the lives of thy wives and of thy children, because thou lovest thy enemies more than thou lovest them. For I see plainly that if Absalom had been saved alive, and all of us had been slain in the battle, it would have pleased thee well. Now, therefore, rise up and come and speak kindly to thy servants, for I tell thee if thou dost not come out to them, they will all go away and leave thee alone, so there will not be a man left with thee this night; and that will be worse for thee than all the evil that has happened to thee from thy youth until now. Then the king arose and went out and sat in the gate of the city. And when the people knew of it they all came to him there.

After this the people who were in Jerusalem sent word to the king, saying, Come back to us, thou and all who are with thee. So David left the city of Mahanaim, and started to go back to Jerusalem.

Now Shimei, who had cursed David, and thrown stones at him when he was fleeing from Absalom, heard how he had gained the victory, and was going back to Jerusalem. Therefore Shimei was afraid for what he had done, and now he came out to meet the king. When he saw him he fell down before him, and said, Let not the king blame me, nor remember what I did wickedly, for I know that I have sinned. Then Abishai, David's nephew, who before had wanted to cut off his head, asked David, saying, Shall not Shimei be put to death because he cursed the king? But David answered that none of his enemies should be put to death that day, since on that day he was once more made king over all the people of Israel. And the king said to Shimei, Thou shalt not die.

And as David went toward Jerusalem, Barzillai, who had brought him wheat, and barley, and flour, also came out to meet him. And David remembered Barzillai's kindness, and he said to him, Come thou with me to Jerusalem, and thou shalt live in my house, and I will take care of thee. But Barzillai answered that he was a very old man, and had not long to live, and that he would not enjoy being in the king's house, or seeing the beautiful things that were there; he would rather go back to his own city, that he might die where his home was, and be buried by the grave of his father and mother. Yet, Barzillai said, that his son might go with David, if David would have him. David answered, He shall go with me, and I will do for him whatever will please thee. Then the king kissed Barzillai and blessed him, and let him return to his own home. So David came back to Jerusalem, and was king as he had been before, and all the people obeyed him.

DAVID MOURNING FOR ABSALOM

But after these things the children of Israel sinned against the Lord, and David also displeased him. For he commanded Joab to go out among the people, and number all the men who could fight in war. We are not told why God was displeased with David for doing this, but we suppose it was because David felt proud of his great army, and trusted in it to keep his kingdom safe, instead of trusting only in the Lord. When he commanded Joab to number the men of Israel, Joab knew it would offend God, therefore he did not wish to do it, but David again commanded him. So he went out to obey the king. It took him and those who were with him, nine months and twenty days to number the people. Then they came back to Jerusalem, and told David that in the tribe of Judah there were five hundred thousand brave men, who could fight with the sword, and in the other tribes there were eight hundred thousand.

But after they had told him, David felt that he had sinned, and he said to the Lord, I have sinned greatly in what I have done; and now, I pray thee, O Lord, forgive my sin. But God chose to punish David and the people, that they might remember how they had disobeyed him, and fear to do so again. Therefore, when David rose up in the morning, the Lord sent the prophet Gad to ask him which of these punishments he would choose: Would he have seven years of famine in the land? Or would he have his enemies come, and, for three months, fight against him and gain the victory over him? Or would he have three days of pestilence among the people? When the prophet asked him this, David answered, I am in great trouble to know what I shall say. Yet I would rather the Lord should punish us himself than that he should send our enemies to do it. David meant that he chose the three days of pestilence.

So the Lord sent an angel that brought a great pestilence among the children of Israel, and there died of them, in three days, seventy thousand men. Now Jerusalem was built upon three small mountains, or hills; one of them was called mount Moriah. On the top of this mountain was a threshing-floor belonging to a man named Araunah. And the angel that the Lord sent stood over Araunah's threshing-floor, and David saw him standing there, between the earth and the sky, having a drawn sword in his hand, stretched out over Jerusalem, as though he would destroy all the people in the city. David and the elders of Israel, who had put on sackcloth, bowed down with their faces to the earth. And David prayed that the Lord would punish him alone, but that the people might be saved. Then the prophet Gad came to David, and told him to go and set up an altar to the Lord at Araunah's threshing-floor.

DAVID SACRIFICES ON MOUNT MORIAH

Now Araunah was threshing his wheat; when he saw the king coming, he went out and bowed down before him, saying, Why has my lord the king come to his servant? David answered, To buy the threshing-floor of thee, that I may build an altar upon it and offer up burnt offerings to the Lord, so that the pestilence may be taken away from the people. Then Araunah told David that he might take the threshing-floor for nothing, and might have his oxen also for a burnt offering. But David said, No, I will buy it of thee for the full price, neither will I offer up as a burnt offering to the Lord that which has cost me nothing.

So David bought the threshing-floor for six hundred shekels of gold, and built an altar there and laid a burnt offering upon it.   Then he prayed to the Lord, and the Lord heard his prayer and sent down fire from heaven that burned up his offering.   And the Lord commanded the angel to cease, and slay the people no more; so the pestilence was taken from among them.

THE BOOKS OF KINGS AND CHRONICLES

1 KINGS I–VII (1–7).   1 CHRON. XXII–XXIX (22–29). 2 CHRON. I–IV (1–4)

DAVID PREPARES FOR THE BUILDING OF THE TEMPLE.   ADONIJAH REBELS. SOLOMON IS MADE KING.   DAVID SPEAKS TO ALL THE PEOPLE: HE DIES. GOD PROMISES SOLOMON WISDOM AND RICHES.   TWO WOMEN COME TO HIM FOR JUDGMENT.   THE TEMPLE IS BUILT.

Now David was old, and the time came near for him to die.   And he remembered what God had said about the house for the ark: that he should not build it, but that his son, who would be king after him, should build it.   Yet David made ready stones and timber and iron for the house, and told where it should be built: the top of mount Moriah, he said, where Araunah's threshing-floor had been, was the spot on which it should stand.

And David set masons to shaping the stones, and carpenters to hewing beams out of cedar trees, and men to making nails out of iron.   He gathered also much gold and silver and brass for the work; for he said, My son Solomon is yet young, and not able to attend to these things, and the house he shall build is to be exceedingly beautiful, and admired among all nations.

David also gathered the priests and the Levites together, and divided them up into different courses, or companies, so that each course might take its turn in attending to God's worship at the house of the Lord, after Solomon should build it.

And David called Solomon, and told him that many years

before, he himself had wanted to build the house, but the Lord had sent him word, because he was a man of war and had shed much blood, that he must not build it. God did not mean to reprove David for going to war, for it was God who had helped him to gain the victory over the enemies of Israel. But God chose that a man of peace, and not a man of war, should build his house. God had promised, David said, that Solomon should be a man of peace, and should be king over Israel, and that he should build his house.

But David had another son, named Adonijah, who wanted to be king, and because his father was now old and weak, he thought he might be. Therefore he made a great feast for his friends, and persuaded them to go with him to make him king. When David heard of it, he commanded his servants to take his own mule and cause Solomon to ride upon it to a fountain called Gihon, that was near Jerusalem; there, David said, they should anoint Solomon. Then they should blow the trumpet and cry out, God save King Solomon! Afterward they should bring him to the house where David's throne was, that he might sit on the throne and be king over Israel. For on account of what Adonijah had done, David said he would make Solomon king while David himself was yet alive.

So David's servants did as he commanded. They took Solomon, and made him ride on the king's mule, and brought him to Gihon: there they anointed him, and blew the trumpet, and all the people rejoiced and cried, God save King Solomon! And Adonijah, and the men who were with him, heard them, and said, What meaneth this noise among the people in the city? While they were speaking some one came in and told them that David had made Solomon king, and that all the people were shouting for joy. Then Adonijah was troubled, for he knew that he had done wickedly, and he feared that Solomon would kill him. And it was told Solomon that Adonijah was afraid. But Solomon said that if he would show himself a good man, no harm should be done to him; and he commanded Adonijah to go to his own house.

David, before he died, called all the princes and chief men

of his kingdom to Jerusalem. And he told them how the Lord, many years before, had chosen Solomon to build the house for the ark. The Lord had promised, David said, that if Solomon would obey his commandments, he and his descendants should continue to be kings over Israel. And David said to the princes and great men, Do you also be very

DAVID TELLS SOLOMON THAT HE SHALL BE KING

careful to obey the commandments of the Lord, so that you may keep this good land which he has given you, and leave it to your children when you die. Then David spoke to Solomon before them all, saying, And thou, Solomon, my son, obey the God of thy father, and serve him with all thy heart; for the Lord looks at the heart, and knows all the thoughts. If thou serve him he will be thy friend, but if thou turn away from serving him he will cast thee off forever.

Then David gave to Solomon patterns of the house for the

ark, and of all the things that were to go into it; for the Lord had given him the pattern of all these things. David gave Solomon also gold for the things that were to be made of gold, and silver for the things that were to be made of silver. And he said to him, Be strong and do not fear to begin the house, for the Lord God, whom I serve, will be with thee to help thee, until thou shalt finish building it.

And David called all the people together and told them that, because he loved to help build the house of the Lord, he had made ready gold and silver, brass, iron, precious stones, and marble, to be used in building it. Beside what he had given out of the spoils taken from his enemies, he gave from his own riches a great deal; as much as three thousand talents of the gold of Ophir, and seven thousand talents of pure silver, to overlay the walls with; and gold and silver also for the vessels of the temple. He asked the people if any among them were willing to give. Then they, too, brought gold and silver, brass and precious stones, and gave them to the Lord.

And David thanked the Lord, before all the people, for making him and the people willing to give. All they gave, he said, was the Lord's; for they were only giving back to the Lord what he had first given to them. And David prayed very earnestly for the people, and for Solomon his son, that the Lord would help them to keep on loving him, and obeying his laws. Then David said to all the people, Now thank the Lord your God. And they all bowed down their heads and worshipped. The next day they offered up sacrifices, burnt offerings and peace offerings: a thousand bullocks, a thousand goats, and a thousand lambs. And they held a feast on the flesh of their peace offerings, and ate and drank before the Lord with great joy and gladness. Then they anointed Solomon again, and made him king again, over the children of Israel. So Solomon sat on the throne and was king instead of David, his father; and all the princes and mighty men, and all the people, obeyed him.

David was king for forty years, and he died, being an old man and honored by all the people; and they buried him in the city of Jerusalem.

Solomon feared God, and was careful to do no evil. And God spoke to him in a dream at night, and offered him anything that he desired to have. God said to him, Ask what I shall give thee? Solomon answered, Give thy servant wisdom, that I may be able to rule well over thy people, the children of Israel. God was pleased with the answer that Solomon made, and told

SOLOMON'S JUDGMENT

him that because he had not asked for riches, or a long life, or the victory over his enemies, he would give him the wisdom he asked for, and beside this, riches and honor, more than any of the kings who had been before him, or who should be after him; and if he would obey his commandments, God promised to give him a long life also.

And there came two women to king Solomon, and stood before him. They lived together in one house; and one of them spoke to the king, and said, O my lord, this woman and I live in one house, and we each of us had a little son. This woman's child died in the night, and she rose up at midnight, while I slept, and took my son from me, and laid it in her bed, and laid her dead child in my bed. When I woke in the morning to feed my child, it was dead; but when I looked upon it, I saw it was not my child.

After this woman was done speaking, the other contradicted her, saying, No, the living is my son, and the dead is thine. Then the king called out to his servants, Bring here a sword! And they brought it. And the king said, Cut the living child in two, and give half to one and half to the other. Then the true mother of the child, because she loved it, and would not have it killed, said, O my lord, give her the living child, and on no account slay it. But the other, who pretended to be its mother, said, Yes, cut it in two. The king, when he had heard them, commanded that the child should be given to the woman who had pity upon it, because he knew that it must be hers. It was to find out this that he called for the sword, not because he intended to slay the child.

All the people heard of what the king had done, and were willing to serve him, because they saw that God had given him wisdom to judge aright. King Solomon was ruler not only over the children of Israel, but also over other nations that lived near them. They obeyed him, and brought presents of precious things. For David had, long before, made those nations his servants, and now God kept them from rebelling against Solomon, so that he might have peace in his kingdom as the Lord had promised him. And God gave Solomon great wisdom and riches; he had many officers and servants, and many great men came to visit him in his palace. Every day there were killed for his table and the table of his servants, ten oxen that had been fatted in the stable, twenty oxen brought in from the field, and a hundred sheep; beside roe-bucks, deer, and fatted fowls. He had also forty thousand horses for his chariots, and twelve thousand horsemen.

Now Solomon made ready to build the house for the ark on mount Moriah, at the place where Araunah's threshing-floor had been. He asked Hiram, king of Tyre, who had been David's friend, to send his servants into the forests to cut down trees for the building, because Hiram's servants knew better than Solomon's how to cut wood and hew timber. So Hiram sent out men into the forest, on a mountain called Lebanon, where cedar trees grew. Solomon sent many thousands of his own servants

SOLOMON HAD MANY CHARIOTS AND HORSES

also, and Solomon's servants and Hiram's servants worked together in cutting down trees. Afterward they brought them to the sea, which was not far off, and made them into rafts and floated them along the shore till they came near to Jerusalem.

And Hiram sent to Solomon a man who was skilful to work in gold and silver, in brass, iron, wood, and fine linen, that he might help him in building the house for the ark. Solomon gave Hiram corn, and oil, and wine for his servants. And Hiram's servants and Solomon's servants made ready great stones and timbers; and Solomon began to build the house according to the pattern which David had given him. It was to be about a hundred feet long, thirty-three feet wide, and fifty feet high. In front of it was to be a porch, with its top built up like a steeple, or tower, far above the rest of the house. This tower was to be about two hundred feet high. The house had

HEWING THE WOOD AND STONE FOR SOLOMON'S TEMPLE

narrow windows in it. Against the walls, on the outside, were built chambers, three stories of them, one above the other, for the priests to live in, while they should stay attending to God's worship there.

The house was built of stone; yet each stone was hewn into its proper shape, and made ready to go in the wall, before it was brought to the place where the house was to stand; so that no noise of a hammer, or of an axe, or any tool of iron was heard in the house all the time it was building.

When the walls were built up, Solomon covered them on the inside with boards of cedar which were carved with the shapes of flowers. Then he covered the flowers over with gold. The floor of the house and the inside of the porch he covered over with pure gold. And he hung up inside of the house a curtain of blue, and purple, and crimson, called the veil, to make two rooms there, as had been done in the tabernacle. The innermost of these rooms was for the ark, and was called the most holy place. The walls inside of the most holy place were covered with wood, carved into shapes of cherubim, and palm trees, and flowers. These Solomon covered with gold, and the floor also. And he made two cherubim fifteen feet high, first out of the wood of the olive tree, and then he covered them with gold. They stood in the most holy place, with their faces turned to the wall, and with their wings spread out, reaching from one side of the room to the other.

And he made doors for the house out of wood of the fir tree, and carved upon them shapes of cherubim, and palm trees, and open flowers, and afterward covered them with gold fitted upon the carved work. In different parts of the house he set precious stones to make it more beautiful.

And Solomon made two great pillars of brass, each over thirty feet high, to stand in front of the house, one on the right hand and the other on the left. And he made a brass altar, which was four times as large as the one that Moses had made for the tabernacle. He made also a great basin, or sea of brass, that rested on the backs of twelve brass oxen. This was to hold water for the priests to wash their hands and their feet with, whenever they should go into the house, or offer up sacrifices on the altar, as the Lord had commanded them. And he made ten lavers of brass, which were set upon wheels, and could be moved from one place to another. These were to hold water for the sacrifices to be washed in.

And Solomon made ten candlesticks of gold, and stood them in the house to give light there. He made also the table of gold for the shew-bread, and basins and spoons, and censers of pure gold, and hinges of gold for the doors of the house. And

THE BUILDING OF SOLOMON'S TEMPLE

he made a court for the priests, around the house, in which the altar of burnt offering, and the sea that rested upon twelve oxen, and the ten lavers, were placed; and another court also, outside of this one, for the people of Israel. He was more than seven years in doing the work, until all of it was finished.

---

1 KINGS VIII–XII (8–12). 2 CHRON. V–X (5–10)

THE TEMPLE IS DEDICATED TO THE LORD. THE QUEEN OF SHEBA VISITS SOLOMON. SOLOMON MARRIES HEATHEN WIVES, WHO PERSUADE HIM TO WORSHIP IDOLS. HIS DEATH. THE TEN TRIBES REBEL, AND CHOOSE JEROBOAM FOR THEIR KING.

SOLOMON called all the elders and chief men of Israel to Jerusalem, that they might be there when the ark should be brought into the house. And the elders and chief men came and gathered together with the king, and all the people before the ark. And the priests took up the ark and carried it into the house, into the most holy place, and set it under the wings of the cherubim which Solomon had made. The two tables of stone, with the ten commandments written on them, were in the ark. And when the priests came out of the most holy place, after they had left the ark there, a cloud filled the house of the Lord, so that the priests could not go into it, because the glory of the Lord filled the house of the Lord.

Then the king stood up before the people, and thanked God for helping him to build the house; and he asked God to take that house for his Temple. And Solomon kneeled down before all the people, and spread out his hands toward heaven, and prayed to the Lord that he would hear and answer all the prayers which the children of Israel should make in that house. If ever their enemies should come, and gain the victory over them because of their sins, or if the Lord should punish them by not sending rain on their fields, so that their seed, their vines, and their fruit would not grow; if pestilence should come into the land, or locusts, or caterpillars, to eat their grain; whatever trouble or whatever sickness they might have, Solomon asked that, when the people should come to that house and spread forth their hands in prayer, the Lord would hear them.

After Solomon had finished speaking, there came down fire from heaven, and burnt up the offering which lay on the altar. When all the children of Israel saw the fire come down, and saw the glory of the Lord in the house, they bowed with their faces to the ground, upon the pavement, and worshipped the Lord, saying, For he is good; for his mercy is with us forever.

SOLOMON BRINGS THE ARK INTO THE TEMPLE

Then the king and all the people offered sacrifices. Solomon gave, for peace offerings, twenty-two thousand oxen and a hundred and twenty thousand sheep. So the king and all the people dedicated, or gave, the house to the Lord, that it might be his Temple, where his ark should be kept and where sacrifices should always be offered up to him. Solomon held a great feast for fourteen days and invited all the people to it; and they came and feasted on the flesh of the peace offerings which he had given. Afterward he sent them to their homes, and they went away with joyful hearts, thanking the Lord for his kindness to king Solomon, and to all the children of Israel.

And the Lord spoke to Solomon in the night, and said that he had heard his prayer, and would take the house to be his Temple. And he promised that when the children of Israel should sin against him, and he should punish them for their sin, if they would repent and come to that house and pray to him, he would forgive them and take their punishment away. And he promised again that if Solomon would obey him, he should be king as long as he lived, and his descendants should be kings over Israel after him.

Yet, the Lord said, that if Solomon and the people should turn away from serving him and go to serve other gods, he would bless them no longer, but would drive them out of the good land which he had given them; and that house which was so glorious and beautiful now, he would no more have for his temple, but would destroy it, so that all who should pass by it would be astonished, and ask, Why has the Lord done such things to this land and to this house? And the answer would be, Because the people disobeyed the Lord God of their fathers, who brought them up out of Egypt, and chose other gods and worshipped them and served them.

Beside building the temple, Solomon built a palace for himself in Jerusalem. He built store cities also, in which to keep his riches and goods; and cities for his chariots. He made the heathen people, who were still left in the land, his servants; but of the men of Israel he made soldiers, and captains, and horsemen.

And Solomon sent to the temple the different courses, or companies, of the priests and the Levites which his father had appointed to attend to God's worship there; and he sent the porters to watch at the gates. He commanded that sacrifices should be offered up on the morning and evening of each day, on the Sabbath days, and at the three great feasts which the children of Israel were commanded to keep every year: the feast of the passover, the feast of harvest, and the feast of tabernacles.

The queen of a far-off country, called Sheba, heard of his wisdom and his knowledge of the true God. And she came to visit him. She brought with her a great company of servants, with camels carrying costly spices, such as grew in her country, and gold and precious stones. And she talked with Solomon and asked him hard questions about things that she wanted to know. Solomon answered all her questions, and explained to her every-

THE QUEEN OF SHEBA VISITS SOLOMON

thing that she asked him. And when she looked on the pal-ace that Solomon had built, and the costly food that was upon his table; the number of his servants that waited on him, and the beautiful pathway he had made to go up to the temple; she wondered at all these things, and said that she had not believed what she heard in her own land of his riches and wisdom, but now she saw that the half was not told her. And she gave to Solomon presents of gold and spices, and precious stones, and

Solomon gave her costly presents also. Then she turned, she and her servants, and went back to her own land.

Solomon was wiser than all the other kings of the earth, and they came to him to be taught of his wisdom. He made a great throne of ivory and overlaid it with pure gold; there were six steps leading to the top of the throne, and a footstool of gold was fastened upon it. On the steps were the figures of twelve

SOLOMON WORSHIPS IDOLS

lions, six on one side and six on the other. There was not such a throne made in any other kingdom. And all the cups that Solomon drank out of, and all the vessels that were in his house, were made of pure gold. For his ships sailed to a far country, called Tarshish, and every three years came back, bringing him gold and silver, ivory, apes, and peacocks.

But Solomon had many wives, and he took for his wives heathen women, whom the Lord had commanded the children of

Israel not to marry.   And when he grew old, his wives persuaded him to worship idols, so that he did not continue serving God, as David his father had done.   For David, after he had sinned, repented and asked to be forgiven, and worshipped the Lord alone. But Solomon went with his heathen wives after their idols, and he even built temples to worship those idols in.   And the Lord was angry with him, and said that because he had done these things, his son should not be king over the children of Israel after Solomon himself should die.   Yet, for David's sake, the Lord would not take away all of the kingdom from Solomon's son, but would make him king over two of the tribes of Israel. And the Lord raised up enemies against Solomon, to trouble him because of his sin.

Now there was among the children of Israel a young man named Jeroboam.   One day, as he went out of Jerusalem, a prophet met him; he was wearing a new garment, and they two were alone in the field.   And the prophet took hold of the new garment that he wore, and tore it in twelve pieces.   Then he told Jeroboam to take ten of the pieces, because the Lord was going to make him king over ten of the tribes of Israel.   When Solomon heard this he tried to kill Jeroboam, but Jeroboam fled into Egypt and stayed in that land.

Solomon was king over Israel forty years, and he died and was buried in Jerusalem.   And when the people saw that he was dead, they sent word to Jeroboam, in Egypt, and Jeroboam came back to the land of Israel.   Then he and all the people came to Rehoboam, Solomon's son, to make him their king.   But first they talked with him, and complained that his father had ruled over them harshly and treated them cruelly, and they asked Rehoboam if he would not treat them more kindly than his father had done; if he would do so, they said, they would serve him.   Rehoboam told them to go away and come to him again in three days, and then he would tell them what he would do. So they went away.

After they had gone Rehoboam asked advice from the old men who had been friends of his father.   And they advised him to speak gently to the people, and promise that he would be kind to them; if he would do this, they said, the people would choose him for their king, and be his servants forever. But Rehoboam was not satisfied with the good advice that the old men gave him; he asked the young men also, who had grown up with him, what they would advise him to do. And the young men told him to speak roughly to the people, and say that if his father had been cruel to them, he would be yet more cruel,

REHOBOAM REFUSES TO FOLLOW THE ADVICE OF THE OLD MEN

and if his father had punished them a little, he would punish them a great deal.

So the people came again in three days, and Jeroboam was with them. And Rehoboam spoke roughly to them, as the young men had advised him; he cried, If my father has been cruel to you, I will be yet more cruel, and if he punished you a little, I will punish you a great deal. Then the people went away in great anger, and said that Rehoboam, Solomon's son, should not rule over them, but Jeroboam should be their king. Yet the tribe of Judah still kept Rehoboam for their king, and the tribe of Benjamin also. But the other tribes chose Jeroboam. So Jeroboam was made king over ten tribes, as the prophet had told him.

When Rehoboam saw that the ten tribes had gone from him, he sent a messenger to them, asking them to come back and be his servants; but they stoned the messenger with stones and killed him. Then Rehoboam made haste and called together all the men of Judah and of Benjamin, one hundred and eighty thousand of them, and gathered them into an army to go out and fight against the ten tribes. But God sent a prophet to tell them that they should not fight against their brethren, the children of Israel, but should go to their own homes. And they obeyed the Lord and went to their own homes again.

So now there were two kings ruling over the children of Israel. Until this time, one king had ruled over them all, first Saul, then David, and then Solomon. But now Solomon's son, Rehoboam, was king over the tribes of Judah and Benjamin, and Jeroboam was king over the other ten tribes. Rehoboam's kingdom was called the kingdom of Judah, and Jeroboam's, the kingdom of Israel.

THE STORY OF THE KINGDOM OF ISRAEL

1 KINGS XII–XVII (12–17)

JEROBOAM SETS UP GOLDEN CALVES FOR THE PEOPLE TO WORSHIP. A PROPHET FORETELLS JOSIAH'S BIRTH. THE PROPHET IS SLAIN BY A LION. JEROBOAM DIES. NADAB, BAASHA, ELAH, ZIMRI, OMRI, AND AHAB REIGN OVER ISRAEL. ELIJAH FORETELLS A FAMINE. THE RAVENS FEED HIM. HE RAISES THE WIDOW'S SON TO LIFE.

As soon as the ten tribes had chosen Jeroboam king, they left Rehoboam and went away to their own homes. Then Jeroboam said to himself, If the people of the ten tribes shall go up to Jerusalem to offer sacrifices, and worship at the temple, they will some day put me away from being their king. For at Jerusalem they will see Rehoboam, Solomon's son, and will want to serve him, but me they will put to death. Therefore Jeroboam

made two calves of gold, and set them up in that part of the land
which belonged to the ten tribes.   Then he said to the people, It
is too far for you to go to Jerusalem to worship.   See these idols
of gold, they are your gods; worship them, for it was they that
brought your fathers up out of Egypt.

And he built houses for the idols, one at Bethel and the other
at Dan, in different parts of the land, and the people went there

WORSHIPPING THE GOLDEN CALF AT BETHEL

to worship them.   He made a feast also for the people to keep
at Bethel, instead of the feasts which the Lord had commanded
them to keep at Jerusalem.   And Jeroboam chose wicked men
as priests for his idols, to stay at the idols' houses and offer up
sacrifices to them, but he would not allow the priests of the Lord
to offer up sacrifices to God.   Therefore, all the priests and the
Levites who were living in the land of the ten tribes, left that
land and came to Jerusalem to live; and many other persons

who would not worship the calves, came with them and chose Rehoboam for their king.

Jeroboam did very wickedly, for he prevented the people of the ten tribes from going to Jerusalem, where God had commanded them to worship, and he taught them to worship the golden calves which he had set up. And the people also sinned with him, for they willingly obeyed him, and worshipped the calves, and did not any more go to Jerusalem to worship the Lord.

And one day Jeroboam was standing in his idol's house, by the altar of incense, to burn incense to the calf which was at Bethel. And there came to him a prophet out of the land of Judah, who said that a king should be born in Judah, named Josiah, who would come and burn men's bones on that altar, to defile, or spoil it, and make it unclean. This was not to happen for many years, and yet, that Jeroboam might know it would surely come true, the prophet said, the altar should be broken and its ashes emptied on the ground that very day.

Then Jeroboam was angry at what the prophet said, and stretched out his hand to take hold of him; but while it was stretched out, the Lord made it grow stiff and withered, in a moment, so that he could not draw it back to him again. The altar was broken also, as the prophet had said, and its ashes were scattered on the ground. When Jeroboam saw what the Lord had done to him, he begged the prophet to pray that his hand might be made well. And the prophet prayed for him, and his hand was made well. Then Jeroboam said to the prophet, Come home with me and rest thyself, and I will give thee a reward. But the prophet answered, Though thou shouldst give me half of all the riches in thy house, I will not go with thee, neither will I eat bread nor drink water in this place. For so the Lord commanded me, saying, Eat no bread nor drink water there, nor come back by the same way that thou goest.

So the prophet turned to come back by another way, to the land of Judah. Now there was living at Bethel an old man who was also a prophet. And his sons came and told him of all that the prophet from Judah had done. Then the old prophet at Bethel asked them which way he went, for his sons had seen the road he had taken. When he heard, he said to them, Saddle the ass for me; and they saddled it, and the old man followed after the prophet.

And he came up with him, and found him sitting under an oak, and said to him, Art thou the prophet that came from Judah? He answered, I am. Then the old man said, Come home with me and eat bread. But the prophet from Judah said, I may not go with thee, nor eat bread nor drink water in this place, for the Lord has commanded me, saying, Thou shalt eat no bread nor drink water there, nor come back by the way that thou goest. Then the old man said to him, But I also am a prophet, and an angel spoke to me, saying, Bring him back with thee to thy house, that he may eat bread and drink water. Yet the old prophet lied to him, for no angel had spoken these words.

Now the prophet from Judah ought not to have listened to what the old man said, for the Lord himself had commanded the prophet from Judah what he must do. Yet he listened to the old man's words and went back with him, and did eat bread and drink water in his house. Then the Lord was angry at his disobedience, and while they sat at the table, the Lord made the old man speak to the prophet from Judah, and tell him that because he had disobeyed the Lord and come back to Bethel, and had eaten bread and drunk water there, he should not, when he died, be buried in his father's sepulchre.

So after he had eaten and drunk, he started to go back to the land of Judah. But as he went, a lion met him and slew him, and his dead body lay in the road, and the ass on which he had ridden stood by it, and the lion also. Some men who passed that way, saw the dead body in the road and the lion standing by it. Then they came and told it in Bethel, where the old prophet lived. When he heard it, he said, It is the prophet from Judah who disobeyed the command of the Lord, therefore the Lord has given him to the lion, which has slain him, so that he shall not be buried in the sepulchre of his fathers, as the Lord said.

And the old man spoke to his sons, saying, Saddle the ass

for me; and they saddled it.   Then he went to the place where
the prophet had been slain, and found his dead body lying in
the way, and the ass and the lion standing by it.   The lion
had not eaten the body nor killed the ass.   And the old man
took up the prophet's dead body, and laid it upon the ass and
brought it to Bethel, where he buried it in his own grave.   Then
he said to his sons, When I am dead, bury me in the sepulchre

A LION KILLS THE PROPHET FROM JUDAH

where the prophet of Judah is buried; lay my bones beside
his bones, for the words that he spoke against the altar in Bethel
shall surely come true.

At that time the son of king Jeroboam grew sick, and Jeroboam said to his wife, Put on other raiment, that no one may
know thee, and go to Shiloh, to the prophet who told me I
should be king; take him a present of ten loaves of bread and
a cruse of honey, and he will tell thee whether the child shall

get well. And Jeroboam's wife did as he said. She put on other raiment and went to Shiloh, and came to the prophet's house. Now the prophet was old and could not see, for his eyes were dim. But the Lord had told him that the wife of Jeroboam was coming to ask about her son.

So when he heard the sound of her feet, as she came in at the door, he said, Come in, thou wife of Jeroboam; why dost thou pretend to be another woman? For I have to tell thee sad tidings. Go, say to Jeroboam, thus saith the Lord, I raised thee up from among the people, and made thee king over ten of the tribes of Israel; I took those ten tribes away from Solomon's son and gave them to thee. Yet thou hast not obeyed my commandments, but hast done wickedly, for thou hast turned away from serving me and made other gods. Therefore I will send evil upon thee and thy family, until not one of them is left alive. And after they are dead they shall not be buried in the grave, as the families of other kings are buried; but those that die in the city the dogs shall eat, and those that die out in the field the birds of the air shall eat; for so the Lord has said it shall be. Go back, therefore, to thy own house, and as thou goest, thy child shall die. And all the people shall mourn for him and bury him; for he is the only one of Jeroboam's family who shall be buried in the grave.

So Jeroboam's wife rose up and went from the prophet's house to her own home, and as she came in at the door the child died. And they buried him, and all Israel mourned for him as the prophet had said. Jeroboam reigned, that is, he was king, for twenty-two years; then he died, and Nadab, his son, was made king in his place.

Nadab did not serve God, but worshipped the golden calves which his father had set up. He went with his army against the Philistines and besieged one of their cities. To besiege a city is to set soldiers around it, who will let no one come out or go in; but will fight against it, and prevent food or help from being brought to the people, until the city is taken. And Nadab besieged a city of the Philistines. While he was there and after he had been king for two years, a man named Baasha rebelled against him and slew him; and Baasha was made king over the ten tribes of Israel.

Baasha put every one of Jeroboam's family to death; so the words of the prophet came true, which he spoke to Jeroboam's wife, when he told her that the Lord would bring evil on Jeroboam and his family, until not one of them was left alive. Yet Baasha did not kill them because they were wicked, nor because

NADAB BESIEGES A CITY OF THE PHILISTINES

the Lord's prophet had spoken these words, but because he wanted to rule over the people himself. For Baasha was wicked also, and he too worshipped the golden calves. He was king for twenty-four years; and he died, and Elah, his son, was made king in his place.

Elah lived in the city of Tirzah, where his father had lived. He reigned for two years. One day, he was drinking himself drunk in the house of his chief servant; when Zimri, the captain of half his chariots, came into the house and killed him; and Zimri made himself king. Now the men of Israel were away, fighting against the Philistines at this time, but as soon as they heard what Zimri had done, they said that he should not rule over them, so they chose Omri, their captain, for king. Then Omri and the men of Israel came to Tirzah, where Zimri was, and besieged it. When Zimri saw they were about to gain the victory over him and take the city, he went into the king's palace, and setting it on fire, burnt himself up there. Zimri was king for only seven days.

Omri, after he was made king, bought a hill called the hill of Samaria, for two talents of silver; and he built a city on it which he called the city of Samaria. In this city Omri lived, and the kings of Israel, who reigned after him, continued to live there as long as their kingdom lasted—for nearly two hundred years. But Omri also sinned, for he worshipped the golden calves, and encouraged the people to worship them. He was king for twelve years, and he died, and was buried in Samaria, the city which he had built; and Ahab his son was made king in his stead.

Up to this time, six kings had ruled over the ten tribes of Israel, and every one of them had been wicked. But the Bible tells us that Ahab, Omri's son, was more wicked than all who had ruled before him. He took for his wife the daughter of a heathen king. Her name was Jezebel, and she worshipped the idol Baal. Ahab built a house, or temple, for the idol in the city of Samaria. He chose wicked men also to stay there and offer up sacrifices to the idol. These men he called priests, or prophets, of Baal. Ahab also set up an image and an altar, and he made the people of Israel worship Baal as the heathen nations did.

And the Lord was displeased with Ahab, and sent the prophet Elijah to tell him that there should not, for years, be any more rain in the land of Israel. No rain should come there, the Lord said, until Elijah should ask for it. As this would make Ahab very angry with Elijah, the Lord told the prophet, after he had spoken these words, to flee away where Ahab could not find him. Go, the Lord said, and hide by a brook that is in the wilderness.

Thou shalt drink of the water of the brook, and I have commanded the ravens to feed thee there. So Elijah went and hid by the brook; and he drank of the water, and the ravens brought him bread and meat in the morning, and bread and meat in the evening. But after a while, because there had been no rain, the brook dried up and a great famine came in the land.

ELIJAH FED BY THE RAVENS

Then the Lord said to him, Arise, and go to the city of Zarephath, for I have commanded a widow woman there to feed thee. And Elijah arose and went. When he came to the gate of the city, the woman was gathering sticks, and he called to her and said, Bring me, I pray thee, a little water in a cup, that I may drink. As she was going he called to her again, and said, Bring me, I pray thee, a piece of bread in thy hand. She answered, As surely as the Lord thy God liveth, I have no bread, but only a handful of meal in a barrel, and a little oil in a cruse; and now I am gathering a few sticks that I may go in and bake it, for me and my son to eat, before we starve.

But Elijah said to her, Fear not; go and bake it, as thou hast said, but make a little cake for me first and bring it. After that make more for thee and thy son. For the Lord says that

ELIJAH ASKS THE WIDOW FOR BREAD

although there is but little of the meal and of the oil, yet they shall last until the famine ceases in the land. Then she went and did as Elijah commanded; and afterward she, and he, and her son did eat for a whole year, and the Lord made the meal and the oil last all that time.

After this the son of the woman grew sick, and his sickness

was so great that he died. When she told Elijah of it, he said, Give me thy son. And he took him out of her arms, and carried him up into his own chamber and laid him on his bed. And Elijah cried to the Lord, and said, O Lord, hast thou

ELIJAH RAISES THE WIDOW'S SON

brought evil upon the woman in whose house I stay, by slaying her son? I beseech thee, O Lord, let the child's soul come into him again. And the Lord heard Elijah's prayer, and sent the soul of the child into him again, so that he lived. Then Elijah took him, and brought him down out of his chamber and gave him to his mother.

1 KINGS XVIII, XIX (18, 19)

ELIJAH SHOWS HIMSELF TO AHAB. HE SLAYS BAAL'S PROPHETS AT MOUNT
CARMEL, AND PRAYS FOR RAIN. JEZEBEL SEEKS TO SLAY ELIJAH. HE
FLEES INTO THE WILDERNESS. GOD SPEAKS TO HIM AT HOREB. ELIJAH
CALLS ELISHA TO FOLLOW HIM.

Now there were in the land of Israel many other prophets of
the Lord beside Elijah, whom the Lord had sent to teach
the people. But Jezebel, the wicked wife of Ahab, hated them
and tried to kill them. Then Obadiah, the chief servant in
Ahab's house, because he was a good man and feared the Lord,
took a hundred of the Lord's prophets and hid them in caves,
where Jezebel could not find them; there he sent them bread
to eat and water to drink.

After the famine had lasted for more than three years, the
Lord spoke to Elijah, and said, Go, show thyself to king Ahab,
and I will send rain on the land. Then Elijah started to go.
But Ahab did not know that Elijah was coming, or that the
Lord was going to send rain. So he called Obadiah, his chief
servant, and said to him, Go, and look wherever there are any
brooks or springs of water, perhaps we may find grass enough
there to save the horses and mules alive, that we lose not all
of them by the famine. And Ahab and Obadiah went out
to search through the land: Ahab went one way by himself,
and Obadiah went another way by himself.

Now as Obadiah went on his way, Elijah met him, and Obadiah knew him, and fell on his face, and said, Art thou, my lord,
Elijah? Elijah said, I am. Go tell king Ahab that Elijah is
here. But Obadiah answered, There is no nation nor kingdom where Ahab has not sent to seek thee. And now, as soon
as I have gone to tell him that thou art here, the Lord will carry
thee away, I know not where, and hide thee, and when Ahab
shall come and cannot find thee, he will kill me. But Elijah
answered, As surely as the Lord liveth, I will show myself to
Ahab this day. So Obadiah went and told Ahab, and Ahab
came to meet Elijah. When he saw him, he said, Art thou he
that troubleth the people of Israel? He said this because he
blamed Elijah for the famine. But Elijah answered, I am not

the one who troubles Israel, but thou and thy family, because you have forsaken the Lord and have served Baal.

Then Elijah told Ahab to send and gather all the people at mount Carmel, and to bring there also all the priests, or prophets of Baal, four hundred and fifty men. So Ahab sent word to all the people, and gathered them and Baal's prophets together, at mount Carmel. And Elijah came there and spoke to the people, saying, How long will you be in deciding whom you will serve? If the Lord be God, obey him; but if Baal be God, then obey him. And the people heard what Elijah said, but they answered him not a word.

Then Elijah told the people that he was the only prophet of the Lord who was left in the land, because all the rest had been killed or made to flee away for their lives, but Baal's prophets, he said, were four hundred and fifty men. And Elijah said, Bring two bullocks, and let Baal's prophets choose one of them and kill it and lay it on Baal's altar, but not put any fire under it. And I will take the other bullock and kill it, and lay it on the Lord's altar, and not put any fire under it. Then they shall pray to Baal to send down fire from heaven, and I will pray to the Lord; and the one that sends down fire to burn up his offering, he shall be God. And all the people answered that it should be as Elijah said.

And Baal's prophets chose their bullock and killed it, and laid it on the wood on the altar, but put no fire under it. Then they cried out to their idol from morning till noon, saying, O Baal, hear us! And they leaped up and down at their altar. But no voice answered them, neither did any fire come down to burn up their offering. And, at about noon, Elijah mocked them, and said, Call louder upon your god, for perhaps he is talking to some one and cannot hear, or has gone away from his home on a journey, or is asleep and must be awaked. And they cried to Baal until the evening, and cut themselves with knives till the blood gushed out, as the heathen nations used to do, hoping it would make their idols answer them. But no answer came.

Then Elijah called all the people to come near to him, and they came near. And he took twelve stones and built up the altar of the Lord which had been broken down, and he made a trench, or trough around it. And he put the wood on the altar, and cut the bullock in pieces, and laid it on the wood. And he said to the people, Fill four barrels with water, and pour it on the burnt sacrifice and on the wood. When they had done it, he said, Do it a second time. And they did it a second time. And he said, Do it a third time. And they did it the third time. And the water ran down over the sacrifice and over the wood, and filled the trench around the altar.

And in the evening, at the time when the priests at the temple used every day to offer up a lamb for a burnt offering, Elijah came near to the altar and prayed to the Lord, saying, Hear me, O Lord, hear me, so that this people may know thou art the true God, and that thou dost call them from serving idols to serve thee again. Then the fire of the Lord fell from heaven upon the altar, and burnt up the bullock and the wood, and the stones of which the altar was made, and licked up the water that was in the trench. When all the people saw it, they fell on their faces, and said, The Lord, he is God! The Lord, he is God! And Elijah said to them, Take the prophets of Baal, let not one of them escape. And the people took them; and Elijah brought them down to the brook Kishon and slew them there; for so the Lord commanded it should be done to all those who taught the people to serve idols and forsake him.

Then Elijah spoke to king Ahab, and told him that now he might go and eat and drink, for the rain was coming and the famine would soon be ended. So Ahab went to a place a little way off on the mountain, to eat and drink there. But Elijah went up to the top of mount Carmel, and kneeled down with his face to the ground, and prayed that God would send the rain. After he had prayed, he said to his servant, Go up now and look toward the sea. And the servant went up to a place still higher on the mount, and looked, but came back and said, I see nothing. Elijah said, Go again seven times. And at the seventh time he came, saying, There rises up out of the sea, a little cloud as large as a man's hand.

Then Elijah knew that the Lord was sending the rain. So

he said to his servant, Go, say unto Ahab, Make ready thy chariot and get thee down from the mountain, lest the rain stop thee. While his servant was going, the little cloud rose up from the sea, and grew larger, till all the sky was black with clouds and wind, and there was a very great rain. And Ahab rode in his chariot and went to the city of Jezreel. And the Lord gave Elijah strength to run before the chariot till he came to the gate of the city.

Ahab told his wife, Jezebel, of all that Elijah had done, and how he had slain the prophets of Baal with the sword. Then Jezebel was very angry, and she sent word to Elijah, saying, Let the gods (that is, the idols which she worshipped) slay me also, if I do not put thee to death by to-morrow about this time. When Elijah heard these words he was greatly afraid, and made haste to flee for his life, and came to the city of Beer-sheba in the land of Judah. There he left his servant, but he went on another day's journey to hide in the wilderness.

And he sat down under a juniper tree, and asked that he might die, saying, Now, O Lord, take away my life. For he was weary of fleeing from his enemies. But he did wrong in asking that he might die. God had sent the ravens to feed him in the famine, and had saved him from Ahab, and the wicked prophets of Baal. Elijah should have remembered these things, and not been afraid, but willing to wait patiently until the Lord was ready to take him to heaven. We shall see afterward what glorious things he would have missed if the Lord had allowed him to die, as he asked, there alone in the wilderness.

And he fell asleep. As he lay sleeping under the juniper tree, an angel came and touched him and said to him, Arise and eat. And Elijah looked, and saw a cake that was baked on some coals of fire near him, and a cruse of water by his head. And he ate and drank, and lay down and slept again. Then the angel of the Lord came a second time and touched him, and told him to eat, so that he might have strength for the journey that was before him. So he rose up and ate and drank; and the Lord gave him strength from that food to go forty days and forty nights, until he came to mount Horeb.

And he went into a cave on the mountain, and lay down and slept there. And the Lord spoke to him, saying, What doest thou here, Elijah? Elijah answered, The children of Israel have broken their promise to obey thy law, and have thrown down thy altars, and slain thy prophets with the sword; I am the only one left, and they seek to slay me also. Then the Lord

ELIJAH FED BY THE ANGEL

passed by the cave where Elijah was. But first there came a great and strong wind before him, that tore up the earth on the mountain, and broke the rocks in pieces; but the Lord was not in the wind. And after the wind came an earthquake that shook the ground; but the Lord was not in the earthquake. And after the earthquake came a fire; but the Lord was not in the fire. And after the fire came a still, small voice. When Elijah heard it he knew that God was there; and he wrapt his face in his mantle, for he was afraid to look upon God. And God called him to come out and stand upon the mountain. And Elijah went out and stood at the mouth of the cave.

And the Lord asked him, as he had done before, What doest thou here, Elijah? Elijah answered, The children of Israel have broken their promise to obey thy law; they have thrown down thine altars and slain thy prophets with the sword; I am the only one left, and they seek to slay me also. But the Lord told Elijah that he was not the only one left who served him. I have yet seven thousand persons in the land of Israel, the Lord said, who have never bowed their knees to the idol Baal. Then the Lord commanded Elijah to leave the cave and go back, by the way that he came, toward the wilderness of Damascus, and as he went, to anoint Elisha to be prophet in his place; because the time was coming near when the Lord would take Elijah up to heaven.

ELIJAH HEARS THE VOICE OF THE LORD

So Elijah went back as the Lord commanded him; and on the way he saw Elisha ploughing with his oxen in the field. Elijah came near to him, and as he passed by, threw his mantle, or coat, on Elisha. And the Lord made Elisha understand that this meant he should leave his home and go with Elijah. Then Elisha left the oxen and ran after Elijah, and said to him, Let me go first, I pray thee, and kiss my father and my mother farewell, and then I will come with thee. So Elisha returned to his home to bid his father and mother farewell, but afterward he came to Elijah and went with him and waited on him, and was his servant.

ELIJAH THROWS HIS MANTLE ON ELISHA

1 KINGS XX–XXII (20–22). 2 KINGS I (1)

AHAB GAINS THE VICTORY OVER THE SYRIANS, BUT LETS BENHADAD GO.
HE TAKES NABOTH'S VINEYARD. JEHOSHAPHAT GOES OUT TO BATTLE
WITH AHAB. AHAB IS SLAIN. AHAZIAH REIGNS. HE SENDS SOLDIERS
TO TAKE ELIJAH, AND THEY ARE BURNED UP BY FIRE FROM HEAVEN.
AHAZIAH'S DEATH.

BENHADAD, the king of a country called Syria, gathered
all his army together and went up to fight against the city of
Samaria, where Ahab, the king of Israel, lived. And he sent

messengers to Ahab, saying, Thy silver and thy gold, thy wives
and thy children, even those thou lovest best, are mine. When
Ahab heard this he was afraid, and answered that Benhadad
might take all those things. Then Benhadad sent messengers
again to Ahab, and said, Although thou wilt give me all thy silver
and gold, and thy wives and thy children, these are not enough.
But to-morrow I will send my servants, and they shall search thy
house, and whatever they find there that thou dost value most,
they shall take away from thee, and bring to me. Then Ahab
called all the elders of Israel to him, and told them the words
Benhadad had spoken. And the elders answered that Ahab
should not allow Benhadad to do as he said.

When Benhadad heard this, he sent word to Ahab that he
had with him a great army, and that he would come and take
the city of Samaria. But Ahab replied that he should not
boast beforehand, as if he had already gained the victory. Then
Benhadad was very angry, and said to his soldiers, Make ready
for the battle. And they made ready. And the Lord sent a
prophet to Ahab, who told him not to fear, but to go out against
the Syrians with only seven thousand men. So Ahab went out
against them, as the prophet said. Benhadad and his captains
were drinking themselves drunk in their tents. And Ahab and
his seven thousand men fought against them, and the Syrians
fled. When Benhadad saw that his army had fled, he escaped
on a horse with some of his horsemen.

And the prophet spoke to Ahab a second time, and told him
that Benhadad would come up again the next year against
Samaria. What the prophet said proved true. For Benhadad's
servants persuaded him to gather together another army as great
as the first, and they came up and spread over the whole country. But the men of Israel, when they went out against him,
seemed only like two little flocks of kids, there were so few of them.
After seven days the battle began, and the Lord gave the men of
Israel the victory this time also, for they slew of the Syrians a hundred thousand men. The rest escaped to the city of Aphek, and
there a great wall fell down and killed many more of them. But
Benhadad fled into the city and hid in a secret chamber.

And his servants came to him and said, We have heard that the kings of Israel are merciful kings, let us, we pray thee, put on sackcloth, to show that we humble ourselves, and then go out to the king of Israel and ask him to save thy life; perhaps he may let thee live. So they put on sackcloth, and came to Ahab, saying, Thy servant Benhadad says, I pray thee let me live. Ahab answered, Was he not killed in the battle? When he heard that he was yet alive, he told them to go and bring him. Then Benhadad came out to him, and Ahab took that wicked king up into his chariot, and because Benhadad promised to give him some cities, Ahab allowed him to return to his own land. But God was angry with Ahab for doing this. He had given Ahab the victory over Benhadad that Ahab might put him to death. And now God sent a prophet to Ahab who spoke to him, and said, Because thou hast let this man go, whom I meant thou shouldst utterly destroy, therefore thy life shall go for his life and thou shalt be slain instead of him.

After this there was a man named Naboth, who had a vine yard in the city of Jezreel. Now Ahab, the king, had a palace in that city, and as Naboth's vineyard was near it, Ahab spoke to him, saying, Sell me thy vineyard, that I may have it for a garden to plant herbs in, and I will give thee a better vineyard for it, or else, if thou wouldst rather, I will give thee what it is worth in money. But Naboth did not want to sell his vineyard. It had belonged to his father, who, when he died, left it to him; therefore it was Naboth's inheritance. And Naboth would not let Ahab have it; he said, The Lord forbid that I should sell the inheritance of my fathers to thee.

When Ahab heard this, he came home to his house sad and displeased. He lay down upon his bed, and turned away his face, and would eat no food. Then Jezebel, his wife, came to him, saying, Why art thou so sad that thou wilt eat no food? And Ahab answered, Because I spoke unto Naboth, and said to him, Sell me thy vineyard for money, or else, if thou wouldst rather, I will give thee another vineyard for it, but he answered, I will not give thee my vineyard. Jezebel said to him, Art thou now the king of Israel, and wilt thou be treated so? Rise up, eat thy food, and be merry; I will give thee the vineyard of Naboth the Jezreelite.

Then she wrote letters, and signed them with Ahab's name, and sealed them with his seal, and sent them to the elders of the city of Jezreel, where Naboth lived. In the letters she commanded them to find some wicked men who would tell lies about Naboth, and say that they had heard him speak evil of God and

NABOTH REFUSES TO SELL HIS VINEYARD

the king. And the elders did as Jezebel commanded; for they found two men who bore false witness, that is, who lied against him, saying, Naboth did blaspheme, and speak evil of God and the king. Now, as we have read, the Lord had commanded that whoever blasphemed his name should be stoned. So they took Naboth out of the city and stoned him with stones until he died, and the dogs came and licked up his blood. Then they sent word to Jezebel, saying, Naboth is stoned and is dead.

When Jezebel heard it she said to Ahab, Arise, and take the vineyard of Naboth for thine own, for Naboth is not alive, but dead. So Ahab arose, and went down to the vineyard of Naboth to take it for his own. And the Lord commanded Elijah to go and meet him there, and say to him, Hast thou killed Naboth and taken his vineyard? I tell thee that in the place where the dogs licked up the blood of Naboth, shall dogs lick thy blood,

ELIJAH CONDEMNS AHAB TO DEATH

even thine. And Elijah went to meet Ahab; when Ahab saw him, he said to him, Hast thou found me, O my enemy? Elijah answered, I have found thee because thou hast given thyself up to sin against the Lord.

Then Elijah told Ahab that the Lord would send evil on him and on his family, and that they should all be destroyed, as the family of Jeroboam had been, until not one of them was left alive. Of Jezebel also, the Lord said, The dogs shall eat Jezebel by the wall of Jezreel. For there was none so wicked as Ahab, who gave himself up to do evil, and whose wife, Jezebel, tempted him to sin more and more. He did very wickedly also in worshipping idols, like the heathen nations that the Lord had driven out of Canaan before the children of Israel.

And Jehoshaphat, the king of Judah, came down to Samaria to visit Ahab. Then Ahab told him that Benhadad, king of Syria, was keeping one of the cities from him, and Ahab asked Jehoshaphat to go out with him to take it again. Now Jehoshaphat was a good man and feared the Lord, therefore he told Ahab to inquire first whether the Lord was willing they should go.

And Ahab gathered his prophets together, about four hundred men, and said to them, Shall I go up against the city to battle, or shall I not go? They answered, Go up, for the Lord will give it into thy hand. But Jehoshaphat did not believe these men, for they were false prophets, who said whatever they thought would please Ahab. And Jehoshaphat said, Is there not here a prophet of the Lord, beside these, whom we may ask? Ahab answered, There is yet one, a man named Micaiah, but I hate him, because he does not prophesy good to me, but evil. Jehoshaphat answered, Let not the king say so.

Then Ahab called an officer, and told him to make haste and bring Micaiah there. And the king of Israel and the king of Judah, having put on their royal robes, sat each of them on a throne in an open place by the gate of Samaria. And all Ahab's false prophets were speaking before them, telling them to go out to battle, for they should have the victory.

And the messenger came back, bringing Micaiah to the king. Then Ahab asked him, Shall we go to battle against the city, or shall we not go? At first Micaiah said, Go. But the king saw that he did not mean what he said. And Ahab said to him, How often must I ask thee before thou wilt tell me what is true? Then Micaiah answered, I saw all the children of Israel scattered upon the hills, like a flock of sheep that is lost and has no shepherd. Micaiah meant that the Lord had shown him Ahab's army, as it would be after the battle, when Ahab himself would be killed and his army would have no one to lead them.

Ahab said to Jehoshaphat, Did I not say to thee truly that he would prophesy no good about me, but evil? And Ahab was angry, and commanded his servants, saying, Take Micaiah to the governor of the city, and say, Thus saith the king, Put this fellow in prison, and feed him on bread and water, and treat him cruelly, until I come back safe from the battle. Micaiah answered, If thou come back safe at all, then the Lord has not told me what I should answer thee.

AHAB IS WOUNDED BY AN ARROW

Yet the king of Israel and the king of Judah went up to fight against the city. And Ahab said to Jehoshaphat, I will put on another dress, that no one may know me, and will go among the soldiers and fight in the battle, but put thou on thy royal robes and let them see thou art a king. Now, before the battle began, Benhadad, king of Syria, had commanded all his captains to try and kill Ahab; and when they saw Jehoshaphat in his robes, they said, Surely it is king Ahab, and they came to fight against him. Then Jehoshaphat cried out; and when they saw it was not Ahab, they turned back from following him. It was the Lord who made them turn back, because Jehoshaphat was his servant, and the Lord was watching over him, to save him from them.

But a man in Benhadad's army shot an arrow, not aiming at any one, nor knowing where it would strike, and the Lord made it strike Ahab and go in between the pieces of armor that covered his breast. Then Ahab said to the driver of his chariot, Turn back, and carry me out of the host, for I am wounded. The battle lasted all that day, and Ahab was held up in his chariot that he might see it, and send orders to his soldiers, but he died in the evening. And about the time the sun was going down, word was sent through all the host of Israel that every man should flee to his own home.

So the men of Israel fled, and Ahab was slain, as the prophet told him he would be, when he let Benhadad go, after the Lord had given that wicked king into his hand. And they carried Ahab's dead body to Samaria and buried it there. As a man was washing the blood from the king's chariot, in a pool of water that was near the city, the dogs came and licked up his blood, as Elijah said they should, when the dogs licked up the blood of Naboth at the city of Jezreel.

And Ahaziah, the son of Ahab, was made king in his place. He did wickedly, as his father had done. And he fell down from an upper chamber in his palace and was hurt, and made sick. Then he sent messengers to Baal-zebub, the idol of the Philistines, to ask whether he would get well of his sickness. And the angel of the Lord said to Elijah, Go up to meet the messengers of Ahaziah, and say to them, Is it because there is no God in Israel that you are going to ask Baal-zebub, the idol of the Philistines? Now, therefore, the Lord says that Ahaziah shall not rise up from that bed on which he is laid, but shall surely die.

Elijah met the messengers, and spoke to them the words that the Lord had commanded. And they came to Ahaziah again, and he said to them, Why are you come back so soon? They answered, There came a man to meet us, who said, Go back to king Ahaziah and say to him, thus saith the Lord: Is it because there is not a God in Israel that you send to inquire of Baal-zebub, the idol of the Philistines? Therefore know now that you shall not rise up from the bed on which you are laid, but shall surely die. The king said to the messengers, What sort of a man was he that met you and told you these words? They answered, He was a hairy man, with a girdle of leather about his loins. And Ahaziah said, It is Elijah.

Then the king was displeased, and sent a captain of his army, with fifty soldiers, to take Elijah, and bring him to the king. And they came, and found him sitting on the top of a hill; and the captain called to him, and said, Thou prophet, the king commands thee to come down. Elijah answered, If I be a prophet, let fire come down from heaven and burn up thee and thy fifty men. And there came down fire from heaven, and burned up the captain and the fifty men who were with him.

And Ahaziah sent another captain with fifty men, and he came to Elijah and called to him, saying, Thou prophet, the king commands thee to come down quickly. Elijah answered, If I be a prophet, let fire come down from heaven and burn up thee and thy fifty men. Then fire came down again from heaven, and burned up the captain and his fifty men. And Ahaziah sent a third captain with fifty men more. But when he came to the place where Elijah was, he fell on his knees before him, and said, O prophet, I pray thee, save my life and the lives of these fifty men, thy servants. Let not the fire come down from heaven and burn us, as it burned the two captains, with their men, who were here before us.

And the angel of the Lord said to Elijah, Go with him, be not afraid. So Elijah went with him to the king. And Elijah said to the king, Thus saith the Lord, Because thou hast sent messengers to inquire of Baal-zebub, the idol of the Philistines, instead of sending to me, the God of Israel, therefore thou shalt not rise up from the bed on which thou art laid, but shalt surely die. So Ahaziah died, as Elijah told him, and Jehoram, his brother, was made king over the ten tribes of Israel.

2 KINGS II–IV (2–4)

ELIJAH IS TAKEN UP TO HEAVEN. ELISHA MAKES THE WATERS AT JERICHO
PURE. LITTLE CHILDREN MOCK HIM AND ARE SLAIN BY BEARS. HE
COMMANDS DITCHES TO BE DUG, AND THESE ARE FILLED WITH WATER.
THE WIDOW POURS OIL INTO EMPTY VESSELS. THE SHUNAMITE'S KIND-
NESS TO ELISHA. HE RAISES HER SON TO LIFE.

AND it was so, when the Lord was going to take Elijah up to
heaven, that Elijah went with his servant Elisha to a place
called Gilgal. Now Elijah wanted to be alone when the Lord
should take him up, so he said to Elisha, Stay here, I pray thee,
at Gilgal, for the Lord has sent me to Bethel. But Elisha said,
As surely as the Lord liveth, and as thou art living, I will not
leave thee. So they went down to Bethel. And the young men
who went to the schools that were taught by the prophets at
Bethel, came to Elisha, and said to him, Knowest thou that the
Lord will take away thy master from thee to-day? He answered,
Yes, I know it, hold ye your peace.

And Elijah said to Elisha, Stay here at Bethel, I pray thee,
for the Lord has sent me to Jericho. But Elisha said, As surely
as the Lord liveth, and as thou art living, I will not leave thee. So
they came to Jericho. And the young men who were in the schools
of the prophets at Jericho, came to Elisha, and said to him, Knowest thou that the Lord will take away thy master from thee to-day?
He answered, Yes, I know it, hold ye your peace.

And Elijah said to Elisha, Stay here, I pray thee, at Jericho,
for the Lord has sent me to the river Jordan. But Elisha answered, As surely as the Lord liveth, and as thou art living, I
will not leave thee. And they two went on. And fifty young
men from the schools of the prophets followed them, to look, a
good way off. And Elijah and Elisha stood by the side of the
river. Then Elijah took his mantle and wrapt it together, and
struck the waters with it, and the waters were parted before
them, so that they two went over on dry ground.

When they had gone over, Elijah said to Elisha, Ask what I
shall do for thee, before I be taken away from thee. And Elisha
asked that he might have more of God's Spirit in his heart, as
Elijah had. Elijah answered, Thou hast asked a hard thing; yet

if thou see me when I am taken from thee, thou shalt have what thou askest for; but if not, thou shalt not have it.

And as they walked on and talked together, behold, there came a chariot of fire, with horses of fire, that took Elijah away from Elisha, and he went up in the chariot to heaven. Elisha saw it, and cried out, My father, my father, the chariot of Israel and the horsemen thereof. He called Elijah father, for so they called the prophets in those days. And he called him

ELIJAH IS TAKEN UP TO HEAVEN

the chariot of Israel and the horsemen thereof, because Elijah would have been better than chariots and horses to help the people, and gain the victory for them over their enemies, if they had only been willing to obey him. After that Elisha saw Elijah no more; and he took hold of his own clothes and rent them in two pieces. And Elisha took up the mantle of Elijah that fell from him, and with it he struck the waters of the river, and they parted for him as they had done for Elijah, and Elisha went over alone, on dry ground.

And the fifty young men from the schools of the prophets, who had followed afar off, came to meet him, and bowed themselves down to the ground before him. And they said to Elisha, Let us go, we pray thee, and look for thy master; perhaps the Lord has taken him away and left him on some mountain, or in some valley. But Elisha answered, Ye shall not go. Then they begged him, till Elisha was ashamed to refuse any longer, and he said to them, Go. They went, therefore, and searched three days for Elijah, but could not find him. Then they came to Jericho and told Elisha, and he said to them, Did I not say to you, Do not go?

And the men of Jericho said to Elisha, Our city is pleasant to live in, as thou seest, except that the water is not good to drink, and it makes the ground barren, so that nothing will grow here. Elisha said to them, Bring me a new cruse, and put some salt in it; and they brought it to him. And he went to the spring from which the water flowed, and threw the salt in there, and said, Thus saith the Lord, I have made these waters pure; they shall not any more cause the people to be sick, or the ground to be barren. So the waters were made pure from that day.

And Elisha went from Jericho to Bethel; as he was going, there came forth little children out of the city, and mocked him, and cried after him, saying, Go up, thou bald head; go up, thou bald head. So they made sport of him, because he was bald, and told him to go up, as Elijah had gone up, when God took him to heaven. And Elisha turned back, and as he looked on them, asked the Lord to punish them for their sin. And there came forth two bears out of the wood, and tore forty-two children of them.

After this Jehoram, king of Israel, gathered his army together to fight against the Moabites. And he sent word to Jehoshaphat, the king of Judah, saying, The king of Moab has rebelled against me; wilt thou go with me against him to battle? Jehoshaphat answered, I will go: and the king of Edom also went with them. So these three kings set out with their armies, and they marched seven days, and found no water for the host, nor for the cattle that they had brought with them to eat by the

BEARS DESTROY THE MOCKING CHILDREN

way. Then the king of Israel was afraid, because his soldiers had no water to drink, and he said, Alas, the Moabites will gain the victory over us.

Now Jehoram, the king of Israel, served idols that could not help him; but Jehoshaphat served the Lord, and he asked, saying, Is there no prophet here, who can inquire of the Lord for us what we shall do? One of the king of Israel's servants answered, Elisha is here, who was the servant of Elijah. Jehoshaphat said, He is a prophet of the Lord; let us go to him. So Jehoram, king of Israel, and Jehoshaphat, king of Judah, and the king of Edom, went to Elisha. And when Elisha saw the king of Israel, he said, Why dost thou come to me? Go to the false prophets of thy father Ahab, and thy mother Jezebel; let them help thee. The king of Israel answered that he had come because he was afraid of the Moabites, lest they should gain the victory over them. Elisha said to him, As surely as the Lord of hosts liveth, if it were not for Jehoshaphat, the king of Judah, who is with thee. I would not look toward thee nor see thee.

Then the Lord commanded Elisha to tell the men of Israel to dig the valley, in which their camp was, full of ditches; for the Lord said that although there should be no wind nor rain, yet the ditches should be filled with water, that they and their cattle might drink. And the Lord will not only do this for you, Elisha said, but he will give you the victory over the Moabites, and you shall destroy their cities, and cut down their trees, and fill up their wells, and spoil the best of their land. And the words of Elisha came true, for the next morning the Lord caused water to flow into the valley, so that the ditches were filled with it.

When the Moabites heard that the kings of Israel, of Judah, and of Edom had come up against them, they gathered all their army together and came near the camp of Israel. And the sun shone on the water in the ditches, and made it look red. Then the Moabites thought that their enemies had been fighting with one another, and that this was their blood. And they said, Let us go and take the spoil they have left. So they came near the camp; but when they saw the armies that were there, they were afraid and fled. And the men of Israel rose up and followed them, even into their own country. There they cut down the trees and destroyed the cities; they filled up the wells, and on every good piece of ground threw great quantities of stones and spoiled it, as Elisha had said they should. Afterward the men of Israel came back to their own land.

And a woman, who was the wife of one of the scholars, or (as they were called at that time), the sons of the prophets, cried to Elisha, saying, My husband is dead, and thou knowest that he served the Lord. But he owed money that he was not able to pay; and now the man to whom he owed it has come to take my two sons and make them his bondmen. Elisha said to her, What shall I do for thee? Tell me, what hast thou in thy house? She answered, I have not anything except a pot of oil. Then he said to her, Go, borrow empty vessels of all thy neighbors, and bring them into thy house and shut the door, and pour out of the pot of oil that thou hast, into the vessels thou hast borrowed, and set to one side those that are full.

So she went and borrowed empty vessels, and carried them into her house and shut the door. Then her sons brought the empty vessels to her, while she poured out of the pot of oil into them, and the oil kept on coming until they were all full. But she did not know they were all full, and she said to her son, Bring me another vessel. He answered, There is not one more. Then she came and told Elisha, and he said, Go, sell the oil, and pay the man what thy husband owed him, and take the money that is left to buy food for thee and thy children.

After these things, as Elisha journeyed through the land, he came to a city called Shunem, where lived a rich and great woman, and she begged him to stop at her house and eat food. She was so kind to him that whenever he passed by that way he stopped there and did eat. Then she said to her husband, I see that this is a prophet of the Lord who passes by us so often. Let us make a little chamber for him in our house, and put in it a bed, a table, a stool, and a candlestick; and whenever he comes to us he shall stay there. So they made it as she said.

And it happened one day that Elisha came with his servant,

whose name was Gehazi, and went into the chamber, and lay down there to rest. And he said to Gehazi, Call this woman. When Gehazi had called her, she came and stood before him. And Elisha told him to say to her, Thou hast been very kind to us, what shall be done for thee? Is there anything thou wouldst have me ask for thee from the king, or from the captain of the army? But she answered that she was satisfied with the things that she had; and she went away again. Then Elisha said to Gehazi, What is to be done for her? Gehazi answered, She has no child. And Elisha said, Call her. When Gehazi called her she came again and stood in the door. Then Elisha told her that the Lord would give her a son. And the words that Elisha spoke came true, for after these things the Lord gave her a son.

When the child was grown, he went out one day in the field to his father, among the reapers. And while he was there he grew sick, and cried to his father, My head, my head. His father said to one of the young men, Carry him to his mother. When the young man had carried him to her, the boy sat in her lap till noon, and then died. And she took him up to the chamber which she had made for Elisha, and laid him on the bed, and shut the door and went out. And she called to her husband, saying, Send me, I pray thee, one of the young men, and one of the asses, that I may make haste to the prophet and come back again. Now her husband did not know that the boy was dead, and he said to her, Why wilt thou go to the prophet to-day? This is not a feast day nor the sabbath. She answered, It is well for me to go. Then she rode on the ass, and said to the servant who went with her, Drive on, and make haste, and do not stop till I bid thee. So she came to Elisha at mount Carmel.

When Elisha saw her a good way off, he said to Gehazi, his servant, Look, yonder comes that Shunamite. Run to meet her, and say, Is it well with thee? Is it well with thy husband? Is it well with the child? And Gehazi ran and asked her. She answered, It is well. When she came to Elisha, she kneeled down, and caught him by the feet, and Gehazi came near to thrust her away. But Elisha said, Let her alone, for her soul is troubled within her, and the Lord hath not told me what her trouble is. And the woman said to Elisha, Did I ask that I might have a son? Then he knew that the boy was dead.

And he said to Gehazi, Make ready, take my staff in thy hand and go to the child. Go in haste; if thou meet any man

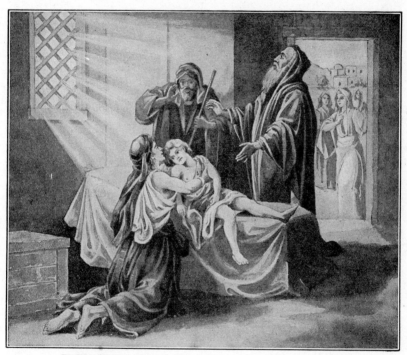

ELISHA BRINGS TO LIFE THE SON OF THE SHUNAMITE WOMAN

by the way, do not stop to speak with him, and if any man speak to thee, do not stop to answer him; and lay my staff upon the face of the child. But the woman said to Elisha, As surely as the Lord liveth, and as thou art living, I will not go without thee. Then he rose up and went after her. Now Gehazi had gone on before them, and he came to the woman's house and went up into the prophet's chamber and laid the staff on the face of the child. But the child did not speak, nor hear; therefore

Gehazi turned back to meet Elisha, and he came to him and said, The child has not awaked.

When Elisha came into the house the child was dead, and lying upon the bed. He went into the chamber, therefore, and shut the door and prayed to the Lord. And he got up on the bed, and lay upon the child, and put his mouth upon the child's mouth, and his eyes upon the child's eyes, and his

THE BOY GOES OUT WITH HIS MOTHER

hands upon his hands; and he stretched himself upon the child, and the child's flesh grew warm. Then Elisha came out of the chamber, and walked for a while up and down in the house. And he went up and stretched himself again upon the child; and the child sneezed seven times, and opened his eyes and came to life again. And Elisha spoke to Gehazi, saying, Call this Shunamite. So Gehazi called her; and when she had come into the chamber, Elisha said to her, Take thy son.

Then she bowed down to the ground in thankfulness, and took her son and went out.

And Elisha came to Gilgal. While the sons of the prophets who lived there were sitting before him, he said to his servants, Set the great pot on the fire, and boil pottage for the sons of the prophets to eat. And one of them went out into the field to gather herbs for the pottage, and found a wild vine which was poisonous; but he did not know that it was poisonous, and he gathered his lap full of it, and when he came into the house, sprinkled it into the pot. After the pottage was cooked, they poured it out for the men to eat. But as they were eating, they tasted the vine and cried, O thou prophet, there is poison in the pot! And they could not eat of it. Elisha said to them, Bring here some meal. And they brought it, and he cast it into the pot; then he said, Pour out now, that you may eat. And they ate of it, and it did them no harm.

And there came a man with a present for Elisha of twenty loaves of bread, and some ears of corn. Then Elisha told his servant to give them to the sons of the prophets, for they wanted food, because there was a scarceness of bread in the land. But the servant said, What, shall I set so small a quantity before a hundred men, that they may eat? Elisha answered, Set it before them, for thus saith the Lord, They shall all have enough, and some shall be left. Then the servant obeyed, and as the food was divided among the people, the Lord caused the twenty loaves of bread and the ears of corn to increase so that there was enough for them all. And after they had eaten, some was still left.

---

2 KINGS V–VII (5–7)

ELISHA HEALS NAAMAN OF HIS LEPROSY. GEHAZI TAKES A PRESENT FROM NAAMAN. ELISHA MAKES THE AXE FLOAT IN JORDAN. BENHADAD'S ARMY IS STRUCK WITH BLINDNESS AT DOTHAN. THE SYRIANS BESIEGE SAMARIA. IN THE FAMINE A WOMAN EATS HER SON. ELISHA FORETELLS THE END OF THE SIEGE.

Now Naaman, the captain of the army of the Syrians, was a great man with his master, the king of Syria, because he had gone out to war against the king's enemies, and gained the victory over them. Naaman was also a mighty and brave soldier, but he was a leper. And the Syrians had brought away captive out of the land of Israel a little maid who waited on Naaman's wife. And one day she said to her mistress, I wish that my master could see the prophet that is in Samaria, for he would cure him of his leprosy. And it was told Benhadad, the king of Syria, what the little maid said. Then the king spoke to Naaman, saying, Thou shalt go to Samaria, and I will give thee a letter to the king of Israel who lives there.

So Naaman started to go, and took with him ten talents of silver, six thousand pieces of gold, and ten changes of raiment, that he might have a present for the man who should make him well. And he came to the city of Samaria, and brought the letter to Jehoram, king of Israel. Benhadad's letter said, I have sent Naaman my servant, to thee, that thou mayest cure him of his leprosy. When the king of Israel had read the letter, he was troubled, and rent his clothes, and said to his servants, Have I the power of God, that I can cure this man of his leprosy? See now, how Benhadad is seeking for an excuse to make a quarrel against me.

But when Elisha heard that the king had rent his clothes and was troubled, he sent word to him, saying, Why hast thou rent thy clothes? Let the man come now to me, and he shall know that there is indeed a prophet in Israel. So Naaman came with his horses, and with his chariot, and stood at the door of the house of Elisha. And Elisha sent out a messenger to him, saying, Go, wash seven times in the river Jordan, and thou shalt be clean; that is, made well.

But when the messenger came to Naaman, and told him these words, he was angry, and said, I thought the prophet would surely come out to me himself, and pray to the Lord his God, and put his hand upon me and make me well. Are not the rivers in my own country better than all the rivers in the land of Israel? So he turned and went away in a rage. But his servants came near to him and said, My father, if the prophet had bid thee do some hard thing that thou mightest be made well, wouldst thou not have done it? How much better then it would be to obey him, when he tells thee only to wash, and be clean.

Then Naaman went down and dipped himself seven times in the river Jordan, and his flesh grew pure and clean as the flesh of a little child, and he was made well of his leprosy. And he went back to the house of Elisha, he and all the men who were with him, and he said, Now I know there is no other God

NAAMAN DIPS SEVEN TIMES IN THE RIVER JORDAN

in all the earth, but the God of Israel? Then he said to Elisha, I pray thee take a present from thy servant. But Elisha answered, As surely as the Lord liveth, I will take no present from thee. And Naaman begged him, but he would not.

Then Naaman asked permission to take from the land of Israel some earth, as much as two mules could carry, that he might make an altar with it, when he should go back to his own land; for he said, that he would never again offer a burnt offering to any other god but to the Lord. Now Naaman's

master, the king of Syria, was an idolater; he worshipped idols
And Naaman said that when his master should go into the
idol's house to worship, he would want Naaman to go also, that
he might lean on Naaman's arm. And Naaman asked Elisha
whether the Lord would forgive him when he went into the idol's
house with his master, and bowed down with his master before
the idol, if he did not worship it in his heart? And Elisha told
him to go in peace.

And Naaman left Elisha's house to go back to his own land.
But when he had gone a little way, Gehazi, the servant of Elisha,
said to himself, My master would take no present from this
Naaman, but as surely as the Lord liveth, I will run after him
and take something for myself. So Gehazi followed Naaman,
and when Naaman saw him running after him, he stopped his
chariot and came down to meet him, and said, Is all well? Ge
hazi answered, All is well; but my master sent me to tell thee,
that since thou didst leave him, there are come to him two young
men who are sons of the prophets; and he asks thee to give them
a talent of silver and two changes of garments. Naaman answered, I pray thee, take two talents. And Naaman took two
talents of silver bound in two bags, and two changes of raiment,
and gave them to two of his servants to carry for Gehazi, because they were heavy; and they carried them before him.
But when they came to Elisha's house, Gehazi took them from
the servants' hands and hid them in a secret place; and the men
went back to Naaman again.

Then Gehazi came in and stood before his master. Now the
Lord had told Elisha what Gehazi had done; so when he
came and stood before him, Elisha said, Where hast thou been,
Gehazi? Gehazi answered, Thy servant has been nowhere.
Elisha said, Did I not know it, when Naaman came down from
his chariot to meet thee? Is this a time for us to take money, and
garments, and riches? Therefore, because thou hast done this
thing, the leprosy which Naaman has been cured of shall be
on thee and on thy children forever. And as Elisha spoke,
the leprosy came on Gehazi, and he went out from him covered
with it, as white as snow.

And the sons of the prophets spoke to Elisha, saying, Behold now the house in which we live is too small for us. Let us go, we pray thee, to the river Jordan and cut down trees, and take each of us, a beam, and build a larger house in which we may live. And one of them said to Elisha, I pray thee go with us. Elisha said, I will go. Then he went with them, and when they came to Jordan they cut down trees there. But while one of

ELISHA MAKES THE AXE FLOAT

them was doing it, the head of his axe flew off from the handle and fell into the water. And he came to Elisha and said, Alas, master, for it was borrowed. Elisha said, Where did it fall? The young man showed him the place. Then Elisha cut down a stick from a tree, and threw it into the river where the axe had fallen, and the iron axe rose and floated on the top of the water. And Elisha said to the young man, Take it up. And he put out his hand and took it.

After this Benhadad, king of Syria, made war against Israel, and commanded his soldiers where they should go to find Jehoram, king of Israel, and take him captive. But when they came to the place, Jehoram had fled, because Elisha had told him the Syrians were coming there. And so it happened wherever the Syrians went to find Jehoram. Then Benhadad was greatly troubled about this thing, for he knew not who told the king of Israel, but thought it must be one of his own servants. Therefore Benhadad called his servants to him, and asked them, saying, Will you not tell me which of you is on the king of Israel's side? One of them answered, None of us is on his side, O king; it is Elisha the prophet, who tells him where thou dost send us; he tells him also the words thou dost speak, even when thou art shut up in thy bed-chamber.

Then the king of Syria said, Go, and inquire where Elisha is, that I may send and take him. When they had inquired, they came and told Benhadad that he was in the city of Dothan. Therefore Benhadad sent horses and chariots and soldiers to Dothan, and they came by night and spread themselves around the city. In the morning, when Elisha's servant had risen up early and gone out of the house, he saw them. And he came to Elisha, saying, Alas, my master, what shall we do? Elisha answered, Fear not, for we have more on our side than the king of Syria has on his. Then Elisha prayed that the Lord would make his servant able to see who were there to take care of him. And the Lord made the servant see; and, behold, the mountain on which the city stood was full of horses and chariots of fire, that the Lord had sent to guard Elisha.

When Benhadad's soldiers came to the city to take him, Elisha prayed that the Lord would send blindness upon them. And the Lord did as Elisha asked, and made them blind, so that they groped about, needing some one to lead them. And Elisha went to them, and said, Come after me, and I will bring you to the man you seek. Then he led them to the city of Samaria, where the king of Israel lived. After they had come there, Elisha prayed to the Lord that he would open their eyes. And the Lord opened their eyes, and they saw where Elisha had led them.

Then Jehoram, king of Israel, said to Elisha, Shall I now smite them and slay them? Elisha answered, Thou shalt not slay them, but shalt set bread and water before them, that they may eat and drink, and go back to their own land. And Jehoram did as Elisha said. He made food ready for them, and when they had eaten and drunk, he sent them away; and they went back to their master, Benhadad, the king of Syria.

But not long after this, Benhadad gathered his army together and went up to fight against the city of Samaria. His soldiers besieged it, and would let no bread be brought in for the men of Israel, and there was a great famine in the city. And as the king of Israel walked among his soldiers on the top of the wall, a woman called out to him, saying, Help me, O king! He said, What aileth thee? She answered, This woman who is with me, said to me the other day, Give thy little son, that we may eat him to-day, and I will give my son to-morrow. So we killed my son and did eat him. And I said to her the next day, Give thy son that we may eat him; and she would not, but took him and hid him.

When king Jehoram heard the words of the woman, he rent his clothes, for it grieved him to know that the famine was so dreadful in the city, and that such a thing had been done among the people. But Jehoram was a wicked man, like Ahab, his father. It was for his sins, and the sins of the people, that God sent these troubles upon them. Jehoram should have repented, and asked God to take his troubles away. Instead of this, he blamed them on Elisha, and said that the prophet should be put to death that very day. But Elisha knew the king would send a messenger to kill him. And when the messenger came to his house, Elisha commanded the men who were with him to shut the door, so that he might not come in.

Then the king himself came to Elisha's house, leaning on the arm of one of his officers. And Elisha told them that the Lord said the famine should cease, and that on the morrow there would be plenty of food in the city. But the officer, on whose arm the king leaned, would not believe it. Then Elisha told him that, because he did not believe the words of the Lord, he should see those words come true, but should not taste of the food which the Lord would send.

Now four men of the children of Israel, who were lepers, sat together by the gate of the city. And they said to one another, Why do we sit here until we starve? If we go into the city the famine is in the city, and we shall die there. If we sit still here, we have nothing to eat, and we shall die here also. Come, therefore, let us go out to the army of the Syrians. If they do not kill us we shall live, and if they kill us we shall but die. So they rose up in the evening, and went out to the camp of the Syrians, but when they came to it no man was there. For the Lord had made the Syrians think that they heard the noise of chariots, and horses, and a great army, coming out against them. Therefore they had risen up, as it grew dark, and left their tents and their horses, and everything that was in their camp, and fled for their lives.

When the lepers had gone all through the camp and seen no man, they went into one of the tents and ate and drank of the food that was there. They also took silver and gold and raiment that they found, and went away and hid them. And they came again and went into another tent, and carried away more silver and gold, and hid it also. Then they said to one another, We are not doing right, because we have good news for the people, yet do not tell them. If we stay here till morning, some punishment will be sent upon us. Now, therefore come, let us go and tell the king of Israel.

So they came to the city, and called to the porters who watched at the gate, saying, We have been to the camp of the Syrians, and found no man there, but horses tied, and asses and tents, just as they were left. Then the porters went and told the king. And the king rose up in the night, and said to his servants, I will tell you now what the Syrians have done. They know that we are hungry; therefore they have gone from the camp a little way, and hid themselves, so that when we shall come out of the city to get food, they may rise up and take us captives.

And one of the king's servants answered him, saying, Let us take some of the horses that are left alive and go out and see.

They took, therefore, two chariot horses; and the king sent men with them to go and look for the army of the Syrians. And the men went as far as the river Jordan, and could not find them. But all the road was strewed with garments and vessels that the Syrians had thrown away in their haste. So the men came back to Samaria and told the king.

When the people heard it, they went out to the camp of the Syrians, and brought away all the flour and the grain that the Syrians had left. So the famine was ended, and there was plenty of food in the city. And the king sent that officer on whose arm he leaned, and who would not believe the words of Elisha, to stand at the gate and keep the people in order. But the people crowded on him in such numbers, that he was trodden under foot and killed. So it happened to him as Elisha had said; he saw the famine ended, but did not taste of the food that God sent for the people.

------

2 KINGS VIII–X (8–10), XIII (13)

ELISHA TELLS THE SHUNAMITE OF THE COMING FAMINE. HE PROPHESIES THAT HAZAEL WILL BE KING OVER SYRIA. JEHU IS ANOINTED KING OF ISRAEL. JEHORAM AND JEZEBEL ARE SLAIN. THE REIGNS OF JE-HOAHAZ AND JEHOASH. ELISHA DIES.

AFTER these things, Elisha spoke to the woman whose son he had brought to life again, saying, Go, thou and thy family, to live a while in some other land, for the Lord is going to send a famine on the land of Israel which shall last seven years. And the woman did as Elisha told her; she went with her family into the land of the Philistines, and lived there for seven years. Then she came back again into the land of Israel, but found that, while she was gone, another person had taken her house and her fields.

And she went with her son to king Jehoram, to beg of him that they might be given back to her. When she came to the king's house, Gehazi, the servant of Elisha, was there; the king was talking with him, and said to him, Tell me, I pray thee, of all the great things that Elisha has done. While Gehazi was telling how Elisha had brought a dead body to life, the woman and her son came in to speak with the king. And Gehazi said, My lord, O king, this is the woman, and this is her son whom Elisha brought to life again. And when the king asked her about it, she told him it was true. Then he commanded one of his officers, saying, Give back to this woman her house and her land, and enough money also to pay for the fruit and the grain that have grown in her fields, since she has been in the land of the Philistines.

Elisha came to Damascus, where Benhadad, the king of Syria, lived, and it was told the king that he had come. Now Benhadad was sick, and when he heard that Elisha had come to the city, he said to Hazael, one of his officers, Take a present with thee, and go to meet Elisha, the prophet, and tell him to ask of God for me whether I shall get well of my sickness. So Hazael went to meet Elisha, and took a present with him, some of all the good things of Damascus, as much as forty camels would carry.

Then he came and stood before Elisha, and said, The king of Syria has sent me to ask thee whether he shall get well of his sickness? Elisha answered, Go and tell him that he is not so sick but that he might get well, and yet the Lord has shown me that he will die. Then Elisha looked at Hazael, without speaking, until Hazael was ashamed; and Elisha wept. Hazael said, Why weepeth my lord? Elisha answered, Because I know the evil things that thou wilt do to the children of Israel; their cities thou wilt set on fire, their young men thou wilt slay with the sword, and their women and little children thou wilt cruelly put to death. Then Hazael was astonished, and said, What, is thy servant a dog, that he should do these things? Elisha answered, The Lord has shown me that thou shalt be king over Syria.

So Hazael went back to king Benhadad, who asked him, saying, What said Elisha to thee? Hazael answered, He told me that thou shouldst surely get well. But the next day Hazael took a thick cloth and dipped it in water, and brought it into the chamber where the king was sick. And he spread it over the king's face, so that he could not breathe, and

Benhadad, the king of Syria, died; and Hazael made himself king of that land.

Now Jezebel, the wicked wife of Ahab, was still living in the city of Jezreel, and Jehoram, her son, the king of Israel, was there with her.

And Elisha called a young man, who was one of the sons of the prophets, and said to him, Carry some oil with thee, and go to the city of Ramoth-gilead, and there look for Jehu, who is a captain in the king of Israel's army. When thou hast found him, take him into a secret chamber alone, and pour the oil on his head, and say, The Lord has anointed thee to be king over Israel. Then open the door and flee, stay not. So the young man went to Ramoth-gilead, and found there the captains of the army sitting together, and Jehu was with them. And the young man went to them, and said, I have a message for thee, O captain. Jehu said, For which one of us? The young man answered, For thee.

Then Jehu rose up, and went with him into the house, and the young man poured the oil on his head, and said to him, Thus saith the Lord, I have anointed thee to be king over Israel. And after thou art made king, thou shalt put to death all who are left of the family of Ahab, that I may punish them for killing my prophets, and for the death of all my servants whom the wicked Jezebel has slain. For the whole family of Ahab shall be destroyed, as the family of Jeroboam was destroyed, till not one of them is left. The dogs shall eat Jezebel in the city of Jezreel, and there shall be no one to bury her. When the young man had spoken these words to Jehu, he opened the door of the house and fled.

And Jehu came out again to the captains of the army, and one of them asked him, saying, What did this mad fellow say to thee? He answered, He told me that the Lord anointed me to be king over Israel. Then the captains all made haste and blew with trumpets, and cried out, Jehu is king! So they made Jehu king instead of Jehoram.

And Jehu said to the captains, Let no one go to Jezreel to tell king Jehoram of what we have done, for I myself will go there.

24

Then Jehu made ready his chariot, and rode to Jezreel. As he came near the city, the watchman, who stood on the tower over the gate, saw him and the men who were with him. And the watchman told king Jehoram of it. Jehoram said, Send out a horseman to ask whether they are coming for peace or for war? So there went out a man on horseback to meet Jehu, and when he met him, he asked, Are you coming for peace or for war? But Jehu would not answer him; he commanded the man to go behind his chariot, and follow after it.

Then Jehoram sent out another man, who came and asked the same question. And Jehu would not answer him, but commanded him also to go behind his chariot and follow after it. When Jehoram saw that the men did not come back to tell what Jehu said, he got into his chariot, and rode out himself to meet him. And he came to him and said, Is it peace, Jehu? Jehu answered, How can there be peace while the sins of thy mother Jezebel are so many? When Jehoram heard this, he turned the horses of his chariot to flee, for he saw that Jehu had come to fight against him. But Jehu drew a bow with all his might, and shot an arrow at Jehoram, that went into his heart, and he fell down dead in his chariot. Then Jehu commanded his captain to throw Jehoram's dead body on the ground. The place where he threw it was in the vineyard that Ahab, Jehoram's father, had taken from Naboth; for Naboth's vineyard was at the city of Jezreel.

Then Jehu came into the city. And Jezebel, Jehoram's mother, heard of it, and she put on her ornaments, and painted her face, and looked out at a window. And as Jehu came in at the gate of the city, she spoke to him. But he looked up at the window, and said to the men in the house with her, Who is on my side? And there looked out to him two or three officers. Then Jehu said to them, Throw her down. So they threw her down, and her blood was sprinkled on the wall, and the horses of Jehu's chariot trod her under their feet. After Jehu had come out of his chariot, and had eaten and drunk, he said to his servants, Go, see now where the dead body of that wicked woman is, and bury her, for she was a king's daughter. And they went to bury her, but could find only her skull and her feet and the palms of her hands, for the dogs had eaten her flesh.

And Jehu caused all the family of Ahab to be put to death. So the words of Elijah came true, which he spoke fifteen years before, when Ahab took from Naboth the vineyard which his

THE DEATH OF JEZEBEL

father had left him. At that time Elijah told Ahab that the Lord would send evil upon him and his family, until not one of them was left alive. And of Jezebel Elijah said, The dogs shall eat Jezebel by the wall of Jezreel. Yet Jehu did not do these things because he wanted to obey the Lord, but, like Baasha, who slew the family of Jeroboam, Jehu did them because he wanted to be great, and to make himself king. For he took no care in other things to obey the Lord with all his heart, but did wickedly like the kings who had lived before him. He reigned for twenty-eight years; and he died, and Jehoahaz, his son, was made king over Israel.

Jehoahaz disobeyed God as his father had done, and God was angry with him and the people of Israel. He sent against them Hazael, king of Syria. We have heard how Hazael murdered his master by spreading a wet cloth over his face while he was sick, and so made himself king. But God often sent wicked kings as a punishment against the children of Israel; and now he sent Hazael, the king of Syria. And Hazael did to them as Elisha had said he would do; he burned their cities and put their young men and women to death. He destroyed the army of Israel also, and allowed Jehoahaz to have only fifty horsemen, ten chariots, and ten thousand foot-men, so that he might not be able to rebel against him. Jehoahaz reigned seventeen years, and he died, and Jehoash his son was made king.

Now Elisha was sick and about to die. And king Jehoash came to see him, and stood by his bed and wept over him, and cried out as Elisha had cried to Elijah, O my father, my father, the chariot of Israel and the horsemen thereof. Elisha said to king Jehoash, Take a bow and arrows. And he took them. Elisha said to the king, Put thy hand on the bow. And he put his hand on it; and Elisha put his hands upon the king's hands. And he said, Open the window toward the east. And he opened it. Elisha said, Shoot; and the king shot. Then Elisha told the king what that arrow meant; he said it meant that Jehoash should gain the victory over the Syrians, and set the children of Israel free from them.

And Elisha spoke to the king again, and told him to take the arrows in his hand, and strike with them on the ground. And the king struck with them three times and stopped. And Elisha was angry, and said, Thou shouldst have struck five or six times, for then thou wouldst have smitten the Syrians till they were destroyed; but now thou shalt smite them only three times.

KING JEHOASH SHOOTS THE ARROW

And Elisha died and they buried him.   After this the Moabites came into the land to rob the men of Israel.   And as some
of the people were carrying out a dead man to bury him, they
saw a band of the Moabites coming, then, because they were
afraid, they did not go to the grave that was made ready for
the man, but lowered him in haste into Elisha's sepulchre.   And
when the dead body touched the bones of Elisha the man came
to life again, and stood up on his feet.

2 KINGS XIII–XVII (13–17).   AMOS

JEHOASH DIES AND JEROBOAM REIGNS.   THE PROPHETS AMOS AND HOSEA
ARE SENT.   THE REIGNS OF ZACHARIAH, SHALLUM, MENAHEM, PEKA-
HIAH, PEKAH, AND HOSHEA.   THE TEN TRIBES ARE CARRIED AWAY
CAPTIVE.

AFTER Elisha was dead, king Jehoash fought against the
Syrians and gained the victory over them three times, as Elisha
had told him he should, but he was not able wholly to destroy
them.   Jehoash was king for sixteen years, and he died, and
they buried him in the city of Samaria; and Jeroboam, his son,
was made king in his place.

The Lord was kind to Jeroboam and the people of Israel,
for he saw the sufferings which their enemies caused them, and
he pitied them.   He helped Jeroboam as he had helped Jehoash, his father, in fighting against the Syrians, so that Jeroboam
took from them two of their cities, Damascus and Hamath.
But the men of Israel did not thank God for his kindness.
Although he helped them in their trouble, and saved them from
their enemies, they still worshipped the golden calves.

Then the Lord sent Amos the prophet to speak to them.
Amos came and said that they were the only people in all the
earth whom the Lord had chosen for his own, yet, instead of
serving him, they served idols, and disobeyed his commandments.   They were cruel to the poor, they deceived and robbed
one another when they sold corn and wheat, they hated those
persons who did justly and told the truth, but took bribes from
the wicked and allowed them to go on in their wickedness.

The Lord had seen all their sins, Amos said, and had kept

back the rain from their fields, and sent famine and pestilence into their land, to show them he was angry; still they would not turn from their evil ways. Therefore a greater punishment should be sent upon them. There would be weeping and wailing in their streets, and their vineyards; for an enemy should come who would gain the victory over them, and treat them cruelly, and they should be carried away captives to other lands. Yet, Amos told them that if they would repent and obey the Lord, the Lord would forgive them.

· But woe, or sorrow, Amos said, should come to those who would not think of their sins, or of the punishment that was coming on the people; who put all such thoughts out of their minds, and cared only to enjoy themselves; who lay on rich couches, and on beds of ivory; who ate lambs out of the flock, and fatted calves from the stall; who sang to instruments of music, and drank wine out of bowls. Those persons should be among the first to be carried away captives.

After Amos had spoken these things to the people, Amaziah, who was the chief priest at the idol's temple at Bethel, sent to king Jeroboam, saying, Amos is speaking against thee. He says that thou shalt be slain, and the people carried away captive. Amaziah spoke to Amos also, and said to him, Go out of our land into the land of Judah, and prophesy to the people there, but do not prophesy any more here in Bethel. For this is the place where king Jeroboam lives, and where he worships the golden calves.

Then Amos answered Amaziah, saying, I was not always a prophet, neither was I the son of a prophet; I was only a herdsman and gatherer of wild figs. But as I was driving my flock out in the field, the Lord said to me, Go, prophesy to the children of Israel. Hear then, Amaziah, what the Lord commands me to say to thee. Thou tellest me not to prophesy to the people, when the Lord has sent me to prophesy to them. Now, therefore, the Lord will send his punishment upon thee also: thy wife shall go away from thy home and leave thee alone; thy sons and thy daughters shall be slain by the sword, and thou thyself shalt die in a heathen land.

King Jeroboam and the people heard the words of Amos, which the Lord had sent him to speak; and not the words of Amos only, but of the prophet Hosea also, who came and told them of their sins, and of the great punishment which the Lord would send; he, too, begged them to repent, that the Lord might forgive them. Yet they would not listen to the words of the prophets, neither would they repent as the Lord commanded. Jeroboam was king forty-one years, and he died, and Zachariah, his son, was made king in his stead.

Zachariah was king in the city of Samaria but six months. Then Shallum rebelled against him and killed him, and made himself king. But after Shallum had reigned only one month, Menahem came to Samaria and slew him, and Menahem was made king.

Menahem reigned ten years, and all that time he did evil. And Pul, the king of Assyria, came up against him. Then Menahem was afraid, and promised to pay Pul a thousand talents of silver if he would be his friend and help him, and allow him still to be king. Menahem had not this money himself, but he forced the rich men of his kingdom to give it to him, and when they had given it, he paid it to Pul. So Pul took the thousand talents and allowed Menahem still to be king over Israel. And Pul went back to his own land. After this Menahem died, and Pekahiah, his son, was made king in his place.

The Bible tells us that Pekahiah sinned as Jeroboam, the first king of Israel, had done. We have read that Jeroboam was the one who first set up the golden calves as idols, and told the people that these were their gods that brought them up out of Egypt. And Pekahiah, when he was made king, did not put down these idols, but he went to their temples to worship them, and taught the people to go there, instead of going to Jerusalem to worship God. After he had been king for two years, Pekah, the son of one of his captains, came into the king's palace in the city of Samaria, and killed him; and Pekah was made king.

Pekah also did wickedly. He went up to Jerusalem to fight against that city, but was not able to take it. And the king of

Assyria came with an army and made war against him, and carried away many of the people. After Pekah had been king twenty years, Hoshea rebelled against him and killed him, and made himself king.

Hoshea was king for nine years, and he did evil and displeased the Lord. Against him also the king of Assyria came up, and Hoshea promised to be his servant and obey him, and to

THE KING OF ASSYRIA DEMANDS TRIBUTE

pay him tribute money each year. But he did not keep his promise, for after the king of Assyria had gone back to his own land, Hoshea sent word to the king of Egypt, asking that king to help him against the king of Assyria; neither did Hoshea send the king of Assyria tribute money as he had done in years before. Then the king of Assyria bound Hoshea and put him in prison, and came up with an army against Samaria and besieged it for three years, until he took the city.

We have seen, by what we have now read, how wicked the people of Israel had been. Ever since they separated from the tribes of Judah and Benjamin, and made a kingdom of their own, they had been sinning against God. For instead of doing as he taught them, they chose to do as the heathen nations did that lived around them. Those nations would not serve God, because he commanded them to be pure and holy; they served false gods, who, they pretended, allowed them to do everything that was wicked. The Bible tells us they worshipped their false gods in the high places. These were places where altars and images were set up. The heathen people made them on mountains and hills, and there they worshipped their false gods.

And the people of Israel did like them. They, too, made high places on the mountains and hills, and they made them in their cities also. We are not told how they made them in their cities. Perhaps they were mounds of earth heaped up, or platforms of wood or stone, we cannot tell. All we know about them is that idols and altars were placed there. And there the people burnt incense and offered sacrifice to the idols. They kindled fires also, as the heathen nations used to do, and made their sons and their daughters go through the fires and be burned, because, they said, the idols would be pleased with it.

And God was very angry with the people of Israel for these things. Yet he waited long for them to turn from evil ways; as we have read, he sent famine and pestilence and war into their land to show them he was angry. When they still continued to disobey him, he sent his prophets to warn them. We have been told how those prophets came and preached to the people, telling them of the punishment that was coming upon them, and begging them to repent and cease doing evil, so that God might forgive them, and keep them for his children: but they would not. So at last God did to them what his prophets had said he would do. He drove the people of Israel out of Canaan, as he had driven out the heathen nations that lived there before them. For the king of Assyria, after he had shut up Hoshea in prison, went through all the land of Israel and took the people and carried them away captive to the land of Assyria. There he gave them cities to live in; but he would not let them come back to the land of Israel again.

So the kingdom of Israel was ended. It had lasted two hundred and fifty-four years, ever since the ten tribes chose Jeroboam for their king. Nineteen kings had ruled over them during that time, every one of whom did evil and disobeyed the

THE PEOPLE CARRIED AWAY CAPTIVE TO ASSYRIA

Lord. The king of Assyria sent people from his own land to live in the cities of Israel, where the ten tribes had lived; and they came and lived there, and took those cities for their own. But we do not read that the ten tribes ever returned, and no one can tell what afterward became of them.

We have now finished the story of the kingdom of Israel, and will go back two hundred and fifty-four years, to begin the story of the kingdom of Judah.

THE STORY OF THE KINGDOM OF JUDAH

1 KINGS XII–XXII (12–22).   2 CHRON. XI–XXI (11–21)

REHOBOAM, HAVING GROWN RICH AND STRONG, DISOBEYS GOD AND WORSHIPS
IDOLS.   THE KING OF EGYPT COMES UP AGAINST HIM.   THE REIGNS OF
ABIJAH, ASA, AND JEHOSHAPHAT.

WE have read that Rehoboam, Solomon's son, was made
king over the tribes of Judah and Benjamin, and that he lived
at Jerusalem, where the temple stood which his father had built.
We have read also that Jeroboam would not allow the people
of the ten tribes to go to Jerusalem to worship at the temple,
as God had commanded; but he set up two golden calves in
that part of the land where the ten tribes lived, and taught the
people to worship them.

Yet the priests and the Levites, who were living among the
ten tribes at that time, would not worship the golden calves.
They came, with many other persons, to live at Jerusalem,
and chose Rehoboam for their king. They made his kingdom
greater and stronger by coming, because there were so many of
them, and because they were the ones whom the Lord would
bless. And for three years Rehoboam and his people did what
was right and obeyed the Lord.

But when he grew rich and strong, and was no longer in fear
that his kingdom would be taken from him, he ceased obeying
the Lord. For he and all the people of Judah began to worship idols, and, like the people of Israel, they built high places
in the cities, and on every high hill, and there they set up their
idols and worshipped them. Then the Lord sent the king of
Egypt against Judah. That king brought with him twelve
hundred chariots, and sixty thousand horsemen, and a very great
army. He took many cities in the land, and afterward came
up to Jerusalem. And Rehoboam and the princes of the people
were afraid of him.

Then there came a prophet who said to them, Thus saith the
Lord, You have left off serving me, therefore I will not help you
against the king of Egypt. When Rehoboam and the princes

heard this, they bowed their heads, and confessed that the Lord did right to punish them. Then the Lord sent his prophet again to tell them that, because they humbled themselves before him, the king of Egypt should not destroy them, and yet, because they had done wickedly, he should make them his servants. So the king of Egypt came with his army into Jerusalem, and took away much gold and silver out of the temple, and out of the king's palace. But afterward he returned to his own land.

Rehoboam was forty-one years old when he was made king; he reigned seventeen years; then he died, and was buried in Jerusalem, and Abijah, his son, was made king in his place.

There was war between Abijah, king of Judah, and Jeroboam, king of Israel. Abijah made ready for the battle with an army of four hundred thousand men, but Jeroboam had eight hundred thousand. Before the battle began, Abijah stood on a mountain where Jeroboam and his men could hear him, and he said to them, Hear me, Jeroboam, and all you men of Israel, do you not know that God made David and his sons to be kings over the children of Israel forever? Yet Jeroboam has rebelled, and made himself king. And he has brought out wicked men to fight with us. You are a great multitude, and have with you the golden calves which Jeroboam made for your gods, but we worship the Lord: he is with us, and is our captain. O, then, you men of Israel, do not fight against the Lord, for if you do you shall not prosper.

But while Abijah was speaking, Jeroboam led out his army and the battle began. And the men of Judah cried to the Lord for help, and the priests who were with them blew on their trumpets. Then the men of Judah gave a shout, and as they did so, God helped them, and Jeroboam and his army fled away. And Abijah and his people followed them, and fought against them, and a great number of the men of Israel fell down slain. So the men of Judah gained the victory, because they trusted in God. And Abijah pursued Jeroboam into the land of the ten tribes, and took cities from him. Jeroboam was never able to bring out an army against Abijah again. Abijah reigned for three years, then he died, and Asa, his son, was made king.

Asa did what was right, and pleased the Lord. And the Lord gave the people rest from war. Then Asa said to them, Let us build more cities in our land, with walls around them, and towers, and gates, and bars, so that our enemies cannot take them from us. And they built more cities, and their kingdom grew strong and prospered.

Asa had an army of three hundred thousand men out of the tribe of Judah that carried shields and spears, and of two hundred

JEROBOAM'S ARMY DRIVEN AWAY BY THE MEN OF JUDAH

and eighty thousand out of the tribe of Benjamin that carried bows and arrows; all these were brave soldiers. Yet the king of Ethiopia made war against him with an army much greater than his. And Asa came out of the battle, and he cried to the Lord, and said, It is no trouble for thee to help us whether we have many soldiers or few; help us, O Lord, our God, for in thy name we go out against this great multitude. O Lord, let them not gain the victory over us. So the Lord helped the men of Judah in the battle, and gave them the victory; and they took much spoil from the Ethiopians, and carried away great numbers of their sheep and camels. Afterward, Asa and his army came back to Jerusalem.

And the Lord sent a prophet who spoke to them, saying, Hear me, Asa, and all you men of Judah and Benjamin: The Lord will be with you, to help you, as long as you shall serve him; but if you forsake him he will forsake you. Therefore fear not to do what is right, and you shall be rewarded. When Asa heard these words, he took courage, and put away the idols that the people had set up through the land, and repaired and made new the altar of burnt offering that stood in the court of the temple; for the people had allowed it to go to decay. Then he gathered all the people together at Jerusalem, and he offered up, out of the spoil that had been taken from the Ethiopians, seven hundred oxen and seven thousand sheep. And the people made a covenant with the Lord, and promised to serve him with all their heart and with all their soul; and they said that whoever would not serve him should be put to death, whether he was rich or poor, whether it was a man or a woman.

After Asa had been king over Judah for thirty-five years, Baasha, the king of Israel, came up to make war against him. Then Asa, instead of praying to the Lord for help, took silver and gold out of the temple, and out of his own palace, and sent it to the king of Syria, saying, Behold, I have sent thee a present of silver and gold. Go, therefore, and make war against Baasha, king of Israel, so that he may not fight against me. And the king of Syria did as Asa asked him. He sent his army against some of the cities of Israel, and when Baasha heard of it he returned to his own land, and fought against Asa no more.

But the Lord sent a prophet to reprove Asa for seeking help from the king of Syria instead of from him. Were not the Ethiopians a great army, the prophet asked, with very many chariots and horsemen? Yet, because thou didst trust in the Lord, he gave thee the victory over them. For the eyes of the Lord look up and down through the whole world, to watch over those who love him, that he may help them. Thou hast done foolishly. Therefore, from this time thy enemies shall make war against thee. But Asa was angry with the prophet, and shut him up in prison for speaking these words.

After he had been king for thirty-eight years, there came a disease in his feet. It grew worse until it was very great. Yet in his sickness, he did not ask the Lord to heal him, but trusted only in his physicians. He was king forty-one years, when he died. And his servants laid him in a bed filled with sweet-smelling spices, that the apothecaries had made ready. And they buried him in a sepulchre which he had made for himself, in Jerusalem; and Jehoshaphat, his son, reigned in his stead.

The Lord was with Jehoshaphat, because from the time he was made king he did what was right. Therefore, the Lord gave him the kingdom to keep it; and all the people brought him gifts, and he had riches and honor in plenty. In the third year of his reign he sent men through all the cities of Judah, with the book which had God's laws written in it, that they might teach them to the people. And the Lord made the heathen nations afraid to come out to war against Jehoshaphat. The Philistines brought him presents and tribute money; and the Arabians brought him flocks, as many as seven thousand seven hundred sheep, and seven thousand seven hundred goats. And he became very great and had a great army. He built castles, and store cities also, in which to keep his riches.

But after this he went down to the city of Samaria, to visit Ahab, king of Israel. And Ahab killed sheep and oxen, and made a feast for him, and persuaded him to go out to war against the king of Syria. We have read how Jehoshaphat put on his royal robes, and went into the battle, and how the Syrians thought it was Ahab, and tried to kill him. But when he cried out, they turned away from following him, because God would not let them come near to put him to death. When the battle was over Jehoshaphat came back to Jerusalem.

And the Lord sent a prophet to meet him, who said, Was it right for thee to help the wicked Ahab, and to go out to war with men who hate the Lord? Therefore, the Lord is angry with thee. Yet thou hast done well in other things: in taking away the altars and the high places, where the people worshipped idols, and in making thy own heart ready to serve God. After this Jehoshaphat went no more to the city of Samaria, but lived in Jerusalem; and he went out through the land of Judah, commanding the people to put away their idols. He set judges, also, in all the cities of Judah to punish those who did wrong, and to save the innocent from harm. He said to the judges, Be careful that you act justly, for you must give account, not to me, but to the Lord, who sees all you do. Therefore, fear him.

And the Moabites, the Ammonites, and the Edomites came up to fight against Jehoshaphat. When he heard of it, he sent word to all the people that they should eat no food, but should fast and pray. And the people came out of all the cities of Judah to the temple at Jerusalem, and prayed for help. Then Jehoshaphat stood up before them, and said, O Lord, art thou not our God, who didst drive out the heathen from this land, and give it to thy people, the children of Israel? We have lived here, and we have built a temple in which to worship thee, and pray to thee. But now the Ammonites, the Moabites, and the Edomites have gathered together to drive us out of the land which thou hast given us. Wilt thou not punish them? For we are not able to fight with the great army they are bringing against us. And we know not what to do, but are looking up to thee. While Jehoshaphat prayed, all the people stood up before the Lord, with their little babes, their wives, and their children.

Then the Lord sent a prophet to speak to Jehoshaphat and the people, saying, Be not afraid of this multitude. To-morrow go out against them. You will find them by the brook in the wilderness. And you need not fight with them; only stand still, and you shall see how the Lord will save you. O men of Judah and Jerusalem, fear not, for the Lord will help you. When the prophet had spoken these words, king Jehoshaphat bowed his face to the ground, and all the people of Judah and Jerusalem fell down and worshipped.

Early in the morning they went out to meet their enemies. As they were going, Jehoshaphat said to his soldiers, Trust in the Lord and believe what his prophet has said; then you shall have the victory. And Jehoshaphat set men in front of the army to sing praises to God. As these began to praise him, God helped the men of Judah, for he caused the Moabites, the Ammonites, and the Edomites to fight with each other, and slay one another. And when the men of Judah came near, they saw their enemies lying dead upon the ground. Then they went among the slain, and gathered from their dead bodies gold and silver, and precious jewels, more than they could carry away.

JEHOSHAPHAT TELLS HIS SOLDIERS TO TRUST IN THE LORD

They were three days in gathering the spoil, there was so much of it. On the fourth day they met together in a valley near by, and blessed and thanked the Lord for giving them the victory. Therefore that valley was called the valley of Berachah, which means, the valley of Blessing. Then Jehoshaphat and all the men of Judah returned with the music of harps and trumpets to Jerusalem, and to the temple.

After this the heathen nations feared to come out against

him, and God gave him and his people rest from war. Yet Jehoshaphat did wrong again, in joining with the king of Israel to send ships to a land called Ophir, that they might bring back gold for him. And a prophet came and told him that because he had joined with that wicked king, his ships should be broken. And what the prophet said came true, for his ships were broken and wrecked at Ezion-geber, where they were built, so that they could not go to that far-off land.

Jehoshaphat reigned twenty-five years, and did what was right and pleased the Lord; then he died and was buried in Jerusalem.

---

2 KINGS IX–XIV (9–14). 2 CHRONICLES XXI–XXV (21–25)

JEHORAM SLAYS HIS BRETHREN. THE EDOMITES REBEL AGAINST HIM. THE REIGNS OF AHAZIAH, ATHALIAH, JOASH, AND AMAZIAH.

JEHOSHAPHAT left seven sons. To six of them he gave presents of silver and gold, and other precious things; he made them rulers also over some of the cities of Judah; but Jehoram, his eldest son, he made king.

Jehoram was not like his father, he did not serve God. He cared only to get the kingdom, and to keep it for himself. Because he feared that his brethren might take it from him, he killed them. He killed also some of the princes of the land, who, he thought, were not his friends.

Now the Edomites had been servants to the kings of Judah for many years before this time, but while Jehoram was king, they rebelled against him and chose a king of their own. Then Jehoram went out with all his war chariots, and fought against them in the night, but he could not overcome them and make them his servants again. For the Lord did not help him, because he had turned away from serving the Lord.

Jehoram did very wickedly. He built high places in the mountains, for the people to worship idols there, and he made the people of Judah to sin, as the kings of Israel made their people. For Jehoram had for his wife the daughter of Ahab, the wicked king of Israel. And there came a letter to him from Elijah, the prophet, saying, Thus saith the Lord,

Because thou hast not obeyed me, as Jehoshaphat thy father did, but hast done wickedly, and made the people do wickedly, and hast slain thy brethren who were better than thou art; therefore I will send trouble on thy people, thy wives, and thy children, and a great sickness shall come upon thee.

And the Lord sent the Philistines, and the Arabians against Jehoram. They came up to Jerusalem and went into his house and took away his riches. They carried away his wives also, and his sons, as captives, so that he had not one son left, save Ahaziah, the youngest. After all this the Lord sent a dreadful disease upon him, as Elijah had said. He was sick two years, and grew worse and worse, for he could not be cured. Jehoram reigned eight years, and he died, but the people did not mourn for him. They buried him in Jerusalem, but not in the sepulchre where the kings of Judah were buried. Then they made Ahaziah, his son, king in his place.

Ahaziah reigned only one year; like his father, he did wickedly; for his mother, who was the daughter of Ahab, taught him to sin. He went down to visit Jehoram, king of Israel, at Jezreel. While he was there, he rode out with Jehoram to meet Jehu, each in his chariot. We have read how Jehu drew a bow with all his might, and shot an arrow at Jehoram that went into his heart, and Jehoram fell down dead. Then Ahaziah turned his horses to flee, but Jehu followed him, saying to his servants, Kill him also in the chariot; and they killed him. Afterward the servants of Ahaziah brought his dead body in a chariot to Jerusalem, and buried him there, in the sepulchre of the kings.

When his mother, whose name was Athaliah, saw that he was dead, she took Ahaziah's sons (who were her own grandchildren) and slew them, to make herself queen. But one of his sons, a little boy named Joash, was stolen away from her, and hidden with his nurse in the temple. He was hidden there six years, for Jehoiada, the high priest, watched over him, and Athaliah, the queen, knew nothing of it. But when the six years were ended, Jehoiada showed him to the Levites and told them that he ought to be king. And the priests and Levites talked in secret together, and agreed to make Joash king.

Now there were at the temple some spears and shields that had belonged to king David; these the priests gave to the Levites. And on the day that the high priest appointed, the Levites came to the temple, and kept guard all around it with their spears in their hands, that no one might go in. And they brought Joash, who was but seven years old, out of the chamber

THE CROWNING OF JOASH

where he was hidden, and, pouring oil on his head, they anointed him; and they put the crown upon his head, and made him king over Judah; then they clapped their hands, and cried, God save the king!

When the queen heard the noise of the people running, and shouting, she came to the temple and looked in, and saw the king, standing by a pillar, with the crown on his head. The princes of the land stood by him, and all the people rejoiced, and blew on trumpets, and the singers in the temple sang to instruments of music. Then the queen was angry; she rent her clothes, and cried out, Here is rebellion! Here is rebellion! But the high priest said to the Levites, Take her out from the temple, for she must not be slain in the house of the Lord. So they took hold of her and brought her out, near to the king's palace, and slew her there.

Afterward the high priest made a covenant with king Joash, and with all the people, and they promised to serve the Lord. For the queen had served Baal, and kept a house with images of the idol in it, but the temple of the Lord she had allowed to go to decay. She had allowed her sons also to break into the temple, and carry away the sacred vessels of gold and silver, and put them into the house of Baal. But when the queen was dead all the people went to Baal's house, and tore it down, and broke the altars and images, and killed the priest of Baal. Then Jehoiada, the high priest, sent the priests of the Lord and the Levites to the temple, to attend to the worship of God there; he set porters also to watch the gates, so that no one who was forbidden might enter.

When Joash grew older and saw how the temple was broken and decayed, he called the priests and Levites to him, saying, Go out through all the cities of Judah, and gather money from the people, to mend and repair the house of the Lord. And see that you make haste in doing it. But the Levites did not make haste. Then the king sent for Jehoiada, the high priest, and said to him, Why do not the Levites bring the money to repair the house of the Lord?

So Jehoiada took a chest and bored a hole in the lid of it,

HALF SHEKEL

Upper side.   Lower side.

and set it before the door of the temple. And word was sent through all the land that every man should bring a piece of silver money, called a half shekel, as an offering to the Lord. Then all the princes and the people brought the money willingly, and cast it into the chest. As soon as much had been cast in, the high priest and the king's officer came, and emptied it out and counted it, and put it in bags and gave it to the men who were set over the carpenters, the masons, and the builders that were mending the house.

After the work was done, and the house was finished, these men brought the money that was left and gave it to the king and Jehoiada; and they had spoons and vessels of gold and silver made of it, to take the place of those which had been carried away by the sons of queen Athaliah. And Jehoiada, the high priest, caused sacrifices to be offered up at the temple every day. He persuaded the king also to obey the Lord; for though Joash had taken pains to repair the temple, he did not love God in his heart. Yet as long as Jehoiada lived he did what was right. But Jehoiada, when he was a hundred and thirty years old, died. And they buried him in Jerusalem in the same sepulchre where the kings were buried, because he had done good in Judah, obeying the Lord himself and teaching the people to obey him.

Now the princes of Judah were wicked men; for although they had worshipped at the temple while Jehoiada was alive, it was only because Jehoiada had persuaded the king to worship there, and they went to the temple with him. As soon as Jehoiada was dead they came to the king, and said that they wanted to worship at the temple no more. And the king, whose own heart was wicked, gave them permission to stay away. Then they went and worshipped idols.

And Zechariah, the priest, the son of Jehoiada, when he saw the wickedness of the princes and the people, spoke to them, saying, Why do you disobey the commandments of the Lord, and so bring trouble on the land? for you cannot prosper while you disobey him. But king Joash was angry with Zechariah for saying this, and commanded the people to stone him; then they took stones and stoned him to death, even in the court of the temple. So Joash forgot how kind Jehoiada, Zechariah's father, had been to him in making him king, and he slew Zechariah, Jehoiada's son. Zechariah, as he was dying, said to the people, The Lord will see what you have done, and will punish you for it

And what Zechariah said came true, for at the end of the year the Syrians made war against Judah. They came into Jerusalem, and slew the princes, and took away their silver and gold, and sent it to the king of Syria at Damascus. For the king of Syria had not come up himself against Jerusalem, nor sent a great army there. He had sent only a small company of men;

KING JOASH TELLS THE PEOPLE TO STONE ZECHARIAH

and the Lord gave them the victory over a great multitude of the men of Judah, because the men of Judah had ceased to obey him. So the Lord punished king Joash, and the people, for their sins. A great sickness came upon Joash also, and, after the Syrians were gone, his own servants rebelled against him, and slew him while he lay in his bed. And they buried him in Jerusalem, but not in the sepulchre of the kings. He had reigned forty years. And Amaziah, his son, was made king over the land.

Amaziah, after he was made king, gathered together a great army out of the tribes of Judah and Benjamin, three hundred thousand men, who could fight with spear and shield. He hired also a hundred thousand more brave and strong soldiers from the kingdom of Israel, and paid them a hundred talents of silver, to go with the men of Judah and Benjamin against the Edomites. But there came a prophet to him, saying, O king, let not the men of Israel go with thee to the battle, for the Lord is not with them to help them. And if they go, he will not aid thee; for God has power to help thee against thy enemies, or to give them the victory over thee. Amaziah said to the prophet, But what shall I do for the hundred talents of silver, which I have paid to the men of Israel? The prophet answered, The Lord is able to give thee back much more than this, if thou wilt trust in him. Then Amaziah obeyed the command of the Lord, and sent the men of Israel to their own homes. And they left in great anger, because they could not go out to war with the men of Judah and Benjamin.

Amaziah went with his army against the Edomites, and the Lord gave him the victory over them. But when he came from the battle he brought with him the idols of the men of Edom, and set them up to be his gods. Therefore the Lord was displeased with Amaziah, and sent a prophet to speak with him, saying, Why dost thou worship the idols of Edom that could not help the Edomites themselves, when thou didst go up to fight against them? But Amaziah was angry with the prophet, and said to him, Art thou the one to tell me what I should do? Be silent, lest I punish thee. Then the prophet spoke to him about the idols no more; yet he said to Amaziah, I know that God has determined to destroy thee, because thou hast done this wicked thing, and wilt not cease, although he has sent thee word.

After this Amaziah sent messengers to the king of Israel, saying, Come, let us look one another in the face: he meant that they should come out with their armies and fight with each other. But the king of Israel answered him, and said, Because thou hast gained the victory over the Edomites, therefore thou art proud and ready to boast. But stay now at home; why shouldst thou meddle with me, and so bring trouble on thyself, and on all the people of Judah with thee? But Amaziah would not listen to the king of Israel, because the Lord meant to punish him, and the people of Judah, for worshipping the idols of Edom.

So Amaziah went out with the army of Judah, and the king of Israel came out against him; then the men of Judah were afraid and fled. And the king of Israel took Amaziah captive, and brought him back to Jerusalem, and broke down the wall of the city. He went into the temple and took the vessels of gold and silver that were there, and the treasures that were in the king's palace, and carried away some of the people, as captives, to his own city of Samaria. After this the people of Jerusalem rebelled against Amaziah, and when he tried to escape from them they followed him and killed him. Then they brought his dead body upon horses to Jerusalem, and buried him there. He had been king over Judah for twenty-nine years.

---

2 CHRONICLES·XXVI–XXXI (26–31). ISAIAH

UZZIAH OBEYS GOD AND PROSPERS. HIS GREAT ARMY. HE GROWS PROUD AND ENTERS THE TEMPLE. THE REIGN OF JOTHAM. ISAIAH IS SENT. THE REIGN OF AHAZ AND PART OF HEZEKIAH'S REIGN.

Now all the people of Judah took Uzziah, Amaziah's son, and made him king. He was sixteen years old when he began to reign, and at first he did what was right; for he had a good and wise counsellor, named Zechariah, whose advice he followed, and as long as he did right the Lord caused him to prosper. He built towers by the gates of Jerusalem, and made them ready for war. He owned a great many cattle, and had wells dug for them out in the fields where they fed, and towers built there for his herdsmen to go into and be safe from robbers. He loved to sow grain and plant vineyards, and he had husbandmen to work for him, both on the plains and in the mountains.

He had also a great army of three hundred and seventy thousand men, and he made for them shields and spears, helmets and bows, and slings to throw stones. He built in Jerusalem curious

engines, which he put in the towers and on the walls, to shoot
arrows and stones against his enemies when they should come
to make war on the city. And God helped him in fighting
against the Philistines, so that he took cities from them; the
Ammonites brought him gifts, and all the nations heard of him,
for he became very great and strong.

THRESHING IN THE EAST.   OXEN TREADING OUT THE GRAIN

But when he was strong he grew proud and disobeyed the
Lord; for he went into the temple, where the priests only were
allowed to go, and took a censer in his hand to burn incense on the
golden altar.   Then Azariah, the high priest, and eighty other
priests with him, who were not afraid to reprove the king, went
into the temple after him, and said to him, It is not right for thee,
Uzziah, to burn incense to the Lord, but only for the priests, the
descendants of Aaron, who are commanded to burn incense.   Go
out of the temple, for thou hast sinned, neither will the Lord

be pleased with thee for doing this thing.   But Uzziah was angry with the priests for speaking these words, and while he was angry, suddenly the leprosy came on his forehead, and the priests saw it there as he stood beside the golden altar.   Then they took hold of him and thrust him out of the temple; yes, he himself

UZZIAH IS STRICKEN WITH LEPROSY AND DRIVEN FROM THE TEMPLE

made haste to go, because the Lord had sent this punishment upon him.

And Uzziah, the king, was never cured, but was a leper till his death; he lived in a house by himself, because God had said that no leper should live with the rest of the people; and Jotham, his son, ruled for him, over the land.   Uzziah was king for fifty-two years, and he died, and they buried him in Jerusalem; and then Jotham was made king.

Jotham was twenty-five years old when he began to reign, and he reigned sixteen years in Jerusalem.   He built cities in the mountains of Judah, and in the forests he built castles and towers. He went out to war against the Ammonites, and made them his servants. They gave him each year a hundred talents of silver, ten thousand measures of wheat, and ten thousand measures of barley. And he became very great, because in all that he did he tried to please the Lord.

But though he served the Lord, the people did wickedly; and God sent Isaiah the prophet to speak to them. Isaiah came and told them that even the dumb ox remembered his master, who was kind to him and fed him, but the children of Israel did not remember the Lord, who gave them every good thing that they had. For the land was full of idols, and the people worshipped them, though they had made them out of pieces of wood with their own hands. The Lord asked them why they offered up sacrifices to him at the temple, when they went away afterward to worship idols, and disobey all his commandments? He did not care for their sacrifices any more, he said, and when they should pray to him, he would not hear them. If they would cease to do evil and learn to do good, then, the Lord said, he would forgive them and bless them.

But they would not do this, for their priests, their princes, and all the men of Judah did wickedly. Because of their sins, Isaiah told them, the Lord was very angry with them, and he would call their enemies from far-off countries to punish them. These enemies would come swiftly with sharp spears and arrows; they would be fierce as lions, and no man could save the people out of their hands. For the people of Judah should be carried away captive, their land would be left lonely and desolate, briars and thorns should grow over it, the cities should have no one living in them, and Jerusalem and the temple would be destroyed. But after many years, Isaiah said, they should be rebuilt, for the Lord would raise up a great king, named Cyrus, who would command that the city and the temple should be built again.

Isaiah lived more than seven hundred years before our Saviour came on the earth, yet he prophesied about him as descended from king David, and born as a little child; he told also how he would grow up to have sorrow and suffering, and afterward be put to death for the people's sins. And Isaiah spoke of John the Baptist as the one who would come before the Saviour, and preach to the people out in the wilderness, telling them to make ready for the Saviour's coming by repenting of their sins.

But the people of Judah would not listen to the preaching of Isaiah, and God took away their good king from them, for Jotham died. And Ahaz, his son, was made king.

Ahaz was twenty years old when he began to reign. He did not serve God as his father had done, but served idols and offered up sacrifices to them on the high places and the hills, and under the shade of trees; and made his sons pass through the fire before them as the heathen nations did. And the Lord sent the kings of Syria and Israel against him. They came up to Jerusalem and besieged the city. The king of Syria took many of the people captive, and carried them away to his own city of Damascus; and the king of Israel killed a hundred and twenty thousand of the men of Judah in one day. He took away also great numbers of the women and children, and brought them to the city of Samaria where he lived.

And not only the kings of Syria and Israel made war against Ahaz, but the Edomites and the Philistines came up and fought against him. Then Ahaz took some of the silver and gold out of the temple, and some of the treasures out of his own palace, and sent them to Tiglath-pilezer, king of Assyria, and asked that king to help him against his enemies. And Tiglath-pilezer took the present of gold and silver and did as Ahaz asked him, for he fought against the Syrians, and took the city of Damascus from them; but it did Ahaz little good, because the Lord was against him on account of his sins.

And Ahaz went to Damascus to meet Tiglath-pilezer. While he was there he saw an idol's altar that greatly pleased him. And he sent the pattern of it to the high priest in Jerusalem, commanding him to make one like it. The high priest did so and put the altar he had made in the court of the temple. When Ahaz returned to Jerusalem he went to it and offered sacrifices on it: he even took away the altar of the Lord from its place in the court, to make room for the idol's altar.

After this Ahaz did still more wickedly. For he took to pieces the lavers which Solomon had made, to stand and hold water in the court of the temple; he took down the great sea of brass, from the backs of the twelve oxen on which it rested, and set it on the pavement of the court. He also carried out

THE KINGS OF SYRIA AND ISRAEL TAKE JERUSALEM

from the temple the sacred vessels of gold and silver and cut them in pieces. Then he shut up the doors of the temple, so that no one could go there to worship; but in every corner of Jerusalem he set up his idols, and in every city of the land he made high places on which to burn sacrifices to them. And the Lord was very angry with Ahaz and the people of Judah for their wickedness.

Ahaz was king for sixteen years, and he died, and was buried in Jerusalem, but they did not bury him in the sepulchre of the kings. And Hezekiah, his son, was made king in his place.

Hezekiah did what was right and served the Lord. As soon as he was made king he opened the doors of the temple, which his father Ahaz had shut up, and he called the priests and Levites who had been sent away from the temple, to come and cleanse it and put it in order, so that God might be worshipped there again. For he said, Our fathers have done wrong; they have shut up the doors of the temple, and have put out the lamps, and not burned incense, nor offered burnt offerings. And the Lord has been angry with us and sent us trouble, and shame, as you have seen; our men have been killed by our enemies, and our sons and daughters have been led away captive on account of these things.

And now, Hezekiah said, I want to make a promise and a covenant with the Lord, to obey him, so that he may not be angry with us any more. Therefore, ye priests and Levites, be diligent and make haste to cleanse, and open the house of the Lord; for you are the ones whom he has chosen to go into his house, and attend to his worship. Then the priests, when they heard what the king said, went into the inner part of the temple, and brought out all the uncleanness that they found there, and the Levites took it and emptied it into the brook Kidron. They began this work on the first day of the month, and on the sixteenth day they came to the king, saying, We have cleansed all the house of the Lord, and the altar that is in the court, and the table on which is set the shewbread; and the vessels of gold and silver, which Ahaz took away, we have put there again, and all things are ready.

Then king Hezekiah rose early in the morning and called the rulers of the city, and they went up together to the temple. They took with them seven bullocks and seven rams, seven lambs and seven goats; and Hezekiah commanded the priests to offer these up on the altar as a sacrifice for all the people's sins. And Hezekiah set the priests and the Levites in the temple, to play on instruments and sing praises to the Lord. When the offering began to burn on the altar, the songs of praises began, with music from the cymbals, the harps, and the trumpets that the priests and Levites held in their hands. And all the people worshipped and the singers sang and the trumpets sounded, until the burnt offering was finished.

After the offerings which the king and the rulers had brought were offered up, Hezekiah invited the people to bring their offerings: and they brought seventy bullocks, a hundred rams, and two hundred lambs. The priests offered up these also. And the king rejoiced, and the people with him, because the Lord had made them willing to bring their offerings to him, and because the Lord's worship was begun at the temple once more.

And Hezekiah wrote letters to all the people in Judah, and to the people of the ten tribes of Israel also, asking them to come to Jerusalem and keep the feast of the passover; for it had been many years since the people kept that feast as the Lord commanded them to keep it. And the messengers whom the king sent, went out among the people, carrying the king's letter, which said, Ye children of Israel, who have been disobeying the Lord, turn now and obey him; then he will turn to you and bless you. Be not like your fathers and your brothers, who have gone on sinning against him, and been carried away captive for their sins; but obey his commandments, and come to his temple and serve him, that he may take away his anger from you. If you will do this, he will remember those who have been taken captive, and will make their enemies kind to them, so that they will allow them to come back to their own land.

So the messengers with the king's letters went out through all the land. But when they came into the land of Israel, the men of the ten tribes would not listen to them; they mocked them and laughed them to scorn. Yet not all the men of Israel did this, for some of them confessed their sins and were sorry for them, and came to Jerusalem. But in the land of Judah, the Lord made all the people willing to come. So there came to Jerusalem a very great company of people to keep the feast. But before they began to keep it, they went out through the city and took away all the idols' altars that were still left there, and cast them into the brook Kedron.

26

Then they made ready to keep the feast of the passover; each man took a lamb, and brought it to the temple; there it was killed before the altar. Afterward the man took it to his own house, and it was roasted with fire, and he and his family ate of it in the night, as the children of Israel did on the night that they came out of Egypt. For the Lord wanted the people to remember that night, how he had saved them from Pharaoh and the cruel Egyptians; therefore he commanded them to keep this feast every year. But they had neglected to do so, and now Hezekiah called them to Jerusalem to keep it again, so that they might obey the Lord, and he might be pleased with them and bless them.

We have read that when the children of Israel kept the passover the first time in Egypt, they were commanded to eat only one kind of bread, called unleavened bread; and for seven days afterward they were allowed to eat no other bread but this. So now, and for seven days after they had eaten the lamb, they ate unleavened bread. And they kept the feast through all those seven days with gladness. The priests and the Levites sang praises every day, playing on harps and trumpets. And the Levites went out among the people and taught them the law of the Lord, that they might know his law, and take care to obey it. King Hezekiah spoke kindly to the Levites who were doing this work, and encouraged them to go on in it.

Through the seven days of the passover the people feasted on the flesh of the peace offerings which they had brought to the temple, and they confessed their sins to the Lord. And after they had kept these seven days, they all agreed to stay seven days more, praising God. And king Hezekiah and the princes gave them great numbers of cattle for sacrifices, two thousand bullocks and seventeen thousand sheep. All the people of Judah, with the priests and Levites, and the men of Israel also, who had come to keep the feast with them, rejoiced; for since the time when Solomon lived no such feast had been kept in Jerusalem.

When the feast was over, the people went out to the different cities of the land and broke in pieces all the idols that they found there, and destroyed the high places and the altars that had been made to worship idols on. They did this both in the land of Judah and in the land of Israel. Afterward they returned every man to his own home.

And Hezekiah sent the different courses, or companies, of the priests and Levites to the temple, as king David had appointed them, to take turns in attending to the worship of the

LEVITES READING THE LAW TO THE PEOPLE

Lord; and he gave them sacrifices to be offered up every day, in the morning and evening, and on the sabbath, and feast days. The king told the people, also, to bring a tenth part of all that grew in their fields to the priests and Levites for food, as Moses had commanded; for the people had long neglected to do this. But now they obeyed the king and brought these things to the temple. Not only the people of Judah did so, but many who lived in the land of Israel. In the third month they began to bring them, and they kept on bringing until the seventh month.

When the king and the princes came to the temple, and saw the great heaps of food that had been brought, they thanked the Lord who had made the people willing to bring so much. Then Hezekiah asked the priests and the Levites how it happened that there was so much. Azariah, the chief priest, answered him, saying, Ever since the people began to bring their offerings, the priests and Levites have had enough to eat, and not only enough, but plenty to spare; for after eating all they wanted, these heaps are left. For the Lord has not only made the people willing to bring offerings, but he has blessed their fruit and their grain out in the field, making them grow well, so that the people have had large offerings to bring.

Then Hezekiah commanded that some chambers, or storerooms, should be made ready, near the temple, where the heaps of food could be brought and kept safe. And they made the chambers ready and brought the food into them. And Hezekiah appointed some of the Levites to take care of it, and to give to all the priests and Levites as much as they needed for themselves and their families to eat: not only to those whose turn it was to stay in the temple, but to those also who were resting at home, or teaching the laws of God to the people in different parts of the land.

---

2 KINGS XVIII–XXI (18–21). 2 CHRON. XXXII, XXXIII (32, 33). ISAIAH XXXVII–XXXIX (37–39). MICAH

THE KING OF ASSYRIA COMES INTO THE LAND OF ISRAEL. AN ANGEL DESTROYS HIS ARMY. THE WICKEDNESS OF THE PEOPLE. MICAH, THE PROPHET, IS SENT. REIGN OF MANASSEH AND AMMON.

AFTER these things, the king of Assyria came into Judah with his army, and took some of the cities of the land. When Hezekiah heard of it he built up the walls of Jerusalem, where they had been broken down, and made shields and darts in abundance. And he gathered the men of Judah together, and set captains over them and spoke to them, saying, Be strong and brave, fear not the king of Assyria nor the multitude that is with him, for there are more on our side than on his. He has men to fight for him, but we have God to fight for us. Nevertheless, Hezekiah, because he was afraid of the king of Assyria, sent him a great deal of gold and silver, so that he should not fight any more against Judah. Then the king of Assyria took the gold and silver, and returned to his own land. But afterward, he wickedly came back with his army into the land of Judah, and made war against it.

And he stopped at a city called Lachish, to besiege it, but he sent his servants on before him to Jerusalem, to tell the people he was coming there also. And his servants came and said to the people, Thus saith the king of Assyria, Do not listen to Hezekiah when he tells you that he is able to fight against me, and that the Lord will save you out of my hand. Listen not to his words, but make an agreement with me; pay me now tribute money of gold and silver, and come out and be my servants. Then I will do you no harm, but will let you alone until I return to take you to another land. Then the servants of the king of Assyria cried with loud voices to the people who were on the walls of Jerusalem, to frighten them and make them willing to give up the city. And they spoke against God, as though he were like the idols that the heathen nations worshipped.

When Hezekiah heard what they said, he rent his clothes and put on sackcloth, and went up to the temple to pray to the Lord. And he sent priests and elders to Isaiah, the prophet, telling him of the message of the king of Assyria, and asking him to pray for the people. And the priests and elders came and told Isaiah. Then Isaiah sent word to king Hezekiah, saying, Thus saith the Lord: Be not afraid of the words which the king of Assyria has spoken against me; for I will send a great punishment upon him, and he shall turn and go back to his own land, and there I will cause him to be put to death with the sword.

So Hezekiah would not obey the command of the king of Assyria to give up the city. And that king's servants went back to their master, and told him what Hezekiah said. Then the king sent his servants again to Hezekiah, with a letter, saying, Do not let thy God make thee believe that I cannot take Jerusalem. Thou hast heard how the kings of Assyria have destroyed other nations; their gods were not able to save them, and can thy God save thee?

When Hezekiah read the letter which the king of Assyria had sent, he was in great trouble, and he took it and went up to the temple, and there spread it open before the Lord. And Hezekiah prayed and said, O Lord, thou art the only God over all the kingdoms of the earth; for it was thou who didst make the heaven and the earth. Lord, open thine eyes and see, and turn thine ears and hear the words which the king of Assyria has spoken against thee. It is true that he has destroyed the other nations, and cast their gods into the fire, for those gods were only dumb idols, made out of wood and stone; therefore he was able to destroy them. But now, O Lord, he is seeking to destroy Jerusalem. Save us, I pray thee, out of his hands, so that all the kingdoms may know that thou art not like the idols of the heathen nations, but that thou art the Lord, and that there is no other God beside thee.

And the Lord heard Hezekiah's prayer, and commanded Isaiah, the prophet, to send a messenger to him, saying, Thus saith the Lord, I have heard the words which thou hast prayed to me against the king of Assyria, and I will do to him as thou hast asked. He shall not come before the city with shields and spears, nor build forts around it, neither shall he shoot an arrow into it. By the way that he came he shall return again, for I will save Jerusalem out of his hands. And what Isaiah said came true, for that night the Lord sent his destroying angel into the camp of the Assyrians, and the angel slew a hundred and eighty-five thousand of them. Then the king of Assyria went back with shame to his own land. There, while he was worshipping in the house of his idol, two of his own sons put him to death. So the Lord saved Hezekiah and the people of Judah from the king of Assyria, and from all their other enemies.

In those days king Hezekiah was sick, and the prophet Isaiah went to him, and said, The Lord hath sent thee word to make all

KING HEZEKIAH, CLOTHED IN SACKCLOTH, SPREADS OPEN THE LETTER BEFORE THE LORD

things ready, for thou shalt die and not live. After the prophet had spoken these words, he came out from Hezekiah's chamber. Then Hezekiah turned his face to the wall and prayed, saying, O Lord, remember, now, how I have served thee with all my heart, and have done those things that pleased thee. And Hezekiah wept greatly. And the Lord commanded Isaiah to go back to Hezekiah, and say, Thus saith the Lord, I have

THE DESTROYING ANGEL SLAYS THE ASSYRIANS

heard thy prayer, and seen thy tears; behold, I will make thee well; in three days thou shalt go up to the temple, and I will add to thy life fifteen years. So Isaiah went back and spoke these words to the king. And he said to the king's servants, Take a lump of figs and lay it upon the boil. And they took the figs, and laid them upon the boil of which the king was sick, and he grew well again.

And king Hezekiah had great riches and honor. He made

for himself treasuries, or strong chambers, in which to keep his gold and silver, his jewels and precious stones. He built store-houses also for his corn, and wine, and oil; and made stalls for his horses and cattle, and cotes, or pens, for his flocks of sheep; for he had great numbers of all these things. And the Lord helped him, so that he prospered in all that he did.

ANCIENT SHEEP PEN

Yet Hezekiah did not keep humble and thankful to God for his blessings; he grew proud of his riches and power. And the king of Babylon heard of his greatness, and sent messengers with letters and a present for him. When the messengers came to Jerusalem, Hezekiah received them gladly, and in his pride, showed them his silver and gold, his horses and armor, and all the great things of his kingdom.

Then Isaiah, the prophet, came to Hezekiah, and said, What did these men say? And from whence did they come? Hezekiah answered, They came from a far country, from Babylon. **And** Isaiah said, What have they seen in thy house? Hezekiah answered, All that is in my house they have seen; there is nothing among my treasures that I have not shown them. Then Isaiah

HEZEKIAH SHOWING HIS TREASURES

said, Hear what the Lord says to thee, The day is coming when all the riches that are in thy house, which thou and thy fathers have laid up, shall be carried to Babylon; nothing shall be left. And some of thy own descendants also shall they take away and make them servants in the palace of the king of Babylon. Hezekiah answered, All that the Lord will do is right; yet it is good in him not to send these troubles while I live, but to send peace and truth in my days.

We have read how Hezekiah persuaded the people to put

away their idols and serve the Lord, but they did this only for a time; then they went back to serving idols again. And God sent the prophet Micah to speak to them. Micah came and said that God asked what he had done to make them weary of serving him? He had brought them up out of Egypt, from being servants to Pharaoh, and had sent Moses and Aaron to guide them through the wilderness. And afterward, when the king of Moab sent for Balaam to curse them, he made Balaam bless them instead. What did the Lord ask of the children of Israel, except to do justly, to be kind and merciful to each other, and humble and obedient to the Lord?

But they would not do this, Micah said. Their rich men were cruel to those who were poor; their judges, who should punish the wicked, were wicked themselves. Scarcely any good men were left in the land; all were ready to rob and to kill, so that friends could not trust one another; and even brothers and sisters, and fathers and mothers, had come to be enemies, and to hate one another. On account of these things, Micah told them, the Lord would send a great punishment upon them. The people should be carried away to Babylon, and Jerusalem, their beautiful city, should be destroyed. Instead of houses in it there would be only heaps of stone. The temple also should be thrown down and taken away, until nothing was left of it, and the place where it stood should be ploughed over like a field where the farmer sows his grain.

Micah, like Isaiah, prophesied of the Saviour, telling where he should be born, that it would be in the city of Bethlehem. And not only Micah and Isaiah, but almost all the prophets that God sent, spoke or taught about him, so that the children of Israel might know the Saviour was coming; and so that we, who are living now, after he has come, may know that he is the Son of God, and that it was God who sent him.

Hezekiah was king over Judah twenty-nine years, and he died, and they buried him in Jerusalem, in the best of the sepulchres of the kings; and Manasseh his son was made king in his place.

Manasseh was twelve years old when he was made king, and

he did wickedly. The Bible tells us that he worshipped all the host of heaven, that is, the sun, the moon, and the stars. He built up again the high places, which his father Hezekiah had destroyed, and made idols' altars in the courts around the temple, and even set up an idol in the temple itself. He made his children pass through the fire before his idols, and he talked with familiar spirits, which the Lord had commanded the

MANASSEH LED AWAY CAPTIVE

children of Israel not to do.   He put to death also many inno- cent persons in Jerusalem, who had done no wrong; so that he did more wickedly, and caused the people to do more wickedly, than the heathen nations used to do, that lived in Canaan before the children of Israel came there.

And the Lord spoke to Manasseh and to the people, by his prophets, about their sins, but they would not hear.   Therefore the Lord brought against them the captains of the army of the king of Assyria, who came and took Manasseh, as he was hiding from them among some bushes and thorns; and they bound him with chains, and carried him to Babylon. When he was there, far away from home, and in affliction, he remembered his sins, and repented of them. He prayed with all his heart to the Lord; and the Lord heard him, and was kind to him and brought him back to Jerusalem. Then Manasseh knew that the Lord was the only true God, and he took away the idol which he had set up in the temple, and all the altars that he had built in the courts around the temple, and cast them out of the city; he also repaired the altar of the Lord, and offered up sacrifices upon it.

Manasseh was king over Judah for fifty-five years, and he died, and they buried him in the garden of his palace in Jerusalem, and Ammon, his son, was made king.

Ammon was twenty-two years old when he began to reign, and he did evil; for he offered up sacrifices to all the carved images that his father, Manasseh, had made; yet he did not afterward repent and put them away, as his father had done, but he went on sinning more and more. After he had been king for two years, his servants rebelled against him and killed him, and the people of the land chose Josiah, his son, for their king.

---

2 KINGS XXII–XXV (22–25). 2 CHRON. XXXIV–XXXVI (34-36). JER. II–XI, XVIII, XXXVI, XXXVIII, XXXIX (2-11, 18, 36, 38, 39)

THE REIGNS OF JOSIAH, JEHOAHAZ, JEHOIAKIM, JEHOIACHIN, AND ZEDEKIAH, AND THE END OF THE KINGDOM OF JUDAH.

JOSIAH was eight years old when he was made king. He reigned thirty-one years, and did what was right; for while he was yet a boy he began to serve the Lord. He went out through all the land of Judah, and also among the people who were living in the land of Israel (for the ten tribes had been carried away captive before this time), and he made his servants destroy the altars of Baal wherever he found them, and tear down the images that were set up above the altars, and break them in pieces. Then he came back to Jerusalem, and set men at work to repair the temple where it had been allowed to go to decay; and the people brought money to the temple to pay the workmen for doing this.

And Josiah sent one of his servants, saying, Go up to the high priest, and tell him to count the money which the people have brought and let it be given to the carpenters, the builders, and the masons, who were at work repairing the temple. And the servant went and told the high priest, who did with the money as the king commanded. Then the high priest said to the servant, I have found in the temple the book of the law.

In the olden times men did not know how to print books as we do now. Instead of printing, they wrote with pen and ink, on long rolls of paper, or parchment, and these rolls were called books. We have read that Moses, before he died, wrote down in a book the laws which God had given him; and he commanded that once in seven years those laws should be read out loud to all the people. But the wicked kings and people of Judah had not cared to hear God's laws, and had neglected the book until it was lost and forgotten, and Josiah had never seen it. But now, while the temple was being repaired, the high priest found it again. And he gave it to the king's servant, who took it to Josiah and said, The high priest has given me a book. And he read it to the king.

When king Josiah heard his servant read the words of God's law, and heard him read also of the punishments which God said he would send on the people for not obeying that law, he rent his clothes and wept. And he spoke to the high priest, saying, Go, and ask for me, what the Lord will do to us; for he is very angry, because our fathers have not obeyed the commands that are written in the book. Then the high priest went to a woman named Huldah, who was a prophetess, and asked her the question. She answered, The Lord says, I will send upon Jerusalem and upon the people who live there, all the punishments that are written in the book, because they have turned away from serving me, and gone to serve other gods. But as

JOSIAH HEARING THE BOOK OF THE LAW

for king Josiah, who sent you, go and say to him, Thus saith the Lord, Because thou wast grieved for the sins of the people, and didst humble thyself and weep before me, I will not send those punishments in thy days, and thou shalt not see all the evil that is coming upon Jerusalem. So the high priest came back and told king Josiah what the prophetess said.

Then Josiah sent and gathered the priests, the Levites, and all the people together, and went up to the temple; and he read to them the words that were written in the book which the high priest had found. The king stood by a pillar, and made a covenant with the Lord, and promised to obey his commandments with all his heart and with all his soul. He also caused the people to promise that they, too, would obey them.

The wicked kings of Judah, who lived before Josiah, had made spoons, and forks, and vessels to be used in offering up sacrifices to Baal, and they had taken these things into the temple. They had set up an idol, also, in the court of the temple, and appointed men as priests, to burn incense to it, and burnt offerings. But now Josiah put down these priests and would have them no more; and he sent the priests of the Lord to bring out from the temple all the vessels that had been used in worshipping Baal, and the image that had been set up there; and he took the image and the vessels outside of the city and burnt them. And Josiah punished, or sent out of the land, all those persons who talked with familiar spirits. He sent men also to the valley of Hinnom, where the people used to make their children pass through the fire, before the idol Molech, and he defiled, or spoiled the valley, so that they should not use it in this way any more.

And Josiah went to Bethel, where Jeroboam, the king of Israel, had set up one of the golden calves which he made for the people of the ten tribes to worship. We have read how Jeroboam was burning incense on an altar to his idol, when a prophet came there and told him that a king should be born in Judah, named Josiah, who would burn men's bones on that altar, to defile it and make it unclean. It had been more than three hundred years since the prophet spoke those words. Jeroboam had long since been dead, and the people of the ten tribes had been carried away captive; yet now the prophet's words came true. For Josiah went to Bethel to break down the idol's altar, which was still there, and as he turned around, he saw sepulchres in the mountain near that place. Then he sent and took men's bones out of the sepulchres and burned them on the altar.

We have read how Hezekiah, while he was king, sent for the people to come to Jerusalem and keep the feast of the passover, which they had not kept for many years. Yet, after Hezekiah died, the people again neglected to keep it. But now Josiah called them to Jerusalem to keep that feast. And he gave them, out of his own flocks, thirty thousand lambs and kids, and three thousand bullocks, that they all might have sacrifices to offer. But, although they obeyed the command of the king, and came to keep the feast, the people did not truly love God nor sincerely worship him, for in their hearts they still trusted in their idols.

And Jeremiah, the prophet, came to them, and said that God had brought them up out of Egypt by his mighty power, and given them that good land which he had promised to their fathers, but they had not thanked him for this, neither had they obeyed any of his commandments. God had seen their wickedness, Jeremiah told them, and was angry with them. Yet if they would turn from their evil ways he would forgive them, and keep back the punishments which were coming upon them. But the people would not hear what the prophet said to them. No man repented of his evil acts. They all went on in their wickedness, and sinned more and more. While Jeremiah was yet speaking to them, they said one to another, Let us kill him. But God saved him out of their hands.

After these things, the king of Egypt came up with his army into the land of Israel, and Josiah went out against him. Then the king of Egypt sent word that he had not come to fight with Josiah, but was going to make war against the king of Assyria, and he told Josiah to let him alone. But Josiah would not turn back; he took off his own garments and put on others, that no one might know him, and went into the battle. And the archers of the king of Egypt shot their arrows at him and struck him; then he said to his servants, Take me out of the battle, for I am sore wounded. And they took him out of his chariot and put him into another that was near, but he died; and they brought him in a chariot to Jerusalem, and buried him in the sepulchre of the kings. All the people mourned for him; and they made Jehoahaz, his son, king over Judah.

Jehoahaz was twenty-two years old when he was made king, and he reigned but three months. He did not do right, as his father had done, neither did the people obey God. And Pharaoh, king of Egypt, came up against them; he took Jehoahaz and bound him with fetters, and carried him away to Egypt: there he kept him until he died. And Pharaoh made Jehoiakim, the brother of Jehoahaz, king in his place. But he forced Jehoiakim, and the people of Judah, to pay him a great sum of money—a hundred talents of silver, and a talent of gold. After Pharaoh had gone, Nebuchadnezzar, king of Babylon, came up against Judah, and Jehoiakim was not able to fight against him, so he promised to obey him and be his servant. And Nebuchadnezzar took some of the sacred vessels out of the temple, and carried them to Babylon, and put them in the house of his idol there.

In the fourth year that Jehoiakim was king, the Lord spoke to the prophet Jeremiah, and commanded him to write down in a book all the punishments that were coming on the children of Israel. For the Lord said that when the people should hear of those punishments, perhaps they would repent, so that he might, even yet, forgive them. Then Jeremiah called to him a man named Baruch, who was a scribe, or writer; and Baruch wrote down the words as Jeremiah spoke them. Afterward Jeremiah told him to go and read them to the people. Then Baruch took the book up to the temple and read it, where all the people could hear.

And the princes, who sat in the king's palace, heard of the book, and sent for Baruch to come and read it to them. So he took the roll in his hand and went to them. And they said to him, Sit down now and read it to us. When they heard all the things that the Lord had spoken against the children of Israel, and of the punishments that he was going to send upon them, they were afraid, and said, Tell us now how didst thou write these words? Baruch answered, Jeremiah spoke them to me with his mouth, and I wrote them down with ink in the book. Then the princes said to Baruch, We will tell the king. But go and hide, thou and Jeremiah, and let no man know where you are, lest the king be angry with you and seek to harm you.

BARUCH WRITING THE BOOK

So they told king Jehoiakim of the book, and he sent his servant to bring it. And his servant brought it, and read it before the king, and before all the princes who stood beside him. Now the king sat by the fire that was burning on the hearth, for it was winter. And as soon as his servant had read three or four leaves of the book, the king took his penknife and cut them out, and threw them into the fire; so he did till all the book was burned. Some of the princes who were with him begged him not to burn it, but he would not listen to them; neither was he troubled, nor afraid when he heard of all the evil that was coming upon the people for their sins. Yet he was angry with Jeremiah and Baruch for writing the book, and sent his servants to take them, but the Lord hid them from him.

Then the Lord commanded Jeremiah to take another roll and write in it all the words that were written in the one which the king had burned. And Jeremiah took another roll and gave it to Baruch, and repeated to him the words that had been written in the first roll, and beside these many more that the Lord spoke to him. But the people hated Jeremiah for telling them of their sins, and he complained to the Lord, saying, Though I have done them no evil, yet every one of them doth curse me. Then the Lord promised that when the enemies of Jerusalem should come to take the city, they should not harm Jeremiah. Truly, the Lord said, I will cause them to treat thee kindly.

Jehoiakim reigned eleven years, and he died, and Jehoiachin, his son, was made king in his place.

Jehoiachin was eighteen years old when he was made king, and he reigned three months in Jerusalem. Then Nebuchadnezzar, king of Babylon, came up against him, as he had come up against his father. And Jehoiachin promised to obey him. Then Nebuchadnezzar went into the temple, as he did when he came up before, and carried out more of the vessels of gold which Solomon made, and he cut them in pieces; he came also into the king's palace and took away the treasures that were there. And he took king Jehoiachin, his mother, his wives, and the princes of Judah; also the builders, the smiths, and the carpenters, and all the strong and brave soldiers that were in Jerusalem, and carried them to Babylon.

After they had gone to Babylon, the prophet Jeremiah wrote a letter to them, telling them to build houses and plant gardens, and be contented in that land, because the Lord said they should stay there and serve the king of Babylon for seventy years. But when the seventy years were ended, and they should repent of their sins and pray to be forgiven, then, Jeremiah said, the Lord would bring them back to their own land.

As for the people who were still left in the land of Judah, Nebuchadnezzar made Zedekiah, the brother of Jehoiakim, king over them. But Zedekiah was the servant of the king of Babylon, and had to promise before the Lord that he would obey him. Yet, after Nebuchadnezzar had gone back to Babylon, Zedekiah rebelled against him; the priests and the people of Judah, also, did wickedly. Then Nebuchadnezzar came up again with all the army of the Chaldeans, and made forts around Jerusalem, from which they shot darts and arrows at the men of Judah, who were on the walls and towers of the city; and Jerusalem was besieged, so that no one could go out or come in.

Now Jeremiah, the prophet, was shut up in Jerusalem, with the rest of the people. And king Zedekiah, because he was afraid of the Chaldeans, sent word to him, asking him to pray to God that Jerusalem might be saved. But the Lord commanded Jeremiah to tell the king that the Chaldeans should

JEREMIAH LET DOWN INTO THE DUNGEON

certainly take the city and burn it with fire. Yet, Jeremiah said, if the people would bear the punishment which the Lord was sending upon them, and would go out to the king of Babylon and be his servants, without fighting any more against him, they should not be put to death. Whoever would go out should be saved alive, but whoever stayed in the city would be killed by the sword, the famine, or the pestilence. For the Lord said that Jerusalem should be taken by the king of Babylon, and he would burn it with fire, because the Lord would punish the people for their sins.

But some of the princes of Judah came to king Zedekiah, and said, We pray thee, let Jeremiah be put to death, for he makes the people afraid, because he says the Lord will send famine and pestilence upon us, and will give the city to the king of Babylon. And the king told the princes they might do with Jeremiah as they chose. Then they took him and let him down with cords into a deep pit, or dungeon, that was in the prison; at the bottom of the dungeon was mire, so Jeremiah sank in the mire.

But one of the officers at the king's palace, when he heard what had been done, went to the king, and said, My lord, the king, these men have done wickedly in putting Jeremiah into the dungeon, for he may die there of hunger. Then the king commanded the officer, saying, Take thirty men with thee, and bring Jeremiah out of the dungeon, that he die not. So the officer took men, and they carried with them some pieces of old clothes and rags, and let these down by cords into the dungeon to Jeremiah. And the officer called to him, saying, Put now these pieces of clothes and rags under thy arms, that the cords may not hurt thee. Jeremiah did as the officer said, and they drew him up by the cords out of the dungeon. Yet they did not set him free, for he was still kept in another part of the prison.

Then king Zedekiah sent to Jeremiah again, after he had been taken up out of the dungeon, and he brought him into the entry of the temple, where he might talk with him secretly. And the king said to him, I will ask thee a question; do not hide the answer from me. Jeremiah answered, If I tell thee, wilt thou promise not to put me to death? The king said, As surely as the Lord liveth I will not put thee to death, neither will I give thee to the men who want to kill thee.

Then Jeremiah answered, saying, Thus saith the Lord, If thou

JEREMIAH TELLS THE KING THAT JERUSALEM SHALL BE TAKEN

wilt go out to the king of Babylon and be his servant, thou and thy family shall be saved alive, and this city shall not be burned. The king said, I am afraid if I shall go out to the Chaldeans, that they will give me back to the Jews (that is, to the men of Judah) who have turned against me, and that they will treat me cruelly. Jeremiah answered, The Chaldeans shall not give thee back to them. Do not be afraid, but obey, I beseech thee, the command of the Lord, so that it may be well with thee, and thou shalt be saved alive. But if thou refuse to go out to the king of Babylon, thy wives and thy children shall be given to the Chaldeans; thou thyself shalt not escape from them, and this city also shall be burned with fire.

But king Zedekiah would not obey the command of the Lord, and go out to the king of Babylon. Therefore the Chaldeans fought against Jerusalem, and after they had besieged it for eighteen months the bread was all gone in the city; there was no more left for the people to eat. And in the night Zedekiah fled out of the city with his army. But the Chaldeans followed after him and caught him, and brought him to the king of Babylon. Then that cruel king killed Zedekiah's two sons, before his eyes; after he had done this he put out Zedekiah's eyes, and bound him with chains and carried him to Babylon. There he kept him in prison till he died.

And the captain of Nebuchadnezzar's army burnt the temple at Jerusalem, and the palace of the king, and the houses of the people, and broke down the walls all around the city. He carried away to Babylon the two pillars of brass, which Solomon had made to stand before the temple, and the sea of brass that stood on the backs of twelve oxen in the court of the temple, and whatever vessels of gold and silver were still left there. The people of Jerusalem who were not slain, he carried away captive, except some of the poor of the land, whom he left to work in the fields and vineyards. Over these Nebuchadnezzar set Gedaliah to be their governor.

So the kingdom of Judah was ended, as the kingdom of Israel had been, on account of the sins of the people. It had lasted three hundred and eighty-eight years, ever since Rehoboam was made king over the tribes of Judah and Benjamin; nineteen kings and one queen had ruled over the people during that time; of these, we are told, that fifteen did wickedly and five served the Lord. But even while they had good kings, the people worshipped idols. And though the Lord waited long, and gave them time to repent, and sent his prophets to warn and persuade them, they would not obey him, and cease doing evil. Therefore, at last, he sent the people of Judah, as he had before sent the people of Israel, out of the land of Canaan.

JEREMIAH XXXIX–XLIII (39–43)

THE CHALDEANS TREAT JEREMIAH KINDLY. GEDALIAH IS SLAIN. THE JEWS, TAKING JEREMIAH WITH THEM, FLEE INTO EGYPT.

WE have read the promise which the Lord made to Jeremiah, that the Chaldeans would treat him kindly when they should come to take Jerusalem. And now the Lord made his promise come true, for, after the city was taken, the king of Babylon commanded the captain of his army, saying, Take Jeremiah and be good to him, a..d do him no harm, but do unto him whatever he shall ask of thee. So the captain sent and took Jeremiah out of prison, where the men of Judah had left him, and he said to him, If it please thee to come with me to Babylon, come; and I will take care of thee; but if thou wouldst rather stay here, do not come. All the land is before thee to go wherever it shall please thee to go; or thou canst go and live with Gedaliah, whom the king has made governor over the cities of Judah. Then the captain gave Jeremiah money and food, and let him go; and Jeremiah went and lived with Gedaliah, because he wanted to stay with the people that were still left in the land.

Now some of the Jews had fled out into the fields, and away to other countries, when the Chaldeans took Jerusalem; therefore they were not taken captive with those that went to Babylon. And when they heard that Nebuchadnezzar had left some of the people still living in the land, and had made Gedaliah governor over them, they came back to the land of Judah, to the city of

Mizpeh, where Gedaliah lived; for he could not live in Jerusalem because it was destroyed. And Gedaliah spoke kindly to the Jews who came to him and said to them, Do not be afraid to come back and live in your own land. For if you will stay here and sow your seed, and gather in your grain, and serve the king of Babylon, you shall be happy, and it shall be well with you. So the people came and lived in the land, and gathered in much fruit and grain from their fields.

EASTERN PLOUGHMAN

Then some men came to Gedaliah and spoke to him, saying, Dost thou not know that the king of the Ammonites has sent Ishmael, one of the princes of Judah, to slay thee? And one of the men who came to tell him this spoke secretly to Gedaliah, and said, Let me go therefore and put Ishmael to death, and no one shall know of it; for why should he slay thee and cause all the people who are left in the land to be scattered and destroyed? But Gedaliah would not believe what the man said; he answered him, saying, Thou shalt not put Ishmael to death, for what thou tellest me about him is not true.   Yet what the man said was true; for after that, Ishmael came, and ten men with him, to Gedaliah's house, pretending that they wanted only to eat at his table.   But after they had eaten they rose up and slew him; and Ishmael fled away into the land of the Ammonites. Then all the people were afraid lest the king of Babylon should come and punish them, because Gedaliah, whom he had made governor over them, was slain.

And they came to Jeremiah, and said, Pray to the Lord for us that he may show us where we shall go and what we shall do. Jeremiah answered, I will pray for you as you ask me, and whatever the Lord shall tell me, I will tell you; I will hide nothing from you.   Then they said to Jeremiah, All that the Lord shall command us, we will do; whether it be good or whether it be bad for us, we will obey the voice of the Lord, so that he may help us and take care of us.

And Jeremiah prayed to the Lord, and after ten days the Lord answered him, and told him what he should say to the people.   So Jeremiah called them to hear, and he said to them, Thus saith the Lord, If you will stay in this land I will bless you.   Be not afraid of the king of Babylon, for I am with you to save you from harm, and I will make him kind to you, so that he shall let you live in your own land.   But if you disobey me and say, We will not live in this land, but will go into Egypt, because there we shall have bread enough to eat, and shall have no more war, then, after you have gone, the war and the famine, that you fear, shall follow you; there in Egypt you shall die, and you shall see your own land no more.

When the people heard these words, all the proud and wicked men among them answered Jeremiah, saying, Thou speakest falsely, for the Lord did not tell thee to say that we should not go down into Egypt, but thou dost want us to stay here, that the Chaldeans may come and put us to death, or carry us away captives to Babylon.   So they would not obey the commandment of the Lord, but they took all the people, the men, the women, and the children, who were left in the land of Judah, and Jeremiah also, and brought them down into the land of

Egypt. Then those words came true that the prophet Isaiah had spoken more than a hundred years before, when he said that the land of Judah should be left lonely and desolate; that briars and thorns should grow over it, and that the houses should have no one living in them.

THE BOOK OF EZEKIEL

CHAPTERS I–VIII (1–8)

EZEKIEL, IN A VISION, IS COMMANDED TO SPEAK TO THE CAPTIVES BY THE RIVER CHEBAR. HE MAKES KNOWN BY SIGNS THE COMING DESTRUCTION OF JERUSALEM. IN A SECOND VISION HE IS CARRIED TO THE TEMPLE, AND SHOWN THE IDOLATRY OF THE JEWS.

WE have read that while Jehoiachin was king in Jerusalem, Nebuchadnezzar, king of Babylon, came up and besieged the city. And Jehoiachin, because he was afraid of Nebuchadnezzar, went out to him and promised to be his servant. Then Nebuchadnezzar took Jehoiachin, his mother, his wives, and the princes of Judah; the builders also, and carpenters, and all the strong and brave soldiers that were in Jerusalem, and carried them away as captives. Yet Nebuchadnezzar did not at that time destroy Jerusalem, nor take all the people away; he left some of them, and made Zedekiah their king. But he took many of the Jews to his own land, and there gave them a place where they might live by the river Chebar. The Lord allowed Nebuchadnezzar to take them, because he was punishing them for their sins.

Yet even after they had been carried away captive, the Jews would not obey the Lord. We have read how Jeremiah, the prophet, wrote a letter to them from Jerusalem, telling them to serve the king of Babylon, and be contented in the land to which he had taken them, because the Lord said they should stay there for seventy years. But instead of doing as Jeremiah told them, they found fault, and complained, and wanted to go back to Jerusalem; for they would not believe that the city was to be destroyed, and that the Jews who were still living there were to be carried away captive too. The prophets of the Lord had told them so, but they chose to believe the false prophets who said that these things should not happen.

Now among the captives by the river Chebar was a priest named Ezekiel. And in the fifth year after they were carried away, Ezekiel had a vision. He looked, and behold a whirlwind came out of the north, and with the whirlwind a cloud; and out of the midst of the cloud came four cherubim. Above the wings of the cherubim was a throne, and on the throne Ezekiel saw a form like the form of a man, yet not made of flesh; it seemed to be of fire, or as if fire were burning within it: and around it were bright colors like a rainbow. This form that Ezekiel saw, sitting upon a throne, with a rainbow around it, was a likeness of the glory of the Lord. And when he saw it he turned away his eyes, and fell on his face to the ground.

Then the Lord said to him, Stand upon thy feet. And when he had risen up, the Lord commanded him to go and speak to the Jews who were captives with him by the river Chebar. I send thee to them, the Lord said, because they are a disobedient people; both they and their fathers have disobeyed me. Yet thou shalt tell them my message, whether they will hear or whether they will not hear. And be not thou afraid of them, though they be fierce as serpents and scorpions; or like briars and thorns that would tear thy flesh; fear them not, for I will make thee strong and brave when thou standest before them, and thou shalt speak all the words that I tell thee to speak against them.

After this, the Lord commanded Ezekiel to take a flat, earthen tile, and to draw upon it a picture of Jerusalem. And he was to set this picture of the city on the ground, with an iron pan for its wall. And before it he was to build a little fort, in the shape of the forts which soldiers used to build around cities that they besieged in those days. Then Ezekiel was to lie down on the ground, upon his side, before the picture of Jerusalem, with his face toward it; and there he was to stay many days. And while he lay there he was to eat only a little coarse bread, and to drink only a little water, every day.

The Lord commanded Ezekiel to do these things that the people might see him; for in this way the Lord intended to teach them what would happen to Jerusalem; how Nebuchadnezzar would come up with his army against the city, and build forts around it, and besiege it for many days. And when the people

EZEKIEL SHOWS BY SIGNS THE COMING SIEGE OF JERUSALEM

should see Ezekiel taking only a little coarse bread, and a little water every day, they would understand how the Jews who were still in Jerusalem were to suffer from famine, and how they would have hardly enough food to keep them from starving, while the Chaldeans were fighting against them.

And the Lord commanded Ezekiel to take a barber's razor, and with it to shave off the hair of his head and his beard. After he had done this he was to take a pair of scales, and weigh out the hair into three equal parts. Then he was to go to the place where he had left the picture of Jerusalem; and one part of the hair he was to burn there, as though it were burned in the midst of the city; one part he was to cut up into small pieces with a knife; and one part he was to hold out in his hand and let the wind blow it away on every side.

And the Lord told Ezekiel that so it should be done to the people in Jerusalem. For the Lord had chosen them to be his people before all other people, yet they had sinned against him more than any other people; therefore he was going to punish them as he had never punished any people before. A third part of them, he said, should die with the pestilence and the famine, in the midst of the city, like the hair that Ezekiel was to burn with fire; a third part should be killed by their enemies around and outside of the city, like the hair that he was to cut into pieces with a knife; and a third part should be carried away from their own land, and scattered over all the earth, like the hair that Ezekiel was to hold out in his hand, for the wind to blow it away on every side.

For the time had come, the Lord said, to punish the children of Israel for their sins, and very soon their punishment should come upon them. For he would send the worst of the heathen nations against them, who would destroy Jerusalem and go into the temple, even into the most holy place, and take away its precious and holy things. Then, the Lord said, the men of Israel would be weak with fear, and unable to fight against their enemies. And they would bring out their gold and silver and throw it into the streets; for it could do them no good, but would increase their trouble, because they had loved it more than they loved God, and had so often broken his laws in getting it.

In the sixth year after Jehoiachin was taken captive, Ezekiel saw again, the form like the form of a man, which he had seen before, sitting on a throne above the wings of the cherubim. And Ezekiel thought that a hand was stretched out from it, and that the hand took hold of a lock of his hair and lifted him up between the earth and the sky, and carried him away from the river Chebar to the gate of the temple in Jerusalem. There the Lord spoke to him, saying, Look now toward the north. So Ezekiel looked, and he saw, near the altar of burnt offering, an idol set up. And the Lord said, Dost thou see what the children of Israel have done, how they set up an idol, even in this holy place, to offend me, and make me go far away from my temple?

But turn away from this, and thou shalt see still greater wickedness. Then the Lord brought Ezekiel near to the court of the temple, and when he looked, he saw a hole in the wall. And the Lord said to him, Dig now through the wall. When Ezekiel had done so, he saw a door that led into a dark chamber. And the Lord said, Go into this chamber and see the things that are done there. So Ezekiel went in, and there, on the walls around him, he saw pictures of unclean beasts and creeping things, and of all the idols that the children of Israel worshipped. Before these pictures stood seventy of the elders of Israel, each with a censer in his hand, burning incense to the idols; and a thick cloud of smoke went up from the incense through the chamber. And the Lord said to Ezekiel, Seest thou what the elders of Israel are doing, every man worshipping his idol in the dark? For they say, The Lord does not see us, he has gone away from the earth.

Then the Lord said to Ezekiel, Turn away again, and thou shalt see yet more of their sin. And he brought him to the inner court of the temple, and there Ezekiel saw about twenty-five men with their backs turned toward the temple, and their faces toward the east, where the sun rose up in the sky; and they were bowing down to the sun and worshipping it. And the Lord said, Dost thou see this? Is it a little thing for the men of Judah to do all the evil they are doing here? For they have filled the whole land with wickedness, and now they have come back to the temple to sin against me and provoke me to anger. Therefore I will punish them in my anger, neither will I pity them; and though they shall cry out to me in their suffering I will not hear.

After the vision was over, Ezekiel thought that he was lifted up again between the earth and the sky, and brought away from Jerusalem, back to the river Chebar. When he had come there he told the captives, who were living by the river, of all the things he had seen in the vision. But they would not believe what he told them; for they still chose to believe the false prophets who said that the people in Jerusalem should not be punished, and that the city should not be taken by the king of Babylon.

CHAPTERS XII, XXIV, XXXIII, XXXVII (12, 24, 33, 37)

EZEKIEL SHOWS, BY SIGNS, THAT JERUSALEM SHALL BE TAKEN.   THE VISION OF THE VALLEY OF DRY BONES.   THE TWO STICKS JOINED FOR ISRAEL AND JUDAH.   GOD PROMISES THAT THE JEWS SHALL RETURN TO THEIR OWN LAND AND STAY THERE ALWAYS.

THE Lord commanded Ezekiel to make ready all the things that were in his house, and to carry some of them out of his door to another place, like a person who is moving.   He was to do this in the day time.   But when the evening should come, he was to dig an opening through the wall of his house, and was to go out through the opening, carrying more of his things upon his shoulder.   At the same time he was to cover his face as if he were in trouble, and did not wish other persons to know him.

Then Ezekiel did as the Lord commanded; he made his things ready and carried a part of them out of the door of his house in the day time, and took them and left them in another place. And in the evening he digged through the wall and brought out more of them, through an opening in the wall, carrying them upon his shoulder; and he covered his face like a person in trouble who did not wish others to know him.   The people who were captives with him, saw him doing all this.

The next morning the Lord spoke to him, saying, Do they not ask thee what these things mean?   Tell them they are to show what will happen to king Zedekiah and all the people in the land of Israel.   As thou hast taken the things out of thy house, and moved them to another place, so shall they be carried away captive to other lands.   And king Zedekiah shall go also. His servants shall break through the wall, and he shall flee out of the city in the evening, carrying a burden upon his shoulder, and he shall cover his face to keep the Chaldeans from knowing him.   Yet he shall not escape, for I will give him into their

28

hands and they shall take him to Babylon. But although he shall go into that land, and die there, he shall not see it. The Lord meant that Zedekiah would not be able to see the land into which he was taken, because king Nebuchadnezzar would put out his eyes before he should go there.

And the Lord commanded Ezekiel, when he should eat bread and drink water, to tremble, like a person who was afraid that his enemies were coming to take it from him. Then he was to tell the people that so the Jews in Jerusalem, and in the land of Israel, would tremble and be afraid, when their enemies should come to fight against them. Because their enemies should come, the Lord said, to destroy their cities and carry away the people and leave the whole land lonely and desolate.

And in the ninth year, in the tenth month, and on the tenth day of the month, the Lord told Ezekiel to write down the day, so that it might be remembered; for on this day, he said, the king of Babylon has gone up against Jerusalem to besiege it.

After these things some of the captives to whom Ezekiel was speaking, came to him and said, If we must be punished for all the sins we have done, and if the Lord is determined to destroy us for them, what can we do, and who can save us? Ezekiel answered them, This you can do: Repent of your sins and cease doing evil. For thus saith the Lord: As truly as I live, I have no pleasure in punishing the wicked man, or in putting him to death for his sin; but would rather he should turn from his wickedness and live. Turn ye, turn ye from your evil ways; for why will ye die, O ye children of Israel?

And in the twelfth year, in the tenth month, and on the fifth day of the month, a man who had escaped out of Jerusalem, came to Ezekiel at the river Chebar, and said that the city was taken. Then when the captives heard this, they knew that Ezekiel had told them only those words that the Lord had spoken to him, but that the false prophets had deceived them when they said that the men of Israel should not be punished for their sins, and that Jerusalem should not be taken by the king of Babylon. For now all Ezekiel's words had come true. The king of Babylon had taken Jerusalem, and had broken down the walls of the city, and burned the houses, and the king's palace, and the temple with fire. He had taken king Zedekiah also and put out his eyes, and carried him and the people away to Babylon; and the whole land was left lonely and desolate.

EZEKIEL IN THE VALLEY OF DRY BONES

And yet, although the Lord had sent all these troubles upon the children of Israel, he did not mean wholly to destroy them, but only to punish them for a time, until they should repent; then he intended to bless them and take them for his people again. He commanded Ezekiel to tell them that the day was coming when he would seek for them in all the lands where they were carried away captive, as a shepherd seeks for his sheep that are lost, and that he would bring them back to their own land, where they had lived before.

Once more the Lord showed Ezekiel a vision. Ezekiel thought that he was carried out into a valley where the ground was covered with dead men's bones. And he walked about among the bones and looked on them, and saw they had no flesh on them, but were very dry. And the Lord spoke to him and asked him, saying, Can these bones be made alive again? Ezekiel answered, O Lord God, thou knowest. The Lord said to him, Speak to them and say, O ye dry bones, listen to the command of the Lord; for he says that flesh shall come upon you, and breath shall come into you, and you shall live.

So Ezekiel spoke the words that the Lord commanded. After he had spoken, he heard a noise among the bones, and saw a shaking among them; they began to move and come together, each bone to the one belonging to it. And as soon as they had come together, flesh grew upon them, and skin, until the bones all became bodies again. But there was no breath in them; they were still dead.

Then the Lord spoke to Ezekiel and commanded him to speak to the winds, and say, Come ye winds and blow upon these dead bodies, that they may have breath, and live. And Ezekiel spoke to the winds, and the winds blew upon the dead bodies, and breath came into them; they breathed and were alive, and all stood up on their feet like a very great army.

Then the Lord explained to Ezekiel why he had shown him this vision, and what it meant. He told him that all the people of Israel complained because of their punishment and their trouble; they said they were like bones that were dry and dead, and that they had lost all hope of ever being happy, or of seeing their own land again. But the Lord said he would raise them up out of their troubles, as he had raised those dry bones to life, and that he would bring them back to their own land. When he had saved them from their troubles, and put his Spirit in their hearts, and brought them back to their own land again, then the children of Israel would know that it was the Lord who had spoken these words to them, and that he had made his words come true.

The Lord commanded Ezekiel to take two sticks and give each of them a name; one was to be named for the kingdom of

Israel, and the other for the kingdom of Judah. And Ezekiel was to write its name upon each stick. Then he was to hold the two sticks close together; and while he was holding them, the Lord said, they would grow into one stick in his hand.

When the people should see this and ask him what it meant, Ezekiel was to answer them, Thus saith the Lord, I will take the children of Israel away from the nations where they have gone captive, and will bring them back to the land of Canaan. And after they come there, they shall not be divided into two nations any more, but I will make them one nation. Neither shall they worship idols nor do wickedly; for I will put my Spirit into their hearts and make them holy, and they shall be my people and I will be their God. They shall live in the land where their fathers lived, and their children, and their children's children shall live there always. And I will be kind to them and will give them a king who shall rule over them forever.

We have read, before this, that the prophet Jeremiah told the people they should stay in Babylon seventy years, and then go back to Jerusalem. And what Jeremiah told them came true. When the seventy years were ended, the Jews did go back to Jerusalem and to Canaan, and lived in their own country, but this was not the going back that Ezekiel meant. For after they had gone back they sinned yet more than they had ever sinned before, and made God more angry with them than he ever had been, because they crucified his Son. Therefore he sent them out of Canaan again, and scattered them among all nations, as they are scattered at this day.

But Ezekiel tells us, in the words we have just read, that the Lord means to bring them back into Canaan once more, and that when he shall do so, they will stay there always. For then they will not sin any more, but will repent of their wickedness in crucifying God's Son, and will believe on him, and obey him, and take him for their Saviour.

The time for this to happen to the Jews has not come yet, and we cannot tell when it may come. But we are sure that it will come, because God, by his holy prophet, has told us so.

THE BOOK OF DANIEL

CHAPTERS I, II (1, 2)

DANIEL, SHADRACH, MESHACH, AND ABEDNEGO ARE TAKEN TO BABYLON
BY KING NEBUCHADNEZZAR.   THEY REFUSE TO EAT THE FOOD WHICH
IS SENT THEM BY THE KING.   THEY COME AS SERVANTS INTO THE KING'S
PALACE.   DANIEL INTERPRETS NEBUCHADNEZZAR'S DREAM OF THE
GREAT IMAGE.

WHILE king Nebuchadnezzar was in Jerusalem, he commanded the chief of his officers to choose some of the princes of the children of Israel, that he might take them to be servants in his palace at Babylon. None should be chosen, the king said, who had any fault in them, but only such as were young and beautiful and quick to learn. For he wanted them to be taught in all the wisdom of the Chaldeans, and to learn also the language that the Chaldeans spoke. After they had been instructed in these things for three years, they were to come to the palace, and stay there and wait on the king.

Among those that were chosen by the chief officer were four young men, named Daniel, Shadrach, Meshach, and Abednego. These four were brought to Babylon, and teachers were set over them, that they might be taught as king Nebuchadnezzar commanded. And the king sent them, each day, meat and wine from his own table, intending so to feed them until they should come to live at the palace and wait upon him.

Now the Chaldeans worshipped idols, and offered up sacrifices of animals, and drink offerings of wine to them; and they ate of the sacrifices, and drank of the wine that had been offered to their idols. But Daniel did not wish to eat what had been offered to idols, lest he might offend the Lord; and beside, some of the animals that the Chaldeans ate, the Lord had commanded the children of Israel not to eat; they were called unclean. Therefore Daniel said to himself that he would not eat of the meat, nor drink of the wine that the king sent him, and the three young men who were with him said they also would not.

And Daniel spoke to the chief officer, who had the care of him, about this thing, and asked his permission not to eat the

food which the king sent. Now the Lord had made the chief
officer love Daniel, yet he dared not do as Daniel asked him;
he answered, saying, I am afraid it will displease the king, who
sends you your meat and your drink. For if, after a while, he
should see your faces look paler and thinner than the faces of
the other young men who eat food from the king's table, he may
be angry with me, and put me to death.

DANIEL AND HIS THREE FRIENDS REFUSING THE KING'S FOOD

And the chief officer gave Daniel and his friends to the care
of the steward. Then Daniel came and said to the steward,
Try us, I beseech thee, ten days: give us, for that time, only
pulse (that is, vegetables) to eat, and water to drink. Afterward
look at our faces, and then at the faces of the other young men,
who eat of the king's food, and if we look not as well as they,
give us whatever thou shalt think best to eat.

So the steward gave them pulse for ten days, and at the end

of that time, their faces were fatter and fairer than the faces of all the other young men who ate food from the king's table. Then he took away the meat and the wine that were sent to them, and gave them only pulse to eat. And God helped these four young men to get knowledge and wisdom, and he made Daniel to understand visions and dreams.

After they had been taught for three years, the chief officer brought them into the palace of the king. And king Nebuchadnezzar talked with them, and found that among all those who had been chosen for his servants, none were like Daniel, Shadrach, Meshach, and Abednego; therefore they stayed at the palace and waited on the king. And to all the questions which the king asked them, they replied with wisdom and understanding, and he found them ten times better than all the wise men in his kingdom. Daniel lived in Babylon for more than seventy years.

One night King Nebuchadnezzar dreamed a dream that troubled him, so that he could not sleep. Then he commanded his servants to call all the wise men of Babylon; and the wise men came and stood before him. And the king said, I have dreamed a dream and am troubled because of it. Then the wise men spoke to the king, and said, O king, live forever: tell us what thy dream was, and we will interpret it for thee. The king answered, and said to the wise men, The thing is gone from me, and I cannot remember it: if you will not tell me what my dream was, and the interpretation of it, you shall be cut to pieces, and your houses shall be torn down and made into heaps. But if you tell me my dream and interpret it for me, you shall have great riches and honor. Therefore tell me my dream and the interpretation of it.

The wise men answered again, and said, If the king will tell us his dream, we will tell the interpretation of it. The king answered, I know that you want to deceive me and gain time, until some evil has happened to me, so that you need not tell me at all; therefore tell it to me now, and when you tell me what my dream was, I will know that you can tell me the interpretation. The wise men answered the king, and said, There is not a man on the earth who can tell the king his dream; therefore there is no king or ruler who would ask such a thing of any wise man. For it is a strange thing that the king asks of us —to tell him his dream, when he himself has forgotten it; and none can tell him what it was, except the gods, who do not live on the earth.

Then the king was very angry, and he commanded that all the wise men of Babylon should be destroyed. And the commandment went forth that they should be slain. Now Daniel and his three friends had not been called before the king; but as they were among the wise men, the king's servants sought for them, that they also might be put to death. When Daniel heard of it, he said to the king's captain who had come out to slay the wise men, Why is the command made in such haste by the king? Then the captain told Daniel of all that had happened. And Daniel went into the palace to the king, and promised that if time should be given him, he would show the interpretation of the dream. And the king gave him the time that he asked for.

Then Daniel went to his house, and told his three friends to pray that God would show him what the king's dream was, so that they might not be slain. Therefore, his three friends prayed to God as Daniel asked them. And in a vision of the night, God showed Daniel the dream and the interpretation of it. Then Daniel praised God, and said, I thank thee and praise thee, O thou God of my fathers, because thou hast heard our prayer, and told me the things that the king desires to know. Therefore Daniel went to the captain of the king's soldiers, and said to him, Destroy not the wise men of Babylon, but bring me in before the king, and I will tell him the interpretation of his dream.

Then the captain brought Daniel in haste before the king, and the king said to him, Art thou able to make known to me the dream that I have dreamed, and the interpretation of it? Daniel answered, The secret which the king has asked, no wise man on earth can tell him, but there is a God in heaven that telleth secret things; in thy dream he has made known to thee what shall happen in the times to come. And God has told it to me, not because I am wiser than any one else, but that I should tell it to thee, and show thee that he is the true God, who is worshipped by the captives from Judah.

Then Daniel told king Nebuchadnezzar his dream: he said, Thou sawest in thy dream, O king, a great image. The form of it was terrible, and it shone with exceeding brightness as it stood before thee. Its head was made of fine gold, its breast and arms were of silver, the rest of its body was of brass; its legs were of iron, and its feet were part of iron and part of clay. Thou sawest it, until, as thou wast looking, there came a stone cut out of a mountain, that struck the image upon its feet and broke them to pieces. Then the image fell, and the iron, the brass, the silver, the gold, and the clay were all broken up together by the stone, into pieces as small as the dust which is left on the threshing-floor, after the farmer has been threshing his grain; and the wind blew them away, no one could tell where. Afterward the stone that had broken the image, grew to be a great mountain and filled all the earth. This was the king's dream.

Then Daniel told the king the interpretation of it. The gold, the silver, the brass, the iron, and the clay that were in the image, all meant different kingdoms. The head of gold meant Nebuchadnezzar himself, Daniel said, because God had given him the greatest of the kingdoms, and made him greater than all the other kings who were upon the earth. But after he should die, new kingdoms would arise: the silver, the brass, the iron, and the clay, meant these. Last of all, Daniel said, the Lord would set up one kingdom more, which should never be destroyed, but should break in pieces all the kingdoms that were before it, as the stone cut out of the mountain had broken the image in Nebuchadnezzar's dream. This stone meant the kingdom of Christ.

After Daniel had told the king his dream, and the interpretation of it, the king fell on his face before Daniel, and said to him, It is true that your God is a God of gods, and a King of kings, and can tell all secret things, because he has told thee this dream. Then the king made Daniel a great man, and gave him many gifts, and appointed him ruler over the province of

Babylon, and the chief governor over all the wise men. And, because Daniel requested it, he made his three friends also rulers in the land. But Daniel stayed at the palace of the king.

SHADRACH, MESHACH, AND ABEDNEGO WILL NOT WORSHIP THE GOLDEN IMAGE

CHAPTERS III, IV (3, 4)

SHADRACH, MESHACH, AND ABEDNEGO ARE CAST INTO THE FIERY FURNACE. DANIEL INTERPRETS THE KING'S DREAM OF THE GREAT TREE. NEBU-CHADNEZZAR IS DRIVEN OUT TO LIVE WITH THE BEASTS.

NEBUCHADNEZZAR, the king, made an image of gold, and set it up on a plain in the province of Babylon. Then the king sent and called the princes, the governors, the captains, the judges, and all the rulers of his kingdom; and these great men came and were gathered together before the image that Nebuchadnezzar had set up. Then one of the king's servants called out in a loud voice to them, and said, It is commanded that as soon as you hear the sound of the harp, the flute, the trumpet, and all kinds of music, you shall fall down and worship the golden image that Nebuchadnezzar, the king, has set up. And whosoever falleth not down and worshippeth, shall that same hour be cast into the midst of a burning, fiery furnace. Then the king commanded the musicians to play, and as soon as the people heard the sound of the music, they all fell down and worshipped the golden image.

But some of the Chaldeans came to the king, and spoke against the Jews, saying, O king, live forever! Thou, O king, hast made a law that every man who shall hear the sound of the flute, the harp, the trumpet, and all kinds of music, shall fall down and worship the golden image, and that whosoever falleth not down and worshippeth, shall be cast into the burning, fiery furnace. There are some Jews whom thou hast set over the province of Babylon, named Shadrach, Meshach, and Abednego, and these men, O King, have not obeyed thee, they serve not thy gods, nor worship the golden image which thou hast set up.

Then Nebuchadnezzar, because these men had not obeyed him, commanded that they bring Shadrach, Meshach, and Abednego; and they brought them before the king. Nebuchadnezzar spoke to them, and said, Is it true, O Shadrach, Meshach, and Abednego, that ye do not serve my gods, nor worship the golden image that I have set up? Now, if you be ready when you shall hear the sound of the harp, the flute, the trumpet, and all kinds of music, and fall down and worship the image I have made, no harm shall be done to you; but if you worship not, you shall be cast, the same hour, into the midst of a burning, fiery furnace; and who is the God that is able to save you out of my hands?

Then Shadrach, Meshach, and Abednego answered and said to the king, We are not afraid to tell thee what we will do in this matter. If thou wilt cast us into the burning, fiery furnace, our God, whom we serve, is able to save us from death, and he will save us out of thy hand, O king. Yet even if he let us burn, we tell thee, O king, that we will not serve thy gods, nor worship the golden image that thou hast set up.

Then was Nebuchadnezzar full of fury. He looked in fierce anger on Shadrach, Meshach, and Abednego, and said to his ser-

SHADRACH, MESHACH, AND ABEDNEGO IN THE FIERY FURNACE

vants, that they should heat the furnace seven times hotter than it was heated before. And he commanded the most mighty soldiers in his army to bind Shadrach, Meshach, and Abednego, and cast them into it. Then these three men were bound, in their coats, their hats, and their other garments, and were thrown into the burning, fiery furnace. And because the furnace was exceeding hot, and the king made them go near to it, the flame killed the men who cast Shadrach, Meshach, and Abednego in; and these three men, Shadrach, Meshach, and Abednego, fell down, bound, into the midst of the fire. But soon they rose up, and walked in the fire; for God would not let it burn them.

Then Nebuchadnezzar, the king, was astonished, and he said in haste to the rulers and great men who were with him, Did we not cast three men bound, into the midst of the fire? They answered, We did, O king. And he said, Lo, I see four men, loose and walking in the midst of the fire, and they are not hurt. And the form of the fourth is like the Son of God. Then Nebuchadnezzar came near to the mouth of the burning, fiery furnace, and cried out and said, Shadrach, Meshach, and Abednego, ye servants of the Most High God, come out and come here. Then Shadrach, Meshach, and Abednego came out of the midst of the fire. And the princes, the governors, and the captains, who were gathered together, saw these men whom the fire had not hurt, nor was a hair of their heads burned, neither were their coats changed, nor was the smell of the fire upon them.

Then Nebuchadnezzar spoke and said, Blessed be the God of Shadrach, Meshach, and Abednego, who has sent his angel and saved his servants that trusted in him. Therefore I make a decree and a law, that every nation and people which shall speak evil of the God of Shadrach, Meshach, and Abednego, shall be destroyed, and their houses shall be torn down and made into heaps; for there is no other God that can save like him. Then the king made Shadrach, Meshach, and Abednego greater than they had been before, in the province of Babylon.

Now Babylon was a very great city. The river Euphrates ran through the midst of it, so that part of the city was on one side of the river, and part on the other. The walls around Babylon were sixty miles long. They had in them one hundred gates, all made of brass. Built up above the walls were high towers. The palace of king Nebuchadnezzar was of great size, and ornamented with statues of men and animals, with vessels of gold and silver, and with many other costly and beautiful things which he had taken from the nations that he made to serve him.

Near to his palace were large gardens, called The Hanging

Gardens, because they were raised high up in the air, on the sides of a hill. We read (not in the Bible, but in other books which tell us about him) that Nebuchadnezzar made these gardens to please his wife. She had lived, while she was young, in a hilly country. When the king married her and brought her to Babylon, which stood on a wide, level plain, she longed for hills and woods, like those in the land where she was born. Then Nebuchadnezzar had this great hill made, four hundred feet high, and planted its sides with trees, and bushes and flowers. Steps led up to its top, and water was drawn from the river that flowed through the city, to water the gardens that were planted upon it. From a distance it looked like a mountain covered with woods.

And Nebuchadnezzar lived in Babylon. He was a mighty king, and had princes and rulers for his servants, who, because they wanted to please him, told him of his greatness and praised everything that he did; so that he forgot God, and thought only of his own riches and power. Then God was displeased, and sent a strange punishment upon him. But after he had been punished, Nebuchadnezzar repented of his sins, and he sent to all the people of his kingdom, and to all the nations of the earth, an account of what God had done to him.

He said, I thought it right to tell you of the wonderful things that God has done to me. I had gained the victory over my enemies, and was at rest in my palace, with nothing to trouble me, when I had a dream that made me afraid. Therefore I called all the wise men of Babylon and told them my dream. But they could not interpret it. At last came Daniel before me, in whom is the spirit of the holy gods; and I told him my dream. I said to him, I saw a tree that stood in the midst of a wide plain, and the height of it was great. The tree grew and was strong, and it reached up to heaven, and its branches spread out to the ends of the earth. The leaves of it were green, and the fruit plentiful. The beasts of the field lay down under its shadow, and the birds of the air made their nests in its branches, and everything that lived came to it for food.

And I saw in my dream a holy angel come down from heaven.

He cried with a loud voice, Hew down the tree, and cut off its branches, shake off its leaves and scatter its fruit. Let the beasts get away from under it, and the birds from its branches. Yet leave the stump of the tree in the ground, where the dew shall fall upon it and wet it. Let it be with the beasts out in the field, until seven years are past. This dream I, Nebuchadnezzar, have seen. And I said, O Daniel, tell me the interpretation of it, because all the wise men of my kingdom are not able to make it known to me. But thou art able, for the Spirit of God is in thee.

Then Daniel was troubled, and afraid to answer the king. But the king said to him, Let not the dream trouble thee, and do not fear to tell me the interpretation of it. Then Daniel said, The tree which thou sawest, which grew and was strong, whose height reached to heaven, under which the beasts lay down, and among whose branches the birds built their nests— that tree means thee, O king, who hast grown great and full of power, and whose kingdom reaches to the end of the earth. And as thou didst see a holy angel coming down from heaven, and saying, Cut down the tree and destroy it, yet leave the stump of its roots in the earth, and let it be wet with dew, and be with the wild beasts of the field, till seven years pass over it, this is the interpretation, O king, and this is what God has said shall be done to thee, Thou shalt not stay in thy palace to be waited on by thy servants and to live among men. But they shall drive thee out to live with the beasts of the field; thou shalt eat grass like oxen, and lie upon the ground like them, and be wet with the dew, till thou hast learned that God rules over all the nations of the earth, and makes whomsoever he will to be king.

And all of Daniel's words came true. At the end of twelve months, Nebuchadnezzar was walking in the palace of the kingdom of Babylon. And as he looked out upon that mighty city, its walls, its temples, its palaces, and its gardens, his heart was filled with pride; he forgot that it was God who had made him to be king, and he said, Is not this great Babylon that I have built, by my own power and for my own honor and majesty?

While the words were yet in the king's mouth, there came a voice from heaven, saying, O king Nebuchadnezzar, to thee it is spoken, the kingdom is taken from thee. And they shall drive thee from men, and thou shalt live with the beasts of the field: they shall make thee eat grass like oxen, and seven years shall pass over thee, until thou knowest that God rules over all the nations of the earth, and makes whomsoever he will to be king.

In that same hour, God took from king Nebuchadnezzar his reason, so that he was no longer fit to rule over his kingdom, or to live among men. And he was driven out and did eat grass like oxen, and lay upon the ground, and his body was wet with the dew, till his hairs were grown like eagles' feathers, and his nails like birds' claws.

But when the seven years were ended, king Nebuchadnezzar said, I looked up to heaven, and my reason came back to me, and I praised God and honored him who lives forever, and whose kingdom shall have no end. He doeth what he will, in heaven and on earth, and no man can hold back his hand, or ask why he doeth anything. And when my reason came back to me, so did my honor and my kingdom. For the rulers and governors sought for me, and I was made king again, and all my greatness was given me. Now I, Nebuchadnezzar, praise and honor God, the king of heaven, who doeth only what is just and true; and those that are proud he is able to bring down.

CHAPTERS V, VI, IX (5, 6, 9)

DANIEL INTERPRETS THE WRITING ON THE WALL. BELSHAZZAR IS SLAIN, AND DARIUS TAKES THE KINGDOM. DANIEL IS CAST INTO THE DEN OF LIONS; HIS PRAYER FOR THE RETURN OF THE JEWS TO THEIR OWN LAND. THE ANGEL GABRIEL SPEAKS TO HIM.

AFTER these things Nebuchadnezzar died, and Belshazzar reigned over the kingdom of Babylon. He made a feast to a thousand of his lords, and drank wine with them in his palace. Belshazzar, while he tasted the wine, commanded his servants to bring the gold and silver vessels which his father, Nebuchadnezzar, had taken out of the temple in Jerusalem. Then they

29

brought the golden vessels, and the king and his princes, and his wives, drank out of them. They drank wine, and praised their idols of gold and silver, of brass, of iron, of wood, and of stone.

And while they were feasting, and making merry, there came a man's hand, and wrote words upon the wall of the king's palace, in the room where the king and his lords held their feast. But the writing was in a language they could not understand. And the king saw the hand that wrote. Then his face was changed, for his thoughts troubled him and he was filled with fear, so that his knees trembled and smote one against another. And he cried out aloud to his servants that they should bring in the wise men before him. When the wise men came, he said to them, Whoever shall read this writing, and tell the interpretation of it, shall be clothed with scarlet, and have a chain of gold about his neck, and shall be the third ruler in the kingdom. But none of the wise men could read the writing, or tell the interpretation. Then the king was troubled yet more, and his lords were astonished at what had been done.

Now the queen, when she heard what the king had said, came in before him and spoke to him, saying, O king, live forever; let not thy thoughts trouble thee, nor let thy face be sad. There is a man in thy kingdom in whom is the spirit of the holy gods, and in the days when thy father, Nebuchadnezzar, lived, great wisdom was found in him, and the king, Nebuchadnezzar, thy father, made him master over all the wise men of Babylon; because he had knowledge and understanding for interpreting dreams, and telling of secret things. Now let Daniel be called, and he will tell the interpretation.

Then was Daniel brought in before the king. And the king spoke to him, and said, Art thou that Daniel who was brought captive with the children of Israel, out of Judah? I have heard of thee that the spirit of the gods is in thee, and that thou hast understanding and excellent wisdom. And now the wise men have been brought in before me, that they should read this writing, and make known to me the interpretation, but they cannot. And I have heard of thee that thou canst interpret and tell secret things. Now if thou canst read the writing, and

BELSHAZZAR'S FEAST

make known the interpretation of it, thou shalt be clothed with scarlet and have a chain of gold about thy neck, and shalt be the third ruler in the kingdom.

Then Daniel answered, and said before the king, Keep thy gifts for thyself, and give thy rewards to another. Yet will I read the writing to the king, and make known to him the interpretation. O thou king, the most high God gave Nebuchadnezzar, thy father, a kingdom and glory and honor. And because God made him so great, all nations trembled and feared before him. Whom he would he slew, and whom he would he kept alive; whom he would he set up, and whom he would he put down.

But when his heart was full of pride, so that he forgot God, he was made to come down from his throne, and his greatness was taken from him. He was driven out from his palace, and from living among men, and was made like the beasts and lived with the wild asses. They fed him with grass like oxen, and his body was wet with the dew, till he learned that God rules over the nations of the earth, and maketh whomsoever he will to be king.

And thou, his son, hast not humbled thy heart, though thou knewest all this, but hast been proud, and sinned against God; and they have brought the vessels of the temple of God before thee, and thou and thy lords, and thy wives, have drunk wine in them. Thou hast praised the idols of silver and gold, of brass, iron, wood, and stone, which cannot see, nor hear, nor know anything; but the true God who lets thee live, and gives thee all things, thou hast not praised. Therefore has he sent this hand, and this writing was written; and these are the words of it: MENE, MENE, TEKEL, UPHARSIN. This is the interpretation: Thy kingdom is ended, God has taken it from thee. He tried thee as king, but thou hast not obeyed him. He has given thy kingdom to the Medes and the Persians.

When Daniel had interpreted the dream, then Belshazzar commanded his servants to clothe him with scarlet, and to put a chain of gold about his neck, and the king made a decree that he should be third ruler in the kingdom. That same night came Cyrus, with the army of the Medes and Persians, into

Babylon, and Belshazzar, the king of the Chaldeans, was slain, and Darius, the Mede, took the kingdom.

After Darius was made king, it pleased him to set over the people one hundred and twenty princes. Over these princes he set three presidents, and Daniel was the first of them. So Daniel was the chief one of all the presidents and princes, because of the wise and good spirit that was in him. And Darius

DANIEL PRAYS TO GOD BESIDE THE OPEN WINDOW

thought to make him ruler over the whole kingdom. Then the presidents and the princes hated Daniel, because he was greater than they, and they tried to find out some evil concerning him, that they might speak against him to the king. But they could find none, for he was faithful, and no fault nor error was to be found in him. Therefore these men said, We shall not be able to complain of this Daniel to the king, unless it be about something that he does in serving his God.

Then they gathered together and came to the king, and said, King Darius, live forever. All the presidents of thy kingdom, the governors, the princes, and the captains, want a law and a decree to be made, that whosoever shall ask help of any god or man, for thirty days, except of thee, O king, shall be cast into the den of lions. Now, O king, make this law and this decree, and sign the writing, so that it cannot be changed; for the law of the Medes and Persians changes not. Therefore king Darius signed the writing and the decree.

Now, when Daniel knew that the writing was signed, he went into his house, and the windows of his chamber being opened toward Jerusalem, he kneeled upon his knees three times a day, and prayed and gave thanks to his God, as he had always done. Then these men gathered together, and found Daniel praying and asking help of God. And they went to the king, and said, Hast thou not signed a decree, that whoever shall ask help of any god, or man, for thirty days, except of thee, O king, shall be cast into the den of lions? The king answered, The decree is signed, and is made a law of the Medes and Persians, which changes not. Then answered they, and said, That Daniel, who is one of the captives of Judah, obeys thee not, O king, or the decree that thou hast made, but prays and asks help of his God three times a day.

Then the king, when he heard these words, was displeased with himself for having made the decree, because he did not want to punish Daniel. And he set his heart on having him excused, and tried until the evening to save him from punishment. But the presidents and the princes gathered together to the king, and said to him, Thou knowest, O king, that it is the law of the Medes and Persians, that no decree nor law which the king has made can be changed. Then king Darius commanded his servants, and they brought Daniel, and cast him into the den of lions. But the king spoke to Daniel, and said to him, Thy God, whom thou servest continually, he will deliver thee. And a great stone was brought and laid upon the mouth of the den.

Then the king went home to his palace, and would eat no food, but passed the night fasting. Neither were the instruments

of music played before him as at other times; and he could
not sleep. And he arose very early in the morning and came in
haste to the den of lions, and cried with a mournful voice unto
Daniel, saying, O Daniel, thou servant of the living God, is thy
God, whom thou servest continually, able to deliver thee from
the lions? Then said Daniel to the king, O king, live forever.
My God has sent his angel, and shut the lions' mouths that they

DANIEL IN THE LIONS' DEN

have not hurt me, because I have not sinned against him; and
also, unto thee, O king, I have done no wrong. Then was the
king exceedingly glad for him, and he commanded that they
should take Daniel up out of the den. So Daniel was taken
up, and no hurt was found upon him, because he trusted in his
God.

And the king commanded that those men be brought who
had spoken against Daniel, and cast into the den of lions—
them, their children, and their wives—and the lions leaped

on them, and broke all their bones in pieces, as soon as they came into the bottom of the den. Then king Darius wrote to all the people and nations of the earth, saying, I make a decree that in every part of my kingdom men tremble and fear before the God of Daniel. For he is the living God; his kingdom is the one that shall not be destroyed, and his power shall never end. He is the God who can save from danger, who has saved Daniel from the mouths of the lions. So Daniel prospered in the reign of Darius, and in the reign of Cyrus, who was made king after Darius was dead.

While Daniel was in Babylon, he read in a book the words which the Lord had commanded the prophet Jeremiah to write, saying, that after the Jews had been captive for seventy years, they should go back to their own land. And when those seventy years were nearly ended, Daniel fasted, and prayed to the Lord, for the people of Judah, that they might go back, and for the city of Jerusalem, that it might be built again. He said, O Lord, we have done wickedly and have disobeyed thy law, and would not listen to thy prophets whom thou didst send to tell us of our sins. We, and our kings, and our princes, and all the children of Israel have disobeyed thee. Therefore that punishment is come upon us which Moses said should be sent. And now, O Lord, who didst bring thy people up out of Egypt, I beseech thee be not angry against us any more; for, because of our sins, Jerusalem, and thy people, the children of Israel, are made to be ashamed before all the nations that are around us. O Lord, forgive us, and make haste to help us; for we do not ask this of thee because we deserve to be forgiven, but because thou art merciful.

While Daniel was praying, the angel Gabriel flew by him swiftly, and touched him: it was in the evening, about the time when the priests used to offer up a lamb for a burnt offering at the temple in Jerusalem. And the angel said, O Daniel, I am come to tell thee of things that shall happen. At the beginning of thy prayer I was commanded to come unto thee, for thou art greatly loved of God. Therefore, understand the words that I shall speak. Then the angel told Daniel that the Jews should go back to their own land and build up Jerusalem, and that four hundred and eighty-three years afterward the Saviour would be born. But, the Saviour, the angel said, would be put to death, and then enemies would come and destroy Jerusalem and the temple again.

THE BOOK OF EZRA

CHAPTERS I–VI (1–6)

CYRUS, KING OF PERSIA, SENDS THE JEWS BACK TO THEIR OWN LAND. THEY BEGIN TO REBUILD THE TEMPLE, BUT ARE STOPPED BY THE SAMARITANS. THE PROPHET HAGGAI REPROVES THEM FOR THEIR DELAY, AND THE TEMPLE IS FINISHED IN THE REIGN OF DARIUS.

AND now the seventy years that the Jews were to spend in captivity had passed, and the time for them to go back to their own land had come. Therefore God made Cyrus, who was king in Babylon, willing to let them go. Then those words came true which the prophet Isaiah spoke, when he was alive, saying, That God would raise up a great king, named Cyrus, who would send the people back to build up Jerusalem and the temple again. It had been nearly two hundred years since Isaiah spoke those words. Cyrus was not born at that time; neither had the Jews yet been sent away from their own land. But God knew of all that would happen, and he told his prophet to foretell these things.

And king Cyrus made a proclamation, or decree, and sent it through all his kingdom, saying, Thus saith Cyrus, king of Persia, The Lord has commanded me to build up his house in Jerusalem. Who is there among the captives from Judah that wishes to go back to his own land? Let him go now and build up the house of the Lord; and let the people of my kingdom help those who go, by giving them silver and gold, and cattle, and raiment, to take with them.

Then the chief men of the Jews, and the priests and the Levites, and all those whom the Lord made willing to go, prepared to start on their journey. And many persons gave them vessels of silver and gold, and cattle, and raiment, as the king had com-manded.   And king Cyrus brought out the vessels which Neb-uchadnezzar had taken from the temple, and he counted them and gave them to the prince of Judah, who was going back with the people.   The name of this prince was Zerubbabel; he was descended from king David.   The number of all the vessels of gold and silver that Cyrus gave to him, was five thousand and four hundred.

So Zerubbabel took the vessels and carried them to Jerusalem. And there went with him forty-two thousand, three hundred and sixty persons of the children of Israel, beside their servants, who were seven thousand, three hundred and thirty-seven more.   They had with them, seven hundred and thirty-six horses, two hun-dred and forty-five mules, four hundred and thirty-five camels, and six thousand, seven hundred and twenty asses.   When they came to Jerusalem, they found it in ruins, as the army of Nebuchadnezzar had left it so many years before.   The walls of the city, the houses, and the temple had been broken down and burned.

And the people built again the altar of the Lord, which stood in the court of the temple.   They made haste to build it that they might worship God, and ask for his help, because they were afraid of the heathen nations around them.   As soon as the altar was built they offered up burnt offerings on it every day, a lamb in the morning, and a lamb in the evening, as the children of Israel used to do, before they were carried away to Babylon.

Then they made ready to rebuild the temple, and hired men of Tyre, as Solomon had done, to cut down cedar trees on mount Lebanon, and make rafts of them and float them, by the sea, near to Jerusalem.   They gave these men meat, and drink, and oil while they worked for them; and they paid money to car-penters, and masons who began to build the house.   When the first stones of it were laid, the priests and Levites played on trumpets and cymbals, and sang songs of praise to the Lord. And the people were glad and shouted with a great shout, because the building of the temple was begun.   But many of the old men, who remembered the beautiful temple which stood there before, wept with a loud voice. So that the sounds of shouting and the sounds of weeping went up together, and were heard afar off.

We have read that after the king of Assyria carried away the ten tribes of Israel as captives, he sent people from his own land

THE REBUILDING OF THE TEMPLE

to live in the cities which they had left. These people, who were called Samaritans, had been living there ever since that time. They worshipped idols, though they pretended to serve God. But now, when they heard that the people of Judah had come back to their own land, and were rebuilding the temple, they came to Zerubbabel, and the rulers of the Jews, and said to them, Let us help you, for we are the servants of God as well as you, and have offered up sacrifices to him ever since the king of Assyria sent us to live in the land of Israel.

Zerubbabel and Jeshua, the high priest, and the chief men of Israel, answered the Samaritans, and said, You have nothing to do with the building of the Lord's house. We will build it ourselves, as Cyrus, king of Persia, has commanded us. At this answer the Samaritans were angry, and did all they could to stop the Jews, and hired men to speak to the king's officers against them. They did this as long as Cyrus lived.

After Cyrus died Artaxerxes was made king, and they wrote a letter to him, saying, We want thee to know, O king, that the Jews who came from Babylon are now at Jerusalem, which is a wicked city, and they are building it up again and setting up its walls. And if this city be built and the walls set up, they will not pay thee tribute as thy servants ought to do, but will rebel against thee. Now, because we do not want the king to be disobeyed by them, we send him word, so that he may inquire and find out whether the city of Jerusalem was not always a rebellious city, which gave trouble to the kings that reigned in the old time; for on this account Jerusalem was destroyed.

And the king did as the Samaritans asked him. Afterward he sent an answer to them, saying, The letter which you wrote me has been read before me, and I have inquired, and do find that Jerusalem was a rebellious city which gave trouble to the kings of old time. Therefore I tell you to go and command the men of Judah that they cease, and that the city be not built until permission shall be given them. Then the Samaritans went in haste to Jerusalem, and made the people cease building. So the work of building the temple was stopped as long as Artaxerxes was king.

After this Artaxerxes died, and Darius was made king. But now, although the men of Judah knew there was another king in Babylon, they did not send and ask permission of him to go on building the temple. For since the Samaritans had stopped them in building it, they had been building houses for themselves, and had become more interested in this than in finishing the house of the Lord; so they put off the building of the temple. Therefore the Lord was displeased with them, and sent Haggai, the prophet, who came and said: Thus saith the Lord, You say, It is not yet time for the Lord's house to be built. But is it time for you to be living in beautiful houses of your own, while my house lies in ruins? It is because you have left it unbuilt, and have made haste, every man, to build his own house, that I have not blessed you, and that you have not prospered and been happy. Now, therefore, go up to the mountains and cut wood, and build the house, and I will be pleased with it.

Then the people obeyed the command of the Lord, and began to build the house. But when the Samaritans saw it, they came again to Zerubbabel and to Jeshua, the high priest, and said to them, Who has commanded you to go on building the temple? Zerubbabel and Jeshua answered them, King Cyrus commanded us to come back to our own land, and to build this house. And he gave us the vessels of gold and silver which Nebuchadnezzar had taken out of the temple, and said to us, Go, carry them to Jerusalem, and let the temple be built there.

Then the Samaritans wrote a letter to king Darius, at Babylon, and told him what the people of Judah said. And they asked the king to inquire and see whether it was true that Cyrus had commanded them to build the temple. When Darius read the letter, he told his servants to search in the books where all the decrees were written down, which the different kings of Babylon had made. And a book was found with these words written in it: In the first year that Cyrus was king, he made a decree, saying, Let the house of the Lord, where the Jews used to offer up sacrifices, be built again at Jerusalem; let the foundations of it be strongly laid, and let the money that it shall cost be given out of the king's treasury. Also let the gold and silver vessels, which Nebuchadnezzar took out of the temple, be taken back to Jerusalem and put into the temple that shall be built there.

As soon as king Darius found this decree, which Cyrus had made so many years before, he sent word to the Samaritans to let the men of Judah build the house of the Lord, and not to disturb them. And Darius said, I make a decree that some of the king's tribute, which the Samaritans should pay to the king, they shall pay to the Jews instead, so that the Jews may go on building the temple: and that young bullocks, and rams, and lambs be given them for burnt offerings; and wheat and salt, and wine, and oil, whenever the priests may ask for them. Let these things be given them day by day, without fail, so that they may offer sacrifices unto God, and pray for the king and his sons. King Darius said also, Whoever shall alter this law and decree, that I have made, shall have the timber pulled out of his house, and a gallows shall be built of it, and he shall be hanged thereon. Then his house shall be torn down and made into heaps.

When the Samaritans and their chief men heard this decree, they feared to disobey the king. Therefore they ceased troubling the Jews, and gave them young bullocks, and rams, and lambs for burnt offerings, and also wheat, and salt, and wine, and oil, as the king commanded. So the men of Judah went on building the house until it was finished. Then they dedicated it to the Lord and offered up sacrifices to him, a hundred bullocks, two hundred rams, four hundred lambs, and twelve goats. And they sent the priests and Levites to the temple to attend to the worship of God there. And in the first month the people kept the feast of the passover for seven days, with joy; because the Lord had made them glad, and had caused the king of Persia to be kind to them, and to help them in finishing the temple.

CHAPTERS VII–X (7–10)

EZRA, AND THE JEWS WHO ARE WITH HIM, GO UP TO JERUSALEM. HE IS TOLD THAT MANY OF THE PEOPLE THERE HAVE TAKEN HEATHEN WIVES. HE COMMANDS THOSE WHO HAVE SINNED IN THIS THING TO PUT THEIR WIVES AWAY.

AFTER these things, and while Artaxerxes was king of Persia, there lived in Babylon a Jew, named Ezra. He was a priest and teacher of the laws which God had given to Moses, and was a learned and holy man. Now Ezra loved the Jews, and was very anxious they should obey God and have his blessing. Therefore he asked permission of Artaxerxes, the king, to go to Jerusalem that he might teach God's laws more perfectly to the Jews who were there, and see also that they obeyed them.

And Artaxerxes gave Ezra permission to go. He not only did this, but he and his princes gave him presents of gold and silver to take with him, as offerings to God. And the king gave Ezra a letter which said, I make a law and a decree, that all the people of Israel who are still in Persia, and who want to go up to Jerusalem, may go with Ezra, because he is sent to inquire and see whether the law of his God is obeyed there;

THE KING GIVES EZRA A LETTER

and to carry up the silver and gold which the king, and his princes, and the people of Babylon shall give him as an offering to the God of Israel.

And thou, Ezra, shalt take the money that is given thee, and go up, and buy with it bullocks, rams, and lambs as sacrifices, and shalt offer these on the altar, at the house of your God which is in Jerusalem. The vessels, also, which are given thee to be used at the temple, do thou carry with thee. And whatever more thou mayest need for the temple of thy God, shall be taken out of the king's treasure-house. And I, Artaxerxes, the king, do command all the treasurers who have the care of my money in the provinces where Ezra is going, to give him, whenever he shall ask for it, as much as a hundred talents of silver, a hundred measures of wheat, a hundred portions of wine, and of oil, and salt as much as he shall want, without waiting to measure it. And whatever God shall command to be done for his temple, let it be done diligently, so that he may not be angry and send punishment upon my kingdom.

And do thou, Ezra, choose men for judges in the land of Judah, that they may judge the people who have learned the law of thy God; and let those who have not learned it, be taught it. And whoever will not obey the law of thy God, and the command of the king, let him be punished with the punishment he deserves, whether it be by putting him to death, or by sending him away to some other land, or by taking away his riches from him, or by shutting him up in prison.

After the king had given this letter to Ezra, Ezra thanked God for putting into the king's heart such kind feelings toward him, and for making the king willing to let him go up to Jerusalem, that he might teach God's laws to the people. Then Ezra called some of the chief men of the Jews who were yet in Babylon, and some of the priests and Levites, and gathered them together by the river of Ahava. There they set up their tents and stayed three days. And Ezra told them to fast, and pray to the Lord, so that the Lord might show them the right way for them to go, and might take care of them, and their little children, and of the treasures they would carry with them, while they were on their journey. For Ezra was ashamed to ask the king to send soldiers with them, to guard them by the way; because he had told the king that the Lord himself would guard all those who obeyed him, but would punish those who sinned against him. So Ezra and all the people who were with him, fasted and prayed to God, and God heard their prayers.

Then Ezra called to him twelve of the priests, and he weighed out to them the silver, the gold, and the vessels which had been given by the king, and the princes, and the people as offerings to the temple. He found there were six hundred and fifty talents of silver, and of silver vessels a hundred talents, and of gold a hundred talents; also twenty basins of gold, and two vessels of fine copper as precious as gold. And Ezra said to the priests, This silver and gold is an offering to the Lord. Be careful of it and watch over it to keep it safe, until you shall bring it to Jerusalem, and there weigh it out again and give it to the priests and Levites at the temple.

Then the priests took the silver, the gold, and the vessels, to bring them to the temple. And Ezra, and all the people who were with him, started from the river of Ahava on the twelfth day of the first month. They had to go through a wild, desert country, and enemies were waiting to rob them as they passed by. But the Lord watched over them, and would not allow their enemies to harm them. So they went on their journey, and in about four months safely reached Jerusalem. After coming into the city they rested for three days. Then they went up to the temple, and there the silver, the gold, and the vessels, which they had brought, were weighed again, to see that none had been lost; and afterward, were given to the priests and Levites at the temple.

And now all the Jews who had come from Babylon with Ezra, and whom the Lord had saved from their enemies by the way, offered up sacrifices to God, twelve bullocks, ninety-six rams, seventy-seven lambs, and twelve goats. And Ezra gave the letters which the king had written, to the governors who ruled over the provinces in that part of the kingdom; and the governors obeyed the words of the king, and gave to Ezra and the people such things as the king commanded.

After this, some of the chief men among the Jews, came to Ezra, and told him that the people of Jerusalem, and also the priests and the Levites, had disobeyed the Lord; for they had made friends with the heathen nations around them, and taken heathen women for their wives. And the princes and rulers, the men said, had been the principal ones in committing this sin. When Ezra heard their words, he was filled with sorrow; he

30

rent his clothes, and plucked off the hair of his head, and sat down in great distress. Then all those persons who served God, and who were afraid lest he might punish the people for their wickedness, came to Ezra. But Ezra sat still in his grief, until the time when the evening sacrifice of a lamb was being offered up at the temple.

Then he kneeled down and spread out his hands, and prayed, saying, O my God, I am ashamed to lift up my face to thee; because the sins of the children of Israel are so many and so great, that they are like a mountain reaching up to the skies. All our lives we have been sinning against thee, and because of our sins thou hast let the heathen nations gain the victory over us, and they have killed our people with the sword, and made us their captives, as we are at this day.

But thou, our God, hadst pity upon us, and madest the kings of Persia kind to us, so that they allowed us to come back to our own land, and to build up the temple again. Yet after all this, we have disobeyed thy commandments, which said, You shall not make friends with the wicked nations of Canaan, nor take wives from among them for ever. O Lord, thou art good to us because thou hast not destroyed us for this, but dost allow us still to live. And now we are come before thee with our sins upon us; for we have no excuse to make.

When Ezra had prayed, and confessed the wickedness of the people, there came to him great numbers of men and women and children, who were weeping on account of the sins that had been done. Then one of the men of Israel, whose name was Shecaniah, spoke to Ezra and said, We have sinned against God and taken wives from among the heathen nations. Yet, now, that he may forgive us, let us promise him to put away our wives from us, as thou hast told us we should. Rise up, Ezra, for thou hast power to make us obey thee; and we also will help thee; fear not then, but do it.

Then Ezra rose up and made the priests, the Levites, and all the people promise to do as Shecaniah said. And word was sent through all the land of Judah, that the people should come to Jerusalem, and that whoever would not come within three days, should have his money, his goods, his cattle, and all that he had, taken from him; and should not any longer be counted as one of the children of Israel. So the people came within three days. And they were gathered together in the street near to the temple, afraid and trembling on account of their sin; at the same time a great rain was falling upon them.

Then Ezra stood up and spoke to them, saying, You have disobeyed God and taken heathen wives, and so have brought still greater guilt upon the children of Israel. Now, therefore, confess your guilt to God, and do what will please him. Be no longer friends with those wicked nations, and put away your heathen wives from you. Then all the people answered with a loud voice, saying, As thou hast commanded, so we will do. Yet, they said, we cannot stand without, in the rain; neither can we all of us put away our wives in one day, or in two days, for a great many of us have sinned in this thing. Let our rulers, therefore, meet together, and let all those who have taken heathen wives come before them, that the rulers may judge them, and command each one what he shall do, so that the anger of our Lord may be turned away from us.

And Ezra did as the people said. For he, and some of the chief of the elders, went on the first day of the tenth month, and sat down at a place where the men of Israel could come to them. And all who had taken heathen wives came and confessed their sin, and promised to put them away. So many persons did this, that it took Ezra, and the elders who were with him, three months to question them all and hear what they had to say, and to tell each one what it would be right for him to do.

THE BOOK OF ESTHER

CHAPTERS I–IV (1–4)

KING AHASUERUS MAKES A GREAT FEAST TO HIS SERVANTS IN HIS PALACE
VASHTI, THE QUEEN, REFUSES TO OBEY HIM.   ESTHER IS MADE QUEEN.
HAMAN, BECAUSE MORDECAI WILL NOT BOW TO HIM, TRIES TO DESTROY
ALL THE JEWS IN THE KINGDOM.

ALL the Jews had not come back to Jerusalem with Zerubbabel and Ezra: many of them still lived in the land of Persia.
The name of the king who reigned over Persia at this time
was Ahasuerus.   In the third year of his reign, he made a
great feast for his servants in the court, or garden of his palace,
that was in the city of Shushan, where the kings of Persia lived
during the winter.   Around the court were hung curtains of
white and green and blue, which were fastened by cords and
silver rings, to pillars of marble.   The beds in the palace were
made of gold and silver, and the pavement was of red and blue,
and white and black marble.   The persons at the feast drank out
of vessels of gold, and the king's wine was given in abundance, so
that every man might drink as much as he wanted.

Vashti, the queen, also made a feast for the women in the
palace of king Ahasuerus.   And on the seventh day of the king's
feast, after he had drunk wine and was merry, he sent to bring
Vashti before him, with the crown upon her head, that the princes
and people might see her beauty.   Now in Persia the women
lived in a separate part of the house, by themselves, and never
came out before men unless they wore veils.   And when the king
Ahasuerus sent for Vashti, the queen, to come before all the
princes and people, that they might see her face unveiled, she
refused to obey the king's command.

Therefore the king was angry, and said to his wise men,
What shall we do to queen Vashti, and how shall she be punished, because she has not obeyed the command of the king?
One of the wise men answered, Vashti has done wrong, not only
to the king, but also to all the princes and people of thy kingdom.   For all the women of Persia will no more obey their husbands, when they hear that king Ahasuerus commanded Vashti,

the queen, to come in before him and she came not. Therefore let the king make a decree, and let it be written among the laws of the Medes and Persians, which cannot be changed, that Vashti shall come no more before the king; and let the king choose another woman for queen who is better than she. Then, when this decree shall be known throughout the kingdom, all the wives, both of rich men and of poor men, will obey their husbands.

These words pleased the king and his princes, and the king did as the wise man had told him. For he sent letters through all the different provinces of his kingdom, commanding that every man should be ruler in his own house, and that this law should be made known to all the people. Then the king's servants came to him, saying, Let the king send officers to all the provinces of his kingdom, that they may gather together all the beautiful young women of Persia into the palace at Shushan; and let the one who pleaseth the king best, be queen instead of Vashti. And the king did as his servants said.

Now there was among the servants at the palace a Jew, named Mordecai, who had a cousin named Esther. She was a Jewess. Her father and mother were dead, but when they died Mordecai took Esther to his house, and since that time had brought her up as his own daughter. And the maid was fair and beautiful.

And it happened, when the king's command was made known through the land, and many young maidens were gathered together at Shushan, the palace, that Esther was brought there among them, and given to the care of the king's officer who had the charge of the women. The officer was pleased with Esther, and gave her a present, and also seven young maidens to wait on her; and he put her and her maidens into the best part of the house of the women. But Esther did not let it be known that she was a Jewess, for Mordecai had advised her not to tell it.

When king Ahasuerus saw Esther, he loved her more than all the other maidens who were brought before him, so that he set the royal crown upon her head, and made her queen instead of Vashti. Then the king made a great feast that was called Esther's feast, and he gave gifts to his servants for her sake. But Esther was still careful to do all that Mordecai told her, for she obeyed him now, although she was made queen, as willingly as when she lived in his house and was brought up as his own daughter.

THE CROWNING OF ESTHER

In those days, two of the king's officers, because they were angry with the king, wanted to lay hands on him and kill him. But Mordecai, who was a watchman at the king's gate, heard what they said, and told Esther, and Esther told the king. When the officers were examined their guilt was found out, and they were both hanged on a gallows. And what Mordecai had done to save the king's life, was written down in a book, where an account was kept of all the principal things that happened in the kingdom.

Now there was at the palace a servant named Haman. After these things, king Ahasuerus made Haman a great man, and set him above all the princes who were at the palace with him.

MORDECAI WILL NOT BOW DOWN BEFORE HAMAN

And all the king's servants, who watched by the king's gate, bowed down and did reverence before Haman, for so the king commanded them to do. But Mordecai would not bow down before him. Then the king's servants said to Mordecai, Why dost thou not obey the king's command? And after they had spoken to him day by day, and he would not listen to them, they told Haman of it.

When Haman saw that Mordecai bowed not, nor did him reverence, he was very angry and determined to punish him. But he was not satisfied to punish Mordecai alone, he thought he would punish, and destroy, all the Jews that were in Persia; for the king's servants had told him that Mordecai was a Jew.

So Haman spoke to king Ahasuerus against the Jews. He said, There are some of them living in all the provinces of thy kingdom, and they have laws of their own which are different from the laws of thy people, neither do they obey the king's laws. Therefore it is not well for the king to let them live. And if the king will make a decree that they shall be destroyed, I will pay ten thousand talents of silver into the king's treasury.

King Ahasuerus listened to what Haman said, and took his ring from his finger and gave it to Haman. Now the ring was what the king used when he made a law, or decree; he sealed the writing with his ring instead of signing it with his name, as we do now, and that was what made it one of the laws of the Medes and Persians which could not be changed. When he gave Haman his ring, he meant that Haman should make such a decree as he chose against the Jews, and seal it with his ring; for then it would be the same as if the king himself had made it. The king told Haman also that he need not pay the ten thousand talents of silver into his treasury, but he might do with the Jews as he pleased.

Then Haman called the king's scribes, or writers, together, and they wrote for him a decree that, on the thirteenth day of the twelfth month, the people of Persia should kill and destroy all the Jews in the kingdom, both young and old, little children and women. And whoever should kill them, had permission to take their houses, their lands, and their money, and to keep these things for his own. Haman sealed the decree with the king's ring, and copies of it were sent by messengers to the governors and rulers of all the provinces, so that it might be made known to all the people of Persia. And the messengers went out in haste, according to the king's commandment. After they had gone, the king and Haman sat down to drink wine together.

When Mordecai heard of the decree that Haman had made, he was filled with sorrow; he rent his clothes, and put on sackcloth, and went out into the streets of the city, and cried with a loud and bitter cry. He came even before the king's gate, though he might not pass through there, because it was forbidden that any one should pass through the king's gate who was clothed in sackcloth. And in every province where the messengers brought the decree, there was great mourning among the Jews, and fasting, and weeping, and wailing; and many lay down in sackcloth and ashes because of their grief.

Now Queen Esther had not heard of the decree, but her maids came and told her that Mordecai was clothed in sackcloth, and that he cried in the streets of the city. Then Esther was very sorry, and she sent new garments to him, that he might take off the sackcloth and put the new garments on. But he would not. Therefore Esther called one of the king's officers who waited on her, and sent him to Mordecai to ask why he was troubled. So the officer went to the street before the king's gate, where Mordecai was, and asked him. Then Mordecai told the officer of all that had happened, and of the money that Haman had promised to pay into the king's treasury, if he might be allowed to destroy the Jews. Mordecai gave the officer also a copy of Haman's decree, to show Esther; and he asked the officer to tell the queen that she should go into the palace to the king, and pray and beseech him to save the Jews.

And the officer came and told Esther what Mordecai said. Then Esther sent word to Mordecai, saying, All the king's servants, and all the people of Persia know, that whosoever shall go in before the king without being called, whether it be man or woman, must be put to death, unless the king shall hold out the golden sceptre. But I have not been called to come unto the king these thirty days; how then can I go and speak with him?

And the officer went and told Mordecai. But Mordecai sent again to Esther, and said to her, Do not think, because thou art queen, that our enemies will spare thee when they kill all the Jews. For if thou wilt not try to save thy people at this time, some one else shall save them, but thou and thy relations shall be destroyed. And who can tell whether thou hast not been made queen on purpose for this time, so that thou mightest save them? Then Esther sent word to Mordecai, saying, Go and gather together all the Jews that are in the city, and let them fast for me, and neither eat nor drink for three days, night or day; I also, and my maidens, will fast, and then I will go in and speak with the king, though he has not called for me. And if I be put to death, I am willing to die. So Mordecai went and called all the Jews together, and they did as Esther commanded.

CHAPTERS V–IX (5–9)

ESTHER COMES IN BEFORE THE KING, WHO RECEIVES HER KINDLY. SHE INVITES THE KING AND HAMAN TO HER BANQUET. HAMAN IS HANGED UPON THE GALLOWS THAT HE MADE FOR MORDECAI. THE JEWS DESTROY THEIR ENEMIES.

On the third day Esther dressed herself in her royal robes and went into the inner part of the king's palace. She stood where the king, as he sat on his throne, could see her. And it was so, when he saw her, that God made him feel kindly toward her, and he held out his golden sceptre to Esther. So she came near to him, and touched the top of the sceptre. Then said the king to her, What is thy desire, queen Esther, and what is thy request? It shall be given thee, even to the half of my kingdom. Esther answered, If the king be willing, I want the king and Haman to come to-day to a banquet that I have made ready for him. Then the king spoke to his servants, saying, Tell Haman to make haste, that he may do as the queen has said. So the king and Haman came to the banquet that Esther made ready.

Now the king knew that Esther had invited him because she wanted to ask some favor of him, and as they sat at the banquet, he said to her again, What is thy desire? It shall be given thee, even to the half of my kingdom. Esther answered, My desire is, if the king be willing, that the king and Haman come to another banquet which I shall make ready for them to-morrow, and then I will tell the king what it is I would ask of him. So the king and Haman went from the queen's house that day. And Haman's heart was filled with pride because he had been to the queen's banquet, and was invited to her house again on the morrow. But as he went out, and passed Mordecai at the king's gate, and saw that he did not bow to him, nor do him reverence, he was filled with anger, yet he said nothing.

When he came to his home, he sent and called for his friends and for his wife. And Haman boasted to them of his riches and greatness, and told them how the king had set him above all the princes, and above all the king's other servants. He said also, Yes, and Esther the queen allowed no man to come in

ESTHER TOUCHES THE GOLDEN SCEPTRE

with the king to the banquet that she had made ready, excepting myself. And to-morrow I am invited to come again with the king to her house. Yet all these things cannot make me happy while I see Mordecai, the Jew, sitting in the king's gate. Then his wife, and all his friends, said to him, Let a gallows be made, fifty cubits high, and to-morrow ask the king that Mordecai may be hanged on it; then, after that, go thou in merrily to the queen's banquet. And Haman was pleased with what they said to him, and he went out and commanded the gallows to be made.

That night the king could not sleep. And he told his servants to bring him the book, in which was written down an account of the principal things that had happened in his kingdom. And the book was brought and read before him, and there it was found written that Mordecai had, a long while before, saved the king's life by telling of two of the king's officers who had intended to kill him.

Then king Ahasuerus said to his servants, What reward has been given Mordecai, or what honor has been done to him, because he did this? They answered, There has been nothing done for him. While the king was speaking to his servants, some one came into the court of the palace. And the king said, Who is it in the court? Now Haman had just come there that he might speak with the king, and ask his permission to have Mordecai hanged on the gallows which was made ready for him. Then the king's servants answered, It is Haman who stands in the court. The king said, Let him come in.

So Haman came in, and the king said to him, What shall be done for the man whom the king wants greatly to honor? Then Haman said to himself, The king means me: I am the one whom he wants greatly to honor. Therefore he answered the king, saying, Let the royal robes that the king wears, and the horse that he rides, and the crown that is set on his head, be brought to the man whom the king wants greatly to honor. Let him wear the king's robes, and his crown, and let him ride upon the king's horse; and let one of the king's most noble princes lead the horse through the streets of the city, while he cries out to all the people, Thus shall it be done to the man whom the king delighteth to honor!

Then the king said to Haman, Make haste and take the robes and the horse, and the crown, and do to Mordecai, the Jew, as thou hast said; leave nothing that thou hast spoken undone. Then Haman, because he dared not disobey the king, took the king's robes, his horse, and his crown, and brought them to Mordecai, and led him on horseback through the streets of the city, and cried out before him to all the people, Thus shall it be done to the man whom the king delighteth to honor. After all this, Mordecai came and sat down again, humbly, in his place at the king's gate. But Haman made haste to his home, full of shame, with his face covered, so that no one might know him. And he told his wife and all his friends what had

MORDECAI RIDES UPON THE KING'S HORSE

happened to him. While he was yet talking with them, the king's messenger came to bring him to the banquet that Esther had made ready.

So the king and Haman came to the banquet of Esther, the queen. And the king said, again, to Esther, What is thy petition, queen Esther? And what is thy request? For it shall be given thee, even to the half of my kingdom. Esther answered, If the king be pleased with me, this is my request, that the king will save my life, and the lives of all the Jews. For evil things have been spoken against us, which are not true, and I and my people have been sold to be destroyed, to be slain, and to perish. King Ahasuerus said, Who is the man that has dared to do these things? Esther answered, Our enemy is this wicked Haman.

Then Haman was afraid before the king and queen. And the king arose from the banquet in great anger, and went out into

HAMAN BEGS FOR HIS LIFE

the palace garden. When he came again into the banqueting-room, Haman had fallen down before the queen to beg for his life. But one of the king's officers said to the king, Behold the gallows, fifty cubits high, which Haman made ready for Mordecai who saved the king's life, is standing by the house of Haman. And the king said, Hang him upon it. So they hanged Haman on the gallows that he had made ready for Mordecai; and the king's anger went from him.

On the same day, king Ahasuerus gave to Esther the house in which Haman had lived. And Mordecai was called in before the king, for Esther told him that Mordecai was her relation, and how kind he had been to her. Then the king took off his ring, which he had before given to Haman, and gave it to Mordecai. And Esther made Mordecai ruler over the house that had belonged to Haman.

But Esther was still troubled, because the decree which Haman had written and sealed with the king's ring, had been sent out to all the provinces, telling the governors, the rulers, and the people of Persia, that on the thirteenth day of the twelfth month, they should kill and destroy the Jews in every city, and take away whatever belonged to them. Therefore Esther came again to the king, though he had not called for her, and she fell down at his feet and wept there. Then the king held out the golden sceptre toward her. So she arose and stood before him, and begged that the decree of Haman might be changed, for, she said, How can I bear to see my people perish?

Now the king himself could not change the decree which he had allowed Haman to make, because, as we have read, no law, nor decree, of the Medes and Persians might ever be changed. But king Ahasuerus told Esther and Mordecai that they might make another decree concerning the Jews such an one as should please them, and might seal it with the king's ring. Then Mordecai called the king's scribes together, and commanded them to write another decree, saying, That the Jews had permission, on the thirteenth day of the twelfth month, to gather themselves together in every city, and to slay and destroy all who should try to harm them.

And Mordecai sent copies of this decree to the different provinces of the kingdom, by messengers on horseback, and by riders on mules, camels, and young dromedaries. And the messengers went out in haste, according to the king's command, for the decree was made at Shushan, the palace. And Mordecai, after he had done talking with the king, came out from the palace clothed in royal garments, such as the king himself wore, of blue and white, and with a crown of gold upon his head. All the people of Shushan were glad, and everywhere the Jews were filled with joy, and they feasted and were happy.

On the thirteenth day of the twelfth month the Jews took their swords, and gathered themselves together in every city, to

A MESSENGER RIDING A SWIFT CAMEL

fight for their lives; and they gained the victory over all who came out against them. But on the fourteenth and fifteenth days they rested from fighting against their enemies. So God saved Esther and her people from those who had hoped to destroy them. Then Esther and Mordecai sent letters to all the Jews, telling them to keep the fourteenth and fifteenth days of the twelfth month, every year, as a time of feasting and gladness, when they should rejoice together, and give presents to one another and gifts to the poor. Because at that time they had been saved from their enemies, and their sorrow and mourning had been turned into joy.

THE BOOK OF NEHEMIAH

NEHEMIAH IS SENT TO BUILD UP THE WALLS OF JERUSALEM. THE PEOPLE
BEGIN TO BUILD, AND ARE OPPOSED BY THEIR ENEMIES. THE POOR JEWS
COMPLAIN AGAINST THE RICH. THE WALL IS FINISHED AND DEDICATED
EZRA TEACHES THE PEOPLE.

IT had now been ninety years since Zerubbabel, and those who
were with him, went up to Jerusalem. Artaxerxes was king
over Persia, and Nehemiah, a Jew, was his cup-bearer, who
carried his wine-cup to him when he wanted to drink. While
Nehemiah was in the palace at Shushan, some men came there
from the land of Judah; and Nehemiah asked them about the
Jews in that land, and about Jerusalem. The men told him
that the Jews were in great affliction; that the walls of Jerusalem were still in ruins, and that the gates of the city had
never been set up.

When Nehemiah heard this he wept. And he fasted and
prayed for the Jews: he prayed also that God would make
king Artaxerxes willing to do what he should ask of him; for
Nehemiah was going to ask the king to send him to Jerusalem,
that he might build up the walls of the city, and help the Jews
who were there.

After this, as king Artaxerxes was sitting one day in his
palace, Nehemiah took the wine-cup and handed it to him to
drink. And Nehemiah looked sad; the king noticed it, and
said to him, Why is thy face sad, seeing thou art not sick?
Surely thou hast some sorrow in thy heart. Nehemiah answered,
Let the king live forever: should I not look sad while Jerusalem, the city where my fathers are buried, is left without
walls, and its gates are burned with fire? The king said to
him, What dost thou ask of me? What is thy request? At
first Nehemiah did not answer, but silently, in his heart, he
prayed again that God would make the king willing to do what
he should ask. Then he answered the king, saying, If it
please thee, I pray thou wilt send me to Jerusalem, that I
may build up its walls. The king said (while the queen was
sitting by him), How long will thy journey take thee? And how

31

soon wilt thou return? When Nehemiah had told him, the king gave him permission to go.

And Nehemiah said, If it please the king, let letters be given me to the governors of the provinces through which I shall pass, telling them to help me; and a letter also to the keeper of the king's forest which is near Jerusalem, that he may give me timber to make beams for the walls and gates of the

NEHEMIAH FINDS THE WALLS OF JERUSALEM BROKEN DOWN

city. And the king gave the letters, because the Lord made him willing, in this thing also, to do as Nehemiah asked him. Then Nehemiah started on his journey, and the king sent soldiers and horsemen with him to guard him by the way. When he came to the governors of the provinces that were near to the land of Judah, he gave them the letters which the king had sent. Now there were with the governors two wicked men, named Sanballat and Tobiah, who were enemies to the Jews.

When they heard, therefore, that the king had sent a man to help the Jews, it grieved them exceedingly.

But Nehemiah came safely to Jerusalem. After he had been there three days, he rose up secretly in the night, so that his enemies might not know it, and went out to examine the walls of the city, to see if what had been told him about them were true; and he found that it was true, for they were broken down and in ruins. Afterward he spoke to the people, saying, You see the danger and distress we are in, with no walls to guard us. Come, let us build them up, that we be no longer afraid of our enemies. Then he told the Jews of the kind words that the king had spoken to him. And they said to one another, Let us rise up and build. So they began to build the walls. The priests, the Levites, the people, and even some of the women of Israel, helped in the work.

But when Sanballat heard of it, he was angry, and mocked them, saying, What are these weak Jews doing? Will they try to build a wall around Jerusalem? And where will they find stones enough among the heaps of rubbish that were left by their enemies, after they had burned the city? Then Tobiah, who was with Sanballat, answered him, saying, Such a wall as they can build, even a fox, if he should go up on it, would break down. But the Jews went on with the work, till they had built the wall up to half of its height all around the city, and the two ends of it were joined together.

Then Sanballat, and Tobiah, and all the enemies of the Jews, spoke secretly to one another, and said, We will go and fight against them; but we will go suddenly, so that they may not know we are near, until we come among them and slay them, and cause the work to cease. But the Jews were told of their coming; and Nehemiah set the men of Israel behind the wall, with their swords, their spears, and their bows. And he said to them, Be not afraid; remember that the Lord will help you. Fight, therefore, for your wives, your children, and your homes. When their enemies heard that the Jews had made ready for them, they did not come against the city.

After that, half of the men of Israel worked on the wall,

while the other half watched, with swords, and spears, and bows. Even those who were building, carried their swords with them. And Nehemiah kept a trumpeter near him, whom he commanded to blow on his trumpet if their enemies should come in sight. For, he said, the wall is very long, and while we are at work we are separated far from one another. Therefore, so soon as you shall hear the sound of the trumpet in any place, make haste to

REBUILDING THE WALLS OF JERUSALEM

help the men who are there. So the people labored in the work from morning till evening. And neither Nehemiah, nor the men who were with him, took off their clothes, by day or by night, except when they took them off for washing.

Now about this time the Jews had trouble among themselves. For some of those who were poor, complained against the rich. We and our children are many, they said, and we have had to buy bread, and to pay the king's tribute money also. To do this, we were forced to borrow money; yes, and even to sell our children for slaves. And now the rich men, who lent us money, have taken away our lands and our vineyards, and we have nothing left. Neither are we able to buy back our children, that we may bring them to their homes again. Yet we are Jews as well as the rich princes and rulers who have taken our lands from us, and we love our children as much as they love theirs.

When Nehemiah heard what the poor Jews said, he was angry, and called all the people together; and he spoke to the princes and rulers before them, saying, You do wrong to your poor brethren, and are cruel to them. Give back to them, I pray you, this day, their houses, their lands, and their vineyards; and also the money, the corn, the wine, and the oil that you are taking from them. The princes and rulers answered him, saying, We will do what thou dost command. Then Nehemiah called the priests, and made the princes and rulers promise them, before the Lord, that they would surely do as they had said.

Now when Sanballat and Tobiah heard that Nehemiah, and the men of Israel, were still at work on the wall, and that it was built up all around the city, they were afraid to go into Jerusalem. So they sent word to Nehemiah, saying, Come down to one of the villages on the plain, and meet us there, for we wish to talk with thee. But Nehemiah knew that they wanted only to do him harm. So he sent messengers back to them, saying, I am doing a great work, and I cannot come down. Ought I to leave that work, and cause it to cease, while I go and talk with you? Yet these men sent to him four times, asking him to come; and Nehemiah answered them each time in the same way.

Then Sanballat sent his servant again, with a letter in his hand. The letter said, Some persons have told me that the Jews who are in Jerusalem are going to rebel against the king of Persia, and that thou dost want to make thyself their king, and therefore thou art building up the wall around the city. Now before the king of Persia shall hear of this, thou hadst better come out and talk with me about what thou hast done. But Nehemiah sent an answer to Sanballat, saying, The things thou speakest of are not true, and thou knowest they are not; thou art only pretending them out of thy own evil heart. Then Nehemiah prayed to the Lord to help him, so that the work on the wall should not be stopped by his enemies.

When Sanballat and Tobiah found that they could not persuade Nehemiah to come out of Jerusalem, they hired a man in the city to try and deceive him, and make him afraid. The man's name was Shemaiah. He shut himself up in his house and pretended that the Lord had spoken to him, and sent a message by him to Nehemiah. And Nehemiah went to his house and talked with him; and Shemaiah said, Come, let us go into the temple and shut to the doors, for thy enemies are coming to slay thee; yes, in the night they are coming to slay thee. But Nehemiah answered him, saying, Ought a man who is doing work for the Lord, to leave that work unfinished and flee? And who that knows he is obeying the Lord, as I do, would go into the temple and hide there to save his life? I will not go in. For Nehemiah saw that the Lord had not spoken to Shemaiah at all, but that Sanballat and Tobiah had paid that wicked man to tell him an untruth. Then Nehemiah prayed to the Lord that he would remember how Sanballat and Tobiah were trying to stop him in his work, and that the Lord would not let them succeed.

So Nehemiah and the people kept on working at the wall, and they finished it in fifty-two days. Afterward they dedicated it. The priests, the Levites, and the people went up on the top of it in two great companies. One company went one way, and the other went the other way. And they walked around the city, on the top of the wall, with trumpets and harps, singing praises, until they met. Then they came down from the wall and marched together up to the temple, and offered sacrifices there with joy and gladness. So the wall was dedicated, or given to the Lord, that it might be his, to guard his temple and his people from their enemies.

And Nehemiah set rulers over the city, and said to them, Let

the gates be shut at night, and not opened in the morning till
the sun has risen high up in the heavens. And cause the men
of the city to watch upon the walls, every one taking his turn
there, to guard against our enemies.

We have read that while the children of Israel were in the wilderness, the Lord commanded silver trumpets to be made for the
priests to blow when they were about to start on their journeys.

THE PEOPLE MARCH ON THE WALL IN TWO GREAT COMPANIES

These trumpets were to be blown also at the coming of the new
moon, or on the first day of each month. But on the first day
of the seventh month, the trumpets were to be blown and all the
people were to meet together to worship. No work was to be
done on that day, and the children of Israel were to hold a feast
to the Lord; it was called the Feast of Trumpets.

And now the first day of the seventh month having come, the
people met together to worship, as the Lord commanded. And
they asked Ezra, the priest, to bring out of the temple the book

of the law which Moses had written.   Then Ezra brought out
the book, and he stood on a pulpit of wood, where all the people
could see him, for he was above them all.   And he opened the
book before them and read out of it to the men, the women, and
the children, from morning till noon; and the priests and Levites explained what was read.

When the people heard the words of God's law, and remembered how often they had disobeyed it, they were troubled and
wept.   But the Levites said to them, Do not weep, for this is the
day for a feast to the Lord, when you are to be glad, and to thank
him.   Go, therefore, to your homes, and eat and drink of the
good things which he has given you, and send some of those
things to the poor, who have none of their own.   So all the
people went away to eat, and drink, and send gifts to the poor,
and to be glad and rejoice; because the Lord was kind to them,
and because they had understood the words that were read to
them out of his law.

The next day they came to Ezra again, that he might teach
them still more.   And he read out of the book, that God commanded them to keep the feast of tabernacles that same month.
Go up, the book said, on the mountains, and cut down olive
branches, and pine branches, and myrtle branches, and make
booths.   So the people went up and cut branches from the trees,
and made themselves booths on the flat roofs of their houses, in
their yards, in the courts of the temple, and in the streets of
Jerusalem; and they all came out of their houses, and lived in
the booths for the seven days of the feast.   And there was great
joy and gladness among them; because no such feast had been
kept in Jerusalem for hundreds of years.

And yet, although the people kept the feast and rejoiced,
because the Lord was so good to them, they did not forget that
they had often disobeyed him, and that he was still punishing
them for their sins.   Therefore on the twenty-fourth day of the
month they met together again, to fast and confess their sins to
him, and they put on sackcloth to show their grief.

Then some of the Levites stood up before them, and prayed,
saying, Remember, we pray thee, O Lord, all the troubles that

have come upon us since the time when we were carried away captives, until this day. Yet it was just in thee to punish us, and thou hast done right, but we have done wickedly. Therefore thou hast given our land to the Assyrians, and they rule over us and our cattle, and do with us as they please, and we are in great distress. But now we want to be thy servants; and here we promise to obey thee, and we do also write down our promise,

THE PEOPLE LIVE IN BOOTHS DURING THE FEAST OF TABERNACLES

and our priests and Levites, and chief men, will sign the writing for us with their names, and seal it with their seals.

Then Nehemiah, the governor, and some of the priests, and many of the chief men of Israel, signed the writing which the people had made. And the people promised, before the Lord, to obey all his commandments; that they would not make friends with the heathen nations, nor take wives from among them; that they would keep holy the sabbath day; that they would give a tenth part of all that grew in their fields, to the priests and the Levites, and would bring the first of their grain and of their fruits, each year, to the temple, as an offering to the Lord. All these things the people promised to do.

After this Nehemiah went back to Persia, as he had promised the king. We are not told how long he stayed there, but when he returned to Jerusalem, he found that the people had already forgotten their promise to obey God's law. They had again made friends with the heathen nations around them, and had taken wives from among the heathen women; they had ceased giving to the priests and the Levites a tenth of their fruit and their grain, so that the Levites had gone away from the temple to work in the fields, and raise food for themselves. Then Nehemiah was grieved, and he called the priests and Levites back to the temple, saying, Why is the house of God forsaken?

And Nehemiah saw the people loading their asses on the sabbath, and bringing their grain in from the fields; they brought grapes and figs, and all kinds of burdens into Jerusalem on that day. Then he spoke to the rulers, and said, Why do ye so wickedly? Did not God punish our fathers for doing these things, by destroying this city?

On the evening before the sabbath, when it began to grow dark, Nehemiah commanded that the gates of the city should be shut, and not opened again till the sabbath was past. And he set some of his servants to watch that no burden should be brought into the city on the sabbath day. Then those men who came from other places, with fish, and all kinds of goods, to sell on the sabbath, when they found the gates shut, lay down outside the walls, and slept there all night. The next sabbath they came, and did the same. Nehemiah spoke to them, saying, Why do ye lodge before the wall? If ye do so again I will take hold of you, and punish you. Therefore they came no more on the sabbath. He spoke also to the men who had married heathen women, and said, Was not Solomon a great and wise king? Yet when he took heathen wives, they tempted even him into sin. Shall we then listen to you, when you would persuade us to disobey God, and do this great wickedness?

CONNECTION BETWEEN
THE OLD AND NEW TESTAMENTS

HISTORY OF THE JEWS

FROM THE TIME WHEN THE OLD TESTAMENT ENDS, TO THE
TIME WHEN THE NEW TESTAMENT BEGINS

THE chapter which we last read ends the Old Testament, and
the Bible tells us no more about the Jews for over four hundred years. From other books, we learn that they continued to be
servants to the king of Persia, for nearly a hundred years after
Nehemiah returned from Babylon. Then Alexander, a great
general, who was at war with Persia, brought an army, and took
Jerusalem, and the Jews served him for nine years.

After his death they were servants to the kings of Egypt for
more than a hundred years. Some of these kings treated the
Jews kindly; but, at last, one of them came to Jerusalem, and
seeing how beautiful the temple was, determined to go into,
not only its courts, but even the building itself, where the priests
alone were allowed to go. The priests begged him not to disobey God by doing this, and the people cried out with fear and
sorrow when they saw him enter; still he went on until he came
to the holy place. But while he was there, God sent such great
terror and weakness upon him, that he had to be carried out
like one almost dead. In his anger at not being permitted to do
as he wished, he treated the Jews very cruelly, making slaves
of some, and putting others to death.

After this the Jews refused to obey the kings of Egypt, and
served the kings of Syria for over thirty years. The one whom
they first served, was good to them as long as he lived. But
after he died, his son, Antiochus, hearing they had rebelled
against him, came with an army and took Jerusalem, not spar-
ing the people, but putting both old and young to death. In
three days forty thousand of them were slain, and as many
more sold to be captives. The king then went into the temple
and took away the golden altar, the golden table, the golden
candlestick, and all the treasures that were kept there.

Two years afterward, he sent Apollonius, one of his generals, with twenty-two thousand men, against Jerusalem. Apollonius came into the city, and waiting until the Sabbath-day, when he knew the Jews would not fight against him, he set his soldiers upon the people, commanding them to kill the men, to take the women and children captive, to rob the houses, and to throw down the city walls. The soldiers obeyed his commands, putting so

ELEAZAR FORCED TO EAT SWINE'S FLESH

many of the Jews to death, that the streets of the city, and the courts of the temple, ran with their blood.

But, not satisfied with what he had already done to show his fury against them, the king of Syria afterward made a decree forbidding the Jews to offer up sacrifices to God, or to obey God's laws, or to keep the Sabbath day. He sent an officer to Jerusalem, who drove them away from the temple, and made it a place to worship idols in. Heathen altars were set up in every city of the land, and the Jews who would not sacrifice upon them were punished. One of their elders, an old man named Eleazar, was forced by the king's servants to take swine's flesh into his mouth, which the Lord had commanded the Jews not to eat. When he spat it out he was beaten to death.

Seven brothers, with their mother, were taken by the king and scourged, to make them eat swine's flesh. But the eldest brother

A MOTHER AND HER SEVEN SONS PUT TO DEATH

spoke to the king, saying, We will not eat of it, for we would rather die than disobey the laws of God. Then the king, in great anger, commanded that his tongue should be cut out, and parts of his feet and hands cut off, and afterward that he should be burned slowly over a fire as long as there was any life in him. As soon as he was dead, the other brothers were asked whether they would obey the king; and as they refused, were one by one tortured and put to death. When the mother had seen her seven sons die, she also was slain.

There was at this time among the Jews, a family called the Maccabees. The father, who was a priest, had five sons. He loved the worship of God, and hated the worship of idols. He killed one of the king's servants for setting up an idol's altar in the city where he lived. Then he fled with his sons to the

THE MACCABEES RECEIVE THEIR FATHER'S BLESSING

mountains. There many of the Jews came to him, until he had gathered around him a little army, with which he fought against their enemies.

But, being an old man, he could not bear the hardships of war, and feeling that the time was near for him to die, he called his sons to give them his blessing. And he told them not to fear the Syrians, but to be brave, and go out to battle against them, trusting in God, and obeying the words of his law.

The sons, after their father was dead, obeyed his command.

They led the people against their enemies and drove them away from the temple. Then the Jews came back to the temple, and destroyed the idol's altar which the Syrians had built; and they cleansed the temple and began to worship God there again. After this they gained more victories over their enemies, until they were free; and they had kings of their

THE JEWS DESTROY THE IDOL'S ALTAR IN THE TEMPLE

own, of the family of the Maccabees, to rule over them for nearly a hundred years.

But now, when God had helped them and made them free once more, they forgot him, and, instead of obeying his command to love one another, they grew proud and selfish, and had wars and battles among themselves. At last while two brothers, the sons of their former king, were quarrelling as to which should rule over the people, the Romans came with an army and took Jerusalem, and broke down its walls; and the Jews were made servants to the Romans, as they had been before to the Egyptians, and the Syrians.

The Romans sent a general, named Herod, to be their king. He was not one of the children of Israel, yet he pretended to believe in their religion and to worship God as they did. He was, in truth, a fierce and a cruel man who cared only to be ruler over the people, and to keep all the power to himself. That he might do this, he put many persons to death, among them his wife and two of his own sons.

After he had been king eighteen years, finding that the Jews hated him for his wickedness, he determined to build up the temple anew, by doing which he hoped to please them, and make them more willing to have him rule over them. The temple, which then stood on mount Moriah, was the one built by the Jews after they had returned with Zerubbabel from Babylon. It was nearly five hundred years old, and much broken and decayed. Herod took it down, a part at a time, and built it up again with great stones of white marble. These stones he covered, in some places, with plates of silver and gold. The building was very splendid, and shone so brightly under the morning sun that it dazzled the eyes of those who looked on it.

The inside of the temple was divided, as it had been before, by the curtain, called the veil, into two rooms: one of them being the holy place, where the golden altar, the golden table, and the golden candlestick stood; and the other, the most holy place, where the ark used to stand. But the ark had been lost long before (as we suppose), when the Jews were carried captive to Babylon on account of their sins. They had no ark now to bring into the most holy place, and we are told that this was empty, except that a stone lay on the spot where the ark should have been.

Outside of the temple was the court, called the court of the priests, where the altar of burnt offering and the laver stood. And outside of this court was another, called the court of Israel, where the men of Israel might come. Beyond this was a third court, called the court of the women, because the women of Israel might go there. And outside of this, and around all the others, was a very large court, called the court of the Gentiles, because the Gentiles, that is, the people of other nations beside the Jews, were allowed to go into it.

Nine large and splendid gates opened into these courts; one, more splendid than the rest, was called the Beautiful Gate. It

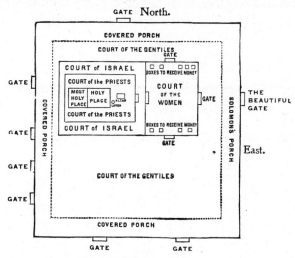

PLAN OF HEROD'S TEMPLE

was seventy-five feet high, and covered with Corinthian brass, which, at that time, was more costly than silver or gold. Around the different courts, walls were built; that around the court of the Gentiles was twenty-five feet high. On the inside of this wall were wide porches with flat roofs, which rested on marble pillars, so large that three men with their arms stretched out could hardly reach around one of them. The floor of the porches was paved with different colored marble. One of the porches was called Solomon's, because it stood over a very high wall which Solomon had built up from the valley below. These porches made a beautiful covered walk for the people, in hot or stormy weather; while in pleasant weather they could go upon their flat roofs, from which they had a view of the temple, the city, and the mountains that were around Jerusalem.

The Jews did not go into the temple itself to worship; only

32

the priests were allowed to go there. The people worshipped
in the courts of the temple, and when they said they were going
up to the temple, they meant they were going up to its courts.
The way up to these, on the top of mount Moriah, was by high
flights of steps.

Herod had eighteen thousand men at work on the temple and
its courts, and it took him over nine years to build them.

END OF CONNECTION BETWEEN OLD AND NEW TESTAMENTS

THE NEW TESTAMENT

THE GOSPELS

MATT. II (2). LUKE I, II (1, 2)

THE BIRTHS OF JOHN THE BAPTIST AND OF JESUS. THE ANGELS APPEAR
TO THE SHEPHERDS. WISE MEN FROM THE EAST COME TO BETHLE-
HEM. HEROD SLAYS THE CHILDREN THERE. THE FLIGHT INTO EGYPT.
JESUS ATTENDS THE PASSOVER.

AND now the time was near for the Saviour to come upon
earth. We have read how God promised, when Adam and
Eve first sinned in the garden, that a Saviour should come.
We have read also how the prophets, who lived afterward, told
the children of Israel that he was coming. But before he came,
they said, John the Baptist would be sent to tell the people to
make ready for him by repenting of their sins.

499

While Herod was king in Judea, there lived a priest named Zacharias. His wife was named Elizabeth. They were both of them old, and the Bible tells us, were righteous and careful to obey all God's commandments. But God had never given them a child.

Zacharias belonged to the company of priests which was called the company, or course, of Abia, for the priests were still divided into different courses, or companies, as king David had divided them. There were twenty-four of these courses. Each one took its turn in staying for a time, at the temple, to attend to God's worship there.

Very early every morning, before it was light, the priests at the temple began the work of the day. Some of them went to the altar of burnt offering, and cleaned it, taking away the ashes that had been left there from the day before, and putting fresh wood on the fire, which was never allowed to go out. Other priests went into the temple, and trimmed the lamps on the golden candlestick, and cleaned the golden altar of incense. Afterward one of the priests offered up a lamb on the altar of burnt offering, and another burned incense on the golden altar. The lamb was offered up, and the incense burned, about nine o'clock in the morning, and again about three o'clock in the afternoon. These were called the hours of prayer. At these hours the people came up to the temple to worship, and stood in the court, praying, while the incense was burning in the holy place.

Every day, before the priests began their work, lots were cast for them, to see what part of the work, or service, each one was to do. On the day we are reading about, the part of Zacharias was to burn incense on the golden altar; therefore he went into the holy place, to burn incense at the hour of prayer.

And while he was in the temple, he saw an angel standing beside the golden altar. When he saw him he was afraid. But the angel said, Fear not, Zacharias, for God will give to thee and thy wife, Elizabeth, a son, and thou shalt call his name John. He shall not drink wine, nor any strong drink, and shall be filled with God's Holy Spirit from the time he is born. He shall tell

THE ANGEL APPEARS TO ZACHARIAS IN THE TEMPLE

the children of Israel of the Saviour who is coming, and shall teach many of them to repent of their sins and obey him. Then Zacharias said to the angel, But how shall I know that these things will be? The angel answered, I am the angel Gabriel.

I live in heaven and stand before God, to do whatever he commands me, and he has sent me to tell thee this good news. But now, because thou hast not believed it, thou shalt be punished by being dumb and unable to speak until the words I have spoken come true.

And the people, who were waiting in the courts of the temple for Zacharias to come out of the holy place, wondered what

THE ANGEL APPEARS TO MARY

kept him so long. When he came they saw that he could not speak. But he made them understand, by signs, that he had seen a vision.

Six months after this, God sent the angel Gabriel into the city of Nazareth, to a young woman named Mary. She was a cousin of Elizabeth, the wife of Zacharias, and was descended from king David. When Mary saw the angel she was troubled, for she knew not why he had come. But he said, Fear not, Mary·

for God has greatly blessed thee. Thou shalt have a son, and shalt call his name JESUS. He shall have no father upon earth, but shall be the Son of God. And God will make him king over those who love him, forever. To thy cousin Elizabeth, also, God has promised a son. Mary answered the angel, saying, I am the servant of the Lord, let it be done to me as thou hast said. And the angel departed from her.

THE NAMING OF JOHN THE BAPTIST

Then Mary made haste and went into the land of Judah, to the house of Zacharias and Elizabeth, to visit her cousin, and she stayed with Elizabeth about three months. Afterward she came back to her own home. Now Mary's husband was named Joseph. He also was descended from king David; yet they were both poor, and Joseph was a carpenter.

And God gave to Zacharias and Elizabeth the son he had promised them. When the child was eight days old, their neighbors and relations came together, to dedicate, or give him to the Lord, and also to decide what his name should be. And they called him Zacharias, after the name of his father. But his mother said, Not so; he shall be called John. They said to her, None of thy relations are called by this name. And they made signs to his father, asking what he would have him called. He asked for a writing table, because he could not yet speak, and wrote, saying, His name is John. Then they were all astonished; for Zacharias had not yet told them that the angel had given him this name in the temple.

As soon as Zacharias had written these words, God gave him power to speak again; and he spoke, and praised God. All the people in that part of the land heard of what had been done, and they said, What sort of a child shall this be? And the boy grew, and the Lord blessed him. He lived in the lonely wilderness, away from the rest of the people, until he was a man, and the time had come for him to preach to the Jews and tell them about Jesus. For this little child, whom God had given to Zacharias and Elizabeth, was John the Baptist.

We have read that the Jews were servants to the Romans: they had to obey whatever the emperor of Rome commanded. And now he made a decree that all the Jews should be enrolled, or have their names written down, and he commanded each one of them to go to the city where his fathers had lived, so that the Roman officers might take down his name there. Therefore every one went to his own city. And Mary, with Joseph, her husband, went out of Nazareth, where their home was then, to Bethlehem, where David used to live, because they were descended from king David. When they came to Bethlehem, there was no room for them at the inn: it was already full, and they went into the stable to sleep. And while they were there, God gave to Mary the son which the angel had promised her. It was in the stable at Bethlehem that the infant Jesus was born. And Mary, his mother, wrapped him round with swaddling clothes, or bands, and laid him in a manger.

There were in that country shepherds, who stayed out in the field watching over their flocks all night. And the angel of the

THE ANGEL SPEAKS TO THE SHEPHERDS

Lord came down to them, and a bright light shone around them, and they were afraid. But the angel said, Fear not, for I bring you good news which shall give joy to all people. Because there is born for you this day, in the city of David, a Saviour, who is Christ the Lord. And this is the way you shall know him: You shall find him wrapped in swaddling clothes,

THE SHEPHERDS COME TO SEE THE INFANT SAVIOUR

and lying in a manger. When the angel had said this, suddenly there was a multitude of angels with him, who praised God, saying, Glory be to God on high, and on earth peace, good will toward men.

After the angels had gone from them up into heaven, the shepherds said one to another, Let us go now to Bethlehem, and see these things of which the angel has told us. And they came with haste, and found Mary and Joseph, and the babe lying in a manger. And they saw the child, and afterward went out and told others what the angel had said to them about him. All whom they told wondered at what they said. Then the shepherds returned to their flocks again, praising God for what they had seen and heard.

When the babe was eight days old, his parents called his name Jesus, as the angel had commanded; and they dedicated him to the Lord. For although he was the Son of God, yet he came on the earth to be like one of us, and to set us an example in all things, of what we ought to do.

After this Joseph and Mary brought him to Jerusalem, and took him to the temple, and offered up a sacrifice of turtle-doves, or young pigeons. There was a man in Jerusalem named Simeon. He was a good man, who feared God, and who was expecting Jesus to come into the world because of what the prophets had written about him. The Holy Spirit had promised Simeon that he should not die until he had seen Jesus. And now the Spirit told Simeon to go into the temple, and when Joseph and Mary brought in the child, Simeon took him up in his arms, and said, Now, Lord, thy promise has come true, and I can die in peace, because I have seen the Saviour.

And there was a woman named Anna, a prophetess. She was a widow of great age, who lived near to the temple, so that she might worship there day and night. While Simeon was speaking, she also came into the temple where Jesus was, and thanked God because he had let her see him. Then she went out, and spoke of him to others who were looking for the coming of the Saviour.

And there came to Jerusalem wise men from some far off eastern country, who asked the people, saying, Where is he that is born to be king of the Jews? for we have seen his star in the sky, and are come to worship him. God had sent a star that shone over the land where these wise men lived, so they might know that Jesus was born; and they had come to Jerusalem seeking him. But when they reached there they did not see Jesus; therefore they asked the people where they might find him.

Herod heard what they said, and was troubled because they

called Jesus, King. He was afraid that the child which was born, might some day be made king over Judea instead of himself. Therefore, he also wanted to know where Jesus was. And he gathered together some learned men who he knew had studied the Scriptures, and asked them to tell him where Christ should be born. They answered, In the city of Bethlehem, for so the prophet has said. Then Herod called the wise men to

THE WISE MEN BRINGING PRESENTS TO JESUS

him, and sent them to Bethlehem, saying, Go and look diligently for the young child, and when you have found him, bring me word, that I may come and worship him also. But he said this, not because he wanted to worship Jesus: it was because he wanted to put him to death.

After Herod had spoken to them, the wise men departed from Jerusalem, and went toward Bethlehem. And as they went, the star, which they had seen in their own land, appeared to them again. When they saw the star, they were filled with joy, for it moved on before them, and showed them the way, till it came and stood over the house where the young child was. Then they went into the house and saw the young child, with Mary, his mother, and they bowed down and worshipped him.

THE ANGEL WARNS JOSEPH TO FLEE INTO EGYPT

In those days, persons who came to visit kings, brought presents with them. So the wise men brought presents for Jesus, of such things as were precious in the country where they lived. And when they had opened these things, they gave to him gifts of gold, and frankincense, and myrrh. But God spoke to them in a dream, and commanded them not to go back to Herod; therefore they returned to their own country by another way.

When Herod found that the wise men had disobeyed him, he was very angry, and sent his servants to Bethlehem and slew all

the little children there, that were two years old or younger, for
he hoped that among them Jesus would be slain. But before
Herod's servants came, the angel of the Lord told Joseph to

THE FLIGHT INTO EGYPT

take the young child and his mother and flee into Egypt. And
Joseph arose in the night and fled into Egypt; and he stayed
there till Herod was dead. Then the angel spoke to him again,
saying, Arise, and go back into the land of Israel, for they are
dead who sought to destroy the young child. And Joseph did
as the angel commanded, and he and Mary and the young child
came and lived in the city of Nazareth.

Joseph and Mary used to go every year to Jerusalem, to keep
the feast of the passover; and when Jesus was twelve years old,
he also went with them. After the days of the feast were ended,
they started on their journey back to Nazareth. Now people
who went to the passover, used to travel in companies; friends

and neighbors would go up to Jerusalem together: some of them rode on mules and horses, perhaps, but many of them walked all the way. It was with such a company as this that Joseph and Mary started to return to Nazareth, and they thought that Jesus was among those who journeyed with them. So they went on till evening; then they looked for him, but could not find him. Therefore they left the company they journeyed with, and went

JESUS IN THE TEMPLE TALKING WITH THE DOCTORS

back to Jerusalem. They had been one day in coming to the place where they missed him; it took them one day more to go back to Jerusalem, but on the next, or the third day, they found him at the temple, talking with the doctors, or wise men, hearing what they said, and asking them questions.

And all who heard Jesus were astonished at the words that he spoke, for he was only a child, but those whom he talked with were men of great learning. And his mother said to him,

Son, why hast thou treated us so? Thy father and I have sought thee, sorrowing. He answered, Why have you looked for me? Did you not know that I must be about my Father's business? He meant that he must be doing what his Father in heaven had sent him on earth to do. For God had sent him to teach men, and explain the Scriptures to them, before he should die on the cross for their sins. Joseph and Mary did not understand what he meant by the words that he spoke to them, but his mother kept these sayings in her heart.

Then Jesus returned with his parents to their home in the city of Nazareth, where he lived with them, and obeyed what they said to him. And as he grew, God blessed him, and those who were with him loved him.

MATT. III, IV, XIV (3, 4, 14). MARK I, VI (1, 6). LUKE III, IV (3, 4). JOHN I–IV (1–4)

JOHN PREACHES IN THE WILDERNESS; HE BAPTIZES JESUS, WHO IS AFTER-
WARD TEMPTED BY SATAN. JESUS TURNS WATER INTO WINE. HE
DRIVES THE TRADERS OUT OF THE TEMPLE. HE TALKS WITH NICODEMUS.
JOHN IS PUT TO DEATH. JESUS COMES TO NAZARETH.

AFTER what we have read in the last chapter, the Bible tells us nothing more about Jesus, nor about John the Baptist, for many years. During those years, while Jesus was living with his parents in the city of Nazareth, he grew up to be a man. The people did not know that he was the Son of God, and John the Baptist had not yet preached to them about him. John was still living in the wilderness. His clothes were made of the coarse hair that grows on the back of the camel, and were fastened around his waist by a girdle, or belt of leather. He had for his food the insects called locusts, which he found out in the wilderness, and the honey which the wild bees left among the rocks and in the hollow trees.

But now the time had come for John to preach to the people, and God commanded him to go and tell them to make ready for the Saviour, by repenting of their sins. Then he went into the lonely country near to the river Jordan, and a great multitude came there to hear him. And he preached to them, and told them that the Saviour, who had been promised, was soon coming among them, and that he would save the righteous, but destroy the wicked. The Jews must not think, John said, that their sins would be forgiven, because they were descended from a good

JOHN PREACHING IN THE WILDERNESS

man like Abraham; they must obey God themselves. And many who heard John preach, repented, and were baptized by him in the river Jordan.

Now baptism means, or represents, the washing away of our sins. Yet it does not mean that they are washed away by the water on our bodies, but by the Holy Spirit sent into our hearts. John spoke to the people who came out to hear him, and said, I indeed baptize you with water, but the Saviour, who is coming after me, is greater than I; he will baptize you with the Holy Ghost. John meant to tell the people that although he baptized them with water, he could not wash their sins away;

but that Jesus, because he had power to send the Holy Spirit into their hearts, could really wash away their sins for them.

Then Jesus came out from his home in Nazareth for John to baptize him also. But when John saw him he did not wish to baptize him; John said, I have need to be baptized by thee, and dost thou come to be baptized by me? John felt that he had need to have his own sins washed away. But Jesus had no sins to be washed away; why then should he be baptized? It was because he had come on earth to obey all of God's commandments, for us, and in our place, so that if we believe in him we may be rewarded for his obedience.

When John refused to baptize Jesus, Jesus told him that although he could not understand it now, yet it was right that he should baptize him. Then John consented, and went down with him into the river Jordan, and baptized him there. And while Jesus was coming up out of the water, praying to God, the sky above him opened, and there came down from heaven what seemed to be a dove, and it lighted on him. It was the Holy Spirit that came down in the form of a dove. At the same time God's voice spoke out of heaven, saying, This is my beloved Son with whom I am well pleased. Jesus was now about thirty years of age. And he went out into the wilderness and stayed there alone, forty days and forty nights. All that time he ate nothing, but fasted and prayed to God: and afterward he was hungry.

We have read how Satan tempted Eve to disobey God, and so caused us all to have wicked hearts and be sinners. And now when Satan saw Jesus had come to give us new hearts, and make us righteous, he thought he would try and prevent him. Therefore he went out into the wilderness to tempt Jesus, as he had tempted Eve in the garden of Eden. And he came to him and said, If thou art the Son of God, change these stones that are lying on the ground into bread, so that thou mayest have food, because thou art hungry. But Jesus knew why Satan had come, and he would not make the stones into bread to obey him. He told him it was written in the Bible that we must be more careful to obey God, and do what is right, than even to get bread when we are hungry.

33

Then Satan took Jesus into Jerusalem, and up on to a very high part of the temple. And he said to him, If thou art the Son of God, cast thyself down, for it is written in the Bible that the angels shall hold thee up as thou art falling, lest thou be dashed against a stone. But Jesus said it was also written in the Bible, that we must not put ourselves in danger, only to try whether God will save us from harm.

SATAN TEMPTS JESUS

Then Satan set before Jesus his principal temptation. He took him up on to a high mountain, and showed him all the kingdoms of the world at the same time, with their beautiful cities, their mighty armies, and their great riches: and he said to him, All these will I give to thee for thine own, if thou wilt kneel down and worship me. It was to try and make Jesus do this that Satan had come out in the wilderness.

He cared little whether Jesus turned the stones into bread, or cast himself down from the temple. But he cared a great deal that Jesus should be willing to obey him, and take him for his master. This was the reason why he promised to give him all the kingdoms in the world, (though they were not his to give), if he would only kneel down and worship him. But Jesus answered him, saying, Go from me, Satan, for it is written in the Bible, Thou shalt worship the Lord thy God, and him only shalt thou serve. When Satan saw that he could not make Jesus obey his words, he departed from him, and behold, angels came and waited on him.

Then Jesus returned to the river Jordan where John was. When John saw him coming, he said, Behold the Lamb of God! He called Jesus the Lamb of God, because he was to be offered up as a sacrifice on the cross, as lambs were offered up on the altar. And two men who heard John say this, followed Jesus. He spoke to them, and took them to the place where he dwelt, and one of them, named Andrew, brought his brother Peter also. The next day two others, named Philip and Nathaniel, followed him. All these men came to Jesus that he might teach them; therefore they were his disciples, for a disciple is a person who learns something from another.

Jesus went into the city of Cana, which was in that part of the land called Galilee, and there was a marriage in the city. The mother of Jesus was there, and both Jesus and his disciples were invited to the marriage. And a feast was made ready for all who should come. Food was prepared for them to eat, and wine for them to drink; but before the end of the feast, the wine was all gone. And when they wanted more, the mother of Jesus said to him, They have no wine. Then she said to the servants, Whatever he tells you to do, do it.

Now there were in the house six water-pots made of stone, such as the Jews kept to hold water. Jesus said to the servants, Fill the water-pots with water. And they filled them up to the brim. Then he said, Take some out now, and carry it to the chief man of the feast. And when they did so, the water was changed into wine. But the chief man, or ruler of the feast, did not know that Jesus had changed it into wine, (yet the servants knew), therefore, when he tasted of the water that was made wine, he called the bridegroom to him and said, Other persons, when they give a feast, set the good wine on the table first, and after men have had enough, they bring out that which is worse;

JESUS CHANGES THE WATER INTO WINE

but thou hast kept the good wine until now. This was the first miracle that Jesus did to show his power to the people. And when his disciples saw it, they believed that he was the Son of God.

The time was near for the feast of the passover, and Jesus went up to Jerusalem to keep it. When he came to the temple, he found in the court of the Gentiles, men who had brought oxen and sheep and doves there, to sell for sacrifices; and other men who had tables on which were pieces of silver money. This money was Jewish money, and was called the half shekel. We are told that each Jew gave one of these half shekels to the priests, every year, to buy sacrifices with, or whatever else was needed at the temple. The men at the tables were money-changers; they exchanged, or sold, the half shekels to those Jews who wanted to give them to the priests. But Jesus was much displeased to find men selling in the court of the temple, and he made a scourge, or whip of small cords, and drove them all out, and also the sheep and the oxen. Then he poured out the changers' money on the ground, and threw down their tables,

JESUS DRIVES THOSE WHO BUY AND SELL OUT OF THE TEMPLE

and said to those who sold doves, Take them away; my Father's house is a place for prayer, not a place to buy and sell in. And while he was at the feast of the passover, many believed on him when they saw the miracles that he did.

There was a man named Nicodemus, who was one of the rulers of the Jews. He came to Jesus in the night, and said to him, Master, we know that God has sent thee to teach us what is right, for no man could do the miracles that thou doest if God

were not with him. Jesus answered Nicodemus, and told him,
that unless he was born again, that is, unless he had a new
heart, he could not be one of God's children.

We have read that while the children of Israel were journeying
through the wilderness they sinned, and fiery serpents came
into the camp, and bit them. Then God told Moses to make a
serpent of brass and lift it up on a pole, and when any one who

CHRIST AND NICODEMUS

had been bitten looked at that serpent, he was made well. And
now Jesus said to Nicodemus, As Moses lifted up the serpent in
the wilderness, so must I be lifted up. Jesus meant that he was
to be lifted up on the cross, that we might look up to him, and
be forgiven our sins. For, he said, God loved us so much, that
he sent his only Son into the world to die for us, so that whoever looked up to him in faith, should not be punished, but
forgiven and taken to heaven.

Now Herod, who slew the little children in Bethlehem, was dead, and his son Herod was ruler over that part of the land called Galilee. This Herod, like his father, was a wicked man. He had married Herodias, his brother's wife, while his brother was yet alive. When John the Baptist told Herod that this was wrong, the woman, whose name was Herodias, was angry, and

THE BURIAL OF JOHN THE BAPTIST

would have persuaded Herod to kill him, but she could not. For Herod was afraid to kill John, because he had heard him preach, and knew that he was a holy man. Yet to please Herodias, he took John and bound him, and shut him up in prison. While John was in prison, Herod, on his birthday, made a great feast for the lords, high captains, and chief men of Galilee. And Salome, the daughter of Herodias, came in and danced before them. Then Herod was greatly pleased with her, and said, Ask of me whatever thou wilt, and it shall be given thee, even to the half of my kingdom.

And Salome went to her mother and said, What shall I ask? Her mother answered, Ask the king to command that John the Baptist's head be cut off, and brought to thee here in a large dish. And Salome came back in haste to the king, saying, I want thee to give me presently, in a large dish, the head of John the Baptist. Then Herod was very sorry, yet because he had promised her, and because the men who were with him had heard him do so, he would not refuse. And immediately he sent one of his soldiers, who cut off John's head in the prison, and brought it in a large dish to Salome, and she gave it to her mother. When John's disciples heard of it, they came and took up his dead body and laid it in a tomb, and went and told Jesus.

Jesus and his disciples went into a part of the land called Galilee. On the way there, they came to a city named Sychar. Just outside of the city was a well, called Jacob's well, where the people came to get water. It was in the hot part of the day, and Jesus, being wearied with his journey, sat down by the well. His disciples had gone into the city to buy food, and had left him alone.

And a woman came out of the city, carrying her pitcher to draw water. Now this woman was a sinner. She did not love God in her heart, and had done many things to displease him. Jesus knew this, for he sees all our hearts and knows of everything that we have done. And he talked with the woman, and told her of some of the things she had done, long ago, to displease God. Then she was surprised, and said, Sir, I see thou art a prophet. She meant that he was a person whom God told of things which other people did not know. And she said to Jesus, I know that the Saviour is coming into the world. When he comes he will tell us all things. Jesus said to her, I that speak to thee am he.

Then the woman left her pitcher and made haste back to the city, and said to the people, Come and see a man who told me all the things that ever I did. Is not this the Saviour?

And the people went out and saw Jesus, and begged him to come into their city. So he came there and stayed with them three days. And they listened to the things that he taught

JESUS TALKS TO THE WOMAN AT THE WELL

them. Then they said to the woman, Now we believe on him, not because thou didst tell us about him, but because we have heard him ourselves, and know that he is the Saviour who has come down from heaven.

From that time Jesus began to teach all the people in the land of Israel, telling them that the Judgment day was coming, and that they should repent of their sins and believe in him.

After this he went again to the city of Cana, where he had changed the water into wine. And a nobleman who lived in another city came to him, and begged him to heal his son who was very sick. The nobleman said, Sir, come quickly, before my child dies. Jesus said to him, Go to thy house, thy son is made well.

And the man believed what Jesus said, and left him to go to his home. But before he reached there, his servants met him and said to him, Thy son is well. He asked at what time he began to get better. They answered, Yesterday, at the seventh hour the fever left him. Then the man knew that it was at the same hour when Jesus said to him, Thy son is made well. And the nobleman and all his family believed that Jesus was the Son of God.

The Jews, as we have read, offered up their sacrifices only at one place, which was the temple in Jerusalem. But they had houses in every city, where they met together to worship, when they did not want to offer up sacrifices, or to go to Jerusalem. These houses were called synagogues. On the Sabbath days the Jews met there to pray and read the Scriptures. Their Scriptures were the same as ours, excepting the part called the New Testament, which was not written until after Jesus was crucified.

As they did not yet know how to print, as we do now, they used to copy the different books of the Scriptures with pen and ink, on rolls of paper, or parchment. These rolls were kept in the synagogue, in a box or chest, called the ark, because it was shaped like the ark that used to stand in the most holy place in the temple. When the people met together in the synagogue on the Sabbath day, the chief officer or, as he was called, the ruler of the synagogue, sometimes asked one of them to read the Scriptures, and speak to the rest.

Jesus came to Nazareth, where he had been brought up, and he went into the synagogue on the Sabbath day. And the roll on which was written the book of the prophet Isaiah, was handed him, that he might read to the people. When he had opened the roll, he read to them from the part where Isaiah told the children of Israel of the Saviour, who was coming into the world. After he was done reading, Jesus closed the roll and sat down; and the eyes of all who were in the synagogue were fixed on him. Then he said to them that those words of the prophet had come true, and that he was the Saviour, the Son of God, of whom Isaiah had spoken. But when he said this, all the men in the synagogue were filled with anger, for they would not believe that he was the Saviour. And they rose up and led him out to the top of a steep hill, on which their city was built, that they might cast him down and kill him. But Jesus, because he had the power of God, went out from among them, and they could do him no harm.

MATT. IV–XII (4–12). MARK I–III (1–3). LUKE IV–VI (4–6). JOHN V (5)

JESUS TEACHES THE MULTITUDE BY THE SEA-SIDE, CALLS PETER, ANDREW, JAMES, AND JOHN TO FOLLOW HIM, PRAYS IN THE WILDERNESS, PREACHES THE GOSPEL, HEALS THE LEPER AND THE PARALYTIC, CALLS MATTHEW, HEALS THE IMPOTENT MAN, CHOOSES THE TWELVE APOSTLES, PREACHES THE SERMON ON THE MOUNT.

JESUS went down to Capernaum, which was a city by the sea of Galilee, and great numbers of people came there to hear him. As he stood by the sea, they crowded upon him. And he saw two boats on the shore, but the fishermen had gone out of them and were mending their nets. Then Jesus went into one of the boats, which was Peter's, and asked him to push it out a little way from the land. And he sat down, and taught the people out of the boat.

When he had done teaching them, he said to Peter and to Andrew, his brother, Sail out now on the sea, and let down your nets into the water to catch fish. Peter answered, Master, we have been laboring all night, and have caught nothing; yet at thy command, I will let down the net. When they had done this they caught a great multitude of fishes, so that the net broke. Then they beckoned to their partners, who were in the other boat, by the shore, that they should come and help them. And they came, and filled both boats with the fish, until they began to sink.

When Peter saw the miracle which Jesus had done, he kneeled down and worshipped him, saying, I am a sinful man, O Lord. For he was astonished, and so were his partners, James and John, at the multitude of fishes they had taken. Jesus did this miracle so that these men might see it, and believe on him and know that he was the Son of God, because he had chosen them to be his disciples, and to go with him wherever he should go. And he said to them, Come with me. Then they left their boats and their nets and all that they had, and followed him.

On the Sabbath day, Jesus went into the synagogue and taught the people. And a man was there who had an evil spirit. We have read before of evil spirits—how one of them

THE NET WAS FILLED WITH FISHES

went into king Saul, when he cast his spear at David to kill him. And this man who was now in the synagogue, had an evil spirit, and he cried out to Jesus, saying, Let us alone: what have we to do with thee, thou Jesus of Nazareth? Art thou come to destroy us? I know thee, that thou art the Son of God. Jesus said to the evil spirit, Be still, and come out of him. Then the spirit threw the man down, and cried with a loud voice, and came out of him. All the people who were in the synagogue were astonished, and said among themselves, What does this mean? for even the wicked spirits obey him.

When they had come out of the synagogue, Jesus went into the house where Andrew and Peter lived. James and John also were there. And Peter's wife's mother was sick of a fever, and they begged Jesus to heal her. Then he stood by her bed, and commanded the fever to come out of her. And immediately she was made well, and she rose up and waited on them. In the evening when the sun had set, the people of the city brought many who were sick, and who had evil spirits, to the house where Jesus was, and a great multitude were gathered about the door. And he healed the sick, and cast out the evil spirits from those who had them.

In the morning, rising up a great while before it was light, he went out to a lonely place in the wilderness, and there prayed to God. For although he was God's Son, yet he had come on the earth to be a man; and while he was on earth, he felt pain and hunger and sorrow like men. Therefore he prayed to God for help, as men do; and now he went out into the wilderness where he would be alone, and prayed there.

But after he had gone, the people came to Peter's house to seek him. Then Peter and the other disciples followed Jesus, and when they found him, they said, All the people are seeking for thee. Jesus answered, I must go and preach the gospel in other cities also. And he went through all Galilee, teaching in the synagogues and preaching the gospel to the people. Gospel means good news. What good news was it that Jesus preached? It was this: That he had come into the world to be punished for our sins, in our place and instead of us; so that, if we repent of those sins and believe on him, we shall not be punished at the Judgment day, but forgiven and taken up to heaven where we shall be happy forever.

And there came to him a man with the leprosy, who kneeled down before him and said, Lord, if thou wilt thou canst make me clean. Jesus pitied him, and put out his hand and touched him, saying, I will: be thou clean. And immediately the leprosy went from him, and he was made clean. Then Jesus sent him away, and commanded him to tell no man who had healed him, but to go to the priest at the temple, and offer up a sacrifice, as Moses had commanded those persons to do who were cured of the leprosy. Yet the man, as soon as he was gone, told all the people what Jesus had done for him.

EASTERN HOUSE-TOP

Now there were among the Jews some men called Scribes, and others called Pharisees, who pretended to be very holy. They studied the Scriptures and explained them to the rest of the people; but they did not themselves do as the Scriptures said. For although they obeyed some of the commandments, and were careful not to work on the Sabbath, and made long prayers in the synagogues, and even at the corners of the streets, yet they did this that others might see them and praise them for doing it. For these men were hypocrites, that is, persons who pretended to be good, while in their hearts they were wicked. Therefore, when Jesus came, telling them they must repent of their sins, and obey God, they hated him, and did all they could to keep the people from believing on him.

Jesus went again into the city of Capernaum; and when the

JESUS CURES THE MAN WITH THE PALSY

people heard of it they gathered together at the house where he was, and he preached to them there. The houses of the Jews were usually square, and but one story high. The roofs were flat, with a wall, or railing around them, so that persons might safely walk there. In the center of the house was a large square room called the court. Over this, the roof was left open, but in time of rain, or much heat, an awning or covering of some kind, was stretched across the opening. It was into such a house as this that Jesus had now come. And some men brought a man who was sick of the palsy and unable to walk, for Jesus to heal him. When they could not come in at the door, on account of the crowd, they went up on the roof, (perhaps through the next house), and taking off the covering, let the man down on his bed or mattress, into the room below, where Jesus was.

When Jesus saw how much faith they had, he spoke to the sick man, saying, Thy sins are forgiven thee. But some of the Scribes and Pharisees, who were sitting there, said to themselves, Who is this, that pretends he is able to forgive sins, as if he were God? Jesus knew their thoughts, and said to them, Why do you think these things in your hearts? Is it not as easy

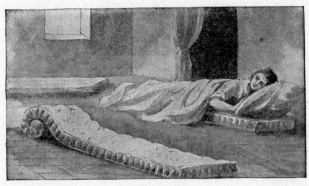

EASTERN BEDS

for me to forgive this man his sins, as it is to cure him of his palsy? But to show you that I have power to forgive sins, I will make him well. Then he said to the sick man, Stand up on thy feet, and take up thy bed and go to thy house. Immediately the man rose, stood on his feet, took up his bed, and went out before them all. The people who saw it were astonished, and said, We never saw such things done before.

We have read that the Jews had to pay taxes, or tribute money, to the Romans. There were men in each city who took these taxes from the people. They were called publicans. The Jews hated them, not only because they took their money for the Romans, but also because most of them were unjust and cruel men, taking more than was right. Yet the publicans did not all do this. And as Jesus passed by, he saw one of them, named Matthew, sitting at the place where the people came to pay him the tribute money. Jesus spoke to him, and said, Follow me. Then Matthew obeyed, and rising up, left all and followed Jesus. From that time he was one of his disciples.

After this there was a feast of the Jews, and Jesus went up to Jerusalem. Now there was at Jerusalem, by the sheep gate, a

JESUS CURES THE SICK MAN AT THE POOL OF BETHESDA

pool of water called the pool of Bethesda. Around it were built five porches, in which lay a great number of persons who were sick, or blind, or lame. They waited there, because at certain times the water moved, as if some one had stirred, or troubled it. And they thought that whoever went into it first, after it was troubled, was made well of whatever disease he had.

And a man was there who had been sick thirty-eight years. Jesus saw him, and knowing how long he had been sick, pitied

34

him. And he said to him, Wilt thou be made well? The man answered, I have no one, when the water is troubled, to help me into the pool; but while I am trying to get down to it, another steps in before me, and I am too late. Jesus said to him, Rise, take up thy bed, and walk. And immediately the man was made well, and took up his bed and walked. Now it was the Sabbath day. And the Jews, wishing to find fault, said to him, It is wrong for thee to carry thy bed on the Sabbath. The man

JESUS AND HIS DISCIPLES WALK THROUGH THE CORN

answered, He that cured me, told me to take up my bed and walk. They asked him, Who is it told thee? The man said it was Jesus. Then did the Jews persecute Jesus and try to kill him, saying he had broken the Sabbath day.

But Jesus talked with them, and told them that the miracles which he did, showed that God had sent him, and the prophets also he said had spoken about him, though the Jews would not believe in him. Yet he said, he was the Son of God, and had power to raise the dead, as only God had, and that the hour was coming when all who were in their graves should hear his voice, and come forth. And then he would judge them. Those who had done good should be rewarded for their obedience, and those who had done evil should be punished for their sins. Because his Father had made him the Judge of all men, so that all men should worship and obey Jesus, as they worshipped and obeyed God.

Jesus walked on the Sabbath day, with his disciples, through

JESUS HEALS THE MAN WITH A WITHERED HAND

the fields of corn. And they, being hungry, picked some of the ears, and rubbed out the grains with their hands and did eat them. When the Pharisees saw it they found fault, and said that the disciples were working on the Sabbath. But Jesus told them that he was not to be judged for what he did on that day, because he was the Lord, or Master, of the Sabbath.

On another Sabbath day he went into the synagogue, and a man was there whose hand was withered, so that he could not open it or stretch it out. And the Pharisees watched Jesus, to see whether he would heal the man on the Sabbath, that they might accuse him of doing wrong. But Jesus knew their thoughts, and said to them, If one of you have a sheep which should fall into a pit on the Sabbath, would you not lay hold of it and lift it out? And if it be right to do good to a sheep, how much more is it to do good to a man. Therefore I tell you it is right to do good on the Sabbath day. Then he said to the man, Stretch out thy hand. And he stretched it out, and it was made well like the other.

Then the Pharisees were filled with madness against him, and they went out of the synagogue, and talked with one another about some way of putting him to death. When he knew of it, he left that place, with his disciples, and came to the sea of Galilee. And many persons from Jerusalem, and Judea, and from countries far off, when they heard of the wonderful works that he did, came to him. And those that were sick crowded around him, that they might, by only touching him, be made well; and he healed them all.

After this, he went out to a desert place alone, and stayed there all night praying to God. When it was morning he called his disciples, and chose twelve of them that they might be with him, and that he might send them out to preach, and give them power also to do miracles, to heal those that were sick, and to cast out devils. These twelve he called apostles, which means Messengers. They were Peter and Andrew his brother, James and John his brother, Philip and Bartholomew, Thomas and Matthew the publican, James and Lebbeus, Simon and Judas Iscariot.

And seeing the multitude that followed him, he went up on to a mountain, and when he was set down, his disciples came to him, and he taught them there. He told them what persons were truly happy; he called them the blessed ones. He said:

Blessed are the poor in spirit, for theirs is the kingdom of heaven.

By the poor in spirit, Jesus meant those who are humble on account of their sins, and who feel that God only can forgive them, and save them from punishment. Jesus called these

persons blessed, or happy, because they are the ones whom he
brings into his kingdom here on earth, and whom he will take
to live with him in heaven after they die.

And he said, Blessed are those who mourn, for they shall be
comforted.

To mourn is to weep and lament because we have trouble. It
is hard to bear trouble, yet if we are troubled on account of

THE SERMON ON THE MOUNT

our sins, God is pleased with us and he will take our trouble
away.

Blessed are the meek, for they shall inherit the earth.

To be meek is to be patient, and not to get angry when others
insult us, and try to do us harm. When Jesus was on earth,
wicked men did so to him, but he bore it meekly and patiently.
And those who follow his example shall inherit, or have for
their own, the happiest earthly lot.

Blessed are those who hunger and thirst after righteousness, for they shall be satisfied, or filled.

We hunger and thirst after righteousness when we are as anxious to do right, and to please God, as we are to get food when we are hungry, and water when we are thirsty. If we desire to do right as much as this, God will help us do it, and we shall be satisfied in pleasing him.

Blessed are those who are merciful to others, for they shall have mercy shown to them.

Blessed are the pure in heart, for they shall see God.

Blessed are the peacemakers, (that is, those who will not quarrel themselves, and who try to keep others from anger and strife), for they shall be called the children of God.

Jesus told his disciples that when they were treated cruelly, and persecuted, for his sake, they should not be sorry, but glad, for great would be their reward in heaven. And they were not the only ones, he said, who had been treated so. Even the prophets, those holy men whom God sent in the old times, were treated in the same way.

And he said to his disciples that they must let their light shine; he meant they must not be afraid to let others know that they loved and obeyed God. Instead of hiding this they must let others see it. Then, perhaps by their example, they might be led to love and obey God also. For Jesus said that if we do the things that God commands, and teach others to do them, we shall be called great in the kingdom of heaven. But if, like the Scribes and Pharisees, we only teach those things without doing them, we cannot enter into the kingdom of heaven.

And he said to the people, Your teachers have told you that if you should kill another person, you would be in danger of being punished. But I tell you that if you are even angry with another, who has done you no harm, you will be in danger of punishment.

Then he told his disciples that when they were going up to the temple to worship God, they must try and remember whether they had done wrong to any other person; whether they had taken anything that belonged to him, or had said what was not true about him, or in any other way had done him harm.   And if they had, they must go and do what was right to that person.   For God would not accept, or care for, their worship while there was some sin in their hearts that they had not repented of.

We must be pure and good, Jesus says, in all we do and say, and must not even think an impure or bad thought.   And if the thought that is impure offends God, how greatly will the impure word, or act, displease him!

When others are unkind to us, and do us harm, we must not do harm to them again.   Instead of this we must do good to them, and pray for them, and love them; then, Jesus says, we will be the children of our Father in heaven.   For he is kind even to those who do not obey him or love him.   And we must try to be like him, perfect in all things.

And Jesus commanded his disciples to be careful, lest when they did what was right, they should do it only for other persons to see them and praise them.   For this was not the reason why they should do right, because they wanted to be praised. They should do it because they wanted to please God.   When they gave anything to the poor, they must not go about telling it; when they prayed to God, they must not choose a place where others could see them, but must go into their chamber and shut the door, so that no one but God could see them. Then God would answer their prayers.

And when they should fast, they must not look sad, as the hypocrites did, on purpose to let others know they were fasting; but they must look as cheerful then as at other times, so that no one but their heavenly Father would know it; then their heavenly Father would reward them.

And Jesus said that we must not want to be rich, and to lay up a great deal of money in this world, but must lay up riches in heaven.   He did not mean that we could lay up money in heaven.   We shall not want any money there.   Jesus meant that we should be trying all the time to live so that at last we shall get to heaven.   For in heaven we shall have more things to make us happy than all the money in the world could buy.

Then he said to the people, You cannot obey God and Satan,

too. We cannot do this, because if we obey God we will do right, but if we obey Satan we will do wrong. Therefore, we cannot obey both; and we must choose which one to obey.

And he told his disciples not to judge other persons; he meant that we should be careful how we find fault with others, and blame them. For perhaps they never did the thing that we blame them for; or even if they did it, did not mean any harm. We cannot see their hearts and tell how they felt while they were doing it; only God can tell that, and perhaps he does not blame them. And how often we ourselves do the very things we blame others for doing. Jesus said we should first stop doing wrong ourselves, and then we would be able to tell others of their faults.

And he told the people who were listening to him, and he tells you and me, that whatever we want other persons to do to us, we must do to them. If we want them to treat us kindly and justly, we must treat them kindly and justly too.

And he said, Strive earnestly to go in at the strait, or narrow gate, for wide is the gate and broad is the way that leadeth to destruction. He meant that the good and the bad ways are like two gates in our path, for us to choose which one we will go through. The good way is like a small and narrow gate, that we cannot see till we look carefully after it. The bad way is like a wide gate which stands open directly before us. This wide gate leads down to hell, and many go in there. The narrow gate leads up to heaven, and there are few who find it.

Not every one, Jesus said, who called him Lord, or Master, would be taken up to heaven, but only those who obeyed his Father in heaven. Many persons who had not done this, would come to him at the Judgment day, and would call him Lord, Lord, and would say they had worked for him, and had taught other persons about him. But he would tell them they had never truly been his disciples. And he would send them away, with all those who had been wicked.

Then he spoke about two men, who, each of them, built a house. One chose a rock to build his upon. When it was done there came a great storm, and beat against it. But the rain could not move the rock, nor the wind blow it away; therefore his house stood firm, and the storm did it no harm. The other man built his house in a place where there was nothing but sand. And the storm came against it also. And the rain washed the sand away from underneath it, and the wind blew against it, and it fell and was destroyed.

THE HOUSE ON THE ROCK AND THE HOUSE ON THE SAND

Then Jesus said that all those persons who listened to his teaching, and did what he taught them, were like the wise man who built his house upon the rock. But those who listened to his teaching and would not do as he taught them, were like the foolish man who built his house upon the sand. He meant that those who obeyed what he taught them, would be saved, but those who disobeyed him would be lost. For the two men who built the houses meant the righteous and the wicked; and the storm meant the Judgment day.

MATT. VIII–XIII (8–13). MARK IV, V (4, 5). LUKE VII, VIII–XII (7, 8–12)

JESUS HEALS THE CENTURION'S SERVANT; RAISES THE WIDOW'S SON; IS ANOINTED; IS MINISTERED TO; SPEAKS THE PARABLE OF THE RICH FOOL; TELLS HIS DISCIPLES NOT TO FEAR WANT; THE PARABLES OF THE SOWER, THE TARES, THE MUSTARD SEED, THE PEARL, AND THE FISHERMEN. HE STILLS THE STORM, AND HEALS THE DEMONIAC.

THERE was at Capernaum, a centurion, or captain in the Roman army; he had a servant whom he loved, and who was sick and about to die. When the centurion heard that Jesus was there, he sent some of the elders of the Jews who were his friends, to ask him to come and heal his servant. And the elders came and begged Jesus earnestly, saying, Although this centurion is not a Jew, but a Roman, yet he loves the Jews, and has been kind to us; for with his own money he has built us a synagogue.

Then Jesus went with them toward the centurion's house. But before he came there, the centurion sent some more of his friends with a message to Jesus: the message was this, That the centurion had not come himself to speak with Jesus, because he thought he was not good enough. And now he sent word that he did not think himself good enough for Jesus even to come into his house. But if Jesus would only say that his servant should get well, without coming, the centurion was sure that he would get well. For I have soldiers under me, the centurion said, and I say to one, Go; and he goes where I tell him. To another I say, Come; and he comes. So, I know that the disease which my servant has, will obey thee and go out of him, if thou wilt command it to go.

When Jesus heard these words he was astonished, and said to those who were with him, I have not found any one, even among the children of Israel, who has so much faith in me as this Roman has. And I tell you that at the last day, many of the people of other nations who have believed in me, shall be taken up into heaven, while the children of Israel, because they will not believe, shall be shut out. And when the centurion's friends returned to his house, they found the servant made well.

The next day Jesus went into a city called Nain. As he came near to the gate of the city, the people were carrying out a dead man to bury him. He was the only son of his mother, and she was a widow; and many of her friends were with her. When Jesus saw her, he pitied her, and said, Weep not. And he came and touched the bier on which the body lay, and those who car-

JESUS RAISES THE WIDOW'S SON

ried it stood still. Then Jesus said, Young man, I say unto thee, arise. And he that was dead sat up, and began to speak, and Jesus gave him to his mother. And all who saw it were afraid, and they praised God, and said that he had sent a great prophet among them.

We have read that the people in eastern countries wore sandals instead of shoes. These they took off when they came into the house, and a servant brought water for them to wash their feet.

The people of those countries also used oil, or ointment, to put upon their heads and their beards, and sometimes over their whole bodies. This was called anointing. They did it because it made the skin smooth and soft, and, they thought, kept away disease: also because the smell of the ointment was sweet and pleasant. Men considered it a kindness to have their heads anointed by the person at whose house they were visiting.

A WOMAN ANOINTS THE FEET OF JESUS

A Pharisee, named Simon, asked Jesus to his house. Jesus went there, and sat down with him to eat. And a woman who lived in the city, and who had been a sinner, when she heard that Jesus was there, came with an alabaster box of ointment and bowed down at his feet. And because she was sorry for her sins, and wanted to be forgiven, she wept and washed the feet of Jesus with her tears, and wiped them with the hairs of her head; and she kissed his feet and anointed them with the ointment.

Now the Pharisee knew that the woman was a sinner, and he said to himself, If this man had come from God, he would know what sort of a woman this is, and would send her away: for the Pharisees thought themselves too holy to let sinners touch them. But Jesus knew what was in his heart, and he said to him, Simon, I have something to say to thee. He answered, Master, say on. Then Jesus said, Two men owed another man money; one owed him a great deal, and the other owed him a little. But as neither of them had any thing to pay with, he freely forgave them both. Tell me, now, which of them will love him the most? Simon answered, I suppose the one whom he forgave most. Jesus said, Thou hast answered rightly. And he turned to the woman, and said unto Simon, Seest thou this woman? I came into thy house, and thou gavest me no water to wash my feet; but she has washed my feet with tears, and wiped them with the hairs of her head. Thou gavest me no kiss, but this woman, since I came in has not ceased to kiss my feet. My head with oil thou didst not anoint, but she has anointed my feet with ointment. Therefore I say unto thee, her sins which are many, are forgiven; for she loved me much, but those who have little forgiven, love but little. And Jesus said to the woman, Thy sins are forgiven thee, go to thy home in peace.

After this Jesus went through every city and village preaching the gospel to the people; and the twelve apostles were with him. And he was poor, for though he might have been rich, (for everything in the world was his), yet he chose to be poor and to suffer for our sakes, to save us from being punished for our sins. And because he was poor, some of the women whom he had healed of sickness, and out of whom he had cast evil spirits, gave to him such things as he needed. One of them was named Mary Magdalene, another Joanna, and another Susanna; beside these there were many others.

And he spoke a parable to the people. A parable is a story which has a meaning to it, and which helps us to understand and remember something we are learning. Jesus told the people this parable that they might know how foolish and wicked it was for them to put their trust in riches. He said, There was a rich man who had fields and vineyards. When harvest-time came, and he gathered in his fruits, there were so many that his barns would not hold them. Then he said to himself, What shall I do? for I have no room where I can put my fruits. And he answered, This will I do. I will pull down my barns and build larger ones, and there I will put away all my fruits and my goods. Then I will say to myself, Now I

THE RICH MAN CANNOT FIND ROOM FOR HIS FRUITS

can eat and drink and be merry, for I have enough riches laid up to last me for many years.

But when the rich man had spoken these words, God said to him, Thou foolish man, this night thou must die. Who then shall have those things which thou hast laid up for many years? So, Jesus said, it will be with all those persons who care only to lay up riches for themselves in this world, but do not care to please God. Death will come when they are not expecting it, and then they will have to leave their riches for others, and go away themselves to a world where nothing has been laid up for them.

And Jesus told his disciples not to be afraid, because they were poor, lest they might want food to eat, and clothes to wear. Think of the birds, he said; they do not sow seed in the fields, nor reap grain and carry it to the barn to lay it up there, yet they always have enough to eat, because God feeds them. And God cares more for you than he does for the birds. And look at the flowers, how they grow. They do not work like men to make raiment for themselves, and yet they are more beautifully

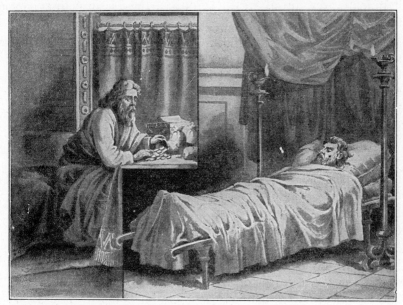

THE RICH MAN COUNTS HIS MONEY   HE DIES

clothed and have brighter colors upon them, than Solomon when he was king over Israel. If then, God gives such beautiful clothing to the flowers, which are of so little value that one day they are growing up in the field, and the next are cut down and burned, he will be more careful to clothe you, though now you are afraid to trust in him. Therefore do not be anxious lest you may want things to eat, and to drink, and to wear, for your heavenly Father knows that you need these things. But seek first to obey him and be his children, and then he will give all these things to you.

While Jesus walked by the seaside, great multitudes came to him, so that he went into a boat and sat down to teach them, and the whole multitude stood on the shore. And he spoke a parable, saying, A farmer went out in the field to sow his seed, and he scattered it by handfuls over the ground. Some of the seed fell upon the hard, beaten path, that ran along by the edge of the field, and the birds flew down and ate it. Some fell upon stony places, where there was only a little earth. There it quickly grew up above the ground; but because there was not earth enough to make larger roots, in a few days it withered away. And some fell along the side of the field where briars and weeds were growing; and the briars grew up and choked it. But the rest of the seed fell upon good ground that had been ploughed and made ready to receive it. And the rain fell on it and watered it there, and the sun shone upon it, and it sprang up and bore grain, a hundred times as much as the farmer had planted.

When Jesus was alone, his disciples came and asked him to explain this parable to them. He answered, that the seed meant the words which he preached. Some of the people who heard those words did not understand what he said, nor care to remember them. Then Satan came and made them think of other things, and took his words out of their hearts as quickly as the birds ate up the seed that fell on the pathway. And some who heard him, remembered his words and tried for a little while to obey them. But it was only for a little while. As soon as they had trouble, or were blamed by others for doing it, they ceased trying and forgot them. This was the seed that fell on the stony ground, and that sprang up at first, but in a few days withered away. And some heard Jesus preach, and were glad to hear what he said, but afterward they went away and paid more attention to their houses, their riches, and their pleasures, than they did to the things he had taught them. This was the seed that fell among thorns, and the thorns grew up and choked it. But there were some who listened to all that he taught, and remembered it in their hearts, and tried every day to do as he told them. This was the good seed that took root and grew, and bore a hundred times as much as the farmer had planted.

AN ENEMY SOWS TARES

And Jesus spoke another parable about a man who sowed seed in his field. But while his servants were asleep, an enemy came and sowed tares, or weeds, among the wheat, and then went away so that the servants knew nothing of it. When the time had come for the wheat to grow up, the servants went out in the field to look at it, and there they saw tares growing among the wheat. Then they came back to the owner of the field and said

THE REAPERS BURN THE TARES

to him, Was it not good seed that was sowed in thy field? Why then are tares growing among the wheat? He answered, An enemy has done this. Then the servants asked, Shall we not go and pull up the tares? He said, No, lest while you pull up the tares, you root up the wheat also with them. Let both grow together until harvest; and then I will say to my reapers, Gather together first the tares, and bind them in bundles to burn them, but gather the wheat into my barn.

And Jesus explained this parable also to his disciples. The field, he said, meant the world, the owner of the field meant Jesus himself; the good seed meant the words that he preached; the wheat that grew up meant the persons who listened to those words and obeyed them. The enemy that sowed the bad seed meant Satan; and the tares in the field meant wicked men. As the owner of the field allowed the wheat and the tares to grow together until the harvest, so Jesus will allow good and bad men to live together in the world until the Judgment day. Then he will send forth his angels to gather up the good and take them to heaven, but the bad will be sent away to be punished.

And Jesus spoke a parable about the mustard seed, which is among the smallest of seeds; yet when a man takes it, and plants it in the ground, it grows up to be the largest of herbs, and the birds come and lodge in its branches. So it is with our love to God. At first it seems very small. But if we are truly his children, it will go on growing stronger and greater, until we love him more than we love any one else, and try harder, in all that we do, to please him.

Jesus also told the people about a merchantman who was looking for pearls to buy. He went to every person who had any to sell, hoping to find some that would suit him. At last he found one that was larger and more beautiful than any he had ever seen before. But its price was so great that he had not the money to buy it. Therefore, he went away and sold everything he had, so that he might come back and buy that one precious pearl. This is the way that persons feel who want their sins forgiven. They cannot be happy till it is done, and they are willing to give up every sinful pleasure, and everything that offends God, so that they may come to him and ask him to forgive their sins for them.

Then Jesus spoke of the fishermen with their net. They carry it out in their boat on the sea, and cast it into the water, and afterward drag it slowly to the shore. When they come there, and draw it up out of the water again, they find a great number of fishes in it. But the fishes are of many different kinds. Some are good: these they gather into baskets to keep; and some are bad: these they throw away. So, Jesus said to his disciples, it would be at the end of the world. For, he told them again, the angels would then come forth and separate the righteous from the wicked, and would send away to be punished those who had not obeyed him.

And there came to Jesus a Scribe, or teacher of the law of Moses, who said to him, Master, I want to stay with thee and go with thee wherever thou goest. Jesus answered him, saying, The foxes have holes in the ground and the birds have nests, but I have not where to lay my head. Jesus meant that he was poorer even than the foxes and the birds. For they had homes of their own in which they might stay, but he had no place where he might go when he was weary, and lie down to rest.

In the evening, after he had spoken these things, both Jesus and his disciples went into a boat, to sail over to the other side of the sea of Galilee. As they were going, a great storm arose, and the waves dashed into the boat and filled it with water, so that it was ready to sink. But Jesus was asleep in the hinder part of the boat, with his head on a pillow. And his disciples came and awakened him, saying, Lord, save us, or we shall perish. Jesus rose up, and spoke to the winds and the sea, and said to them, Peace, be still. And the wind ceased to blow, and the sea was still and calm. Then he said to his disciples, Why were you afraid? How is it that you have so little faith?

And they sailed over to the other side of the sea. When Jesus was come out of the boat, there met him a man who had an evil spirit. He had torn off his clothes and was very fierce, so that no one could pass by that way. His friends had often bound him with chains, to keep him at home; but he broke the chains, and went and lived in the caves, that had been hollowed out of the sides of mountains for tombs. And always, night and day, he was wandering in the tombs and mountains, crying out and cutting himself with stones. But when he saw Jesus a good way off, he ran to him and fell down at his feet and worshipped him, saying, What have I to do with thee, Jesus, thou Son of God? I beseech thee, punish me not.

Now there was near the mountains a herd of swine feeding, and the evil spirits that were in the man, (for more than one had gone into him), begged Jesus, that if he commanded them to come out, he would let them go into the swine. Jesus said to them, Go. And when they had come out of the man, they went into the herd of swine; and the whole herd (there were about

JESUS ASLEEP IN THE STORM

two thousand of them) ran swiftly down a steep place into the sea, and were drowned in the waters. And the men who took care of them, fled into the city and told what they had seen. Then all the people came out to meet Jesus. When they saw the man who before had evil spirits, sitting down, quiet and clothed, and in his right mind, they were afraid, and asked Jesus to go away from their country.

And when he was come into the boat to leave that place, the

man out of whom he had cast the evil spirits, begged that he might go with him. But Jesus said to him, Go home to thy friends, and tell them what great things the Lord has done for thee. Then the man went, and began to tell all the people how he had been made well.

MATT. IX–XIV (9–14). MARK V, VI (5, 6). LUKE VIII, IX (8, 9). JOHN VI (6)

JESUS HEALS THE WOMAN WHO TOUCHES HIS GARMENT, RAISES THE RULER'S DAUGHTER, HEALS TWO BLIND MEN AND A DUMB MAN, SENDS OUT HIS APOSTLES TO PREACH THE GOSPEL, FEEDS THE FIVE THOUSAND, WALKS ON THE WATER, AND HEALS THE SICK.

JESUS went into Capernaum. And one of the rulers of the synagogue came to him, and kneeling down at his feet, begged him earnestly, saying, My little daughter is sick and ready to die: I pray thee, come and lay thy hands on her, that she may live. Jesus went with him, and so did his disciples. And many people followed after him and crowded around him. Among them was a woman who had suffered for twelve years from a disease which no physician could cure; for she had asked many, and given them all the money she had, yet she was no better, but rather grew worse. When she heard that Jesus was there, she said to herself, If I can but touch his garment, I shall be made well. So she came in the crowd behind him, and touched him; and as soon as she had done it she felt that her sickness was cured.

Then Jesus, turning toward the people that followed him, said, Who touched me? His disciples answered, Thou seest the multitude pressing against thee, and askest thou, Who touched me? But he looked around to see her who had done this thing. When the woman saw that he knew it, and that she could not be hid, she came trembling, and falling down at his feet, told before all the people why she had touched him, and how in a moment she was made well. Jesus said to her, Daughter, be not afraid; because thou hadst faith in me, thou art healed.

While he yet spoke to the woman, there came to the ruler

of the synagogue a messenger, saying, Thy daughter is dead; therefore trouble not the Master any further. But Jesus said to him, Fear not; only have faith, and she shall live. When they came to the ruler's house, Jesus saw the people weeping and wailing greatly. He said to them, Why do you weep? the child is not dead, but sleeping. He meant that she should soon rise up from the dead, like one who waked out of sleep. But they

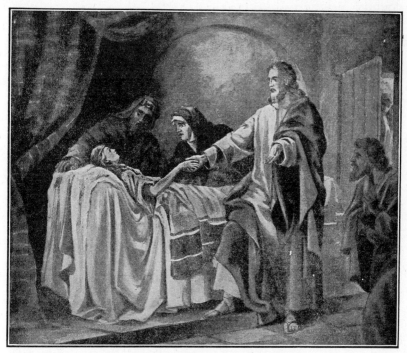

JESUS RAISES TO LIFE THE RULER'S DAUGHTER

would not believe him, and laughed him to scorn. Then Jesus put them all out, and took three of his apostles—Peter, James, and John—and the father and the mother of the child, and went into the room where she lay. And he took her by the hand, and said, I say to thee, arise. And the child, who was twelve years of age, arose and walked. All those who saw it wondered; and he commanded that food should be given her.

As Jesus went away from the ruler's house, two blind men

followed him, and cried after him, saying, Thou son of David, have mercy on us. They called him this, because he was descended from king David. Jesus said to them, Do you believe that I am able to make you well? They answered, Yes, Lord. Then he touched their eyes, and immediately they could see. Jesus said to them, Tell no man what I have done to you. But when they left him, they told the people through all that country how he had healed them.

They brought to him a dumb man who could not speak, because an evil spirit had entered into him. And Jesus cast out the evil spirit, and the man spoke. Then all the people wondered, and said, We have never seen such things done before in the land of Israel. But the Pharisees hated Jesus, and told the people that he was able to cast out devils, because Satan, the prince of the devils, helped him.

Jesus came again to Nazareth, where he had been brought up, and he went into the synagogue on the Sabbath day, and taught the people. And they were astonished at his words, and said, Where did this man get such great wisdom, and power to do such wonderful works? Is he not the son of Joseph, the carpenter? Is not his mother named Mary, and are not his brethren and his sisters here with us? So they would not believe on him; and because they would not, he did no miracles there, except that he put his hands on a few sick persons and healed them.

Jesus called his twelve apostles to him, that he might send them out through all the land, to preach the gospel. Yet he told them not to go into the cities where the Samaritans, or the Gentiles lived, but to go only among the children of Israel. He told them this because the children of Israel were God's chosen people, and the gospel was to be preached to them first.

And before the apostles went, Jesus gave them power to do miracles, so that all who should see them do those wonderful works might believe the gospel that they preached. He said to them, Wherever you shall go among the people, heal their sick, make their lepers well, raise their dead; and tell them that Christ has come to save all who believe on him. But do not expect them to treat you kindly for doing these things; as they have treated me, so they will treat you. They will take you before their courts to try you, and scourge you, because you preach to them about me. Yet do not fear them, they are able only to kill your bodies; rather fear God, who is able to destroy both soul and body in hell.

Jesus also told the apostles not to take any money or food with them for their journey; for all they should need would

JESUS FEEDS THE MULTITUDE

be given to them, because they were working for him. He said, You know that two sparrows are sold for a farthing; they are worth so little that men care nothing for them. Yet God cares for them; he feeds them, and not one of them ever dies without his knowing it. Fear not then that he will forget you, for you are of more value than many sparrows. He remembers the smallest thing about you, and knows even the number of the hairs upon your head. And he will remember also those who are kind to you, for when any one shall be kind to you, it will be the same as if he were kind to me; and whoever gives you a cup of cold water only, because you are my disciples, shall be rewarded for doing it.

When Jesus had done commanding his twelve apostles, they went out through the cities and towns, preaching to the people and healing those who were sick. Afterward they came back to him, and told him of all they had done. And he said to them, Come, let us go to some place apart, where you may rest awhile; for there were so many coming and going, they had no time even to eat. Then they went into a boat, and sailed to the other side of the sea of Galilee, that they might be alone. But when the people heard of it, they followed them on foot, walking around by the side of the sea and coming where Jesus was.

In the evening his apostles came to him, saying, This is a desert place where there is nothing to eat, and the day is now passed: send the people away, that they may go into the villages and buy themselves food. Jesus said, They need not go away, give you them something to eat. The apostles answered, Shall we go and buy two hundred pennyworth of bread, and give them to eat? and even this would not be enough, for each one of them to take a little. He said to them, How many loaves have you? Go, and see. When they knew, they answered, Five, and two small fishes.

And he commanded his apostles to make all the people sit down in companies on the green grass. And Jesus took the five loaves and the two fishes, and looked up to heaven and thanked God for them. Then he broke the loaves in pieces, and gave them to the apostles; the fishes also he divided among them. And the apostles gave them to the multitude. And Jesus made those few loaves and fishes to increase, as they were given to the people, so that there was enough for them all. When they had eaten, he said, Gather up what is left, that nothing be lost. And they gathered up of the pieces that were left, twelve baskets full. Those that had eaten were about five thousand men, beside women and children.

The people, when they saw this great miracle which Jesus

did, wanted to make him their king, but he left them and went up on a mountain alone, to pray. The apostles he sent away in a boat, to go across the sea toward Capernaum. And in the evening they were out on the middle of the sea, rowing, for the wind was against them, but Jesus was alone on the shore. From there he could see them toiling in rowing, for the waves were rough and stormy. And in the night he went out to them,

CHRIST WALKS ON THE SEA

walking on the sea. When they saw him, they were afraid, and said, It is a spirit: and they cried out with fear. But Jesus spoke to them, saying, Be not afraid, It is I.

Then Peter answered out of the boat, and said, Lord, if it be thou, bid me come to thee on the water. Jesus said to him, Come. And Peter came down out of the boat, and walked on the water to go to Jesus. But when he heard the noise of the wind and saw the great waves dashing around him, he was afraid, and began to sink, and he cried, Lord, save me.

Immediately Jesus stretched out his hand, and caught him, and said to him, O thou of little faith, why didst thou doubt? When Jesus, and Peter had come into the boat, the wind was still; and in a moment the boat was at the land where the apostles wanted to be. Then they worshipped him, saying, Truly, thou art the Son of God.

JESUS HEALS MANY SICK PERSONS

As soon as they were come on the shore, the people knew him, and ran through all that country, and began to carry about in beds those that were sick, to the place where they heard he was. Wherever he went into villages, or cities, they laid the sick in the streets, and begged that they might touch, if it were only his garment; and as many as touched him were made perfectly well.

MATT. XV–XVIII (15–18).   MARK VII–IX (7–9).   LUKE IX–XVII (9–17).   JOHN VI (6)

JESUS TEACHES THE PEOPLE; CASTS OUT AN EVIL SPIRIT; HEALS THE DEAF,
THE BLIND, AND THE DUMB; FEEDS THE MULTITUDE; FORETELLS HIS
DEATH; IS TRANSFIGURED; PROVIDES MONEY IN THE FISH'S MOUTH.
PARABLE OF THE UNFORGIVING SERVANT.   JAMES AND JOHN WOULD
DESTROY THE SAMARITANS.   TEN LEPERS HEALED.

JESUS came again to Capernaum, and went into the synagogue and taught the Jews. And they asked him, saying,
What shall we do to please God? He answered, Believe that I
am the Saviour whom God was to send into the world. But the
Jews had expected the Saviour, when he should come, to be a
great soldier, who would set them free from the Romans, and
make them into a kingdom, and rule over them like the kings
of other nations. Therefore when Jesus came as a poor man,
telling them to repent of their sins and obey God's commandments, not promising to reward them in this world, but in
heaven, they were displeased with him, and refused to believe
that he was the Saviour.

Then he said to the twelve apostles, Will you also go away,
and leave me? Peter answered him, Lord, if we leave thee, to
whom shall we go to be saved? Jesus answered, I have chosen
you twelve to be my apostles, and one of you is my enemy. He
meant Judas Iscariot, who he knew was going to betray, and sell
him, to the chief priests and elders of the Jews, that they might
put him to death. The chief priests were the chief, or principal,
ones in the different courses of priests that served by turns at
the temple. There were twenty-four chief priests. Like the
Scribes and Pharisees, they hated the Saviour, and did all they
could to keep the people from believing on him.

Jesus went out of the land of Israel and came near the
cities of Tyre and Sidon. The people of those cities were not
Jews, but Gentiles. Yet a woman who lived there, when she
heard that Jesus had come, went to him and begged him to cast
an evil spirit out of her daughter. At first he turned away as
if unwilling to hear her, because she was not a Jew; but he did

this only to try whether she truly believed in him. Then she prayed the more earnestly, and fell at his feet and worshipped him, saying, Lord, help me. Jesus answered and said to her, Because thou hast faith in me, thy daughter is made well. And when she came to her house she found the evil spirit gone out, and her daughter laid upon the bed.

Jesus came again into the land of Israel, by the sea of Galilee. There the people brought to him a man that was deaf. and could hardly speak, and they asked him to lay his hands on the man that he might be healed. Then Jesus took him aside from the multitude and put his fingers into the deaf man's ears, and spit and touched his tongue, and looking up to heaven, said, Be opened. And immediately the man was made well, so that he could both hear and speak.

Many persons came to him, bringing those who were lame, and blind, and dumb, and laid them down at his feet that he might heal them. Jesus healed them all, so that the people wondered when they saw the lame to walk, the dumb to speak, and the blind to see. And they thanked God for what had been done to them.

The multitude being very great, Jesus fed them again with only a few loaves and fishes, for they had been with him three days, and had nothing to eat. He said to his disciples, If I send them away to their homes without food, they will grow weary and faint by the way, for many of them have come from far. And he asked, How many loaves have you? His disciples answered, Seven, and a few little fishes. Then he commanded the people to sit down on the ground. And he took the seven loaves and the fishes, and thanked God for them, and gave them to his disciples to give to the people. And they all ate and had enough. Afterward they took up of the pieces that were left seven baskets full. Those that had eaten were about four thousand persons; and Jesus sent them away.

And he came to the city of Bethsaida, and they brought a blind man and begged Jesus to touch him. He took him by the hand and led him out of the town; and when he had spit on his eyes and put his hands on him, he asked if he could see. The blind man answered, I see men, yet they do not look like men, but like trees walking. Then Jesus put his hands again on the man's eyes, and made him look up, and he saw everything clearly.

As Jesus came with his apostles toward the city of Cesarea, he asked them, Who do the people say that I am? They answered, Some say that thou art John the Baptist, risen from the dead,

JESUS CURES A BLIND MAN

some that thou art the prophet Elijah, and others the prophet Jeremiah, come back to the earth again. Then Jesus asked, But who do you say that I am? Peter answered, Thou art the Christ, the Son of God. Peter meant to tell Jesus that the apostles believed him to be the Saviour, whom God had promised to send into the world.

We have read that the Jews expected this Saviour, when he should come, to set them free from the Romans and make them into a kingdom, and to reign over them like other earthly kings.

Even the apostles who were with Jesus all the time, and believed that he was the Saviour, thought he was going to set up an earthly kingdom. For although they saw he was now a poor man, they did not think he would stay so, but expected he would soon become rich and great, and would make them great too. Like the rest of the Jews, they had not yet learned that he had come to rule only in their hearts, and to have his kingdom there; and that instead of fighting battles for them, and ruling over them as a king, he was going to die on the cross for their sins.

But from this time he began to tell them what was really going to happen to him; that he must go to Jerusalem, and there be cruelly treated by the chief priests, the scribes, and the elders of the Jews; and that he would be killed by them, but would rise from the dead on the third day. When Peter heard this he was surprised, and said, No, these things shall not happen to thee. Yet it was to suffer these things that Jesus had come into the world, and when Peter said they should not happen to him, it seemed as if he wanted Jesus to live, and set up an earthly kingdom, rather than die to save the people from their sins. Therefore, Jesus was much displeased with Peter, and called him his enemy, because Peter did not want him to do the things that would please God, but the things that would please Peter himself.

Then Jesus said that if any man wanted to be his disciple, he must not seek his own pleasure, but must take up his cross every day, and follow him. Jesus meant that his disciples must follow his example, and do what is right, no matter how hard and painful it may be. For, he asked, what good would it do any one to have all that he wanted in this world, or even to have everything in the world for his own, as long as he lived, if, after he died, he should lose his own soul.

After six days Jesus took Peter, James, and John, three of his apostles, and went up on a high mountain to pray. While he prayed, his face was changed, so that it shone bright like the sun, and his raiment glistened, and was white as snow. And suddenly two men were with him. They were Moses and Elijah, who had come back to this world to talk with him about his being crucified at Jerusalem. The Bible says they appeared in glory; this means, we suppose, that they looked beautiful and glorious, as they may look in heaven.

The apostles knew that it was Moses and Elijah, and they wanted to stay there on the mount with them, and not go down any more. Peter said, Master, it is good for us to be here; if thou art willing, let us make three tents, one for thee, one for

JESUS IS TRANSFIGURED ON THE MOUNT

Moses, and one for Elijah. While he was speaking, there came a bright cloud and covered them, and God's voice spoke out of the cloud, saying, This is my beloved Son, hear him. When the apostles heard it, they bowed down with their faces to the ground, and were greatly afraid. But Jesus came and touched them, and said, Arise, be not afraid. When they had risen up and looked around, Moses and Elijah were gone, and they saw no one except Jesus. Jesus said to them, Tell no man

36

of the things you have seen, until I be risen from the dead. But they did not understand him when he spoke of rising from the dead, and they asked one another what that saying could mean.

The next day, when they had come down from the mountain, many people were waiting to see Jesus. And there came a man who kneeled to him, saying, Master, I beseech thee, look upon my son; for he is my only child, and an evil spirit has gone into him, that often makes him fall into the fire and into the water, to destroy him. And I took him to thy disciples that they might heal him, but they could not. Jesus answered, Bring him to me. As they brought him, the spirit threw him down, and he rolled on the ground and foamed at the mouth. Jesus asked his father, saying, How long ago did this come upon him? He answered, When he was a child. And Jesus said to the evil spirit, I command thee to come out of him, and go no more into him. Then the spirit, crying with a loud voice, shook the young man greatly and came out of him, but left him weak, like one dead, so that many said, He is dead. But Jesus took him by the hand and lifted him up, and he stood upon his feet and was well.

And they went into Capernaum. Now the Jews who lived in the different cities of the land used to send money to the priests at the temple, to buy sacrifices with. And the men who took this money in the city of Capernaum, came to Peter and asked whether his Master would give them any. Jesus knew what the men had asked, and when Peter came into the room where he was, Jesus said to him, Go thou to the sea of Galilee, and cast a hook into the water, and take up the fish that is first caught, and when thou hast opened its mouth thou shalt find there a piece of money. Give that to the men for me and for thee. Peter did as Jesus commanded, and found the piece of money, and gave it to the men.

Now, although Jesus had told the apostles plainly what was going to happen to him, how he would be cruelly treated, and put to death at Jerusalem, yet they had never understood him when he spoke of these things. They still expected, whatever he might have to suffer, that afterward he would set up an earthly kingdom and become very great, and that then they would become great also.

And while they walked by the way, they began to dispute with one another as to which of them should be greatest. Jesus knew what they said, and when they came into the house, he asked them saying, What is it that you disputed among yourselves by the way? But they were ashamed and did not

THE EXAMPLE OF A LITTLE CHILD

answer him. Then he called a little child and set him in the midst of them, and told them that unless they should put away their pride, and their desire to rule over one another, they could not belong to the kingdom which he was going to set up. Whoever, therefore, he said, should be most humble and willing to obey like that little child, would be the greatest in his kingdom.

And he said, If thy hand or thy foot cause thee to do wrong, cut them off, and cast them from thee; he meant, that if his disciples were committing any sin, which they loved so much that it seemed as hard to part with even as a hand or a foot, still they must cease committing it and put it away from them. For, he said, it would be better for them to part with that sin, and at the day of Judgment be taken up to heaven, than to keep on committing it, and be punished.

And Jesus told his disciples that whenever they should meet together in any place to worship him, though only two or three of them might be there, he would be with them; he meant that his Spirit would be with them. And he said that if one of them should sin against another, and afterward confess his fault, the one he had sinned against must forgive him. Peter asked how many times they should forgive, whether as often as seven times. Jesus answered that they should forgive one another not only seven times, but seventy times seven; he meant always.

Then he spoke to them a parable. He said, There was a king who wanted to take an account of the money that his servants owed him. And one was brought who owed him a very great sum, as much as ten thousand talents. But as he had nothing to pay with, the king commanded that he, and his wife, and his children should be sold as slaves, so that the money they were sold for might be paid to him for the debt. Then the servant fell down on his knees before the king, and prayed that he would have patience with him till he could earn the money, or get it from those who owed it to him, Then, he said, I will pay thee all. The king, when he saw his distress, pitied him, and was kind to him, and forgave the debt altogether.

But that same servant went out and found one of his fellow-servants who owed him only a hundred pence. And he came to him, and caught him by the throat and said, Pay me what thou owest. And his fellow-servant fell down at his feet, and begged him, saying, Have patience with me, and I will pay thee all. And he would not, but went and cast him into prison, to be kept there till he should pay the debt.

Therefore, the king's other servants who saw what he had done, were very sorry, and they came and told the king. Then the king, when he had called him, said to him, O thou wicked servant. I forgave thee all thy debt because thou didst ask me. Shouldst thou not, also, have pitied thy fellow-servant as I pitied thee? And the king was greatly offended, and sent him to be punished till he should pay all that he owed him.

In this parable the king means God, and the servant who owed him ten thousand talents means us, because we have sinned so often against him. As the king punished that wicked servant because he would not forgive his fellow-servant, so, Jesus says, God will punish us if we do not forgive one another our tres-passes.

As Jesus journeyed toward Jerusalem, he sent some of his disciples on before him, to make ready a place where he might stop and rest by the way. And they came to a village of the Samaritans, but the men of that village would not let Jesus stop there, because he was a Jew, and was going toward Jeru-salem. Then the apostles James and John were very angry, and asked him if they might not call down fire from heaven to destroy those men, as the prophet Elijah had called down fire to burn up the captain, with his fifty men, whom the king of Israel sent to take him. But Jesus was displeased with James and John for asking this; he said to them, I did not come on the earth to destroy men's lives, but to save them. And they went on to another village.

As they went, there came ten men who were lepers to meet Jesus. These men stayed with each other because they were all sick with the same dreadful disease, and were not allowed to come near persons who were well. Therefore, they did not come near Jesus and his disciples, but stood a good way off and cried out, saying, Jesus, Master, have mercy on us. Now, as we have read, Moses had commanded every leper who was healed, to go and show himself to the priest, that the priest might give him permission to live among the people again. When Jesus heard these poor men crying out, he said to them, Go, show yourselves to the priest. And as they went they were healed. And one of them, when he saw that he was healed, turned back, and with a loud voice praised God, and came and knelt down at the feet of Jesus, giving him thanks; the man was a Samaritan. Jesus said, Were there not ten cleansed? Where are the other nine? Only this Samaritan comes back to thank God for what has been done to him.

LUKE X, XI (10, 11). JOHN VII–XI (7–11)

JESUS TEACHES THE JEWS; ANSWERS THE LAWYER'S QUESTION; SPEAKS THE PARABLE OF THE GOOD SAMARITAN; VISITS BETHANY; TEACHES THE LORD'S PRAYER; CHOOSES THE SEVENTY DISCIPLES; HEALS A BLIND MAN; SAYS HE IS THE GOOD SHEPHERD; RAISES LAZARUS.

JESUS went up to the temple, and the Jews came to him, and he sat down and taught them. He said to them, Yet for a little while I will be with you, and then I will go back to my Father who sent me. After I have gone you shall look for me but shall not find me, and where I go you cannot come. You will not believe that I am the Son of God, and therefore you shall die without having your sins forgiven. But if any man will believe on me he shall never die. Jesus meant that his soul should never die, but the Jews thought he meant that the man's body should not die. And they answered him, saying, Abraham has died, and the prophets, and yet thou sayest that if a man believe in thee he shall never die. Art thou greater than Abraham and the prophets?

Then Jesus told them that Abraham, when he was alive, believed on him, and knew that he was coming on the earth; and that Abraham wanted to see the day when he should come, and in his heart, and by faith, he did see it, though it was then a long way off: and Jesus said that it made Abraham glad. The Jews answered, Thou are not yet fifty years old, and hast thou seen Abraham? Jesus told them that he was living in heaven before Abraham was born. At this they were angry, and took up stones to cast at him, but he passed out from among them, and they could do him no harm.

On another day while he was teaching the people, a lawyer stood up to ask him questions, saying, Master, what must I do to be saved? Jesus said to him, What does God's law command thee to do? The lawyer answered that it commanded him to love God with all his heart, and his neighbor as himself. Jesus said, Thou hast answered right; do these things and thou shalt be saved. But the lawyer, because he wanted to excuse himself, said, And who is my neighbor?

Then Jesus spoke this parable, saying, A certain man went down from Jerusalem to the city of Jericho, and as he went, got among thieves, who stripped him of his clothing and wounded him, and went away leaving him half dead. While he lay on

THE GOOD SAMARITAN HELPS THE WOUNDED MAN

the ground too weak to rise, there came by chance a priest that way. As this priest was a minister, and a teacher of God's law, we might suppose that he would have shown kindness to the wounded man. But instead of this, he crossed over to the other side of the road and went by, pretending that he did not see him. And after the priest came a Levite. He also was one of those who attended to God's worship at the temple: yet when he looked at the man, he passed on as the priest had done, without offering to help him.

But after the priest and the Levite had gone, a Samaritan, as he journeyed, came to the place. Now the Jews hated the Samaritans, and would have no dealings with them. Therefore we would not be surprised to hear that this Samaritan had refused to help the wounded Jew. Yet it was not so, for when he saw him he pitied him, and went to him and bound up his wounds, pouring in oil and wine to make them heal. Then he lifted him up, and setting him on his own beast, took him to an inn and nursed him there. The next day when he left he took out money, and gave it to the owner of the inn, saying, Take care of him; and whatever more thou shalt spend for him after I am gone, when I come again I will pay thee.

Jesus, after he had told this parable, said to the lawyer, Which now of these three thinkest thou was neighbor unto him that fell among thieves? The lawyer answered, The one that showed kindness to him. Then Jesus said to him, Go thou, and do likewise: that is, to every one who needs thy help, do as the Samaritan did. So Jesus taught the lawyer, and so he teaches us, that whoever does good to another person is that person's neighbor.

Jesus came to a village called Bethany, which was a little way from Jerusalem; and a woman named Martha asked him to her house. She had a sister named Mary, who, when Jesus had come, sat down at his feet, that she might listen to what he taught about the way we are to be saved, and taken to heaven. Then Martha, because she had all the work to do, was displeased with her sister, and she came to Jesus, saying, Lord, dost thou not care that Mary has left me to do the work alone? Bid her therefore, that she come and help me. Jesus answered, Martha, Martha, thou art careful and troubled about many things; yet only one thing is needful. Mary has chosen that, and it shall never be taken away from her. He meant that Mary had chosen religion, which, when we come to die, will be the only thing that we need, and the only thing that shall not be taken from us.

Jesus taught his disciples what they should say when they prayed to God. He said, When you pray, say, Our Father, who art in heaven, Hallowed be thy name. Thy kingdom come.

Thy will be done on earth as it is in heaven. Give us this day
our daily bread. And forgive us our trespasses, as we forgive
those who trespass against us. And lead us not into temptation,
but deliver us from evil; for thine is the kingdom, the power,
and the glory forever. Amen.

Jesus told his disciples to ask God for those things that they

JESUS AT THE HOUSE OF MARY AND MARTHA

needed, and God would give them. For, he said, if one of your
children should ask you for bread, would you give him a stone?
or if he asked for a fish, would you give him a serpent? If
you, then, who are sinful men, know how to give good things to
your children, how much more certain is it that your heavenly
Father will give the Holy Spirit to them that ask him. Jesus
said that God would give us the Holy Spirit, because that is the
best gift he can give us; for it is the Holy Spirit who comes

into our hearts and changes them into new hearts, and so makes us God's children.

Jesus chose seventy more of his disciples, beside the twelve apostles, and sent them out two and two, into every city and town where he himself expected to come, that they might heal the sick, and preach the gospel to the people. And the seventy went and did as Jesus commanded. Afterward they returned to him, full of joy, because they had been able to do miracles in his name. But he told them not to rejoice because they had power to do miracles, but rather because their names were written down among those whose sins were forgiven, and who should be taken up to heaven.

As he came from the temple, he saw a man who had been blind ever since he was born. And Jesus spat on the ground, and making clay of the spittle, put it upon the eyes of the blind man, and said to him, Go, wash in the pool of Siloam. He went therefore and washed, and when he came back, could see. Then the neighbors, and those who before had known that he was blind, said, Is not this he who sat and begged? Some said, This is he: others said, He is like him; but the man himself said, I am he.

Therefore they asked him, saying, How were thine eyes opened? He answered, A man that is called Jesus made clay and put it upon my eyes, and said to me, Go to the pool of Siloam and wash; and I went and washed, and after that I could see. They said to him, Where is he? He answered, I know not.

And they brought the man who had been blind to the Pharisees. It was the Sabbath day when Jesus made clay and opened his eyes. And the Pharisees also asked him how he had been made well. He answered, He put clay on my eyes, and I washed and do see. Then some of the Pharisees said, The man that cured thee cannot be one who obeys God, because he did it on the Sabbath day; and they asked him what he thought of Jesus. The man said, I think he is a prophet.

But the Jews would not believe that the man had really been blind, until they called his parents and asked them, saying, Is this your son who, you say, was born blind? How is it then that he can now see? His parents answered, We know that this is our son and that he was born blind, but how it is that he now sees, we cannot tell; he is old enough to speak for himself, ask him. The parents were afraid to say that it was Jesus who cured their son, because the Jews had agreed together that if any man said Jesus was the Saviour, he should not come into the synagogue. Therefore they answered, Our son is old enough to speak for himself, ask him.

Then the Pharisees again called the man who had been blind, and said to him, Thank God for curing thee, and not the man who put clay on thine eyes, for we know that he is a sinner. The man answered, Whether he is a sinner or no, I know not: one thing I know, that I used to be blind, but now I see. They said to him again, What did he do to thee? How did he open thine eyes? The man said, I have told you already and you would not hear me. Why do you want to hear it again? Will you also be his disciples? Then they abused him, and said, Thou art his disciple, but we are Moses' disciples. We know that God sent Moses, but as for this fellow we know not who sent him.

The man answered, Why this is a strange thing, that you know not who sent him and yet he has opened my eyes. Since the beginning of the world, such a thing was never heard of before, as that a man should give sight to one that was born blind. If God had not sent this man, he could not have cured me. Then the Pharisees were filled with anger, and they answered him, saying, Thou wast born altogether a sinner, and wilt thou try to teach us? And they forbade him to come any more into the synagogue. Jesus heard what the Pharisees had done, and when he found the man, he said to him, Dost thou believe on the Son of God? The man answered, Who is he, Lord, that I may believe on him? Jesus said, It is he that talketh with thee. And the man said, Lord, I believe. And he worshipped him.

Jesus said to his disciples, I am the good shepherd, and know my sheep. He meant that he was like a shepherd to his disciples, and they were like his flock of sheep. In that country the shepherds went before their flocks, and the sheep followed them. Each sheep had its name, and knew the shepherd's voice and came when he called it. The shepherd stayed with his sheep by night, as well as by day, to keep them from

THE GOOD SHEPHERD

being lost, and to guard them from wild beasts. So Jesus is always with his disciples to guard them from Satan, and show them the way to heaven.

As he walked in the temple, in Solomon's porch, the Jews came round about him, and said, If thou art the Son of God.

who, the prophets said, should come into the world, tell us so plainly. Jesus answered, I have told you already, but you would not believe because you are not of my sheep. My sheep listen to my voice and follow me, and I will give them eternal life; they shall never be lost, neither shall any man take them away from me. My Father gave them to me, and no man can take them out of his hand. I and my Father are one. Jesus meant that he was God; yet not God the Father, but God the Son; as good and as great as God the Father, and to be loved and worshipped as much.

Then the Jews took up stones to cast at him because he said that he was God, but he escaped from them and went out of Jerusalem, beyond the river Jordan, to the place where John had baptized; and the people came to him and many believed on him there.

Now Mary and Martha, who lived in the town of Bethany, had a brother named Lazarus, and he was sick. Therefore his sisters sent word to Jesus, to tell him their brother was sick. Jesus loved Martha and her sister and Lazarus, yet when he heard their message, he did not go to them, but stayed two days longer in the place where he was. Afterward he said to his disciples, Let us go to Bethany, for our friend Lazarus sleepeth and I go to awake him out of his sleep. Jesus meant that Lazarus was dead, and that he was going to raise him up from the dead. But his disciples thought he meant that Lazarus was taking rest in sleep. Then Jesus told them plainly, saying, Lazarus is dead.

Now Bethany was near to Jerusalem, about two miles off, and many of the Jews had gone there to be with Martha and Mary, and comfort them in their trouble. Martha, as soon as she heard that Jesus was coming, went out to meet him, but Mary sat still in the house. Then Martha, when she met Jesus, said to him, Lord, if thou hadst been here my brother had not died. But I know that even now, whatever thou wilt ask of God, he will give it thee. Jesus said to her, Thy brother shall rise again. Martha answered, I know that he shall rise again at the Judgment day.

Then Martha went back to her home and called Mary, saying, The Master is come, and asks for thee. As soon as Mary
heard this she rose quickly to go to him, and when she saw
him she kneeled down at his feet and said, Lord, if thou hadst
been here my brother had not died. When Jesus saw her
weeping and the Jews weeping with her, he was troubled, and
said, Where have you laid him? They answered, Lord, come
and see. Jesus wept. Then the Jews, when they saw him

JESUS RAISES LAZARUS FROM THE DEAD

weeping, said, See how he loved him. And some of them
asked, Could not this man, who opened the eyes of the blind
have saved Lazarus from dying?

Jesus came to the grave. It was a cave, and a stone was rolled
to the mouth of it. Jesus said, Take away the stone. Martha,
the sister of Lazarus, said to him, Lord, by this time his body
is decayed, for he has been dead four days. Jesus answered her,
Did I not tell thee that if thou wouldst believe in me, thou
shouldst see how great God's power is? Then they took away

the stone. Now the Jews, when they buried their dead, wrapped the body in linen, and tied up the head in a napkin. So they had buried Lazarus. And after the stone was taken away from the mouth of the cave, Jesus cried with a loud voice, Lazarus, come forth! Then he that was dead came forth, with his hands and feet bound in grave-clothes, and his face bound around with a napkin. Jesus said to them, Loose him, and let him go.

And many of the Jews who had come to visit Martha and Mary, when they saw this great miracle which Jesus did, believed on him. But some went to the Pharisees and told them of what they had seen. Then the Pharisees and chief priests gathered together, and said one to another, What shall we do? for this man worketh many miracles. If we let him alone, all the people will believe on him and make him their king; and then the Romans will be angry, and come and take away our city and destroy our nation. From that time they talked with one another about some way of putting him to death.

MATT. XIX, XX (19, 20). MARK X (10). LUKE XIII-XVIII (13-18)

JESUS HEALS A WOMAN ON THE SABBATH. HE TELLS WHAT IS NEEDED IN A DISCIPLE. THE PARABLES OF THE LOST SHEEP, THE GREAT SUPPER, THE LOST PIECE OF SILVER, THE PRODIGAL SON, THE RICH MAN AND LAZARUS, THE UNJUST JUDGE, THE PHARISEE AND PUBLICAN. HE BLESSES LITTLE CHILDREN.

JESUS was teaching in one of the synagogues on the Sabbath. And a woman was there who, for eighteen years, had been bent down with disease, so that she could not straighten herself nor lift herself up. When he saw her he called her to him, and said, Woman, thou art made well of thy sickness. Then he laid his hands on her, and immediately she lifted herself up and was made straight, and she spoke, praising God.

But the ruler of the synagogue was angry because Jesus had healed her on the Sabbath day. He said to the people, There are six days in which men ought to work; if any of you want to be healed, come then, and not on the Sabbath. Jesus answered him, Thou hypocrite, doth not each of you, on the Sabbath, take his ox or his ass from the stable, and lead him out to water him? And if it is right to do what is needful for the ox or the ass, is it not right that this woman, who has been suffering for eighteen years, should be made well on the Sabbath day? When he said this his enemies were ashamed; but the people were glad for the miracles that were done by him.

THE GREAT SUPPER

On another Sabbath, Jesus went into the house of one of the chief Pharisees, and, while there, he spoke a parable about a man who made a great supper. When everything had been set on the table, the man sent his servant to those who were invited, saying, Come, for all things are now ready. But they began with one accord to make excuse. The first said, I have bought a piece of ground and must go and see it; I pray thou wilt have me excused. Another said, I have bought five yoke of oxen, and am going to try them; I pray thee have me excused. And another said, I have married a wife, and therefore, I cannot come.

So the servant came and told his master these things. Then the master, being angry, said to him, Go out quickly into the streets and bring into my house the poor, the lame, and the blind. And the servant did as he was commanded. Afterward he came to his master, saying, I have done as thou hast commanded, and there is room for still more. The master said, Go again, through the streets and lanes of the city, and make the people come in, that my house may be filled; for none of those men who were first invited shall taste of my supper.

In this parable the man who gave the supper means God; the supper itself means the good news of the gospel. The servant means God's ministers who preach that gospel; and the men who were first invited, and would not come, mean the Jews, because the gospel was preached to them first, and they would not believe it. The men who were brought into the supper afterward mean the people of other nations, who have heard the gospel since that time, and obeyed it. And the command to go out into the streets and lanes and bring them in means that not only the rich and great, but also the poor and despised, are invited to come and be saved.

And great multitudes came to hear Jesus. But he said to them, that although a man might come and listen to his words, yet if he did not in his heart, care more for him than for any one else in the whole world, he could not be his disciple. And if he did not take up his cross, that is, deny himself things that were wrong, as Jesus himself did, he could not be his disciple.

For which of you, he asked, who intends to build a house or a tower, does not first sit down and count how much it will cost, and find out whether he has enough money to build it? Lest after he has begun, and built only a little way, he may have to stop, and all that see it mock him, saying, This man began to build, but was not able to finish. Or what king who is going to make war against another king, does not before he sets out, consider how large an army his enemy has, lest his own army

37

be too small to fight against it? So, Jesus said, that any man who wanted to follow after him, must think first of what he would have to do. For unless he was willing to give up all that he had, if Jesus commanded it, he could not be his disciple.

Then the publicans, or tax-gatherers, and other men who were sinners, came near to hear him. Therefore the Scribes and Pharisees found fault with Jesus, saying, He keeps company with wicked men, and eats with them. But Jesus answered, Which of you, having a hundred sheep, if he lose one of them, does not leave all the rest and go after that which is lost till he find it? And when he has found it, he takes it up on his shoulders and carries it home, rejoicing. When he comes there, he says to his neighbors and friends, Rejoice with me, for I have found my sheep which was lost.

Or what woman who has ten pieces of silver, if she lose one piece, does not light a candle, and sweep the house, and look carefully till she find it. And when she has found it, she says to her friends and her neighbors, Rejoice with me, for I have found the piece which was lost. Jesus meant, by these parables, to teach the Scribes and Pharisees, that the publicans and sinners who came to hear him were like the lost sheep, and the lost piece of silver, because they were wicked. Yet he would not for this reason, send them away; but would rather seek for them, and encourage them to come to him, so that he might teach them to repent. For he said, that even the angels in heaven were glad whenever one of those wicked men repented. and began to serve God.

And he spoke a parable, saying, There was a man who had two sons; and the younger one said to his father, Father, give me my share of the riches which thou hast laid up for thy children. And his father gave him his share. Not many days after, the younger son took all that he had, and went away into a far country, and there wasted what his father had given him, among wicked companions. When he had spent all, there came a great famine in that land and he began to want bread to eat. Then he went and hired himself to a man of that country, who sent him into his fields to feed swine. And he would have been glad to have enough of the coarse food which the swine ate, but the man did not give it to him.

And after he had suffered awhile, he said to himself, In my father's house, at home, how many hired servants there are who have plenty to eat, and more than they want, while I stay here starving with hunger. I will arise and go to my father, and

THE PRODIGAL SON RETURNS TO HIS FATHER

will say to him, Father, I have sinned against God and done wickedly to thee, and do not deserve any more to be called thy son; let me come back to thy house, and treat me as one of thy hired servants.

So he left that country to go back to his father. But as he went, while he was yet a good way off, his father saw him and pitied him, and ran out to meet him, and put his arms around his neck and kissed him. Then the son said to him, Father, I have sinned against God and done wickedly to thee, and do not deserve any more to be called thy son. But his father said to the servants, Bring out the best robe and put it on him, and put a ring on his hand and shoes on his feet; and bring here the fatted calf and kill it, and let us eat and be merry; for this my son had left me and is come back again; he was lost, and is found. And they began to be merry.

Now the elder son was out in the field, and when he came near to the house, he heard music and dancing. And he called one of the servants, and asked him what these things meant. The servant answered, Thy brother is here, and thy father has killed the fatted calf, because he has come back safe and sound. Then the elder son was angry and would not go in; therefore his father came out to him and begged him. But he answered his father, and said, For a great many years I have served thee, neither did I ever disobey thy commandments, yet thou never gavest me a kid that I might make a feast for my friends. But as soon as this thy son was come, who has wasted thy money in doing wickedly, thou hast killed for him the fatted calf. The father answered, My son, I have always loved thee, and everything I have is the same as though it were thine. Yet it is right that we should be glad and rejoice, for this thy brother had left us, and is come back again; he was lost, and is found.

In this parable Jesus taught the proud Scribes and Pharisees, who blamed him for preaching to sinners, that God loved those sinners and was willing to forgive them, and take them for his children again, if they would only cease doing evil and obey him.

And he spoke another parable to those persons who loved to be rich, and to spend their time only in enjoying themselves, but did not care to obey God. He said, There was a rich man who was dressed in the most beautiful garments, and ate the nicest of food every day. And there was a beggar named Lazarus, who was sick, and covered with sores. And because he was poor, and had nothing to eat, his friends carried him and laid him down every day at the rich man's gate, so that he might get the crumbs and pieces of food that were left from the rich man's table. And even the dogs seemed to pity him, for they came and licked his sores.

And the beggar died, and was carried by the angels to heaven. He was not poor there, neither had he to beg his food. He ate

LAZARUS BEGS FOR CRUMBS FROM THE RICH MAN'S TABLE

at the table with Abraham, and leaned upon Abraham's bosom. Afterward the rich man died also, but his soul went where the wicked go. And in hell, while he was being punished for his sins, he looked up and saw Abraham afar off, and Lazarus leaning on his bosom. Then he cried, saying, Father Abraham, have pity upon me, and send Lazarus that he may dip the tip of his finger in water, and come with it and cool my tongue; for I am tormented in this flame. But Abraham said to him, Remember that in thy lifetime thou hadst good things, and Lazarus evil things; but now he is comforted, and thou art tormented. Beside this, there is between us and you a great gulf which no one can pass, so that those who would go from us to you cannot, and those who would come to us from you cannot come.

Then the rich man said, If Lazarus cannot come to me, I pray thee send him to my father's house, for I have five brethren living there, that he may tell them to repent and obey God, so that they come not, when they die, to this dreadful place. Abraham answered, They have the Scriptures to read, let them learn to

LAZARUS IS CARRIED TO HEAVEN

repent from them. And the rich man said, Nay, Father Abraham, but if one from the dead shall go and speak to them, they surely will repent. Abraham answered him, If they will not hear what God says to them in the Scriptures, they would not be persuaded to obey him, even though one rose from the dead.

And Jesus spoke yet another parable, when he wished to teach his disciples that they should continue to pray, and not be discouraged, although God did not at first seem to answer their prayers. He said, There lived in a city a wicked judge, who did not fear God, nor care to act justly toward men. And in the same city lived a poor widow, who kept coming to him, and asking that he would punish a man who was her enemy. For a while the judge would not listen to her, but afterward he said to himself, Though I will not do it because I fear God, or care to act justly toward men, yet because this woman wearies me, I will

THE PHARISEE AND THE PUBLICAN

do what she asks. Then Jesus said, Hear what this judge saith. If he, who was a wicked man, would do what the widow wished because she asked him so often, will not God, who is holy, and who loves his children, give them what they pray for by day and by night, though he seem for a while not to hear them?

And Jesus spoke a parable to those persons who thought themselves more righteous than others. He said, Two men went up to the temple to pray, one of them was a Pharisee and the other a publican. The Pharisee chose a place where the people would see him; there he stood up proudly, and prayed in this way: God, I thank thee that I am not like other men, who are unjust, and who take more than belongs to them. I thank thee that I am not a sinner like this publican. I fast twice in the week; I give to the priests and Levites a tenth part of all that I get. But the publican, who felt himself to

JESUS BLESSING LITTLE CHILDREN

be wicked and was sorry for it, stood where he hoped no one would notice him, and bowing down his head, he beat upon his breast in great distress, saying, God be merciful to me a sinner. Then Jesus told those who listened to him, that this publican went back to his home forgiven more than the Pharisee. For he said, Every one who is proud and thinks much of himself, shall be put down, but he that is humble and confesses his sin shall be raised up higher.

The people brought little children to Jesus, that he might put his hands on them and bless them. And his disciples found fault with those who brought them, and would have sent them away. But Jesus was much displeased with his disciples, and said, Let the little children come unto me, and forbid them not, for of such is the kingdom of heaven. He meant that only those persons who are humble and loving, like little children, shall come into his kingdom. Then he took the little children up in his arms, and put his hands upon them, and blessed them.

And as they journeyed together, he took the twelve apostles aside by themselves, and told them they were going up to Jerusalem, and that when they should come there, all those things would happen to him which the prophets had spoken. He would be mocked and scourged, and spit upon, and crucified; and the third day he would rise again. But the apostles, because they still expected that he was going to set up an earthly kingdom, could not understand him when he spoke of those things.

MATT. XXI–XXIII (21–23).   MARK X–XII (10–12). LUKE XVIII–XXI (18–21).   JOHN XII (12)

JESUS COMES TO JERICHO, HEALS BLIND BARTIMEUS AND VISITS ZACCHEUS. HE ENTERS JERUSALEM RIDING ON AN ASS, HEALS THE BLIND AND LAME, CURSES THE BARREN FIG-TREE, SPEAKS THE PARABLES OF THE VINEYARD AND OF THE MARRIAGE FEAST, TELLS WHICH IS THE GREATEST COMMANDMENT, AND COMMENDS THE WOMAN WHO GAVE TWO MITES.

WHEN Jesus came to Jericho a great number of people followed him. A blind man, named Bartimeus, sat there by the way-side begging; and hearing the multitude, he asked what it meant. They told him that Jesus of Nazareth was passing by. As soon as he heard this he began to cry out with a loud voice, saying, Jesus, thou son of David, have mercy on me! When the people heard him crying out, they told him to be silent. But he cried a great deal the more, Thou son of David, have mercy on me! Jesus stood still, and commanded him to be called. And they called him, saying, Be of good comfort, rise, he calleth for thee. Then the blind man rose up in haste, and threw away his outer garment, that he might go the more quickly to Jesus.

Jesus said to him, What wilt thou have me do for thee? The blind man answered, Lord, that thou wouldst give me my sight. Jesus said, Because thou hast faith thou art made well. And immediately he could see; and he followed Jesus, praising God for what had been done to him.

There was in Jericho a man named Zaccheus, who was the chief one among the publicans, or tax-gatherers; and he was rich. As Jesus passed through the streets of the city, Zac-

JESUS TELLS ZACCHEUS TO COME DOWN

cheus tried to see who it was, but could not for the crowd, because he was not so tall as the rest of the people. Then he ran on before, and climbed up into a sycamore tree, for Jesus was to pass that way. When Jesus came to the place he looked up and saw him, and said to him, Zaccheus, make haste and come down, for to-day I must stay at thy house. And he made haste and came down, and, going with Jesus, received him into his house joyfully.

Now the publicans, who took the people's money for the

king, were often unjust and cruel men. They were unjust to poor persons, taking from them more than it was right to take. And it is very likely that Zaccheus did this before Jesus came to his house. But when Jesus had come, he believed that God sent him, and he listened to his teaching, and obeyed his words.

And Zaccheus stood up before all the people who were there, and told Jesus that he would be unjust no more. He would be kind to the poor, he said, and would give them half of all the money he had. And if he found he had taken anything that did not belong to him, he would give back four times as much to the person he took it from.

When Jesus saw how Zaccheus repented of his sins, and obeyed what he taught him, he told Zaccheus that all his sins were forgiven. But the Jews found fault with Jesus for going to the house of a publican; they said that he had gone to stay with a man who was a sinner. Then Jesus told them that he had come into the world on purpose to go among sinners, so that he might teach them to repent, and save them from being punished for their sins.

Now the feast of the passover was near, and many of the people went up to Jerusalem to keep it. Then they looked for Jesus, and as they stood in the courts of the temple, spoke to one another, saying, What think you, will he not come to the feast? For both the chief priests and the Pharisees had given a commandment, that if any man knew where Jesus was, he should tell them. And six days before the passover, Jesus came to Bethany, where Lazarus lived, whom he had raised from the dead. The Jews knew that Lazarus was there, and they came to Bethany, not to see Jesus only, but Lazarus also. Then the chief priests talked with one another, seeking some way to put Lazarus to death; because many of the Jews, after they had seen him, believed on Jesus.

And Jesus left Bethany to go to Jerusalem. When he was come to the mount of Olives, he sent two of his disciples, saying, Go into the village which is near you, and you shall find there a colt tied, on which no man ever yet rode. Loose him, and bring him to me. If any man asks, Why do you this?

you shall say, Because the Lord has need of him; and immediately he will send him. So the two disciples went and found
the colt, as Jesus had said. As they were loosing him, the
owners asked, Why loose you the colt? They answered, The
Lord has need of him. Then they let them take him. And
they brought him to Jesus; and the disciples put their garments
upon the colt and Jesus sat on him.

JESUS ENTERS JERUSALEM

As he rode toward the city a great multitude took off their
outer garments and spread them in the way. Others cut down
branches from the trees and strewed them in the way, that he
might ride over them. They did this to honor him, for so the
people used to do when a king rode through their streets. And
the multitude that went before and that followed after, cried
with a loud voice, praising him, and saying, Hosanna! Blessed
is he that has come to us, sent by the Lord. Yet Jesus knew

that although they now praised him, they did not love him in
their hearts, and that in a few days they would be crying out
to crucify him. As he came near to Jerusalem, he looked on
it and wept, when he thought of the sufferings that were coming
upon the Jews. Their enemies would bring an army, he said,
and make a camp around the city, and besiege it and destroy it;
every house would be thrown down, so that not one stone would
be left standing upon another; because, although he had come
from heaven to save them, the Jews would not believe on him,
and were now going to put him to death.

Jesus came into Jerusalem, and went up to the temple, and
the blind and the lame were brought to him, and he healed
them. But when the chief priests and the Scribes saw the miracles that he did, and heard the children in the temple praising
him and crying out, Hosanna, they were much displeased.

In the evening he went out of the city, to Bethany, and slept
there. In the morning, as he came back to Jerusalem, he was
hungry, and seeing a fig-tree on the way, he went to it to eat of
the fruit, but found only leaves on the tree. Then he said to it,
Let no more fruit grow on thee forever; and the disciples heard
his words. The next day, as they passed by again, they saw that
the fig-tree was dried up from the roots, for it was dead. And
remembering the words that Jesus had spoken, they said, How
soon has the fig-tree withered away.

And Jesus spoke this parable. He said, There was a man who
planted a vineyard, and set a hedge or fence around it, and dug
a cistern to hold the juice of the grapes, when they were pressed
to make wine. He built a tower also, for the servants who
should stay to guard it against wild animals and robbers. After
everything was finished, he rented his vineyard to husbandmen
who were to give him a part of the fruit. Then he went away
to a far country.

When the time had come for the fruit to be ripe, he sent one
of his servants to the husbandmen, that they might give him his
share. But the husbandmen caught the servant and beat him,
and sent him away without any. And the owner of the vineyard sent another servant; at him they cast stones and wounded

him in the head, and sent him away cruelly treated. Afterward
he sent yet more servants, and some of these they beat and some
they killed. Then the owner of the vineyard, having one son
whom he loved, sent him, saying, Surely they will fear to harm
my son. But the husbandmen, when they saw him, said, This
is the son, who, when his father dies, will have the vineyard.
Come, let us kill him and take it for our own. So they caught
him, and cast him out of the vineyard and slew him. Then

WINE PRESS IN AN EASTERN VINEYARD

Jesus said to the people who heard him, When the owner of the
vineyard comes, what will he do to the husbandmen? The people answered, He will destroy those wicked men, and let out his
vineyard to others, who will give him his share of the fruit.

In this parable the owner of the vineyard meant God, and the
wicked husbandmen meant the Jews. God had chosen them for
his people, and given them the land of Canaan; he had taught
them his laws, and they had promised to obey him. When they
did not do this he sent his prophets to warn and persuade them.
But they had persecuted those prophets and slain them. Then,

at last, God sent his only Son, Jesus. And now they were going to kill him also, as the wicked husbandmen had killed the son of the owner of the vineyard. When the chief priests and the Pharisees heard this parable, they knew that Jesus had spoken it about them; and they were angry and wanted to put him to death.

Jesus spoke another parable to the people. He said, There was a king who made a marriage-feast for his son. And he sent out his servants, telling those who were invited to come: and they would not. Then he sent to them again, saying, My oxen, my fatted calves, and my sheep, have been killed for my dinner, and all things are ready, therefore come to the marriage. But some turned away and would not hear, and others took the servants, and treated them cruelly and slew them. When the king heard of it he was angry, and sent out his soldiers and destroyed those murderers and burned up their city. Then he said to his servants, The wedding-feast is ready, but those who were invited cannot come. Go out, therefore, into the streets and lanes and ask all whom you meet to the marriage. So the servants went out and gathered all the people they could find and brought them in.

Now the king had provided new and beautiful garments for those who should sit down to his feast, and one of these garments was offered to each person as he came into the house, and he was commanded to put it on. But when the king went into the room where the feast was held, he saw there a man that had not on a wedding garment. And he said to him, Friend, how camest thou in here not having on a wedding garment? And the man was silent, for he had refused to take it when it was offered him. Then the king, being angry, said to the servants, Bind his hands and his feet, and take him away, and cast him into the dark dungeons where those persons are kept who will not obey me.

In this parable the king who gave the feast means God, and the king's son for whom it was given, means Jesus. Those who were first invited to it and would not come, mean the Jews, because they were first asked to believe in Jesus, but they would not. The people who were brought into the feast afterward, mean those of other nations who have believed in him since that time. And the man without the wedding garment means any one who pretends to believe, but in his heart does not. Such a person may seem to obey God's word, and thus deceive others, but God sees our hearts, and nothing we can do will hide them, even for a moment, from him.

A Pharisee, who was also a teacher of the laws of Moses, came to Jesus and asked him a question: he said, Master, which is the first, or principal one, of all God's commandments? Jesus answered, Thou shalt love the Lord thy God with all thy heart, and with all thy soul, and with all thy mind. This is the first and great commandment. And the other one that is like it is, Thou shalt love thy neighbor as thyself. Then Jesus said, On these two commandments hang all the law and the prophets; he meant that all the other commandments in the Bible come from these two. For if we obey the first, we shall do all our duty to God, and if we obey the last, we shall do all our duty to our neighbor; and so we shall do everything that the Bible commands us to do.

Jesus spoke to the Scribes and Pharisees and called them hypocrites, because they loved to sit in the chief seats in the synagogues and to make long prayers there, that the people might see and praise them for doing it; while, at the same time, they were unjust to other persons and cruel to the poor, taking for their own what did not belong to them. Because they did these things, Jesus said, they should receive the greater punishment at the Judgment day.

And he sat in the court of the temple where the chests, or boxes, were placed, into which the people cast the money that they gave to buy sacrifices. And many persons who were rich gave much. But there came a poor widow who gave only two mites, which were less than a penny. Then Jesus called his disciples to him, and told them that the small sum of money the poor woman had put into the box seemed more to God than all that the rich men had given. For they, Jesus said, had much left for themselves, because they gave only a very small part of the riches they possessed. But the poor widow had nothing left for herself, because she gave all that she had, even to live upon.

THE WIDOW'S OFFERING

MATT. XXIV–XXVI (24–26).   MARK XIII, XIV (13, 14). LUKE XXI (21).   JOHN XII (12)

JESUS FORETELLS THE DESTRUCTION OF THE TEMPLE. THE PARABLES
OF THE TEN VIRGINS AND OF THE TALENTS. JESUS SPEAKS OF THE
JUDGMENT-DAY. HE GOES TO BETHANY, WHERE MARY ANOINTS HIS
FEET. JUDAS AGREES TO BETRAY HIM FOR THIRTY PIECES OF SILVER.

ALTHOUGH the Jews had seen Jesus do so many miracles, they would not believe that he was the Saviour, because their hearts were wicked. Yet many of their rulers believed on him, but were afraid to confess it, lest the Pharisees should forbid them to come into the synagogue; for they cared more to have men think well of them than they did to please God.

We have read that Herod had built up the temple anew with stones of white marble. He had richly adorned it, so that it was one of the largest and most splendid buildings in the world. The houses, for the priests to live in, were built near to the temple; we have read also of the different porches, with great marble pillars, which stood around the court of the Gentiles. As Jesus was going away from the temple, one of his disciples came to him and said, Look, Master, at the great stones and beautiful buildings that are here. Jesus answered him, Dost thou see these great buildings? Verily, (that is, Truly), I say unto thee, the day is coming when they shall all be thrown down, so that not one stone of them will be left standing upon another. Jesus said this because he knew that the Jews were going to crucify him, and that afterward God would punish them by sending their enemies against them, who would destroy their city and their temple.

And Jesus told his disciples to be always ready for the Judgment day, because they could not tell how soon that day would come. Then he spoke a parable to them about ten virgins who went out to meet the bridegroom. For in that country when a man was married, he brought his bride home to his house in the night, and some of his friends, each one carrying a lamp, or torch, used to go out to meet him. These ten virgins, in the parable, had made ready to go out and meet the bridegroom. They

38

had lighted their lamps, but because the bridegroom stayed longer than they expected, they sat down to wait until he should come. And they all fell asleep. Now five of them were wise, and brought oil in vessels with them, beside the oil that was in their lamps, so that if their lamps should go out, they would have enough to fill them again. But five were foolish, and brought no oil except what was in their lamps.

THE MARRIAGE-FEAST

And at midnight the people who were watching, cried, The bridegroom is coming, go ye out to meet him. Then all the virgins rose up in haste and trimmed their lamps. And the foolish said to the wise, Give us some of your oil for our lamps have gone out. But the wise answered, saying, We have not enough for us and for you; go therefore to those that sell, and buy more for yourselves. While they were gone the bridegroom came, and those that were ready went in with him to the marriage-feast; and the door was shut. Afterward came the other virgins, saying, Lord, Lord, open to us. But he answered and said, I know you not; and he refused to let them come in.

In this parable the bridegroom means Jesus coming back to the earth on the Judgment day. The ten virgins mean those of us who call ourselves his disciples, and who expect to be ready to meet him then. The oil that was burned in the lamps means religion in our hearts; if we have not enough of this to keep our lamps burning, that is, to keep us loving Jesus and obeying his commandments, we shall not, when he comes again, go with him to heaven. But, like the foolish virgins whose oil was all gone, we shall find the door shut, and will never be allowed to enter there.

Jesus spoke another parable of a man who took a journey into a far country. But before he went, he called his servants and gave them some money, that they might take it and earn more with it for him, while he was gone. To one servant he gave five talents, to another two, and to another only one. He gave to each servant as much as he thought that servant would know how to use. When he had done this, he went away on his journey. Then the servant who had five talents took them and traded with them, until he earned for his master five talents more. And the one who had two talents, did the same, till he had earned two talents more. But the servant with one talent, because he had no love for his master, did not care to work for him. Therefore he went and digged in the ground, and hid his lord's money, to keep it till he should come.

After a long time the master returned, and called his servants to give an account of what they had done. So he who had the five talents came to him, saying, Master, thou gavest me five talents, see, I have earned beside them five talents more. His master said, Well done, thou good and faithful servant; thou hast been industrious and careful with the few things that I gave thee, I will now give thee many things; thou shalt come and live in my house and be happy with me there. He also who had the two talents came, and said, Master, thou gavest me two talents, I have earned two other talents beside them. And the master said, Well done, thou good and faithful servant; thou hast been industrious and careful with the few things that I gave thee, I will now give thee many things; thou also shalt come and live in my house and be happy there.

Then he who had the one talent came, and said, Master, I knew that thou wast an unjust man, taking what was not thine own, and using what did not belong to thee; and I was afraid lest I might lose thy money, and be punished for it. Therefore I went and hid it in the earth, where no one could steal it from me. And now I have brought it again; there it is; take it, for it is thine. The master answered him, Thou disobedient and slothful servant, even if I were an unjust man, it was no reason why thou shouldst neglect thy duty, and be idle while I was gone. Therefore thou art only making an excuse for thy own wickedness. Then he said to his other servants, Take the one talent from him, and give it to him who earned five talents. For to every one who has earned something, I will give more; but from him who has earned nothing, I will take away even the little that he has.

In this parable the master means Christ, who has gone to heaven to stay for a time, we know not how long, but is coming back on the Judgment day. The servants are all of us whom he has left to work for him in this world. The talents mean whatever he has given us to work with. Some of us have many talents, and some of us have few, but each one has as many as he knows how to use. When Jesus comes again, he will reward those who have used their talents in working for him, but he will punish those who have not used them, or who have used them only in working for themselves.

Jesus also told his disciples of what would happen on the Judgment day. On that day he will come in his glory, and all the holy angels will be with him. Then he will sit on his throne, and the dead of all nations shall rise up from their graves and stand before him to be judged. And he will separate the righteous from the wicked, as a shepherd separates his sheep from the goats; he will set the sheep on his right hand, but the goats on the left.

Then he will say to those on his right hand, Come, ye

children of my Father, into the kingdom which has been made ready for you from the beginning of the world. For when I was hungry you gave me food; when I was thirsty you gave me drink; when I was poor and naked you clothed me; when I was sick you visited me; when I was in prison you came to me and comforted me. Then the righteous shall answer him, saying, Lord, when saw we thee hungry and fed thee, or thirsty and gave thee drink? When saw we thee poor, and naked, and clothed thee, or sick, or in prison, and comforted thee? And Jesus shall answer them, Whenever you did these things to any poor and suffering person who loved me on earth, it was the same as if you did it to me.

Then shall he turn to the wicked on his left hand, and say, Depart from me, ye cursed, for I was hungry and you gave me no food; I was thirsty and you gave me no drink; I was naked and you clothed me not; sick and in prison, and you visited me not. Then shall they also answer him, saying, Lord, when saw we thee hungry, or thirsty, or naked, or sick, or in prison, and did not help thee? And he shall answer them, Because ye did not do it to any of the poor and the suffering people who loved me on earth, it was the same as if ye did not do it to me. And these shall go away into everlasting punishment, but the righteous into life eternal.

When Jesus had spoken all these things to his disciples, he told them that in two days would be the feast of the passover, and then he would be betrayed to be crucified. Now the chief priests and scribes were anxious to take him; and they met together at the house of the high priest, to plan how they might do this by cunning, and afterward put him to death. But, they said, we cannot do it on the feast day, when all the people will be gathered together, lest they be angry and it cause a disturbance among them.

And Jesus came to Bethany, the town where Mary, Martha, and Lazarus lived. They made him a supper there, and Martha waited on him, but Lazarus was one of those who ate at the table. Now the Jews at their meals, did not sit upright on chairs as we do; they reclined, or lay down on couches which were placed around the table instead of chairs. They reclined on these couches, leaning upon their left arms and feeding themselves with their right hands, while their feet were stretched out, away from the table, on the couches behind them.

As Jesus was reclining in this way, Mary took a pound of ointment, called spikenard, which was very costly, and bowing down at his feet, she anointed them with it and wiped them with her hair; and the house was filled with the sweet smell of the ointment. One of his apostles, named Judas Iscariot, who

RECLINING AT MEALS

afterward betrayed him, said, Why was not this ointment sold for three hundred pence, and the money given to the poor? Judas said this, not because he cared for the poor, but because he was a thief, and carried the bag in which the money was kept, and he wanted to take it for his own. But Jesus answered him, saying, Let her alone; why do you find fault with her? She has done a good work on me. For you have the poor with you always, and whenever you will you may do them good, but you will not have me always. And Jesus said to his disciples, that wherever his gospel should be preached over the whole world, this thing that Mary had done to him, should be told, that it might be remembered of her.

Then Judas Iscariot went to the chief priests, and said to them, What will you give me, if I bring you to the place where he is, so that you may take him? And they promised to give him thirty pieces of silver. From that time he tried to find Jesus alone, that he might betray him to them.

THE APOSTLES FOLLOW THE MAN INTO THE HOUSE

MATT. XXVI (26). MARK XIV (14). LUKE XXII (22). JOHN XIII–XVIII (13–18)

JESUS AND HIS APOSTLES EAT THE PASSOVER. THE APOSTLES DISPUTE AS TO WHICH SHALL BE GREATEST. JESUS WASHES THEIR FEET; EATS OF THE LORD'S SUPPER WITH THEM; GOES WITH THEM TO GETHSEMANE; PRAYS IN THE GARDEN; AND IS BETRAYED BY JUDAS.

Now the day was come when the Jews made ready for the feast of the passover. To do this, each man among them took a lamb to the temple and killed it, as a sacrifice, before the altar. Then the priests burned its fat on the altar, but the rest of the lamb the man took to his home; there it was roasted with fire, and he and his family ate of it in the night; for, as we have read, the feast of the passover was eaten in the night.

Jesus and his apostles were going to keep this feast together, and the apostles came to him and asked at what place they should make it ready. He answered, Go into Jerusalem, and there shall meet you a man carrying a pitcher of water; follow him into the house where he is going, and say to the man who lives there, The Master wants thee to show us the chamber where he shall come to eat the feast of the passover with his disciples. And the man will show you a large upper room, furnished; there make ready the feast. The disciples did as Jesus commanded, and the man showed them the room and they made the feast ready there.

In the evening Jesus came with his twelve apostles, and reclined with them at the table. And he said to them, I have greatly desired to eat this passover with you before I die, for I say unto you, I will not any more eat of the lamb that has been sacrificed, until I myself have been sacrificed for the sins of the people. But the apostles did not understand him when he spoke of being sacrificed for the people. They still thought he was going to set up an earthly kingdom, and that now the time for him to do this was coming near. And they began to dispute among themselves, as they had done before, about which of them should be greatest in that kingdom. Then Jesus told them that among the people of this world, those who were great ruled over the rest. But, he said, it shall not be so with you. For whoever among you will be the greatest, let him be the most humble, and the one who will be chief, let him be as if he were the servant of all.

Then Jesus asked them which was the greatest, the person who ate at the table, or the one who served him while he was eating. Yet, he said, I am among you as the one who serves. And he arose from the table, and laid aside his outer garment, and took a towel and girded himself with it. After that he poured water into a basin, and began to wash the disciples' feet and to wipe them with the towel with which he was girded. And he came to Peter. Now Peter did not wish Jesus to wash his feet as though Jesus were his servant, and he said to him, Lord, wilt thou wash my feet? Jesus answered, Thou dost not understand why I do it now, but thou shalt know afterward. Peter said, Thou shalt never wash my feet. Jesus answered him, If I wash thee not thou canst not be one of my disciples. Then Peter said, Lord, wash not my feet only, but also my hands and my head. Jesus said to him, He that is washed needs only to wash his feet.

JESUS WASHES THE APOSTLES' FEET

So after he had washed their feet, and put on the garment which he had laid aside and come to the table again, he said to them, Do you know what I have done unto you? You call me Master and Lord, and you say well, for so I am. If I, then, your Lord and Master, have washed your feet, you ought to wash one another's feet, for I have given you an example that you should do as I have done to you.

And as they ate of the passover, Jesus said to them, Verily, I say unto you, one of you who are eating with me shall betray me. Then the disciples were filled with sorrow, and they looked on one another wondering of whom he spoke. Now there was leaning on Jesus' bosom one of his disciples whom Jesus loved.

Peter therefore motioned to him that he should ask Jesus of whom he spoke. He then that leaned on Jesus' breast said to him, Lord, who is it? Jesus answered, It is he to whom I shall give a piece of bread when I have dipped it in the dish. And when he had dipped the bread he gave it to Judas Iscariot. After that, Satan went into Judas. Then Jesus said to him, What thou art going to do, do quickly.

Now no man at the table knew what Jesus meant by these words. Some of them thought, because Judas carried the bag in which the money was kept, that Jesus commanded him to go and buy those things of which they had need, or else that he should give something to the poor. Then Judas went out from the house where Jesus and the apostles were. And it was night. When he was gone, Jesus said to them, I will be with you only a little while. Before I leave you I give a new commandment unto you: it is that you love one another; as I have loved you, so shall ye also love one another. By this every one shall know that you are my disciples, if you have love one to another.

And Jesus told the apostles that they would all be tempted to leave him that night. Peter answered, Though all the rest shall leave thee I never will, for I am ready to go to prison and be put to death with thee. Jesus said, I tell thee, Peter, that this night, before the cock crows twice, thou shalt three times deny that thou knowest me. But Peter answered the more confidently, Though I should die with thee, I will not deny thee. And so they all said.

And as they were eating together, Jesus took bread and blessed it, and broke it in pieces and gave it to his apostles, saying, Take and eat, for this is my body which is broken for you. He meant that the bread was like his body, and represented it, because his body was soon to be broken, and crucified, and offered up on the cross for them. Then he took some wine in a cup, and when he had thanked God, he gave it to them and they all drank of it. And he said to them, This wine is my blood, which is shed for the forgiveness of sins. He meant that the wine was like his blood, and represented it, because his blood was very soon to be shed, like the blood of the sacrifices at the altar, so that all who believed in him might have their sins forgiven. Then he commanded his apostles to meet together, after he should be put to death, and to eat the bread and drink the wine in the same way that he had shown them; and as often as they did it to remember him.

This is the Communion, or Lord's Supper, that his disciples have still. It was Jesus who told us to have it. Whenever

JESUS GIVES HIS APOSTLES THE BREAD AND WINE

we see the broken bread in that Supper it means his body, wounded and nailed to the cross. And whenever we see the wine it means his blood, poured out of the wounds in his hands and his side. Those who love him will keep on having this Supper until he comes to the earth again. Every time they eat of it they think of the sins they have committed that he was punished for on the cross; and they repent of those sins and determine to commit them no more.

And as they sat at the table Jesus talked with his apostles, and told them not to be troubled because he was to be taken away from them. He was going to heaven, he said, to make ready a place for them there; afterward he would come and take them, so that where he was, they might be. And he said to them, Obey my commandments, for it is he who obeys my commandments that loves me; and whoever loves me my Father will love. Then he promised them that his Father would send the Holy Spirit into their hearts, to make them remember and understand every thing he had told them; and to teach them also what they should teach others. The Holy Spirit would stay with them, and be their Comforter, while he was away from them.

Jesus also said, I am the vine and ye are the branches; he meant that he was like a vine, and the apostles were like branches growing out of the vine. The good branches, he said, that bore fruit, his Father took care of, and made stronger, so that they would bear more fruit; but the bad branches, that bore no fruit, were cut off and thrown into the fire. And if the apostles wanted to bear fruit, that is, if they wanted to do the good works that Jesus told them to do, they must keep on loving and obeying him, for without his help they could do nothing that was good.

Then he told the apostles that he had chosen them to bear fruit, and do good works among the people. Yet they must remember what he had before told them, that the people would not love them for doing these things, but would hate them and persecute them. And now, he said, you have sorrow, because I am to be taken away from you, but after I have risen from the dead I will see you again, and then you shall have joy.

And he commanded them when they asked anything from God, to ask it in his name and for his sake. Before that time they had never prayed in this way, but now they were to do it, and God would always hear and answer their prayers. God would answer the disciples when they prayed in Jesus' name, because Jesus was the one who had borne the punishment for their sins.

Then he lifted up his eyes to heaven and prayed for his disciples, and for all those who should believe in him from hearing the words that his disciples preached. He prayed that they might be kept from sin, and might love one another; and he said that he wanted them to be with him in heaven, where they could see his glory which his Father had given him.

After these things Jesus and his apostles sang a hymn together, and then they went out from the house where they had eaten the passover, and came to the mount called the mount of

JESUS PRAYS IN THE GARDEN OF GETHSEMANE

Olives, which was a little way from Jerusalem; and they went into a garden that was there, called the garden of Gethsemane. Jesus said to his apostles, Sit ye here while I go yonder and pray. Then he went a little way from them, and kneeled down and prayed. And now, because he was being punished for our sins, and knew that in a few hours he would be crucified, he was in an agony, and his sweat was like great drops of blood falling down to the ground; and an angel came and comforted him. When he rose up from prayer and went back to his disciples, he found them sleeping, and he said to them Why sleep ye? Arise and pray, lest you be tempted to do wrong. And he went away and prayed again, and came and found them sleeping. But when he came the third time, he said, Rise up, and let us be going; behold, he who will betray me is coming near.

JUDAS BETRAYS JESUS

Now Judas had been watching when Jesus went to the garden. And because it was night and only a few of his disciples were with him, Judas thought it the best time to betray his Master. Therefore he went to the chief priests and elders and told them, and they gave him a band of men to go with him to take Jesus; now Judas was bringing the men to the garden, and Jesus knew it, yet he did not flee, but waited to let them take him, because the time had come for him to die.

And while he was yet speaking with his apostles, and telling them that one who would betray him was near, Judas came, and with him the band of men carrying swords and staves, and lanterns.

Judas had given them a sign, saying, The one that I shall kiss is he; take him and hold him fast. Then he came to Jesus, and said, Hail, Master, and kissed him. Jesus said to him, Judas, dost thou betray me with a kiss? Then the men laid their hands on Jesus and took him. When the apostles saw them take Jesus, they said to him, Lord, shall we fight them with the sword? And Peter, having a sword, drew it, and struck a servant of the high priest and cut off his ear. But Jesus said, Put thy sword back again into the sheath. Might I not now pray to my Father that he should send me quickly many thousands of angels to fight for me, and save me from death? But how then could the words of the prophets come true, which say that I am to die for the people? Then Jesus touched the servant's ear and healed it. And he said to the men that took him, Have you come out with swords and staves, as though I were a thief, to take me? I sat daily with you, teaching in the temple, and you did nothing to me. Then all his apostles, being afraid, left him and fled.

MATT. XXVI, XXVII (26, 27). MARK XIV, XV (14, 15).
LUKE XXII, XXIII (22, 23). JOHN XVIII, XIX (18, 19)

JESUS IS LED BEFORE THE HIGH PRIEST. PETER DENIES HIS MASTER. JESUS
IS BROUGHT BEFORE THE COUNCIL; IS CONDEMNED TO DEATH; HE COM-
MITS HIS MOTHER TO JOHN'S CARE; HE DIES ON THE CROSS.

THE men that took Jesus led him away to Caiaphas, who was the high priest that year. In the high priest's palace were gathered together all the chief priests, the scribes, and the elders, and they brought Jesus before them. Now Peter had followed Jesus, a good way off, hoping that no one would know him, and he came into the high priest's palace, and sat down among the servants, by a fire that was burning there; for he wanted to see what would be done.

And a young woman came to him, and said, Thou wast with Jesus of Galilee. But Peter denied it, and said he was not.

Then he went out on the porch, and the cock crew. There another maid saw him, and said to those who stood by, This fellow also was with Jesus of Nazareth. And again Peter denied it, saying, I do not know the man. After a while, one of the servants of the high priest, who was a relation of him whose ear Peter had cut off, said, Did not I see thee with him in the garden? Then Peter denied it again: and the second time the

PETER DENIES THAT HE IS JESUS' DISCIPLE

cock crew. And Jesus turned and looked upon Peter. And Peter remembered the words which Jesus had spoken to him, saying, Before the cock crow twice thou shalt three times deny that thou knowest me. And when he thought of it, he went out and wept bitterly.

Then the high priest asked Jesus about his disciples, and about the gospel that he preached. Jesus answered, I taught in the synagogue and in the temple, where the Jews always go, and in secret have I taught nothing. Why askest thou me?

ask those who heard me, what I said to them; they know what I said. When he had spoken these words, one of the officers that stood by struck him with the palm of his hand, saying, Answerest thou the high priest so? Jesus said to him, If I have spoken evil, tell those who should punish me; but if I have spoken well, why strikest thou me?

CHRIST BEFORE THE HIGH PRIEST

Now the chief court of the Jews, which tried persons who disobeyed the law, used to meet in a room near the temple. It was called the Court, or Council, of the Sanhedrim, and was made up of seventy men. The high priest was among them, and the chief priests, and many of the scribes and elders. These men were the rulers of the Jews, and they punished in different ways persons who had disobeyed the law of Moses. But whenever they wanted to punish any one by putting him to death, they had to ask permission of the Roman governor; for the Jews,

39

being servants to the Romans, were not allowed to put any one to death without the governor's consent.

As soon as it was morning the men who had taken Jesus brought him before the council. There the chief priests, and scribes and elders, tried to find false witnesses to speak against him. At last two false witnesses came, who said, This fellow said, I am able to destroy the temple and to build it up again in three days. But Jesus did not answer them. Then the high priest arose, saying, Answerest thou nothing? But Jesus was silent. And the high priest said, I ask thee to tell us whether thou art the Christ, the Son of God? Jesus answered, I am. And I say unto you, Hereafter you shall see me sitting on the right hand of God, and coming back to earth again in the clouds of heaven.

Then the high priest rent his clothes and said, What need have we of any more witnesses against him? You have heard the wicked blasphemy he speaks. What do you say his punishment should be? And all the men in the council said he should be put to death. Then they did spit in his face, and mock him; and when they had blindfolded him they struck him with the palms of their hands, saying, Tell us, thou Christ, who it is that struck thee?

And after they had bound him, all the council rose and led Jesus to Pontius Pilate, the Roman governor. When they brought him into Pilate's house they began to accuse him before the governor, saying, We found this fellow teaching the Jews to rebel against the Romans; forbidding them to pay tribute to the emperor, and saying that he himself is Christ, a king. Pilate asked him, Art thou a king? Jesus answered, I am; but my kingdom is not of this world, for then would my servants fight to save me from the Jews.

And Pilate said to the chief priest and to the Jews who had brought him, I find no fault in this man. But they were the more fierce, and cried out, saying, He stirs up the people to do wrong throughout all Judea, from Galilee to Jerusalem. When Pilate heard them speak of Galilee, he asked if Jesus came from there; and after they had told him that he came out of Galilee, he sent him to Herod, who was governor over that part of the land; for Herod was in Jerusalem at this time.

When Herod saw Jesus, he was glad, for he had long wanted to see him because he had heard many things of him. He hoped, also, to see some miracle done by him. And Herod asked Jesus many questions; but Jesus answered him nothing. And the chief priests, and scribes, stood by and bitterly accused him. Then Herod with his soldiers made sport of him and mocked him, and put on him a purple robe, because he had said he was a king;

CHRIST IS MOCKED

for kings dressed in purple. Afterward Herod sent him back to Pilate again. Then Pilate called together the Jews, with the chief priests and rulers, and said to them, You have brought this man to me as one that stirs up the people to do wrong; but I, having questioned him before you, have found no fault in him. Neither has Herod; for I sent you to him, but nothing for which he ought to die has been proved against him.

Now every year, when the feast of the passover was held in

Jerusalem, if any of the Jews were shut up in prison for disobeying the Romans, the Roman governor used to set one of
them free, and he allowed the Jews to say which prisoner it
should be. He did this to please them, and to make them more
willing to let him rule over them. There was at this time in
prison a Jew, named Barabbas, who had been put there for
murder. And the people began to ask the governor to do for
them as he had always done before, and set one of the prisoners
free. Then Pilate said, Which one shall it be? Barabbas, or
Jesus, who is called Christ? For he knew they had brought
Jesus to be punished only because they hated him. While Pilate
was speaking with them, his wife sent word to him, saying, Do
no harm to that just man, for I have been much troubled this day
in a dream concerning him.

But the chief priests persuaded the Jews to ask that Barabbas
might be set free. Pilate answered, What then shall I do with
Jesus, who is called Christ? They all said, Let him be crucified. Pilate said, Why, what evil has he done? But they cried
out the more with loud voices, Crucify him! When Pilate saw
that he could not persuade them to ask for Jesus, he took some
water and washed his hands before the people, saying, I am not
to blame for the death of this just man; see you to it. Then,
answered all the Jews, Let the blame be on us and on our children. But Pilate, by washing his hands, did not take the blame
from himself. The sin was in his heart, because when he knew
that Jesus was innocent, he would not let him go, but gave him
up to be crucified, for fear the Jews might be offended and want
some one else for their governor.

Now the Romans, before they crucified a man, used to scourge
him. He was stripped to the waist, his hands were bound to a
low post, or pillar, in front of him, so as to make him stoop forward; and while he stood in this way, he was cruelly beaten with
rods, or cords. Pilate, therefore, took Jesus and scourged him.

Then the soldiers, who were to put him to death, led him into
a room in the governor's palace, and called together the whole
band of soldiers to which they belonged. There they took off
his outer garment, and to mock him, as Herod had done before,

they put on him a purple robe. And when they had plaited a wreath of thorns, they put it on his head instead of a crown; and instead of a golden sceptre, such as kings held, they put a reed, or stick, in his right hand. Then they bowed down before him, pretending he was a king, and saying, Hail, King of the Jews! And they spat upon him, and took the reed, and struck him upon the head, and smote him with their hands.

PILATE SAID, BEHOLD THE MAN

After Jesus had suffered all these things, Pilate hoped that the Jews might be willing to let him go. Therefore he spoke to them again, saying, I bring him out to you, to tell you once more that I find no fault in him. Then came Jesus out before the multitude, wearing the crown of thorns and the purple robe. And Pilate said to them, Behold the man! But when the chief priests and officers saw him, they cried out, Crucify him! Crucify him! Pilate said to them, Take him yourselves, then, and crucify him, for I find no fault in him. The Jews answered, We have a law, and by our law he ought to die, because he has said that he was the Son of God.

When Pilate heard them say this he was the more afraid to put Jesus to death, and he said to him, From what place didst thou come? But Jesus gave him no answer. Then said Pilate, Wilt thou not speak to me? Knowest thou not that I have

JUDAS BRINGS BACK THE MONEY

power to crucify thee, and power to let thee go? Jesus answered, Thou canst do only that to me which God will let thee do. From that time Pilate tried to set him free. Now the emperor of Rome was named Cæsar. He was a jealous and cruel man, and Pilate feared him. When the Jews saw that Pilate wanted to set Jesus free, they cried out, If thou let this man go thou art not Cæsar's friend, because he said he was king instead of Cæsar. After they said this Pilate was afraid to let Jesus go, lest the Jews might tell Cæsar. Therefore he gave him up to them to be crucified.

And Judas Iscariot, who had betrayed him, when he saw that Jesus must die, was afraid for what he had done, and he brought the thirty pieces of silver back to the chief priests and elders, saying, I have sinned, because I have betrayed one who is innocent. They answered, What is that to us? See thou

CHRIST IS TAKEN TO CALVARY

to that. Then Judas threw down the thirty pieces of silver in the court of the temple, and went away and hanged himself. The chief priests took the silver pieces, and said to one another, It is against the law to put them into the treasury at the temple, because they were paid for betraying a man who is to be put to death. Therefore they bought with them the potter's field to bury strangers in.

And the soldiers took off the purple robe from Jesus and put his own clothes on him, and led him away to put him to death. They made a man named Simon, whom they met coming out of the country, help him carry the cross. And there followed him a great multitude of people, and of women, who mourned and wept for him. But Jesus, turning to them, said that they should not weep for him, but for themselves and for their children, because of the sorrows that were coming on the Jews.

And they brought him to a place called Calvary, which was a little way outside of the gates of Jerusalem. There they nailed his hands and his feet to the cross and crucified him. While they were crucifying him Jesus prayed for them, saying, Father, forgive them, for they know not what they do! He meant that they did not know how great their sin was in crucifying him, the Son of God—or how fearful the punishment would be. And they gave him vinegar to drink mixed with gall. This was given to persons who were crucified to make them sleep, and feel their pains less. But when Jesus had tasted it he would not drink, because he was suffering those pains for us, that we might be forgiven, and he was willing to bear them all. And with him they crucified two thieves, one on his right hand and the other on his left.

Now persons who were crucified did not die at once; they lived for many hours, hanging on the cross. So Jesus, although he was crucified in the morning, hung in agony until the afternoon. And the soldiers who had crucified him, sat down and watched him there. They also took his garments and divided them among themselves; but for his coat they cast lots. And upon the cross, above his head, Pilate set up this writing, JESUS OF NAZARETH, THE KING OF THE JEWS. These words, then, were read by many of the Jews, for the place where he was crucified was near the city. And those that passed by felt no pity for him, but shook their heads at him, saying, If thou be the Son of God, come down from the cross. The chief priests and the scribes also mocked him, and said, He trusted in God, let God help him now if he will have him.

And one of the thieves who were crucified with him spoke wickedly to Jesus, saying, If thou art the Christ, save thyself

THE CRUCIFIXION

and us. But the other thief answered him, and said, Dost thou not fear God, seeing thou also art soon to die? We deserve to die for our wicked acts, but this man has done nothing wrong. Then he said to Jesus, Lord, remember me when thou comest into thy kingdom. Jesus answered him, To-day shalt thou be with me in Paradise. Jesus meant that his sins were forgiven, and that as soon as he should die, even on that very day, his soul would go to the happy place where Jesus himself was going.

Now there stood by the cross of Jesus, his mother, and the apostle whom Jesus loved, who leaned on his breast at the table while they were eating the feast of the passover. And because he was going to die and leave her, Jesus wanted that apostle to take care of his mother. Therefore he told him to let her be the same to him, from that time, as if she were his own mother. And he told his mother to let that apostle be to her as if he were her son. From that hour the apostle, whose name was John, took her to his own home to take care of her, and give her all that she needed.

Now from the sixth hour there was darkness over all the land till the ninth hour; that is, from twelve until three o'clock. When the sun shines brightest on other days, it was dark over all the land on that day. God sent the darkness because his Son was being put to death by wicked men. And about the ninth hour Jesus cried out with a loud voice, My God, My God, why hast thou forsaken me? He said this, because, as we believe, God seemed then to turn away from him, displeased, as our father turns away displeased from us when we have disobeyed him. Yet Jesus had not disobeyed God. But we have done so, and he was taking our blame upon himself. Therefore God turned away from him as though Jesus himself had sinned. And when Jesus saw this it grieved him more than all his sufferings, and he cried out.

Then one of the men who were standing near, when he heard him cry, ran and took a sponge and filled it with vinegar, and lifted it up on a reed to his mouth, and gave him to drink. When Jesus, therefore, had taken the vinegar, he said, It is finished. He meant that the work which he had come to do, and the punishment which he had come to bear, for us, were finished. And he bowed his head and died. Then the curtain, called the veil, which hung in the temple, was torn in two from the top to the bottom; the earth shook, the rocks were broken in pieces, and the graves were opened. Many of those persons who, while they lived, had served the Lord, arose and came out of their graves after Jesus himself had risen from the dead; and they went into Jerusalem, and were seen by many there.

When the Roman soldiers who were watching Jesus saw these things that were done, they feared greatly, and said, Surely this man was the Son of God.

MATT. XXVII, XXVIII (27, 28).   MARK XV, XVI (15, 16).
    LUKE XXIII, XXIV (23, 24).   JOHN XIX–XXI (19–21).
    1 COR. XV (15).   ACTS I (1)

THE THIEVES ARE PUT TO DEATH.   JOSEPH OF ARIMATHEA BURIES JESUS.
A WATCH IS SET AT THE SEPULCHRE.   AN ANGEL ROLLS AWAY THE
STONE FROM THE DOOR, AND JESUS RISES FROM THE DEAD.   HE APPEARS
TO HIS APOSTLES, AND ASCENDS TO HEAVEN.

Now the Jews who were in the city did not know that Jesus was dead, and because the next day was the Sabbath, they were unwilling to let the bodies hang upon the cross on that day. Therefore they begged Pilate to send and kill Jesus, and the two thieves who were crucified with him, so that they could be taken down and buried before the Sabbath began. Then Pilate commanded the soldiers, and they went and broke the legs of the two thieves, to kill them, but when they came to Jesus, and saw that he was dead already, they broke not his legs. But one of the soldiers with a spear pierced his side, and there came out from it blood and water.

At the place where Jesus was crucified was a garden, and in the garden a new sepulchre in which no one had ever been buried It was a cave cut out of the rock, and belonged to a rich man named Joseph, who came from the city of Arimathea. Joseph was a disciple of Jesus, though he had never before let it be known, because he was afraid of the Jews. But now, after

Jesus was dead, he went boldly to Pilate and begged for his body. Then Pilate commanded that the body should be given him. Joseph took it down from the cross and wrapped it in new, fine linen that he had bought, and laid it in the sepulchre. A great stone was rolled to the door and left there to close it. Mary Magdalene, and Mary the mother of James, the apostle, were sitting near the sepulchre and saw where Jesus

THE BURIAL OF JESUS

was laid. And they went away to rest during the Sabbath, intending to come back with spices and ointments to put upon his body; because the Jews, when they buried their dead, used to prepare the bodies in that way.

After Jesus was buried, the chief priests and the Pharisees came to Pilate, saying, Sir, we remember that while that deceiver was yet alive, he said, After three days I will rise again. We pray thee therefore that the sepulchre may be watched and made safe, until the third day, lest his disciples should come in the night and steal him away, and then go and tell the people he had risen from the dead. Pilate answered, You shall have soldiers to guard the sepulchre, go and make it as sure as you can. So they went and made the sepulchre sure, setting soldiers to watch it, and sealing the stone that was rolled to the door.

But that night the angel of the Lord came down from heaven,

THE WOMEN AT THE SEPULCHRE

and rolled back the stone from the door, and sat upon it. His face was bright like lightning, and his garments were as white as snow; the soldiers trembled for fear of him, and were weak and helpless as dead men. And they left the sepulchre and went into the city again.

But very early in the morning, as soon as it began to be light on the first day of the week, Mary Magdalene and the other Mary, and Salome, came to the sepulchre, bringing the spices which they had made ready. As they were coming, they said one to another, Who shall roll away the stone for us from the door of the sepulchre? for it was very great. But when they came near, they found the stone was rolled away. And going into the sepulchre they saw an angel clothed in a long white garment, and they were affrighted. He said to them, Be not affrighted: You seek Jesus who was crucified. He is not here, he is risen. See the place where they laid him. But go tell his disciples that he is risen from the dead, and that he will go before you into Galilee; there shall you see him.

Then they went out quickly, and fled from the sepulchre with fear and yet with great gladness, and ran to bring his disciples word. As they went Jesus met them and spoke to them, saying, Rejoice. And they came and held him by the feet, and worshipped him. He said to them, Be not afraid; but tell my brethren that they go into Galilee; there shall they see me.

And the women came and told all these things to the eleven apostles, and to the disciples who were with them. And Peter and John, when they heard what the women said, came in haste to the sepulchre. They ran both of them together, but John did outrun Peter and came first to the sepulchre; there stooping down and looking in at the door, he saw the linen clothes lying which Jesus had worn, yet he did not go in. But Peter, when he came, went into the sepulchre and saw the linen clothes, and the napkin which had been wrapt about the head of Jesus, not lying with the linen clothes, but folded together in a place by itself. Then John went in also, and he saw and believed that Jesus was risen. For before that time they did not understand the words which he had spoken to them while he was yet alive, saying that after three days he would rise from the dead. And the apostles went away to their own homes.

Now after Jesus was risen, some of the soldiers who had guarded the sepulchre went to the chief priests, and told them of all that had happened. Then the chief priests and elders gave them a large sum of money, and said to them, Go you and tell the people that his disciples came at night, and stole him away while you slept. If the governor should hear of it and want to punish you for sleeping, (because the Roman soldiers were put to death if they slept while on guard), we will persuade him to pardon you. So the soldiers took the money and did as the chief priests told them; therefore the Jews, since that time, have always said that the disciples of Jesus came and stole him away in the night, while the soldiers were asleep.

JESUS MEETS THE DISCIPLES GOING TO EMMAUS

On the first day of the week when Jesus was risen from the dead, two of his disciples were walking together to a village called Emmaus, which was about seven miles from Jerusalem. And they talked with one another of all the things that had been done. And it was so, that while they were talking, Jesus came near and went with them. But he was changed so that they did not know him. And he said to them, What is it that you are saying to one another as you walk, and are sad? One of them, whose name was Cleopas, answering, said to him, Art thou only a stranger in Jerusalem, that thou hast not heard of the things which have happened there in these days? He said, What things? They answered him, Concerning Jesus of

Nazareth, who was a prophet, and did great miracles before all the people; how the chief priests and the rulers have taken him and crucified him. But we hoped that he was the one who would set the children of Israel free from the Romans; and beside all this, to-day is the third day since he was put to death. Yes, and some of the women who belong to our company, and who went early to the sepulchre, have made us astonished by

JESUS WALKED ON AS THOUGH HE WOULD GO FURTHER

saying that his body was not there, and that they saw a vision of angels who told them he was alive. Some of the men also who were with us, went afterward to the sepulchre and found it was as the women had said; but him they saw not.

Then Jesus answered the two disciples, and told them that the things which had happened in Jerusalem seemed strange to them, because they did not understand what the prophets had written. For was it not to be expected, Jesus asked, from what the prophets had said about Christ, that he should be put to death, and afterward would rise from the dead, and go up to heaven? Then he began and explained to them what was written about himself in all the Scriptures. But still the two disciples did not know him.

And as they came near the village to which they were going, he walked on, as though he would leave them and go further. But they, supposing him to be some traveller, said to him, Come

THE DISCIPLES KNOW JESUS IN BREAKING THE BREAD

and stay with us to-night, for it is near evening and the day has almost gone. Then he went with them into the house. And while they were at supper Jesus took bread, and after he had thanked God for it, he broke it and gave it to them. But as he did this they knew him; and suddenly he was gone out of their sight.

Then they said to one another, Did not our hearts warm to him while he talked with us by the way, and explained to us what the prophets have written? And they rose up that same hour and went back to Jerusalem; there they found the eleven

40

apostles gathered together, and others with them. The two disciples told them how they had seen Jesus, and talked with him, and how they had known him as he was breaking the bread. While they were speaking, Jesus himself stood in the midst of them, and said, Peace be unto you. But they were frightened, for they thought it was a spirit. Then he said to them, Why are you troubled? And why does fear come into your hearts? Look at my hands and my feet; touch me, and see that it is I, myself, for a spirit has not flesh and bones as you see me have. When he had spoken these words he showed them his hands and his feet, with the marks of the nails in them. And while they could hardly believe for joy, and wondered, he said to them, Have you here any food? And they gave him a piece of a broiled fish and of an honey-comb, and he took it and did eat before them.

Jesus said to them, I told you while I was yet with you that all those things must be fulfilled which are written in the Scriptures about me. Then he made the apostles understand those parts of the Scriptures which said he should die for the people, and rise again from the dead. For although they had read those parts before, they never, till now, had been able to understand them.

And Jesus said to them, Thus it was written about me, and therefore it was needful for me to suffer death, and to rise up from the dead on the third day, so that the people of all nations might be told how I have died for them; and that if they will repent and believe on me, they shall have their sins forgiven. And you, my apostles, are the ones who know of these things; on that account I send you forth to tell the nations about them. Go you, therefore, into all the world and tell this good news to every creature. Whoever believes in me and is baptized, shall be saved; but he that believes not shall be lost.

Now Thomas, one of the apostles, was not with the others when Jesus came. They therefore told him, afterward, that they had seen the Lord. But Thomas answered, Except I shall see in his hands the marks of the nails, and thrust my hand into the wound that the spear made in his side, I will not believe it was he.

Eight days afterward the apostles were again gathered together, Thomas also being with them, and the doors of the
room were shut. Then came Jesus and stood in the midst, and

THOMAS BELIEVES

said, Peace be unto you. Then saith he to Thomas, Reach hither
thy finger and touch my hands, and reach hither thy hand and
thrust it into my side, and be not faithless, but believe that I
have risen again. When Thomas heard his voice and knew
that it was Jesus, he said, My Lord and my God. Jesus said
to him, Thomas, because thou hast seen me thou hast believed;
but I say unto thee, Blessed are those who are willing to believe
even though they have not seen me.

After these things Jesus showed himself again to his disciples at the sea of Galilee. There were together there Peter and
Thomas, Nathaniel, James and John, and two other of his disciples. Peter said to them, I am going a-fishing. They answered,
We will go with thee. They went, therefore, into a boat and
sailed out on the sea, but that night caught nothing. When the

morning had come, Jesus stood on the shore; but the disciples did not know it was Jesus. And he spoke to them, saying, Have you any food? They answered, No. He said, Cast the net on the right side of the boat and you shall find some. They did as he commanded and then were not able to draw up the net, because of the multitude of fishes that were caught in it.

Therefore that disciple whom Jesus loved said to Peter, It is

JESUS APPEARS TO THE APOSTLES BY THE SEA OF GALILEE

the Lord. When Peter heard it was the Lord, he fastened his fisherman's coat around him and cast himself into the sea, that he might hasten to the shore. The other disciples came in the boat, dragging the net with fishes. As soon as they had come to land they saw a fire burning there, and fishes laid upon it, and bread. Jesus said to them, Bring some of the fish which you have caught. Then Peter went and drew the net up on the land, and it was full of great fishes, a hundred and fifty and three; yet, although there were so many, the net was not broken. Jesus said to them, Come and eat. And none of the disciples dared ask him, Who art thou? For they knew that it was the Lord. This was the third time he had shown himself to them since he had risen from the dead.

At another time he met them on a mountain in Galilee, where he had told them to go, that they might see him, and when they

JESUS ASCENDS TO HEAVEN

saw him they worshipped him. And he spoke to them, saying, God has given me all power, both in heaven and in earth. Go you, therefore, and preach the gospel to the people of all nations, baptizing them in the name of the Father, and of the Son, and of the Holy Ghost; teaching them to do all those things that I have commanded you.

Not only to his disciples did Jesus show himself, but he

was seen also by more than five hundred of those who believed on him, at one time. And when forty days were past after he had risen from the dead, Jesus met his apostles again at Jerusalem. When he had talked with them, and commanded them to wait there until the Holy Spirit should be sent upon them, he led them out as far as to Bethany. Then he lifted up his hands and blessed them. And it was so, that while he blessed them, he was taken from them and carried up into heaven; and he went into a cloud out of their sight. While they looked toward heaven as he went up, behold, two angels stood by them, in white garments, who said, Ye men of Galilee, Why stand you gazing up into heaven? This same Jesus who is taken up from you into heaven, shall come down again, in the clouds, as you have seen him go up into heaven.

THE ACTS OF THE APOSTLES

CHAPTERS I–V (1–5)

THE APOSTLES RETURN TO JERUSALEM. MATTHIAS IS CHOSEN IN PLACE OF JUDAS. THE HOLY SPIRIT IS SENT UPON THE DISCIPLES. PETER HEALS A LAME MAN AT THE TEMPLE. AN ANGEL OPENS THE PRISON DOORS, AND SETS THE APOSTLES FREE. ANANIAS AND SAPPHIRA FALL DEAD. THE APOSTLES ARE IMPRISONED AND SCOURGED.

AFTER Jesus was taken up into heaven the apostles returned to Jerusalem, as he had commanded, to wait there until the Holy Spirit should be sent upon them. And they gathered together in an upper room, where they prayed and gave thanks to God. Other disciples also were with them, the number of those who met together being about a hundred and twenty.

Then Peter stood up among them and said, Men and brethren, the words which the prophet spoke about Judas must come true, for it is written of him in the Scriptures that he should be put away from being an apostle, and another should take his place. Therefore, of these men who have believed in Jesus, and been with him ever since he was baptized by John, until he was taken up into heaven, one must be chosen who can go with us, and preach to the people about Jesus, and tell them that he has risen up from the dead. And the disciples agreed to what Peter said. Then they took two men, named Joseph and Matthias, and prayed, saying, Thou Lord, who canst see every man's heart, show us which of these two thou hast chosen. And they cast lots to know which one it would be; and the lot fell on Matthias: after that he was counted with the eleven apostles.

THE HOLY SPIRIT COMES ON THE APOSTLES

When the day for the feast of harvest, or Pentecost, was come, the disciples were all met together in one place. And suddenly they heard a sound, like the rushing of a great wind from heaven, which filled the house where they were sitting. And there appeared in the room what seemed to be flames of fire, in the shape of tongues, and one of these flames rested on the head of each of the disciples. Then the Holy Spirit came into them, as Jesus had promised, and they all began to speak in other languages, such as they had never understood before. The Holy

Spirit made them able to do this, so that they might go to far off countries and preach the gospel there.

Now there were at that time in Jerusalem, Jews who had come from the countries where those languages were spoken; and when they heard the disciples, they were astonished, and asked, Do not all these men live in Galilee? How, then, are they able to speak the languages of those countries where we were born? Others, who did not understand the words that the disciples spoke, mocked them, and said they had been drinking wine, and were drunken.

But Peter, standing up with the other apostles, said to the people, These men are not drunken as you suppose, but God has sent his Holy Spirit into them. Therefore listen, ye men of Israel, to what I now say: Jesus of Nazareth, who did great miracles among you, which showed that God had sent him, you have taken and wickedly have put to death. But he has risen up from the dead, for it is written in the Scriptures that God would raise him up. And we, his apostles, have seen him since he rose. Therefore you, and all the children of Israel, may surely know that this same Jesus, whom you have crucified, is the Saviour that was to come into the world.

When the Jews heard these words they were filled with sorrow for what they had done, and they said to Peter and the other apostles, Men and brethren, what shall we do? Peter answered them, Repent of your sins, and be baptized, and the Holy Ghost shall be given to you also; for God has promised to send him to you, and your children, and to all who hear and obey him when he calls. Then great numbers believed on the Lord Jesus, so that about three thousand persons were baptized that same day. These all came and met together with the apostles, and with the rest of the disciples; and such as had money, gave to those who had none. They also went to the temple to worship there, and did eat together in each other's houses, being full of joy: God made all the people kind to them, and every day, others who repented and believed, came to the apostles and were baptized.

Now Peter and John went up together to the temple at the

hour of prayer. And a poor man, who had been lame ever
since he was born, was carried every day by his friends, and laid
at the gate, called the Beautiful Gate of the temple, that he
might ask alms, or gifts, of those who came up to worship. This

PETER HEALS THE LAME MAN

man, seeing Peter and John about to go into the temple, asked
them for alms. Peter, fixing his eyes upon him, said, Look on
us. And the man attended, for he supposed they would give
something to him. Then Peter said, I have no silver and gold,
but what I have I will give to thee. I tell thee, in the name of
Jesus Christ of Nazareth, to rise up and walk. And Peter took
him by the right hand and lifted him up, and immediately his
feet and ankle-bones were made strong, and he, leaping up, stood
and walked and went with them into the temple, walking, and
leaping, and praising God.

All the people saw him, and knew that it was he who had

sat asking for alms at the Beautiful Gate of the temple. And they were filled with wonder at what had been done, and ran together to the place where the apostles stood. Then Peter spoke to them, saying, You men of Israel, why wonder you at this? Or why do you look so earnestly on us, as if we had made this man to walk? It is Jesus who has given us the power to make him well. Therefore, brethren, repent, and believe on Jesus, that when he shall come again at the Judgment day, your sins may be forgiven.

Now there was among the Jews a sect, or society of men, called Sadducees, who did not believe there would ever be any Judgment day, or that the dead would ever rise up from their graves. Some of the Sadducees belonged to the Council of the Sanhedrim, and were rulers over the people. And while Peter and John were speaking at the temple, they came there, being angry, because the apostles preached about Jesus and the resurrection, that is, the rising up from the dead. Then they put them in prison to keep them till the next day, for it was now evening. Yet many of the people who heard the apostles, believed, so that the number of them was about five thousand.

The next day all the council met together. And when they had brought in Peter and John, they asked them, saying, By what power did you heal the lame man? Peter answered, Ye rulers of the people, and elders of Israel, If you ask us about the good deed done to the lame man, and how he was healed, we tell you that he was made well by the power of Jesus of Nazareth, whom you crucified. For though you counted Jesus as nothing while he was on the earth, yet God has made him to be the ruler over us all. Neither is there any other person in all the world who can save us from being punished for our sins, except him.

When the rulers saw that Peter and John were poor and unlearned men, and yet were bold, and without fear, in speaking before them, they were astonished. But seeing the man who had been healed standing near them, they could not deny what the apostles had done. Then, commanding them to go for a little while out of the council, they talked among themselves, saying,

What shall we do to these men, for that they have done a great miracle is known to all the people in Jerusalem, and we cannot contradict it. But that the news of it may spread no further, let us say that we will punish them if they preach any more to the people. Then they called Peter and John, and commanded them not to speak at all, nor teach about Jesus. But Peter and John answered them, saying, Whether it is right for us to obey you more than God, you yourselves, may judge; for we cannot help teaching the people about Jesus, and telling them of the things that we have heard him speak, and seen him do. So when the rulers had threatened again to punish them, they let them go, because they could not prove any evil against them.

After being let go, Peter and John went to the other apostles, and to the disciples who were with them, and told of what the rulers had said. Then they all prayed together, saying, Lord, help us, that we may not be afraid to preach the gospel; and give us power to do miracles also in Jesus' name. And when they had prayed, the place was shaken where they were gathered together. In this way God let them know that he heard their prayer, and would give them what they asked him for. And they went out and preached again to the people, with boldness, not fearing what the rulers could do to them. Many heard them, and believed, and all who believed met together, helping and loving one another; and as many as had houses or lands sold them, and brought the money to the apostles that they might give alms to those who were poor.

But a man named Ananias, and Sapphira his wife, having land, sold it, and agreed together that they would bring part of the money to the apostles, and tell them that they brought all. They did this to deceive the apostles, and make them believe they were the disciples of Jesus, while, in their hearts, they were not. But God told Peter of what they had done. Therefore when Ananias came with the money, and told Peter this lie, Peter said to him, Ananias, was not the land thy own before it was sold, so that thou didst not have to sell it? And was not the money thy own after the land was sold, to keep if thou didst want it? Why hast thou let Satan tempt thee to lie to the Holy

Ghost? Peter said that Ananias had lied to the Holy Ghost, because the Holy Ghost was with Peter and the other apostles, helping them to teach the disciples, and to set up Christ's kingdom on earth.

THE DEATH OF ANANIAS

Then Peter told Ananias that when he lied to the Holy Ghost he lied to God. Peter said this, because the Holy Ghost is God; not God the Father, nor God the Son, but one with them, God the Holy Ghost. As soon as Peter had spoken these words, Ananias fell down dead. So the Lord punished him for his sin. And when the disciples saw that he was dead, the young men who were there took him and put grave-clothes upon him, and carried him out and buried him.

About three hours afterward, his wife, Sapphira, not knowing what had happened, came to the place where the disciples were. And Peter asked her, saying, Tell me, was the money thy husband brought us, all that you received for the land? She answered, Yes. And Peter said to her, Why have you agreed together to try and deceive the Spirit of the Lord? Behold, the men are at the door who have just buried thy husband, and they shall also carry thee out. Then she fell down at Peter's feet and died; and the young men came in and found her dead, and carrying her forth, buried her by her husband.

And great fear came upon all who heard of these things, so that no others dared try to deceive the apostles as Ananias and Sapphira had done. After this the apostles preached to the people and did miracles among them, and many believed, both of men and women. And they brought out sick persons on beds and couches, and laid them in the streets, that if Peter could not touch them, at least his shadow might fall on them as he passed by, to make them well. There came also a multitude out of the cities around Jerusalem, bringing with them those who were sick and who had evil spirits, and they were every one healed.

Then the high priest, and the Sadducees, being angry with the apostles, took hold of them and put them in the common prison. But in the night, the angel of the Lord came down and opened the prison doors, and brought them out, saying, Go up to the temple and preach the gospel to the people. And they did as the angel commanded; for early in the morning they went up to the temple and preached there. But the high priest and the Sadducees, not knowing what the angel had done, called the council together, and sent to the prison to have the apostles brought. And the officers went to the prison, but did not find them. Then they came back to the council, saying, The prison, truly, we found shut, and the guards were keeping watch before the doors, but the men for whom you sent us were not there.

Now the rulers in the council wondered what this could mean. But while they were in doubt about it, there came a messenger who said, The men whom you put in prison, are standing in the temple, teaching the people. Then the officers went and brought the apostles, yet without doing them any harm, lest the people should be angry. And when they had set them before the council the high priest asked them, saying, Did we not command you to speak no more about Jesus? But you have not obeyed us. Then Peter and the other apostles answered, and said, We ought to obey God rather than men. That Jesus whom you persecuted, and cruelly put to death on the cross, God has raised up again, as a Saviour, to give the Jews new and penitent hearts, and forgive them their sins. And we, his apostles, are sent to tell you of these things.

When the high priest and the rulers heard what the apostles said, they were filled with madness against them, and talked with one another about putting them to death. Then stood up one of the rulers, a learned man named Gamaliel, who was much thought of by all the Jews, and he commanded that the apostles should be sent out of the council for a little while. When they had gone, Gamaliel said, Ye rulers of Israel, be careful what you do to these men. For a good while ago, a man named Theudas rose up, pretending that he was some great person, and about four hundred men followed him and obeyed what he told them. But before long he was slain, and all who had obeyed him separated from one another. Afterward another man, named Judas, of Galilee, persuaded many persons to follow him, but he also perished, and those who had gone with him were scattered. And now, I say to you, let these men alone and do them no harm; for if what they teach be untrue it will soon come to nothing; but if God has indeed sent them to speak to the people you cannot stop them, for if you try to do so you will be fighting against God.

And all the men in the council agreed to what Gamaliel said. Yet they scourged the apostles, and commanded them not to preach any more, before they would let them go. Then the apostles went out of the council rejoicing that they were allowed to suffer pain for Jesus' sake. For by this time they had learned that Jesus did not come to be an earthly king, and that they would not be made rich and great by preaching his gospel, but would continue to be poor and humble men. They would also be persecuted like him, and afterward rewarded when he should take them to heaven to dwell with him forever.

CHAPTERS VI–IX (6–9)

SEVEN MEN ARE CHOSEN AS DEACONS. STEPHEN IS STONED. THE DIS-
CIPLES FLEE TO OTHER COUNTRIES. PHILIP PREACHES IN SAMARIA;
HE BAPTIZES THE EUNUCH. SAUL IS CONVERTED, HE PREACHES THE
GOSPEL. PETER HEALS ENEAS OF THE PALSY, AND RAISES DORCAS
FROM THE DEAD.

WE have read that the disciples who had houses or lands, sold them and brought the money to the apostles, that they might give alms to the poor. Now there were among the disciples some poor widows, who complained that their share of the alms was not given them. Then the apostles called all the disciples together and said, It is not right that we should leave off preaching the gospel to attend to giving out alms; therefore do you choose, from among yourselves, seven men who are honest and prudent, and full of the Holy Spirit, and let them take the money, instead of us, and attend to this business. But we will spend all our time in preaching and praying to God.

What the apostles said pleased the disciples, and they chose seven men who were called deacons. Their names were Stephen and Philip, Prochorus and Nicanor, Timon, Parmenas, and Nicolas. These seven the disciples brought to the apostles, who prayed for them, that God would help them and give them wisdom in attending to the work they were chosen for. When they had prayed for them they laid their hands on the heads of each one of them, for so the apostles used to do to those persons whom they sent out to work, and preach among the people.

After this many were baptized, and great numbers of the priests believed. And Stephen, one of the seven deacons, not only waited on the poor, but he preached to the people and did great miracles among them. Then some of the Jews who would not believe, being angry, took him before the council. There they brought false witnesses to accuse him, who said, This man ceaseth not to speak wicked words against the temple, and God's law. And the high priest asked him, saying, Are these things so? Stephen answered, Men and brethren, listen to me. A great while ago God spoke to our father Abraham, and told him to go away from the land where he was born, and where he then lived, to another land which God said he would show him. Then Abraham left his own land and came into the land of Canaan, where you now dwell. And God promised to give this land to him, and to his descendants, after he should die. God said, also, that Abraham's descendants should live in a country that was not theirs four hundred years, and that the people would treat them very cruelly. Yet God told Abraham he would punish the people who treated them so, and afterward would bring Abraham's descendants back to the land of Canaan.

And God made a covenant, or agreement, with Abraham and his descendants, and promised to be their God. And he gave Abraham a son whose name was called Isaac. And Isaac had a son called Jacob; and Jacob had twelve sons who were called the twelve patriarchs, of whom Joseph was one. Joseph's brethren, because they were jealous of him, sold him to the Ishmaelites, who carried him down into Egypt. But God was with him, and caused Pharaoh, the king of Egypt, to be kind to him; and Pharaoh made Joseph governor over Egypt.

Now there came a great famine in Egypt and Canaan, and Joseph's brethren had nothing for themselves or their families to eat. But Jacob, their father, heard there was corn in Egypt, and he sent them into that land to buy food. When they came there Joseph knew them, and he told Pharaoh of them. Then Joseph sent them to bring their father, their wives, and their children down into Egypt. Jacob, (who was also called Israel), came into Egypt and died there, and afterward was carried back into Canaan to be buried in the sepulchre which Abraham had bought of Ephron the Hittite.

But Joseph and his brethren still lived in the land of Egypt; there, after many years, their descendants grew to be a great many people. And another king ruled over Egypt who had never known Joseph. This king was very cruel to the Israelites and commanded his servants to take their little children and kill them. At that time Moses was born; he was very beautiful and his mother loved him. She hid him for three months so that

the Egyptians might not take him. Then when she could hide
him no longer, she laid him in an ark beside the river. There
Pharaoh's daughter found him; she pitied him and took him
to her house to bring him up as her own son; and he was
taught in all the learning of the Egyptians.

But when he was forty years old he went out to visit his
brethren, the children of Israel. And seeing an Egyptian treat

STEPHEN BEFORE THE COUNCIL

one of them cruelly, he killed the Egyptian and hid his body in
the sand; for Moses thought the children of Israel would under
stand that God had sent him to set them free from the Egyptians, but they understood not. When Pharaoh heard what
Moses had done he tried to kill him, but Moses fled into the
land of Midian where Pharaoh could not find him.

After he had been in that land forty years he saw on mount
Sinai a flame of fire in a bush, yet the bush was not burned.
When Moses saw it he wondered at the sight. And as he turned

to look at it God spoke to him out of the bush, saying, I am the God of thy fathers, the God of Abraham, and the God of Isaac, and the God of Jacob.   Moses trembled and hid his face, for he was afraid to look upon God.   And God told him that he had seen the affliction of the children of Israel, and had come down to deliver them.   God also commanded Moses to go and bring the children of Israel out of Egypt, and he made Moses ruler over them.

Moses did as God commanded; he went into Egypt, and when he had called down great punishment on Pharaoh and his people, he brought the children of Israel out of that land through the Red Sea; and afterward led them forty years through the wilderness.   This is that Moses, Stephen said, who received God's laws on mount Sinai that he might teach them to our fathers.   Yet our fathers would not obey him; they tried to put him away from ruling over them, and wanted to go back into Egypt.   For while he was on mount Sinai they asked Aaron to make an idol for them, saying, As for this Moses, the man that brought us up out of Egypt, we know not what has become of him.   Aaron made them a golden calf, and they offered up sacrifices to it and worshipped it.   Then God was angry with them and allowed them to go on worshipping idols, but he said that they should be carried away, as captives, to Babylon.

After Stephen had spoken these things to the rulers in the council, and told them about the wickedness of their fathers, he said to them, You are like your fathers.   Which of the prophets did they not persecute?   They killed those who were sent to tell them that Jesus was coming, and now you have slain that Just One himself.

When the men in the council heard these words, they were filled with rage against Stephen, and gnashed on him with their teeth like wild beasts.   But he, looking up toward heaven, saw a glorious light there, and Jesus standing at the right hand of God.   And he said, I see the heavens opened, and Jesus standing at the right hand of God.   Then they cried out with loud voices against him, and stopped their ears that they might not

hear his words; and they brought him out of the city and stoned
him.   While they were stoning him, he kneeled down on the
ground and prayed, saying, Lord forgive them for this sin.

Now whenever a man was stoned by the Jews, the persons
who had borne witness against him always cast the first stone.
And so the false witnesses who had spoken against Stephen, cast
the first stones at him.   They took off their outer garments that

THE STONING OF STEPHEN

they might use their arms more freely in doing this, and they
laid those garments down on the ground by the feet of a young
man named Saul, for him to keep them safe till they were ready
to put them on again.

After this there was a great persecution against the disciples.
But good men took Stephen's dead body, and mourned over him,
and buried him.   As for Saul, the young man who had kept the
clothes of the witnesses, he did much harm; for he went into

every house to find those who believed on Jesus, and when he had found them, he took them, both men and women, and put them in prison.   Therefore the disciples fled out of Jerusalem to different parts of the land, and to other countries; but wherever they went, they preached the gospel to the people.

And Philip, another of the seven deacons, went down to the city of Samaria, and preached to the people there; and they listened to him, seeing the miracles he did.   For unclean spirits, crying with loud voices, came out when he commanded them, and persons who were sick with the palsy, or lame, he made well. Therefore there was great joy in the city and many believed and were baptized, both of men and women.   When the apostles in Jerusalem heard this they sent Peter and John, who came to Samaria and prayed that the Holy Spirit might be given to the persons who believed.   Then they laid their hands on the heads of those persons, and God sent his Holy Spirit into them.

Now there was at Samaria a man named Simon, who before that time had deceived the people, pretending he could do things for them by magic; and they all listened to his words, and said, This man has power given to him from God.   But when Philip preached the gospel in that city, and many believed and were baptized, Simon came and said that he believed, and asked to be baptized also.   Then Philip baptized him.   Afterward he stayed with Philip, wondering at the miracles that he did.

And when Peter and John had come from Jerusalem, and Simon saw that by laying on of their hands the Holy Spirit was given to those who believed, he went to them and offered to pay them money if they would give him power, by laying on of his hands, to bring down God's Holy Spirit from heaven.   But Peter told him he had done very wickedly in thinking that what God gave to those who loved him, could be bought for money; and he said to Simon, Repent of thy sin, and ask to be forgiven, for I see thou art yet a wicked man, and a servant of Satan.   Then Simon answered, Pray you to the Lord for me, that he may not send his punishment upon me.

And the angel of the Lord spoke to Philip, and commanded him to leave Samaria, and go through the wilderness toward the city of Gaza. Philip obeyed and went. As he was going, a man from the land of Ethiopia, who was an eunuch, or officer of great power under the queen of Ethiopia, and who took care of all her treasure, came by that way. He had been up to Jerusalem to worship at the temple, and now, as he sat in his chariot returning to his own land, he read the Scriptures. The part he

PHILIP EXPLAINS THE SCRIPTURES TO THE QUEEN'S TREASURER

read was where the prophet Isaiah told the children of Israel that a Saviour was coming into the world to die for their sins.

When Philip saw this man the Holy Spirit commanded him, saying, Go near to the chariot and speak with him. Then Philip ran and came near to the chariot, and he heard him reading aloud the words which the prophet had written. Philip spoke to him, and said, Dost thou understand what thou readest? The officer answered, How can I, except some man should explain it to me? And he asked Philip to come and sit with him in the chariot. Philip did so; and the treasurer said, I pray thee, tell me what the prophet meant when he wrote these words? Whether he was speaking about himself or some other man? Then Philip began and explained the Scriptures. and preached to him about Jesus.

As they went on their journey, they came to a place where there was water, and the officer said, See, here is water; what is there to keep me from being baptized? Philip said, If thou believest with all thy heart, thou mayest. The officer answered, I believe that Jesus Christ is the Son of God. And he commanded the chariot to stand still; and they two went down into the water, both Philip and the eunuch, and Philip baptized him. When they had come up again the Holy Spirit took Philip away, so that the officer saw him no more. And the man went on his journey back to his own land, full of joy, because he had heard about Jesus and been made one of his disciples. Afterward Philip was found at a city called Azotus, and leaving there, he preached in all the cities till he came to Cesarea.

Now Saul, being full of anger and hatred against the disciples, went to the high priest at Jerusalem, and asked for letters to the rulers of the synagogues in the city of Damascus, that he might go to that city, and if he found any disciples there, bind them with fetters, whether they were men or women, and bring them to Jerusalem to be punished. So the high priest gave him the letters he asked for, and he started on his journey to Damascus. But when he came near that city, suddenly there shone around him a great light from heaven, and Jesus appeared to him. Then Saul was afraid, and fell down on the ground. And he heard a voice, saying, Saul, Saul, why persecutest thou me? Saul said, Who art thou, Lord? The voice answered, I am Jesus, whom thou persecutest. It was Jesus speaking to Saul, and he meant to say, that when Saul persecuted his disciples, it was the same as if he persecuted him.

Then Saul, trembling and astonished, said, Lord, what wilt thou have me to do? The Lord said, Arise, and go into the city, and it shall be told thee what thou must do. All the men who were with him stood silent; they heard the voice but could

not understand the words that were spoken. When Saul rose
from the earth he could not see, for the light had blinded him;
and those who were with him led him by the hand, and brought
him into Damascus. And he was for three days without sight,
and did neither eat nor drink.

There was living at that time, in Damascus, a disciple named
Ananias. And the Lord spoke to him, and said, Ananias; he

SAUL IS BLINDED BY THE SHINING LIGHT

answered, I am here, Lord. The Lord said to him, Arise, and
go into the street which is called Straight, and ask at the house
of Judas for a man named Saul. He is now praying to me, and
has seen thee in a vision, coming to him and putting thy hand
on him, that he may receive his sight. Ananias answered, Lord,
I have heard many speak of this man, and of the great evil he
has done to thy people in Jerusalem; and he has come here with
letters from the chief priests, giving him power to bind in fetters
all who believe on thee. But the Lord said, Go, as I have told

thee, for I have chosen him to preach my gospel to the Gentiles, and to kings, and to the children of Israel. And I will show him what great sufferings he must bear for my sake.

Then Ananias obeyed and went into the house of Judas, and, putting his hands on Saul, said, Brother Saul, the Lord Jesus, who appeared to thee as thou wast coming to Damascus, has sent me to put my hands on thee, that thou mayest receive thy sight and be filled with the Holy Ghost. And immediately Saul's eyes were opened and he could see; and he rose up and was baptized. After he had eaten some food his strength came to him again.

SAUL (OR, PAUL) ESCAPES FROM DAMASCUS

Then he stayed with the disciples who were in Damascus, and went into the synagogues, and preached about Christ to the people, telling them that he was the Son of God.

But all who heard him were amazed, and said, Is not this the man who persecuted those who believed, in Jerusalem, and came here that he might bind the disciples and carry them to the chief priests to be punished? Yet Saul preached more and more earnestly, and proved, out of the Scriptures, to the Jews at

Damascus that Jesus was the Saviour; so that, although they would not believe, they could not deny what he said. And after many days had passed, the Jews, being filled with anger, talked with one another, about some way of killing him. And they watched by day and by night, to take him when he should go out through the gates of the city. But the disciples heard of it, and took him by night, and let him down in a basket from a window that was over the wall, so that he escaped out of Damascus, and afterward went to Jerusalem.

When he had come to Jerusalem he went to the disciples who were there, because now, instead of hating them, he loved them and wanted to be with them; but they were all afraid of him, and would not believe that he himself had been made a disciple. Then Barnabas, one of the men who had sold their land and given the money to the poor, brought him to the apostles, and told them how Saul had seen Jesus as he journeyed, and afterward preached the gospel boldly at Damascus. So the apostles took Saul, and he stayed with them, and preached in Jerusalem. But some of the Jews at Jerusalem, like those at Damascus, determined to slay him. When the apostles knew of it, they sent him away to a city called Tarsus, (which was not in the land of Israel, but in a country called Asia Minor), where Saul was born. After this, the Bible says, the Churches had rest, that is, no one troubled, or persecuted them. By Churches are meant the congregations, or companies, of disciples that met together in different places, not the buildings, or houses, in which they met.

As Peter went through different parts of the land, visiting the churches there, he came to the city of Lydda. And he found in that city a man named Eneas, who had the palsy, and had lain on his bed for eight years. Peter said to him, Eneas, Jesus Christ maketh thee well. Rise up, and make thy bed. And he arose immediately. Many of the people who lived at Lydda and in the country around it, saw Eneas after he was made well; and they believed on Jesus.

At Joppa, which was a city not far from Lydda, there was a disciple named Dorcas. This woman was full of good works and kind acts, which she did to the poor. At that time she fell sick and died. Then they washed her dead body, and made it ready for burial, laying it in an upper chamber. And because Lydda was near to Joppa, and the disciples heard that Peter

DORCAS IS RAISED TO LIFE

was there, they sent two men asking him to make haste and come to them. Peter arose, and went. When they had brought him to the house, they took him into the upper chamber where the body of Dorcas lay. And all the poor widows whom she had helped, stood by him, showing the coats and garments which she had made for them while she was alive. But Peter put every one out, and kneeled down and prayed; then turning to the dead body, he said, Dorcas, arise! And she awaked like one who had been asleep, and when she saw Peter, sat up. He reached out his hand and helped her to rise and called those who were in the house, and gave her to them. Peter stayed many days in Joppa, at the house of Simon, a tanner.

CHAPTERS X–XIV (10–14)

THERE was a man in the city of Cesarea named Cornelius, a centurion in the Roman army. He was not a Jew; yet he was a good man, who feared God and taught his family to

PETER'S VISION

fear him, giving much alms to the poor, and praying to God always. Cornelius saw in a vision, about the ninth hour of the day, an angel coming to him who said, Cornelius. When he saw the angel he was afraid, and said, What is it, Lord? The angel answered, God has heard thy prayers, and seen the alms which thou hast given. Now send men to Joppa for a man named Peter, who is staying in the house of Simon, a tanner, which is by the sea-side; when he has come, he will tell thee what thou oughtest to do. After the angel had gone,

Cornelius called two of his servants who waited upon him, and also a soldier who feared God, and whom he kept with him continually. When he had told them what the angel said, he sent them to Joppa.

The next day, as they went on their journey and came near to the city, Peter, who did not know they were coming, went up on the house-top to pray; for as we have read, the houses in which the Jews lived, had flat roofs, and oftentimes a little room was built upon them, where any one of the family could go and be alone, to pray to God. And Peter went up on the house-top to pray, about the sixth hour. As he prayed, he grew very hungry, and wanted to eat; then he had a dream, or vision. He saw the sky above him open, and something like a great sheet, held up at the four corners, let down to the earth before him. In this sheet were all kinds of wild beasts, and creeping things, and birds of the air. At the same time there came a voice, saying, Rise, Peter, kill and eat.

We have read how Moses commanded the children of Israel not to eat any of the animals that were called unclean. Now some of these animals were in the sheet. Therefore, when the voice told Peter to kill and eat them, he answered, I cannot do it, Lord, for I have never eaten anything that is forbidden, or unclean. Then the voice spoke again, saying, What God has made clean, do not thou call forbidden, or unclean. These words were spoken three times, and then the sheet was lifted up toward heaven again.

It was God who sent the vision to Peter, and the reason he sent it was this: The Jews thought, because God had chosen them for his people, that they were better than other nations, and that Jesus came to save them alone. They called other nations unclean, and did not want to preach the gospel to them. But now God taught Peter that this was wrong. For the animals that he saw in the vision, meant those other nations, and God intended in this way, to show Peter that he should not call them unclean any more, nor refuse to teach them, but should preach to them just as he preached to the Jews; because God had made those nations, as well as the Jews, and had sent Jesus to save them also.

PETER VISITS CORNELIUS

While Peter was wondering in himself what the vision could mean, the servants of Cornelius came to Simon's house and stood before the gate and asked if Peter was there. Then the Holy Spirit spoke to Peter, saying, Behold, three men are looking for thee. Arise and go with them, without fear, for I have sent them. And Peter went down to the men, and said to them, Behold, I am he whom you seek; for what reason have you come? They answered, Cornelius, the centurion, who is a just man and one that fears God, and is well thought of by all the Jews, was told by a holy angel to send for thee to come to his house, that he might hear the words which thou wouldst speak. Then Peter called the men into Simon's house, and kept them that night; on the morrow he went with them, and some of the disciples who lived at Joppa went also.

The next day they came to Cesarea. Cornelius was expecting them, and had invited his relations and near friends to be with him when Peter should come. And as Peter entered into his house, Cornelius fell down and worshipped him. But Peter spoke to him, saying, Stand up; for I am only a man like thyself. Then Peter went in with him and found there many persons gathered together, who, like Cornelius himself, were not Jews, but Gentiles. And Peter said to them, You know that the Jews say it is wrong for them to make friends with the men of other nations, because the Jews think themselves better, and call others common and unclean. But God has taught me, in a vision, not to call the men of other nations common or unclean. Therefore I came to you as soon as you sent for me, and now I ask for what reason you wanted me to come?

Cornelius answered, Four days ago I was fasting and praying in my house, and, behold, an angel stood before me in bright clothing, and said, Cornelius, God has heard thy prayers, and seen thy kind acts to the poor. Send, therefore, to Joppa for a man named Peter. He is staying in the house of Simon, a tanner, by the sea-side. When he comes, he will tell how thou and all thy family can be saved. Immediately then I sent for thee, and thou hast done kindly to come. Now, therefore, we are all met together to hear what God has commanded thee to say.

Then Peter spoke to them, and said, Truly I see that God does not choose one nation to be his people more than another, but in every nation those persons who fear him, and do what is right, he takes for his children. You have heard of the words that are preached to the children of Israel about Jesus: how God sent him into the world, and how he went about doing good. Yet the Jews took him and put him to death. But God raised him up again on the third day, and showed him to us, his apostles, who did eat and drink with him after he had risen. And he commanded us to go and preach to the people, and tell them that God has appointed him to be the Judge of all men. For he is the one of whom the prophets said, that all those who believe in him shall have their sins forgiven.

While Peter was yet speaking, the Holy Ghost came upon Cornelius, and the other Gentiles who were with him. And the Jews who had come with Peter from Joppa, were astonished: for, before that time, they thought that God did not care for the Gentiles, but now they saw that he sent his Holy Spirit upon them, and they heard the Gentiles speaking in other languages which they had never understood before, the Holy Spirit giving them power to do so. Then Peter said, Ought not these men to be baptized, to whom the Holy Ghost has been sent as well as to us? And he commanded them to be baptized in the name of Jesus. Then they begged him to stay with them for some days.

The apostles and disciples at Jerusalem heard that Peter had gone to visit Cornelius and his friends at Cesarea. And when Peter came to Jerusalem they found fault with him, saying, Thou wentest into the house to visit men who are Gentiles, and didst eat with them. But Peter told them of all that had happened to him, how God had taught him by the vision, that he was to preach the gospel to the Gentiles also, and had commanded him to go with the men whom Cornelius sent. And, Peter said, while I was preaching to Cornelius and his friends, the Holy Ghost came upon them as he did upon us, who are Jews, at the day of Pentecost. Therefore, as God sent his Spirit upon them, what was I, that I should oppose him? When the apostles and disciples heard these things, they ceased to blame Peter, and gave thanks, saying, Then has God given to the Gentiles also new hearts, that they may be saved as well as we.

Now some of the disciples who fled from Jerusalem at the time Stephen was put to death, went to a city called Antioch, in the land of Syria, and there preached to the Gentiles, and God helped them, so that great numbers believed. When news of this reached Jerusalem, the apostles sent Barnabas to Antioch, who, having come there and seen how many believed, was glad; and he spoke kindly to them, persuading them to go on, earnestly serving the Lord. For Barnabas was a good man, whose heart was full of the Holy Ghost and of faith; and through his preaching many more persons believed in Jesus.

Then Barnabas went to Tarsus to look for Saul, and when he found him, he brought him to Antioch; and they stayed with the church in that city (that is, with the disciples who met together there) for a whole year, preaching the gospel to many people. It was in Antioch that the disciples were first called by the name of Christians.

In those days some men who were prophets came to Antioch from Jerusalem. And one of them, named Agabus, stood up and said that a great famine was coming in all lands. Then the disciples at Antioch determined to send help to the Christians at Jerusalem, and they sent alms to them by Barnabas and Saul, each disciple giving as much as he was able.

About that time, Herod, the king, began to persecute the Christians; he killed James, one of the apostles, with the sword, and because he saw it pleased the Jews, he took Peter also, and put him in prison. Herod set soldiers to watch over him, by night and by day, that he should not escape; intending, after the feast of the passover, to bring him out to the people and put him to death. Peter, therefore, was kept in prison, but prayer was made continually by the church in Jerusalem for him. On the night before he was to be brought out, Peter was sleeping between two soldiers, being bound with two chains that were fastened to the soldiers' hands, so that if he moved they would know it.

And, behold, an angel came to him, and a light shone in the

THE ANGEL COMES TO PETER IN PRISON

prison. And the angel touched Peter's side and wakened him, saying, Rise up quickly. But the soldiers did not waken. Then the chains fell off from Peter's hands, and the angel said to him, Dress thyself, and put on thy sandals and follow me. And Peter followed him; but he thought it was only a dream, or vision. When they had passed the guard of soldiers they came to the iron gate that led into the city, which opened to them of its own accord. And they went out, and walked on through the first street, and there the angel left him.

When Peter had time to think of what had been done he said to himself, Now I know surely that the Lord has sent his angel to save me from Herod and from the Jews, who expected to kill me. And he went to the house of Mary, the mother of the disciple whose name was Mark, where many Christians were gathered together praying. As Peter knocked at the gate, a young woman came to listen, named Rhoda, who, when she heard his voice, was so full of gladness that she forgot to open the gate for him, but ran back and told those who were in the house that Peter was there. They said to her, Thou art mad; Peter is in prison. Yet she declared the more earnestly that it was he. Then they said, It must be his spirit. Still Peter continued knocking; and when they opened the door and saw him, they were astonished. But he, motioning with his hand that they should be still, told them how the Lord had brought him out of prison. And he said, Go tell these things to the other apostles. And he left them, and went to another place.

Now as soon as it was morning, the soldiers wondered where Peter had gone, for the angel (as we suppose) had made them fall into so deep a sleep that they saw nothing of what had been done. And when Herod called them to him and questioned them, but found they could not tell what had become of Peter, he commanded that they should be put to death.

After this there was a day when Herod, dressed in his royal robes, sat on his throne and made an oration, or speech, to the people, who as they heard him, gave a shout, and cried, It is the voice of a god and not of a man! And Herod, being filled with pride, was not offended at these wicked words; but was pleased

when he heard them, and willing that the people should worship
him as if he were a god. Therefore the Lord was angry, and
sent his angel to punish him. There came a dreadful disease
upon him, and he was eaten by worms till he died.

And Barnabas and Saul brought the alms which had been
sent by the disciples at Antioch, and gave them to the poor

PAUL PREACHING AT ANTIOCH

Christians in Jerusalem. Afterward they returned to Antioch,
taking with them the disciple whose name was Mark.

Now there were in Antioch, other preachers and teachers beside Barnabas and Saul. And while they were worshipping the
Lord, the Holy Spirit spoke to them, and told them to send
Barnabas and Saul away from Antioch, to other countries, that
they might preach the gospel to the people who lived there. So
after they had all fasted and prayed together, the rest laid their
hands on the heads of Barnabas and Saul, and sent them away

Then these two left Antioch, and sailed away in a ship to the island of Cyprus. At Salamis, the chief city of that island, they went into the synagogue and taught the Jews. For the Jews were living not only in the land of Judea, but in all the countries around that land; and wherever they lived they built synagogues to worship in. The disciple named Mark was with Saul and Barnabas. They had brought him not to preach, but to help them in other ways, while they were on their journey.

And they came to another city in the island, called Paphos. There they found a Jew, named Elymas, who was a false prophet. He was with the governor of the country. Now the governor was a wise and prudent man, and he sent for Barnabas and Saul that they might come and explain the gospel to him. But Elymas spoke against them, and tried to keep the governor from believing what they taught. Then Saul, who was also called Paul, looked on Elymas, saying, O thou, who art full of all mischief, thou child of the devil, wilt thou not cease speaking evil of those things which the Lord has commanded us to teach? And now, behold, the Lord has sent a punishment upon thee, and thou shalt be blind, not seeing the sun for a time. And immediately his sight was taken from him, and he groped about like a person in the dark, seeking some one to lead him by the hand. Then the governor, when he saw the miracle that Paul had done, believed what the apostles said.

And they sailed away from Paphos, and came to the city of Perga, in the country called Asia Minor. There Mark left them, and went back to Jerusalem. He did this because he was unwilling to go with them, and help them any further on their journey. But Barnabas and Paul went on to the city of Antioch; not that Antioch from which they first set out, but another city of the same name, in Asia Minor. And they came into the synagogue on the Sabbath day, and sat down. After the Scriptures had been read the rulers of the synagogue sent word to them saying, Brethren, if you have any words to say to the people, speak on.

Then Paul stood up and said, Men of Israel and all you who fear God, listen to me. The God of the children of Israel chose our fathers to be his people, and by his mighty power set them free, when they were living as strangers in the land of Egypt. Afterward he took care of them for about forty years, while they wandered in the wilderness; and when he had destroyed the wicked nations of Canaan, he divided that land among them by lot. There he gave them judges to rule over them, for about four hundred and fifty years, until the time when Samuel, the prophet, lived. Then the people asked for a king, and God gave them Saul; and when he had taken Saul away, he gave them David.

And now, Paul said, according to his promise, he has sent you Jesus, who was descended from David. But the people of Jerusalem, and their rulers, because they did not know him, put him to death. Yet God raised him up from the dead, and he was seen for many days after he had risen, by his apostles, who are sent to preach to the people about him. And we have come to you to tell you the good news, that this Jesus is the Saviour who was promised, and that you shall be forgiven all your sins if you will believe in him. Be careful, therefore, lest after you have been told of him, you do not believe and so at last perish.

When the Jews had gone out of the synagogue, the Gentiles who were there, begged Paul and Barnabas that those words might be preached to them again. And on the next Sabbath almost the whole city came to hear them. But when the Jews saw such multitudes coming they were displeased, and spoke against the things that Paul said, contradicting them and blaspheming. Then Paul and Barnabas spoke boldly to the Jews, saying, It was right for us to preach the gospel to you first, but seeing you will not hear it, and do not care to be saved, we will now preach it to the Gentiles. Because so God has commanded us; for he said that Jesus should be a Saviour, not to the Jews only, but to all the nations upon earth. When the Gentiles heard this they were glad. But the Jews stirred up the chief men and the rulers, and raised a persecution against Paul and Barnabas, until they were driven out of Antioch; and they came to the city of Iconium.

At Iconium they went together into the synagogue and taught the people, and God gave them power to do miracles so that great numbers, both of the Jews and the Gentiles, believed. But in this city also, the Jews who would not believe, stirred up the people until they were about to stone the apostles. Then Paul and Barnabas fled to another city, called Lystra, and preached there. And a man who had been lame ever since he was born,

THE PEOPLE OF LYSTRA PREPARE TO SACRIFICE TO THE APOSTLES

and had never walked, sat near the place where Paul preached, and heard him. And Paul, seeing that the man had faith to believe that he could make him well, said with a loud voice, Stand up on thy feet. And he leaped up and walked.

When the people of Lystra saw the miracle which Paul did, they cried out in the language of that country; These are gods who have come down to us from heaven, looking like men. And they called Barnabas, Jupiter, and Paul, Mercury, which were the names of their idols. Then the priests from the idols' temple brought oxen covered with wreaths of flowers, intending to sacrifice them to the apostles, in the same way that they sacrificed them to their idols. But when Barnabas and Paul saw it they rent their clothes, to show their displeasure, and ran in among the people, crying out, Sirs, why do you these things? For we also are men like yourselves, and have come to preach to you, and persuade you to turn from worshipping idols, and to worship only the true God, who made heaven and earth, and the sea, and all that are in them. He is the God who sends us rain and sunshine, and makes the earth to bring forth fruit, so that all men may have food to eat and be glad. Yet even after the apostles had spoken these words to the people, they could hardly keep them from offering up sacrifices as they had intended.

But after this, some of the Jews who had driven them from Antioch and Iconium, came to Lystra, and said that Barnabas and Paul were wicked men, who were trying to deceive the people. Then immediately the people of Lystra, who before had wanted to worship them, tried to kill them. And they stoned Paul and dragged him out of the city, thinking he was dead. But while the disciples were standing around him, he rose up and came into the city again.

The next day he went with Barnabas to another city, called Derbe. When they had preached there, they went again through all the cities where the people had persecuted them, and they spoke to the disciples who lived in those cities, persuading them still to believe in the Lord Jesus, and telling them that we must bear trouble, and sorrow, if we would serve God, and be among those who enter into his kingdom. And after they had set men, called elders, over the churches in the cities they passed through, the apostles came back to that Antioch from which they first started out on their journey. There they called all the members of the church together, and told how they had preached the gospel to the Gentiles, as well as to the Jews, in the places where they had been. And they stayed a long while with the disciples in Antioch.

CHAPTERS XV–XVIII (15–18)

SOME MEN TELL THE DISCIPLES THEY MUST KEEP THE LAW OF MOSES.
THE APOSTLES MEET TOGETHER TO DECIDE THIS QUESTION. PAUL
AND BARNABAS PART FROM ONE ANOTHER. PAUL AND SILAS VISIT
LYSTRA; THEY ARE PUT IN PRISON. THE JAILER IS CONVERTED. PAUL
PREACHES IN ATHENS AND VISITS CORINTH.

CERTAIN men came from Jerusalem to Antioch, who told
the disciples there that they could not be saved, unless they
obeyed the law of Moses, which commanded the children of
Israel to offer up animals in sacrifice. We have read that for
many hundred years before Jesus came on earth, such sacrifices
were offered up to show that he was coming. But when he had
come, there was no more need of them; for we do not need
anything to remind us that a person is coming, after he is here
and we have seen him for ourselves. Therefore Paul and
Barnabas talked with these men, and tried to make them understand that sacrifices were needed no longer. When they could
not do this, they agreed to go with them up to Jerusalem, to
inquire about the matter. So they went with them, and after
they had come there, the apostles and elders met together to
decide this question. Then the Holy Spirit told them that
now, since the Saviour had been offered up, it was not necessary
to offer up any more animals as a sacrifice.

And the apostles and elders chose two men, named Judas and
Silas, to go back with Paul and Barnabas to Antioch. And they
wrote a letter for these men to carry with them, and give to the
Christians in Antioch, and other cities, telling them that they
need no longer offer up lambs, or oxen, or goats to the Lord.
For the time was past when the Lord cared that the people
should worship him in this way. What he wanted them to do
now was to obey the words of the gospel, which said that they
should repent of their sins, and believe in his Son, Jesus; loving
him in their hearts and obeying his commandments.

So Paul and Barnabas, and Judas and Silas, left Jerusalem and
came to Antioch; there they called all the disciples together and
gave them the letter which the apostles and elders had sent. And
the disciples were glad when they read it, and learned that now

they could worship God as well in the places where they lived, as if they should go to Jerusalem and offer up sacrifices at the temple.

After these things Paul said to Barnabas, Let us go again and visit our brethren in all the cities where we have preached the gospel, and see how they do. And Barnabas was willing to go, and he wanted to take Mark with them; but Paul thought it not best to take Mark, who, when they took him before, left them, and was unwilling to stay with them to the end of their journey. So they disagreed about this matter, and their disagreement was so great that they parted from one another. Then Barnabas took Mark and sailed to the island of Cyprus, but Paul chose Silas and went into Syria, visiting the churches in that land.

And he came to Lystra, the city where he had healed the lame man. There he found a young man named Timothy whose mother was a Jewess, and a disciple of Jesus, but his father was a Gentile. And Timothy was well spoken of by the Christians at Lystra, for from the time he was a little child, he had been taught to know what was in the Scriptures, and to obey the Lord. When Paul saw how wise and good a young man he was, he chose him to go with himself and Silas, so that Timothy might learn to be a minister, and preach the gospel.

They came to Troas, a city near the sea; and there in the night Paul had a vision. He saw a man standing before him, who said, Come over to Macedonia and help us. Macedonia was a country on the other side of the sea; so Paul, and those who were with him, sailed in a ship from Troas, and came to a city of Macedonia, called Philippi.

On the Sabbath day they went a little way out of the city, to a place by the side of a river, where the Jews used to meet together to pray; and they sat down and talked with the women who came there. And a woman named Lydia, who was a seller of purple cloth, heard them. Then the Lord sent his Spirit into her heart, so that she attended to what Paul said and believed in Jesus. When she and her family had been baptized, she begged Paul and his friends, saying, If you think I am a believer, come and stay at my house. And she persuaded them till they went.

And a young woman who had an evil spirit, and who earned

much money for her masters, by pretending to tell persons what would happen to them in the future, followed Paul and his companions, and cried out, saying, These men are the servants of God, who show us the way we may be saved. This she did for many days. But Paul, being troubled that she followed them, turned and said to the evil spirit, I command thee, in the name of Jesus Christ, to come out of her. And the spirit came out that same hour.

When the masters of the young woman saw that she was made well, and could no longer earn money for them by repeating what the evil spirit said, they were angry, and caught Paul and Silas, and brought them before the rulers, saying, These men, who are Jews, do greatly trouble our city, and teach the people things which it is not right for them to do. Then the people of Philippi rose up against them, and the rulers commanded that they should be scourged. And after they had beaten them with many stripes they put them in prison, telling the jailer to keep them safely. He therefore took them into the inner prison and made their feet fast in the stocks, or heavy pieces of wood, so they might not escape.

In the middle of the night Paul and Silas prayed, and sang praises to God, and the other prisoners heard them. And suddenly there was a great earthquake, which shook the whole prison, and immediately all the doors opened, of their own accord, and the chains that bound the prisoners fell from them. And the keeper of the prison, waking out of his sleep, and seeing the prison doors open, and fearing that he would be put to death for allowing the prisoners to escape, drew out his sword and would have killed himself, supposing they had fled. But Paul cried to him, with a loud voice, saying, Do thyself no harm, for we are all here.

Then the jailer called for a light, and came trembling into the dungeon where Paul and Silas were, and kneeling down before them, cried, Sirs, what must I do to be saved? They answered him, Believe on the Lord Jesus Christ, and thou shalt be saved. Then they told him and all who were in his house, about the Saviour, and preached the gospel to them. And they believed, and were all of them baptized. That same hour of the night the jailer took Paul and Silas, and washed the wounds that had been made when they were beaten. He brought food also, and set it before them, that they might eat. And the jailer was filled with joy, because he and his family were made Christians, and had their sins forgiven.

In the morning the rulers sent some officers to the prison who said to the jailer, Let those men go. Then the jailer told Paul,

THE DOORS OF THE PRISON ARE OPENED

saying, The rulers have sent to let you go. Now the Jews, as we have read, were servants to the Romans. Yet Paul's father, although he was a Jew, had been made free. We are not told whether he bought his freedom for money, or received it as a reward from the emperor, for doing something that pleased him. But because his father was made a free Roman, Paul also was one. And it was against the law to scourge a free Roman. So when the rulers sent officers to say he might go, Paul answered, They have taken us who are Romans, and although no harm has been proved against us, have beaten us before all the people. If then, they want us to go, let the rulers come themselves and take us out, so that the people may know we were unjustly scourged and cast into prison.

When the rulers heard that Paul was a Roman, they were afraid lest they might be punished for what they had done to him; and they came and begged him earnestly to go out of the city. Then he and Silas left the prison and came into the house of Lydia; after they had met with the disciples there, and talked with them, to comfort them, they departed from Philippi and went on their journey.

And they came to another city of Macedonia called Thessalonica, where was a synagogue. And Paul, for three Sabbath days, went into it and preached to the Jews, as he used to do in every city; explaining the Scriptures to them and showing, from what the prophets had written, that Jesus was the Saviour. And some of them believed, and many of the Gentiles also.

But the Jews, who would not believe, being angry because they saw others believing, took wicked men with them and made an uproar in the city, and went to the house where Paul and Silas stayed, to bring them out to the people. When they could not find them, they caught the man to whom the house belonged, whose name was Jason, and brought him before the rulers, saying, The men called Christians, who have made such trouble and confusion in other places, have come here also. They disobey the decrees of Cæsar, and say there is another king named Jesus. Yet Jason has taken them into his house. Then the rulers made Jason promise that Paul and Silas should cause no more disturbance among the people, and afterward they let him go. But the brethren, that is, the men who were Christians in Thessalonica, sent Paul and Silas away by night to another city called Berea.

When they came there they went into the synagogue to preach to the Jews. Now the Jews in Berea were more willing to learn than those in Thessalonica, for they listened to the gospel, and after hearing it, they read every day, in the Scriptures, to see whether the things that Paul and Silas told them out of the prophets were true. Therefore many of them believed, and of the Gentiles also, both men and women, not a few. But when the Jews who had driven Paul away from Thessalonica, heard that he was preaching in Berea, they came there to stir up the people against him. Then the brethren sent him away from Berea, but Silas and Timothy stayed there still.

And the men who went with Paul brought him to Athens,

PAUL PREACHING AT ATHENS

which was the chief city of a country called Greece. The people of Athens were considered the wisest people living at that time, and were known all over the world for their learning; yet they worshipped false gods. They made beautiful statues of these, and built splendid temples and altars to them in different parts of their city. But among the altars was one with these words on it, TO THE UNKNOWN GOD. For though they had many gods, the people felt there was one God whom they had never learned about. Therefore, they built this altar to him.

And as Paul passed through the streets of Athens he saw that the city was full of idols. This grieved him at his heart; and he preached not only to the Jews in their synagogues, but he went every day to the market-place, where the people of the city met, and explained the gospel to them. When the philosophers, or wise men of Athens, heard him, some of them asked, What is it that this fellow says? Others answered, He seems to be telling about some new and strange gods. They said this, because he preached about Jesus and the resurrection. Then they took him and brought him to the place where the chief court of Athens met, on a hill called Mars' Hill, in the centre of the city; and they said to him, Tell us now what this gospel is which thou art preaching; for thou dost speak strange words, and we would like to know what they mean. For the people of Athens spent all their time in doing nothing else but either in telling, or hearing, some new thing.

Then Paul stood up, and said, Ye men of Athens, I see that you think a great deal about the gods which you worship; for as I walked through your city, looking at your temples, your altars, and your images, I saw there an altar with these words written on it: TO THE UNKNOWN GOD. That God, therefore, whom you worship without knowing him, I now want to tell you of.

Paul told them that God, who made the world, and made all things, did not live in temples such as they had built, neither was he like the idols of gold, silver, and stone, which were made by men's hands. While the people knew no better than to worship such idols, Paul said, God had not destroyed them for doing it, but had allowed them to live, and had given them food and clothing and everything that they needed. But now he told all men to worship idols no more, commanding them to repent of their sins and believe on Jesus, because he had appointed a day when he would send him to judge them; and God had given them a proof that he would do this, by raising Jesus up from the dead.

When the men of Athens heard Paul speak of the resurrection, or the rising up from the dead, some of them would not listen to his words, and mocked him, but others said, We will hear thee speak again of this matter. Yet a number of those who had heard him, believed, among whom was Dionysius, one of the members of the chief court of Athens, and a woman named Damaris, and others with them.

After these things, Paul left Athens and came to the city of Corinth. And he found there a Jew named Aquila, with his wife Priscilla. The Jews used always to teach their sons some business, or trade, while they were young, so that they would be able when they grew older to support themselves. Paul had been taught while young to be a tent-maker; and though now he was an apostle, whenever he was in want, he made tents for his living. And because Aquila was also a tent-maker, Paul went to stay and work with him. But every Sabbath day he came into the synagogue and taught the people, persuading both the Jews and the Gentiles to believe in the Saviour. When the Jews contradicted him, and spoke wickedly of Jesus, he said to them, I have done my duty in telling you of him. If you will not be saved, the fault is your own; from this time I will go and preach to the Gentiles.

Now Corinth, like Athens, was a great city, but the people who lived there were wicked. Yet the Lord spoke to Paul in the night, in a vision, and told him that many of them should become Christians; and he commanded Paul to preach boldly and without fear; For, the Lord said, I am with thee to take care of thee, and no man shall hurt thee. Paul stayed in Corinth a year and six months, preaching to the people. But the Jews of that city, who would not believe, rose up against him and brought him before the governor, saying, This fellow teaches men to worship God in a way that is wrong.

When Paul was going to answer them, the governor said to those who brought him, If this man had done something that was really wicked, it would be right that I should hear what you have to say against him. But if it be only a question about your worship, you may attend to it yourselves, for I will not be a judge between you in such matters. And he drove them away. Then the Gentiles, being angry with the Jews for persecuting Paul, took the chief ruler of the synagogue and beat him, even before the governor. Yet the governor did not stop them, for he cared about none of those things.

CHAPTERS XIX–XXIII (19–23)

SOME IDLE JEWS ATTEMPT TO CAST OUT EVIL SPIRITS. DEMETRIUS STIRS UP THE WORKMEN. PAUL PREACHES AT TROAS; RAISES EUTYCHUS FROM THE DEAD; SENDS FOR THE ELDERS AT EPHESUS; VISITS TYRE AND CESAREA. AGABUS PREDICTS PAUL'S IMPRISONMENT. PAUL IS TAKEN AT THE TEMPLE; IS SENT TO CESAREA.

AFTER this Paul stayed in Corinth for a good while. Then he bade farewell to the brethren there, and sailed away to the land of Syria, and came to the city of Ephesus. He was in Ephesus for three years preaching the gospel, until all the people in that part of Asia, both Jews and Gentiles, heard it. And God gave him power to do wonderful miracles, so that handkerchiefs, or aprons, which he had touched, when taken to persons who were sick, or had evil spirits, made them well.

Then some idle Jews, who spent their time in wandering about from one place to another, pretended they could cast out evil spirits also; and they spoke to them as Paul did, saying, We command you, in Jesus' name, to come out. There were seven brothers who did this; but the evil spirit answered them, and said, Jesus I know, and Paul I know; but who are ye? And the man in whom the evil spirit was, leaped on them and beat them, so that they fled out of the house wounded and with their clothes torn from them. And all the people heard of it, and many who had been wicked, believed, and came to Paul confessing the evil they had done. Others who before that time had deceived the people, pretending they could work by magic, brought the books which taught about such things, and burned them where all the people could see it. And when they had counted up the cost of the books, they found it to be fifty thousand pieces of silver. Yet the men to whom they belonged were willing to destroy them, rather than continue to use them in doing what they knew would offend God.

Now the people of Ephesus worshipped an image of a false goddess, named Diana, which they pretended had fallen down from heaven. They had in their city a very splendid temple where this idol was kept. The temple was built of cedar and cypress-wood, marble and gold. The people were two hundred and twenty years in building it. It was known among all nations, and persons from every land came to visit it; for it was thought to be one of the most beautiful and wonderful things in the world.

There were men at Ephesus who made little copies of this temple out of silver, with an image of Diana inside. These were called shrines. The men who made them sold them to the people, and in this way earned much money. One of the men was named Demetrius. When he heard Paul telling the people that they should not worship idols, and saw that many were obeying what Paul said, Demetrius called together all the workmen who made silver shrines for Diana, and said to them, Sirs, you know that it is by making these we get our wealth. Now you have heard that both here in Ephesus, and in almost every other city of Asia, this Paul has persuaded many persons, telling them that those are false gods which are made with men's hands. So there is danger, not only that we cannot sell our shrines, but also that the great goddess Diana shall not be worshipped any longer, and that the people will come to her beautiful temple no more.

When the workmen heard what Demetrius said, they were filled with rage and cried out, saying, Great is Diana of the Ephesians! And the whole city was soon in confusion. Then the workmen, having caught Gaius and Aristarchus, two men who had come with Paul to Ephesus, rushed all together into the theatre. When Paul wanted to go in and speak with them, the disciples would not let him, fearing that harm might be done to him. Some of the chief men of the city also, who were his friends, sent him word not to go. For the people were in a great uproar, some of them crying one thing and some another; yet many who had followed the workmen into the theatre did not know why they had come. The Jews also came there to speak against Paul; and one of them, named Alexander, stood up and motioned with his hand for the people to be still and listen to what he said; yet they would not, but all the multitude cried out together, for about two hours, Great is Diana of the Ephesians!

43

Then one of the chief officers of the city, called the town-clerk, came in among them, and, as soon as they were quiet, spoke to them saying, Ye men of Ephesus, what man is there among you who does not know that the people of our city are worshippers of the great goddess Diana, and of her image that fell down from heaven? Now as no one denies this, you ought to be careful, and do nothing in anger. For you have brought here the men called Christians, who have not robbed your temple, nor spoken evil of your goddess. Therefore if Demetrius, and the workmen who are with him, have any complaint to make against them, let him go before the court and prove what evil they have done. For we are in danger of being blamed by our rulers for this day's disturbance, because we can give no reason why it should have been made. When the town-clerk had spoken these words, he sent the people away.

After they were gone, Paul called to him the disciples, and bidding them farewell, left them, and went again into the land of Macedonia. When he had preached in the different cities of that land, he came again to Troas, in Asia. And on the first day of the week, when the disciples came together to eat of the bread and drink of the wine, as Jesus had commanded, Paul preached to them, for he was going to leave Troas the next day. There were many lights in the upper chamber where they met together, and Paul continued speaking till the middle of the night.

And there sat in a window, listening to him, a young man named Eutychus, who, as Paul was long preaching, slept, and while asleep, fell from the third story and was taken up dead. But Paul went down to him and putting his arms around him, said to those who stood by, Do not be troubled; he has come to life again. And the young man's friends, when they saw that he was alive, took him up and were comforted. When Paul had returned to the upper chamber and eaten with the disciples, and talked with them a long while, even till it was morning, he left them to go from Troas.

And he and the brethren who were with him, sailed to the city of Miletus, which was not far from Ephesus. And because

PAUL PARTING WITH THE ELDERS AT MILETUS

675

he did not wish to go to Ephesus at that time, he sent for the elders of the church there, to come and meet him. When they had come, he spoke to them, saying, You know, from the first day that I came among you, and for the three years that I stayed with you, how I lived at all times; serving the Lord humbly, yet having many sorrows and trials because of the Jews, who were always seeking to do me some harm. And you know that when I preached to you, I did not keep back anything that it was best for you to hear, even though it were something that might offend you; but I taught you in the synagogue and in your own houses, telling both the Jews and the Gentiles, that they should repent of their sins and believe in the Lord Jesus Christ.

And now I am going up to Jerusalem not knowing what shall happen to me there, except that in every city the Holy Spirit tells me, bonds and afflictions are waiting for me. Yet none of these things make me afraid, neither do I care even though I be put to death, so that I may die with joy, and finish the work which the Lord Jesus has given me, as his minister, to do. And now I know that all of you who have heard me preach the gospel so often, shall see my face no more. Therefore before I go, I want you to confess that if any of you be lost at the Judgment day, the fault will not be mine; for I have not neglected to tell you how you may be saved, as God sent me to tell you.

After Paul had said these things, he kneeled down and prayed with them. And they all wept greatly, and put their arms around his neck and kissed him, sorrowing most of all for the words which he spoke, that they should see his face no more. And they went with him to the ship in which he sailed away from Miletus.

Paul came to the city of Tyre, for there the ship was to unload her burden. Finding some disciples there he stayed with them seven days. As he was about to leave them, they, with their wives and children, came with him to the shore; and they all kneeled down together and prayed. And when they had bidden each other farewell, Paul and the brethren who journeyed with him, went into the ship, and the disciples returned to their own homes. And Paul came to the city of

Cesarea, and went into the house of Philip, one of the seven deacons on whom the apostles had laid their hands; it was that Philip who preached the gospel to the eunuch, as he rode in his chariot going back from Jerusalem to Ethiopia.

While Paul was in Philip's house, a prophet, named Agabus, came there, who took Paul's girdle, and bound his own hands and feet with it, saying, The Holy Ghost has told me that the Jews at Jerusalem shall so bind the man who owns this girdle, and shall give him to the Gentiles to be punished. When the disciples who were with Paul heard these words, they wept, and begged him earnestly not to go up to Jerusalem lest some evil should happen him. But he said to them, Why do you weep, to trouble me and break my heart? For I am ready not only to be bound, but also to die at Jerusalem, if they will kill me for preaching about Jesus. When they saw that he would not be persuaded to stay, they begged him no more, but said, Whatever the Lord will, let it be done.

After this Paul and his company left Cesarea and went up to Jerusalem; and the brethren of Jerusalem welcomed him gladly. The day afterward he went to the house of James, one of the apostles, and all the elders of the church were there to meet him. Then Paul told them of the places to which he had been, and how God had helped him, so that by his preaching many Gentiles believed. When they heard these things they rejoiced and thanked God for what had been done.

And Paul went up to the temple. But while he was there, some Jews from Asia saw him and took hold of him, crying out to all the people, Men of Israel, help us! This is the man who teaches the people everywhere not to obey the law of Moses, nor to worship here; and, beside this, he has brought with him into the temple Gentiles, who are not allowed to come in this holy place. Soon all the city was in an uproar, and the people ran together and took Paul and brought him away from the temple; and immediately the gates leading into the courts of the temple were shut. As they were about to kill him, some person went and told the chief captain of the Roman soldiers, who stayed in a castle near the temple to guard it and keep order there.

Then the chief captain, taking some of his soldiers with him, ran down among the people, who, when they saw him coming, stopped beating Paul. And the chief captain took him from them and commanded him to be bound with two chains, and asked who he was and what he had done. And some of the multitude cried one thing, and some another, so that no one could tell what they said. Then the chief captain ordered him to be taken into the castle. And when they came upon the stairs which led up to the castle, the soldiers carried Paul, to save him from the people, for they followed after him, crying out, Away with him! Kill him!

But as the soldiers were leading Paul off to shut him up in the castle, he said to the chief captain, May I speak to thee? Now there had been, before this time, a man from Egypt who deceived the Jews. Pretending that he was a prophet, he persuaded them to follow him out into the wilderness, and caused many of them to be slain. When the chief captain saw the people so angry, he thought Paul was that man. Therefore he said to him, Art thou not that Egyptian who did lead men out into the wilderness? Paul answered, No, I am a Jew who was born in Tarsus, which is a well-known city, and I beseech thee let me speak to the people.

When permission had been given him, Paul stood on the stairs where the people could see him, and motioned with his hands for them to be still. As soon as there was silence among them he spoke to them in the Hebrew language, which he knew the Jews would understand. He said, I am in truth a man that is a Jew, who was born in Tarsus, but brought up in this city of Jerusalem; and I was taught by a learned Jew, named Gamaliel, all the laws which Moses spoke to our fathers. And I was as anxious that every one should obey those laws as you are this day; for I persecuted and wanted to put to death, all who believed in Jesus, binding them and sending them to prison, both men and women. The high priest, and all the Council of the Sanhedrim, will tell you that what I say is true, for they gave me letters to the Jews at Damascus, that I might go and bind the Christians whom I found there, and bring them to Jerusalem to be punished.

But as I went on my journey and came near to Damascus, about noon, suddenly there shone from heaven a great light around me. And I fell down to the ground, and heard a voice, saying, Saul, Saul, why persecutest thou me? I answered, Who art thou, Lord? He said, I am Jesus of Nazareth, whom thou persecutest. The men who were with me saw the light and were afraid, but could not understand the words that were

PAUL IS BOUND BY THE ROMAN SOLDIERS

spoken. And I said, What shall I do, Lord? The Lord said unto me, Arise, and go into Damascus, and there it shall be told thee what thou must do.

And when I could not see, because the brightness of that light had blinded me, I was led by the hand and came into Damascus. After three days a disciple there, named Ananias, who feared God and was well thought of by all the Jews, came and stood by me, and said, Brother Saul, receive thy sight. And immediately I could see him. And he said to me, God has allowed thee to see Jesus and hear him speak, so that thou shouldst go and preach to all nations about him. And three years after that time, when I was in Jerusalem, and was praying in the temple, I saw Jesus again, in a vision, and heard him say, Make haste; go quickly out of Jerusalem, for the Jews will not believe what thou tellest them about me, and I will send thee far away to preach among the Gentiles.

And all the multitude of the Jews, to whom Paul was speaking, listened until he had spoken these words about preaching to the Gentiles; then they cried out with loud voices, Kill him! For such a fellow is not fit to live. As they said this, and in their rage cast off their outer garments, and threw dust in the air, the chief captain commanded that Paul should be brought into the castle and scourged, to make him confess what evil he had done.

But as they bound him with cords, and made ready to scourge him, Paul said to the centurion who stood near by, Is it lawful for you to scourge a man that is a free Roman, before any evil has been proved against him? When the centurion heard this he went and told the chief captain, saying, Be careful what thou doest, for this man is a Roman. Then the chief captain came and said to Paul, Tell me, art thou a Roman? He answered, Yes. The chief captain said, I paid a great sum of money to be made a free Roman. Paul answered, But I was born free. He said this because his father was a freeman, as we have read. Then the men who were about to scourge him, went away and left him; and the chief captain also, after he heard that Paul was a Roman, was afraid lest he might be punished for having bound him.

The next day, when the chief captain wanted to know certainly what the Jews accused him of, he commanded all the Council of the Sanhedrim to meet together, and brought Paul down and set him before them. And Paul, looking earnestly upon them, said, Men and brethren, I have done only those things that my conscience told me were right, until this day. Then Ananias, the high priest, ordered those who stood near Paul to smite him on the mouth. Paul said, God shall smite thee, thou hypocrite, for pretending to try me according to the law, and yet commanding me to be smitten before I am proved guilty, which is against the law. The Jews said to him, Dost thou insult the high priest? Paul answered, I did not know, brethren, that he was the high priest, for it is written in the Bible that we must not speak evil of the one who rules over us.

Then Paul tried again to speak to the men in the council, but soon there arose such a great uproar among them that the chief captain, fearing he might be torn in pieces, commanded the soldiers to go and take him from them, by force, and bring him into the castle.

The next night, while Paul was kept a prisoner, the Lord Jesus came and stood by him, and said, Fear not, Paul, for as thou hast spoken about me to the people here in Jerusalem, so shalt thou also speak about me in the city of Rome. And in the morning some of the Jews agreed together, and promised one another solemnly, that they would neither eat bread, nor drink water, till they had killed Paul. There were more than forty who made this promise. Then they went to the chief priests and elders, and said to them, We have agreed with one another that we will not eat, nor drink, till we have slain Paul. Now, therefore, do you tell the chief captain to bring him down to-morrow before the council, as though you wanted to ask some more questions of him; and while he is being brought, we will come upon him and kill him.

But Paul's sister's son heard what the Jews said, and he went into the castle and told Paul. Then Paul called one of the centurions to him, saying, Bring this young man to the chief captain, for he has something to tell him. So the centurion took him to the chief captain, and said, Paul the prisoner begged me to bring this young man to thee.

Then the chief captain took him by the hand, and led him to a place alone and asked him, saying, What is it thou hast to tell me? The young man answered, The Jews have agreed to ask thee to bring Paul down to-morrow, before the council, pretending they wish to inquire something more of him. But do not thou bring him, for there will be hidden, by the way, more than forty of them, who have promised each other solemnly that they will neither eat, nor drink, till they have killed him.   And they are now waiting, hoping that thou wilt do as they ask.   Then the chief captain let the young man go, saying, See thou tell no one that thou hast spoken these things to me.

The Roman governor of Judea was named Felix.   He did not live at Jerusalem, but at the city of Cesarea, which was on the sea coast, about sixty miles from Jerusalem.   When the chief captain heard that the Jews wanted to kill Paul, he determined to send him to the governor.   So he called to him two centurions, and said to them, Make ready two hundred foot soldiers, and seventy horsemen, and two hundred spearmen, to go to Cesarea at the third hour of the night.   And send also beasts for Paul, and the men who are with him, to ride upon, that he may be taken safe to Felix, the governor of Judea.

And the chief captain wrote a letter to the governor, saying, The man whom I send to thee was taken by the Jews, who were about to kill him: then I went with soldiers and took him from them, for I heard he was a Roman.   And because I wanted to know what evil they accused him of, I brought him before their council, and found that he had not done anything for which he ought to be put to death.   When it was told me that they were still determined to kill him, I sent him to thee, and commanded the Jews who accused him, to go and tell thee what they had against him.   Farewell.

Then the soldiers took Paul, and brought him by night to the town of Antipatris, which was on the way to Cesarea.   There the foot-soldiers left him, and returned to the castle at Jerusalem, but the horsemen brought him the next day to the governor at Cesarea; and they gave the governor the letter which the chief captain had sent.   After reading the letter, the governor asked Paul in what part of the empire he was born; when Paul had told him, the governor said to him, I will hear what thou hast to say for thyself, when the Jews who accuse thee shall also come to Cesarea.   And he commanded that Paul should be kept in prison till they came.

CHAPTERS XXIV–XXVIII (24–28)

THE JEWS ACCUSE PAUL, WHO DEFENDS HIMSELF BEFORE FELIX AND AGRIPPA.
HE APPEALS TO CÆSAR; IS SENT TO ROME; HE IS SHIPWRECKED ON THE
WAY. AT ROME HE PREACHES THE GOSPEL. THE SUPPOSED MANNER
OF HIS DEATH.

AFTER five days, Ananias, the high priest, and some of the
council, came down from Jerusalem to Cesarea. They brought
with them also a lawyer, named Tertullus, that he might
speak against Paul before the governor. And when Paul was
brought out of the prison to be tried, Tertullus began to accuse
him, saying, We have found this fellow to be a wicked man,
who is stirring up trouble and disorder among the Jews all over
the world; and he is a chief one among those who believe in
Jesus of Nazareth. He has also brought Gentiles into the temple, who are not allowed to go there. And we would have tried
him according to our law, to see what his punishment should be,
but the chief captain came with soldiers and took him from us
by force, commanding us to come before thee and accuse him.
Now, therefore, we are here, ready to prove all the things that
we speak against him. When Tertullus had finished, the Jews
who were with him said that all he had spoken was true.

Then Paul, after the governor had given him permission,
answered, saying, It is now but twelve days since I went up
to Jerusalem to worship, and they found me in the temple, yet
not disputing with any man, nor trying to stir up the people;
neither can they prove the things which they speak against
me. But this I confess to thee, that I worship God in a way
different from them, although I believe everything that is
written in their Scriptures. And I expect the dead, both the
bad and the good, to rise up at the last day, as the Jews themselves say that they will. And believing this, I am trying
all the time to do nothing that my conscience tells me is wrong,
either to God or to man.

Now after being away from Jerusalem for many years, I
came back at this time to bring alms to the poor Jews there,
and also an offering to God. And some Jews from Asia found

me in the temple, yet not with a multitude, nor causing any disturbance. And they are the ones who should have been here to tell if they had anything against me. Or let these Jews who are here now, say whether they found any evil in me when I was taken before the council in Jerusalem, unless they will say it was wrong for me to preach about the dead rising up from their graves at the Judgment day.

After Paul had spoken these things, Felix would hear no more, but he sent the Jews away, saying, When the chief captain shall come down I will ask him all about your matters. And he commanded the centurion to keep Paul in prison, but to let him walk out, and to see any of his friends who should come to visit him.

Now, Drusilla, the wife of Felix, was a Jewess. And after some days, Felix sent for Paul to come and speak to him and Drusilla, and explain the gospel to them. And as Paul spoke to them, persuading them to obey God, and not to listen to temptation, and told them how they must be judged at the last day, Felix thought of his sins and was afraid, so that he trembled. Yet he did not repent of those sins, but sent Paul back to prison, saying, At some other time, when it shall be more convenient, I will send for thee again to tell me about these things. Felix hoped also that Paul would offer him money to let him go free, and on that account he sent for him the oftener to talk with him. But after two years, when another governor, named Festus, came to take Felix's place, instead of letting Paul go, Felix left him in prison.

When Festus, the new governor, was come to Cesarea, the Jews asked of him that Paul might be sent to Jerusalem to be tried; for they intended now, as they did before, to have men hidden by the way who would rise up and kill him. But Festus answered them, and said, Paul shall stay in Cesarea, and those who wish to accuse him, may come here and say what they have against him. So when they had come, the governor commanded Paul to be brought before them, and the Jews stood and accused him of many things. But Paul answered for himself, saying, Neither against the laws of the Jews, nor against the temple.

nor against Cæsar, have I done anything wrong. Then Festus, because he wanted to please the Jews, answered Paul and said, Art thou willing to go up to Jerusalem, and there be tried for the things they accuse thee of?

PAUL BEFORE KING AGRIPPA

Now it was a law, that any Roman who was going to be put to death, might ask to be taken before Cæsar, the emperor, for the emperor to say whether he should die, or be allowed to live. And when Festus asked Paul if he were willing to go up to Jerusalem to be tried before the Jews, who he knew were determined to kill him, Paul answered, saying, Jerusalem is not the place where I ought to be tried; for I have done no wrong to the Jews, as thou very well knowest. I ask to be taken before Cæsar. Then Festus said, Hast thou asked to be taken before Cæsar? Unto Cæsar shalt thou go. He meant that Paul should be taken to the city of Rome, where the emperor Cæsar lived.

Some days after this, Agrippa, who was king over another part of the land of Israel, came with his sister Bernice, to visit Festus at Cesarea. And Festus told him about Paul, saying, There is a man here in prison, whom the chief priests and elders of the Jews have asked me to put to death. Now Agrippa was a Jew, and when the governor told him that the Jews wanted to put Paul to death, he said, I myself would like to hear what the man says. The governor answered, To-morrow thou shalt hear him.

The next day Agrippa came, and Bernice, dressed in their royal robes, with the chief captains and principal men of the city around them. And Festus sent for Paul to be brought out of prison. So he came with the chains, such as prisoners wore, fastened upon him. Then Festus told Agrippa that this was the man whom the Jews wanted to kill. And Agrippa spoke to Paul, saying, Thou hast permission to speak for thyself, and to answer the things which the Jews say against thee. Then Paul stood up, and told king Agrippa he was very glad that he might make his answer to him, because he was sure that the king had learned all about the laws of the Jews, and would understand what he was now going to say before him.

Then Paul said, The Jews themselves know very well how I have lived, and what I have done, ever since I was a child. For I also am a Jew, and if they would speak the truth they would say that I used to be one of the strictest among them. I, too, thought that I ought to do many things against Jesus of Nazareth. Many of his disciples I shut up in prison, and when they were tried and put to death, I was one of those who spoke against them. I punished them in every synagogue, and did all I could to make them speak against their Saviour. And being full of rage against them, I went even to other cities to seek for them

But as I was going to Damascus, when I came near that city, I saw, in the middle of the day, a light from heaven, brighter than the sun, that shone around me and the men who were with me. And we were all afraid and fell to the earth.

Then Paul told Agrippa and Festus, and all who were listening to him, how Jesus spoke to him at that time, and said that he had come to make Paul a minister, and send him to preach the gospel to the Gentiles, so that they might repent and have their sins forgiven. And when I had heard his voice, Paul said, I did not disobey what the Lord commanded, but went and preached to the Jews at Damascus, and at Jerusalem, and also to the Gentiles, telling them to repent and obey God. And because I did this, the Jews caught me in the temple and were about to kill me. But God saved me from them. Therefore, since God helped me, I have kept on preaching till this day to all the people, both the poor and the rich. Yet I have told them only those things which the prophets said should happen; that Jesus would be put to death, and afterward would rise up from the dead, and be a Saviour both to the Jews and the Gentiles.

While Paul was speaking, Festus, the governor, said with a loud voice, Paul thou art beside thyself; much learning doth make thee mad. He meant that Paul had lost his reason, or his senses, because he had read and thought so much about what was written in the Scriptures. But Paul answered, I am not mad, most noble Festus; but am speaking only words that are true. And king Agrippa understands what I say; for I am sure he has heard of all these things. Then Agrippa said to Paul, Thou dost almost persuade me, too, to be a Christian. Paul said, I wish that not only thou, but also all these persons who are listening to me this day, were Christians such as I am, except that they might not have to wear these chains.

When Paul had spoken these words, Agrippa rose up, and Festus, and the chief men of the city who were with them, and they went apart to talk with one another, saying, This man has not done anything for which he should be put to death, or kept in prison. Then Agrippa said to Festus, He might have been set at liberty if he had not asked to be taken to Rome, before Cæsar.

When the time came for Paul to be sent to Rome, Festus gave him, and some other prisoners that were to go there, into the care of a centurion, who took soldiers with them to guard them by the way. Then they went into a ship that sailed from Cesarea, and came the next day to the city of Sidon. Here they stopped for a while, and the centurion, whose name was Julius, treated Paul kindly, letting him go to the shore to visit some of his friends in that city.

After leaving Sidon they came to the city of Myra. There the centurion took his prisoners on board of another ship, in which they sailed toward Rome. After sailing slowly many days they reached a place called the Fair Havens, in the island of Crete. And now as it was winter, and the time for storms on the sea had come, Paul said to the men on the ship, Sirs, I see that while we are on this voyage there will be great danger, not only to the ship, but also to our lives. But the master of the ship, because he did not believe what Paul said, nor think the Fair Havens a good harbor to stay in for the winter, determined to leave it and try to reach a place called Phenice. And when there came a wind that blew softly from the south, the sailors thought they would be able to do this. Therefore they left the Fair Havens and sailed out on the sea again.

But soon there arose a fierce wind, that beat against the ship; and when the sailors could steer no longer, they let her go wherever the wind might drive her. And they came near to an island called Clauda, and there could hardly save the little boat that was fastened behind the ship from being washed away; but when they had taken it up out of the water, they wound cables, or chains, about the ship, underneath and all around it, to keep it from breaking to pieces. And being greatly tossed by the tempest, the next day they threw out into the sea some of the cargo, to make the ship lighter, and save it from sinking. On the following day they threw over all the ropes and sails that could be spared.

When the wind kept on blowing for many days, and they

could see neither sun, nor moon, nor stars, because of the dark clouds that covered the sky, the people in the ship gave up all hope, thinking they would surely be lost. But after they had eaten nothing for a long time, Paul stood up among them, and said, Sirs, you should have listened to me and stayed at the island of Crete, then you would not have come into this great danger.

SHIPWRECK OF PAUL

Yet now I beg you be not afraid, for there shall be no loss of any man's life among you; but only of the ship. For this night the Lord sent his angel, who spoke to me, saying, Fear not, Paul, thou shalt come safely to Rome and be brought before Cæsar; and, for thy sake, God will save the lives of all the men who are with thee in the ship. Therefore, sirs, be cheerful;

44

for **I** believe what the angel told me. Yet we shall be wrecked on some island.

And when the fourteenth night had come, as the ship was driven along by the wind, the sailors thought they were near some land; and after they had sounded, that is, measured the depth of the water, they found that it was so. And fearing they would strike on the rocks at the bottom of the sea, they dropped four anchors out of the ship to keep it from being driven any further, and then wished for the morning. But the sailors, supposing the ship would soon be broken to pieces, let down the little boat into the water, intending to escape in it, and leave the others to be drowned. But Paul said to the centurion, Except these sailors stay in the ship, the rest cannot be saved. Then the soldiers cut off the ropes that held the boat, and let it float away without any one in it.

When it was near morning, Paul begged them all to take something to eat, saying, This is the fourteenth day since the storm came upon us, and you have eaten hardly anything. Therefore, I pray you, take some food, that you be not made sick; for there shall not the least harm happen to any one of you. When he had said this he took bread, and thanked God for it before them all, and began to eat. Then were they all cheerful, and did eat with him. There were altogether two hundred and seventy-six persons in the ship. And after they had eaten, they threw into the sea some of the cargo of wheat, with which the ship was loaded, to lighten it.

When it was day they saw the shore, though they could not tell to what land they had come; and seeing a creek a little way off, they determined, if they were able, to push the ship into it. After they had taken up the anchors, and hoisted the sail, they steered toward that place; but before they reached it the ship ran aground, and the forepart was held fast on the bottom of the sea, and could not be moved; but the hinder part was broken by the great waves that dashed against it. Then the soldiers advised the centurion to have the prisoners killed, for fear some of them might escape. But the centurion, wishing to save Paul, forbade them to do the prisoners any harm; and commanded

that those who could swim, should first cast themselves into the
sea, and get to the shore.   The rest, some on boards, and some
on broken pieces of the ship, came afterward.   So it was that
they all safely reached land.

When they had come there they found it was an island called
Melita.   The people of the island showed them great kindness,
and kindled a fire for them, because of the rain that was falling,

PAUL IS NOT HARMED BY THE SERPENT

and because of the cold.   Then Paul gathered a bundle of sticks
and laid them on the fire, but after he had done so, a poisonous
snake came out of the heat, and fastened on his hand.   When the
people of the island saw it hanging upon his hand, they said
among themselves, No doubt this man is a murderer, who though
he has escaped drowning in the sea, is yet punished by the bite of
the snake for the evil he has done.   But Paul shook off the snake
into the fire and felt no harm.   Then they looked at him a long
while, expecting that his arm would swell, or that he would fall

down dead suddenly, but when they saw no harm come to him, they changed their minds and said that he was a god.

The chief man of the island, whose name was Publius, invited Paul and those who were with him, to his house, and they went and stayed three days, being kindly treated there. Now the father of Publius was sick of a fever, and Paul laid his hands on him and made him well. When he had done this, others who were sick in the island, came and were healed. And they showed their gratitude by giving to Paul and his friends presents of such things as they needed.

After three months, the centurion took Paul, and the other prisoners, into a ship that had been waiting at the island till the winter was over, and they sailed away to the city of Puteoli, where they stayed seven days with some disciples who lived there; then they journeyed by land toward Rome. When the Christians at Rome heard Paul was coming, they went out to meet him at a place called the Three Taverns. After he had seen them, he gave thanks because he had been saved from so many dangers; and he felt in his heart that God would still take care of him.

When they came to Rome, the centurion gave the prisoners into the care of the captain of the guard, but Paul was allowed to live in a house by himself, with the soldier who watched over him: yet the chains that he had worn so long, were not taken off from him. After three days, he sent for the chief men among the Jews who lived at Rome, and said to them, Men and brethren, though I have done no wrong to the Jews, nor disobeyed the laws which Moses spoke to our fathers, yet the Jews at Jerusalem gave me as a prisoner to the Romans, who, when they examined me, would have let me go, because I had done nothing for which I deserved to die. But when the Jews still wanted to kill me, I asked to be taken before Cæsar. Therefore I have sent for you to come, that I might see you, and speak with you, for it is because I believe in that Saviour about whom the prophets have written, that I am bound with this chain.

When he said this the Jews answered, We have had no

letters sent to us about thee, neither do those Jews who have come from Jerusalem, speak any harm of thee. Yet we would like to hear what it is thou dost preach; for, as for these Christians, we know that everywhere they are spoken against. So after they had appointed a day, many of the Jews came to Paul's house and he taught them, explaining what the prophets had written about Jesus, from morning till evening. And some believed the things he spoke, and some believed not. While they differed among themselves, he told them that the prophet Isaiah had spoken the truth when he said, that although a message from God should be brought to the people of Israel, they would not listen to it, because their hearts were wicked and they did not want to be his children. Therefore Paul told them, that the gospel which the Jews refused to believe should be preached to the Gentiles, and the Gentiles, he said, would obey it.

Paul stayed two whole years in Rome, and lived in a house which he hired for himself. There he welcomed all those persons who came to hear him, and he taught them about Jesus, without fear, for no man tried to prevent him.

The Bible does not tell us where Paul went after this, or how he died at last. But from accounts given in other books, it is thought that when he was set free at Rome, he went back to Jerusalem, and then travelled through other countries preaching the gospel, till he came to Rome again. Not many years after this time, there was a great fire at Rome which continued burning for six or seven days. The people believed that their wicked emperor, Nero, had ordered the city to be set on fire. To save himself from the blame, Nero accused the Christians of doing it. Then the people rose up in great fury against the Christians, and put many of them to death. Among those who were killed, we are told, were the apostles Peter and Paul. Paul, it is said, was beheaded, and Peter crucified.

We suppose that Paul was beheaded, and not crucified, because it was against the law to crucify a Roman, for that was the way in which they put slaves to death; and no Roman might be treated as a slave, even when they were putting him to death. But Peter was not a free Roman, and him, we are told, they crucified. It made no difference to these holy men how they died; they knew that afterward they would be taken to heaven. And so we, who hope to meet them, will be taken there, if, like them, we are the disciples of Jesus. But if we are not his disciples, then he says to us, as he said to the Jews who would not believe on him, Where I am, there you cannot come.

THE EPISTLES

AFTER the Acts of the Apostles, come the Epistles. An epistle is a letter, and the Epistles in the New Testament are letters which were written by the apostles; some of them to particular churches; some of them to all the churches that were then in the world; and some of them to persons who were living at that time.

When Jesus sent out the apostles to teach the people of all nations, he meant that they should do it not only by speaking to them, but also by writing to them. And he gave them the Holy Spirit to tell them both what they should speak, and what they should write. What the apostles spoke is forgotten; for they have long since been dead, and so have the persons who heard them. But what they wrote, we can still read in the Epistles.

There are twenty-one epistles. Paul wrote fourteen of them, Peter two, John three, James one, and Jude, or Thaddeus one. Like the rest of the Bible, the Epistles are a message from God, not from men; and they were intended as much for us, as for those to whom they were sent at the time they were written. Whatever they teach we are to believe, remember, and obey.

We are taught in the Epistles that all the people in the world, being born with wicked hearts, have sinned against God; and that they all would be punished for their sins, had not God loved them so much as to send his only Son, Jesus, to be punished in their place. Yet not all of them are forgiven on this account, but only those who believe in Jesus. And how can we tell who believes in him? For a person may say he believes when he does not. We can tell by the way he acts. If he believes in Jesus he will love him, and obey his commandments, that is, he will be a Christian.

And we are told in the Epistles how Christians ought to live, and what sort of people they should be. They should be honest, industrious, sober, humble; good to the poor; kind to those who are unkind to them; speaking evil of no one; loving and forgiving one another; trying to persuade others to be Christians; thankful for their blessings; patient when they have trouble; full of joy, because they are saved; hating what is wicked; loving what is good; earnest in prayer, striving in every word and act to please God.

But Christians cannot do these things by themselves, for although they desire to do them, Satan is always tempting them to sin. He is their great enemy, who, we are told, is going about like a roaring lion, seeking to destroy them. Yet they have a friend who is stronger than he. For that same Jesus who came on the earth to die for them, now looks down from heaven and watches over them. He hears their prayers, and helps them to fight against Satan's temptations. And when they are overcome, and fall into sin, if they mourn and repent of it, he asks God to forgive them.

He does more than this. Because they have no righteousness, nor goodness of their own, to make God pleased with them, he gives them his righteousness, and God counts it the same as if it were theirs, and as if they had never sinned. And at the last day God will accept all those who have this righteousness, and will take them up to heaven where Jesus is, and where they will never be tempted to sin any more.

The Epistles tell us that as the end of the world draws near, there will be scoffers, or persons who mock at the Bible as though it were not true. They will say, If Jesus is coming again to judge the world, as the Bible says he is, why is he so long in coming? They will not believe the true reason—that God is waiting to give wicked men time to repent, because he is not willing that any should perish, but that all should repent of their sins and have everlasting life.

But although God has waited so long, he will not wait always. For we are told that the day of the Lord, that is, the day of Judgment, shall come as a thief comes in the night, when no one is expecting it. Then the world, with its mighty kingdoms, its splendid cities, and all the great and beautiful things that men have made, will be burned up, but the people who have lived in it, will rise up out of their graves to be judged. And now, since God has told us of this, how careful we who are Christians should be to live holy lives, so that when the day of the Lord does come, and Jesus descends to the earth again, we may be ready to meet him.

We have read in the Gospels, and in the book of the Acts, that Jesus is God, and that the Holy Ghost is God. We are taught this again in the Epistles. We are taught there that God the Father, God the Son, and God the Holy Ghost, are three persons who rule over all things. Yet they are not three Gods, but the three together are one God. We cannot understand this any more than we can understand how God never had any beginning, or how he is in every place at one time; but we can believe it, because the Bible tells us that it is so. It is God the Father who made us; it is God the Son who died for us; it is God the Holy Ghost who comes into our hearts and makes us love, and obey the Father and the Son—that is, who makes us Christians. We need not be afraid, therefore, of worshipping one more than the other, for they are all of them God. When we pray to Jesus, we pray to God. When we pray to the Holy Ghost, we pray to God. And when we pray to God, we pray to the Father, the Son, and the Holy Ghost.

THE REVELATION OF ST. JOHN

THE last Book in the Bible is called the Revelation. It was written by the Apostle John. One of the wicked emperors of Rome, being angry because he preached the gospel, sent John to a lonely island named Patmos. There, we are told, he was

JOHN IN THE ISLAND OF PATMOS

treated cruelly and made to work in the mines, though he was a very old man at the time.

But while he was at Patmos the Saviour appeared to him, in a vision, and showed him those things that are written in the Book of Revelation. John says, I heard behind me a great voice like a trumpet, and I turned to see who it was that spoke to me, and saw Jesus clothed in a garment that reached down to his feet, and around his breast was a golden girdle. When John saw him he was afraid, and fell down like one dead; but Jesus laid his right hand upon him, saying, Fear not, I am he that was crucified; but, behold, I am alive again, and will live for-evermore. And Jesus talked with John, and gave him mes-sages to seven different churches in the land of Asia, and told him to write down the messages in a book, and send them to the seven churches for which they were intended.

Afterward, John saw a door opened in heaven, and a voice called to him, saying, Come up hither, and I will show thee what will happen hereafter. And he heard the voices of a great mul-titude of angels praising the Saviour, and calling him The Lamb that was slain. Then, in the vision, John was shown many wonderful things, which were meant to teach him what would happen to Christians on the earth, from that time until the end of the world. He was shown how wicked nations and kings would persecute them, and kill them, hoping that none of them might be left. But he was shown also how the Lord would de-stroy those nations and kings, and save his people, so that at last no enemy could hurt them.

After this John saw a great white throne in heaven, and Jesus sat upon it. And he saw the dead risen up from their graves; and they came and stood before the throne to be judged. Then the books were opened in which was written down every-thing they had done while they were living on the earth. And they were judged out of the books according to what was written there. And another book was opened, called the book of life, in which were written the names of those who had believed in Jesus. And whoever had not his name written in the book of life, was cast into the lake of fire.

And after the Judgment was past, John saw new skies, and a new earth, for the earth and the skies that had been there before, were burned up. And he saw a beautiful city, called the New Jerusalem, coming down out of heaven, and heard a voice, say-ing, God is coming to live with men. Around the city was a great and high wall, with twelve gates. At each gate was an angel to guard it. The city was built of pure gold; in its walls were all kinds of precious stones, and its gates were made of pearls. There was no need of sun or moon to lighten it, for God was there, and the Lord Jesus, and the glory that shone around them made it light. The people whom Jesus had saved out of all nations were to come and live in it. The gates should never be shut, for there will be no night there. And none of the wicked shall go into it, but only those whose names are written in the Lamb's book of life.

And John saw also a pure River of water, called the water of life. By its side, as it flowed through the streets of the city, grew the tree of life, that bore twelve different kinds of fruit which ripened every month. And those who shall live in the city and drink of the waters of the River, and eat of the fruits of the tree of life, shall see the Lord's face and be with him and serve him. He will wipe away all tears from their eyes, and there shall be no more death, neither sorrow nor crying; neither shall there be any more pain, for all these things will have passed away forever. And Jesus spoke to John, saying, Blessed are those who obey God's commandments, that they may enter in through the gates into the city.

INDEX